Classic Readings in American Politics

SECOND EDITION

EDITED BY

Pietro S. Nivola

University of Vermont

David H. Rosenbloom

Syracuse University

With Forewords by
Nelson W. Polsby
and
Theodore J. Lowi

St. Martin's Press New York

Senior Editor: Don Reisman
Development Editor: Cathy Pusateri
Project Editor: Bruce Glassman
Text design: Levavi & Levavi
Graphics: G&H Soho
Cover design: Darby Downey
Cover art: Star Spangled Banner by Milton Bond from Jay Johnson America's Folk Heritage Gallery, New York City

Library of Congress Catalog Card Number: 88-63045

Manufactured in the United States of America.
8 7 6 5
g f e d

For information, write:
St. Martin's Press, Inc.
175 Fifth Avenue
New York, NY 10010

ISBN: 0-312-02014-7

Acknowledgments

Acknowledgments and copyrights are continued at the back of the book on page 524, which constitutes an extension of the copyright page.

Edward C. Banfield, "Influence and the Public Interest." Reprinted with permission of The Free Press, a Division of Macmillan, Inc., from POLITICAL INFLUENCE by Edward C. Banfield. Copyright © 1961 by The Free Press.

James D. Barber, "Adding it Up," THE PRESIDENTIAL CHARACTER, third edition (NJ: Prentice-Hall, Inc., 1985), pp. 500–528. Reprinted by permission of the author.

Alexander M. Bickel, "Establishment and General Justification of Judicial Review, from THE LEAST DANGEROUS BRANCH: THE SUPREME COURT AT THE BAR OF POLITICS by Alexander M. Bickel (Reissued by Yale University Press, 1986). Copyright, Josephine Ann Bickel. Reprinted by permission.

Walter Dean Burnham, "The Turnout Problem," in James A. Reichley, Ed., ELECTIONS AMERICAN STYLE (Washington, D.C.: The Brookings Institution, 1987), pp. 97–133. Reprinted by permission of The Brookings Institution.

Edward S. Corwin, "The 'Higher Law' Background of American Constitutional Law," HARVARD LAW REVIEW, vol. XLII (1928–1929), pp. 149–185, 365–409. Copyright © 1928, 1929 by the Harvard Law Review Association. Reprinted by permission.

Thomas E. Cronin, "Everybody Believes in Democracy Until He Gets to the White House," LAW AND CONTEMPORARY PROBLEMS (Volume 35, no. 3, summer 1970). Copyright 1970, Duke University School of Law. Reprinted by permission of The Duke University School of Law and the author.

For our sons and daughters,
Adrian, Alessandro, Lila, Joshua, Sarah, and Leah

Preface

The favorable reaction to the first edition of *Classic Readings in American Politics* surpassed our highest expectations. The book was very widely adopted. Evidently, political scientists at many colleges and universities throughout the United States shared our belief that the teaching of American government would benefit from a volume dedicated to works of enduring value, works that would, as Theodore J. Lowi suggested in the Foreword, help "lift the discourse" in political science instruction. We are gratified to have conceived a book that has been welcomed by so many of our colleagues.

Nonetheless, there was room for improvement. Students in introductory classes sometimes found certain selections—those containing arcane language, advanced concepts, or unfamiliar references—beyond their comprehension. Feedback from extensive surveys of faculty who had used *Classic Readings* suggested that we, as editors, could make some helpful revisions, while still maintaining a high level of quality control. The second edition, therefore, contains two sorts of changes. A number of the original selections have been deleted, and ten substitutes have been added. The new material is no less important or valuable, but it tends to be more intellectually accessible to the beginner. The new table of contents reveals a leaner, and more readable book, without compromising a commitment to "classic" themes and treatments.

We have also sought to assist our readers by including headnotes for each piece and explanatory footnotes wherever references, terms, or concepts may be too obscure for most undergraduates. These devices, in addition to our revised introductions for each section, should help students get off to a smoother start with each of the readings and to help place the various readings and authors in context. We are grateful to Casey Cleary-Hammarstedt for her hard work on our new headnotes and footnotes. We are also grateful to the following instructors who offered suggestions for the second edition. They are: W. F. Abboushi, University of Cincinnati; Thomas J. Baldino, Juniata College; Anthony J. Brunello, Eckerd College-University of New Mexico; Alice-Catherine Carls, Lambuth College; James Carpenter, Boston University; Donald Chisholm, Ohio State University; Bernard F. Condon, Jr., Iona College; Albert Cover, SUNY-Stony Brook; Burnet V. Davis, Alma College; Sybil M. Delevan, Pennsylvania State University; Matthew J. Dickinson, Harvard University; Gavan Duffy, University of Texas at Austin; Edgar Dyer, Coastal Carolina College-University of South Carolina; M. Lauren Ficaro, California State University at Fullerton;

Brian L. Fife, SUNY-Binghamton; Henry Flores, St. Mary's University of Texas; Ed Fuchs, University of Texas at El Paso; James M. Gerhardt, Southern Methodist University; Robert M. Gill, Radford University; Paul A. Gough, University of Mississippi; Peg Griffin, Northern Kentucky University; Roger Hamburg, Indiana University-Southbend; Susan Hammond, American University; Gordon Henderson, Widner University; James F. Herndon, Virginia Polytechnic Institute and State University; John Hevrman, University of Minnesota; James R. Hurtgen, SUNY-Fredonia; Curtis Johnson, Lewis and Clark College; Gary L. Jones, University of Nevada at Las Vegas; Ellis Katz, Temple University; Michael Keefe, Michigan State University; Matthew R. Kerbel, University of Michigan; Jeff Kraus, Keuka College; Jan Leighley, Washington University at St. Louis; Tim Luther, California Baptist College; Richard G. Martin, Troy State University at Dothan; Pamela A. Mason, University of North Carolina at Chapel Hill; Nancy Maveety, Tulane University; William Mishler, University of South Carolina; Rita Moniz, Southeastern Massachusetts University; Glenn Morris, University of Colorado at Denver; Ruth Mitchell Pitts, University of North Carolina at Chapel Hill; P.H. Pollack, III, University of Central Florida; Andrew Polsky, CUNY-Hunter College; Barbara Ryan, Trenton State College; Jose R. Sanchez, SUNY-Old Westbury; Robert Schmuhl, University of Notre Dame; Edward Schneier, CUNY-City College; Stephen Schneck, Catholic University of America; Jeffery Leigh Sedgwick, University of Massachusetts; Robert Shapiro, Columbia University; Henry Sirgo, McNeese State College; David R. Smedley, Temple University; Thomas Smith, CUNY-Brooklyn College; Kerry N. Stephenson, Purdue University-West Lafayette Campus; William J. Teague, University of Texas at Dallas; Stella Z. Theodoulou, California State University at Northridge; W.A.P. Thompson, Jr., University of Texas at Dallas; A. Worden, Michigan State University.

Like the first edition, this one remains, in our view, a rich anthology of original writings that can be used independently of, or as a complement to, most standard texts in the field. It also remains, in our opinion, unique in its emphasis: giving contemporary undergraduates a sample of the very best that scholars of American politics, past and present, have had to offer.

Pietro S. Nivola
Washington, D.C.

David H. Rosenbloom
Syracuse, New York

CONTENTS

II. FEDERALISM 57

III. ELECTIONS AND POLITICAL PARTIES 105

VIII. THE JUDICIARY 427

IX. THE POLICY PROCESS 481

FOREWORD

TO THE SECOND EDITION

BY

NELSON W. POLSBY

Education—higher education not excepted—is all about the transfer of information between generations. The purpose of a book of readings of this kind is to provide members of a student generation with information about some of the sign-posts their elders have been using to guide themselves through the world of politics. "Classic" readings aspire not merely to give facts and figures, although many of them do that. Many of these essays and excerpts also embody ideas that have been influential in guiding thought, in sorting out categories of causes and relating them to categories of effects. The expression of key ideas that readers—sometimes a great many readers—have found so useful gives articles like those reprinted here their capacity to "stick to the ribs" and entitles them to be considered "classics."

It is not required, however, that the articles be right. Some of the ideas in these writings have been superseded by time, some have been ably rebutted, and some were never strongly supported by evidence. Some are, thus, to put it mildly, regarded as scientifically controversial. It is characteristic of the social sciences that even with controversy, many such contributions remain very much a part of the literature if the proposals they make about how social and political life are organized are sufficiently interesting. So it is important for readers to read this book critically, attentively, and skeptically—as they should any work of political science.

That a collection of important works about the American political system should show great diversity is no surprise. Although it is unfashionable even to entertain such a thought, it seems to me plain enough that the American experiment in self-government, now a remarkable 200 years old, has properties that make it unique. Seen in a comparative perspective, the United States is one of the world's few federal systems, one of the world's few separation-of-powers systems, and one of the world's few systems embodying a written, legally enforced Bill of Rights. All three of these features, when taken together, have produced over time a political system that is unusual in the extreme—indeed singular.

The American political system is singular in its capacity to absorb change, and, hence, has proven to have unusual adaptability and, therefore, longevity, as constitutional orders go. No doubt it has helped enormously that the United States has grown extremely rich, has been geographically isolated from rival powers during its development as a nation, and has been militarily strong. But the very diversity of its inhabitants has provided much material for internal combustion, as the Civil War illustrated. And so it is not entirely inappropriate that we look inward for sources of adaptation.

Two such sources are embodied in the party system and in the judicial system. A Western European parliamentarian from a nation a little less than one-quarter the size of the United States once asked me how a nation as large and diverse as the United States made do with only two major political parties when other democratic nations had three, four, or more parties regularly represented in their Parliaments. Surely, he conjectured, we must be suppressing major strands of opinion by having so narrow a set of realistic alternatives.

It seems to me a fascinating question. One possible response is to agree that our two-party democracy does indeed suppress broader expressions of opinion. If we were to seek independent confirmation of the factual premise of this explanation, however, especially as compared with other, smaller, multi-party democracies, we would, I think, come up short. A second possibility, equally implausible, is that a smaller variety of opinions actually exist in America—that Americans are more homogeneous than Spaniards or Italians or Swedes. That a continental multi-ethnic nation of a quarter of a billion souls should be less varied than seven million or so Swedes seems a dubious proposition indeed.

A third possible explanation suggests itself. Perhaps we do not really have a two-party system at all, but rather two party labels, under which many parties group themselves. Parties in America have a devolved, state-by-state, legal, and ideological basis. State parties are not franchises of a central, national party, like so many fast-food restaurants serving the same menu everywhere. Rather, they are fried clams in New England and catfish in the south, intimately expressive of sectional ideas and histories, of local populations and cultures. This is possible because we are a federal system, and hence have not a two-party but a hundred-party system (more or less).

A claim like this one deserves a longer exposition, and a more careful defense, than can be supplied here. If it turns out to have merit, however, it might explain how the federal structure of the union supplies some of the extraordinary flexibility and adaptiveness that our political system undeniably seems to have.

A second possible source of adaptiveness is a feature of the American political system that is frequently criticized: its litigiousness. The existence of a Bill of Rights, guaranteeing citizens protection against the government, to a large extent also guarantees a strong form of judicial review. These rights provide incentives to litigate, and rather soon in our constitutional history produced a political system deeply influenced by lawyers and legalities. Many commentators have observed that other democratic political systems make do with fewer lawyers and with less-influential judges. And so they do. But they are also systems far more capable of solving problems concerning the assignment of prerogatives and responsibilities through the strength of their status systems. The American legal system, in part, is a response to the weakness of social status as a means of giving Americans their place in the world. It provides, in effect, for the renegotiation of status, and a capacity to renegotiate is a form of adaptiveness.

If the American political system is unusually long-lasting and unusually adaptive, as I believe, it seems to be so because it is unusually complex, providing numerous alternative points of entry, access, and innovation for those fortunate enough to be able to take advantage of them. The observant reader of the pages that follow will find numerous examples of the exercise of power, exercised by a wide range of actors who are diversely situated in the system. These actors can sometimes act alone, but more frequently they must persuade, lobby, build coalitions, and engage in cooperative behavior. These are signs of a complex political system, one which requires the mastery of process in order to understand it, or influence it. Actors in the American political drama, no matter how compelling, are, in the end, the creatures of process. And there are a great many of them. The sheer size of the cast of players in the American political system makes it unusual in a comparative perspective. Each and every one of the fifty state capitals has a full complement of political actors who make policy pertaining to health, welfare, education, transportation, the maintenance of public order, local economic growth, and other issues of intimate day-to-day public concern. And then there are the thousands of policy-makers—large and small—executive, legislative, and judicial, who influence the outcomes of national government.

The sheer size of American government, over and above its great complexity, has no real analogue anywhere in the world. Nations larger than our own—and there are only three—are governed by relatively tiny oligarchies. Nations smaller than ours are mostly governed by oligarchies as well, but those nations that are democracies are nevertheless served by rather small and close-knit political classes. It is common to find in the annals of these democratic nation-states that political rivals of the same generation were school-mates—the relationships among key actors in the political class having been cemented long before any of them came to power. The analyst of American politics who expects to find a similar close-knit framework in the United States will be disappointed.

One consequence of the extraordinary properties of the American political system is that it requires a great deal of attention from analysts. Analogies with the rest of the systems of the world will usually not do. And as a literature on American politics has developed, some contributions have proven to be especially helpful in getting a grasp on how this sizeable, long-lasting, complex, and adaptive system works—and how its parts fit into a whole. Some of those contributions are among the articles reprinted here.

FOREWORD

TO THE FIRST EDITION

BY

THEODORE J. LOWI

In music, the term *classic* refers to the age of Haydn and Mozart because that was the period when musical forms, instruments, and ensembles became standardized, providing the framework for most subsequent Western musical composition and performance. *Classic* was not intended to refer to superior results; nor was it intended to distinguish between serious music and popular music. As one music historian put it, "To group all music which does not come under the head of popular music as classical is a mark of lack of cultivation."

This musical usage is consistent with the *Oxford English Dictionary*, where, although the primary definition identifies *classic* as referring to things of the highest quality, the brief history of its usage affirms that the meaning of *classic* arises out of references to "classes of colleges or schools." It is probable that this notion influenced the extension of the word to the ancient authors themselves, as studied in school or college. It is also probable that "the transference of the epithet from the first-class or standard writers in Greek and Latin to these languages themselves has been partly owing to the notion that the latter are intrinsically excellent or of the first order, in comparison to the modern tongues." Thus, a musical composition or an essay is referred to as "classic" if it is thought to perform as the model or standard for other works in a school of thought or a discipline.

But here's the rub. If a work qualifies as "classic" only when it is loyally imitated by all successors, then not even the masterpieces of the great Haydn or Mozart would fit the definition because significant departures from their model occurred even before they were cold in the grave. The classical era of music was rather quickly replaced by the romantic era. What we can say, however, is that the works of Haydn and Mozart were classic because, as the models, they set the terms of discourse, even for the dissenters and the innovators.

How are the essays in this volume classics? Each is considered something of a classic because it has helped shape the terms of discourse in political science. Each has served as a kind of jumping off point for other scholars. Actually, I should say jumping *on* point, since many scholars have found it useful to criticize one or more of these works as a way of distinguishing their own. In other words, a work can become a classic regardless of its weaknesses. The hundreds of citations of these works in the footnotes of others indicate how influential they have been. To cite another author's work does not mean it is being used as the authority to clinch the argument. More often, a work is cited because it has been integrated into the thought on that subject. Even a cursory reading of the essays in this volume shows that the authors were seeking to be part of a discourse outside the confines of their own research by saying something lasting about the conditions of political life—especially about the conditions of that most delicate of all political specimens, institutionalized democracy.

In the introduction to his own classic work, *American Capitalism*, John Kenneth Galbraith characterized the U.S. economy by observing that "such are the aerodynamics and wing-loading of the bumblebee that, in principle, it cannot fly. It does, and the knowledge that it defies the august authority of Issac Newton and Orville Wright must keep the bee in constant fear of a crack-up."[1] Such a comparison is more appropriate for the American polity, because it has been relatively stable for over two hundred years despite the fact that American society and the American economy have been unstable. To add to the mystery, American democracy itself was built on contradictions: How is it possible to balance free thought and free choice with the requirements of public order? In a representative legislature? But is it possible to set up a legislature that gives equality of access to policymaking and still makes important decisions in time to meet the collective needs of an immensely complex society? And how can we have intelligent policymakers if a very substantial fraction of the American electorate is ignorant of the issues? Or an accountable bureaucracy without giving its leader, the president, powers far in excess of what a legislature can oversee or the people or the courts will accept?

Political scientists address themselves to these difficult issues with one hand tied behind their backs; that is, they are trying to study with scientific precision matters as complex and ever-changing as the institutions of government. Science requires analysis, it has its own language—that of variables and hypotheses—and it holds to its own standards of truth, which presume strict canons of evidence and demonstration, and an attitude of utmost objectivity. Few political scientists want to reject the scientific method, but they use it at a heavy cost. While being scientific, political scientists sacrifice at least some concern for the questions of history, context, and value, which attend all political issues. Does this mean that we yield to others the joy of confrontation with big questions, even when our findings may bear on them?

The authors in this collection have indicated an unwillingness to yield. But this does not mean they have abandoned their discipline. An outstanding characteristic of these selections, especially those drawn from the professional political science of the twentieth century, is that each started on a fairly solid evidentiary base and each *lifted the discourse* from that base to an entirely different

[1]John Kenneth Galbraith, *American Capitalism*, second edition, revised (Boston: Houghton Mifflin, 1956), p. 1.

language—from a language of variables to a language of argument, from a language of causes to a language of consequences. That, to me, is the secret of a classic, whether it succeeds or whether it fails; and that is the only way to make political science interesting.

Lifting the discourse toward the larger consequences that are of concern to the whole political community also makes authors more vulnerable than if they stayed within the confines of what has been carefully studied. As Woodrow Wilson said in 1911 in his address as president of the American Political Science Association, "There is no such thing as an expert in human relationships."[2] Inevitably, those who seek to engage in the larger, continuing discourse concerning human—and political—relationships must go a considerable distance beyond their professional competence.

Not everyone wants to take such a risk, but those who do have something in common: They are both teachers and scholars. Although four of the six pre-twentieth century authors represented here—Madison, Hamilton, Chief Justice Marshall, and de Tocqueville—were not academicians, they were, in their own way teachers of politics. For example, Madison and Hamilton addressed their arguments in *Federalist* #10 and #78 to the New York voters and the members of the New York State Assembly who were polarized over whether to ratify the new Constitution. Alexis de Tocqueville wrote about democracy in the America of the 1830s but aimed his argument at the French public. All the others, including the late nineteenth-century authors Woodrow Wilson and Lord Bryce, were card-carrying academic political scientists (with the exception of a half dozen who took Ph.D.s in some related academic field but addressed a large number of their writings to political scientists); and all but one had a career in college teaching.

Is this dominance by teacher-scholars merely a reflection of editorial bias? I doubt it, because the primary interest of the editors is to provide selections, regardless of the source or author, most likely to be considered essential reading by the largest segment of the relevant market, namely, the professors who select books and students who are assigned to purchase and read them. I think the explanation is to be found in the creative contradiction faced by college teachers who embrace their discipline by carrying on a parallel career in research and writing. Writing for the discipline of political science subjects the author to the anonymous, professional peer review process of scholarly journals and book publishing. The college classroom subjects the teacher to the contrary pressure of trying to transcend the methods and results of research in the discipline by explaining its value to students. College students require of their teachers at least some concern for consequential argument as well as causal analysis. They want to know "So what?" In the classroom, professors rarely can talk down to their students; generally they have to talk *up* to their students because they have the difficult task of bringing specialized research and unspecialized students to a community of common concern: how we govern ourselves.

[2]Raymond Seidelman, with the assistance of Edward J. Harpham, *Disenchanted Realists: Political Science and the American Crisis* (Albany: State University of New York Press, 1985).

A teacher's attempt to be memorable by being consequential is the important bridge between the down-to-earth science of our research and the more elevated argument of our teaching. The contradiction between the stringencies of science and the goal of a higher, more consequence-oriented level of discourse is not only creative, it is also invaluable. If in the process we reveal our incompetence, that is in itself good teaching, because it encourages students to join the process as bona fide participants.

In the preface to his intellectual history of political science (*The Tragedy of Political Science,* 1984) David Ricci observes that with the rise of academic political science, "The line of first-rate thinkers in the Western tradition came to an end." Those whose writings form the basis for the history of political science—from Plato and Aristotle to Marx and Mill—were not the product of an academic environment, though some of them did teach for a living. As Ricci put it, "The longer I thought about the declining number of great thinkers and the growing prominence of universities, the more I was convinced that these two trends must be significantly related."[3] It is difficult to disagree with Ricci's contention that the twentieth century has yet to produce a single political thinker of the stature of a Marx or Mill, the last of the great thinkers before political writing and teaching became organized into the discipline of political science. But it would be equally difficult for him to disagree with the contention that in the 2,000-plus years between Plato and Mill, *no* country or century—not even the Greece of classical antiquity—could lay claim to many great thinkers. Great thinkers just don't come along very often. And it's even possible that their appearance may drop still further because of the tendency of both democracy and science to reduce issues to manageable proportions, while thinkers tend to magnify issues. America's greatest thinkers all appeared at the time of our founding, with the possible exception of Abraham Lincoln and a half dozen members of the U.S. Supreme Court—and all for the same reason: They confronted issues too big to trivialize, and they crafted their responses accordingly.

Modern academic political scientists from Woodrow Wilson to the present, including all the contemporary authors in this volume, have overcome many of the constraints of science and democracy, and although there are still no Aristotles or Rousseaus, we can consider ourselves keepers of the flame. If enough political scientists can transcend the discipline without unsciencing it, we can maintain a discourse worthy of the great thinkers to come—who may be in our classrooms at this very moment. We cannot yet know who they are, and we cannot create them. But we can encourage them by exposing them to the best thinking our field of study can offer.

[3]David Ricci, *The Tragedy of Political Science: Politics, Scholarship, and Democracy* (New Haven: Yale University Press, 1984).

PART ONE

POLITICAL CULTURE AND TRADITIONS

American and foreign observers have long considered government and politics in the United States to be unique. This uniqueness is suggested by structural features such as a written constitution, a two-party system, an elaborate separation of powers, a bicameral legislature, federalism, and judicial review—features that are not found together in other political systems. But the unique qualities of the American polity reach well beyond structures and institutions; they go to the very core of the United States' political culture.

Political culture involves the ways in which the members of a political community think about and evaluate their government and politics. Although different scholars have stressed various keys to understanding the United States' political culture, the classic interpretations tend to stress two related elements—equality and constitutionalism.

The first selection on political culture is drawn from the seminal work of Alexis de Tocqueville, whom some consider still the keenest observer of the American political community. In *Democracy in America* (Vol. I, 1838; Vol. II, 1840), this visitor from France identified equality as the fundamental aspect of the developing American political culture. In perhaps his best-known words, Tocqueville wrote, "The great advantage of the Americans is that they have arrived at a state of democracy without having to endure a democratic revolution; and that they are born equal, instead of becoming so." Equality stemmed from the attitudes and values of the early settlers, from an abundance of land, and from the Americans' laws of inheritance, which encouraged the division of estates among heirs. Unlike European societies, there were no fixed stratifications, such as aristocrats and peasants. Moreover, in Tocqueville's view, there was great mobility among Americans: "In America," he writes, "most of the rich men were formerly poor. . . ." But equality extended beyond wealth; it included education and social conditions generally. For the most part, Tocqueville was comparing the equality among American citizens to the inequality among Europeans. However, in passages not reprinted here, he noted that racial inequality posed a threat to the United States and that men and women were expected—indeed, required—to play different roles and to engage in separate pursuits.

Although Tocqueville presents a sound beginning for the student of American political culture, Louis Hartz is correct in pointing out that "no school of American historians has ever come out of the well known work of the greatest foreign critic America ever had—Tocqueville." Hence, while frequently rooted in Tocqueville's work, intellectual traditions concerning American political culture have frequently moved beyond his formulations in addressing additional dimensions.

In his *Liberal Tradition in America* (1955), Hartz argues that what sets America apart from other countries is its liberal consensus. Although "liberalism" eludes a precise definition, Hartz uses it to refer to a democratic ethos stressing individual rights, political equality, and limited government. In his view, this liberalism developed naturally from the absence of a feudal past in America. Essentially, a nonfeudal society lacks both a genuine revolutionary tradition and a tradition of reaction; these conditions make it possible for what would be revolutionary elsewhere (liberalism) to be a matter of consensus in a political community such as the United States.

Seymour Martin Lipset also addresses the unique qualities of the American political experience. In *The First New Nation* (1963), he compares the emergence of the United States as an independent state in the eighteenth century to the experiences of new nations in the twentieth century. He finds some fundamental similarities in the challenges facing all states upon gaining independence. However, several elements set the newly formed United States apart. Perhaps most important, in Lipset's view, was "the fact that the weight of ancient tradition which is present in almost all of the contemporary new states was largely absent. It was not only a new nation, it was a new society, much less bound to the customs and values of the past than any nation of Europe." Lipset believes that the values of the new society were proclaimed in the preeminent document of the American Revolution—the Declaration of Independence—and that these values have continuously influenced American social and political behavior.

The Constitution is the cornerstone of U.S. government and politics. An early recognition of the role the Constitution could play, or a "constitutionalist" approach, was manifested in the writings of "Publius," the pseudonym Alexander Hamilton, James Madison, and John Jay used in writing *The Federalist Papers* (1787–1788). Regardless of the particular topic under discussion, Publius' basic assumption is that a written constitution can serve to structure both the operation of a nation's government and the nature of its politics. *The Federalist Papers* included here state what can be taken as the Founders' general theory of government and politics. In their treatment of republicanism, the separation of powers, and the nature of executive power, they reveal a great deal about the theories and concerns held by the Constitution's framers, as well as their views of human nature and the ambitions and motives of politicians.

1

ALEXIS DE TOCQUEVILLE

EQUALITY OF CONDITION

Alexis de Tocqueville (1805–1859), a French aristocrat, visited the United States for nine months in 1831. Ostensibly his purpose was to study American prison systems. Actually, Tocqueville was keenly interested in studying the strengths and weaknesses of American democracy, which was unlike any European political system. The French Revolution of 1789 had altered the status and future of the French aristocracy and deeply touched Tocqueville's life. He sought to understand how democracy could function and what its impact on American political, economic, and social life had been. The Jacksonian era, during which he visited, was characterized by egalitarianism and the rule of the "common man." During this era, several restrictions on male suffrage had been removed and property requirements for officeholding had been rescinded. Tocqueville discussed his observations of every aspect of American life in the two volume Democracy in America *(Vol. I, 1835; Vol. II, 1840). He also wrote* The Old Regime and the Revolution *(1856), which enhanced understanding of the French Revolution. In the following selection, composed of excerpts from* Democracy in America, *Tocqueville marvels at the equality of the citizenry and discusses obstacles to the development of an American aristocracy. He comments on how much easier it is to establish democracy when men are born politically equal and there is no landed aristocracy to dismantle.*

Among the novel objects that attracted my attention during my stay in the United States, nothing struck me more forcibly than the general equality of conditions. I readily discovered the prodigious influence which this primary fact exercises on the whole course of society, by giving a certain direction to public opinion, and a certain tenor to the laws; by imparting new maxims to the governing powers, and peculiar habits to the governed.

I speedily perceived that the influence of this fact extends far beyond the political character and the laws of the country, and that it has no less empire over civil society than over the government; it creates opinions, engenders sentiments, suggests the ordinary practices of life, and modifies whatever it does not produce.

The more I advanced in the study of American society, the more I perceived that the equality of conditions is the fundamental fact from which all others seem to be derived, and the central point at which all my observations constantly terminated. . . .

The emigrants who fixed themselves on the shores of America in the beginning of the seventeenth century, severed the democratic principle from all the principles which repressed it in the old communities of Europe, and transplanted it unalloyed to the New World. It has there been allowed to spread in perfect freedom, and to put forth its consequences in the laws by influencing the manners of the country.

* * *

THE STRIKING CHARACTERISTIC OF THE SOCIAL CONDITION OF THE ANGLO-AMERICANS IS ITS ESSENTIAL DEMOCRACY

Many important observations suggest themselves upon the social condition of the Anglo-Americans; but there is one which takes precedence of all the rest. The social condition of the Americans is eminently democratic; this was its character at the foundation of the colonies, and is still more strongly marked at the present day.

I have stated . . . that great equality existed among the emigrants who settled on the shores of New England. The germ of aristocracy was never planted in that part of the Union. The only influence which obtained there was that of intellect; the people were used to reverence certain names as the emblems of knowledge and virtue. Some of their fellow-citizens acquired a power over the rest which might truly have been called aristocratic, if it had been capable of invariable transmission from father to son.

This was the state of things to the east of the Hudson: to the southwest of that river, and in the direction of the Floridas, the case was different. In most of the states situated to the southwest of the Hudson some great English proprietors had settled, who had imported with them aristocratic principles and the English law of descent.* I have explained the reasons why it was impossible ever to establish a powerful aristocracy in America; these reasons existed with less force to the southwest of the Hudson. In the south, one man, aided by slaves, could cultivate a great extent of country: it was therefore common to see rich landed proprietors. But their influence was not altogether aristocratic as that term is understood in Europe, since they possessed no privileges; and the cultivation of their estates being carried on by slaves, they had no tenants depending on them, and consequently no patronage. Still, the great proprietors south of the Hudson constituted a superior class, having ideas and tastes of its own, and forming the centre of political action. This kind of aristocracy sympathized with the body of the people, whose passions and interests it easily embraced; but it was too weak and too short-lived to excite either love or hatred for itself. This was the class which headed the insurrection in the south, and furnished the best leaders of the American revolution.

At the period of which we are now speaking, society was shaken to its centre: the people, in whose name the struggle had taken place, conceived the desire of exercising the authority which it had acquired; its democratic tendencies were awakened; and having thrown off the yoke of the mother-country, it aspired to independence of every kind. The influence of individuals gradually ceased to be felt, and custom and law united together to produce the same result.

But the law of descent was the last step to equality. I am surprised that ancient and modern jurists have not attributed to this law a greater influence on human affairs. It is true that these laws belong to civil affairs: but they ought nevertheless to be placed at the head of all political institutions; for, while political laws are

*_Law of descent:_ law governing the transference of property, such as by inheritance. Distinguished from law governing the acquisition of property through purchase.

only the symbol of a nation's condition, they exercise an incredible influence upon its social state. They have, moreover, a sure and uniform manner of operating upon society, affecting, as it were, generations yet unborn.

Through their means man acquires a kind of preternatural power over the future lot of his fellow-creatures. When the legislator has once regulated the law of inheritance, he may rest from his labour. The machine once put in motion will go on for ages, and advance, as if self-guided, toward a given point. When framed in a particular manner, this law unites, draws together, and vests property and power in a few hands: its tendency is clearly aristocratic. On opposite principles its action is still more rapid; it divides, distributes, and disperses both property and power.

* * *

In the United States [the law of inheritance] has nearly completed its work of destruction, and there we can best study its results. The English laws concerning the transmission of property were abolished in almost all the states at the time of the revolution. The law of entail* was so modified as not to interrupt the free circulation of property. The first having passed away, estates began to be parcelled out; and the change became more and more rapid with the progress of time. At this moment, after a lapse of little more than sixty years, the aspect of society is totally altered; the families of the great landed proprietors are almost all commingled with the general mass. In the state of New York, which formerly contained many of these, there are but two who still keep their heads above the stream; and they must shortly disappear. The sons of these opulent citizens have become merchants, lawyers, or physicians. Most of them have lapsed into obscurity. The last trace of hereditary ranks and distinctions is destroyed—the law of partition† has reduced all to one level.

I do not mean that there is any deficiency of wealthy individuals in the United States; I know of no country, indeed, where the love of money has taken stronger hold on the affections of men, and where a profounder contempt is expressed for the theory of the permanent equality of property. But wealth circulates with inconceivable rapidity, and experience shows that it is rare to find two succeeding generations in the full enjoyment of it. . . .

It is not only the fortunes of men which are equal in America; even their acquirements partake in some degree of the same uniformity. I do not believe there is a country in the world where, in proportion to the population, there are so few uninstructed, and at the same time so few learned individuals. Primary instruction is within the reach of everybody; superior instruction is scarcely to be obtained by any. This is not surprising; it is in fact the necessary consequence of what we have advanced above. Almost all the Americans are in easy circumstances, and can therefore obtain the first elements of human knowledge.

**Law of entail:* law limiting the succession of property to specified heirs rather than to all heirs.
†Law of partition: law guiding the division of real or personal property among joint owners.

In America there are comparatively few who are rich enough to live without a profession. Every profession requires an apprenticeship, which limits the time of instruction to the early years of life. At fifteen they enter upon their calling, and thus their education ends at the age when ours begins. Whatever is done afterward, is with a view to some special and lucrative object; a science is taken up as a matter of business, and the only branch of it which is attended to is such as admits of an immediate practical application.

In America most of the rich men were formerly poor: most of those who now enjoy leisure were absorbed in business during their youth; the consequence of which is, that when they might have had a taste for study they had no time for it, and when the time is at their disposal they have no longer the inclination.

There is no class, then, in America in which the taste for intellectual pleasures is transmitted with hereditary fortune and leisure, and by which the labours of the intellect are held in honour. Accordingly there is an equal want of the desire and the power of application to these objects.

A middling standard is fixed in America for human knowledge. All approach as near to it as they can; some as they rise, others as they descend. Of course, an immense multitude of persons are to be found who entertain the same number of ideas on religion, history, science, political economy, legislation, and government. The gifts of intellect proceed directly from God, and man cannot prevent their unequal distribution. But in consequence of the state of things which we have here represented, it happens, that although the capacities of men are widely different, as the Creator has doubtless intended they should be, they are submitted to the same method of treatment.

In America the aristocratic element has always been feeble from its birth; and if at the present day it is not actually destroyed, it is at any rate so completely disabled that we can scarcely assign to it any degree of influence in the course of affairs.

The democratic principle, on the contrary, has gained so much strength by time, by events, and by legislation, as to have become not only predominant but all-powerful. There is no family or corporate authority, and it is rare to find even the influence of individual character enjoy any durability.

America, then, exhibits in her social state a most extraordinary phenomenon. Men are there seen on a greater equality in point of fortune and intellect, or in other words, more equal in their strength, than in any other country of the world, or, in any age of which history has preserved the remembrance.

POLITICAL CONSEQUENCES OF THE SOCIAL CONDITION OF THE ANGLO-AMERICANS

The political consequences of such a social condition as this are easily deducible.

It is impossible to believe that equality will not eventually find its way into the political world as it does everywhere else. To conceive of men remaining for ever unequal upon one single point, yet equal on all others, is impossible; they must come in the end to be equal upon all.

Now I know of only two methods of establishing equality in the political world: every citizen must be put in possession of his rights, or rights must be granted to no one. For nations which have arrived at the same stage of social existence as the Anglo-Americans, it is therefore very difficult to discover a medium between the sovereignty of all and the absolute power of one man: and it would be vain to deny that the social condition which I have been describing is equally liable to each of these consequences.

There is, in fact, a manly and lawful passion for equality, which excites men to wish all to be powerful and honoured. This passion tends to elevate the humble to the rank of the great; but there exists also in the human heart a depraved taste for equality, which impels the weak to attempt to lower the powerful to their own level, and reduces men to prefer equality in slavery to inequality with freedom. Not that those nations whose social condition is democratic naturally despise liberty; on the contrary, they have an instinctive love of it. But liberty is not the chief and constant object of their desires; equality is their idol: they make rapid and sudden efforts to obtain liberty, and if they miss their aim, resign themselves to their disappointment; but nothing can satisfy them except equality, and rather than lose it they resolve to perish.

On the other hand, in a state where the citizens are nearly on an equality, it becomes difficult for them to preserve their independence against the aggressions of power. No one among them being strong enough to engage singly in the struggle with advantage, nothing but a general combination can protect their liberty: and such a union is not always to be found.

From the same social position, then, nations may derive one or the other of two great political results; these results are extremely different from each other, but they may both proceed from the same cause.

The Anglo-Americans are the first who, having been exposed to this formidable alternative, have been happy enough to escape the dominion of absolute power. They have been allowed by their circumstances, their origin, their intelligence, and especially by their moral feeling, to establish and maintain the sovereignty of the people.

* * *

INDIVIDUALISM STRONGER AT THE CLOSE OF A DEMOCRATIC REVOLUTION THAN AT OTHER PERIODS

. . . An aristocracy seldom yields without a protracted struggle, in the course of which implacable animosities are kindled between the different classes of society. These passions survive the victory, and traces of them may be observed in the midst of the democratic confusion which ensues.

Those members of the community who were at the top of the late gradations of rank cannot immediately forget their former greatness; they will long regard themselves as aliens in the midst of the newly composed society. They look upon all those whom this state of society has made their equals as oppressors, whose destiny can excite no sympathy; they have lost sight of their former equals, and feel no longer bound by a common interest to their fate: each of them, standing aloof, thinks that he is reduced to care for himself alone. Those, on the contrary, who were formerly at the foot of the social scale, and who have been brought up to the common level by a sudden revolution, cannot enjoy their newly acquired independence without secret uneasiness; and if they meet with some of their former superiors on the same footing as themselves, they stand aloof from them with an expression of triumph and of fear. . . .

The great advantage of the Americans is that they have arrived at a state of democracy without having to endure a democratic revolution; and that they are born equal, instead of becoming so.

* * *

OF CERTAIN PECULIAR AND ACCIDENTAL CAUSES WHICH EITHER LEAD A PEOPLE TO COMPLETE CENTRALIZATION OF GOVERNMENT, OR WHICH DIVERT THEM FROM IT

. . . These observations explain why the supreme power is always stronger, and private individuals weaker, among a democratic people which has passed through a long and arduous struggle to reach a state of equality, than among a democratic community in which the citizens have been equal from the first. The example of the Americans completely demonstrates the fact. The inhabitants of the United States were never divided by any privileges; they have never known the mutual relation of master and inferior, and as they neither dread nor hate each other, they have never known the necessity of calling in the supreme power to manage their affairs. The lot of the Americans is singular: they have derived from the aristocracy of England the notion of private rights and the taste for local freedom; and they have been able to retain both the one and the other, because they have had no aristocracy to combat.

2

LOUIS HARTZ

THE CONCEPT OF A LIBERAL SOCIETY

The United States is a liberal society in the classical sense. It favors private property and relies on markets rather than on government to coordinate economic activity. In The Liberal Tradition in America *(1955, 1983) Louis Hartz brought a fresh perspective to the understanding of the peculiarities of American liberalism. He examined the liberal political ideology predominant during the founding period and the early evolution of the American state. When contrasted with Europe, he noted, the range of political ideas in American thought and discourse was narrow, with a strong preference for limited government. Despite serious political disagreements on some issues, there was a strong liberal consensus. Because Americans lack a feudal past, he said, they also lack the kind of revolutionary tradition associated with breaking feudal bonds. Americans have been singularly able to build their social and political systems on the basis of individualism, free markets, and limited government. Hartz speculated that a larger American role in the international arena after World War II might prompt Americans to come to terms with political ideas beyond classical liberalism. "The Concept of a Liberal Society," which follows, is the beginning of the 1955 edition of* The Liberal Tradition in America. *Hartz also wrote* The Founding of New Societies *(1964).*

1. AMERICA AND EUROPE

The analysis which this book contains is based on what might be called the storybook truth about American history: that America was settled by men who fled from the feudal and clerical oppressions of the Old World. If there is anything in this view, as old as the national folklore itself, then the outstanding thing about the American community in Western history ought to be the nonexistence of those oppressions, or since the reaction against them was in the broadest sense liberal, that the American community is a liberal community. We are confronted, as it were, with a kind of inverted Trotskyite* law of combined development, America skipping the feudal stage of history as Russia presumably skipped the liberal stage. I know that I am using broad terms broadly here. "Feudalism" refers technically to the institutions of the medieval era, and it is well known that aspects of the decadent feudalism of the later period, such as

**Trotskyite:* follower of the doctrines of Leon Trotsky (1879–1940), a Russian revolutionary and theorist. Trotsky was a strategist of the Bolshevik Revolution of 1917, which transformed Russia into a communist state. Trotsky argued later that the Bolsheviks had replaced one form of domination with another and had betrayed the purposes of the revolution and the workers. Trotsky advocated adherence to the concept of worldwide revolution and socialism. Josef Stalin's (1879–1953) chief rival for leadership after the death of Vladimir Lenin (1870–1924), Trotsky was expelled from Russia in 1927 and murdered at Stalin's instigation in 1940.

primogeniture,* entail, and quitrents,† were present in America even in the eighteenth century.[1] "Liberalism" is an even vaguer term, clouded as it is by all sorts of modern social reform connotations, and even when one insists on using it in the classic Lockian‡ sense, as I shall insist here, there are aspects of our original life in the Puritan colonies and the South which hardly fit its meaning. But these are the liabilities of any large generalization, danger points but not insuperable barriers. What in the end is more interesting is the curious failure of American historians, after repeating endlessly that America was grounded in escape from the European past, to interpret our history in the light of that fact. There are a number of reasons for this which we shall encounter before we are through, but one is obvious at the outset: the separation of the study of American from European history and politics. Any attempt to uncover the nature of an American society without feudalism can only be accomplished by studying it in conjunction with a European society where the feudal structure and the feudal ethos did in fact survive. This is not to deny our national uniqueness, one of the reasons curiously given for studying America alone, but actually to affirm it. How can we know the uniqueness of anything except by contrasting it with what is not unique? The rationale for a separate American study, once you begin to think about it, explodes the study itself.

In the end, however, it is not logic but experience, to use a Holmesian phrase, which exposes the traditional approach. We could use our uniqueness as an excuse for evading its study so long as our world position did not really require us to know much about it. Now that a whole series of alien cultures have crashed in upon the American world, shattering the peaceful landscape of Bancroft§ and Beard,‖ the old non sequitur simply will not do. When we need desperately to know the idiosyncrasies which interfere with our understanding of Europe, we can hardly break away from "European schemes" of analysis, as J. Franklin Jameson** urged American historians to do in 1891 (not that they ever really used them in the first place) on the ground that we are idiosyncratic. But the issue is deeper than foreign policy, for the world involvement has also brought to the

**Primogeniture*: common law rule of inheritance whereby the oldest male child has the right to an ancestor's estate, excluding both younger siblings, and other relatives.

†*quitrent*: rent paid by a tenant after which the tenant is free from any other rent.

‡*Lockian*: based on the theories of John Locke (1632–1704), an English philosopher whose work greatly influenced the Framers of the Constitution. In his most widely read book *Two Treatises of Government* (1690), Locke rejected the monarchy's claim to a divine rule and advocated a government resting on popular consent and natural rights.

§*Charles George Bancroft* (1800–1891): influential American historian noted for his ten-volume *History of the United States (1834–1875)*, *The American Revolution* (1874), and *History of the Formation of the Constitution of the USA* (1886), among others.

‖*Charles A. Beard* (1874–1948): major American historian who often relied on economic interpretation of past events and developments. With his wife, Mary Ritter Beard (1876–1946), he wrote numerous books, including *America in Mid-Passage* (1939) and *A Basic History of the United States* (1944). Other works are *The Supreme Court and the Constitution* (1962) and, perhaps best known, *An Economic Interpretation of the Constitution of the United States* (1913).

***John Franklin Jameson* (1859–1937): noted historian and professor. Among his books are *History of Historical Writing in America* (1891), *A Dictionary of United States History* (1894), and *The American Revolution Considered as a Social Movement* (1926).

surface of American life great new domestic forces which must remain inexplicable without comparative study. It has redefined, as Communism shows, the issue of our internal freedom in terms of our external life. So in fact it is the entire crisis of our time which compels us to make the journey to Europe and back which ends in the discovery of the American liberal world.

2. "NATURAL LIBERALISM": THE FRAME OF MIND

One of the central characteristics of a nonfeudal society is that it lacks a genuine revolutionary tradition, the tradition which in Europe has been linked with the Puritan and French revolutions: that it is "born equal," as Tocqueville* said. And this being the case, it lacks also a tradition of reaction: lacking Robespierre it lacks Maistre, lacking Sydney it lacks Charles II.† Its liberalism is what Santayana‡ called, referring to American democracy, a "natural" phenomenon. But the matter is curiously broader than this, for a society which begins with Locke, and thus transforms him, stays with Locke, by virtue of an absolute and irrational attachment it develops for him, and becomes as indifferent to the challenge of socialism in the later era as it was unfamiliar with the heritage of feudalism in the earlier one. It has within it, as it were, a kind of self-completing mechanism, which ensures the universality of the liberal idea. Here, we shall see, is one of the places where Marx§ went wrong in his historical analysis, attributing as he did the emergence of the socialist ideology to the objective movement of economic forces. Actually socialism is largely an ideological phenomenon, arising out of the principles of class and the revolutionary liberal

Tocqueville: see page 5.

†*Maximilien de Robespierre* (1758–1794): a famed leader of the Jacobins, a radical political group that was active during the French Revolution (1789–1799). The Jacobins believed that the people could not be expected to willingly adopt the goals of the revolution and that the use of force toward that end was justified. The Jacobins ruled France in a dictatorial manner by suspending civil rights and political freedom in what became known as the Reign of Terror. Hundreds of thousands of dissenters were jailed, and over 17,000 people were executed. The Reign of Terror ended when Robespierre himself was executed in 1794. (See *French Revolution*, page 17.) *Joseph Marie, Comte de Maistre* (1754–1821): French essayist and political philosopher. He was skeptical of liberal and democratic ideas and defended the doctrine of the divine right of kings. *Algernon Sydney* (1622–1683): English statesman, wrote *Discourses Concerning Government* (1698), an argument against the monarchy and for democracy. *Charles II* (1630–1685): King of England, Ireland, and Scotland from 1660 to 1685. Like his father Charles I (1600–1649), he believed strongly in the divine right of kings.

‡*George Santayana* (1863–1952): Spanish-born poet and philosopher who wrote extensively throughout his life. Santayana's published verse includes *Lucifer, a Theological Tragedy* (1898) and *The Hermit of Carmel* (1901). His numerous philosophical works include: *The Life of Reason, or the Phases of Human Progress*, in five volumes (1905–1906): *Realms of Being*, in four volumes (1920–1940); and *Dominations and Powers, Reflections on Liberty, Society and Government* (1951).

§*Karl Marx* (1818–1883): German philosopher, sociologist, and economist who, together with Friedrich Engels (1820–1895), developed a revolutionary theory of history predicting that societies would progress through stages of political and economic development from feudalism to capitalism to socialism and communism. Together, Marx and Engels wrote *The Communist Manifesto* (1848), which popularized their ideas. Marx elaborated more thoroughly on his theory in *Das Kapital* (1867), which has come to be known as the "bible of socialism." Marxism has served as the ideological foundation of many revolutionary movements throughout the twentieth century.

revolt against them which the old European order inspired. It is not accidental that America which has uniquely lacked a feudal tradition has uniquely lacked also a socialist tradition. The hidden origin of socialist thought everywhere in the West is to be found in the feudal ethos. The *ancien régime*[*] inspires Rousseau; both inspire Marx.

Which brings us to the substantive quality of the natural liberal mind. And this poses no easy problem. For when the words of Locke are used and a prior Filmer[†] is absent, how are we to delineate the significance of the latter fact? In politics men who make speeches do not go out of their way to explain how differently they would speak if the enemies they had were larger in size or different in character. On the contrary whatever enemies they fight they paint in satanic terms, so that a problem sufficiently difficult to begin with in a liberal society becomes complicated further by the inevitable perspectives of political battle. Take the American Revolution. With John Adams[‡] identifying the Stamp Act with the worst of the historic European oppressions, how can we distinguish the man from Lilburne or the philosophers of the French Enlightenment?[§] And yet if we study the American liberal language in terms of intensity and emphasis, if we look for silent omissions as well as explicit inclusions, we begin to see a pattern emerging that smacks distinctively of the New World. It has a quiet, matter of fact quality, it does not understand the meaning of sovereign power, the bourgeois[‖] class passion is scarcely present, the sense of the past is altered, and there is about it all, as compared with the European pattern, a vast and almost charming innocence of mind. Twain's "Innocents Abroad" is a pretty relevant concept, for the psyche that springs from social war and social revolution is given to far suspicions and sidelong glances that the American liberal cannot easily understand. Possibly this is what people mean when they say that European thought is "deeper" than American, though anyone who tries to grapple with America in Western terms will wonder whether the term "depth" is the proper one to use. There can be an appalling complexity to innocence, especially if your point of departure is guilt.

[*] *ancien régime:* term used to describe the political, economic, and social system of France before the French revolution (1789–1799).

[†] *Sir Robert Filmer* (1590–1653): English writer who defended the doctrine of the divine right of kings in *Patriarcha* (1680). He argued that the separation of religious and civil organizations would be dangerous to the common good.

[‡] *John Adams* (1735–1826): active participant in the Continental Congress, which produced the Declaration of Independence in 1776. He was the first vice-president of the United States (1789–1797) and the second president (1797–1801). Although his earlier political views were considered radical by some, Adams was a conservative by the time he became president. He lost the election of 1800 to the more liberally inclined Thomas Jefferson. Adams' son, John Quincy Adams (1767–1848), was elected president in 1824.

[§] *French Enlightenment:* philosophic movement of the eighteenth century, characterized by a critical stance toward traditional authority and institutions and a belief in the use of reason as the means to progress. The movement prompted changes in religion, politics, science, and education.

[‖] *Bourgeoisie:* term used to describe the middle class, whose economic success and rise to political power under capitalism was based on profits from commercial and industrial enterprises. The bourgeoisie are distinguished from the traditional aristocracy, whose power and prestige were based on heredity and the ownership of land.

Now if the *ancien régime* is not present to begin with, one thing follows automatically: it does not return in a blaze of glory. It does not flower in the nineteenth century in a Disraeli* or a Ballanche,† however different from each other these men may be. I do not mean to imply that no trace of the feudal urge, no shadow whatsoever of Sir Walter Scott,‡ has been found on the hills and plains of the New World. One can get into a lot of useless argument if he affirms the liberalness of a liberal society in absolute mathematical fashion. The top strata of the American community, from the time of Peggy Hutchinson to the time of Margaret Kennedy, have yearned for the aristocratic ethos. But instead of exemplifying the typical Western situation, these yearnings represent an inversion of it. America has presented the world with the peculiar phenomenon, not of a frustrated middle class, but of a "frustrated aristocracy"—of men, Aristotelian-like, trying to break out of the egalitarian confines of middle class life but suffering guilt and failure in the process. The South before the Civil War is the case par excellence of this, though New England of course exemplifies it also. Driven away from Jefferson by abolitionism, the Fitzhughs§ of the ante-bellum era actually dared to ape the doctrinal patterns of the Western reaction, of Disraeli and Bonald.‖ But when Jefferson is traditional, European traditionalism is a curious thing indeed. The Southerners were thrown into fantastic contradictions by their iconoclastic conservatism, by what I have called the "Reactionary Enlightenment," and after the Civil War for good historical reasons they fell quickly into oblivion. The South, as John Crowe Ransom** has said, has been the part of America closest to Old World Europe, but it has never really been Europe. It has been an alien child in a liberal family, tortured and confused, driven to a fantasy life which, instead of disproving the power of Locke in America, portrays more poignantly than anything else the tyranny he has had.

**Benjamin Disraeli, Earl of Beaconsfield* (1804–1881): English statesman who is credited with having led the British conservative (Tory) party toward political reform—including acceptance of broad adult suffrage. Disraeli's conception of Toryism stressed the common interests of the working class and the aristocracy in their struggles with the rising bourgeoisie. Disraeli served as prime minister in 1868 and from 1874 to 1880.

†*Pierre Simon Ballanche* (1776–1847): French Christian philosopher and writer.

‡*Sir Walter Scott* (1771–1832): Scottish poet and novelist who became a baronet in 1820. Scott had a vivid imagination that gave life to his numerous historical novels, among which *Waverly* (1814), *Ivanhoe* (1819), and *The Red Gauntlet* (1824) were the most highly acclaimed. He was famous for his romantic epic poems, including *The Lady of the Last Minstrel* (1805), *Marmion* (1808), and *The Lady of the Lake* (1810).

§*Fitzhughs:* followers of George Fitzhugh (1806–1881), a Virginia lawyer and an ardent supporter of slavery before the Civil War. He argued in *Sociology for the South* (1854) and in *Cannibals All!* (1857) that slavery was normal and preferable to the "failed" system of laissez-faire capitalism practiced in the North and in England.

‖*Louis-Gabriel-Ambroisa, Viscomte de Bonald* (1754–1840): member of the French Chamber of Deputies from 1815–1822, and a persuasive conservative theorist who defended the divine right of the monarchy and the social position of noblemen.

***John Crowe Ransom* (1888–1974): American poet and professor of poetry at Vanderbilt University (1914–1937) and Kenyon College (1937–1958). He is the author of *Two Gentlemen in Bonds* (1927), *I'll Take My Stand* (1930), and *Beating the Bushes* (1972).

But is not the problem of Fitzhugh at once the problem of De Leon?* Here we have one of the great and neglected relationships in American history: the common fecklessness of the Southern "feudalists" and the modern socialists. It is not accidental, but something rooted in the logic of all of Western history, that they should fail alike to leave a dent in the American liberal intelligence. For if the concept of class was meaningless in its Disraelian form, and if American liberalism had never acquired it in its bourgeois form, why should it be any more meaningful in its Marxian form? This secret process of ideological transmission is not, however, the only thing involved. Socialism arises not only to fight capitalism but remnants of feudalism itself, so that the failure of the Southern Filmerians, in addition to setting the pattern for the failure of the later Marxists, robbed them in the process of a normal ground for growth. Could De Leon take over the liberal goal of extended suffrage as Lasalle† did in Germany or the crusade against the House of Lords as the Labor Party did in England? Marx himself noted the absence of an American feudalism, but since he misinterpreted the complex origins of European socialism in the European *ancien régime*, he did not grasp the significance of it.

Surely, then, it is a remarkable force: this fixed, dogmatic liberalism of a liberal way of life. It is the secret root from which have sprung many of the most puzzling of American cultural phenomena. Take the unusual power of the Supreme Court and the cult of constitution worship on which it rests. Federal factors apart, judicial review as it has worked in America would be inconceivable without the national acceptance of the Lockian creed, ultimately enshrined in the Constitution, since the removal of high policy to the realm of adjudication implies a prior recognition of the principles to be legally interpreted. At the very moment that Senator Benton‡ was hailing the rise of America's constitutional fetishism, in France Royer Collard§ and the Doctrinaires were desperately trying to build precisely the same atmosphere around the Restoration Charter of 1814,‖ but being a patchwork of Maistre** and Rousseau,†† that constitutional docu-

**Daniel De Leon* (1852–1914): political activist who came to the United States from Europe in 1872. He joined the Knights of Labor in 1888 and the Socialist Labor party in 1890. As the result of a split in the organization, he led the formation of the Socialist Trade and Labor Alliance in 1895. The organization was a forerunner of the contemporary Socialist party.

†*Ferdinand Lasalle* (1825–1864): German socialist and revolutionary.

‡*Thomas Hart Benton* (1782–1858): Democratic senator from Missouri (1821–1851) and a member of the United States House of Representatives (1853–1855).

§*Pierre-Paul Royer Collard* (1763–1845): French philosopher and statesman who led a small political party, Les Doctrinaires, after the restoration of Louis XVIII in 1814. Les Doctrinaires sought to mediate between factions supporting the divine right of kings on one side, and democracy on the other.

‖*Restoration Charter of 1814:* constitution decreed by Louis XVIII (1755–1824) on his restoration by the Allies in 1814. The Charter created a British-type monarchy and a legislative branch composed of a Chamber of Peers, appointed by the king, and a chamber of deputies, elected by limited male suffrage. A bill of rights, including freedom of religion, speech, and of the press, was also included.

***Joseph Marie, Comte de Maistre* (1754–1821): see footnote, page 13.

††*Jean Jacques Rousseau* (1712–1778): French political philosopher. Among his works is *The Social Contract* (1762), which had an influence on the thought of the Framers of the Constitution. Rousseau favored broad participation in political decision making as a means of attaining a political community's general will.

ment exploded in their faces in the July Revolution.* *Inter arma leges silent.*† If in England a marvelous organic cohesion has held together the feudal, liberal, and socialist ideas, it would still be unthinkable there that the largest issues of public policy should be put before nine Talmudic judges examining a single text. But this is merely another way of saying that law has flourished on the corpse of philosophy in America, for the settlement of the ultimate moral question is the end of speculation upon it. Pragmatism, interestingly enough America's great contribution to the philosophic tradition, does not alter this, since it feeds itself on the Lockian settlement. It is only when you take your ethics for granted that all problems emerge as problems of technique. Not that this is a bar in America to institutional innovations of highly non-Lockian kind. Indeed, as the New Deal‡ shows, when you simply "solve problems" on the basis of a submerged and absolute liberal faith, you can depart from Locke with a kind of inventive freedom that European Liberal reformers and even European socialists, dominated by ideological systems, cannot duplicate. But the main point remains: if Fitzhugh and De Leon were crucified by the American general will, John Marshall§ and John Dewey‖ flourished in consequence of their crucifixion. The moral unanimity of a liberal society reaches out in many directions.

At bottom it is riddled with paradox. Here is a Lockian doctrine which in the West as a whole is the symbol of rationalism, yet in America the devotion to it has been so irrational that it has not even been recognized for what it is: liberalism. There has never been a "liberal movement" or a real "liberal party" in America: we have only had the American Way of Life, a nationalist articulation of Locke which usually does not know that Locke himself is involved; and we did

***July Revolution:* The French Revolution lasted from 1789 to 1799. It transformed French society, and had a lasting effect on the rest of Europe and America as well. Various circumstances contributed to the revolution: financial problems of the government, interest in democracy, and dissatisfaction in the rising middle class. Although the first major event of the revolution, the formation of the National Assembly, occurred in May and June of 1789 at Versailles, *the July Revolution* is notable because it was the first mass action of the French Revolution. On July 14, 1789, a crowd in Paris stormed the Bastille, a fortress and prison, and before long, widespread uprisings against the nobility erupted throughout the countryside.

†*Inter arma leges silent:* Latin phrase meaning "In the midst of arms the laws are silent."

‡*New Deal:* term given to the domestic policies initiated by President Franklin D. Roosevelt (1882–1945) during his first administration (1933–1937). In response to the Great Depression, the federal government intervened broadly in the economy to regulate commercial and labor relations. Among the many New Deal enactments were the National Labor Relations Act (1935), the Social Security Act (1935), and the Fair Labor Standards Act (1937).

§*John Marshall* (1755–1835): chief justice of the United States (1801–1835). Marshall, who is often considered to have been the Supreme Court's greatest chief justice, left a lasting imprimatur on the powers of the national government and the judiciary. His opinion in *Marbury v. Madison* (an excerpt of which begins on page 463) established the power of judicial review—the judiciary's power to rule on the constitutionality of actions by the federal executive, the Congress, or the states. Marshall believed in the concept of a "living" Constitution; that is, interpretation of its content would vary over time. During his tenure on the Court, he wrote approximately one half of the Court's opinions.

‖*John Dewey* (1859–1952): American philosopher, psychologist, and education theorist. His educational theories were especially influential in the first half of the twentieth century.

not even get that until after the Civil War when the Whigs* of the nation, deserting the Hamiltonian tradition, saw the capital that could be made out of it. This is why even critics who have noticed America's moral unity have usually missed its substance. Ironically, "liberalism" is a stranger in the land of its greatest realization and fulfillment. But this is not all. Here is a doctrine which everywhere in the West has been a glorious symbol of individual liberty, yet in America its compulsive power has been so great that it has posed a threat to liberty itself. Actually Locke has a hidden conformitarian germ to begin with, since natural law tells equal people equal things, but when this germ is fed by the explosive power of modern nationalism, it mushrooms into something pretty remarkable. One can reasonably wonder about the liberty one finds in Burke.†

I believe that this is the basic ethical problem of a liberal society: not the danger of the majority which has been its conscious fear, but the danger of unanimity, which has slumbered unconsciously behind it: the "tyranny of opinion" that Tocqueville saw unfolding as even the pathetic social distinctions of the Federalist era collapsed before his eyes. But in recent times this manifestation of irrational Lockianism, or of "Americanism," to use a favorite term of the American Legion, one of the best expounders of the national spirit that Whiggery discovered after the Civil War, has neither slumbered nor been unconscious. It has been very much awake in a red scare hysteria which no other nation in the West has really been able to understand. And this suggests a very significant principle: that when a liberal community faces military and ideological pressure from without it transforms eccentricity into sin, and the irritating figure of the bourgeois gossip flowers into the frightening figure of an A. Mitchell Palmer‡ or a Senator McCarthy.§ Do we not find here, hidden away at the base of the American mind, one of the reasons why its legalism has been so imperfect a barrier against the violent moods of its mass Lockianism? If the latter is nourished by the former, how can we expect it to be strong? We say of the Supreme Court that it is courageous when it challenges Jefferson, but since in a liberal society the

**Whigs:* members of an American political party established in 1836 in opposition to the Democratic party and the policies of President Andrew Jackson (1767–1845). The Whigs successfully backed presidential candidates William Henry Harrison in 1840 and Zachary Taylor in 1848. The party later split over the issue of slavery.

†*Edmund Burke* (1729–1797): British political theorist who is considered to be a founder of modern political conservative thought. In his book *Reflections on the Recent Revolution in France* (1790), Burke critiqued the revolutionary upheaval in France and mounted a thoughtful defense of the institutions of private property, monarchy, and aristocracy. A critic of unfettered individualism, Burke was skeptical of mass democracy, fearing it would uproot essential social and political traditions.

‡*A. Mitchell Palmer* (1872–1936): U.S. attorney general (1919–1921). He directed his agents to conduct what became known as the "Palmer raids" (following the Russian Revolution of 1917) during which thousands of citizens and aliens who were suspected of sympathizing with anarchism or communism were arrested in the United States.

§*Joseph R. McCarthy* (1909–1957): U.S. senator from Wisconsin (1946–1957) who became famous for his virulent anticommunism. After World War II, McCarthy used the power of his office to accuse individuals and organizations of being "Reds." "McCarthyism" refers to the tactic of smearing political opponents by falsely labeling them disloyal to the United States. The McCarthy era (late 1940s to early 1950s) was a period intolerant of political ideas deemed leftist.

individualism of Hamilton is also a secret part of the Jeffersonian psyche, we make too much of this. The real test of the Court is when it faces the excitement both of Jefferson and Hamilton, when the Talmudic text is itself at stake, when the general will on which it feeds rises to the surface in anger. And here, brave as the Court has been at moments, its record has been no more heroic than the logic of the situation would suggest.

The decisive domestic issue of our time may well lie in the counter resources a liberal society can muster against this deep and unwritten tyrannical compulsion it contains. They exist. Given the individualist nature of the Lockian doctrine, there is always a logical impulse within it to transcend the very conformitarian spirit it breeds in a Lockian society: witness the spirit of Holmes* and Hand.† Given the fact, which we shall study at length later, that "Americanism" oddly disadvantages the Progressive‡ despite the fact that he shares it to the full, there is always a strategic impulse within him to transcend it: witness the spirit of Brandeis,§ Roosevelt, and Stevenson.‖ In some sense the tragedy of these movements has lain in the imperfect knowledge they have had of the enemy they face, above all in their failure to see their own unwitting contribution to his strength. The record of Brandeis was good on civil liberties, but anyone who studies his Progressive thought will see that he was, for good or bad, on that score a vital part of the compulsive "Americanism" which bred the hysteria he fought. The Progressive tradition, if it is to transcend the national general will, has got to realize, as it has not yet done, how deeply its own Jacksonian heroes have been rooted in it.

But the most powerful force working to shatter the American absolutism is, paradoxically enough, the very international involvement which intensifies it. This involvement is complex in its implications. If in the context of the Russian Revolution it elicits a domestic red scare, in the context of diplomacy it elicits an impulse to impose Locke everywhere. The way in which "Americanism" brings McCarthy together with Wilson is of great significance and it is, needless to say, another one of Progressivism's neglected roots in the Rousseauean tide it often seeks to stem. Thus to say that world politics shatters "Americanism" at the moment it intensifies it is to say a lot: it is to say that the basic horizons of the

**Oliver Wendell Holmes* (1841–1935): associate justice of the U.S. Supreme Court (1902–1932). Holmes is remembered for his terse opinions, blistering dissents, and his insistence that legal interpretation be based on empirical reality as apart from legal logic and precedent alone.

†*Learned Hand* (1872–1961): U.S. district court judge (1909–1924) and federal appeals court judge (1924–1954) who was an outspoken advocate of liberty and freedom. Many of Hand's papers were collected and published in *The Spirit of Liberty* (1952); his lectures can be found in *Bill of Rights* (1958).

‡*Progressives:* those American political activists who—during the period from 1900 to 1920—believed in the positive use of the state and other social institutions to regulate economic activity and improve the quality of the political process. The Progressive reform movement was decentralized and attempted to institute sweeping changes at all levels of government.

§*Louis D. Brandeis* (1856–1941): associate justice of the U.S. Supreme Court (1916–1939). Earlier in his career Brandeis developed a legal brief, thereafter dubbed a "Brandeis brief," which took account not only of the law but also of social scientific data and analysis that had implications for the relationship between the law and society.

‖*Adlai E. Stevenson* (1900–1965): unsuccessful Democratic party candidate for the presidency, 1952 and 1956; U.S. ambassador to the United Nations, 1961–1965; and son of Adlai E. Stevenson (1835–1914), who was vice-president of the United States under Grover Cleveland.

nation both at home and abroad are drastically widened by it. But has this not been the obvious experience of the recent past? Along with the fetish that has been made of Locke at peace conferences and at Congressional investigations has not Locke suffered a relativistic beating at the same time? You can turn the issue of Wilsonianism upside down: when has the nation appreciated more keenly the limits of its own cultural pattern as applied to the rest of the world? You can turn the issue of McCarthyism upside down: when has the meaning of civil liberties been more ardently understood than now? A dialectic process is at work, evil eliciting the challenge of a conscious good, so that in difficult moments progress is made. The outcome of the battle between intensified "Americanism" and new enlightenment is still an open question.

Historically the issue here is one for which we have little precedent. It raises the question of whether a nation can compensate for the uniformity of its domestic life by contact with alien cultures outside it. It asks whether American liberalism can acquire through external experience that sense of relativity, that spark of philosophy which European liberalism acquired through an internal experience of social diversity and social conflict. But if the final problem posed by the American liberal community is bizarre, this is merely a continuation of its historic record. That community has always been a place where the common issues of the West have taken strange and singular shape. . . .

NOTE

[1]There is no precise term for feudal institutions and feudal ideas as they persisted into the modern period amid the nation states and economic movements which progressively undermined them. The phrases "quasi-feudal" and "ancien régime" are nebulous enough. Some historians speak of "corporate society," but since a good deal more is involved than a congeries of associational units and since "corporate" is often used to describe current fascist states, the term has disadvantages. Under the circumstances it seems best to retain the simple word "feudal," realizing that its technical meaning is stretched when one applies it in the modern era.

3

SEYMOUR MARTIN LIPSET

FORMULATING A NATIONAL IDENTITY

Seymour Martin Lipset, Professor of Political Science and Sociology at Stanford University, has contributed to American political thought by analyzing the interrelationships between polity, society, and economy. "Formulating a National Identity" is an excerpt from his book The First New Nation: The United States in Historical and Comparative Perspective *(1963). Why was the founding of the United States so successful? Why has it been so difficult for contemporary nationalist movements to found democratic, egalitarian societies? Lipset discusses the relatively homogeneous characteristics of the population, with respect to political traditions, language, religion, education, and class. The opportunity to start a new nation without having to face the entrenched interests, existing structures, and ideology of an old order was a unique advantage. Other books written by Lipset include* Political Man: The Social Bases of Politics *(1960, 1981) and* Revolution and Counterrevolution: Change and Persistence in Social Structure *(1988).*

All states that have recently gained independence are faced with two interrelated problems, legitimating the use of political power and establishing national identity. And if it is a democratic polity they seek to establish, they must develop institutional and normative constraints upon efforts to inhibit organized opposition or to deny civil liberties to individual critics of those in power.

. . . National identity was formed under the aegis, first of a charismatic authority figure, and later under the leadership of a dominant "left wing" or revolutionary party led successively by three Founding Fathers. The pressures in new nations to outlaw opposition movements were reduced in America by the rapid decline of the conservative opposition. The revolutionary, democratic values that thus became part of the national self-image, and the basis for its authority structure, gained legitimacy as they proved effective—that is, as the nation prospered.

The need to establish stable authority and a sense of identity led the leaders of the United States to resist efforts by "old states" to involve the young nation in their quarrels. But at the same time that Americans rejected "foreign entanglements," they clearly used the Old World as both a negative and a positive point of reference, rejecting its political and class structures as backward, but nevertheless viewing its cultural and economic achievements as worthy of emulation. The intellectuals in particular expressed this ambivalence, since they played a major role in establishing and defining the state; but they then found that the task of operating and even living in it required them to conform to vulgar populist and provincial values.

In specifying those processes in the evolution of the first new nation that are comparable to what has been taking place in the societies of Asia and Africa in our own time, I am relying upon analogy. It ought to go without saying that: "We cannot assume that because conditions in one century led to certain effects, even roughly parallel conditions in another century would lead to similar effects. Neither can we be sure, of course, that the conditions were even roughly parallel."[1] It is fairly obvious that conditions in the early United States were quite different from those faced by most of the new nations of today. Many of the internal conditions that hamper the evolution of stable authority and a unifying sense of national identity in the new nations of the twentieth century were much less acute in the early United States. But the evidence suggests that despite its advantages, the United States came very close to failing in its effort to establish a unified legitimate authority. The first attempt to do so in 1783, following on Independence, was a failure. The second and successful effort was endangered by frequent threats of secession and the open flaunting of central authority until the Civil War. The advantages which the early United States possessed, as compared with most of the contemporary new states, then, only show more strongly how significant the similarities are.

There were other American advantages that should be mentioned. Although internal conflicts stemming from attitudes toward the French Revolution* disrupted the young American polity, there was no worldwide totalitarian conspiracy seeking to upset political and economic development from within, and holding up an alternative model of seemingly successful economic growth through the use of authoritarian methods. Also the absence of rapid mass communication systems meant that Americans were relatively isolated, and hence did not immediately compare their conditions with those in the more developed countries. The United States did not so urgently face a "revolution of rising expectations" based on the knowledge that life is much better elsewhere. The accepted concepts of natural or appropriate rights did not include a justification of the lower classes' organized participation in the polity to gain higher income, welfare support from the state, and the like. And whatever the exaggeration in the effects frequently attributed to the existence of an open land frontier, there can be little doubt that it contributed to social stability.

Internal value cleavages, which frustrate contemporary new nations, were comparatively less significant in young America. Shils points out that in today's new nations "the parochialism of kinship, caste and locality makes it difficult to create stable and coherent nation-wide parties."[2] None of these parochialisms was as strong in the United States which was formed by a relatively homogeneous population with a common language, a relatively similar religious background (although denominational differences did cause some problems), and a common cultural and political tradition.

American social structure did not possess those great "gaps" which, in the contemporary new states, "conspire to separate the ordinary people from their government."[3] The culture with which the educated identified contrasted less strongly with that of the uneducated. The ideology in the name of which Amer-

*French Revolution: see footnote on page 17.

ica made its revolution was less alien to prevailing modes of thought than some of today's revolutionary creeds. Perhaps most important, the class structure of America, even before the establishment of the new nation, came closer to meeting the conditions for a stable democracy than do those of the new nations of our time—or, indeed, than those of the Old World at that time. Writing shortly before Independence was finally attained, Crèvecoeur,* though sympathetic to the Tory† cause, pointed up the egalitarianism of American society:

> The rich and the poor are not so far removed from each other as they are in Europe. . . . A pleasing uniformity of decent competence appears throughout our habitations. . . . It must take some time ere he [the foreign traveler] can reconcile himself to our dictionary, which is but short in words of dignity, and names of honor. . . . Here man is as free as he ought to be; nor is this pleasing equality so transitory as many others are.[4]

The ability to work the institutions of a democratic nation requires sophistication both at the elite level and the level of the citizenry at large. And as Carl Bridenbaugh has well demonstrated, the America of revolutionary times was not a colonial backwater.[5] Philadelphia was the second largest English city—only London surpassed it in numbers. Philadelphia and other colonial American capitals were centers of relatively high culture at this time: they had universities and learned societies, and their elite was in touch with, and contributed to, the intellectual and scientific life of Britain.

In this respect, the political traditions that the American colonists held in common, were of particular importance since they included the concept of the rule of law, and even of constitutionalism. Each colony operated under a charter which defined and limited governmental powers. Although colonial subjects, Americans were also Englishmen and were thus accustomed to the rights and privileges of Englishmen. Through their local governments they actually possessed more rights than did most of the residents of Britain itself. In a sense, even before independence, Americans met a basic condition for democratic government, the ability to operate its fundamental institutions.[6]

> It requires, not only efficient administration, but an independent judiciary with high professional standards and, in all branches of government, a scrupulous respect for rules, written and unwritten, governing the exercise of power. What these rules are must be known to more people than those who actually have the power supposed to be limited by these rules, and it must be possible to lodge effective complaints against those people who are suspected of breaking the rules. This means that there must be, in the broad sense, constitutional government.[7]

**Michel Guillaume Jean de Crèvecoeur* (1735–1813): French author who popularized the image of America as a melting pot in his *Letters from an American Farmer* (1782). Both that work and his later book, *Sketches of Eighteenth Century America* (1925), were published under the pseudonym J. Hector St. Jean de Crèvecoeur.

†*Tory:* in the American context, a person loyal to the British Crown during the American Revolution. Also a member of the British or Canadian Conservative party today.

In many contemporary new nations, a potentially politically powerful military class, who have a patriotic, national outlook, may use the army to seize power if it becomes impatient with civilian leadership.[8] When the United States was seeking to establish a national authority, it was not bedeviled by such a class. The entire army in 1789 consisted of 672 men; and even after a decade of threats of war, there were only 3,429 soldiers in 1800. The potential military strength was, of course, much larger, for it included various state militia reserves. The latter, however, were simply the citizenry, and as long as the government had the loyalty of the general population, it had no need to fear its professional soldiers.[9]

Of great significance in facilitating America's development as a nation, both politically and economically, was the fact that the weight of ancient tradition which is present in almost all of the contemporary new states was largely absent. It was not only a new nation, it was a new society, much less bound to the customs and values of the past than any nation of Europe. Crèvecoeur well described the American as a "new man," the likes of which had never been seen before.[10]

Religion, of course, may be viewed as a "traditional" institution which played an important role in the United States. But in the first half-decade of the American Republic, as we have seen, the defenders of religious traditionalism were seriously weakened, as the various state churches—Anglican in the South and Congregationalist in New England—were gradually disestablished. Moreover, the new United States was particularly fortunate in the religious traditions which it did inherit. Calvinistic Puritanism,* which was stronger in the colonies than in the mother country, was not as "uncongenial to modernity" as are some of the traditional beliefs inherited by new nations today. A positive orientation toward savings and hard work, and the strong motivation to achieve high positions that derives from this religious tradition, have been seen as causes of the remarkable economic expansion that made possible the legitimation of equalitarian values and democratic government. Max Weber,† the most prominent exponent of the thesis that ascetic Protestantism‡ played a major role in the development of capitalism in the Western world, argued that "one must never overlook that without the universal diffusion of these qualities and principles of a methodical way of life, qualities which were maintained through these [Calvinist] religious communities, capitalism, today, even in America, would not be what it is. . . ."[11] Calvinism's "insis-

Calvinistic Puritanism: belief system espoused by John Calvin (1509–1564), a French theologian and a leader of the Protestant Reformation. Calvinism emphasized predestination, the unquestioned authority of the Bible, and the sovereignty of God. Puritans demanded rigid adherence to religious doctrines and advocated simplicity in both lifestyle and religious worship.

†*Max Weber* (1864–1920): German sociologist and political economist who wrote, among other seminal works, *The Protestant Ethic and the Spirit of Capitalism* (1904–1905). He is well known for his thorough analysis of bureaucratic organizations, authority, and legitimacy. Many of his writings are collected in H. H. Gerth and C. W. Mills, eds., *From Max Weber: Essays in Sociology* (1946).

‡*Protestantism:* religion espoused by Christian churches that formed during the sixteenth century in disaffection with the Catholic Church. The three original branches, Lutheranism, Calvinism, and Zwinglianism, rejected the authority of the church hierarchy and many of the rituals associated with its worship. Max Weber argued that the "Protestant ethic"—a reliance on hard work, individualism, thrift, and rationalism—was conducive to the development of capitalism.

tence that one's works were signs of eternal grace or damnation" has been transformed into a secular emphasis upon achievement.[12]

Other Puritan influences on American development have perhaps not been sufficiently emphasized. As Richard Schlatter has pointed out in a recent summary of the researches on this subject, the Puritan tradition involved a respect for learning which led to the establishment of schools and universities on a scale that surpassed England.[13] The opportunities for learning thus created, and the pressures for widespread education that equalitarian values implied,[14] led to a wide distribution of literacy. The census of 1840 reported only 9 per cent of the white population twenty years old and over as illiterate.[15]

The Puritan tradition may also have made it easier to legitimize American democracy as the rule of law. Tocqueville saw the special need of an egalitarian and democratic society for a self-restraining value system that would inhibit the tyranny of the majority, a function supposedly once fulfilled in the European societies by a secure and sophisticated aristocratic elite. In a democracy only religion could play this role, and therefore the less coercive the political institutions of such a society, the more it has need for a system of common belief to help restrict the actions of the rulers and the electorate. As he put it:

> But the revolutionists of America are obliged to profess an ostensible respect for Christian morality and equity, which does not permit them to violate wantonly the laws that oppose their designs; nor would they find it easy to surmount the scruples of their partisans even if they were able to get over their own. . . . Thus while the law permits Americans to do what they please, religion prevents them from conceiving, and forbids them to commit, what is rash or unjust.[16]

While Tocqueville pointed out that Catholicism* was not necessarily incompatible with democratic or egalitarian values, since "it confounds all the distinctions of society at the foot of the same altar," he describes the "form of Christianity" in early America as "a democratic and republican religion."[17] It would indeed seem that the Calvinistic-Puritan tradition was particularly valuable in training men to the sort of self-restraint that Tocqueville felt was necessary for democracy. By making every man God's agent, ascetic Protestantism made each individual responsible for the state of morality in the society; and by making the congregation a disciplinary agent it helped to prevent any one individual from assuming that his brand of morality was better than others.[18]

Puritanism had been associated with the movement of the squirearchy for political recognition in England. As Trevelyan has put it:

> Under Elizabeth the increasing Puritanism of the squires introduced a new element. The fear and love of God began to strive with the fear and love of the Queen in the

**Roman Catholicism*: the world's largest Christian religion with some 540 million followers. Catholics believe that Jesus Christ founded their church to bring salvation to all people and that the Church is guided by the Holy Spirit sent by Christ to humanity. A distinctive feature of this Christian faith is the existence of the pope, who is the religion's spiritual leader and who governs the Church from the Vatican, an independent state. Catholicism has been a powerful force in world history, with the papacy reaching dominant political power throughout Western Europe in the twelfth century.

> breast of the Parliament men. . . . Protestantism and Parliamentary privilege were already closely connected, before even the first Stuart came to trouble [the] still further seething waters [of Cromwell's rebellion].[19]

So that, as Schlatter has pointed out, the Puritan tradition implied a concern for "constitutionalism and limited government," as well as a belief "that they are a peculiar people, destined by Providence to live in a more perfect community than any known in the Old World. . . ."[20]

In establishing its identity, the new America quickly came to see itself, and to be perceived by others, as a radical society in which conservatism and traditionalism had no proper place. The religious traditions on which it drew stressed that it was to be different from European nations. But its really radical character derived from its revolutionary origins.

The political scientist Clinton Rossiter has described the effects of the revolution on the political ideologies of the nation in explaining why conservatism as a doctrine is weak in America:

> The reason the American Right is not Conservative today is that it has not been Conservative for more than a hundred years. . . .
>
> Conservatism first emerged to meet the challenge of democracy. In countries like England it was able to survive the rise of this new way of life by giving way a little at a time under its relentless pounding, but in America the triumph of democracy was too sudden and complete. It came to society as well as to politics; it came early in the history of the Republic and found the opposition only half dug in. . . . The result was a disaster for genuine, old-country Conservatism. Nowhere in the world did the progressive, optimistic, egalitarian mode of thinking invade so completely the mind of an entire people. Nowhere was the Right forced so abruptly into such an untenable position. If there is any single quality that the Right seems always and everywhere to cultivate, it is unquestioning patriotism, and this, in turn, calls for unquestioning devotion to the nation's ideals. The long-standing merger of "America" and "democracy" has meant that to profess Conservatism is to be something less than "one hundred per cent American"; indeed, it is to question the nation's destiny. Worse than that, this merger has doomed outspoken Conservatism to political failure.[21]

From Tocqueville* and Martineau† in the 1830s to Gunnar Myrdal‡ in more recent times, foreign visitors have been impressed by the extent to which the values proclaimed in the Declaration of Independence have operated to prescribe social and political behavior. And the legitimacy which the American authority structure ultimately attained has been based on the assumption that as a nation it

**Tocqueville*: see headnote on page 5.

†*Harriet Martineau* (1802–1876): English novelist and economist whose works are noted for her ability to explain complex economic and philosophical concepts in accessible terms. She wrote *Illustrations of Political Economy* (1832–1834) and *The Positive Philosophy of Auguste Comte* (1853), among many books.

‡*Karl Gunnar Myrdal* (1898–1987) Swedish sociologist and economist who shared the first Nobel Prize for Economics in 1974 with Friedrich von Hayek of Austria for their work in social and economic theory. Among his numerous books is *An American Dilemma: The Negro Problem and Modern Democracy* (1944, 1962), and *Challenge of World Poverty* (1970).

is dedicated to equality and to liberty, to the fulfillment of its original political objectives.

As Frank Thistlethwaite put it a few years ago:

> In the mid-twentieth century the American people still pursue their Revolutionary ideal: a Republic established in the belief that men of good will could voluntarily come together in the sanctuary of an American wilderness to order their common affairs according to rational principles; a dedicated association in which men participate not by virtue of being born into it as heirs of immemorial custom, but by virtue of free choice, of the will to affirm certain sacred principles; a community of the uprooted, of migrants who have turned their back on the past in which they were born; . . . a society fluid and experimental, uncommitted to rigid values, cherishing freedom of will and choice and bestowing all the promise of the future on those with the manhood to reject the past.[22]

NOTES

[1]Karl W. Deutsch, S. A. Burrell, R. A. Kann, M. Lee, Jr., M. Lichterman, R. E. Lindgren, F. L. Loewenheim, R. W. Van Wagenen, *Political Community and the North Atlantic Area* (Princeton, N.J.: Princeton University Press, 1957), p. 11.

[2]Edward Shils, "The Military in the Political Development of the New States" in John J. Johnson, *The Role of the Military in Underdeveloped Countries* (Princeton, N.J.: Princeton University Press, 1962), p. 14.

[3]*Ibid.*, p. 29.

[4]J. Hector St. John Crèvecoeur, *Letters from an American Farmer* (New York: Dolphin Books, n.d.), pp. 46–47.

[5]Carl Bridenbaugh, *Rebels and Gentlemen, Philadelphia in the Age of Franklin* (New York: Reynal and Hitchcock, 1942).

[6]See John Plamenatz, *On Alien Rule and Self Government* (New York: Longman's, Green, 1960), pp. 47–48.

[7]*Ibid.*, p. 51.

[8]Shils, "The Military. . . ," *op cit.*, p. 40.

[9]James R. Jacobs, *The Beginning of the U.S. Army, 1783–1812* (Princeton, N.J.: Princeton University Press, 1947); see also Deutsch *et al.*, *Political Community and the North Atlantic Area*, p. 26

[10]"What then is the American, this new man . . . ? He is an American, who leaving behind him all his ancient prejudices and manners, receives new ones from the new mode of life he has embraced. . . . He becomes an American by being received in the broad lap of our great *Alma Mater.* The American is a new man, who acts upon new principles; he must therefore entertain new ideas and form new opinions." J. Hector St. John Crèvecoeur, *Letters from an American Farmer* (New York: Dolphin Books), pp. 49–50.

[11]Max Weber, "The Protestant Sects and the Spirit of Capitalism," in *Essays in Sociology*, translated by Hans Gerth and C. W. Mills (New York: Oxford University Press, 1946), pp. 309, 313.

[12]Robin Williams, *American Society* (New York: Alfred A. Knopf, 1957), p. 313.

[13]Richard Schlatter, "The Puritan Strain," in John Higham, ed., *The Reconstruction of American History* (New York: Harper & Bros., 1962), pp. 39–42. See also Bernard Bailyn, *Education in the Forming of American Society* (Chapel Hill: The University of North Carolina Press, 1960), for a discussion of the influence which the multiplication of numerous sects by the eve of the Revolution

had upon the spread of education. The promotional and propagandizing possibilities of education made it an instrument of survival among competing sects. "Sectarian groups, without regard to the intellectual complexity of their doctrine or to their views on the value of learning to religion, became dynamic elements in the spread of education, spawning schools of all sorts, continuously, competitively in all their settlements; carrying education into the remote frontiers." Bailyn, pp. 40–41.

[14]"What strikes one most forcibly about the Puritans' efforts in education is the expectation of uniformity. Every family, without regard to its fortunes and the accomplishment of its head, and every town, without regard to its condition or resources, was expected to provide an equal minimum of education—for who, in what place, should be exempt from the essential work of life? . . . the quest for salvation . . . this was an occupation without limit, in the proper training for which all were expected to join equally, without regard to natural ability and worldly circumstance." Bailyn, *ibid.*, p. 81.

[15]Bureau of the Census, *A Statistical Abstract Supplement, Historical Statistics of the U.S. Colonial Times to 1957* (Washington: 1957), p. 214. The census of 1840 was the first to report literacy.

[16]Tocqueville, *Democracy in America*, Vol. I, p. 316.

[17]*Ibid.*, p. 311.

[18]Williams, *American Society*, p. 312.

[19]G. M. Trevelyan, *History of England* (Garden City, N.Y.: Doubleday Anchor Books, 1954), Vol. II, pp. 143–144.

[20]Schlatter, "The Puritan Strain," *op. cit.*, p. 42.

[21]Clinton Rossiter, *Conservatism in America* (New York: Vintage Books, 1962), pp. 201–202.

[22]Frank Thistlethwaite, *The Great Experiment* (New York: Cambridge University Press, 1955), pp. 319–320.

4

"PUBLIUS" (ALEXANDER HAMILTON, JAMES MADISO AND JOHN JAY)

THE FEDERALIST PAPERS

The Federalist Papers *are a series of 85 letters written to the general public in 1787 and 1788 by "Publius," a pseudonym for three illustrious advocates of the Constitution drafted in 1787: John Jay (1745–1829), James Madison (1751–1836), and Alexander Hamilton (1757–1804).* The Federalist Papers *are classics of American political science for the insight they provide into the Constitution, and for the richness of the political philosophy of its framers. The purpose of the papers was to convince the citizenry to replace the Articles of Confederation with the new Constitution. The papers were originally published in New York City newspapers during the state's debates over ratification. They were quickly reprinted and distributed in other key states as well. Hamilton is credited with the authorship of 51 of the papers. Three of* The Federalist Papers *were jointly authored by Madison and Hamilton. Madison wrote an additional 26, and Jay contributed 5. The characteristics and advantages of a federalist system and the separation of powers among the legislative, executive, and judicial branches are thoroughly discussed by Madison in numbers 10, 39, 46, 47, and 51. In the last selection, number 69, Hamilton explains the powers of the president through comparisons with those of the king of Great Britain and the governor of New York.*

NUMBER 10

Among the numerous advantages promised by a well-constructed Union, none deserves to be more accurately developed than its tendency to break and control the violence of faction. The friend of popular governments never finds himself so much alarmed for their character and fate as when he contemplates their propensity to this dangerous vice. He will not fail, therefore, to set a due value on any plan which, without violating the principles to which he is attached, provides a proper cure for it. The instability, injustice, and confusion introduced into the public councils have, in truth, been the mortal diseases under which popular governments have everywhere perished, as they continue to be the favorite and fruitful topics from which the adversaries to liberty derive their most specious declamations. The valuable improvements made by the American constitutions on the popular models, both ancient and modern, cannot certainly be too much admired; but it would be an unwarrantable partiality to contend that they have as effectually obviated the danger on this side, as was wished and expected. Complaints are everywhere heard from our most considerate and virtuous citizens, equally the friends of public and private faith and of public and personal liberty, that our governments are too unstable, that the public good is disregarded in the conflicts of rival parties, and that measures are too often decided, not according to the rules of justice and the rights of the minor party, but by the superior force of an interested and overbearing majority. However anxiously we may wish that these complaints had no foundation, the evidence of known facts will not permit us to deny that they are in some degree true. It will be found, indeed, on a candid review of our situation, that some of the distresses under which we labor have been erroneously charged on the operation of our governments; but it will be found, at the same time, that other causes will not alone account for many of our heaviest misfortunes; and, particularly, for that prevailing and increasing distrust of public engagements and alarm for private rights which are echoed from one end of the continent to the other. These must be chiefly, if not wholly, effects of the unsteadiness and injustice with which a factious spirit has tainted our public administration.

By a faction I understand a number of citizens, whether amounting to a majority or minority of the whole, who are united and actuated by some common impulse of passion, or of interest, adverse to the rights of other citizens, or to the permanent and aggregate interests of the community.

There are two methods of curing the mischiefs of faction: the one, by removing its causes; the other, by controlling its effects.

There are again two methods of removing the causes of faction: the one, by destroying the liberty which is essential to its existence; the other, by giving to every citizen the same opinions, the same passions, and the same interests.

It could never be more truly said than of the first remedy that it was worse than the disease. Liberty is to faction what air is to fire, an aliment without which it instantly expires. But it could not be a less folly to abolish liberty, which is essential to political life, because it nourishes faction than it would be to wish the annihilation of air, which is essential to animal life, because it imparts to fire its destructive agency.

The second expedient is as impracticable as the first would be unwise. As long as the reason of man continues fallible, and he is at liberty to exercise it, different opinions will be formed. As long as the connection subsists between his reason and his self-love, his opinions and his passions will have a reciprocal influence on each other; and the former will be objects to which the latter will attach themselves. The diversity in the faculties of men, from which the rights of property originate, is not less an insuperable obstacle to a uniformity of interests. The protection of these faculties is the first object of government. From the protection of different and unequal faculties of acquiring property, the possession of different degrees and kinds of property immediately results; and from the influence of these on the sentiments and views of the respective proprietors ensues a division of the society into different interests and parties.

The latent causes of faction are thus sown in the nature of man; and we see them everywhere brought into different degrees of activity, according to the different circumstances of civil society. A zeal for different opinions concerning religion, concerning government, and many other points, as well of speculation as of practice; an attachment to different leaders ambitiously contending for preeminence and power; or to persons of other descriptions whose fortunes have been interesting to the human passions, have, in turn, divided mankind into parties, inflamed them with mutual animosity, and rendered them much more disposed to vex and oppress each other than to co-operate for their common good. So strong is this propensity of mankind to fall into mutual animosities that where no substantial occasion presents itself the most frivolous and fanciful distinctions have been sufficient to kindle their unfriendly passions and excite their most violent conflicts. But the most common and durable source of factions has been the various and unequal distribution of property. Those who hold and those who are without property have ever formed distinct interests in society. Those who are creditors, and those who are debtors, fall under a like discrimination. A landed interest, a manufacturing interest, a mercantile interest, a moneyed interest, with many lesser interests, grow up of necessity in civilized nations, and divide them into different classes, actuated by different sentiments and views. The regulation of these various and interfering interests forms the principal task of modern legislation and involves the spirit of party and faction in the necessary and ordinary operations of government.

No man is allowed to be a judge in his own cause, because his interest would certainly bias his judgment, and, not improbably, corrupt his integrity. With equal, nay with greater reason, a body of men are unfit to be both judges and parties at the same time; yet what are many of the most important acts of legislation but so many judicial determinations, not indeed concerning the rights of single persons, but concerning the rights of large bodies of citizens? And what are the different classes of legislators but advocates and parties to the causes which they determine? Is a law proposed concerning private debts? It is a question to which the creditors are parties on one side and the debtors on the other. Justice ought to hold the balance between them. Yet the parties are, and must be, themselves the judges; and the most numerous party, or in other words, the most powerful faction must be expected to prevail. Shall domestic manufacturers be encouraged, and in what degree, by restrictions on foreign manufacturers? are questions which would be differently decided by the landed and the manufacturing classes, and probably by neither with a sole regard to justice and the public good. The apportionment of taxes on the various descriptions of property is an act which seems to require the most exact impartiality; yet there is, perhaps, no legislative act in which greater opportunity and temptation are given to a predominant party to trample on the rules of justice. Every shilling with which they overburden the inferior number is a shilling saved to their own pockets.

It is in vain to say that enlightened statesmen will be able to adjust these clashing interests and render them all subservient to the public good. Enlightened statesmen will not always be at the helm. Nor, in many cases, can such an adjustment be made at all without taking into view indirect and remote considerations, which will rarely prevail over the immediate interest which one party may find in disregarding the rights of another or the good of the whole.

The inference to which we are brought is that the *causes* of faction cannot be removed and that relief is only to be sought in the means of controlling its *effects*.

If a faction consists of less than a majority, relief is supplied by the republican principle, which enables the majority to defeat its sinister views by regular vote. It may clog the administration, it may convulse the society; but it will be unable to execute and mask its violence under the forms of the Constitution. When a majority is included in a faction, the form of popular government, on the other hand, enables it to sacrifice to its ruling passion or interest both the public good and the rights of other citizens. To secure the public good and private rights against the danger of such a faction, and at the same time to preserve the spirit and the form of popular government, is then the great object to which our inquiries are directed. Let me add that it is the great desideratum by which alone this form of government can be rescued from the opprobrium under which it has so long labored and be recommended to the esteem and adoption of mankind.

By what means is this object attainable? Evidently by one of two only. Either the existence of the same passion or interest in a majority at the same time must be prevented, or the majority, having such coexistent passion or interest, must be rendered, by their number and local situation, unable to concert and carry into effect schemes of oppression. If the impulse and the opportunity be suffered to coincide, we well know that neither moral nor religious motives can be relied on as an adequate control. They are not found to be such on the injustice and violence of individuals, and lose their efficacy in proportion to the number combined together, that is, in proportion as their efficacy becomes needful.

From this view of the subject it may be concluded that a pure democracy, by which I mean a society consisting of a small number of citizens, who assemble and administer the government in person, can admit of no cure for the mischiefs of faction. A common passion or interest will, in almost every case, be felt by a majority of the whole; a communication and concert results from the form of government itself; and there is nothing to check the inducements to sacrifice the weaker party or an obnoxious individual. Hence it is that such democracies have ever been spectacles of turbulence and contention; have ever been found incompatible with personal security or the rights of property; and have in general been as short in their lives as they have been violent in their deaths. Theoretic politicians, who have patronized this species of government, have erroneously supposed that by reducing mankind to a perfect equality in their political rights, they would at the same time be perfectly equalized and assimilated in their possessions, their opinions, and their passions.

A republic, by which I mean a government in which the scheme of representation takes place, opens a different prospect and promises the cure for which we are seeking. Let us examine the points in which it varies from pure democracy, and we shall comprehend both the nature of the cure and the efficacy which it must derive from the Union.

The two great points of difference between a democracy and a republic are: first, the delegation of the government, in the latter, to a small number of citizens elected by the rest; secondly, the greater number of citizens and greater sphere of country over which the latter may be extended.

The effect of the first difference is, on the one hand, to refine and enlarge the public views by passing them through the medium of a chosen body of citizens, whose wisdom may best discern the true interest of their country and whose patriotism and love of justice will be least likely to sacrifice it to temporary or partial considerations. Under such a regulation it may well happen that the public voice, pronounced by the representatives of the people, will be more consonant to the public good than if pronounced by the people themselves, convened for the purpose. On the other hand, the effect may be inverted. Men of factious tempers, of local prejudices, or of sinister designs, may, by intrigue, by corruption, or by other means, first obtain the suffrages, and then betray the interests of the people. The question resulting is, whether small or extensive republics are most favorable to the election of proper guardians of the public weal; and it is clearly decided in favor of the latter by two obvious considerations.

In the first place it is to be remarked that however small the republic may be the representatives must be raised to a certain number in order to guard against the cabals of a few; and that however large it may be they must be limited to a certain number in order to guard against the confusion of a multitude. Hence, the number of representatives in the two cases not being in proportion to that of the constituents, and being proportionally greatest in the small republic, it follows that if the proportion of fit characters be not less in the large than in the small republic, the former will present a greater option, and consequently a greater probability of a fit choice.

In the next place, as each representative will be chosen by a greater number of citizens in the large than in the small republic, it will be more difficult for unworthy candidates to practise with success the vicious arts by which elections are too often carried; and the suffrages of the people being more free, will be more likely to center on men who possess the most attractive merit and the most diffusive and established characters.

It must be confessed that in this, as in most other cases, there is a mean, on both sides of which inconveniencies will be found to lie. By enlarging too much the number of electors, you render the representative too little acquainted with all their local circumstances and lesser interests; as by reducing it too much, you render him unduly attached to these, and too little fit to comprehend and pursue great and national objects. The federal Constitution forms a happy combination in this respect; the great and aggregate interests being referred to the national, the local and particular to the State legislatures.

The other point of difference is the greater number of citizens and extent of territory which may be brought within the compass of republican than of democratic government; and it is this circumstance principally which renders factious combinations less to be dreaded in the former than in the latter. The smaller the society, the fewer probably will be the distinct parties and interests composing it; the fewer the distinct parties and interests, the more frequently will a majority be found of the same party; and the smaller the number of individuals composing a majority, and the smaller the compass within which they are placed, the more easily will they concert and execute their plans of oppression. Extend the sphere and you take in a greater variety of parties and interests; you make it less probable that a majority of the whole will have a common motive to invade the rights of other citizens; or if such a common motive exists, it will be more difficult for all who feel it to discover their own strength and to act in unison with each other. Besides other impediments, it may be remarked that, where there is a consciousness of unjust or dishonorable purposes, communication is always checked by distrust in proportion to the number whose concurrence is necessary.

Hence, it clearly appears that the same advantage which a republic has over a democracy in controlling the effects of faction is enjoyed by a large over a small republic—is enjoyed by the Union over the States composing it. Does this advantage consist in the substitution of representatives whose enlightened views and virtuous sentiments render them superior to local prejudices and to schemes of injustice? It will not be denied that the representation of the Union will be most likely to possess these requisite endowments. Does it consist in the greater security afforded by a greater variety of parties, against the event of any one party being able to outnumber and oppress the rest? In an equal degree does the increased variety of parties comprised within the Union increase this security. Does it, in fine, consist in the greater obstacles opposed to the concert and accomplishment of the secret wishes of an unjust and interested majority? Here again the extent of the Union gives it the most palpable advantage.

The influence of factious leaders may kindle a flame within their particular States but will be unable to spread a general conflagration through the other States. A religious sect may degenerate into a political faction in a part of the Confederacy; but the variety of sects dispersed over the entire face of it must secure the national councils against any danger from that source. A rage for paper money, for an abolition of debts, for an equal division of property, or for any other improper or wicked project, will be less apt to pervade the whole body of the Union than a particular member of it, in the same proportion as such a malady is more likely to taint a particular county or district than an entire State.

In the extent and proper structure of the Union, therefore, we behold a repulican remedy for the diseases most incident to republican government. And according to the degree of pleasure and pride we feel in being republicans ought to be our zeal in cherishing the spirit and supporting the character of federalists.

Publius
(James Madison)

NUMBER 39

The last paper having concluded the observations which were meant to introduce a candid survey of the plan of government reported by the convention, we now proceed to the execution of that part of our undertaking.

The first question that offers itself is whether the general form and aspect of the government be strictly republican. It is evident that no other form would be reconcilable with the genius of the people of America; with the fundamental principles of the Revolution; or with that honorable determination which animates every votary of freedom to rest all our political experiments on the capacity of mankind for self-government. If the plan of the convention, therefore, be found to depart from the republican character, its advocates must abandon it as no longer defensible.

What, then, are the distinctive characters of the republican form? Were an answer to this question to be sought, not by recurring to principles but in the application of the term by political writers to the constitutions of different States, no satisfactory one would ever be found. Holland, in which no particle of the supreme authority is derived from the people, has passed almost universally under the denomination of a republic. The same title has been bestowed on Venice, where absolute power over the great body of the people is exercised in the most absolute manner by a small body of hereditary nobles. Poland, which is a mixture of aristocracy and of monarchy in their worst forms, has been dignified with the same appellation. The government of England, which has one republican branch only, combined with an hereditary aristocracy and monarchy, has with equal impropriety been frequently placed on the list of republics. These examples, which are nearly as dissimilar to each other as to a genuine republic, show the extreme inaccuracy with which the term has been used in political disquisitions.

If we resort for a criterion to the different principles on which different forms of government are established, we may define a republic to be, or at least may bestow that name on, a government which derives all its powers directly or indirectly from the great body of the people, and is administered by persons holding their offices during pleasure for a limited period, or during good behavior. It is *essential* to such a government that it be derived from the great body of the society, not from an inconsiderable proportion or a favored class of it; otherwise a handful of tyrannical nobles, exercising their oppressions by a delegation of their powers, might aspire to the rank of republicans and claim for their government the honorable title of republic. It is *sufficient* for such a government that the persons administering it be appointed, either directly or indirectly, by the people; and that they hold their appointments by either of the tenures just specified; otherwise every government in the United States, as well as every other popular government that has been or can be well organized or well executed, would be degraded from the republican character. According to the constitution of every State in the Union, some or other of the officers of government are appointed indirectly only by the people. According to most of them, the chief magistrate himself is so appointed. And according to one, this mode of appointment is extended to one of the co-ordinate branches of the legislature. According to all the constitutions, also, the tenure of the highest offices is extended to a definite period, and in many instances, both within the legislative and executive departments, to a period of years. According to the provisions of most of the constitutions, again, as well as according to the most respectable and received opinions on the subject, the members of the judiciary department are to retain their offices by the firm tenure of good behavior.

On comparing the Constitution planned by the convention with the standard here fixed, we perceived at once that it is, in the most rigid sense, conformable to it. The House of Representatives, like that of one branch at least of all the State legislatures, is elected immediately by the great body of the people. The Senate, like the present Congress and the Senate of Maryland, derives its appointment indirectly from the people. The President is indirectly derived from the choice of the people, according to the example in most of the States. Even the judges, with all other officers of the Union, will, as in the several States, be the choice, though a remote choice, of the people themselves. The duration of the appointments is equally conformable to the republican standard and to the model of State constitutions. The House of Representatives is periodically elective, as in all the States; and for the period of two years, as in the State of South Carolina. The Senate is elective for the period of six years, which is but one year more than the period of the Senate of Maryland, and but two more than that of the Senates of New York and Virginia. The President is to continue in office for the period of four years; as in New York and Delaware the chief magistrate is elected for three years, and in South Carolina for two years. In the other States the election is annual. In several of the States, however, no explicit provision is made for the impeachment of the chief magistrate. And in Delaware and Virginia he is not impeachable till out of office. The President of the United States is impeachable at any time during his continuance in office. The tenure by which the judges are to hold their places is, as it unquestionably ought to be, that of good behavior. The tenure of the ministerial offices generally will be a subject of legal regulation, conformably to the reason of the case and the example of the State constitutions.

Could any further proof be required of the republican complexion of this system, the most decisive one might be found in its absolute prohibition of titles of nobility, both under the federal and the State governments; and in its express guaranty of the republican form to each of the latter.

"But it was not sufficient," say the adversaries of the proposed Constitution, "for the convention to adhere to the republican form. They ought with equal care to have preserved the *federal* form, which regards the Union as a *Confederacy* of sovereign states; instead of which they have framed a *national* government, which regards the Union as a *consolidation* of the States." And it is asked by what authority this bold and radical innovation was undertaken? The handle which has been made of this objection requires that it should be examined with some precision.

Without inquiring into the accuracy of the distinction on which the objection is founded, it will be necessary to a just estimate of its force, first, to ascertain the real character of the government in question; secondly, to inquire how far the convention were authorized to propose such a government; and thirdly, how far the duty they owed to their country could supply any defect of regular authority.

First.—In order to ascertain the real character of the government, it may be considered in relation to the foundation on which it is to be established; to the sources from which its ordinary powers are to be drawn; to the operation of those powers; to the extent of them; and to the authority by which future changes in the government are to be introduced.

On examining the first relation, it appears, on one hand, that the Constitution is to be founded on the assent and ratification of the people of America, given by deputies elected for the special purpose; but, on the other, that this assent and ratification is to be given by the people, not as individuals composing one entire nation, but as composing the distinct and independent States to which they respectively belong. It is to be the assent and ratification of the several States, derived from the supreme authority in each State—the authority of the people themselves. The act, therefore, establishing the Constitution will not be a *national* but a *federal* act.

That it will be a federal and not a national act, as these terms are understood by the objectors—the act of the people, as forming so many independent States, not as forming one aggregate nation—is obvious from the single consideration: that it is to result neither from the decision of a *majority* of the people of the Union, nor from that of a *majority* of the States. It must result from the *unanimous* assent of the several States that are parties to it, differing no otherwise from their ordinary assent than in its being expressed, not by the legislative authority, but by that of the people themselves. Were the people regarded in this transaction as forming one nation, the will of the majority of the whole people of the United States would bind the minority, in the same manner as the majority in each State must bind the minority; and the will of the majority must be determined either by a comparison of the individual votes, or by considering the will of the majority of the States as evidence of the will of a majority of the people of the United States. Neither of these rules has been adopted. Each State, in ratifying the Constitution, is considered as a sovereign body independent of all others, and only to be bound by its own voluntary act. In this relation, then, the new Constitution will, if established, be a *federal* and not a *national* constitution.

The next relation is to the sources from which the ordinary powers of government are to be derived. The House of Representatives will derive its powers from the people of America; and the people will be represented in the same proportion and on the same principle as they are in the legislature of a particular State. So far the government is *national*, not *federal*. The Senate, on the other hand, will derive its powers from the States as political and coequal societies; and these will be represented on the principle of equality in the Senate, as they now are in the existing Congress. So far the government is *federal*, not *national*. The executive power will be derived from a very compound source. The immediate election of the President is to be made by the States in their political characters. The votes allotted to them are in a compound ratio, which considers them partly as distinct and coequal societies, partly as unequal members of the same society. The eventual election, again, is to be made by that branch of the legislature which consists of the national representatives; but in this particular act they are to be thrown into the form of individual delegations from so many distinct and coequal bodies politic. From this aspect of the government it appears to be of a mixed character, presenting at least as many *federal* as *national* features.

The difference between a federal and national government, as it relates to the *operation of the government*, is by the adversaries of the plan of the convention supposed to consist in this, that in the former the powers operate on the political bodies composing the Confederacy in their political capacities; in the latter, on the individual citizens composing the nation in their individual capacities. On trying the Constitution by this criterion, it falls under the *national* not the *federal* character; though perhaps not so completely as has been understood. In several cases, and particularly in the trial of controversies to which States may be parties, they must be viewed and proceeded against in their collective and political capacities only. But the operation of the government on the people in their individual capacities, in its ordinary and most essential proceedings, will, in the sense of its opponents, on the whole, designate it, in this relation, a *national* government.

But if the government be national with regard to the *operation* of its powers, it changes its aspect again when we contemplate it in relation to the extent of its powers. The idea of a national government involves in it not only an authority over the individual citizens, but an indefinite supremacy over all persons and things, so far as they are objects of lawful government. Among a people consolidated into one nation, this supremacy is completely vested in the national legislature. Among communities united for particular purposes, it is vested partly in the general and partly in the municipal legislatures. In the former case, all local authorities are subordinate to the supreme; and may be controlled, directed, or abolished by it at pleasure. In the latter, the local or municipal authorities form distinct and independent portions of the supremacy, no more subject, within their respective spheres, to the general authority than the general authority is subject to them, within its own sphere. In this relation, then, the proposed government cannot be deemed a *national* one; since its jurisdiction extends to certain enumerated objects only, and leaves to the several States a residuary and inviolable sovereignty over all other objects. It is true that in controversies relating to the boundary between the two jurisdictions, the tribunal which is ultimately to decide is to be established under the general government. But this does not change the principle of the case. The decision is to be impartially made, according to the rules of the Constitution; and all the usual and most effectual precautions are taken to secure this impartiality. Some such tribunal is clearly essential to prevent an appeal to the sword and a dissolution of the compact; and that it ought to be established under the general rather than under the local governments, or, to speak more properly, that it could be safely established under the first alone, is a position not likely to be combated.

If we try the Constitution by its last relation to the authority by which amendments are to be made, we find it neither wholly *national* nor wholly *federal*. Were it wholly national, the supreme and ultimate authority would reside in the *majority* of the people of the Union; and this authority would be competent at all times, like that of a majority of every national society to alter or abolish its established government. Were it wholly federal, on the other hand, the concurrence of each State in the Union would be essential to every alteration that would be binding on all. The mode provided by the plan of the convention is not founded on either of these principles. In requiring more than a majority, and particularly in computing the proportion by *States*, not by *citizens*, it departs from the national and advances towards the *federal* character; in rendering the concurrence of less than the whole number of States sufficient, it loses again the *federal* and partakes of the *national* character.

The proposed Constitution, therefore, even when tested by the rules laid down by its antagonists, is, in strictness, neither a national nor a federal Constitution, but a composition of both. In its foundation it is federal, not national; in the sources from which the ordinary powers of the government are drawn, it is partly federal and partly national; in the operation of these powers, it is national, not federal; in the extent of them, again, it is federal, not national; and, finally in the authoritative mode of introducing amendments, it is neither wholly federal nor wholly national.

Publius
(James Madison)

NUMBER 46

Resuming the subject of the last paper, I proceed to inquire whether the federal government or the State governments will have the advantage with regard to the predilection and support of the people. Notwithstanding the different modes in which they are appointed, we must consider both of them as substantially dependent on the great body of the citizens of the United States. I assume this position here as it respects the first, reserving the proofs for another place. The federal and State governments are in fact but different agents and trustees of the people, constituted with different powers and designed for different purposes. The adversaries of the Constitution seem to have lost sight of the people altogether in their reasonings on this subject; and to have viewed these different establishments not only as mutual rivals and enemies, but as uncontrolled by any common superior in their efforts to usurp the authorities of each other. These gentlemen must here be reminded of their error. They must be told that the ultimate authority, wherever the derivative may be found, resides in the people alone, and that it will not depend merely on the comparative ambition or address of the different governments whether either, or which of them, will be able to enlarge its sphere of jurisdiction at the expense of the other. Truth, no less than decency, requires that the event in every case should be supposed to depend on the sentiments and sanction of their common constituents.

Many considerations, besides those suggested on a former occasion, seem to place it beyond doubt that the first and most natural attachment of the people will be to the governments of their respective States. Into the administration of these a greater number of individuals will expect to rise. From the gift of these a greater number of offices and emoluments will flow. By the superintending care of these, all the more domestic and personal interests of the people will be regulated and provided for. With the affairs of these, the people will be more familiarly and minutely conversant. And with the members of these will a greater proportion of the people have the ties of personal acquaintance and friendship, and of family and party attachments; on the side of these, therefore, the popular bias may well be expected most strongly to incline.

Experience speaks the same language in this case. The federal administration, though hitherto very defective in comparison with what may be hoped under a better system, had, during the war, and particularly whilst the independent fund of paper emissions was in credit, an activity and importance as great as it can well have in any future circumstances whatever. It was engaged, too, in a course of measures which had for their object the protection of everything that was dear, and the acquisition of everything that could be desirable to the people at large. It was, nevertheless, invariably found, after the transient enthusiasm for the early Congresses was over, that the attention and attachment of the people were turned anew to their own particular governments; that the federal council was at no time the idol of popular favor; and that opposition to proposed enlargements of its powers and importance was the side usually taken by the men who wished to build their political consequence on the prepossessions of their fellow-citizens.

If, therefore, as has been elsewhere remarked, the people should in future become more partial to the federal than to the State governments, the change can only result from such manifest and irresistible proofs of a better administration as will overcome all their antecedent propensities. And in that case, the people ought not surely to be precluded from giving most of their confidence where they may discover it to be most due; but even in that case the State governments could have little to apprehend, because it is only within a certain sphere that the federal power can, in the nature of things, be advantageously administered.

The remaining points on which I propose to compare the federal and State governments are the disposition and the faculty they may respectively possess to resist and frustrate the measures of each other.

It has been already proved that the members of the federal will be more dependent on the members of the State governments than the latter will be on the former. It has appeared also that the prepossessions of the people, on whom both will depend, will be more on the side of the State governments than of the federal government. So far as the disposition of each towards the other may be influenced by these causes, the State governments must clearly have the advantage. But in a distinct and very important point of view, the advantage will lie on the same side. The prepossessions, which the members themselves will carry into the federal government, will generally be favorable to the States; whilst it will rarely happen that the members of the State governments will carry into the public councils a bias in favor of the general government. A local spirit will infallibly prevail much more in the members of Congress than a national spirit will prevail in the legislatures of the particular States. Everyone knows that a great proportion of the errors committed by the State legislatures proceeds from the disposition of the members to sacrifice the comprehensive and permanent interest of the State to the particular and separate views of the counties or districts in which they reside. And if they do not sufficiently enlarge their policy to embrace the collective welfare of their particular State, how can it be imagined that they will make the aggregate prosperity of the Union, and the dignity and respectability of its government, the objects of their affections and consultations? For the same reason that the members of the State legislatures will be unlikely to attach themselves sufficiently to national objects, the members of the federal legislature will be likely to attach themselves too much to local objects. The States will be to the latter what counties and towns are to the former. Measures will too often be decided according to their probable effect, not on the national prosperity and happiness, but on the prejudices, interests, and pursuits of the governments and people of the individual States. What is the spirit that has in general characterized the proceedings of Congress? A perusal of their journals, as well as the candid acknowledgments of such as have had a seat in that assembly, will inform us that the members have but too frequently displayed the character rather of partisans of their respective States than of impartial guardians of a common interest; that where on one occasion improper sacrifices have been made of local considerations to the aggrandizement of the federal government, the great interests of the nation have suffered on a hundred from an undue attention to the local prejudices, interests, and views of the particular States. I mean not by these reflections to insinuate that the new federal government will not embrace a more enlarged plan of policy than the existing government may have pursued; much less that its views will be as confined as those of the State legislatures; but only that it will partake sufficiently of the spirit of both to be disinclined to invade the rights of the individual States, or the prerogatives of their governments. The motives on the part of the State governments to augment their prerogatives by defalcations from the federal government will be overruled by no reciprocal predispositions in the members.

Were it admitted, however, that the federal government may feel an equal disposition with the State governments to extend its power beyond the due limits, the latter would still have the advantage in the means of defeating such encroachments. If an act of a particular State, though unfriendly to the national government, be generally popular in that State, and should not too grossly violate the oaths of the State officers, it is executed immediately and, of course, by means on the spot and depending on the State alone. The opposition of the federal government, or the interposition of federal officers, would but inflame the zeal of all parties on the side of the State, and the evil could not be prevented or repaired, if at all, without the employment of means which must always be resorted to with reluctance and difficulty. On the other hand, should an unwarrantable measure of the federal government be unpopular in particular States, which would seldom fail to be the case, or even a warrantable measure be so, which may sometimes be the case, the means of opposition to it are powerful and at hand. The disquietude of the people; their repugnance and, perhaps, refusal to co-operate with the officers of the Union; the frowns of the executive magistracy of the State; the embarrassments created by legislative devices, which would often be added on such occasions, would oppose, in any State, difficulties not to be despised; would form, in a large State, very serious impediments; and where the sentiments of several adjoining States happened to be in unison, would present obstructions which the federal government would hardly be willing to encounter.

But ambitious encroachments of the federal government on the authority of the State governments would not excite the opposition of a single State, or of a few States only. They would be signals of general alarm. Every government would espouse the common cause. A correspondence would be opened. Plans of resistance would be concerted. One spirit would animate and conduct the whole. The same combinations, in short, would result from an apprehension of the federal, as was produced by the dread of a foreign, yoke; and unless the projected innovations should be voluntarily renounced, the same appeal to a trial of force would be made in the one case as was made in the other. But what degree of madness could ever drive the federal government to such an extremity? In the contest with Great Britain, one part of the empire was employed against the other. The more numerous part invaded the rights of the less numerous part. The attempt was unjust and unwise; but it was not in speculation absolutely chimerical. But what would be the contest in the case we are supposing? Who would be the parties? A few representatives of the people would be opposed to the people themselves; or rather one set of representatives would be contending against thirteen sets of representatives, with the whole body of their common constituents on the side of the latter.

The only refuge left for those who prophesy the downfall of the State governments is the visionary supposition that the federal government may previously accumulate a military force for the projects of ambition. The reasonings contained in these papers must have been employed to little purpose indeed, if it could be necessary now to disprove the reality of this danger. That the people and the States should, for a sufficient period of time, elect an uninterrupted succession of men ready to betray both; that the traitors should, throughout this period, uniformly and systematically pursue some fixed plan for the extension of the military establishment; that the governments and the people of the States should silently and patiently behold the gathering storm and continue to supply the materials until it should be prepared to burst on their own heads must appear to everyone more like the incoherent dreams of a delirious jealousy, or the misjudged exaggerations of a counterfeit zeal, than like the sober apprehensions of genuine patriotism. Extravagant as the supposition is, let it, however, be made. Let a regular army, fully equal to the resources of the country, be formed; and let it be entirely at the devotion of the federal government: still it would not be going too far to say that the State governments with the people on their side would be able to repel the danger. The highest number to which, according to the best computation, a standing army can be carried in any country does not exceed one hundredth part of the whole number of souls; or one twenty-fifth part of the number able to bear arms. This proportion would not yield, in the United States, an army of more than twenty-five or thirty thousand men. To these would be opposed a militia amounting to near half a million of citizens with arms in their hands, officered by men chosen from among themselves, fighting for their common liberties and united and conducted by governments possessing their affections and confidence. It may well be doubted whether a militia thus circumstanced could ever be conquered by such a proportion of regular troops. Those who are best acquainted with the late successful resistance of this country against the British arms will be most inclined to deny the possibility of it. Besides the advantage of being armed, which the Americans possess over the people of almost every other nation, the existence of subordinate governments, to which the people are attached and by which the militia officers are appointed, forms a barrier against the enterprises of ambition, more insurmountable than any which a simple government of any form can admit of. Notwithstanding the military establishments in the several kingdoms of Europe, which are carried as far as the public resources will bear, the governments are afraid to trust the people with arms. And it is not certain that with this aid alone they would not be able to shake off their yokes. But were the people to possess the additional advantages of local governments chosen by themselves, who could collect the national will and direct the national force, and of officers appointed out of the militia by these governments and attached both to them and to the militia, it may be affirmed with the greatest assurance that the throne of every tyranny in Europe would be speedily overturned in spite of the legions which surround it. Let us not insult the free and gallant citizens of America with the suspicion that they would be less able to defend the rights of which they would be in actual possession than the debased subjects of arbitrary power would be to rescue theirs from the hands of their oppressors. Let us rather no longer insult them with the supposition that they can ever reduce themselves to the necessity of making the experiment by a blind and tame submission to the long train of insidious measures which must precede and produce it.

The argument under the present head may be put into a very concise form, which appears altogether conclusive. Either the mode in which the federal government is to be constructed will render it sufficiently dependent on the people, or it will not. On the first supposition, it will be restrained by that dependence from forming schemes obnoxious to their constituents. On the other supposition, it will not possess the confidence of the people, and its schemes of usurpation will be easily defeated by the State governments, who will be supported by the people.

On summing up the considerations stated in this and the last paper, they seem to amount to the most convincing evidence that the powers proposed to be lodged in the federal government are as little formidable to those reserved to the individual States as they are indispensably necessary to accomplish the purposes of the Union; and that all those alarms which have been sounded of a meditated and consequential annihilation of the State governments must, on the most favorable interpretation, be ascribed to the chimerical fears of the authors of them.

Publius
(James Madison)

NUMBER 47

Having reviewed the general form of the proposed government and the general mass of power allotted to it, I proceed to examine the particular structure of this government, and the distribution of this mass of power among its constituent parts.

One of the principal objections inculcated by the more respectable adversaries to the Constitution is its supposed violation of the political maxim that the legislative, executive, and judiciary departments ought to be separate and distinct. In the structure of the federal government no regard, it is said, seems to have been paid to this essential precaution in favor of liberty. The several departments of power are distributed and blended in such a manner as at once to destroy all symmetry and beauty of form, and to expose some of the essential parts of the edifice to the danger of being crushed by the disproportionate weight of other parts.

No political truth is certainly of greater intrinsic value, or is stamped with the authority of more enlightened patrons of liberty than that on which the objection is founded. The accumulation of all powers, legislative, executive, and judiciary, in the same hands, whether of one, a few, or many, and whether hereditary, self-appointed, or elective, may justly be pronounced the very definition of tyranny. Were the federal Constitution, therefore, really chargeable with this accumulation of power, or with a mixture of powers, having a dangerous tendency to such an accumulation, no further arguments would be necessary to inspire a universal reprobation of the system. I persuade myself, however, that it will be made apparent to everyone that the charge cannot be supported, and that the maxim on which it relies has been totally misconceived and misapplied. In order to form correct ideas on this important subject it will be proper to investigate the sense in which the preservation of liberty requires that the three great departments of power should be separate and distinct.

The oracle who is always consulted and cited on this subject is the celebrated Montesquieu. If he be not the author of this invaluable precept in the science of politics, he has the merit at least of displaying and recommending it most effectually to the attention of mankind. Let us endeavor, in the first place, to ascertain his meaning on this point.

The British Constitution was to Montesquieu* what Homer has been to the didactic writers on epic poetry. As the latter have considered the work of the immortal bard as the perfect model from which the principles and rules of the epic art were to be drawn, and by which all similar works were to be judged, so this great political critic appears to have viewed the Constitution of England as the standard, or to use his own expression, as the mirror of political liberty; and to have delivered, in the form of elementary truths, the several characteristic principles of that particular system. That we may be sure, then, not to mistake his meaning in this case, let us recur to the source from which the maxim was drawn.

On the slightest view of the British Constitution, we must perceive that the legislative, executive, and judiciary departments are by no means totally separate and distinct from each other. The executive magistrate forms an integral part of the legislative authority. He alone has the prerogative of making treaties with foreign sovereigns which, when made, have, under certain limitations, the force of legislative acts. All the members of the judiciary department are appointed by him, can be removed by him on the address of the two Houses of Parliament, and form, when he pleases to consult them, one of his constitutional councils. One branch of the legislative department forms also a great constitutional council to the executive chief, as, on another hand, it is the sole depositary of judicial power in cases of impeachment, and is invested with the supreme appellate jurisdiction in all other cases. The judges, again, are so far connected with the

**Charles Louis de Secondat, Baron de Montesquieu* (1689–1755): French philosopher and political theorist hailed as one of the founders of modern political science. He was unique in his time for his application of empirical methods to the study of politics. Montesquieu's *The Spirit of Laws* (1734) was studied by the writers of the United States Constitution. He espoused the concept of the separation of powers and the need for checks and balances between the different branches of government.

legislative department as often to attend and participate in its deliberations, though not admitted to a legislative vote.

From these facts, by which Montesquieu was guided, it may clearly be inferred that in saying "There can be no liberty where the legislative and executive powers are united in the same person, or body of magistrates," or "if the power of judging be not separated from the legislative and executive powers," he did not mean that these departments ought to have no *partial agency* in, or no *control* over, the acts of each other. His meaning, as his own words import, and still more conclusively as illustrated by the example in his eye, can amount to no more than this, that where the *whole* power of one department is exercised by the same hands which possess the *whole* power of another department, the fundamental principles of a free constitution are subverted. This would have been the case in the constitution examined by him, if the king, who is the sole executive magistrate, had possessed also the complete legislative power, or the supreme administration of justice; or if the entire legislative body had possessed the supreme judiciary, or the supreme executive authority. This, however, is not among the vices of that constitution. The magistrate in whom the whole executive power resides cannot of himself make a law, though he can put a negative on every law; nor administer justice in person, though he has the appointment of those who do administer it. The judges can exercise no executive prerogative, though they are shoots from the executive stock; nor any legislative function, though they may be advised by the legislative councils. The entire legislature can perform no judiciary act, though by the joint act of two of its branches the judges may be removed from their offices, and though one of its branches is possessed of the judicial power in the last resort. The entire legislature, again, can exercise no executive prerogative, though one of its branches constitutes the supreme executive magistracy, and another, on the impeachment of a third, can try and condemn all the subordinate officers in the executive department.

The reasons on which Montesquieu grounds his maxim are a further demonstration of his meaning. "When the legislative and executive powers are united in the same person or body," says he, "there can be no liberty, because apprehensions may arise lest *the same* monarch or senate should *enact* tyrannical laws to *execute* them in a tyrannical manner." Again: "Were the power of judging joined with the legislative, the life and liberty of the subject would be exposed to arbitrary control, for *the judge* would then be *the legislator*. Were it joined to the executive power, *the judge* might behave with all the violence of *an oppressor*." Some of these reasons are more fully explained in other passages; but briefly stated as they are here they sufficiently establish the meaning which we have put on this celebrated maxim of this celebrated author.

If we look into the constitutions of the several States we find that, notwithstanding the emphatical and, in some instances, the unqualified terms in which this axiom has been laid down, there is not a single instance in which the several departments of power have been kept absolutely separate and distinct. New Hampshire, whose constitution was the last formed, seems to have been fully aware of the impossibility and inexpediency of avoiding any mixture whatever of these departments, and has qualified the doctrine by declaring "that the legislative, executive, and judiciary powers ought to be kept as separate from, and independent of, each other *as the nature of a free government will admit; or as is consistent with that chain of connection that binds the whole fabric of the constitution in one indissoluble bond of unity and amity.*" Her constitution accordingly mixes these departments in several respects. The Senate, which is a branch of the legislative department, is also a judicial tribunal for the trial of impeachments. The President, who is the head of the executive department, is the presiding member also of the Senate; and, besides an equal vote in all cases, has a casting vote in case of a tie. The executive head is himself eventually elective every year by the legislative department, and his council is every year chosen by and from the members of the same department. Several of the officers of state are also appointed by the legislature. And the members of the judiciary department are appointed by the executive department.

The constitution of Massachusetts has observed a sufficient though less pointed caution in expressing this fundamental article of liberty. It declares "that the legislative department shall never exercise the executive and judicial powers, or either of them; the executive shall never exercise the legislative and judicial powers, or either of them; the judicial shall never exercise the legislative and executive powers, or either of them." This declaration corresponds precisely with the doctrine of Montesquieu, as it has been explained, and is not in a single point violated by the plan of the convention. It goes no farther than to prohibit any one of the entire departments from exercising the powers of another department. In the very Constitution to which it is prefixed, a partial mixture of powers has been admitted. The executive magistrate has a qualified negative on the legislative body, and the Senate, which is a part of the legislature, is a court of impeachment for members both of the executive and judiciary departments. The members of the judiciary department, again, are appointable by the executive department, and removable by the same authority on the address of the two legislative branches. Lastly, a number of the officers of government are annually appointed by the legislative department. As the appointment to offices, particularly executive offices, is in its nature an executive function, the compilers of the Constitution have, in this last point at least, violated the rule established by themselves.

I pass over the constitutions of Rhode Island and Connecticut, because they were formed prior to the Revolution and even before the principle under examination had become an object of political attention.

The constitution of New York contains no declaration on this subject, but appears very clearly to have been framed with an eye to the danger of improperly blending the different departments. It gives, nevertheless, to the executive magistrate, a partial control over the legislative department; and, what is more, gives a like control to the judiciary department; and even blends the executive and judiciary departments in the exercise of this control. In its council of appointment members of the legislative are associated with the executive authority, in the appointment of officers, both executive and judiciary. And its court for the trial of impeachments and correction of errors is to consist of one branch of the legislature and the principal members of the judiciary department.

The constitution of New Jersey has blended the different powers of government more than any of the preceding. The governor, who is the executive magistrate, is appointed by the legislature; is chancellor and ordinary, or surrogate of the State; is a member of the Supreme Court of Appeals, and president, with a casting vote, of one of the legislative branches. The same legislative branch acts again as executive council to the governor, and with him constitutes the Court of Appeals. The members of the judiciary department are appointed by the legislative department, and removable by one branch of it, on the impeachment of the other.

According to the constitution of Pennsylvania, the president, who is the head of the executive department, is annually elected by a vote in which the legislative department predominates. In conjunction with an executive council, he appoints the members of the judiciary department and forms a court of impeachment for trial of all officers, judiciary as well as executive. The judges of the Supreme Court and justices of the peace seem also to be removable by the legislature; and the executive power of pardoning, in certain cases, to be referred to the same department. The members of the executive council are made EX OFFICIO justices of peace throughout the State.

In Delaware, the chief executive magistrate is annually elected by the legislative department. The speakers of the two legislative branches are vice-presidents in the executive department. The executive chief, with six others appointed, three by each of the legislative branches, constitutes the Supreme Court of Appeals; he is joined with the legislative department in the appointment of the other judges. Throughout the States it appears that the members of the legislature may at the same time be justices of the peace; in this State, the members of one branch of it are EX OFFICIO justices of the peace; as are also the members of the executive council. The principal officers of the executive department are appointed by the legislative; and one branch of the latter forms a court of impeachments. All officers may be removed on address of the legislature.

Maryland has adopted the maxim in the most unqualified terms; declaring that the legislative, executive, and judicial powers of government ought to be forever separate and distinct from each other. Her constitution, notwithstanding, makes the executive magistrate appointable by the legislative department; and the members of the judiciary by the executive department.

The language of Virginia is still more pointed on this subject. Her constitution declares "the the legislative, executive, and judiciary departments shall be separate and distinct; so that neither exercises the powers properly belonging to the other; nor shall any person exercise the powers of more than one of them at the same time, except that the justices of county courts shall be eligible to either House of Assembly." Yet we find not only this express exception with respect to the members of the inferior courts, but that the chief magistrate, with his executive council, are appointable by the legislature; that two members of the latter are triennially displaced at the pleasure of the legislature; and that all the principal offices, both executive and judiciary, are filled by the same department. The executive prerogative of pardon, also, is in one case vested in the legislative department.

The constitution of North Carolina, which declares "that the legislative, executive, and supreme judicial powers of government ought to be forever separate and distinct from each other," refers, at the same time, to the legislative department, the appointment not only of the executive chief, but all the principal officers within both that and the judiciary department.

In South Carolina, the constitution makes the executive magistracy eligible by the legislative department. It gives to the latter, also, the appointment of the members of the judiciary department, including even justices of the peace and sheriffs; and the appointment of officers in the executive department, down to captains in the army and navy of the State.

In the constitution of Georgia where it is declared "that the legislative, executive, and judiciary departments shall be separate and distinct, so that neither exercise the powers properly belonging to the other," we find that the executive department is to be filled by appointments of the legislature; and the executive prerogative of pardon to be finally exercised by the same authority. Even justices of the peace are to be appointed by the legislature.

In citing these cases, in which the legislative, executive, and judiciary departments have not been kept totally separate and distinct, I wish not to be regarded as an advocate for the particular organizations of the several State governments. I am fully aware that among the many excellent principles which they exemplify they carry strong marks of the haste, and still stronger of the inexperience, under which they were framed. It is but too obvious that in some instances the fundamental principle under consideration has been violated by too great a mixture, and even an actual consolidation of the different powers; and that in no instance has a competent provision been made for maintaining in practice the separation delineated on paper. What I have wished to evince is that the charge brought against the proposed Constitution of violating the sacred maxim of free government is warranted neither by the real meaning annexed to that maxim by its author, nor by the sense in which it has hitherto been understood in America. This interesting subject will be resumed in the ensuing paper.

Publius
(James Madison)

NUMBER 51

To what expedient, then, shall we finally resort, for maintaining in practice the necessary partition of power among the several departments as laid down in the Constitution? The only answer that can be given is that as all these exterior provisions are found to be inadequate the defect must be supplied, by so contriving the interior structure of the government as that its several constituent parts may, by their mutual relations, be the means of keeping each other in their proper places. Without presuming to undertake a full development of this important idea I will hazard a few general observations which may perhaps place it in a clearer light, and enable us to form a more correct judgment of the principles and structure of the government planned by the convention.

In order to lay a due foundation for that separate and distinct exercise of the different powers of government, which to a certain extent is admitted on all hands to be essential to the preservation of liberty, it is evident that each department should have a will of its own; and consequently should be so constituted that the members of each should have as little agency as possible in the appointment of the members of the others. Were this principle rigorously adhered to, it would require that all the appointments for the supreme executive, legislative, and judiciary magistracies should be drawn from the same fountain of authority, the people, through channels having no communication whatever with one another. Perhaps such a plan of constructing the several departments would be less difficult in practice than it may in contemplation appear. Some difficulties, however, and some additional expense would attend the execution of it. Some deviations, therefore, from the principle must be admitted. In the constitution of the judiciary department in particular, it might be inexpedient to insist rigorously on the principle: first, because peculiar qualifications being essential in the members, the primary consideration ought to be to select that mode of choice which best secures these qualifications; second, because the permanent tenure by which the appointments are held in that department must soon destroy all sense of dependence on the authority conferring them.

It is equally evident that the members of each department should be as little dependent as possible on those of the others for the emoluments annexed to their offices. Were the executive magistrate, or the judges, not independent of the legislature in this particular, their independence in every other would be merely nominal.

But the great security against a gradual concentration of the several powers in the same department consists in giving to those who administer each department the necessary constitutional means and personal motives to resist encroachments of the others. The provision for defense must in this, as in all other cases, be made commensurate to the danger of attack. Ambition must be made to counteract ambition. The interest of the man must be connected with the constitutional rights of the place. It may be a reflection on human nature that such devices should be necessary to control the abuses of government. But what is government itself but the greatest of all reflections on human nature? If men were angels, no government would be necessary. If angels were to govern men, neither external nor internal controls on government would be necessary. In framing a government which is to be administered by men over men, the great difficulty lies in this: you must first enable the government to control the governed; and in the next place oblige it to control itself. A dependence on the people is, no doubt, the primary control on the government; but experience has taught mankind the necessity of auxiliary precautions.

This policy of supplying, by opposite and rival interests, the defect of better motives, might be traced through the whole system of human affairs, private as well as public. We see it particularly displayed in all the subordinate distributions of power, where the constant aim is to divide and arrange the several offices in such a manner as that each may be a check on the other—that the private interest of every individual may be a sentinel over the public rights. These inventions of prudence cannot be less requisite in the distribution of the supreme powers of the State.

But it is not possible to give to each department an equal power of self-defense. In republican government, the legislative authority necessarily predominates. The remedy for this inconveniency is to divide the legislature into different branches; and to render them, by different modes of election and different principles of action, as little connected with each other as the nature of their common functions and their common dependence on the society will admit. It may even be necessary to guard against dangerous encroachments by still further precautions. As the weight of the legislative authority requires that it should be thus divided, the weakness of the executive may require, on the other hand, that it should be fortified. An absolute negative on the legislature appears, at first view, to be the natural defense with which the executive magistrate should be armed. But perhaps it would be neither altogether safe nor alone sufficient. On ordinary occasions it might not be exerted with the requisite firmness, and on extraordinary occasions it might be perfidiously abused. May not this defect of an absolute negative be supplied by some qualified connection between this weaker department and the weaker branch of the stronger department, by which the latter may be led to support the constitutional rights of the former, without being too much detached from the rights of its own department?

If the principles on which these observations are founded be just, as I persuade myself they are, and they be applied as a criterion to the several State constitutions, and to the federal Constitution, it will be found that if the latter does not perfectly correspond with them, the former are infinitely less able to bear such a test.

There are, moreover, two considerations particularly applicable to the federal system of America, which place that system in a very interesting point of view.

First. In a single republic, all the power surrendered by the people is submitted to the administration of a single government; and the usurpations are guarded against by a division of the government into distinct and separate departments. In the compound republic of America, the power surrendered by the people is first divided between two distinct governments, and then the portion allotted to each subdivided among distinct and separate departments. Hence a double security arises to the rights of the people. The different governments will control each other, at the same time that each will be controlled by itself.

Second. It is of great importance in a republic not only to guard the society against the oppression of its rulers, but to guard one part of the society against the injustice of the other part. Different interests necessarily exist in different classes of citizens. If a majority be united by a common interest, the rights of the minority will be insecure. There are but two methods of providing against this evil: the one by creating a will in the community independent of the majority—that is, of the society itself; the other, by comprehending in the society so many separate descriptions of citizens as will render an unjust combination of a majority of the whole very improbable, if not impracticable. The first method prevails in all governments possessing an hereditary or self-appointed authority. This, at best, is but a precarious security; because a power independent of the society may as well espouse the unjust views of the major as the rightful interests of the minor party, and may possibly be turned against both parties. The second method will be exemplified in the federal republic of the United States. Whilst all authority in it will be derived from and dependent on the society, the society itself will be broken into so many parts, interests and classes of citizens, that the rights of individuals, or of the minority, will be in little danger from interested combinations of the majority. In a free government the security for civil rights must be the same as that for religious rights. It consists in the one case in the multiplicity of interests, and in the other in the multiplicity of sects. The degree of security in both cases will depend on the number of interests and sects; and this may be presumed to depend on the extent of country and number of people comprehended under the same government. This view of the subject must particularly recommend a proper federal system to all the sincere and considerate friends of republican government, since it shows that in exact proportion as the territory of the Union may be formed into more circumscribed Confederacies, or States, oppressive combinations of a majority will be facilitated; the best security, under the republican forms, for the rights of every class of citizen, will be diminished; and consequently the stability and independence of some member of the government, the only other security, must be proportionally increased. Justice is the end of government. It is the end of civil society. It ever has been and ever will be pursued until it be obtained, or until liberty be lost in the pursuit. In a society under the forms of which the stronger faction can readily unite and oppress the weaker, anarchy may as truly be said to reign as in a state of nature, where the weaker individual is not secured against the violence of the stronger; and as, in the latter state, even the stronger individuals are prompted, by the uncertainty of their condition, to submit to a government which may protect the weak as well as themselves; so, in the former state, will the more powerful factions or parties be gradually induced, by a like motive, to wish for a government which will protect all parties, the weaker as well as the more powerful. It can be little doubted that if the State of Rhode Island was separated from the Confederacy and left to itself, the insecurity of rights under the popular form of government within such narrow limits would be displayed by such reiterated oppressions of factious majorities that some power altogether independent of the people would soon be called for by the voice of the very factions whose misrule had proved the necessity of it. In the extended republic of the United States, and among the great variety of interests, parties, and sects which it embraces, a coalition of a majority of the whole society could seldom take place on any other principles than those of justice and the general good; whilst there being thus less danger to a minor from the will of a major party, there must be less pretext, also, to provide for the security of the former, by introducing into the government a will not dependent on the latter, or, in other words, a will independent of the society itself. It is no less certain than it is important, notwithstanding the contrary opinions which have been entertained, that the larger the society, provided it lie within a practicable sphere, the more duly capable it will be of self-government. And happily for the *republican cause*, the practicable sphere may be carried to a very great extent by a judicious modification and mixture of the *federal principle*.

Publius
(James Madison)

NUMBER 69

I proceed now to trace the real characters of the proposed executive, as they are marked out in the plan of the convention. This will serve to place in a strong light the unfairness of the representations which have been made in regard to it.

The first thing which strikes our attention is that the executive authority, with few exceptions, is to be vested in a single magistrate. This will scarcely, however, be considered as a point upon which any comparison can be grounded; for if, in this particular, there be a resemblance to the king of Great Britain, there is not less a resemblance to the Grand Seignior, to the khan of Tartary, to the Man of the Seven Mountains, or to the governor of New York.

That magistrate is to be elected for *four* years; and is to be re-eligible as often as the people of the United States shall think him worthy of their confidence. In these circumstances there is a total dissimilitude between *him* and a king of Great Britain, who is an *hereditary* monarch, possessing the crown as a patrimony descendible to his heirs forever; but there is a close analogy between *him* and a governor of New York, who is elected for *three* years, and is re-eligible without limitation or intermission. If we consider how much less time would be requisite for establishing a dangerous influence in a single State than for establishing a like influence throughout the United States, we must conclude that a duration of *four* years for the Chief Magistrate of the Union is a degree of permanency far less to be dreaded in that office, than a duration of *three* years for a corresponding office in a single State.

The President of the United States would be liable to be impeached, tried, and, upon conviction of treason, bribery, or other high crimes or misdemeanors, removed from office; and would afterwards be liable to prosecution and punishment in the ordinary course of law. The person of the King of Great Britain is sacred and inviolable; there is no constitutional tribunal to which he is amenable; no punishment to which he can be subjected without involving the crisis of a national revolution. In this delicate and important circumstance of personal responsibility, the President of Confederated America would stand upon no better ground than a governor of New York, and upon worse ground than the governors of Virginia and Delaware.

The President of the United States is to have power to return a bill, which shall have passed the two branches of the legislature, for reconsideration; but the bill so returned is not to become a law unless, upon that reconsideration, it be approved by two thirds of both houses. The king of Great Britain, on his part, has an absolute negative upon the acts of the two houses of Parliament. The disuse of that power for a considerable time past does not affect the reality of its existence and is to be ascribed wholly to the crown's having found the means of substituting influence to authority, or the art of gaining a majority in one or the other of the two houses, to the necessity of exerting a prerogative which could seldom be exerted without hazarding some degree of national agitation. The qualified negative of the President differs widely from this absolute negative of the British sovereign and tallies exactly with the revisionary authority of the council of revision of this State, of which the governor is a constituent part. In this respect the power of the President would exceed that of the governor of New York, because the former would possess, singly, what the latter shares with the chancellor and judges; but it would be precisely the same with that of the governor of Massachusetts, whose constitution, as to this article, seems to have been the original from which the convention have copied.

The President is to be the "commander-in-chief of the army and navy of the United States, and of the militia of the several States, when called into the actual service of the United States. He is to have power to grant reprieves and pardons for offenses against the United States, *except in cases of impeachment*; to recommend to the consideration of Congress such measures as he shall judge necessary and expedient; to convene, on extraordinary occasions, both houses of the legislature, or either of them, and, in case of disagreement between them *with respect to the time of adjournment*, to adjourn them to such time as he shall think proper; to take care that the laws be faithfully executed; and to commission all officers of the United States." In most of these particulars, the power of the President will resemble equally that of the king of Great Britain and of the governor of New York. The most material points of difference are these:—*First*. The President will have only the occasional command of such part of the militia of the nation as by legislative provision may be called into the actual service of the Union. The king of Great Britain and the governor of New York have at all times the entire command of all the militia within their several jurisdictions. In this article, therefore, the power of the President would be inferior to that of either the monarch or the governor. *Second*. The President is to be commander-in-chief of the army and navy of the United States. In this respect his authority would be nominally the same with that of the king of Great Britain, but in substance much inferior to it. It would amount to nothing more than the supreme command and direction of the military and naval forces, as first general and admiral of the Confederacy; while that of the British king extends to the *declaring* of war and to the *raising* and *regulating* of fleets and armies—all which, by the Constitution under consideration, would appertain to the legislature.[1] The governor of New York, on the other hand, is by the constitution of the State vested only with the command of its militia and navy. But the constitutions of several of the States expressly declare their governors to be commanders-in-chief, as well of the army as navy; and it may well be a question whether those of New Hampshire and Massachusetts, in particular, do not, in this instance, confer larger powers upon their respective governors than could be claimed by a President of the United States. *Third*. The power of the President, in respect to pardons, would extend to all cases, *except those of impeachment*. The governor of New York may pardon in all cases, even in those of impeachment, except for treason and murder. Is not the power of the governor, in this article, on a calculation of political consequences, greater than that of the President? All conspiracies and plots against the government which have not been matured into actual treason may be screened from punishment of every kind by the interposition of the prerogative of pardoning. If a governor of New York, therefore, should be at the head of any such conspiracy, until the design had been ripened into actual hostility he could insure his accomplices and adherents an entire impunity. A President of the Union, on the other hand, though he may even pardon treason, when prosecuted in the ordinary course of law, could shelter no offender, in any degree, from the effects of impeachment and conviction. Would not the prospect of a total indemnity for all the preliminary steps be a greater temptation to undertake and persevere in an enterprise against the public liberty, than the mere prospect of an exemption from death and confiscation, if the final execution of the design, upon an actual appeal to arms, should miscarry? Would this last expectation have any influence at all, when the probability was computed that the person who was to afford that exemption might himself be involved in the consequences of the measure, and might be incapacitated by his agency in it from affording the desired impunity? The better to judge of this matter, it will be necessary to recollect that, by the proposed Constitution, the offense of treason is limited "to levying war upon the United States, and adhering to their enemies, giving them aid and comfort"; and that by the laws of New York it is confined within similar bounds. *Fourth.* The President can only adjourn the national legislature in the single case of disagreement about the time of adjournment. The British monarch may prorogue or even dissolve the Parliament. The governor of New York may also prorogue the legislature of this State for a limited time; a power which, in certain situations, may be employed to very important purposes.

The President is to have power, with the advice and consent of the Senate, to make treaties, provided two thirds of the senators present concur. The king of Great Britain is the sole and absolute representative of the nation in all foreign transactions. He can of his own accord make treaties of peace, commerce, alliance, and of every other description. It has been insinuated that his authority in this respect is not conclusive, and that his conventions with foreign powers are subject to the revision, and stand in need of the ratification, of Parliament. But I believe this doctrine was never heard of until it was broached upon the present occasion. Every jurist[2] of that kingdom, and every other man acquainted with its Constitution knows, as an established fact, that the prerogative of making treaties exists in the crown in its utmost plenitude; and that the compacts entered into by the royal authority have the most complete legal validity and perfection, independent of any other sanction. The Parliament, it is true, is sometimes seen employing itself in altering the existing laws to conform them to the stipulations in a new treaty; and this may have possibly given birth to the imagination that its cooperation was necessary to the obligatory efficacy of the treaty. But this parliamentary interposition proceeds from a different cause: from the necessity of adjusting a most artificial and intricate system of revenue and commercial laws, to the changes made in them by the operation of the treaty; and of adapting new provisions and precautions to the new state of things, to keep the machine from running into disorder. In this respect, therefore, there is no comparison between the intended power of the President and the actual power of the British sovereign. The one can perform alone what the other can only do with the concurrence of a branch of the legislature. It must be admitted that in this instance the power of the federal executive would exceed that of any State executive. But this arises naturally from the exclusive possession by the Union of that part of the sovereign power which relates to treaties. If the Confederacy were to be dissolved, it would become a question whether the executives of the several States were not solely invested with that delicate and important prerogative.

The President is also to be authorized to receive ambassadors and other public ministers. This, though it has been a rich theme of declamation, is more a matter of dignity than of authority. It is a circumstance which will be without consequence in the administration of the government; and it was far more convenient that it should be arranged in this manner than that there should be a necessity of convening the legislature, or one of its branches, upon every arrival of a foreign minister, though it were merely to take the place of a departed predecessor.

The President is to nominate, and, *with the advice and consent of the Senate*, to appoint ambassadors and other public ministers, judges of the Supreme Court, and in general all officers of the United States established by law, and whose appointments are not otherwise provided for by the Constitution. The king of Great Britain is emphatically and truly styled the fountain of honor. He not only appoints to all offices, but can create offices. He can confer titles of nobility at pleasure, and has the disposal of an immense number of church preferments. There is evidently a great inferiority in the power of the President, in this particular, to that of the British king; nor is it equal to that of the governor of New York, if we are to interpret the meaning of the constitution of the State by the practice which has obtained under it. The power of appointment is with us lodged in a council, composed of the governor and four members of the Senate, chosen by the Assembly. The governor *claims*, and has frequently *exercised*, the right of nomination, and is *entitled* to a casting vote in the appointment. If he really has the right of nominating, his authority is in this respect equal to that of the President, and exceeds it in the article of the casting vote. In the national government, if the Senate should be divided, no appointment could be made; in the government of New York, if the council should be divided, the governor can turn the scale and confirm his own nomination.[3] If we compare the publicity which must necessarily attend the mode of appointment by the President and an entire branch of the national legislature, with the privacy in the mode of appointment by the governor of New York, closeted in a secret apartment with at most four, and frequently with only two persons; and if we at the same time consider how much more easy it must be to influence the small number of which a council of appointment consists than the considerable number of which the national Senate would consist, we cannot hesitate to pronounce that the power of the chief magistrate of this State, in the disposition of offices, must, in practice, be greatly superior to that of the Chief Magistrate of the Union.

Hence it appears that, except as to the concurrent authority of the President in the article of treaties, it would be difficult to determine whether that magistrate would, in the aggregate, possess more or less power than the governor of New York. And it appears yet more unequivocally that there is no pretense for the parallel which has been attempted between him and the king of Great Britain. But to render the contrast in this respect still more striking, it may be of use to throw the principal circumstances of dissimilitude into a closer group.

-sident of the United States would be an officer elected by the people years; the king of Great Britain is a perpetual and *hereditary* prince. The uld be amenable to personal punishment and disgrace; the person of the is sacred and inviolable. The one would have a *qualified* negative upon the of the legislative body; the other has an *absolute* negative. The one would have a right to command the military and naval forces of the nation; the other, in addition to this right, possesses that of *declaring* war, and of *raising* and *regulating* fleets and armies by his own authority. The one would have a concurrent power with a branch of the legislature in the formation of treaties; the other is the *sole possessor* of the power of making treaties. The one would have a like concurrent authority in appointing to offices; the other is the sole author of all appointments. The one can confer no privileges whatever; the other can make denizens of aliens, noblemen of commoners; can erect corporations with all the rights incident to corporate bodies. The one can prescribe no rules concerning the commerce or currency of the nation; the other is in several respects the arbiter of commerce, and in this capacity can establish markets and fairs, can regulate weights and measures, can lay embargoes for a limited time, can coin money, can authorize or prohibit the circulation of foreign coin. The one has no particle of spiritual jurisdiction; the other is the supreme head and governor of the national church! What answer shall we give to those who would persuade us that things so unlike resemble each other? The same that ought to be given to those who tell us that a government, the whole power of which would be in the hands of the elective and periodical servants of the people, is an aristocracy, a monarchy, and a despotism.

Publius
(Alexander Hamilton)

NOTES

[1]A writer in a Pennsylvania paper, under the signature of Tamony, has asserted that the king of Great Britain owes his prerogative as commander-in-chief to an annual mutiny bill. The truth is, on the contrary, that his prerogative in this respect is immemorial, and was only disputed "contrary to all reason and precedent," as Blackstone, vol. i, page 262, expresses it, by the Long Parliament of Charles I; but by the statute the 13th of Charles II, chap. 6, it was declared to be in the king alone, for that the sole supreme government and command of the militia within his Majesty's realms and dominions, and of all forces by sea and land, and of all forts and places of strength, EVER WAS AND IS the undoubted right of his Majesty and his royal predecessors, kings and queens of England, and that both or either house of Parliament cannot nor ought to pretend to the same.

[2]*Vide* Blackstone's *Commentaries*, Vol. I., p. 257.

[3]Candor, however, demands an acknowledgment that I do not think the claim of the governor to a right of nomination well founded. Yet it is always justifiable to reason from the practice of a government till its propriety has been constitutionally questioned. And independent of this claim, when we take into view the other considerations and pursue them through all their consequences, we shall be inclined to draw much the same conclusion.

PART TWO

FEDERALISM

Relations between the national and state governments have been perhaps the single most persistent source of conflict in American politics. The protracted struggles over such issues as slavery and civil rights, government regulation of business, and the provision of social welfare programs all reflect in one manner or another the underlying tension of the federal system: the conflict between national interests and states' rights. While other nations such as Great Britain have debated how to extend basic rights (such as the right to vote) to certain groups, or to provide forms of social insurance, or to nationalize the railroads, the United States has debated a different question—whether the central government *had the right* to do such things.[1] Even now, after many of these disputes have been resolved—usually with the national government successfully asserting its right to intervene—the states have retained leverage over the final administration of federal programs, ensuring that the distribution of power between levels of government remains in flux.

Complicating American intergovernmental relations is the fact that the Constitution does not always state clearly where federal authority begins and state sovereignty ends. In part, the framers, faced with the difficult task of winning ratification of the document, often found it inexpedient to be precise. But in part, also, it was hard to be precise when creating a novel form of government that, unlike the known models of the past, was to be neither a confederation of loosely allied provinces nor a strictly unitary regime, but rather an unfamiliar admixture of both.

For most of American constitutional history, "dual federalism" was the prevailing theory. It held that the federal government was restricted to some functions, the states to others, and that each was sovereign in its own legal domain. However, by the 1950s, this concept of federalism appeared increasingly antiquated. In 1960, Morton Grodzins advanced the view that American federalism is a system characterized by *mutual* influence among levels of government. Grodzins provided a now-famous analogy: contrary to what the old doctrine of dual federalism suggested, the federal system is not a "layer cake," in which clear functional distinctions can be drawn between the national and subordinate governments, but a "marble cake." "As colors are mixed in the marble cake," Grodzins wrote, "so functions are mixed in the American federal system." Moreover, in the article reprinted here, Grodzins affirmed that the marble cake model was not a recent development, but a suitable description of federal-state relations from the start: " . . . relative to what governments did, intergovernmental cooperation during the last century was comparable with that existing today."

Paul E. Peterson, writing in 1980, accepts Grodzins' critique of dual sovereignty, but he suggests that the marble cake metaphor does not go far enough. In

[1]James Q. Wilson, *American Government: Institutions and Policies* (Lexington, Mass.: D. C. Heath and Company, 1980), pp. 42–44.

Peterson's view, a theory of federalism must clarify the distinctive characteristics of a federal system, specify appropriate activities of central and local governments, and explain recurring patterns of conflict and cooperation among those levels of government. Examining the Great Society programs of the Johnson administration (1963–1969), Peterson notes how the interests of local authorities in financing their jurisdictions and in recruiting their political and administrative leaders can conflict with the national government's goals of promoting social equality. This essay's analysis of the differing economic interests or fiscal motives at various governmental levels—and the intergovernmental tensions that result—focuses on an important aspect of federalism that is often overlooked.

5

MORTON GRODZINS

THE FEDERAL SYSTEM

A political scientist at the University of Chicago during the 1950s to 1960s, Morton Grodzins (1917–1964) devoted the greater part of his career to studying American federalism. Writing in rebuttal to major reform efforts of the period that sought to separate the functions and revenue sources of the levels of government, Grodzins argued that the American system had been designed to promote a sharing of functions and power. The overlapping governmental authority built into the system, he argues, promotes decentralization and local autonomy. As a member of the University of Chicago's Federalism Workshop, Grodzins studied federalism from 1955 until the early 1960s. Always concerned with applying his theoretical work to the resolution of practical problems, Grodzins was a consultant to numerous agencies on issues related to intergovernmental management. The following article, "The Federal System," was Grodzins' contribution to The American Assembly's Goals for Americans: The Report of the President's Commission on National Goals *(1960). He also wrote* Americans Betrayed: Politics and the Japanese Evacuation *(1949),* The Metropolitan Area as a Social Problem *(1958), and a volume published posthumously,* The American System: A New View of Government in the United States *(1966), which is the product of two decades of research and analysis on federalism.*

Federalism is a device for dividing decisions and functions of government. As the constitutional fathers well understood, the federal structure is a means, not an end. The pages that follow are therefore not concerned with an exposition of American federalism as a formal, legal set of relationships. The focus, rather, is on the purpose of federalism, that is to say, on the distribution of power between central and peripheral units of government.

THE SHARING OF FUNCTIONS

The American form of government is often, but erroneously, symbolized by a three-layer cake. A far more accurate image is the rainbow or marble cake, characterized by an inseparable mingling of differently colored ingredients, the colors appearing in vertical and diagonal strands and unexpected whirls. As colors are mixed in the marble cake, so functions are mixed in the American federal system. Consider the health officer, styled "sanitarian," of a rural county in a border state. He embodies the whole idea of the marble cake of government.

The sanitarian is appointed by the state under merit standards established by the federal government. His base salary comes jointly from state and federal funds, the county provides him with an office and office amenities and pays a portion of his expenses, and the largest city in the county also contributes to his salary and office by virtue of his appointment as a city plumbing inspector. It is impossible from moment to moment to tell under which governmental hat the sanitarian operates. His work of inspecting the purity of food is carried out under federal standards; but he is enforcing state laws when inspecting commodities that have not been in interstate commerce; and somewhat perversely he also acts under state authority when inspecting milk coming into the county from producing areas across the state border. He is a federal officer when impounding impure drugs shipped from a neighboring state; a federal-state officer when distributing typhoid immunization serum; a state officer when enforcing standards of industrial hygiene; a state-local officer when inspecting the city's water supply; and (to complete the circle) a local officer when insisting that the city butchers adopt more hygienic methods of handling their garbage. But he cannot and does not think of himself as acting in these separate capacities. All business in the county that concerns public health and sanitation he considers his business. Paid largely from federal funds, he does not find it strange to attend meetings of the city council to give expert advice on matters ranging from rotten apples to rabies control. He is even deputized as a member of both the city and county police forces.

The sanitarian is an extreme case, but he accurately represents an important aspect of the whole range of governmental activities in the United States. Functions are not neatly parceled out among the many governments. They are shared functions. It is difficult to find any governmental activity which does not involve all three of the so-called "levels" of the federal system. In the most local of local functions—law enforcement or education, for example—the federal and state governments play important roles. In what, a priori, may be considered the purest central government activities—the conduct of foreign affairs, for example—the state and local governments have considerable responsibilities, directly and indirectly.

The federal grant programs are only the most obvious example of shared functions. They also most clearly exhibit how sharing serves to disperse governmental powers. The grants utilize the greater wealth-gathering abilities of the central government and establish nationwide standards, yet they are "in aid" of functions carried out under state law, with considerable state and local discretion. The national supervision of such programs is largely a process of mutual accommodation. Leading state and local officials, acting through their professional organizations, are in considerable part responsible for the very standards that national officers try to persuade all state and local officers to accept.

Even in the absence of joint financing, federal-state-local collaboration is the characteristic mode of action. Federal expertise is available to aid in the building of a local jail (which may later be used to house federal prisoners), to improve a local water purification system, to step up building inspections, to provide standards for state and local personnel in protecting housewives against dishonest butchers' scales, to prevent gas explosions, or to produce a land use plan. States and localities, on the other hand, take important formal responsibilities in the development of national programs for atomic energy, civil defense, the regulation of commerce, and the protection of purity in foods and drugs; local political weight is always a factor in the operation of even a post office or a military establishment. From abattoirs and accounting through zoning and zoo administration, any governmental activity is almost certain to involve the influence, if not the formal administration, of all three planes of the federal system.

ATTEMPTS TO UNWIND THE FEDERAL SYSTEM

Within the past dozen years there have been four major attempts to reform or reorganize the federal system: the first (1947–1949) and second (1953–1955) Hoover Commissions on Executive Organization; the Kestnbaum Commission on Intergovernmental Relations (1953–1955); and the Joint Federal-State Action Committee (1957–1959). All four of these groups have aimed to minimize federal activities. None of them has recognized the sharing of functions as the characteristic way American governments do things. Even when making recommendations for joint action, these official commissions take the view (as expressed in the Kestnbaum report) that "the main tradition of American federalism [is] the tradition of separateness." All four have, in varying degrees, worked to separate functions and tax sources.

The history of the Joint Federal-State Action Committee is especially instructive. The committee was established at the suggestion of President Eisenhower, who charged it, first of all, "to designate functions which the States are ready and willing to assume and finance that are now performed or financed wholly or in part by the Federal Government." He also gave the committee the task of recommending "Federal and State revenue adjustments required to enable the States to assume such functions."[1]

The committee subsequently established seemed most favorably situated to accomplish the task of functional separation. It was composed of distinguished and able men, including among its personnel three leading members of the President's Cabinet,* the director of the Bureau of the Budget, and ten state governors. It had the full support of the President at every point, and it worked hard and conscientiously. Excellent staff studies were supplied by the Bureau of the Budget, the White House, the Treasury Department, and, from the state side, the Council of State Governments. It had available to it a large mass of research data, including the sixteen recently completed volumes of the Kestnbaum Commission. There existed no disagreements on party lines within the committee and, of course, no constitutional impediments to its mission. The President, his Cabinet members, and all the governors (with one possible exception) on the committee completely agreed on the desirability of decentralization-via-separation-of-functions-and-taxes. They were unanimous in wanting to justify the committee's name and to produce action, not just another report.

*Cabinet: appointees who direct the administrative departments of government and report to the chief executive. George Washington first instituted the practice of holding meetings with the vice-president and the heads of the executive departments. The original cabinet included only three departments. Today, the fourteen Cabinet departments are: Treasury, Defense, State, Justice, Interior, Agriculture, Commerce, Labor, Health and Human Services, Education, Housing and Urban Development, Energy, Transportation, and Veterans Affairs.

The committee worked for more than two years. It found exactly two programs to recommend for transfer from federal to state hands. One was the federal grant program for vocational education (including practical-nurse training and aid to fishery trades); the other was federal grants for municipal waste treatments plants. The programs together cost the federal government less than $80 million in 1957, slightly more than two percent of the total federal grants for that year. To allow the states to pay for these programs, the committee recommended that they be allowed a credit against the federal tax on local telephone calls. Calculations showed that this offset device, plus an equalizing factor, would give every state at least 40 percent more from the tax than it received from the federal government in vocational education and sewage disposal grants. Some states were "equalized" to receive twice as much.

The recommendations were modest enough, and the generous financing feature seemed calculated to gain state support. The President recommended to Congress that all points of the program be legislated. None of them was, none has been since, and none is likely to be.

A POINT OF HISTORY

The American federal system has never been a system of separated governmental activities. There has never been a time when it was possible to put neat labels on discrete "federal," "state," and "local" functions. Even before the Constitution, a statute of 1785, reinforced by the Northwest Ordinance of 1787,* gave grants-in-land to the states for public schools. Thus the national government was a prime force in making possible what is now taken to be the most local function of all, primary and secondary education. More important, the nation, before it was fully organized, established by this action a first principle of American federalism: the national government would use its superior resources to initiate and support national programs, principally administered by the states and localities.

The essential unity of state and federal financial systems was again recognized in the earliest constitutional days with the assumption by the federal government of the Revolutionary War debts of the states. Other points of federal-state collaboration during the Federalist period concerned the militia, law enforcement, court practices, the administration of elections, public health measures, pilot laws, and many other matters.

The nineteenth century is widely believed to have been the preeminent period of duality in the American system. Lord Bryce,† at the end of the century described

**Northwest Ordinance:* law passed by the Congress of the Confederation of States in July 1787, creating the governing structure of the Northwest Territory, land acquired as a result of the revolutionary war. It provided a framework for the creation of subsequent territories and established guidelines whereby territories could become states. The Northwest Territory included what is now Ohio, Indiana, Illinois, Michigan, Wisconsin, and part of Minnesota.

†*Lord James Bryce* (1838–1922): British historian who served as ambassador to the United States from 1907 to 1913. His essay "Why Great Men Are Not Chosen Presidents," a chapter from his book *The American Commonwealth* (1888), is remembered for its observation that the most unusual thing about American presidents is how "commonplace" they tend to be.

(in *The American Commonwealth*) the federal and state government as "distinct and separate in their action." The system, he said, was "like a great factory wherein two sets of machinery are at work, their revolving wheels apparently intermixed, their bands crossing one another, yet each set doing its own work without touching or hampering the other." Great works may contain gross errors. Bryce was wrong. The nineteenth century, like the early days of the republic, was a period principally characterized by intergovernmental collaboration.

Decisions of the Supreme Court are often cited as evidence of nineteenth-century duality. In the early part of the century the Court, heavily weighted with Federalists, was intent upon enlarging the sphere of national authority; in the later years (and to the 1930s) its actions were in the direction of paring down national powers and indeed all governmental authority. Decisions referred to "areas of exclusive competence" exercised by the federal government and the states; to their powers being "separated and distinct"; and to neither being able "to intrude within the jurisdiction of the other."

Judicial rhetoric is not always consistent with judicial action, and the Court did not always adhere to separatist doctrine. Indeed, its rhetoric sometimes indicated a positive view of cooperation. In any case, the Court was rarely, if ever, directly confronted with the issue of cooperation versus separation as such. Rather it was concerned with defining permissible areas of action for the central government and the states; or with saying with respect to a point at issue whether any government could take action. The Marshall Court* contributed to intergovernmental cooperation by the very act of permitting federal operations where they had not existed before. Furthermore, even Marshall was willing to allow interstate commerce to be affected by the states in their use of the police power. Later courts also upheld state laws that had an impact on interstate commerce, just as they approved the expansion of the national commerce power, as in statutes providing for the control of telegraphic communication or prohibiting the interstate transportation of lotteries, impure foods and drugs, and prostitutes. Similar room for cooperation was found outside the commerce field, notably in the Court's refusal to interfere with federal grants-in-land or cash to the states. Although research to clinch the point has not been completed, it is probably true that the Supreme Court from 1800 to 1936 allowed far more federal-state collaboration than it blocked.

Political behavior and administrative action of the nineteenth century provide positive evidence that, throughout the entire era of so-called dual federalism, the many governments in the American federal system continued the close administrative and fiscal collaboration of the earlier period. Governmental activities were not extensive. But relative to what governments did, intergovernmental cooperation during the last century was comparable with that existing today.

Occasional presidential vetoes (from Madison to Buchanan) of cash and land grants are evidence of constitutional and ideological apprehensions about the extensive expansion of federal activities which produced widespread intergovernmental collaboration. In perspective, however, the vetoes are a more important

**Marshall Court*: see footnote on page 17.

evidence of the continuous search, not least by state officials, for ways and means to involve the central government in a wide variety of joint programs. The search was successful.

Grants-in-land and grants-in-services from the national government were of first importance in virtually all the principal functions undertaken by the states and their local subsidiaries. Land grants were made to the states for, among other purposes, elementary schools, colleges, and special educational institutions; roads, canals, rivers, harbors, and railroads; reclamation of desert and swamp lands; and veterans' welfare. In fact whatever was at the focus of state attention became the recipient of national grants. (Then, as today, national grants established state emphasis as well as followed it.) If Connecticut wished to establish a program for the care and education of the deaf and dumb, federal money in the form of a land grant was found to aid that program. If higher education relating to agriculture became a pressing need, Congress could dip into the public domain and make appropriate grants to states. If the need for swamp drainage and flood control appeared, the federal government could supply both grants-in-land and, from the Army's Corps of Engineers, the services of the only trained engineers then available.

Aid also went in the other direction. The federal government, theoretically in exclusive control of the Indian population, relied continuously (and not always wisely) on the experience and resources of state and local governments. State militias were an all-important ingredient in the nation's armed forces. State governments became unofficial but real partners in federal programs for homesteading, reclamation, tree culture, law enforcement, inland waterways, the nation's internal communications system (including highway and railroad routes), and veterans' aid of various sorts. Administrative contacts were voluminous, and the whole process of interaction was lubricated, then as today, by constituent-conscious members of Congress.

The essential continuity of the collaborative system is best demonstrated by the history of the grants. The land grant tended to become a cash grant based on the calculated disposable value of the land, and the cash grant tended to become an annual grant based upon the national government's superior tax powers. In 1887, only three years before the frontier was officially closed, thus signalizing the end of the disposable public domain, Congress enacted the first continuing cash grants.

A long, extensive, and continuous experience is therefore the foundation of the present system of shared functions characteristic of the American federal system, what we have called the marble cake of government. It is a misjudgment of our history and our present situation to believe that a neat separation of governmental functions could take place without drastic alterations in our society and system of government.

DYNAMICS OF SHARING: THE POLITICS OF THE FEDERAL SYSTEM

Many causes contribute to dispersed power in the federal system. One is the simple historical fact that the states existed before the nation. A second is in the form of creed, the traditional opinion of Americans that expresses distrust of centralized power and places great value in the strength and vitality of local units of government. Another is pride in locality and state, nurtured by the nation's size and by variations of regional and state history. Still a fourth cause of decentralization is the sheer wealth of the nation. It allows all groups, including state and local governments, to partake of the central government's largesse, supplies room for experimentation and even waste, and makes unnecessary the tight organization of political power that must follow when the support of one program necessarily means the deprivation of another.

In one important respect, the Constitution no longer operates to impede centralized government. The Supreme Court since 1937 has given Congress a relatively free hand. The federal government can build substantive programs in many areas on the taxation and commerce powers. Limitations of such central programs based on the argument, "it's unconstitutional," are no longer possible as long as Congress (in the Court's view) acts reasonably in the interest of the whole nation. The Court is unlikely to reverse this permissive view in the foreseeable future.

Nevertheless, some constitutional restraints on centralization continue to operate. The strong constitutional position of the states—for example, the assignment of two Senators to each state, the role given the states in administering even national elections, and the relatively few limitations on their lawmaking powers—[establish[es] the geographical units as natural centers of administrative and political strength. Many clauses of the Constitution are not subject to the same latitude of interpretation as the commerce and tax clauses. The simple, clearly stated, unambiguous phrases—for example, the President "shall hold his office during the term of four years"—are subject to change only through the formal amendment process. Similar provisions exist with respect to the terms of Senators and Congressmen and the amendment process. All of them have the effect of retarding or restraining centralizing action of the federal government. The fixed terms of the President and members of Congress, for example, greatly impede the development of nationwide, disciplined political parties that almost certainly would have to precede continuous large-scale expansion of federal functions.

The constitutional restraints on the expansion of national authority are less important and less direct today than they were in 1879 or in 1936. But to say that they are less important is not to say that they are unimportant.

The nation's politics reflect these decentralizing causes and add some of their own. The political parties of the United States are unique. They seldom perform the function that parties traditionally perform in other countries, the function of gathering together diverse strands of power and welding them into one. Except during the period of nominating and electing a President and for the essential but nonsubstantive business of organizing the houses of Congress, the American parties rarely coalesce power at all. Characteristically they do the reverse, serving as a canopy under which special and local interests are represented with little regard for anything that can be called a party program. National leaders are elected on a party ticket, but in Congress they must seek cross-party support if their leadership is to be effective. It is a rare President during rare periods who can produce legislation without facing the defection of substantial numbers of his own party. (Wilson could do this in the first session of the Sixty-Third Congress;

but Franklin D. Roosevelt could not, even during the famous hundred days of 1933.)* Presidents whose parties form the majority of the Congressional houses must still count heavily on support from the other party.

The parties provide the pivot on which the entire governmental system swings. Party operations, first of all, produce in legislation the basic division of functions between the federal government, on the one hand, and state and local governments, on the other. The Supreme Court's permissiveness with respect to the expansion of national powers has not in fact produced any considerable extension of exclusive federal functions. The body of federal law in all fields has remained, in the words of Henry M. Hart, Jr., and Herbert Wechsler,† "interstitial in its nature," limited in objective and resting upon the principal body of legal relationships defined by state law. It is difficult to find any area of federal legislation that is not significantly affected by state law.

In areas of new or enlarged federal activity, legislation characteristically provides important roles for state and local governments. This is as true of Democratic as of Republican administrations and true even of functions for which arguments of efficiency would produce exclusive federal responsibility. Thus the unemployment compensation program of the New Deal‡ and the airport program of President Truman's administration both provided important responsibilities for state governments. In both cases attempts to eliminate state participation were defeated by a cross-party coalition of pro-state votes and influence. A large fraction of the Senate is usually made up of ex-governors, and the membership of both houses is composed of men who know that their reelection depends less upon national leaders or national party organization than upon support from their home constituencies. State and local officials are key members of these constituencies, often central figures in selecting candidates and in turning out the vote. Under such circumstances, national legislation taking state and local views heavily into account is inevitable.

Second, the undisciplined parties affect the character of the federal system as a result of Senatorial and Congressional interference in federal administrative programs on behalf of local interests. Many aspects of the legislative involvement in administrative affairs are formalized. The Legislative Reorganization Act of 1946, to take only one example, provided that each of the standing committees "shall exercise continuous watchfulness" over administration of laws within its jurisdiction. But the formal system of controls, extensive as it is, does not com-

Hundred days of 1933: first hundred days of Franklin D. Roosevelt's term as the thirty-second president of the United States. Roosevelt (1882–1945), faced with severe economic and social problems, acted swiftly to set the country on a recovery with his New Deal program. Congress granted Roosevelt an extension of executive powers to facilitate the recovery. Numerous laws were enacted that increased the responsibilities and authority of the federal government; these included the Emergency Banking Relief Act, the Federal Emergency Relief Act, the Agricultural Adjustment Act, the Federal Securities Act, the National Industrial Recovery Act, the Banking Act of 1933, and the Farm Credit Act.

†*Henry M. Hart, Jr.* (1904–1969): lawyer, professor at the Harvard Law School, and U.S. government official. *Herbert Wechsler:* law professor emeritus at Columbia University. He also served at the Department of Justice during World War II. Hart and Wechsler wrote *The Federal Courts and the Federal System* (1953).

‡*New Deal:* see footnote on page 17.

pare in importance with the informal and extralegal network of relationships in producing continuous legislative involvement in administrative affairs.

Senators and Congressmen spend a major fraction of their time representing problems of their constituents before administrative agencies. An even larger fraction of Congressional staff time is devoted to the same task. The total magnitude of such "case work" operations is great. In one five-month period of 1943 the Office of Price Administration received a weekly average of 842 letters from members of Congress. If phone calls and personal contacts are added, each member of Congress on the average presented the OPA with a problem involving one of his constituents twice a day in each five-day work week. Data for less vulnerable agencies during less intensive periods are also impressive. In 1958, to take only one example, the Department of Agriculture estimated (and underestimated) that it received an average of 159 Congressional letters per working day. Special Congressional liaison staffs have been created to service this mass of business, though all higher officials meet it in one form or another. The Air Force in 1958 had, under the command of a major general, 137 people (55 officers and 82 civilians) working in its liaison office.

The widespread, consistent, and in many ways unpredictable character of legislative interference in administrative affairs has many consequences for the tone and character of American administrative behavior. From the perspective of this paper, the important consequence is the comprehensive, day-to-day, even hour-by-hour, impact of local views on national programs. No point of substance or procedure is immune from Congressional scrutiny. A substantial portion of the entire weight of this impact is on behalf of the state and local governments. It is a weight that can alter procedures for screening immigration applications, divert the course of a national highway, change the tone of an international negotiation, and amend a social security law to accommodate local practices or fulfill local desires.

The party system compels administrators to take a political role. This is a third way in which the parties function to decentralize the American system. The administrator must play politics for the same reason that the politician is able to play in administration: the parties are without program and without discipline.

In response to the unprotected position in which the party situation places him, the administrator is forced to seek support where he can find it. One ever-present task is to nurse the Congress of the United States, that crucial constituency which ultimately controls his agency's budget and program. From the administrator's view, a sympathetic consideration of Congressional requests (if not downright submission to them) is the surest way to build the political support without which the administrative job could not continue. Even the completely task-oriented administrator must be sensitive to the need for Congressional support and to the relationship between case work requests, on one side, and budgetary and legislative support, on the other. "You do a good job handling the personal problems and requests of a Congressman," a White House officer said, "and you have an easier time convincing him to back your program." Thus there is an important link between the nursing of Congressional requests, requests that largely concern local matters, and the most comprehensive national programs.

The administrator must accommodate to the former as a price of gaining support for the latter.

One result of administrative politics is that the administrative agency may become the captive of the nationwide interest group it serves or presumably regulates. In such cases no government may come out with effective authority: the winners are the interest groups themselves. But in a very large number of cases, states and localities also win influence. The politics of administration is a process of making peace with legislators who for the most part consider themselves the guardians of local interests. The political role of administrators therefore contributes to the power of states and localities in national programs.

Finally, the way the party system operates gives American politics their overall distinctive tone. The lack of party discipline produces an openness in the system that allows individuals, groups, and institutions (including state and local governments) to attempt to influence national policy at every step of the legislative-administrative process. This is the "multiple-crack" attribute of the American government. "Crack" has two meanings. It means not only many fissures or access points; it also means, less statically, opportunities for wallops or smacks at government.

If the parties were more disciplined, the result would not be a cessation of the process by which individuals and groups impinge themselves upon the central government. But the present state of the parties clearly allows for a far greater operation of the multiple crack than would be possible under the conditions of centralized party control. American interest groups exploit literally uncountable access points in the legislative-administrative process. If legislative lobbying, from committee stages to the conference committee, does not produce results, a Cabinet secretary is called. His immediate associates are petitioned. Bureau chiefs and their aides are hit. Field officers are put under pressure. Campaigns are instituted by which friends of the agency apply a secondary influence on behalf of the interested party. A conference with the President may be urged.

To these multiple points for bringing influence must be added the multiple voices of the influencers. Consider, for example, those in a small town who wish to have a federal action taken. The easy merging of public and private interest at the local level means that the influence attempt is made in the name of the whole community, thus removing it from political partisanship. The Rotary Club as well as the City Council, the Chamber of Commerce and the mayor, eminent citizens and political bosses—all are readily enlisted. If a conference in a Senator's office will expedite matters, someone on the local scene can be found to make such a conference possible and effective. If technical information is needed, technicians will supply it. State or national professional organizations of local officials, individual Congressmen and Senators, and not infrequently whole state delegations will make the local cause their own. Federal field officers, who service localities, often assume local views. So may elected and appointed state officers. Friendships are exploited, and political mortgages called due. Under these circumstances, national policies are molded by local action.

In summary, then, the party system functions to devolve power. The American parties, unlike any other, are highly responsive when directives move from the bottom to the top, highly unresponsive from top to bottom. Congressmen and Senators can rarely ignore concerted demands from their home constituencies; but no party leader can expect the same kind of response from those below, whether he be a President asking for Congressional support or a Congressman seeking aid from local or state leaders.

Any tightening of the party apparatus would have the effect of strengthening the central government. The four characteristics of the system, discussed above, would become less important. If control from the top were strictly applied, these hallmarks of American decentralization might entirely disappear. To be specific, if disciplined and program-oriented parties were achieved: (1) It would make far less likely legislation that takes heavily into account the desires and prejudices of the highly centralized power groups and institutions of the country, including the state and local governments. (2) It would to a large extent prevent legislators, individually and collectively, from intruding themselves on behalf of non-national interests in national administrative programs. (3) It would put an end to the administrator's search for his own political support, a search that often results in fostering state, local, and other non-national powers. (4) It would dampen the process by which individuals and groups, including state and local political leaders, take advantage of multiple cracks to steer national legislation and administration in ways congenial to them and the institutions they represent.

Alterations of this sort could only accompany basic changes in the organization and style of politics which, in turn, presuppose fundamental changes at the parties' social base. The sharing of functions is, in fact, the sharing of power. To end this sharing process would mean the destruction of whatever measure of decentralization exists in the United States today.

GOALS FOR THE SYSTEM OF SHARING

The Goal of Understanding

Our structure of government is complex, and the politics operating that structure are mildly chaotic. Circumstances are ever-changing. Old institutions mask intricate procedures. The nation's history can be read with alternative glosses, and what is nearest at hand may be furthest from comprehension. Simply to understand the federal system is therefore a difficult task. Yet without understanding there is little possibility of producing desired changes in the system. Social structures and processes are relatively impervious to purposeful change. They also exhibit intricate interrelationships so that change induced at point "A" often produces unanticipated results at point "Z." Changes introduced into an imperfectly understood system are as likely to produce reverse consequences as the desired ones.

This is counsel of neither futility nor conservation for those who seek to make our government a better servant of the people. It is only to say that the first goal for those setting goals with respect to the federal system is that of understanding it.

Two Kinds of Decentralization

The recent major efforts to reform the federal system have in large part been aimed at separating functions and tax sources, at dividing them between the federal government and the states. All of these attempts have failed. We can now add that their success would be undesirable.

It is easy to specify the conditions under which an ordered separation of functions could take place. What is principally needed is a majority political party, under firm leadership, in control of both Presidency and Congress, and, ideally but not necessarily, also in control of a number of states. The political discontinuities, or the absence of party links, (1) between the governors and their state legislatures, (2) between the President and the governors, and (3) between the President and Congress clearly account for both the picayune recommendations of the Federal-State Action Committee and for the failure of even those recommendations in Congress. If the President had been in control of Congress (that is, consistently able to direct a majority of House and Senate votes), this alone would have made possible some genuine separation and devolution of functions. The failure to decentralize by order is a measure of the decentralization of power in the political parties.

Stated positively, party centralization must precede governmental decentralization by order. But this is a slender reed on which to hang decentralization. It implies the power to centralize. A majority party powerful enough to bring about ordered decentralization is far more likely to choose in favor of ordered centralization. And a society that produced centralized national parties would, by that very fact, be a society prepared to accept centralized government.

Decentralization by order must be contrasted with the different kind of decentralization that exists today in the United States. It may be called the decentralization of mild chaos. It exists because of the existence of dispersed power centers. This form of decentralization is less visible and less neat. It rests on no discretion of central authorities. It produces at times specific acts that many citizens may consider undesirable or evil. But power sometimes wielded even for evil ends may be desirable power. To those who find value in the dispersion of power, decentralization by mild chaos is infinitely more desirable than decentralization by order. The preservation of mild chaos is an important goal for the American federal system.

Oiling the Squeak Points

In a governmental system of genuinely shared responsibilities, disagreements inevitably occur. Opinions clash over proximate ends, particular ways of doing things become the subject of public debate, innovations are contested. These are not basic defects in the system. Rather, they are the system's energy-reflecting life blood. There can be no permanent "solutions" short of changing the system itself by elevating one partner to absolute supremacy. What can be done is to attempt to produce conditions in which conflict will not fester but be turned to constructive solutions of particular problems.

A long list of specific points of difficulty in the federal system can be easily identified. No adequate congressional or administrative mechanism exists to review the patchwork of grants in terms of national needs. There is no procedure by which to judge, for example, whether the national government is justified in spending so much more for highways than for education. The working force in some states is inadequate for the effective performance of some nationwide programs, while honest and not-so-honest graft frustrates efficiency in others. Some federal aid programs distort state budgets, and some are so closely supervised as to impede state action in meeting local needs. Grants are given for programs too narrowly defined, and overall programs at the state level consequently suffer. Administrative, accounting and auditing difficulties are the consequence of the multiplicity of grant programs. City officials complain that the states are intrusive fifth wheels in housing, urban redevelopment, and airport building programs.

Some differences are so basic that only a demonstration of strength on one side or another can solve them. School desegregation illustrates such an issue. It also illustrates the correct solution (although not the most desirable method of reaching it): in policy conflicts of fundamental importance, touching the nature of democracy itself, the view of the whole nation must prevail. Such basic ends, however, are rarely at issue, and sides are rarely taken with such passion that loggerheads are reached. Modes of settlement can usually be found to lubricate the squeak points of the system.

A pressing and permanent state problem, general in its impact, is the difficulty of raising sufficient revenue without putting local industries at a competitive disadvantage or without an expansion of sales taxes that press hardest on the least wealthy. A possible way of meeting this problem is to establish a state-levied income tax that could be used as an offset for federal taxes. The maximum level of the tax which could be offset would be fixed by federal law. When levied by a state, the state collection would be deducted from federal taxes. But if a state did not levy the tax, the federal government would. An additional fraction of the total tax imposed by the states would be collected directly by the federal government and used as an equalization fund, that is, distributed among the less wealthy states. Such a tax would almost certainly be imposed by all states since not to levy it would give neither political advantage to its public leaders nor financial advantage to its citizens. The net effect would be an increase in the total personal and corporate income tax.

The offset has great promise for strengthening state governments. It would help produce a more economic distribution of industry. It would have obvious financial advantages for the vast majority of states. Since a large fraction of all state income is used to aid political subdivisions, the local governments would also profit, though not equally as long as cities are underrepresented in state legislatures. On the other hand, such a scheme will appear disadvantageous to some low-tax states which profit from the in-migration of industry (though it would by no means end all state-by-state tax differentials). It will probably excite the opposition of those concerned over governmental centralization, and they will not be assuaged by methods that suggest themselves for making both state and central governments bear the psychological impact of the tax. Although the offset would probably produce an across-the-board tax increase, wealthier persons, who are affected more by an income tax than by other levies, can be expected to join forces with those whose fear is centralization. (This is a common alliance and, in the nature of things, the philosophical issue rather than financial advantage is kept foremost.)

Those opposing such a tax would gain additional ammunition from the certain knowledge that federal participation in the scheme would lead to some federal standards governing the use of the funds. Yet the political strength of the states would keep these from becoming onerous. Indeed, inauguration of the tax offset as a means of providing funds to the states might be an occasion for dropping some of the specifications for existing federal grants. One federal standard, however, might be possible because of the greater representation of urban areas in the constituency of Congress and the President than in the constituency of state legislatures: Congress might make a state's participation in the offset scheme dependent upon a periodic reapportionment* of state legislatures.

The income tax offset is only one of many ideas that can be generated to meet serious problems of closely meshed governments. The fate of all such schemes ultimately rests, as it should, with the politics of a free people. But much can be done if the primary technical effort of those concerned with improving the federal system were directed not at separating its interrelated parts but at making them work together more effectively. Temporary commissions are relatively inefficient in this effort, though they may be useful for making general assessments and for generating new ideas. The professional organizations of government workers do part of the job of continuously scrutinizing programs and ways and means of improving them. A permanent staff, established in the President's office and working closely with state and local officials, could also perform a useful and perhaps important role.

The Strength of the Parts

Whatever governmental "strength" or "vitality" may be, it does not consist of independent decision-making in legislation and administration. Federal-state interpenetration here is extensive. Indeed, a judgment of the relative domestic strength of the two planes must take heavily into account the influence of one on the other's decisions. In such an analysis the strength of the states (and localities) does not weigh lightly. The nature of the nation's politics makes federal functions more vulnerable to state influence than state offices are to federal influence. Many states, as the Kestnbaum Commission noted, live with "self-imposed constitutional limitations" that make it difficult for them to "perform all of the services that their citizens require." If this has the result of adding to federal responsibilities, the states' importance in shaping and administering federal programs eliminates much of the sting.

**Reapportionment*: process of drawing the boundary lines of legislative districts so that each member of the legislature represents virtually the same number of people in his or her district. Under the Supreme Court's decisions in *Baker v. Carr* (1962) and *Wesberry v. Sanders* (1964), the guiding principle for reapportionment is "one man, one vote."

The geography of state boundaries, as well as many aspects of state internal organization [is] the [product] of history and cannot be justified on any grounds of rational efficiency. Who, today, would create major governmental subdivisions the size of Maryland, Delaware, New Jersey, or Rhode Island? Who would write into Oklahoma's fundamental law an absolute state debt limit of $500,000? Who would design (to cite only the most extreme cases) Georgia's and Florida's gross underrepresentation of urban areas in both houses of the legislature?

A complete catalogue of state political and administrative horrors would fill a sizeable volume. Yet exhortations to erase them have roughly the same effect as similar exhortations to erase sin. Some of the worst inanities—for example, the boundaries of the states, themselves—are fixed in the national constitution and defy alteration for all foreseeable time. Others, such as urban underrepresentation in state legislatures, serve the overrepresented groups, including some urban ones, and the effective political organization of the deprived groups must precede reform.

Despite deficiencies of politics and organizations that are unchangeable or slowly changing, it is an error to look at the states as static anachronisms. Some of them—New York, Minnesota, and California, to take three examples spanning the country—have administrative organizations that compare favorably in many ways with the national establishment. Many more in recent years have moved rapidly towards integrated administrative departments, statewide budgeting, and central leadership. The others have models-in-existence to follow, and active professional organizations (led by the Council of State Governments) promoting their development. Slow as this change may be, the states move in the direction of greater internal effectiveness.

The pace toward more effective performance at the state level is likely to increase. Urban leaders, who generally feel themselves disadvantaged in state affairs, and suburban and rural spokesmen, who are most concerned about national centralization, have a common interest in this task. The urban dwellers want greater equality in state affairs, including a more equitable share of state financial aid; nonurban dwellers are concerned that city dissatisfactions should not be met by exclusive federal, or federal-local, programs. Antagonistic, rather than amiable, cooperation may be the consequence. But it is a cooperation that can be turned to politically effective measures for a desirable upgrading of state institutions.

If one looks closely, there is scant evidence for the fear of the federal octopus, the fear that expansion of central programs and influence theatens to reduce the states and localities to compliant administrative arms of the central government. In fact, state and local governments are touching a larger proportion of the people in more ways than ever before; and they are spending a higher fraction of the total national product than ever before. Federal programs have increased, rather than diminished, the importance of the governors; stimulated professionalism in state agencies; increased citizen interest and participation in government; and, generally, enlarged and made more effective the scope of state action.[2] It may no longer be true in any significant sense that the states and localities are "closer" than the federal government to the people. It is true that the smaller governments remain active and powerful members of the federal system.

Central Leadership: The Need for Balance

The chaos of party processes makes difficult the task of presidential leadership. It deprives the President of ready-made Congressional majorities. It may produce, as in the chairmen of legislative committees, power-holders relatively hidden from public scrutiny and relatively protected from presidential direction. It allows the growth of administrative agencies which sometimes escape control by central officials. These are prices paid for a wide dispersion of political power. The cost is tolerable because the total results of dispersed power are themselves desirable and because, where clear national supremacy is essential, in foreign policy and military affairs, it is easiest to secure.

Moreover, in the balance of strength between the central and peripheral governments, the central government has on its side the whole secular drift towards the concentration of power. It has on its side technical developments that make central decisions easy and sometimes mandatory. It has on its side potent purse powers, the result of superior tax-gathering resources. It has potentially on its side national leadership capacities of the presidential office. The last factor is the controlling one, and national strength in the federal system has shifted with the leadership desires and capacities of the Chief Executive. As these have varied, so there has been an almost rhythmic pattern: periods of central strength put to use alternating with periods of central strength dormant.

Following a high point of federal influence during the early and middle years of the New Deal, the postwar years have been, in the weighing of central-peripheral strength, a period of light federal activity. Excepting the Supreme Court's action in favor of school desegregation, national influence by design or default has not been strong in domestic affairs. The danger now is that the central government is doing too little rather than too much. National deficiencies in education and health require the renewed attention of the national government. Steepening population and urbanization trend lines have produced metropolitan area problems that can be effectively attacked only with the aid of federal resources. New definitions of old programs in housing and urban redevelopment, and new programs to deal with air pollution, water supply, and mass transportation are necessary. The federal government's essential role in the federal system is that of organizing, and helping to finance, such nationwide programs.

The American federal system exhibits many evidences of the dispersion of power not only because of formal federalism but more importantly because our politics reflect and reinforce the nation's diversities-within-unity. Those who value the virtues of decentralization, which writ large are virtues of freedom, need not scruple at recognizing the defects of those virtues. The defects are principally the danger that parochial and private interests may not coincide with, or give way to, the nation's interest. The necessary cure for these defects is effective national leadership.

The centrifugal force of domestic politics needs to be balanced by the centripetal force of strong presidential leadership. Simultaneous strength at center and periphery exhibits the American system at its best, if also at its noisiest. The interests of both find effective spokesmen. States and localities (and private interest groups) do not lose their influence opportunities, but national policy becomes more than the simple consequence of successful, momentary concentrations of non-national pressures: it is guided by national leaders.

NOTES

[1]The President's third suggestion was that the committee "identify functions and responsibilities likely to require state or federal attention in the future and . . . recommend the level of state effort, or federal effort, or both, that will be needed to assure effective action." The committee initially devoted little attention to this problem. Upon discovering the difficulty of making separatist recommendations, i.e., for turning over federal functions and taxes to the states, it developed a series of proposals looking to greater effectiveness in intergovernmental collaboration. The committee was succeeded by a legislatively based, 26-member Advisory Commission on Intergovernmental Relations, established September 29, 1959.

[2]See the valuable report, *The Impact of Federal Grants-in-Aid on the Structure and Functions of State and Local Governments*, submitted to the Commission on Intergovernmental Relations by the Governmental Affairs Institute (Washington, 1955).

6

PAUL E. PETERSON

FEDERALISM AND THE GREAT SOCIETY

Research has shown that federal programs—such as the War on Poverty that was part of the Great Society initiative led by President Lyndon B. Johnson in the 1960s—often fall far short of their goals. The poverty program, for example, was not too effective in eliminating poverty in the United States. Paul E. Peterson, currently a professor of government at Harvard University, argues that the cause of these shortcomings is rooted in structural features of federalism. Local and national governments are charged with different purposes and tap disparate sources of revenue. Consequently, value conflicts arise when the national and local governments jointly implement programs. Peterson is well known for his work in urban politics and intergovernmental relations. He is the author of City Limits *(1981), and co-author of* When Federalism Works *(1986) and* A Case for a National Welfare Standard *(1989). He is the editor of* The New Urban Reality *(1985), and co-editor with John Chubb of* Can the Government Govern? *(1989).*

The problems encountered in the implementation of antipoverty programs in the 1960s—Johnson's Great Society*—were rooted in conflicts inherent in the structural arrangements of a federal system of government. These programs, with their emphasis on special assistance to the poor and needy, demonstrated a stronger commitment to redistribution by the central government of the United States than was evident at any other time in its history, save perhaps for the New Deal.† However, this egalitarian thrust was implemented through a federal system whose local units did not—indeed, could not—share the federal commitment. Research on poverty has repeatedly revealed the limits on the effectiveness of many programs aimed at reducing poverty in the United States. But in general these studies have not appreciated the structural limitations that the federal system itself placed on Great Society programs. To do so would require the reconstruction of a theory of federalism.

We no longer have a theory of federalism. The word has become at once so encompassing and so vacuous that any multitiered decision-making system can be entitled a federation. Even contractual relationships between central governments and private business firms are now considered to be an element of federalism (Elazar et al. 1969). Once the concept of federalism is stripped of any

**Great Society:* President Lyndon B. Johnson's collective policies of domestic reform in the 1960s. Johnson (1908–1973) believed that the federal government should use its resources and expertise to reduce social, political, and economic inequalities and to eliminate poverty. Great Society legislation included: the Civil Rights Act of 1964, the Economic Opportunity Act of 1964, the Voting Rights Act of 1965, Medicare/Medicaid (1965), the Elementary and Secondary Education Act of 1965, and the Model Cities Act of 1966.

†*New Deal:* see footnote on page 17.

distinctive meaning, we no longer have criteria for the appropriate division of governmental responsibilities among layers of government. Federalism is what federalism does. Even more, we have no orienting concepts that can assist us in explaining the patterns of conflict and cooperation among governmental levels.

In this paper, I shall argue that concepts taken from economics provide the opportunity for reviving a structural approach to the study of federalism, thereby providing a more comprehensive explanation for many of the difficulties faced by the antipoverty programs of Johnson's Great Society. Given a federal system of government, central and local governments perform inherently different political functions. The central government is responsible for regularizing relations with foreign countries, for maintaining the nation's prosperity, and for sustaining social welfare and other redistributive services. Local governments concentrate on operating efficiently those services necessary for maintaining a healthy local economy and society. Because of these differing responsibilities, central and local governments often find themselves engaged in value conflicts over matters of domestic policy. Local governments are primarily concerned with the productiveness of their economy, while the central government is more interested in achieving equality.

DECLINE OF DUAL SOVEREIGNTY THEORY

Traditional theories of federalism took as their point of departure the presence of two sovereigns within a single domain. Each sovereign had power over its citizens with respect to the functions for which it was responsible. Neither had power to interfere with the proper role of the other sovereign. A constitution defined the distribution of powers between the dual sovereigns.

Sovereignty was divided between a central state and a local republic in order to avoid both internal and external threats to liberty. Small republics limited the possibility of internal despotism,* because citizens knew and understood affairs of state that touched them closely. They could readily be called upon to participate in the defense of their freedoms. However, the small republic could be easily overcome by external enemies. Only through joining together in a federation with other republics could a common defense be maintained. The permeability of the small republic by external forces justified its relinquishing certain powers to a higher sovereign (Diamond 1969).

This dual sovereign theory of federalism linked governmental structure to political processes and policy outcomes. It provided a rationale for the proper division of powers between the central state and the local republics within a federation. It gave federalism a core definition: the presence of a contractual arrangement—a constitution—that divided powers among the sovereigns. Although changing circumstances would require continuous interpretation of that constitution, the theory provided the necessary conceptual apparatus for doing so.

**despotism:* government characterized by the exercise of absolute power.

In the United States, constitutional interpretations since the Civil War have regularly expanded the range of powers allocated to the central government so the concept of dual sovereignty, which was somewhat forced even in 1789, has become increasingly difficult to sustain. With the expansion of the Commerce clause in the 1930s and the simultaneous acceptance by the courts of grants-in-aid from the central government to the states, hardly a function remained that could not be exercised as readily by the central as by state and local governments. However valid the dual sovereign theory remained in principle, it had little applicability to a country that had come to believe that its liberties were as safe, if not safer, in the hands of the central government as at state and local levels.

The most creative adaptation in federal theory to these constitutional changes was Morton Grodzins's (1966) metaphor of the "marble cake." Grodzins showed that virtually all governmental activities are affected by decisions taken at national, state, and local levels. Power was both widely diffused and widely shared. The overall pattern had become marked more by cooperation and mutual assistance than by confrontations between dual sovereigns. Drawing upon the emergent behavioral tradition, Grodzins showed that governmental interrelations were characterized by endless processes of sharing and exchange. The resulting formation had, like a marble cake, no discernible structure at all. The metaphor diffused rapidly in the literature of federalism. It fitted nicely with the contemporary process-oriented focus of the political science discipline as a whole (Truman 1951, Greenstone 1975), and it seemed to give point and direction to descriptive studies of intergovernmental relationships. More innovative writers added their own metaphoric variations—picket fence, upside-down cake, harlequin ice cream brick, or what have you (U.S. Senate 1969, Wright 1975).

The impact of Grodzins's work was not limited to the academic scholarship of federalism. His ideas also served to justify the Johnsonian experiment in "creative federalism," a phrase repeated by Lyndon Johnson on several occasions, but endowed with little content. One enthusiastic popular commentator (Ways 1969, p. 620), however, expressed in 1965 the meaning of creative federalism:

> Federalism means a relation, cooperative and competitive, between a limited central power and other powers that are essentially independent of it. In the long American dialogue over states' rights, it has been tacitly assumed that the total amount of power was constant and, therefore, any increase in federal power diminished the power of the states and/or "the people." Creative federalism starts from the contrary belief that total power—private and public, individual and organizational—is expanding very rapidly. As the range of conscious choice widens, it is possible to think of vast increases of federal government power that do not encroach upon or diminish any other power. Simultaneously, the power of states and local governments will increase. . . .

Programmatically, the Great Society epitomized the Grodzins view of American federalism. Johnson's zeal for reform in American domestic social policy was accompanied by an equally intense commitment to the execution of these policies through state and local governments. In 1965, Congress enacted 21 new health programs, 17 new educational programs, 15 new economic development programs, 12 new programs to meet city problems, 4 new programs for manpower training, and 17 resources development programs. All were implemented through joint action between the federal and one or more of the lower levels of government (MacMahon 1972, p. 84). Federal intergovernmental transfers to state and local governments increased from $7.7 billion in 1962 to $41.7 billion in 1973. In 1962, intergovernmental transfers constituted 27 percent of the budget of local governments; by 1973, these transfers constituted 37.1 percent (Peterson 1979). The programs were federal: formulated and financed by central departments but administered and executed by state and local governments.

The evidence that Grodzins and other political scientists influenced the shape of "creative federalism" is admittedly only sketchy. In all probability, federally financed social reform was executed through conjoint effort by all levels of government, because ties between Congress and local officials, together with Johnson's own practical sense of what was feasible, precluded any alternative. Perhaps both politicians and scholars were influenced by judicial decisions that no longer treated as significant the assignment of responsibilities to one or another level of government. Yet the marble cake metaphor was at least a useful justification for the burgeoning network of intergovernmental relationships.

This unprecedented network of intergovernmental relationships rapidly expanded without serious debate about the level of government appropriate for carrying out specific tasks. Since power was so widely shared, and since cooperative relationships were already so extensive, it seemed to make little difference what combination of governments performed social services—as long as the federal government paid the bill. The specific structural arrangement for any particular program was, like so many of Johnson's policies, an issue open to bargaining, and a great range of intergovernmental practices soon came into being. Whether he had directly contributed to this outcome or not, Grodzins would have been content with the result.

THE EFFECTIVENESS OF THE GREAT SOCIETY

Time has not treated "creative federalism" generously. Many of the Great Society programs proved to be less in practice than they had in principle promised to become, and research on these programs has revealed that the cooperative partnership between the federal government and state and local governments did not carry out Johnson's objectives with flawless precision. Conflict, confusion, and simple abandonment of original objectives occurred in most of the more visible antipoverty programs.

I do not mean that in the aftermath of the Great Society there was any increase in the level of poverty or even that the absolute level of poverty remained constant. Such conclusions depend on the measure of poverty used, and, as on most politically sensitive issues, it is possible to reach diametrically opposite results. On one hand, taking absolute levels of poverty and including estimates of earnings that take into account unreported income and cash and in-kind income transfers, one can conclude that poverty in America has been all but eliminated (Lynn, Jr. 1977). On the other hand, taking earnings of low-income groups relative to those of median and high-income groups, one can conclude that no significant change has taken place, even a decade after the war on poverty was declared (Haveman 1977). Using still another measure, official poverty statistics reach the moderate conclusion that problems of poverty are being steadily, if slowly, ameliorated (Lynn, Jr. 1977).

For the sake of argument, let us simply accept the more optimistic assessments of changes in the condition of the poor. Even if the overall position of the poor has improved in absolute terms, it remains highly problematic how much of this change has been due to the programs of planned poverty reduction initiated by the Great Society. A highly inflated, wartime economy seems to have had the biggest impact on personal incomes in the late 1960s and early 1970s. And the governmental programs that had the greatest impact on the poor were the highly centralized programs of income redistribution administered by the central government, such as social security, the provision of medicare to the elderly, and the food stamp program.

By far the least successful of government programs aimed at the poor were those complex programs of service delivery financed centrally but administered locally. The Economic Opportunity Act, the Elementary and Secondary Education Act, manpower development programs, model city programs, the "New Towns" program, urban economic development programs, health maintenance organizations, juvenile delinquency prevention policies, and a host of similar schemes were the liveliest, most imaginative, and most highly touted of the government's efforts at redistributing social and economic opportunities in the United States. But these antipoverty programs seem to have had the smallest long-range impact on low-income groups in the United States. Robert Haveman, former director of the Institute for Research on Poverty at the University of Wisconsin and a cautiously optimistic evaluator of the poverty policies of the federal government, has concluded that "while poverty was reduced during the decade (after 1965), it is difficult to attribute this result directly to the programs that were an explicit part of the war" (Haveman 1977, p. 2).

Specific evaluations of particular programs are consistent with this overall assessment. Examining the celebrated community action program,* the most visible of the antipoverty programs, one finds little evidence that it had much impact on the socioeconomic well-being of the poor. After studying five California cities, Kramer (1969) reported that "if one . . . seeks to determine the cumulative influences [of various participatory techniques] on redirecting the focus and content of any part of the social service system, one finds relatively little change in the basic orientation of health, education and welfare agencies" (p. 241). John Strange's (1972) summary, after an extensive review of both pub-

*_Community action programs_ (CAPs): programs established by the Economic Opportunity Act of 1964, commonly referred to as the "War on Poverty," which were charged with empowering disadvantaged groups by involving them in social and political action programs aimed at breaking the cycle of poverty in their communities.

lished and unpublished analyses of community action, is much the same: "In some cases the number of groups participating in the pluralistic contest for power and influence has been expanded. [But] it is generally agreed . . . that no radical redistributions of influence, power, service, rewards, or other benefits has occurred" (p. 660). After reviewing research on a wide range of educational and training programs, Levin (1977) reached even harsher conclusions: "A wide variety of programs were either initiated or expanded during the poverty decade, and the evaluations and relevant research suggest that their effect on the reduction of poverty was minimal" (p. 179). The pattern was little different for housing policy. As Karl Taeuber (1977) has observed, "The gap between planned innovations and actual implementation was as great in Model Cities and other new HUD efforts as in the community action programs. . . ." (p. 362). Even in the area of health care, the one policy area in which the poor seem to have experienced substantially increased access to a valued public service, "those programs with considerable state discretion have not had a . . . record of high performance" (Davis 1977, p. 230).

Some have suggested that these so-called antipoverty programs were never intended to reduce poverty in America. They were only symbolic programs designed to pacify an unruly urban population in a time of social unrest. But this view is contradicted by the evident commitment and capacity of American society to reduce overall levels of absolute poverty. To explain adequately the extent to which antipoverty efforts were singularly unhelpful in achieving their objectives, one must look for more specific sources of goal-displacement and program frustration. In this regard it is notable how little research attention has been given to the fact that almost all of the antipoverty programs were centrally financed and locally administered.

Throughout the reassessment of antipoverty efforts, the premises upon which creative federalism rested have seldom been questioned. The marble cake analogy continues to be the accepted metaphor for the American federal system.

THE SUBSTITUTION OF METAPHOR FOR THEORY

The practical problems faced by Johnson's creative federalism were rooted in structural relationships not adequately comprehended by the marble cake metaphor. However apt and appealing the analogy may be, comparing federalism to a structureless piece of pastry is not theory. It suggests flux, change, and complexity when the purpose of theory is to identify simplicity, pattern, and order. The metaphor directs attention toward individuals, groups, and processes, when the essence of federalism is a stable relationship among structures of government.

Students of federalism since Grodzins have yet to develop a theory of federalism. Their descriptive analyses, persuasive as they sometime are, have (1) failed to give a distinctive meaning to federalism, (2) failed to preserve any distinctions among functions appropriate to each level of government, and (3) failed to identify any pattern to cooperative and conflictual elements in the federal system. Influenced by the process-oriented behavioralism of the discipline of political science at large, they have all but ignored the structural arrangements of the federal system. Instead, they have concentrated research energy on the activities of groups, elites, constituencies, and bureaucrats at all governmental levels. They have so stretched their energies that they cannot now develop a theory of federalism apart from a complete theory of politics.

First, and most important, their definitions of federalism are so vague that it is impossible to distinguish federalism from relationships between central and field offices in a unitary government. Daniel Elazar's (1966) efforts are more careful than most, but even he defines federalism (p. 2):

> as the mode of political organization that unites smaller polities within an overarching political system by distributing power among general and constituent governments in a manner designed to protect the existence and authority of both national and subnational political systems, enabling all to share in the overall system's decision-making and executing processes.

By this all-encompassing definition, even the U.S. Forest Service is a federal system. Its decision-making processes are divided between central and field offices, which are united together by a handbook of rules and regulations that protects the existence and authority of each jurisdictional level. From a different perspective, Kaufman (1960) has judged the Forest Service to be a highly centralized agency of the central government. But certainly the concept of federalism, when applied in this way, begins to encompass almost all political relationships. Perhaps that is Elazar's intent, for he goes on to say that federalism "is more than an arrangement of governmental structures; it is a mode of political activity that requires certain kinds of cooperative relationships through the political system it animates" (p. 2). This free-flowing assertion is certainly in keeping with the current emphasis on political process, but it does little to focus the study of intergovernmental relationships. To be sure, modern interpreters of American federalism are understandably concerned not to define federalism in narrow, constitutional terms. To see the essence of federalism as the division of powers among constituent units as defined by a written constitution places the study of federalism in a straight-jacket at a time when intergovernmental relationships are marked by patterns hardly foreseen by the earliest interpreters of the American Constitution. But modern federal theorists have not supplied a sufficiently focused substitute for traditional definitions of federalism in order that a distinctive, middle-range theory of intergovernmental relationships could emerge.

Second, without a definition of federalism, modern writers have been unable to state the characteristic and appropriate function of each level of government. In a fascinating commentary, Martin Diamond (1969, p. 79) observed that Grodzins "was driven by the difficulty of defining localness toward rejecting any standard for distributing functions between state and national government. He came to argue that 'Local Is As Local Does.' " The theory degenerates into sheer description. And, once again, it becomes impossible to distinguish the federal system from a decentralized administrative structure.

Perhaps it is unkind to suggest that modern theorists are also left without a standpoint from which to study intergovernmental relationships. After all, Grodzins (1966), Elazar (1966), and other of Grodzins's students (Elazar et al. 1969) have commented extensively on the federal "partnership" and have given intelligent accounts of a cooperative sharing of power among governmental levels. But even though their empirical studies are lucid and helpful, general theoretical explanations of the pattern of cooperation and conflict among governmental levels have not been developed. When the concept of the marble cake was first developed, intergovernmental relationships were so poorly understood that sheer descriptive accounts were useful. But the social scientific studies of the "creative federalism" of Johnson's antipoverty programs have hardly improved on early efforts. The results of the Great Society experiment have left many disturbed about the quality of the sharing among federal partners, but few have expressed their uncertainties at a high level of theoretical abstraction.

FEDERAL THEORY AND POVERTY RESEARCH

In the absence of a federal theory to guide research, political analyses of Great Society programs, at their most interesting and provocative, have used other sources for their theoretical power. In the search for an adequate explanation for the limited success of these redistributive programs, three rival hypotheses have been advanced: (1) the power of local ruling elites, (2) the complexity of intergovernmental relationships, and (3) the differential constituencies of the central and local governments. Each offers a plausible but, in the end, inadequate explanation for the regularity with which national programs have been frustrated at local levels.

Local Ruling Elites

In both popular and academic literature, the favored explanation for the difficulties faced by Great Society programs is the power of local ruling elites. Local politics, it is said, has been dominated by power structures consisting of bankers and businessmen who, together with a few conservative labor leaders and politicians beholden to them, dictate the major contours of local policy (Hunter 1953).* More sophisticated versions of this explanation do not claim that the ruling elite makes each and every local decision but only that its presence precludes redistributive issues from reaching the agenda of local politics. Its power is used to keep policies that are of interest to low-income groups and racial minorities from ever reaching a threshold of public awareness in the local community (Bachrach and Baratz 1962).

A study of Baltimore's community action program provided Bachrach and Baratz (1970) with an opportunity to apply this perspective directly to the implementation of the most visible of the antipoverty programs. In this study, they contend that the politics of community action in Baltimore was marked by "non-decision-making." They concluded (pp. 79–80) that the efforts by black leaders:

*For a collection of readings from this literature and a general bibliography, see Hawley and Wirt (1968).

> to transform the covert grievances of the black population into issues was . . . abortive, in part because they lacked arenas where they could practice the politics of conflict as distinct from the politics of confrontation, and in part because they had no access to key centers of decision-making. In short, the prevailing mobilization of bias blocked black leaders' attempts to arouse their would-be constituents to political action and thereby assured that blacks would remain "locked-out" of the political system.

To support this conclusion, they note that Baltimore lacked an open-occupancy ordinance, discriminated against blacks in public and private employment, and funded the antipoverty program only frugally (p. 97).

About some matters Bachrach and Baratz are certainly correct. If Baltimore resembled other local governments, then the civil rights movement and the war on poverty did not dramatically change the course of local public policy to the extent that low-income minorities received greatly expanded benefits from locally financed redistributive programs. On that score, the evidence to the contrary presented below seems conclusive. But the mechanisms precluding achievement of this objective do not seem to square with the "non-decision-making" model. Indeed, the empirical materials in the study testify to the earnestness and persistence with which redistributive issues came to the regular attention of Baltimore's leaders. As the authors point out, "by the end of 1967 the CAA (Community Action Agency), with its black director in the forefront, was operating at full tilt and practically in the open to organize the black poor for political action" (p. 89). Unless one is prepared to accept Bachrach and Baratz's penchant for stretching the concept of "non-decision" so that it coincides with its opposite—the mayor's decision to establish a series of biracial task forces, for example, is labeled "an extremely effective non-decision" (p. 71)—one can hardly claim that a ruling elite excluded issues of race and poverty from the agenda of local politics.

Fundamentally, the ruling elite hypothesis is unable to cope with the signal accomplishment of antipoverty programs: their capacity to open up local political systems to previously excluded groups. Although the socioeconomic impact of the programs was limited, they did improve the opportunities for political participation by blacks and other racial minorities. Led by the "maximum feasible participation" focus of the community action program, most of the Great Society service delivery programs contained features that required the active involvement of representatives of low-income groups and racial minorities in the deliberative process. Although these policies varied by locale and program, the overall impact was greatly to increase both the involvement of minorities as organized supporters of antipoverty programs and their recruitment to positions of administrative responsibility. The war on poverty was most successful in changing the agenda of local politics. Matters of concern to minority groups became regular, if not pervasive, issues in city politics. Even more significant, black leaders and groups representing minority interests became permanent elements in the institutionalized bargaining process through which local policy was formulated (Greenstone and Peterson 1973, Peterson and Greenstone 1977).

Unfortunately, improved access to local politics did not thereby radically alter the socioeconomic well-being of racial minorities and low-income groups (Chicago Urban League 1977). But to attribute this to the power of a ruling elite once again misguides poverty research. If the issue were simply to place on the agenda of local politics the problems of poor minorities, then the programs of the Great Society would certainly have ended poverty and racism in America. But, as we shall see, there are limits inherent in the functions that local governments can perform, and even "maximum feasible" political participation by minorities and the poor does not alter these limits.

Organizational Complexity

Quite another interpretation of the Johnson antipoverty programs derives from an understanding of the variety, the complexity, and the changeability of political and organizational relationships in a pluralist system. From this perspective, intergovernmental relationships do not consist simply of encounters between federal officials and local elites; on the contrary, at all levels of government (federal, regional, state, and local) are numerous public and private agencies, with overlapping jurisdictions and competing clientele, that must be consulted in the course of implementing government policy. Any one of these entities can act as a "veto group" to frustrate the execution of policy—or at least to delay its implementation until the original purposes are substantially modified.

As familiar as this pluralist view of American politics has become (Truman 1951, Riesman 1960, Dahl 1961), Pressman and Wildavsky's (1973) imaginative utilization of these ideas in their analysis of the innovative programs of the Economic Development Administration (EDA) is worthy of special consideration. The study is a detailed analysis of the problems that beset the EDA when it sought to improve minority employment opportunities in Oakland, California by funding a number of public improvement projects in that city. After beginning with high hopes, large projected budgetary outlays, and the appearance of cooperation on the part of both federal and local officials, EDA was frustrated by numerous delays; almost no detectable progress toward the original objective was made. Although the specific problems encountered are discussed in fascinating detail, Pressman and Wildavsky also reach for a more general explanation for the failure of this and other Great Society programs (p. 94):

> What seemed to be a simple program turned out to be a very complex one, involving numerous participants, a host of differing perspectives, and a long and tortuous path of decision points that had to be cleared. Given these characteristics, the chances of completing the program with the haste its designers had hoped for—and even the chances of completing it at all—were sharply reduced.

The problems of the Great Society were thus the problems encountered by any government program in a pluralist political system in which many participants influence policy. Differences must be negotiated, plans must be delayed, and policies must be modified. The solution is either to develop more simple programs, abandon federal efforts to intervene in socioeconomic relationships, or accept that long delays and major revisions are inevitable.

Although the case study is written with incisiveness and energy, in the end the argument cuts too deeply. Inasmuch as it applies to all government programs, it does not provide an adequate explanation for the particular problems encountered by the redistributive programs of the Great Society. In the first place, complexity was not a feature unique to the antipoverty programs of the Johnson administration. Many programs that have become a routinized feature of the federal system—for example, those for highways, rivers and harbors, land reclamation, and airport construction—are equally complex but have nonetheless been incorporated into the ongoing political processes of the federal system. National and local objectives have in these cases been similar enough that, whatever problems they may have encountered in particular cases, few can make the claim that the programs have failed. Indeed, local governments avidly compete for resources for these programs. Complexity is not a sufficient explanation for the diffidence with which localities participated in antipoverty programs.

Second, Pressman and Wildavsky's assertion that programs failed because participants had diverse views with respect to complex phenomena is at best a very low-level theoretical statement (McFarland 1969). In this respect, Pressman and Wildavsky resemble the students of "marble cake" federalism, who find relationships too complicated to identify critical elements patterning the complexity. For example, even though the empirical material in the Oakland study makes it quite clear that the "feds" were concerned primarily with redistribution (e.g., employing minorities) and the "locals" were concerned primarily with obtaining aid for economic development, Pressman and Wildavsky provide no general explanation for this patterning of the differences between the two levels of government. To say that policies fail because they are complex is a beginning, but research on poverty needs to develop more sophisticated tools to help identify the specific complexities that frustrate the effectiveness of redistributive programs.

Differential Constituencies

Constituency theory offers the promise of identifying patterns of conflicts between central and local governments. In its most general formulation, constituency theory argues that political leaders pursue objectives desired by those who select them for office. Regarding the differences between central and local governments, McConnell (1966) has argued that the central government, with a larger constituency, can be expected to serve broader and more diffuse interests. In local government, which has a smaller constituency, it is easier for dominant economic interests to control policy to the exclusion of weaker, less well-organized interests. In governments with a large constituency, the mutual checking of powerful interests and the need to build coalitions of diverse interests permit consideration of weaker, broader, more diffuse concerns, perhaps including even those of the poor. Although McConnell acknowledges (p. 113) that "it should not be expected that a constituency of a given definition will always produce a particular policy," he nonetheless sees essential differences in constituency influences at national and local levels (p. 114):

> Policies generally adhering to maintenance of the status quo and favoring the concrete interests of existing elites will tend to be associated with organizations [such as states and localities] based on small units; alternatively, large units [e.g., the central offices of the national government] will more probably produce policies favoring change directed to the general, diffuse, and widely shared interests of a broad segment of the population.

One of the best case studies of the failure of a Great Society program is quite convincingly interpreted within the tradition of constituency analysis. In her study of the "New Towns In Town" program initiated in late 1967, Derthick (1972) documents in detail the processes by which a program, originally planned to provide low-income housing through low-cost distribution of surplus federal land, failed to build any new homes for the poor at all. In a thoughtful concluding chapter, Derthick emphasizes the differences in the value commitments of national and local governments and then relates them to their differing constituencies (p. 101):

> In shared programs, both the federal government and local governments have a political function: both play a part in defining the objectives of public action and in responding to differences of value, interest, and opinion. The federal government, being removed from particular and parochial conflicts, is better able to express idealistic and progressive objectives. Local governments, more deeply engaged in these conflicts, are better able to respond to the actual preferences of active political interest.

Although Derthick correctly identifies differing value commitments on the part of national and local institutions, she leaves unstated the exact mechanisms by which local constituencies generate demands that differ from national policies. In Derthick's case study, for example, interest groups and constituency pressures, far from constraining policy choice, were notable for their absence. Although some local officials may have anticipated opposition to a low-income housing program, even that hypothetical opposition does not account for the position of big-city mayors, who could also have anticipated support from sizable low-income and minority constituencies.

The constituency thesis is most helpful in accounting for differential local responses to national policy. But what Derthick, Pressman and Wildavsky, Bachrach and Baratz, and other researchers (Murphy 1971, Pressman 1975) have documented is the consistency of conflict between national and local objectives, including those urban locales where local constituencies have every reason to be most supportive of redistributive programs. Even where the poor constitute the bulk of a local electorate, local governments often frustrated the policy objectives of the Johnson administration.

TOWARD A NEW THEORY OF FEDERALISM

The power of local ruling elites, the complexity of intergovernmental relationships, and the differential constituencies at the national and local levels have all been evoked as explanations for the difficulties that Great Society programs faced when being implemented within a federal system. Although all three hypotheses identify local resistance to redistribution, none provides an adequate explanation for the phenomenon. The problem with all of them is that they are theories concerning the relationships among individuals, groups, and organizations. Influenced by behavioral theories of politics and the marble cake metaphor of federalism, all three approaches try to find explanations for structural differences in government institutions in terms of relationships among elements at the national, state, and local levels. We need instead a theory of federalism that will identify the structural features of central and local institutions and link those features to the process of intergovernmental policy formation.

There can be no return to a theory of dual sovereignty; the work of Grodzins (1966) has surely laid that moribund notion to rest. But a new theory, like the traditional theory of dual sovereignty, must do three things. First, it must provide a definition that clarifies the way in which a federal system is distinguished from a decentralized administrative structure. Second, it must specify characteristic and appropriate activities of the central and local governments within the federal arrangement. Third, the theory must account for persistent patterns of conflict and cooperation among the various levels of government. Some of the elements that such a theory might contain are presented below. This presentation draws heavily on concepts better known to economists than to political scientists.

Federalism is a system of government in which powers are divided between higher and lower levels of government in such a way that both levels have a significant amount of separate and autonomous responsibility for the social and economic welfare of those living within their respective jurisdictions. Within the federation, the central government assumes responsibility for relations with foreign countries and determines the exchange relationships among the component units of the federation. The central government may exercise numerous additional powers, but for the system to remain a federation, lower levels of government must have at least two crucial powers.

First, lower levels of government must have a significant amount of control over the recruitment of their own political and administrative leadership. If local leaders are selected by officials of the central government, or if recruitment processes are governed by such stringent, centrally determined criteria that the local community has no effective choice, then local government is without power to take responsibility for the well-being of its inhabitants. Second, local government must have the power to tax its citizens in order to provide a range of government services that can enhance the well-being of the community. If local government is totally dependent upon centrally determined grants, it has very limited responsibility for the determination of the well-being of the local community. It will always be dependent on external sources of funds and, consequently, will always feel a need for more such funds. Because such funds do not come directly from the local community's own resources, the monies require strict central government supervision. Once it is no longer dependent on local resources, the local government loses the capacity to act responsibly on its own behalf, and thus becomes simply an agent of the central government.

Federalism is thus to be distinguished from simple decentralization, which can occur without the granting of either recruitment or financial powers to lower decision-making levels. For example, the U.S. Forest Service grants considerable decision-making autonomy to its field offices, though they do not gather their revenues from local sources or act independently in the recruitment of personnel. Were the central administrators of the Forest Service or any other department or agency to lose these two powers to their district offices, the organization could scarcely be considered a single governmental unit. Indeed, these are precisely the circumstances for which the term federalism is appropriately reserved and that at one time might have been characterized as dual sovereignty.

Within a federal system, the objectives of central and local governments stand in contrast to one another. Local governments are particularly concerned with operating efficiently so as to protect their economic base; the domestic policy structure of the central government is more concerned with redistributing values so as to achieve a more egalitarian distribution. These central-local differences are not a function of any particular political movement or any political party or group that happens to be in power at a specific time. Although partisanship and group pressures may aggravate or alleviate somewhat the tension between the objectives of national and local governments, the local emphasis on economic productivity and the national emphasis on equality is a function of the structural relationship of the two levels within the federal system.

LOCAL GOVERNMENT AND THE LOCAL ECONOMY

When forced to choose between equality and promoting the local economy, local governments in a federal system place greater weight on economic productivity. This choice is not due to a local power elite or to the biases inherent in small constituency politics; instead, it is a function of the external socioeconomic context in which local governments operate. Unlike national governments, local governments have little control over external socioeconomic forces. Just as an individual firm in a competitive economy cannot control its sources of supply or the demand for its products, so local governments cannot control the movement of capital and labor across their boundaries. Local governments are open systems that can be easily permeated by external forces and are therefore particularly sensitive to external changes. In responding to external forces, local governments act to protect an overriding set of interests. Just as a private firm wishes to maximize its profits, so the local community seeks to maximize its economic well-being.

Local leaders can be expected to try to safeguard the economic prosperity of the local community for at least three reasons. First, economic prosperity is necessary for protecting the fiscal base of local government. In the United States, taxes on local sources and charges for local services remain an important source of local government revenues. Although transfers of revenue to local units from federal and state governments increased throughout the postwar period, as late as 1974–1975 local governments still raised almost 60 percent of their own revenue (U.S. Bureau of the Census 1976). Raising revenue from a community's own economic resources requires continuing local economic prosperity. Second, good government is good politics. By pursuing policies that contribute to the economic prosperity of the local community, the local politician selects policies that redound to his or her own political advantage. Third and most important, local officials usually have a sense of community responsibility. They know that, unless the economic well-being of the community can be maintained, local business will suffer, workers will lose employment opportunities, cultural life will decline, and city land values will fall relative to other areas. To avoid such a dismal future, public officials try to develop policies that assist the prosperity of their community—or, at the very least, do not seriously detract from it.

Governments make decisions that maximize this goal within the numerous environmental constraints with which they must contend. As policy alternatives are proposed, each is evaluated according to how well it will help to achieve local economic prosperity. Although information is imperfect and local governments cannot be expected to select the best alternative on every occasion, policy choices will be constrained to those few that can plausibly be shown to be conducive to the community's economic prosperity. Internal disputes and disagreements may affect policy on the margins, but the major contours of local revenue policy will be determined by this larger objective, as shaped by factors in the community's environment.

In attempting to maximize their economic prosperity, local communities are competing with each other. Each must attract productive capital and labor to its area, and to achieve that end the conditions for productive economic activity must be as favorable in one community as they are in competing communities. Otherwise, there will be a net outward flow of productive resources, leaving a community with a declining economic future. Significantly, local governments can do little directly to control the flow of productive resources; for example, they cannot establish tariff walls or control human migration in the same way that nation-states can. Efficiency is all the more important, therefore, in the design of their policies, so that they protect and enhance the productive capacity of the community.

CENTRAL GOVERNMENT AND SOCIAL EQUALITY

Central governments are also concerned about the economic well-being of their society. But by comparison with local governments, central governments are responsible for less permeable socioeconomic systems. The economic constraints on domestic policy choice operate much less restrictively at the national than at the local level, because the national government has at its disposal a range of powers that curb the impact of the external environment on the indigenous society and economy. The most important of these powers is the capacity to issue passports and visas. Through the exercise of these powers, almost all highly industrialized countries have in recent years carefully restricted immigration. Exact formulas vary, but foreigners are allowed permanent residence in an industrialized society only if they either meet highly select personal criteria (marriage or blood relationship to a citizen, for example) or have highly desired skills that will enhance the nation's economy. Without such laws, it would be impossible for these industrialized economies to maintain high wage levels and elaborate systems of social security for their residents. Given the availability of inexpensive transportation, foreigners from less thriving countries would otherwise swamp their social welfare system.

Central governments also protect their economies from worldwide external forces through a host of controls over the movement of capital, goods, and services. Tariffs, quotas, a national currency, control over exchange rates, and the capacity to fund its own indebtedness are among the powers a central government uses to increase its autonomy from external forces. Not all countries can use these devices with equal effectiveness. The United States is particularly fortunate in that foreign exchange amounts to less than 10 percent of its total economic activity. Smaller countries with less self-contained economies have much less scope for autonomous action. But all countries except the smallest and most dependent (perhaps Hong Kong is the limiting case), have less permeable economies than those for which local governments are responsible.

Greater autonomy allows for greater redistribution from the more prosperous to the less so. It may be that even in an entirely self-contained economy, trade-offs remain between efficiency and equality. Too high and too progressive a rate of taxation to finance too elaborate a welfare state may weaken incentives for capital formation. On the other hand, some minimum standard of welfare provision seems necessary to ensure a steady, healthy, capable working population. These are highly debatable issues that are beyond the scope of this analysis (compare O'Connor 1973). But at the very least there is one set of constraints that do not restrict decision-making at the national level. Taxpayers cannot easily flee to other jurisdictions while needy immigrants flood the social-delivery system. Because of their greater control over their boundaries, central governments have much greater capacity to redistribute goods and services than do local governments.

When governments have the capacity to redistribute, political forces in relatively open, pluralist polities will generate demands for redistribution. Political parties that compete for popular favor have every incentive to redistribute income from smaller numbers of high-income groups to larger numbers of lower and lower middle-income groups in the population. Although the surge for redistribution may be episodic, a response to such specific events as the major depression of the 1930s and the mobilization of black discontent in the 1960s, competitive politics in industrialized societies periodically bring redistributive pressures to bear on the policies of central governments.

Once these policies have been promulgated, a governmental agency is charged with the responsibility for implementing a program; the staff then develops a loyalty to the substantive mission of the program (Greenstone and Peterson,

1973). As a constituent element of the central government's governing apparatus, the agency has a legitimate claim on a continuing—and perhaps slightly increasing—portion of the national budget. To perpetuate its program, its staff solicits the backing of organized elements serviced by its program, who campaign on its behalf in Congress, in other parts of the executive, in the news media, and among the public at large. Quite apart from any short-term political calculus, a structure of power supporting a redistributive program develops a national base.

DIFFERENCES IN POLICIES IN CENTRAL AND LOCAL GOVERNMENTS

Because the interests of local and central governments are different, the pattern of public policies promulgated by the two levels of government is different. For one thing, central and local governments tend to rely on contrasting principles for raising revenue. The central government depends largely on the ability-to-pay principle, and therefore raises most of its revenues through a progressive income tax, taxes on corporate earnings, and excise taxes on luxury commodities. Local governments, on the other hand, rely more on the benefits-received principle, which specifies that individuals should be taxed in accordance with the level of services they receive. As a result, over one-fourth of local revenues are raised through user charges, and the remainder is collected through taxes on property, sales taxes, and nonprogressive income taxes (Peterson 1979). One need not posit any local power elite to account for this propensity of local governments to favor more regressive taxes. If local communities were to rely on the ability-to-pay principle, there would be a greater disjunction betwen taxes levied and benefits received, and those paying the most in taxes (who are usually those contributing the most to the local economy) would have strong incentives to migrate elsewhere. Proportional or, preferably, somewhat regressive local taxes come closer to approximating the benefit principle, the principle that is consistent with the economic well-being of the local community.

Second, the expenditures of central and local governments perform different functions. Specifically, the central government assumes the responsibility for financing redistributive policies. As Table 1 shows, 47 percent of the domestic budget of the central government was allocated for redistributive purposes even at the beginning of the 1960s. After the declaration of war on poverty, this percentage increased to more than 55 percent. By contrast, the percentage of local revenues used for redistributive policies was only 12.9 percent in 1962. Significantly, even after the emergence of the civil rights movement and its supposed impact on local service delivery systems (Piven 1976), this percentage increased over the next decade by less than one percent. The role of the states stands midway between that of the central and local governments. States have contributed somewhat less than 35 percent of their budgets to redistributive programs.

The figures in Table 2 are even more dramatic. This table shows the percentage of all expenditures devoted to a particular activity contributed by each level of

TABLE 1. PERCENTAGE DISTRIBUTION AMONG FUNCTIONS OF DIRECT AND INTERGOVERNMENTAL EXPENDITURES BY LOCAL, STATE AND FEDERAL GOVERNMENTS FROM THEIR OWN FISCAL RESOURCES: 1962, 1967 AND 1973[1]

	LOCAL			STATE			FEDERAL (DOMESTIC ONLY)		
	1962	1967	1973	1962	1967	1973	1962	1967	1973
Function	(Percentage of Total Expenditures by Each Level of Government)								
REDISTRIBUTIVE									
Welfare	2.5	2.5	2.0	6.2	6.4	11.2	12.2	11.9	12.6
Hospital & Health	6.1	6.7	8.6	7.4	7.2	6.2	3.3	3.7	3.5
Housing	2.4	1.5	0.9	0.2	0.2	0.4	1.5	1.9	3.4
Social Insurance	1.9	2.2	2.3	14.4	9.4	17.0	29.7	34.0	35.6
ALL REDISTRIBUTIVE	12.9	12.9	13.8	28.2	23.2	34.8	46.7	51.5	55.1
NON-REDISTRIBUTIVE									
Housekeeping	26.8	26.4	28.5	12.4	12.9	8.4	4.6	4.5	3.8
Utilities	13.2	13.1	11.1	—	—	—	—	—	—
Postal	—	—	—	—	—	—	7.0	7.2	5.1
Transportation	8.1	6.6	5.7	17.8	16.0	11.3	6.2	5.8	4.2
Natural Resources	1.1	1.1	0.7	2.9	3.5	2.3	19.3	9.9	7.8
Interest	4.1	4.4	5.6	2.2	2.3	2.7	12.3	12.1	9.9
Education	33.4	35.2	34.2	33.6	39.5	38.4	3.2	7.2	8.2
Other	0.4	0.3	0.4	3.0	2.6	2.2	0.8	1.8	5.8
Total (%)	100.0	100.0	100.0	100.1	100.0	100.1	100.1	100.0	99.9
Total ($m)	33,591	45,853	77,886	29,356	45,288	89,504	58,960	86,852	186,172

[1]Table adapted from Peterson 1979, Table 3. For sources and other notes see citation.

TABLE 2. PERCENTAGE DISTRIBUTION AMONG GOVERNMENTS OF DIRECT AND INTERGOVERNMENTAL EXPENDITURES BY LOCAL, STATE AND FEDERAL GOVERNMENTS FROM THEIR OWN FISCAL RESOURCES, BY FUNCTION: 1962, 1967, 1973[1]

	LOCAL			STATE			FEDERAL			TOTAL		
Function	1962	1967	1973	1962	1967	1973	1962	1967	1973	1962	1967	1973
	(Percentage of Expenditures for Each Function by all Governments)											
REDISTRIBUTIVE												
Welfare	8.5	7.8	4.3	18.4	20.1	28.7	73.1	72.1	67.2	100.0	100.0	100.2
Hospital & Health	33.2	32.2	35.4	35.2	34.0	29.6	31.6	33.8	35.0	100.0	100.0	100.0
Housing	46.7	29.3	9.7	2.5	3.8	4.5	50.7	66.9	85.8	99.9	100.0	100.0
Social Insurance	2.9	2.9	2.2	18.9	12.3	18.2	78.1	84.8	79.6	99.9	100.0	100.0
ALL REDISTRIBUTIVE	10.8	9.7	7.4	20.6	17.2	21.5	68.6	73.2	71.1	100.0	100.0	100.1
NON-REDISTRIBUTIVE												
Housekeeping	58.7	55.4	60.2	23.7	26.6	20.4	17.5	17.8	19.4	99.9	99.8	100.0
Postal	—	—	—	—	—	—	100.0	100.0	100.0	100.0	100.0	100.0
Utilities	100.0	100.0	100.0	—	—	—	—	—	—	—	—	—
Transportation	23.3	19.7	20.1	45.1	47.3	45.0	31.6	33.0	34.9	100.0	100.0	100.0
Natural Resources	3.0	4.7	3.3	6.7	14.9	12.0	90.3	80.4	84.7	100.0	100.0	100.0
Interest	14.9	14.8	17.2	6.9	7.6	9.6	78.2	77.6	73.2	100.0	100.0	100.0
Education	48.9	40.0	34.9	43.0	44.4	45.0	8.1	15.6	20.0	100.0	100.0	99.9
Other	8.6	5.4	2.2	60.1	41.1	15.3	31.3	53.5	82.5	100.0	100.0	100.0

[1]Table adopted from Peterson 1979, Table 4. For sources and other notes, see citation.

government. As the table shows, not only was the local contribution to redistributive programs scarcely more than 10 percent in 1962, but also the percentage has declined since that time. The fiscal role of the federal government, on the other hand, has become especially significant. And if the political pressures for federalizing welfare policy and health care are any sign, this pattern is likely to continue. As the United States continues to become an increasingly integrated political economy, the redistributive function may well become an almost exclusively federal prerogative.

The distinctively redistributive role of the central government is especially evident in programs supported by federal grants-in-aid. Table 3 shows the distribution by function of intergovernmental revenues from the central and state governments to lower governmental levels. The states allocate most of their intergovernmental monies for educational purposes, but the primary role of the central government has been to finance the redistributive activities of states and localities. When local governments do provide welfare, hospital, health, and housing services to low-income groups, these services are generally provided through intergovernmental grants from the federal government. Even in 1973, after the establishment of a revenue-sharing program by the Nixon administration, 40 percent of intergovernmental revenues received by states and localities was specifically designated for a redistributive function. The increase in undesignated revenues in that year came largely at the expense of funds for educational and other purposes, not as a substitute for redistributive activities.

INTERGOVERNMENTAL RELATIONSHIPS

These data on the contrasting functions of central and local governments suggest that the contrasting purposes of the two levels of government affect redistributive policies. But if the two levels of government pursue differing policies, then intergovernmental programs requiring the cooperative action of both levels of government will be subject to considerable tension. On one hand, the departments of the central government will endeavor to pursue a more egalitarian course, seeking to ensure that federal monies are used for redistributive purposes. On the other hand, local governments, eager to sustain their local economies, will wish to use federal monies so that those contributing the most to the local economy will benefit most from local expenditures.

Consider the interests of local governments that are offered the opportunity to secure a grant-in-aid for a complex new governmental program. Of course, it is an opportunity to receive "free" federal funds for the benefit of the local community. These dollars, pumped into the local economy from outside, have a short-term positive effect on the community's economy, no matter what the purpose for which they are expended. Yet the short-term effects are dispersed quickly. Because local economies are not self-contained but involve extensive trading with other sectors of the highly integrated American economy, any "shot-in-the-arm" effects that federal grants have on local prosperity do not necessarily cumulate. As a result, any local government considering a federal grant must weigh

TABLE 3. INTERGOVERNMENTAL EXPENDITURES BY STATE AND FEDERAL GOVERNMENTS, BY FUNCTION, 1962, 1967, 1973.[1]

	INTERGOVERNMENTAL EXPENDITURE					
	STATE			FEDERAL		
	1962	1967	1973	1962	1967	1973
Function	(Per Cent)					
REDISTRIBUTIVE						
Welfare	16.3	15.2	18.4	31.6	28.2	29.0
Hospital & Health	1.8	1.6	2.1	2.2	2.7	4.2
Housing	.3	.4	.4	4.1	4.5	5.1
Social Insurance	—	—	—	6.0	3.8	1.9
ALL REDISTRIBUTIVE	18.4	17.2	20.9	43.9	39.1	40.2
NON-REDISTRIBUTIVE						
Housekeeping	—	—	—	.9	.9	2.1
Transportation	12.2	9.9	7.4	36.3	27.4	13.2
Natural Resources	.2	.2	.2	1.8	1.6	1.6
Education	59.4	62.2	57.1	15.1	26.1	20.8
Other and Undesignated	9.7	10.6	14.4	2.0	4.9	22.0
TOTAL	99.9	100.1	100.0	100.0	100.0	100.0
Dollars (millions)	10,906	19,056	40,822	7,735	15,027	41,666

[1]Table adapted from Peterson 1979, Table 5. See citation for sources and other notes.

more heavily the long-term economic impact of the policy objectives for which the grant is expended (Thompson 1965, Forrester 1969).

If the purpose of the grant is to assist in the development of the local community's economic base, local leaders will have strong incentives to respond favorably. Federal funds for highways, sewers, industrial parks, dams, dredging of canals and harbors, and the renewal of downtown business districts and attractive prizes, eagerly sought and won. So are air force bases and defense contracts. These are "hard" federal dollars that build the economy of local communities. The grants are invested in productive resources that generate a continuing source of local revenue, materially adding to local prosperity.

The redistributive programs of the Great Society, however, seldom had this unequivocally positive effect on local economies. By and large, they were "soft" programs aimed at servicing the poorest segments of the local population, either by providing them with better education, more training for industrial employment, more health care, more legal assistance, or more political power. To the extent that a local community faithfully carries out the intentions of federal policy, the community makes itself a more attractive locale for poor people to live. To the extent that excellent schools providing high-quality instruction are provided to poor minorities, poor minority groups have great incentives to migrate to that community. To the extent that inexpensive but attractive homes are provided for those in need, the community becomes a haven for the homeless. The more redistributive the policies of any local community, the more that community attracts those in need of governmental assistance. Unfortunately, in an economy with less than full employment, redistributive policies contribute little, if anything, to the local economy. On the contrary, they only add to local crime rates, the costs of fire insurance, and other demands on local services.

When given the opportunity to participate in redistributive Great Society programs, local governments consequently have every incentive to accept the monies (for their short-term positive effect on local economies) but then to modify any redistributive impact they might have. The classis case, of course, was urban renewal, which began as a program for housing the needy but ended as a program to improve the industrial and commercial capacities of central cities (Wilson 1966, Greer 1965). In many cases, urban renewal funds were used to build high-quality homes for upper-middle classes so as to attract desirable citizens back to the central city. Apart from urban renewal, local communities have generally resisted the placement of low-income public housing in their neighborhoods, and even the availability of low-cost federal land was not sufficient enticement to participation in federal low-income housing programs (Derthick 1972). Rather than build housing for the poor, local communities have used their zoning powers to exclude residents who "cannot pay their own way"—i.e., those who do not pay in local taxes an amount that covers the cost of services extended to them (Babcock 1966, Mills and Oates 1975). And because local governments are especially interested in economic productivity, officials in Oakland were far more anxious to secure federal funds for the extension of the Oakland harbor than to insist that local employers act affirmatively in minority recruitment (Pressman and Wildavsky 1973).

CONCLUSION

The central government's commitment to reduce poverty and achieve egalitarian welfare distribution has been frustrated by structural features of the American federal system. Numerous studies have documented the difficulties encountered by Great Society programs in the course of their implementation. But most have attributed the difficulties to conservative local elites, to the inherent complexities of intergovernmental programs, or to the differential constituencies of central and local governments. These explanations are incomplete. Local elites seem conservative because the local community must be concerned above all with protecting its economic base. Federal programs become involved in complex bargaining situations, because central and local interests contradict one another. The local constituencies to which local officials listen are those representing the interests of business and property, because they are the interests that must be protected if the economic well-being of the community is to be safeguarded. In sum, the differing functional responsibilities of central and local governments generate value conflicts that impede the implementation of redistributive policies.

Poverty research has not appreciated this important structural element affecting policy outcomes. Future research could usefully address these questions through cross-national comparative studies and through properly designed studies of the process of policy making in the United States. A few suggestions follow rather directly from the foregoing analysis.

Perhaps the most interesting large-scale research would involve cross-national comparative analyses of the policy implications of various types of intergovernmental arrangements. Although research on this issue is virtually nonexistent, redistributive programs among different levels of government in European countries do not appear to encounter the same level of local resistance that they do in the United States. In Great Britain, for example, there is extensive central-local cooperation in the provision of public housing and social services. Although confrontations sometimes occur, the disputes are usually partisan in nature. It is just as likely for local governments, led by Labour leaders, to attempt to thwart a conservative central government policy as it is for conservative local authorities to undermine a redistributive objective. The consistent disjunction between national and local goals, so evident in the United States, does not occur in other structural contexts.

Research on the elements that differentiate the American from European systems could be highly constructive. The most likely differentiating factor is the much greater equalizing role that central subsidies play in local finance in European countries (Griffith 1966). In Great Britain, as in most European countries, local communities raise less than half their local revenues through local taxes; more important, the remainder is distributed among local authorities in such a way as to ensure that all have roughly similar per capita amounts for expenditures, although certain variations in local need are also taken into account. In other words, a decline in the value of local property does not become translated into a substantial loss in local government income. Local policies are therefore not as closely tied to local economies as in the United States.

Other differences may play an important role as well. Local governments service larger, more heterogeneous populations in Great Britain than in the United States. Capital expansion depends not on a local government's capacity to raise revenue in the bond markets but on the approval of a central department. The central government has its own regional policy, which encourages private investment in areas of high unemployment.

Within the United States, one can usefully compare the problems of implementing a policy through a highly centralized administrative structure with the problems encountered in federal arrangements. If the substantive policies are similar but administrative arrangements quite different, the federal theory offered here would have a reasonably clear test.

One might also compare the implementation of redistributive policies with the implementation of developmental policies that promote local economic growth. How do central-local relations differ in the two policy areas? Does one policy seem to be more "complex" than the other? Is central-local conflict greater on redistributive issues and inter-local competition greater on developmental issues?

The collection and routine analysis of data on intergovernmental expenditures are only in their infancy. To what extent is the vastly increasing program of intergovernmental expenditures freeing local governments from a dependence on their local economy? Is resource equalization beginning to occur? To what extent do programs of federal assistance encourage or deter localities from assisting low-income groups in the community? What are the differences among states in state grant-in-aid programs?

The fact that states differ in their relationships with local governments can be exploited for research purposes. Some states have a more "unitary" system, in which substantial state grants-in-aid supplement local budgets, while other states have essentially a "federal" arrangement. What differences do these arrangements make for the implementation of state-initiated programs of redistribution?

There is variation in the degree to which legislation allows flexibility in federal-local relationships. Do local interests have greater scope when the federal mandate is most flexible? The two most substantial studies of policy implementation—the Derthick and the Pressman-Wildavsky studies—both examined programs that had highly imprecise congressional mandates. Can problems of implementation in a federal system be reduced through more detailed legislative enactments?

Without research on these questions, it is possible only to speculate about the precise connections between government structures and redistributive policy. In general, the overriding political problem to which research needs to direct itself is how the federal system can be made compatible with the objectives of reducing poverty and achieving a more equitable distribution of income. Within the marble cake framework, it seemed that any task could be performed by any level of government, or any combination of levels of government. But if the various levels of government have distinct functions, and intergovernmental cooperation is frustrated by their competing interests, then successful efforts to aid the poor through a decentralized social service delivery system may require changes in the structure of government on a scale not seriously considered even among those carrying out basic research in the field.

REFERENCES

Babcock, Richard (1966) *The Zoning Game*. Madison: University of Wisconsin Press.

Bachrach, Peter, and Baratz, Morton S. (1962) Two faces of power. *American Political Science Review* 56:947–52.

Bachrach, Peter, and Baratz, Morton S. (1970) *Theory and Practice*. New York: Oxford University Press.

Chicago Urban League (1977) The Current Economic Status of Chicago's Black Community. Unpublished report 2.

Dahl, Robert (1961) *Who Governs?* New Haven: Yale University Press.

Davis, Karen (1977) A decade of policy developments in providing health care for low-income families. Pp. 197–231 in Robert H. Haveman, ed., *A Decade of Federal Antipoverty Programs*. New York: Academic Press.

Derthick, Martha (1972) *New Towns in Town: Why a Federal Program Failed*. Washington, D.C.: Urban Institute.

Diamond, Martin (1969) On the relationship of federalism and decentralization. Pp. 72–80 in Daniel J. Elazar, R. Bruce Carroll, E. Lester Levine, and Douglas St. Angelo, eds., *Cooperation and Conflict: Readings in American Federalism*. Itasca, Ill. F. E. Peacock.

Elazar, Daniel (1966) *American Federalism: A View from the States*. New York: Thomas Y. Crowell.

Elazar, Daniel J., Carroll, R. Bruce, Levine, E. Lester, and St. Angelo, Douglas, eds. (1969) *Cooperation and Conflict: Readings in American Federalism*. Itasca, Ill. F. E. Peacock.

Forrester, Jay (1969) *Urban Dynamics*. Cambridge, Mass.: MIT Press.

Greenstone, J. David (1975) Group theories. Pp. 243–318 in Fred Greenstein and Nelson Polsby, eds., *Handbook of Political Science II*. Reading, Mass.: Addison-Wesley.

Greenstone, J. David, and Peterson, Paul E. (1973) *Race and Authority in Urban Politics*. New York: Russell Sage.

Greer, Scott (1965) *Urban Renewal and American Cities*. Indianapolis: Bobbs Merrill.

Griffith, J.A.G. (1966) *Central Departments and Local Authorities*. London: George Allen & Unwin.

Grodzins, Morton (1966) *The American System*. Edited by Daniel J. Elazar. Chicago: Rand McNally.

Haveman, Robert H. (1977) Introduction: poverty and social policy in the 1960s and 1970s—an overview and some speculations. Pp. 1–20 in Robert H. Haveman, ed., *A Decade of Federal Antipoverty Programs*. New York: Academic Press.

Hawley, Willis D., and Wirt, Frederick M., eds. (1968) *The Search for Community Power*. Englewood Cliffs, New Jersey: Prentice-Hall.

Hunter, Floyd (1953) *Community Power Structure*. Chapel Hill: University of North Carolina Press.

Kaufman, Herbert (1960) *The Forest Ranger*. Baltimore: Johns Hopkins Press.

Kramer, Ralph (1969) *Participation of the Poor: Comparative Case Studies in the War on Poverty*. Englewood Cliffs, New Jersey: Prentice-Hall.

Levin, Henry M. (1977) A decade of policy developments in improving education and training for low-income populations. Pp. 123–188 in Robert H. Haveman, ed., *A Decade of Federal Antipoverty Programs*. New York: Academic Press.

Lynn, Laurence E., Jr. (1977) A decade of policy developments in the income-maintenance system. Pp. 55–117 in Robert H. Haveman, *A Decade of Federal Antipoverty Programs*. New York: Academic Press.

McConnell, Grant (1966) *Private Power and American Democracy*. New York: Alfred Knopf.

McFarland, Andrew S.(1969) *Power and Leadership in Pluralist Systems*. Stanford, Cal.: Stanford University Press.

MacMahon, Arthur W. (1972) *Administering Federalism in a Democracy*. New York: Oxford University Press.

Mills, Edwin S., and Oates, Wallace E., eds. (1975) *Fiscal Zoning and Land Use Controls*. Lexington, Mass.: D.C. Heath.

Murphy, Jerome T. (1971) Title I of ESEA: the politics of implementing federal education reform. *Harvard Educational Review* 41:35–63.

O'Connor, James (1973) *The Fiscal Crisis of the State*. New York: St. James Press.

Peterson, P. E. (1979) A unitary model of local taxation and expenditure policies in the United States. *British Journal of Political Science* July.

Peterson, Paul E., and Greenstone, J. David (1977) Racial change and citizen participation: the mobilization of low-income communities through community action. Pp. 241–278 in Robert H. Haveman, ed., *A Decade of Federal Antipoverty Programs*. New York: Academic Press.

Piven, Frances (1976) The urban fiscal crisis. In Stephen David and Paul E. Peterson, eds., *Urban Politics and Public Policy*. 2nd ed. New York: Praeger Publishers.

Pressman, Jeffrey L. (1975) *Federal Programs and City Politics*. Berkeley: University of California Press.

Pressman, Jeffrey L. and Wildavsky, Aaron (1973) *Implementation*. Berkeley: University of California Press.

Riesman, David (1960) *The Lonely Crowd*. New Haven: Yale University Press.

Strange, John H. (1972) Citizen participation in community action and model cities programs. *Public Administration Review* 32:655–669.

Taeuber, Karl (1977) Discussions. Pp. 360–63 in Robert H. Haveman, ed., *A Decade of Federal Antipoverty Programs*. New York: Academic Press.

Thompson, Wilbur R. (1965) *A Preface to Urban Economics*. Baltimore: Johns Hopkins Press.

Truman, David (1951) *The Governmental Process*. New York: Alfred Knopf.

U.S. Bureau of the Census (1976) *Local Government Finances in Selected Metropolitan Areas and Large Countries: 1974–75*. Washington: Government Printing Office.

U.S. Senate, Committee on Government Operations, Subcommittee on Intergovernmental Relations (1969) The federal system as seen by federal aid officials. Pp. 331–338 in Daniel J. Elazar,

R. Bruce Carroll, E. Lester Levine, and Douglas St. Angelo, eds., *Cooperation and Conflict: Readings in American Federalism*. Itasca, Ill.: F.E. Peacock.

Ways, Max (1969) "Creative Federalism" and the Great Society. Pp. 619–631 in Daniel J. Elazar, R. Bruce Carroll, E. Lester Levine, and Douglas St. Angelo, eds., *Cooperation and Conflict: Readings in American Federalism*. Itsaca, Il. F.E. Peacock.

Wilson, James Q., ed. (1966) *Urban Renewal, The Record and the Controversy*, Cambridge, Mass.: MIT Press.

Wright, Deil S. (1975) Revenue sharing and structural features of American Federalism. *Annals of the American Academy of Political and Social Science* 419:100–119.

PART THREE

ELECTIONS AND POLITICAL PARTIES

Elections lie at the heart of the democratic process, and because in any large democracy political parties organize electoral competition, a vital party system is essential to democratic politics. On this general proposition, few political scientists would disagree. Opinions differ, however, as to exactly what a vital party system is; whether the United States still has one; and hence, how "democratic" American national elections will be with the passage of time.

In 1950, the American Political Science Association issued a famous report that called for thorough reform of the political parties to promote a "more responsible two-party system." By "more responsible," the authors meant an arrangement analogous to the British model, that is, a system with the following attributes. The parties would offer the electorate a clear choice between alternative platforms; the party garnering a popular majority in a general election could then claim the consent of the people when adopting its announced course of action; and representatives elected to office would deliver on their campaign promises. If the voters grew disenchanted with the governing party's program, they could withdraw their mandate by voting in the opposition at the next election. Until that time, however, the minority party would mostly be in a position to criticize government policies and to articulate alternatives, but not to frustrate continually, or compromise, the policies. Finally, to make the party system dependable and acountable in this fashion, the stature of party leaders would have to improve, the national party organizations would have to be strengthened, and greater party loyalty would have to be encouraged, principally by sharpening the programmatic differences between the contenders.

It is hard to think of a time in American history when the political parties closely approximated this ideal. (To be sure, there have been periods—the election of 1896, for instance—when the ideological breach between Democrats and Republicans was particularly wide. But seldom has party discipline in Congress, for example, resembled that in most European parliaments. Nor is it likely to. The separation of powers provides Congress and the presidency with different constituencies and functions that inevitably hinder party cohesion in ways parliamentary structures do not.) Nonetheless, at least until quite recently, party played a central role in American elections. Not only did the party organizations nominate candidates, simplify the choices before the public, and actively mobilize voters, but party identification also ran deep in the electorate. The large-scale voting study conducted by Angus Campbell and his associates at the University of Michigan's Survey Research Center during the 1950s discovered that no variable better predicted voting decisions than did party affiliation. According to the Michigan researchers' findings,[1] party attachments are formed early in life and internalized; once established, they tend to be remarkably stable. Only the most wrenching

[1]Angus Campbell, Philip Converse, Warren Miller, and Donald Stokes; *"The Development of Party Identification," The American Voter: An Abridgement*, (NY: John Wiley & Sons, 1964).

personal experiences (such as migrations, occupational shifts, or fundamental changes in one's social milieu) or cataclysmic historical events (e.g., the Civil War, the Great Depression) could be expected to alter partisan orientations.

Yet, by the 1970s it became apparent that a dramatic change had occurred—party affiliation was no longer the decisive predictor of the vote it had been formerly. The essays presented here deal with the central issues of voter identification and party responsibility. In "The Responsible Electorate" (1966), V. O. Key, Jr., challenged the prevailing view that the political parties interfered with the voter's ability to vote responsibly. Based on voters' behavior from 1936 to 1948, Key concluded that "We have established patterns of movement of party switchers from election to election and the patterns of stability of the standpatter that lead us to a conception of the voter that is not often propounded. From our analyses the voter emerges as a person who appraises the actions of government, who has policy preferences, and who relates his vote to those appraisals and preferences." Key's findings indicate that the parties are successfully able to convey to the electorate their differences on major issues. Therefore, the parties meet one major condition of party responsibility—that of having identifiable issue positions. Key also suggests that a second fundamental condition is met—that the parties are held accountable for their performance. In his words, ". . . the data make it appear sensible to regard the voter as a person who is concerned with what governments [i.e., governing parties] have done or not done and what they propose to do. . . ." The idea that voters react to what the parties "have done or not done" is the kernel of the important concept that voting is somewhat retrospective and, consequently, that party responsibility is also assessed retrospectively to some extent.

In "The Turnout Problem" (1987), Walter Dean Burnham addresses another facet of the decline of parties and voter identification—voter abstention. Burnham estimates that the electorate is currently comprised of ". . . about 38 percent of American citizens [who] are 'core' or regular voters for major national and state offices; another 17 percent or so are marginals who come to the polls only when stimulated by the dramas of presidential campaign politics; and 45 percent are more or less habitual nonvoters." After reviewing several perspectives and factors related to low turnouts, he concludes that the decline of political parties is a key cause of abstentionism. Moreover, because nonvoters are disproportionately lower class, abstentionism is neither benign nor neutral in its influence on American politics: ". . . the relative disappearance of partisan teams in campaigns and their replacement by personalistic and imagistic appeals to voters creates conditions that make individual utility calculations difficult, if not impossible. If people are left to their own devices in a society with marked inequalities on all relevant dimensions of political consciousness, education, and information, some people will remain far better positioned to make accurate utility calculations than others." Burnham concludes that prerequisites to a reversal of mass abstentionism include a greater organizational role by the parties in the electorate, and a change in the contemporary trend toward a permanent campaign structure.

In another analysis, Morris P. Fiorina considers "The Decline of Collective

Responsibility in American Politics" (1980). He traces the degeneration of political parties during the twentieth century and discusses its impact on the accountability of elected officials. He notes that each of the following has been declining: the strength of party organization, voter identification with the parties, and unified party control of the executive and legislative branches. Among the consequences of the decline of parties (the only instruments that can promote collective responsibility) are immobilism, the increased importance of single-issue politics, and popular alienation from government. Fiorina concludes that "through a complex mixture of accident and intention we have constructed for ourselves a system that articulates interests superbly but aggregates them poorly. We hold our politicians individually accountable for the proposals they advocate, but less so for the adoption of those proposals, and not at all for overseeing the implementation of those proposals and the evaluation of their results."

James L. Sundquist considers the prospects for "Strengthening the National Parties" (1987). He suggests that the American political culture presents a substantial barrier to the emergence of stronger, more responsible parties. Sundquist notes that ". . . the notion that organized parties, rather than unaffiliated and disconnected individuals, should take responsibility for the affairs of government—and be held accountable by voters—has never been fully embraced in the country at large, and the Constitution has not been altered to accommodate it." In his view, "Deliberate attempts . . . to strengthen political parties run counter to deep-seated public attitudes, to the self-interest of the politicians who would have to initiate change, and to the structure of governmental and political institutions, including the electoral system." Nevertheless, he believes that stronger and more responsible parties may emerge "if, when one party again wins single-party control of the presidency and Congress, it succeeds in coping effectively with the problems of the country, the value of the responsible party concept will have been demonstrated and the model will win a wider public acceptance."

7

V. O. KEY, JR.

THE RESPONSIBLE ELECTORATE

In this selection, Professor V. O. Key, Jr. (1908–1963), argues that Americans vote on the basis of past performance of presidents. In other words, voting is retrospective. Key analyzed vote switching and policy preferences in presidential elections from 1936–1948. He used a combination of polling data and historical analysis to identify a distinct relationship between voter policy preferences and the decision to favor or reject particular candidates. Key concludes that the electorate acts responsibly in its capacity to connect issues to candidates. Key authored Southern Politics in State and Nation *(1949),* American State Politics *(1956),* Public Opinion and American Democracy *(1963),* Parties, Politics, and Pressure Groups *(1964), and* The Responsible Electorate *(1966). This selection is an abridged version of Chapter 3 from* The Responsible Electorate *that was published in* American Democracy: Theory and Reality *(1972), edited by Robert Weissberg and Mark V. Nadel.*

The apparent stability of the popular support of the political party dominant at the moment excites the curiosity of students of American politics. For relatively long periods one party or the other commands so consistently the votes of a majority that the country is said to be either normally Republican or normally Democratic. From 1932 to 1952 elections appeared to be only reassertions by the standing majority of its continued faith in Democratic leadership. In 1932 Franklin D. Roosevelt drew 59.1 per cent of the two-party vote and in 1936, in an extraordinary expression of popular confidence, 62.5 per cent. The Democratic proportion of the vote declined in succeeding elections bit by bit: 55.0 per cent in 1940; 53.8 per cent in 1944; and 52.3 per cent in 1948. Yet it seemed as if each election was but an occasion for the New Deal* to muster again its phalanxes only in slightly diminished strength, march them to the polls, and thereby record its claim to power for another four years.

The unbroken series of Democratic victories in the 1930's and 1940's occurred against a background of marked and abrupt innovations in governmental policy. To the extent that interactions between governmental action and public attitudes can be traced, this epoch should be instructive about the processes involved in the maintenance and renewal of a dominant popular coalition. And, thereby, we may also enlarge our information on the behavior of the supposedly errant voter. To speak of these interactions, though, we must recall some of the principal governmental actions of the 1930's. For a substantial part of the population they are by now only vague episodes in a dim and distant history.

The federal government underwent a radical transformation after the Democratic victory of 1932. It had been a remote authority with a limited range of

*New Deal: see footnote on page 17.

activity. It operated the postal system, improved rivers and harbors, maintained armed forces on a scale fearsome only to banana republics, and performed other functions of which the average citizen was hardly aware. Within a brief time it became an institution that affected intimately the lives and fortunes of most, if not all, citizens. Measures of recovery and of reform—as the categorization of the time went—contributed to this fundamental alteration of federal activities. Legislative endeavors to achieve economic recovery from the Great Depression* shaded over into steps toward basic reform; both types of policy touched the interests and hopes of great numbers of people and ignited the fiercest political controversy.

Large-scale measures for the relief of the unemployed made federal policy highly perceptible to millions of destitute persons. Administered at first as direct relief—a dole—by state relief administrations, the program soon came to be conducted by the Works Progress Administration, a federal agency which employed people on projects as diverse as theatricals, road construction, and leaf raking to the accompaniment of a spirited criticism not noticeably shared by those who relied on the WPA for sustenance. Another numerous class of persons received federal assistance through the Home Owners' Loan Corporation, an agency which had $3,000,000,000 to refinance home mortgages to tide necessitous debtors over until a better day. Hard-pressed banks and other business enterprises received infusions of government capital often in the form of loans. Expenditures on a new scale for public works pumped money into the economy. By the Agricultural Adjustment Act, Congress attempted to alleviate the lot of the farmer who had been especially hard hit by the depression. The National Recovery Administration sought, oddly enough, to activate industry by something of a system of legalized cartels,† with the inclusion in the cartel agreements (or industry codes) of standards with respect to minimum wages, maximum hours, collective bargaining‡, and other aspects of the employer-employee relationship.

How might voters be expected to respond to the actions of government and to the campaign oratory of this era? American parties have had historically a multiclass following. Doubtless in 1932, though the data are not available, persons of all classes deserted the Republicans to vote for Franklin D. Roosevelt and a change. The result was that the 1932 Democratic vote probably included large numbers of persons who would not be regarded as "Democratic" in disposi-

**The Great Depression:* economic crisis catalyzed in the United States by the stock market crash of October 29, 1929. The period of extremely low business activity and high unemployment lasted throughout the 1930s. European and other countries were also in the grip of the Depression. The crisis weakened the public's faith in the self-regulating capacity of the market system and increased public support for governmental intervention in the economy. Franklin D. Roosevelt's New Deal programs were the national government's response to the new challenges.

†*Cartel:* arrangement between suppliers of goods to set prices on their products and to restrict entry into an industry. The aim is to limit competition and guarantee market shares for the dominant firms. In practice, cartels are usually of limited success because one or more of the suppliers will sooner or later break ranks and undercut prices to increase sales. Cartels violate antitrust laws in the United States and in most other Western countries.

‡*Collective bargaining:* process by which employees band together, generally as a union, to negotiate hours, wages, and other conditions of work with their employers, broadly regulated in the U.S. by the Wagner National Labor Relations Act (1935). (See footnote, page 115.)

tion. At any rate, it would be plausible to expect that as the New Deal unfolded, persons of upper-class status and of conservative disposition would be drawn from their Democratic posture to the Republican ranks. Moreover, it might be supposed that a counter-tendency would also operate as 1932 Republican voters in the lesser economic categories moved over to the Democratic side of the fence. In short, the impact of governmental actions and political rhetoric would be expected to heighten polarization among class and occupational lines.

Some such movement of voters occurred, evidently on a fairly large scale. Many upper-class Democratic voters defected, while relatively fewer working-class Democrats left the ranks. Scarcely any information is available for the election of 1936, but in the elections of 1940, 1944, and 1948 these differentials in party switching existed. Persons at all economic levels at each election moved away from the Democratic party but at rates varying with level of economic status. The differentials in party defection among economic levels, as estimated from Gallup polls of presidential preference, appear in Table 4. The rankings from "wealthy" to "poor" assigned by the interviewers are doubtless not measures of precision; nevertheless, of the "wealthy" 1936 Democratic voters, in the neighborhood of four out of ten deserted to the Republicans in 1940. At the other extreme, less than one in seven persons on relief took that step.

The countermovement, from Republican in 1936 to Democratic in 1940, was relatively small, yet it had a class bias in that relatively more of the poor than of the better-off 1936 Republicans switched to Democratic in 1940. In 1944 involvement in World War II gave the stimuli of the campaign a less class-oriented tone; yet in lesser degree than in 1940 the same class-tinged pattern of party switching prevailed. In 1948, with the war out of the way, the political battle assumed its older form with a more marked difference in switching among economic levels. Though the rates of switching in party preference shown by the pre-election polls analyzed in Table 4 may exceed the switch in the actual vote, they suggest the existence of quite large movements across party lines in these elections which brought voting alignments toward a closer congruity with income classes.[1]

What would we find if we proceeded directly to motive or attitude and ascertained the relation between vote switching and views on policy? What kinds of relations would be found if we assumed that the voter was a fairly reasonable fellow who voted to promote or to discourage public policies he approved or disapproved, insofar as he could perceive the consequences of his vote? Obviously, all kinds of motives, attitudes, and concerns enter into the voting decision; yet analyses of the available information indicate quite marked correlations between policy attitudes and vote switching. In short, the data make it appear sensible to regard the voter as a person who is concerned with what governments have done or not done and what they propose to do rather than one guided, perhaps unaware, by the imperatives of economic status or the tricks of Madison Avenue.

Our information on the relation of voter switching to policy preferences is not as comprehensive as we might wish. The information on the election of 1936, which was evidently an event of great significance in the reshaping of the American pattern of party loyalties, is especially limited. Nevertheless, in that year the

TABLE 4. PATTERNS OF VOTE SWITCHING IN PRESIDENTIAL ELECTIONS, 1936–1948, IN RELATION TO ECONOMIC STATUS[a]

	1936–40[b]		1940–44[c]		1944–48[d]	
Status	% of 1936 D's, D-R	% of 1936 R's, R-D	% of 1940 D's, D-R	% of 1940 R's, R-D	% of 1944 D's, D-R	% of 1944 R's, R-D
WEALTHY	46	2	35	4	[e]	0
AVERAGE+	30	1	27	5	47	1
AVERAGE	28	4	24	7	32	3
POOR+	20	5	[f]	[f]	[f]	[f]
POOR	18	7	19	8	22	6
OLD-AGE ASSISTANCE	19	4	13	5	18	[e]
ON RELIEF	14	7	11	[e]	[e]	[e]

[a]The table entries are the percentages of those with a recall of a vote for a major-party candidate at the first election of the pair of years who expressed a preference for a major-party candidate in surveys in October just prior to the election of the second year of each pair. In each instance several surveys are combined to obtain larger samples in the individual cells. Economic status was that assigned to the respondent by the AIPO interviewer.

[b]A consolidation of the following AIPO surveys: 215K, 216K, 217, 218K. Roper 22, October 1940, yielded the following percentages of switchers, D-R, in the indicated economic levels: A, 25; B, 24; C, 20; D, 12. The corresponding R-D switches were: 2, 3, 5, 9.

[c]A consolidation of AIPO 330, 331, 332, 333, 334.

[d]A consolidation of AIPO 430 and 431.

[e]Less than 50 cases.

[f]Data obtained from low-income respondents in 1944 and 1948 were coded only in terms of a "poor" category. There was no "poor+" category.

old-age annuity provisions of the Social Security Act turned out to be a major issue. Republicans attacked the act. All citizens would soon be wearing dog tags carrying their social security numbers and less restrained campaign orators treated the system as a fraud. Voters responded with an expression of opinion startling in its clarity. In the neighborhood of four out of ten 1932 Democratic voters who opposed the legislation shifted over to the Republican candidate while about three out of ten of those 1932 Republicans who favored the plan moved to the support of Roosevelt. The details appear in Table 5.[2] Had the social security issue been the only influence on the vote these switches would have been closer to ten out of ten in each direction. It was not, of course, the only issue.[3] Nevertheless, an impressive relation between voting behavior and policy preference on this question prevailed, which raises a presumption that the social security issue had a notable power to wrench voters from their 1932 party positions to a vote in accord with their policy preferences.

As the election of 1940 approached, newspaper headlines tended to focus on the threat of war; yet voters seemed to be more concerned with the grand issues of domestic politics. Those issues turned broadly around the place and power of business in the American system, and the Democratic Administration occupied the role, in the eyes of business, as the enemy of business and, in the eyes of others, as the protagonist of the generality. The tolerant attitude of government toward the sitdown strikes in the automobile industry in 1937 symbolized the situation. As the 1940 polling neared, however, business protests became sharper

TABLE 5. SWITCHES IN PRESIDENTIAL VOTING PERFERENCE, 1932–1936, IN RELATION TO RESPONSE TO QUESTION: *"DO YOU FAVOR THE COMPULSORY OLD-AGE INSURANCE PLAN, STARTING JANUARY FIRST, WHICH REQUIRES EMPLOYERS AND EMPLOYEES TO MAKE EQUAL MONTHLY CONTRIBUTIONS?"*[a]

Response	*% of 1932 D's, D-R*	*% of 1932 R's, R-D*	*% of New Voters, D*[b]
YES, FAVOR	12 (1,630)	30 (643)	61 (626)
NO	40 (483)	7 (535)	45 (245)
NO OPINION	13 (315)	16 (175)	71 (170)

[a]AIPO 53, 9-26-36. This is the only surviving deck of cards for a 1936 survey with a recall of the 1932 vote. Data on the characteristics of the sample are nonexistent, but the addition of the N's to produce a national sample would probably be even more perilous than is the use here made of the data. The N's appear in parentheses. As in other tables, N is the total number of respondents on which the percentage is based. Thus, the figure 1,630 in the first column means that there were 1,630 respondents who recalled having voted for the Democratic candidate in 1932 and who favored the compulsory old-age insurance plan in 1936. Of these 1,630 persons, 12 per cent reported that they intended to support the Republican candidate in 1936.

[b]New voters are respondents who had not voted in 1932, either because they were too young or for other reasons.

as earlier New Deal legislation, made temporarily ineffective by constitutional litigation, began to make its effects felt. The defeat of Roosevelt's plan for the rejuvenation of the Supreme Court heartened business only temporarily. The Court found ways and means to hold major New Deal legislation constitutional contrary to the opinions of most of the corporation lawyers in the country. Employers, thus, began to feel the bite of the Wagner Labor Relations Act.* Wendell Willkie, an erstwhile Democrat and former president of a utility corporation that had had to sell out to the Tennessee Valley Authority, won the Republican nomination and led the forces of protest against the New Deal.

How did the voters respond to the campaign alternatives? Did their response proceed from their preferences about governmental policy? Or did voters react in a random fashion as the winds of the campaign blew them about? To an astonishing degree (that is, a degree astonishing to persons with experience in the analysis of polling data) voters in their movements to and fro across party lines and from an inactive to an active voting status behaved as persons who made choices congruent with their policy preferences. In a sense, the question of more or less government control of business bundled up most of the lesser domestic questions of the campaign into a single great issue. Of those 1936 Democratic voters who felt that there should be less government regulation of business, about half expressed an intent to defect to Willkie in 1940. Of the 1936 Republican voters who thought there should be less business regulation, 98 per cent remained steadfastly Republican (and the 2 per cent desertion to the Democrats is not in excess of error that could have been produced in recording interviews and in

***Wagner Labor Relations Act*: popular name for the National Labor Relations Act of 1935 (NLRA) as amended by the Labor-Management Relations Act of 1947 (see *Taft-Hartley Act* in the following footnote) and the Labor-Management Reporting and Disclosure Act of 1959 (see *Landrum-Griffin Act* in footnote on page 287). The NLRA is the primary labor relations law regulating private sector interstate commerce, exclusive of railroad and airline operations. Administered by the National Labor Relations Board (a federal agency created by the act), the NLRA was designed to protect the interests of employees, employers, and the general public. It encourages collective bargaining and defines and prohibits unfair labor practices by both labor and management.

processing the data). Few 1936 Republican voters favored the existing level of business regulation or more regulation, but those who did succumbed far more frequently to Democratic blandishments; about 15 per cent of them favored Roosevelt. Table 6 contains the details.

An even more marked association prevailed between voter attitudes on farm policy and shifts across party lines. About seven out of ten Democrats of 1936 who became disillusioned about the farm program had a 1940 preference for Willkie. Republican defectors were not numerous but about one out of five 1936 Republicans who approved the Democratic farm program looked favorably on Roosevelt in 1940. Those with the appropriate policy outlooks stood pat in remarkable degree. Only 1 per cent of the 1936 Republicans who disapproved the Administration farm program threatened to vote Democratic. This relationship between policy outlook and vote (shown in detail in Table 7) doubtless reflected to a degree the tendency of a voter on a specific question to improvise policy views that seem to be consistent with the way he planned to vote for other reasons entirely. A steadfast Democratic partisan might have been expected to opine that the "Roosevelt administration has done a good job in handling the farm problem," if the question were put to him in that form. Yet, however such opinions come into being, their supportive function in the political system should be the same.

By 1940 the Supreme Court had held the Wagner Labor Relations Act constitutional; nevertheless, many employers remained hopeful of the ultimate repeal or modification of the act. The only way to fulfill that hope was to defeat Roosevelt. The electorate responded predictably to the impact of the issue. Of the 1936 Democrate who had come to believe that the act should be repealed (which, in the context of the times, was an antilabor move) about one out of two expressed a 1940 Republican preference. Those who thought it should merely be revised defected only about half as frequently. Similarly, Republican loyalties were maintained most steadfastly by those who stood for repeal or revision of the act. Interestingly, in our sample of 1936 nonvoters only nine respondents turned up favoring the repeal of the act; eight of the nine preferred Wilkie. Withal, vote switches occurred in directions consistent with the assumption that voters were moved by a rational calculation of the instrumental impact of their vote. The detailed data are in Table 8.

Roosevelt's candidacy in 1940 ran counter to the two-term tradition, a fact that agitated the citizenry, especially those who opposed him on other grounds anyway. And probably those who supported him on other grounds declined in an especial degree to become exercised about the third-term question. In any case, the great shifts of the electorate had a close relationship to attitude on the third-term question, as may be seen from Table 9. Of the 1936 Democrats who felt that under no condition should a President serve three terms, nearly 90 per cent moved over to a Republican preference in 1940. On the other hand, 1936 Republicans who became 1940 Democrats tended to hold moderate views on the third-term matter. They could see the necessity for exceptions. These relations do not, of course, establish that persons opposed to a third term in principle defected from the Democracy for that reason. An alternative assumption is that

TABLE 6. SWITCHES IN PRESIDENTIAL VOTING PREFERENCE, 1936–1940, IN RELATION TO RESPONSE TO QUESTION: "*DURING THE NEXT FOUR YEARS DO YOU THINK THERE SHOULD BE MORE OR LESS REGULATION OF BUSINESS BY THE FEDERAL GOVERNMENT THAN AT PRESENT?*"[a]

Response	*% of 1936* D's, D-R	*% of 1936* R's, R-D	*% of New* Voters, D[b]
MORE REGULATION	10 (856)[c]	15 (161)	73 (187)
ABOUT SAME	10 (712)	16 (122)	76 (124)
LESS REGULATION	50 (841)	2 (1,263)	32 (229)
NO OPINION	14 (637)	8 (158)	68 (148)

[a]A consolidation of AIPO 215K-T, 10-9-40, and 219K-T, 10-24-40.
[b]New voters consist of those respondents who had not voted in 1936 either because they were too young or for other reasons.
[c]Here is an illustration of how to read the table entries: these two figures mean that, of the 856 poll respondents in 1940 who said they had voted for Roosevelt in 1936 and who wanted more regulation in the 1940's, 10 per cent expressed an intent to defect to Willkie.

TABLE 7. SWITCHES IN PRESIDENTIAL VOTING PREFERENCE, 1936–1940, IN RELATION TO VIEWS ON ROOSEVELT ADMINISTRATION'S PROGRAM FOR HELPING FARMERS[a]

View	*% of 1936* D's, D-R	*% of 1936* R's, R-D	*% of New* Voters, D
APPROVE	7 (978)	23 (131)	83 (242)
DISAPPROVE	69 (202)	1 (529)	16 (134)
NO OPINION	22 (269)	6 (170)	60 (130)

[a]AIPO 215K&T, 10-9-40.

TABLE 8. SWITCHES IN PRESIDENTIAL VOTING PREFERENCE, 1936–1940, IN RELATION TO RESPONSE TO QUESTION: "*DO YOU THINK THE WAGNER LABOR ACT SHOULD BE REVISED, REPEALED OR LEFT UNCHANGED?*"[a]

Response	*% of 1936* D's, D-R	*% of 1936* R's, R-D	*% of New* Voters, D
REVISED	24 (193)	3 (258)	59 (90)
REPEALED	52 (42)	3 (77)	[b]
LEFT UNCHANGED	12 (376)	12 (91)	64 (106)
NO OPINION	22 (497)	5 (283)	59 (192)

[a]AIPO 215K&T, 10-9-40. The analysis is limited to those who said they had "heard of" the Wagner Act.
[b]Only 9 respondents fell in this cell; one reported a Democratic preference.

they adopted that position because they chose to defect from the Democracy. Whatever its origin, the congruence of outlook on the constitutional issue and the direction of the vote is of importance, and it is not unreasonable to suppose that a goodly number of persons may very well have been governed in their candidate choice by their policy outlook.

The opinion surveys during the campaigns of 1944 and of 1948 included few inquiries suitable for the identification of policy-related movements of voters in those elections. From the behavior of persons of different economic and occupational status (presented earlier in Table 4) it is a fair assumption that patterns quite similar to those of 1940 prevailed in 1948 and probably to a lesser extent in

TABLE 9. SWITCHES IN PRESIDENTIAL VOTING PREFERENCE, 1936–1940, IN RELATION TO VIEWS ON THIRD-TERM QUESTION[a]

Views	*% of 1936 D's, D-R*	*% of 1936 R's, R-D*	*% of New Voters, D*
SILLY AND OUTWORN TRADITION	5 (521)	14 (56)	83 (98)
NOT GOOD, BUT EXCEPTIONS	8 (1,390)	20 (243)	15 (369)
UNDER NO CONDITION	88 (332)	0.3 (989)	5 (189)
DON'T KNOW	15 (59)	4 (23)	68 (28)

[a]Based on Roper survey, October 1940. The question was: "With which one of these statements concerning a third term do you come closest to agreeing?
"a) The idea that a President should not hold office for three terms is a silly and outworn tradition.
"b) While it may not generally be a good idea for a President to serve three terms, there should be no rule at a time of national costs.
"c) Never under any conditions should a President hold office for three terms."

1944 when war muted to some extent the divisive issues of domestic policy. One relevant analysis from the 1948 election appears in Table 10 which presents our familiar pattern of switching in its relation to views on the question whether the laws governing labor unions were too strict or not strict enough. By 1948 the Wagner Act had been revised by the Taft-Hartley Act* to the disadvantage of unions. The AFL and CIO exerted themselves in support of Harry S. Truman who urged repeal of the act, a position which by now had become a prolabor position. The evidence from this question supports the conventional view that the campaign of 1948 shaped antagonisms along New Deal and anti-New Deal lines. Those few Dewey† supporters of 1944 who felt that labor laws were too strict deserted to Truman at a rate of about one out of five in 1948. On the other hand, 1944 Roosevelt supporters who thought the labor laws not strict enough switched to Dewey with somewhat higher frequency, as the table indicates.

As the campaign of 1940 approached, the threat of war preoccupied the pundits and the commentators, who doubtless communicated their anxieties to the public. Yet the promises made and expectations raised by the candidates with respect to foreign policy seemed to have far less bearing on the vote than did questions of domestic policy. For a time foreign policy seemed to have been taken out of the campaign, but as the election neared, Willkie, under the prodding of the Republican professionals, stirred up the issue by his forecasts that war would soon come if Roosevelt were re-elected. Democratic campaigners

**Taft-Hartley Act* (Labor-Management Relations Act of 1947): law that amended the National Labor Relations Act of 1935 (see Wagner Labor Relations Act in the preceding footnote) in the following ways: enlarged the National Labor Relations Board from three to five members; excluded supervisory workers from NLRA coverage; provided for an eighty-day "cooling-off period" in the event of a threatened strike that would create or prolong a national emergency; and provided that lawsuits could be brought against unions for contract violations. The act also outlawed "closed shop" arrangements, under which employers were unable to hire non-union members, and allowed states to pass "right-to-work" laws that prohibited contracts requiring employees to become union members. It also created the Federal Mediation and Conciliation Service.

†*Thomas E. Dewey:* Republican presidential nominee in 1944 and 1948.

TABLE 10. SWITCHES IN PRESIDENTIAL VOTE, 1944–1948, IN RELATION TO RESPONSE TO QUESTION: *"AS THINGS STAND TODAY, DO YOU THINK THE LAWS GOVERNING LABOR UNIONS ARE TOO STRICT OR NOT STRICT ENOUGH?"*[a]

Response	*% of 1944* D's, D-R	*% of 1944* R's, R-D	*% of New* Voters, D
TOO STRICT	8 (304)	22 (76)	74 (80)
ABOUT RIGHT	15 (357)	9 (218)	68 (118)
NOT STRICT ENOUGH	27 (232)	6 (318)	51 (87)
NO OPINION	15 (181)	10 (101)	64 (58)

[a]Based on AIPO 432, 11-1-48. Interviews were conducted after the election; the date is the "send-out" date.

probably became more worried about these charges than did the electorate generally. At any rate, the data indicate a comparatively mild relation between attitudes on foreign policy and vote shifting.

The question whether it was more important to keep out of war ourselves or to help England even at the risk of getting into war should have separated persons into the two conflicting camps of the time. Though more of those who thought that we should keep out of war deserted to Willkie, the difference between this figure and the rate of desertion of those who thought we should help England win (Table 11) was not wide enough to indicate that this difference in attitude contributed nearly so heavily to vote switching as did the impact of domestic issues. Similarly, a person's views on the question whether we should have gotten into World War I might be expected to segregate those of isolationist sentiment from their opponents. Those 1936 Democrats who thought our World War I venture was a mistake shifted to Willkie more frequently than did those who held an opposing view; yet again the difference (Table 12) was relatively small.

This is not to say that foreign policy questions invariably command less attention than do domestic questions. Rather in 1940 this seemed to be the case. Probably the more general rule is that the electorate responds most markedly and most clearly to those events it has experienced and observed, vicariously or directly. Voters had enjoyed or not enjoyed eight years of domestic policy of the New Deal and they reacted demonstrably to those experiences. The prospects for the future may generally tend less to engage the voter or to govern his actions. Those prospects tend to be hazy, uncertain, problematic. Voters may respond most assuredly to what they have seen, heard, experienced. Forecasts, promises, predicted disaster, or pie in the sky may be less moving.

A kind word needs to be said for that supposedly benighted fellow, the standpatter, the consistent party voter. So far our attention has centered on the switcher. The evidence indicates that the shifting voter is far more numerous than is commonly supposed. Moreover, his reports of his actions and attitudes indicate that as he navigates his way from party to party he moves in a manner that is sensible in the light of his policy preferences. To be sure, partisan loyalties invest the electoral mass with a degree of inertia and not all voters follow their policy inclinations by moving from candidate to candidate. What of these voters who remain in the party ranks from election to election? Are they obtuse diehards who swallow their principles to stick by their party?

TABLE 11. SWITCHES IN PRESIDENTIAL VOTING PREFERENCE, 1936–1940, IN RELATION TO OPINIONS ON WHETHER MORE IMPORTANT TO KEEP OUT OF WAR OR TO HELP ENGLAND WIN[a]

Attitude	*% of 1936 D's, D-R*	*% of 1936 R's, R-D*	*% of New Voters, D*
KEEP OUT OF WAR	31 (1,975)	3 (1,127)	56 (724)
HELP ENGLAND WIN	19 (2,426)	5 (1,211)	61 (653)
NO CHOICE	25 (166)	0 (76)	72 (68)

[a]A consolidation of AIPO 217, 10-22-40; 220, 10-22-40; 224, 11-19-40. Note that a post-election survey is combined with two pre-election surveys. The question was: "Which of these two things do you think is the more important for the United States to try to do: 1. To keep out of war ourselves, 2. To help England win, even at the risk of getting into war." The schedules carried the "no choice" box, though the meaning of this response is unclear.

TABLE 12. SWITCHES IN PRESIDENTIAL VOTE, 1936–1940, IN RELATION TO RESPONSE TO QUESTION: "*DO YOU THINK IT WAS A MISTAKE FOR THE UNITED STATES TO ENTER THE LAST WORLD WAR?*"[a]

Response	*% of 1936 D's, D-R*	*% of 1936 R's, R-D*	*% of New Voters, D*
YES, MISTAKE	28 (511)	4 (382)	49 (140)
NO	18 (636)	5 (322)	64 (154)
NO OPINION	20 (258)	6 (118)	67 (108)

[a]AIPO 224, 11-19-40.

Almost all the analyses of the preceding pages throw light on the question. On issue after issue those with views consistent with the outlook of their party stood pat in their voting preference. Notably few Republican defections occurred among those who subscribed to sound Republican doctrine. Democratic deserters were uniformly fewest among those who concurred with the pure and orthodox Democratic tenets of the time. No doubt some Republicans and some Democrats adjusted their views to make them conform with their perceptions of the positions of their party. Yet it is the parallelism of vote and policy view that is significant for our analysis, not its origin.

The facts seem to be that, on the average, the standpatters do not have to behave as mugwumps* to keep their consciences clear; they are already where they ought to be in the light of their policy attitudes. Tables 13, 14, and 15 demonstrate this point in another way. Those who vote consistently from one election to the next, the data of those tables indicate, adhere to the party doctrine in high degree. Though partisan groupings of voters are not models of ideological purity, the standpatters of each party manifest fairly high agreement with the party positions as popularly perceived. Thus, well over half of the 1936–1940 D-D's felt that there should be during the next four years about the same degree or more government regulation. Similarly, the Administration's farm program found favor with three fourths of the 1936–1940 D-D's, while only a little more than 10 per cent of the R-R's could bring themselves to approve it. Again far fewer of the 1944–1948 D-D's than of the 1944–1948 R-R's thought that the laws governing labor unions were too strict.[4]

**Mugwumps:* individuals who abandon their political party to support an opposing candidate.

TABLE 13. PATTERN OF PRESIDENTIAL PREFERENCE, 1936–1940, IN RELATION TO DISTRIBUTION OF RESPONSES TO QUESTION: "*DURING THE NEXT FOUR YEARS DO YOU THINK THERE SHOULD BE MORE OR LESS REGULATION OF BUSINESS BY THE FEDERAL GOVERNMENT THAN AT PRESENT?*"[a]

Response	D-D	R-D	O-D[b]	O-R[b]	D-R	R-R
MORE REGULATION	32%	28%	34%	18%	13%	8%
ABOUT SAME	27	23	23	10	11	7
LESS REGULATION	18	34	18	55	63	76
NO OPINION	23	15	25	17	13	9
	100	100	100	100	100	100
n	(2,386)	(85)	(403)	(285)	(660)	(1,619)

[a]A consolidation of AIPO 215K-T, 10-9-40, and 219K-T, 10-24-40.
[b]New voters, i.e., nonvoters in 1936.

TABLE 14. PATTERNS OF PRESIDENTIAL PREFERENCE, 1936–1940, IN RELATION TO DISTRIBUTION OF VIEWS ON ROOSEVELT ADMINISTRATION'S PROGRAM FOR HANDLING FARM PROBLEM[a]

Response	D-D	R-D	O-D[b]	O-R[b]	D-R	R-R
APPROVE	76%	64%	66%	19%	26%	13%
DISAPPROVE	5	13	7	55	51	66
DON'T KNOW	18	21	26	25	22	20
NO ANSWER	1	2	1	1	1	1
	100	100	100	100	100	100
n	(1,191)	(47)	(305)	(207)	(274)	(795)

[a]Based on AIPO 215K&T, 10-9-40.
[b]Nonvoters in 1936.

TABLE 15. PATTERNS OF PRESIDENTIAL PREFERENCE, 1944–1948, IN RELATION TO DISTRIBUTION OF RESPONSES TO QUESTION: "*AS THINGS STAND TODAY, DO YOU THINK THE LAWS GOVERNING LABOR UNIONS ARE TOO STRICT OR NOT STRICT ENOUGH?*"[a]

Response	D-D	R-D	O-D	O-R	D-R	R-R
TOO STRICT	31%	26%	27%	17%	15%	9%
ABOUT RIGHT	33	31	36	31	31	31
NOT STRICT ENOUGH	19	28	20	35	38	46
NO OPINION	17	15	17	17	16	14
	100	100	100	100	100	100
n	(909)	(65)	(220)	(123)	(165)	(648)

[a]Based on AIPO 432, 11-1-48, a post-election survey (interviews were conducted after the election; the date is the "send-out" date).

Party switchers move towards the party whose standpatters they resemble in their policy views, a proposition made apparent by the tables. The D-R's are divided in their policy views in about the same fashion as the R-R's with whom they join in the election, and the R-D's resemble the D-D's to which they attach themselves for the voting. The nonvoters at the preceding election who join the D-D's or the R-R's also have an attitudinal resemblance to the standpatters with whom they ally themselves. Yet, as the tables also indicate, the switchers bear earmarks of their origin. The D-R's are not in quite the same degree as the R-R's attached to the party policy position, and the R-D's also bore traces of their Republican origin. Nevertheless, on balance each of these groups bore far greater resemblance to the standpatters of the party of their destination than to the faithful of the party of their origin.

For those who have persevered to this point, a few preliminary reflections on the significance of the information so far assembled are in order. We have established patterns of movement of party switchers from election to election and the patterns of stability of the standpatter that lead us to a conception of the voter that is not often propounded. From our analyses the voter emerges as a person who appraises the actions of government, who has policy preferences, and who relates his vote to those appraisals and preferences. One may have misgivings about the data and one can certainly concede that the data also indicate that some voters are governed by blind party loyalty and that some others respond automatically to the winds of the environment of the moment. Yet the obtrusive feature of the data is the large number of persons whose vote is instrumental to their policy preferences.

These parallelisms of voting patterns and policy preferences may be dismissed as the meaningless result of the disposition of people to adopt consistent sets of views on interrelated matters. A survey respondent, bedeviled by an interviewer, may express a preference for a Democratic candidate and then, to keep things tidy, adopt a favorable attitude toward Democratic policy positions. He would, though, in our analysis fit into the same pigeonhole of the IBM sorter as the person who arrived at the same consistent constellation of attitudes by a process of anguished thought and reflection. Doubtless both kinds of respondents are encountered by poll interviewers. Yet, however these patterns of consistent voting preferences are formed, they can scarcely be regarded as without political significance. Our correlations, though, should not be taken to mean that the policy attitudes correlated with changes and continuities in voting preference necessarily cause those changes or continuities. Rather they demonstrate the tendency of persons to build up combinations of outlooks and to adopt voting preferences that make sense in the light of those outlooks.

In another direction our data throw light on the interactions between government and public and on the functions of the electorate in the democratic process. A notable element of our tables is the extent to which an Administration seems to lose the votes of its erstwhile supporters who dissent from actions it has taken. The tables seem to verify the journalistic superstition that the people only vote against; never, for. That appearance results in part from the manner in which the facts have been presented; an equally strong case could be made for the proposition that the standpatters stand pat because they are for what has been done. Nevertheless, the fact remains that some erstwhile supporters do vote against and they tend to disagree with actions that have been taken. Few erstwhile enemies are attracted to a dominant party by its actions, though some are. A president may, with justification, be anxious lest a projected action draw down his reservoir of popular good will. He cannot proceed on the assumption that inaction will maintain the loyalty of the faithful by antagonizing no one. Yet to govern he must be prepared to extend some of his good will. And to continue to govern he must attempt to offset those losses by policies that attract support from the opposition or from among the new voters.

The patterns of flow of the major streams of shifting voters graphically reflect the electorate in its great, and perhaps principal, role as an appraiser of past events, past performance, and past actions. It judges retrospectively; it commands prospectively only insofar as it expresses either approval or disapproval of that which has happened before. Voters may reject what they have known; or they may approve whay they have known. They are not likely to be attracted in great numbers by promises of the novel or unknown. Once innovation has occurred they may embrace it, even though they would have, earlier, hesitated to venture forth to welcome it.

These tendencies of the electorate, as they obtrude from our many tables, make plain how completely the minority party is a captive of the majority—and of the situation. Critics of the American party system fret because the minority party does not play the role of an imaginative advocate heralding the shape of a new world. In truth, it gains votes most notably from among those groups who are disappointed by, who disapprove of, or who regard themselves as injured by, the actions of the Administration. The opposition can maximize its strength as it centers its fire on those elements of the Administration program disliked by the largest numbers of people. Thus, as a matter of practical politics, it must appear to be a common scold rather than a bold exponent of innovation, though it may propose new (or old) approaches to old questions. The misfortunes of the Republicans over the period 1932–1952 sprang essentially from the simple fact that they could not lay their hands on an issue on which the Democrats had outraged enough people to vote them out of office.

NOTES

[1]For the technician it should be noted that the differences in switching rates that appear, for example, in the first column of Table 1 could be attributable in part to a variant of the Maccobyean effect, so called for its identification by Eleanor Maccoby, "Pitfalls in the Analysis of Panel Data: A Research Note on Some Technical Aspects of Voting," *American Journal of Sociology*, 61 (1956), 359–362. The effect may result in an overstatement of differences in rates of change between large and small samples. Random errors in recording responses and in punching data into cards may inflate the rates of change for small N's more than for large N's. The odds are that the potential of the effect is negligible for most of our tables, but comparisons between cells with large and with extremely small N's should be regarded with some wariness.

[2]Editor's note [Weissberg & Nadel]: The data in Table 2 do not indicate how important or visible the social security issue was to the members of Dr. Gallup's sample. Some voters, for example, may have duly registered their approval or disapproval of the old-age insurance scheme without really caring very much about its inclusion in the Social Security Act; and Key intended to emphasize that

undoubtedly the social security issue was more salient for some voters than for others during the 1936 campaign. Either a lack of concern over the social security question or a greater concern with other issues among some voters could help explain why the relation between policy attitudes on social security and 1936 voting behavior was not even stronger than it was.

[3]Editor's note: Key intended to elaborate at some length on the relationship in Table 2 between voters' 1936 presidential preference and their attitude toward the old-age insurance program. Attitudes on the social security issue may have had two broad effects on the 1936 voting. In addition to making voters whose position on the issue was not congruent with their previous presidential vote more likely to switch parties in 1936, it also may have made individuals whose previous presidential vote and policy attitude on the social security question were mutually consistent more inclined to stick with the party they had previously supported. Among 1932 Democratic voters, although four in ten of those who opposed the old-age insurance plan switched to the G.O.P. in 1936, only one in eight of the 1932 Democrats who supported federal old-age pensions left the Democratic party at the next presidential election. On the other hand, 1932 Republican voters who supported the insurance plan were much more likely to switch to the Democratic presidential nominee in 1936 than were 1932 Republican voters who opposed the Social Security pension plan. Three in ten of the 1932 Republican voters who supported the plan switched to Roosevelt in 1936; only 7 per cent of the 1932 Republican voters who opposed the plan deserted the G.O.P. in 1936.

[4]Standpatters, the evidence suggests, acquire their policy attitudes in at least two ways. Some persons more or less deliberately affiliate with the party whose policy emphases appear to parallel their own. Other persons, psychologically identified with a party, adopt those policy outlooks espoused by the more prominent spokesmen of their party. In the course of party life, the acceptance of the cues of party leadership may result in alteration of the attitudes of party followers. This flexible conformity with shifting party doctrine probably occurs most markedly among those strongly identified psychologically with the party. See Angus Campbell and Homer C. Cooper, *Group Differences in Attitudes and Votes* (Ann Arbor: Survey Research Center, 1956), pp. 102–104.

8

WALTER DEAN BURNHAM

THE TURNOUT PROBLEM

Walter Dean Burnham is professor of political science at the University of Texas. He is the author of Critical Elections and the Mainsprings of American Politics *(1970),* American Politics and Public Policy *(1978),* The Current Crisis in American Politics *(1982), and* Democracy in the Making *(1986). The relationships between nonvoting, social class, electoral rules, and partisanship are analyzed in "The Turnout Problem" (1987). The United States has a low voter participation rate compared to other advanced democracies. The increasing numbers of nonvoters are disproportionately lower class and former supporters of the Democratic party. Burnham examines aspects of electoral politics and the modern party system that contribute to the problem of nonvoting and concludes that revitalization of the party system is necessary to reverse these trends.*

Elections American style are peculiar in many respects. One of their chief peculiarities today is that so few eligible citizens vote in them. For example, in 1984 there were roughly 167.7 million citizens of voting age, of whom 92.7 million voted for president, while 75 million (44.8 percent) did not.[1] In 1986, with 171.9 million citizens potentially eligible to vote, 64.6 million cast ballots for the highest offices in their states, and 61.3 million voted for members of Congress—turnout rates of 37.6 percent and 35.7 percent. Thus well over three-fifths of potentially eligible Americans failed to vote in 1986. This produced the third lowest midterm election turnout in a century and a half (only 1926 and 1942 showed lower figures). Excluding the southern quarter of the country, with its unique regional political history, the 1986 participation rate fell to the lowest level recorded for an off-year election since 1978.

Today, I would estimate that about 38 percent of American citizens are "core" or regular voters for major national and state offices; another 17 percent or so are marginals who come to the polls only when stimulated by the dramas of presidential campaign politics; and 45 percent are more or less habitual nonvoters. This level of nonvoting is characteristically, almost uniquely, American. Voting participation in other advanced capitalist democracies—the curious anomaly of the Swiss Confederation apart—is much higher than it is here. An off-year congressional election is not, of course, the equivalent of a parliamentary election elsewhere. Still, it is striking that the participation rate in the German Bundestag election of February 1987 was nearly 50 percentage points higher than the American congressional turnout rate in November 1986.[2]

Once upon a time, in the lost Atlantis of nineteenth-century politics, American participation rates in both presidential and midterm elections were very close to current participation rates abroad. The characteristic American participation rate is a singular property of politics in this century.[3] Outside the special southern region, voter turnout in the United States has declined heavily and nearly continuously since 1960, despite educational and structural changes that in themselves should have led to an increase. This decline is skewed very heavily across class lines—the skew becoming more extreme the lower the overall rate falls. The partisan implications of this change are not symmetrical, but are much more concentrated on the Democratic than the Republican side.

One would have thought that political science's research mainstream would long ago have considered turnout issues to represent a real "problem," as many activists and opinion leaders outside academe do. To be sure, "mass apathy" in America presents a certain public relations problem: it doesn't look good, especially in a comparative context. But is turnout really a "problem" in any more fundamental sense? The answer to this question must depend upon the perspectives of the person analyzing the question. In the days of the Cold War synthesis, it was fashionable to dismiss the issue (when nonsouthern turnouts were considerably higher than now) as being the fruit of a "politics of happiness" and beneficent low pressure.[4] For many obvious reasons, such views are less in vogue today.

In what follows, I will be concerned to evaluate the social "incidence" of nonvoting, concentrating (to what many would regard as an excessive degree) on the class dimensions of voting and nonvoting in American elections. Now it is no new doctrine that social class is subjectively a feeble behavioral anchor in a society that is immensely complex in demography, cultural subtraditions, and locally dominant economic sectors. The United States, after all, is noteworthy for having a dominant, single "liberal tradition"* in its political culture, and, very much related to this, for lacking any significant organized socialist or laborite† alternative in its electoral market.[5] Nevertheless, from a systemic perspective social class differentials loom rather larger, especially where participation is concerned. For the old saw remains profoundly true: if you don't vote, you don't count. Consider, for example, formal education, which is so significant as a political sorting-out variable. Viewed at the individual level, there is little reason to challenge the usual view that this is a more powerful discriminator than occupation, income, or other measures of social differentials.[6] Yet the first thing that would occur to one from a structural or systemic perspective is that access to higher education is expensive and therefore tends to be pretty strictly rationed in economic and social terms. It is one of a variety of interrelated functional

*_Liberal tradition:_ public philosophy espousing a social order that exalts the individual's natural rights and gives free rein to individual action and self-expression. Many aspects of American political culture and governmental structure reflect liberal values of the eighteenth century. The role of the state is limited and decentralized, safeguarding basic civil liberties while affording broad latitude to private enterprise. Classic liberalism views private property as a basic right and implies _laissez-faire_ in the realm of individual economic activity and the accumulation of wealth. During the twentieth century, liberalism has come to be associated with greater positive intervention by government to secure wider public goals, in particular equality of opportunity to share in the economic and political advantages of a free society.

†_Laborite:_ individual who belongs to a political party, such as the British Labour party, that promotes the interests of workers.

measures that discriminate quite effectively between the have-mores and have-lesses in a stratified class system.

COMPETING PERSPECTIVES

At the level of explaining individual voting behavior, two sets of perspectives seem to dominate the field today. They are often thought incompatible or incommensurable with each other, but perhaps are not as much so as was once supposed. These are the perspectives derived from survey research on the one hand and post-Downsian rational-actor models on the other.

The survey research approach has found that if respondents strongly identify with a party and are otherwise cognitively "plugged into" the larger world of politics, there is high probability that they will vote. Another particularly strong predictor of participation seems to be the respondents' sense of external political efficacy—that is, their perception that purposive action directed at the political system (such as voting) would or would not produce positive results.[7] Respondents who agree with such statements as "Sometimes I don't think that government officials care what people like me think," or "Parties are only interested in your vote, not in delivering what they promise to you" are more likely at any income, occupation, or education level to abstain than their counterparts who disagree with these statements. Recently, Arthur Hadley has identified another element in the puzzle: do the respondents believe that in their own personal life, purposive actions will succeed in producing desired results, or do they think that life is dominated by chance?[8] According to Hadley, response to this question powerfully discriminates between voters and nonvoters who are at the same socioeconomic or demographic level.

Overall, a survey research perspective suggests that affective relationships to the larger political world interact with other predictors to shape the respondent's decision to vote or abstain. As American surveys have regularly documented, turnout levels also fall—quite precipitously these days—with education levels, and these remain among all the socioeconomic indicators the best predictors of voting and nonvoting.[9] Although there are many nuances that this brief survey cannot capture, a person of low formal education is relatively likely to have weak party identification and a very low cognitive capacity—little information and little sign of ability or willingness to respond to political stimuli on any significant level of issue conceptualization, much less ideology.

All this is well enough known. Equally so is the fact that in other advanced capitalist democracies things work very differently. For example, in Italy in the late 1960s, "mass" respondents viewed the party landscape in ways very similar to the perspectives of party activists and elites.[10] They were in the same story, as they notoriously often are not in the United States.[11] It seems too that in the European context, party identification works differently, so that when an individual decides to shift voting from one party to another, identification tends to change as well.[12] Party identification thus seems to be much more instrumentally viewed by the individual and much less a matter of general affect and family-transmitted social identity than is the case in the United States. Finally, in countries like Italy or Sweden, turnouts basically do not vary along lines of formal education. With a general participation rate in the high 80s or more, this would have to be so in any case. This suggests that a population with a mean formal-education level of six to nine years gets politically educated and involved through means other than the schools. The key intervening factor is clearly the party system, including the capacity of the parties (along with other organizations) to act as political educators and mobilizers.

The second major "school" was essentially founded by Anthony Downs and to a degree by V. O. Key, Jr.[13] It has now ramified and expanded through the literature on "retrospective voting," which has considerable overlap with public-choice theory.* The assumptions of this school are essentially those of neoclassical capitalist economics as translated into the realm of politics.[14] They are in a sense the polar opposite of survey research perspectives rooted in the discipline of social psychology. The individual is viewed in this model as a social atom or monad, whose basic motivation is national utility maximization.†

This reductionist view has obvious shortcomings, but it has analytic power too. It focuses analytic attention squarely on the organization of the electoral market by political entrepreneurs and on the individual's capacity to arrive at a rational judgment as to how maximum utilities are to be achieved through voting. Under conditions of imperfect information, it is parties, party ideologies, images, and promises that provide the necessary nexus for such calculations. As Downs suggests, elites in a two-party system have considerable electoral incentive to converge toward each other, blurring their appeals, and, in doing so, making it harder for individuals to calculate utility differentials between them. In a multiparty system, on the other hand, politicians' incentives are served best by getting out every last voter they can find in their specialized clientele, rather than by attempting to woo "swing voters" at the center—for there is no center, at least of the convergent two-party type.[15] This should produce maximum clarity on issues for voters during the election period and thus, one would anticipate, extremely high normal turnouts—as indeed one usually finds in such electoral systems. On the other hand, the coalition governments that often result from bargaining after the election will deliver far less to any given voting group than "its" party originally promised.

More recently, studies based on survey materials have argued for the presence of a strong component of retrospective voting, that is, voting based on positive or negative judgments about the records of the two parties. This approach was pioneered by V. O. Key, Jr., who argued that there was a sharp analytic difference between weak party identifiers and people who switch their vote from

Public choice theory: blend of political and microeconomic theory. It postulates that societies could benefit from organizing a competitive market system for the provision of public goods and services. Public agencies would be more responsive to citizen demands if they did not enjoy a monopoly over the provision of a given service or good.

†*Rational utility maximization:* economic term for the tendency of people to advance their own welfare, as they define it, maximally through ordering their preferences and calculating the combinations of goods and services that will best meet their needs and desires.

election to election. In recent years the discussion has been extended further, notably by Morris Fiorina, who demonstrates the existence of a powerful element of retrospective judgment in voting, but stresses that for such judgments to be rational sharply identified and responsible parties are necessary:

> What is the future of party identification in a system where each officeholder bears responsibility only for his individual actions, where the actions themselves are differentiated by office? There is none. No party will receive the credits or demerits in the individual's calculus, because the parties become too inchoate to be the focus of evaluations and because the nominal members of either become unable to govern successfully.[16]

Neither Key nor Fiorina discusses changes in voting and abstention in this context; but the argument is certainly implicit, and is made explicitly and extensively in Downs's analyses of the causes and effects of rational abstention.[17] Ultimately, all abstention in this model arises when the citizen can discern no utility difference at all among the rival candidates or parties. The larger the abstention rate, the greater the number of citizens whose search for utilities has been baffled or thwarted by the organization of the electoral market. Thus under this model turnout is closely and sensitively related to the nature and capacities of parties and other entrepreneurial organizers of electoral politics. The kind of situation described by Fiorina—the breakup of electoral coalitions along office-specific lines and the rise of personalistic incentives to replace team incentives—should therefore be systemically associated with a persistent rise of the "party of nonvoters." As I will show in detail below, this is exactly what has occurred over the past generation.

To summarize, there is accumulating evidence that American citizens respond to politics both affectively and instrumentally—that is, both through social-psychological dispositions and through efforts at rational pursuit of personal objectives through voting. Politicians well understand that the public is a "rational god of vengeance and reward" and do what they can to make major election years times of peace and prosperity.[18]

The political information on which voters base their instrumental decisions is, however, significantly limited and shaped by a number of factors. These include, at the least, the comparatively defective mobilizing and educating capacities of today's American major parties (especially the Democrats); certain important and recent transformations of the electoral market and its organization; and the relative absence in American culture of socially solidaristic traditions of the kind that commonly exist in other countries. In a class society with no true Left, the extent to which relevant political information is present or missing is very strongly arrayed along class lines.[19] In this kind of context, one should anticipate that people who believe their lives are dominated by chance and most people who have a low sense of external political efficacy will be concentrated toward the bottom of the class structure. Absence of a genuine Left also leads to political parties that lack the educative and mobilizing functions found in the major parties of other advanced capitalist democracies. This deficiency generally makes the individual's calculation of utilities more difficult than in other systems. The lower the social class, one should anticipate, the greater this difficulty will be.

Dynamically, then, the more electoral politics offers a choice between contending collective wills and engages the public in collective decisions of both psychological and instrumental importance to many individuals, the higher the turnout rate will be, and the less class skew there will be in participation. When these conditions are approximated today, as in Sweden, Italy, and other countries, this is true. Most accounts of critical realignment in American political history also stress that one of the leading criteria of realignment is a major expansion of participation among the electorate. It is at such times that polarization on some collective issue of fundamental importance occurs and potential voters have the greatest incentives to come to the polls and participate in the collective decision.[20]

EFFECT OF ELECTORAL RULES ON TURNOUT

Before filling in the details of this picture, it will be well to consider a related subject that has received an enormous amount of attention: the influence of the rules of the electoral game on participation. No one can doubt that rules of the game have major effects on electoral behavior (including abstention as a form of behavior). These effects are broadly of two types.

One flows from the rules through which votes are translated into political power. Very broadly, these rules can be divided into the system of election by simple plurality from single-member constituencies* on the one hand and various proportional-representation systems† on the other.[21] There is a generally marked relationship between systems and turnouts outside the United States. On average, systems with proportional-representation elements have contemporary participation rates that fluctuate around 85 percent on average, while the mean turnout for single-member constituency is about 10 to 15 percentage points lower (see Table 16).

If one considers that proportional-representation systems by definition come close to eliminating "wasted votes" and are also associated with multiple parties that optimize voters' utility calculations, this differential should not be surprising. Great Britain has a classic "first-past-the-post" electoral regime. Although it now has three major partisan contenders, the third force, the Alliance, lacks a solid geographical base and therefore gets practically no seats for the nearly one-quarter of the popular vote it wins at the polls. Thus in 1983 it required about 33,000 votes to elect a Conservative, 40,000 to elect a Labourite, and 338,000 to

**Single-member constituencies:* districts that elect only one candidate per legislative seat by a plurality of the vote. The legislative body can be a city council, state assembly, or the U.S. House of Representatives. Single-members constituencies result in "winner-take-all" electoral results because the losing political parties within the district receive no representation.

†*Proportional representation systems:* electoral allocation systems in which the seats in a legislative body are distributed among competing parties based on the percentage of the votes cast for them in an election. Proportional representation systems are infrequently used in the United States, though some city governments and states have adopted forms of PR in municipal and primary elections.

TABLE 16. VOTER PARTICIPATION RATES IN SELECTED COUNRTIES, BY TYPE OF ELECTORAL SYSTEM

Percent

Electoral System and Country	*Period*	*Valid Voting Rate*[a]
COMPULSORY VOTING		
Belgium	1971–85	85.9
Luxembourg	1968–79	83.7
Italy[b]	1972–83	87.9
Mean	. . .	85.8
PROPORTIONAL REPRESENTATION OR ELECTION BY DISTRICT WITH RUNOFF		
Austria[c]	1971–83	91.5
Denmark	1971–84	86.3
Finland	1970–83	78.3
France		
Parliament	1973–86	76.4
President	1974–81	84.8
West Germany	1972–83	89.1
Greece	1974–85	78.9
Iceland	1971–83	88.4
Ireland	1973–82	74.5
Israel	1973–84	77.8
Netherlands	1971–86	84.2
Norway	1973–85	82.2
Portugal	1975–85	80.7
Spain	1977–86	72.6
Sweden	1970–85	90.0
Switzerland	1971–83	51.0
Mean	. . .	82.8[d]
ELECTION BY DISTRICT, PLURALITY ON ONE BALLOT		
Canada	1972–84	72.6
Japan	1972–83	70.3
United Kingdom	1970–87	74.6
Mean	. . .	72.5
United States		
Presidential	1972–84	55.5
Off-year	1974–86	39.4

Sources: Inter-Parliamentary Union, *Chronicle of Parliamentary Elections and Developments*, vols. 10–20 (Geneva: International Centre for Parliamentary Documentation, 1975–86), and other sources in the public domain.

[a] Because only the valid vote is universally reported in the United States, that is the figure given here for all countries.

[b] Voting is not compulsory, but nonvoting is noted on individual's documents.

[c] Voting is compulsory in several states making up about one-fourth of the country's electorate.

[d] Excluding the anomalous case of Switzerland.

elect an Alliance member of Parliament. The turnout in that election was 72.7 percent of the potential electorate; it surely would have been considerably higher (and the Alliance vote higher too, in all probability) if the election rules had been governed by proportional representation.

The United States, of course, has single-member constituencies. The "wasted vote" constraint is heavily reinforced at the national level by multiple-member, at-large slates of presidential electors elected by simple plurality. Moreover, unlike the situation in Britain, Canada, or elsewhere, many legislative seats are often unopposed by a second major-party candidate—some 72 of the 435 U.S. House seats in 1986, for example, and considerably more than an absolute majority of seats in both houses of the current Massachusetts legislature. Obviously, this negatively affects turnout. But there is something else too. Former House Speaker Thomas P. O'Neill commented not long ago that in any other country the Democrats would be four or five parties and the Republicans two or three. The fact that the vastly complex United States offers only two significant parties no doubt also increases the number of potential voters who can find no useful difference for their purposes between parties.[22] Still, even though much might be said in the abstract for introducing proportional representation into congressional elections, no such thing is likely to happen soon.

The second broad effect of rules comes through those that control access by citizens to the ballot box, in particular, the uniquely American requirement of personal registration as preliminary to voting. The literature on this and related issues is truly enormous and can hardly be touched upon here. It is enough to note that first-rate empirical work has demonstrated that personal registration systematically reduces turnout. All other things being equal, the participation rate would go up about 10 percent if an enrollment system were adopted where the state rather than the individual bore the responsibility, as in Canada or Britain.[23] It is also known that much depends on what kind of registration system is employed. Some, such as the periodic reregistration requirement used in New York City from 1911 to 1957, or cutting off registration on January 31 of the election years as Texas attempted in the 1960s, are much more burdensome on voters than others.[24]

Historically, American elections were by today's standards extremely informal affairs. In most of the nineteenth century parties printed ballots, and access to the ballot box was legally unconstrained. But reform flowed as society became more complex and anonymous, and as issues of fraud became important to a changing middle-class culture. Thus, with adoption of the Australian ballot in the early 1890s, parties lost their monopoly over the printing and distribution of ballots. Personal registration statutes came into vogue during the Progressive era* a decade or so later. Voter lists were needed, especially in large anonymous urban environments, and personal registration was one way of getting them. Personal registration as an institution continues to be supported by public opinion for two reasons: adoption of state enrollment seems to be regarded as somehow "un-American" (though Canadians live with it well enough); and sensitivity to the potential for fraud—for example, in schemes that permit registration on the day of election—remains quite high.

All rules of the game have explicit or implicit political purposes and assumptions. As more is known about the effect of personal-registration statutes on shaping who votes and who does not, its differential class effects become more

**Progressive era:* see footnote on page 19.

evident and its defense becomes more explicitly—though even today, not very openly stated—a class-linked political choice. Much rhetoric discusses the citizen's "right to vote." But in fact, there always have been a substantial number of Americans who have believed that voting is not a right but a privilege for which individuals must demonstrate their worthiness.[25]

It has been evident for some time that conservatives are less disposed than liberals to making it easier for people to register, though this is by no means a clear-cut partisan issue. Reformers, recognizing that personal registration retains commanding support in American culture, have exercised much ingenuity in finding ways to reduce the effects of this socially differential legal burden on the franchise. Since 1960 there has been substantial relaxation of registration and residence requirements.[26] At the same time, there has been among the American electorate a vast upgrading of levels of formal education—a factor usually held to be closely and positively related to participation. In 1964, 19.5 percent of the electorate had at least some college-level education; twenty years later, this figure had risen to 35.0 percent.[27] Conventional wisdom of either the Downsian or survey research schools would predict that the American participation rate should have accordingly increased, not only in the southern quarter of the country, which was specially affected by the Voting Rights Act of 1965,* but also in the nonsouthern parts as well. If the marginal costs of voting have been reduced, the marginal propensity to vote should go up, all other things being equal. By the same token, a better-educated electorate should vote more, if the significance of the formal-education variable has been properly specified. Obviously, all other things have not been equal. Turnout rates outside the South declined in presidential years from 72.8 percent of eligibles in 1960 to 57.8 percent in 1984 (a loss of more than one-fifth of the 1960 base) and in off-years from 56.8 percent in 1962 to 39.0 percent in 1986 (a loss of nearly one-third of the 1962 base).

It is easy to speak in terms of percentages (though far less easy to derive them). One should not lose sight of the fact that in a country with a large population these percentages convert into millions of individuals. There is no better way of getting some sense of the absolute magnitude of the "hole" that exists in today's American electorate than by looking at the raw numbers of what voting would be under various assumptions (see Table 17). Such measures are obviously crude and subject to various estimation errors, but they give a rough statement of what American turnouts are today and what they might be (or might have been) under other empirical conditions. Long ago, using more sophisticated techniques, I concluded that no more than one-third of the nonsouthern turnout decline between 1900 and 1930 could be accounted for by changes in the rules of the game.[28] Much the same figure is suggested by this array.

**Voting Rights Act of 1965*: law ensuring suffrage for millions of minority group members, primarily African-Americans, by prohibiting state restrictions on voting targeted at them. The Act provides for the monitoring of elections by federal officials, if necessary, and for federal supervision of jurisdictions with particularly low minority voter participation. The Act required such jurisdictions to submit all changes in voting laws to the U.S. attorney general or the Federal District Court of the District of Columbia for approval. The Act was amended in 1970, 1975, and 1982.

TABLE 17. ACTUAL VOTER TURNOUT AND HYPOTHETICAL ADDITIONS TO THE VOTING POPULATION, UNDER VARIOUS ASSUMPTIONS, TOTAL UNITED STATES AND OUTSIDE THE SOUTH, 1984 AND 1986

Voters in millions

Assumption	*Turnout Rate*[a]	*Voters*	*Nonvoters*	*Additional Voters under Assumption*
TOTAL UNITED STATES 1984				
Actual turnout	55.2	92.7	75.1	. . .
Actual turnout plus 10 percent for easier registration	65.2	109.4	58.4	16.7
Turnout if same rate as 1896	82.6	138.6	29.2	45.9
Turnout if same rate as 1960	62.5	104.8	62.9	12.2
Turnout if same rate as 1960 plus 5 percent for more education and easier registration	67.5	113.2	54.5	20.6
1986				
Actual turnout	37.6	64.7	107.2	. . .
Actual turnout plus 10 percent for easier registration	47.6	81.8	90.0	17.1
Turnout if same rate as 1894	68.8	118.2	53.6	53.6
Turnout if same rate as 1962	49.2	84.6	87.3	19.9
Turnout if same rate as 1962 plus 5 percent for more education and easier registration	54.2	93.1	78.7	28.5
OUTSIDE THE SOUTH 1984				
Actual turnout	57.8	69.7	50.9	. . .
Actual turnout plus 10 percent for easier registration	67.8	81.6	38.8	12.1
Turnout if same rate as 1896	86.2	103.9	16.6	34.3
Turnout if same rate as 1960	72.8	87.8	32.8	18.1
Turnout if same rate as 1960 plus 5 percent for more education and easier registration	77.8	93.8	26.8	24.1
1986				
Actual turnout	39.0	48.1	75.4	. . .
Actual turnout plus 10 percent for easier registration	49.0	60.5	63.0	12.4
Turnout if same rate as 1894	74.0	91.4	32.1	43.3
Turnout if same rate as 1962	56.8	70.2	53.4	22.0
Turnout if same rate as 1962 plus 5 percent for more education and easier registration	61.8	76.4	47.2	28.2

Source: Underlying data in Tables 1 and 3, as projected onto potential U.S. citizen electorate in 1984 and 1986.
[a]Estimates of potential electorate for these calculations are based on citizen voting-age population, not total, since aliens are not permitted to register or vote in the United States.

TURNOUT BEFORE 1960

The broad contours of voting participation in American elections across the country's history are now pretty well known. As my focus here is on contemporary American elections, my remarks on pre-1960 history will be of a very summary kind.

Table 18 presents the entire array of election turnouts for the country outside the South, the South, and the country as a whole from 1788 to the present. In the first decade of the republic under the present Constitution, participation by adult males, almost always white, ranged as a rule between one-fifth and one-quarter of the potential electorate. In an age characterized by a "deferential-participant political culture" and a complete absence of political parties, this was what one might expect.[29]

Presidential elections were not democratized until the arrival of Andrew Jackson on the scene in 1828. As late as 1824, no fewer than six of the twenty-four states in the Union still chose their presidential electors through the state legislatures. Even where electors were chosen by popular vote, turnout was always less than for major state offices in the same period.[30] Participation in elections for other offices during the 1800–26 period, on the other hand, expanded substantially to almost one-half of the potential. In this period—marked, in Ronald Formisano's phrase, by parties but *not* by a party system—there was considerable difference between the scale of voter participation in states with established "standing orders," as in New England, and that in the robustly democratic states of the "new frontier" like Kentucky, Tennessee, and Georgia.

The period 1828–40 was marked by the creation of the institutional vehicles through which de Tocqueville's* "democracy in America" was given political expression. The entrepreneurial, mobilizing, and entertainment functions of parties and election campaigns in this era—indeed from then on throughout the nineteenth century—form a commonplace theme for historians' writings. Participation surged forward in two stages. The first, from 1828 through 1836, brought national presidential turnouts of about 57 percent. The second, culminating in the 1840 "Tippecanoe and Tyler Too"† election, saw the creation of the *Whig* party‡ and the full nationalization of party competition. The off-year congressional election of 1838–39 showed a national turnout rate of about 68 percent (10 points higher than in any of the three preceding presidential contests and fully 30 points higher than in 1986). In 1840 the turnout rate surged to one of its all-time highs, 80.3 percent in the country, and 81.6 percent in the nonsouthern states.

Important but marginal ups and downs occurred thereafter. The most significant of these grew out of the Civil War crisis and its aftermath. The period 1860–96 witnessed, by common consent, the historic apex of political parties, especially the Republicans, as articulators of collective will, mobilizers of voters, and, particularly during the crisis proper, effective organizers of governmental power and performance. This achievement was supported by a political culture that was intensely and enthusiastically partisan. One should hardly be surprised that the mean nonsouthern presidential turnout between 1856 and 1896 was 82.2 per-

*de Tocqueville: see page 5.

†*"Tippecanoe and Tyler Too"*: slogan used in support of William Henry Harrison (1773–1841) and John Tyler (1790–1862) in their campaign as the Whig candidates for the presidency in the election of 1840. Harrison, the presidential candidate, was nicknamed Tippecanoe for his leadership of U.S. soldiers against Tecumseh's Indians at Tippecanoe, Indiana, in 1811. Harrison and Tyler won the election. During the inauguration Harrison caught pneumonia, from which he died 31 days later; Tyler then became the tenth president of the United States.

‡*Whig party*: see footnote on page 18.

TABLE 18. VOTER TURNOUT RATES, BY REGION AND TOTAL UNITED STATES, 1789–1986

Percent

Year	*Outside the South*	*South*	*Total United States*	*Year*[a]	*Outside the South*	*South*	*Total United States*
PRESIDENTIAL ELECTION YEARS				*OFF-YEARS*			
1789	11.0	13.5	11.4	1790	n.a.	n.a.	21.1
1792	n.a.	n.a.	2.6	1794	n.a.	n.a.	27.7
1796	n.a.	n.a.	20.4	1798	34.5	35.8	34.6
1800	39.2	28.0	31.4	1802	43.7	57.2	44.2
1804	28.7	11.9	25.3	1806	47.7	37.9	47.3
1808	43.0	17.8	36.9	1810	48.6	49.0	48.6
1812	47.1	17.8	41.6	1814	50.1	75.7	51.5
1816	26.8	8.3	20.5	1818	41.4	77.7	44.5
1820	12.0	3.8	9.8	1822	46.4	56.2	47.2
1824	26.5	27.4	26.7	1826	42.4	67.8	45.7
1828	62.8	42.6	57.3	1830	53.7	72.3	57.5
1832	64.2	30.1	56.7	1834	63.3	61.7	63.0
1836	58.5	49.2	56.5	1838	69.5	62.5	67.9
1840	81.6	75.4	80.3	1842	63.7	64.6	63.9
1844	80.3	74.2	79.0	1846	59.7	58.3	59.4
1848	74.0	68.2	72.8	1850	61.4	58.9	60.9
1852	72.1	59.5	69.5	1854	64.2	75.8	66.5
1856	82.3	67.9	79.4	1858	69.3	66.9	68.9
1860	83.1	76.5	81.8	1862	63.0	n.a.	63.0
1864	76.3	n.a.	76.3	1866	71.7	51.5	71.1
1868	82.8	71.6	80.9	1870	67.3	68.7	67.7
1872	73.7	67.0	72.1	1874	66.1	64.1	65.6
1876	85.0	75.1	82.6	1878	70.4	50.3	65.6
1880	85.5	65.1	80.6	1882	70.0	57.5	67.0
1884	83.1	63.3	78.3	1886	70.5	52.3	66.2
1888	85.5	64.2	80.5	1890	70.3	50.1	65.7
1892	80.7	59.4	75.9	1894	74.0	51.2	68.8
1896	86.2	57.6	79.7	1898	68.5	40.2	62.0
1900	82.6	43.5	73.7	1902	66.2	26.8	57.2
1904	76.5	29.0	65.5	1906	62.9	22.0	53.6
1908	76.1	30.7	65.7	1910	62.6	24.1	53.8
1912	67.7	27.8	59.0	1914	61.4	21.3	52.9
1916	69.1	31.7	61.8	1918	48.4	15.9	42.2
1920[b]	57.3	21.7	49.3	1922[b]	44.7	13.5	37.7
1924	57.5	19.0	48.9	1926	42.5	9.7	35.2
1928	66.7	22.5	56.9	1930	46.7	13.4	39.4
1932	66.2	24.5	57.0	1934	56.3	13.6	46.8
1936	71.4	25.0	61.0	1938	59.3	11.8	48.7
1940	72.9	26.5	62.5	1942	43.7	8.4	35.7
1944	65.1	24.5	55.9	1946	48.6	10.9	40.0
1948	61.8	25.0	53.4	1950	54.0	13.3	44.6
1952	71.4	38.4	63.8	1954	53.0	16.8	44.6
1956	69.2	36.6	61.6	1958	55.0	16.1	45.9
1960	72.8	41.4	65.4	1962	56.8	24.9	49.2
1964	68.6	46.4	63.3	1966	55.5	33.5	49.3

TABLE 18. (CONTINUED)

Percent

Year	Outside the South	South	Total United States	Year[a]	Outside the South	South	Total United States
	PRESIDENTIAL ELECTION YEARS				*OFF-YEARS*		
1968	65.7	51.8	62.3	1970	52.4	36.0	48.4
1972[c]	61.1	45.1	57.1	1974[c]	43.8	27.3	39.5
1976	57.9	47.5	55.2	1978	42.0	30.6	39.0
1980	56.6	48.1	54.3	1982	44.9	33.0	41.6
1984	57.8	48.7	55.2	1986	39.0	34.2	37.6

Sources: These estimates are based on underlying population and election data of varying quality and completeness. The population-denominator files represent the best estimates available. I have not found returns for any office in some states between 1789 and 1820, but such cases form only a minority of the whole country. Federal census material is problematic as a source before 1860 and very much so before 1840. It can often by supplemented, however, by better state-level information, such as state censuses like New York's or lists of taxables (males twenty and over) in Pennsylvania from 1790 to 1841. While I attempt a little more precision than this, it is roughly correct to estimate for the 1790–1830 period that adult white males constitute about one-fifth of the entire population at any given time. From 1870 on, the definition of eligibles, in addition to race and gender (where relevant by state before 1920), excludes aliens in those states where they were (or became) ineligible to vote. From 1924 on, this ban extended to the entire country. Since the alien component of the voting-age population was particularly large in many states between 1890 and 1930, a reasonably accurate picture of the potentially eligible electorate requires excluding it. The estimates used here converge pretty closely for the very early period with the work of Robert J. Dinkin; see his *Voting in Provincial America* (Greenwood, 1977), and *Voting in Revolutionary America* (Greenwood, 1982). A more general treatment of the issues in constructing these estimates is Walter Dean Burnham, 'Those High Nineteenth-Century American Voting Turnouts: Fact or Fiction?" *Journal of Interdisciplinary History*, vol. 16 (Spring 1986), pp. 613–44.
n.a. Not available.
[a] Before 1880 congressional elections were spread out across almost an entire year, rather than being held on the same day. I have calculated each state's electorate in a given year during the period from 1789 until 1880 and then aggregated it to a regional or national total.
[b] General women's suffrage was introduced in 1920.
[c] The vote was extended to eighteen-year-olds in 1971.

cent, with an all-time high of 86.2 percent reached in the critical election of 1896; or that the mean 1858–94 off-year turnout rate outside the former Confederate states* was 69.3 percent.

The South presents a strikingly different picture. Before secession in 1860–61, the South's electorate was only somewhat less participant than that outside this region. Until the political crisis of the 1850s, it had competitive party politics. Secession brought a new government that was nonpartisan by design. Eric McKitrick some years ago analyzed the consequences of this arrangement in a seminal comparative study of Union and Confederate politics in wartime.[31] His main conclusion was that lack of parties in the Confederacy, by releasing Madisionian "ambition pitted against ambition," made a significant contribution to its eventual destruction.

Two points related to McKitrick's essay can be mentioned. First, voting partici-

The Confederacy: group of eleven states that seceded from the United States in 1860–1861 in a dispute over the sovereignty of the states in relation to the central government, precipitating the Civil War. Those states preferred a more limited central government with powers delegated to it by the states in narrow spheres. The Confederate states were opposed to the regulation of slavery, outside the District of Columbia, by the federal government.

pation collapsed in the Confederacy's nonpartisan elections, especially in voting for Congress, eventually reaching levels not far removed from those of the country as a whole in the 1790s or in Southern primaries in the 1920s.[32] Second, it is of course through the political revolution of the 1860s and southern white reaction to it that the South's long-term deviation from the rest of the country across the next century became firmly established. With the semi-violent termination of Reconstruction, southern turnouts fell sharply in two distinct steps. The first of these, during the "redemption era," partially crippled the southern Republicans, partially disfranchised blacks, and produced a mean regional participation rate of 61.9 percent in presidential elections (1880–96) and 52.3 percent in off-year elections (1878–94). Thereafter, in the wake of the Populist* uprising, the "Great Disfranchisements," aimed at blacks but including many whites as well, were carried out. By the early twentieth century, the presidential-year and off-year averages had fallen to 29.8 percent (1904–16) and 22.0 percent (1902–18). They were to fall still further following the enfranchisement of women, hitting all-time presidential-year and off-year lows of 19.0 percent (1924) and 8.4 percent (1942). Particularly in off-year elections, the region's participation rate was not thereafter to climb much from these abysmal depths until the 1960s.

The vast voter demobilization that developed in the long generation after 1896 in the nonsouthern parts of the country has been discussed in detail elsewhere.[33] All that can be affirmed here—in the wake of extensive controversy—is that the high nineteenth century turnouts were real, and not artifacts of either overwhelming census error or universal ballot box stuffing.[34] By the same token, the demobilizations of the early twentieth century were also real and increasingly class-skewed.[35]

Specific technical and historical explanations for this major increase in the nonvoting pool are many and varied. Several factors were clearly at work to produce it. For one thing, the extreme sectionalism produced by the "colony-metropole" cleavages under the "system of 1896" meant that very large parts of the North and West saw less and less genuine party competition in general elections. For another, the cumulative effects of the direct primary reinforced the practical local electoral monopoly of the majority party in many areas.[36] And, it is quite clear, a very large sea change in the political culture occurred around the turn of the century; the collapse of intense partisanship, its replacement by widespread hostility to political parties and political machines, and a parallel shift of campaign styles from the typical militia-drill model of the nineteenth century to the advertising-oriented techniques of the twentieth.[37] The new campaign style was already strongly if marginally evident in the 1904 presidential election. In 1916 Woodrow Wilson's personalistic "he-kept-us-out-of-war" campaign made extensive use of professional advertising techniques. By then, the shift to

**Populist:* term referring to mass political movements that arise from the nonelite sectors of a population. Populist uprisings were quite common in Europe and the United States during the late nineteenth century because of the social changes brought about by rapid industrialization and urbanization. Populism in the United States has largely involved farmers' protest movements.

personality politics had been consummated as far as available mass-media technology and residual cultural lag would allow. Today's politics of the "permanent campaign" thus has much deeper historical roots than is often supposed. It is almost correct to say that since 1916 only the technological resources have undergone basic change.

By the same token, the nineteenth century "state of courts and parties" was already supplemented and increasingly supplanted by a more positive, bureaucratic, and "nonpartisan" state during the first two decades of this century.[38] The transformations here reflect the emergence of a culture oriented toward high mass consumption, which required the development of advertising and survey research of consumer preferences. At the same time, both culture and specific political action during the First World War contributed to the destruction of a socialist third-party alternative that even in its 1912 heyday was probably not as promising or powerful as it seemed to some at the time.

The "system of 1896" reached the logical culmination of its development in the "normalcy era" of 1920–28. Aided by the enfranchisement of women and their relative lack of incorporation into the active electorate before the New Deal realignment, nationwide presidential-year and off-year turnouts during this decade reached their lowest points in a century or more (48.9 percent of estimated citizen electorate in 1924, 35.2 percent in 1926). Perpetuation of a partisan cleavage that was largely rooted in a "horizontal" polarization between the manufacturing and farming economies, coupled with the absence of a genuine industrial-era Left, provided little incentive for the urban manual-labor workforce to participate in elections.[39] Evidence drawn from analysis of turnout reinforces the view that the ascendancy of corporate capitalism and its preferred political vehicle, the Republican party, was based in very large part upon this socially selective voter demobilization. To a remarkable extent, politics in the 1920s had turned into a politics of oligarchy dressed up in the rhetoric and processes of democracy.[40]

The counterpart to this striking state of political affairs in the 1920s, after the collapse of the capitalist free-market economy, was the New Deal realignment of the 1930s. Nonsouthern turnouts swelled very heavily during the transition, as is so often the case with true electoral realignment. This involved a massive reincorporation—overwhelmingly on the Democratic side—of voters, largely concentrated toward the bottom of the class structure, who had been in the ranks of the "party of nonvoters" in the 1920s. A recent account correctly stresses the vital significance of this conversion of former abstainers into mostly Democratic voters to the building of the New Deal coalition and the political overthrow of the old regime.[41]

Politics in the 1920s, as earlier, had little or no visible sign of class polarization independent of other factors (for example, religion in the 1928 election). By 1940 social-class position had become a powerful explanatory variable. Indeed, the 1940 election looms in retrospect as the most class-polarized election in American political history thus far.[42] By this criterion, one would anticipate finding that the story is more complicated on several fronts than most discussions have indicated. These complications can be seen adequately only by measuring change across the range of alternatives (that is, nonvoting, Democratic, Republican, and other-party shares of the potential electorate). For example, while writers from Samuel Lubell onward have noted the "Al Smith surge" in urban-proletarian (largely Catholic) environments in 1928, most have missed the point that in non-Catholic environments there was at least as large a "Hoover surge." During the 1930s there was a very strong mobilizing surge toward the Democrats among working-class voters, but there was also a noteworthy pro-Republican mobilizing surge, missed by most analysts, within the upper reaches of the social structure.

Two exercises in regression estimation* capture some elements of the dynamic picture of voter participation from the early twentieth century through 1960. One is taken from the ward divisions in the city of Pittsburgh and the other from the forty-six cities and towns of eastern Massachusetts that had a population of at least 10,000 in 1940 (see Figures 1 and 2).

These "sociopolitical maps" from two very different northeastern urban areas tell stories that are basically very similar, though significant details such as response to the stimulus of the Hoover-Smith campaign of 1928 differ quite a bit. In both cases, abstention before the realignment "surge" (1928 in Boston, as late as 1936 in Pittsburgh) is always substantially larger at the work-class than at the middle-class end of the social spectrum.[43] In both cases, there are bilateral mobilizations during the realignment sequence: abstention drops at both ends of the social spectrum, while a powerful Democratic surge occurs at one end and a substantial Republican surge at the other. (In the Boston area, the Republican 91.1 percent of estimated potentional vote in hypothetical solid middle-class settings in 1940 represents an all-time high).

But it is also noteworthy that while the class differential in turnout was significantly and enduringly reduced with realignment, it was by no means eliminated. In fact, with competitive mobilizations at each end of the spectrum, the absolute size of the participation gap between top and bottom scarcely closed at all, either in Pittsburgh or in the Boston area. Obviously, politics in the two areas was organized very differently before and after the New Deal realignment. This seems not to matter much at the bottom, where both sets of estimates suggest that the working-class nonvoting floor even in 1940 or 1960 was between one-quarter and one-third of the potential electorate. There is more difference at the top, where middle-class areas show a minimum nonvoting floor of a bit over one-fifth in Pittsburgh, but less than one-tenth in the Boston area.

Even considering the vast numerical disproportion between the relative top and bottom of the occupational structure, the continuation of these class differentials in nonvoting across and beyond the New Deal realignment was nowhere near enough to compensate for the politicial overthrow created in 1928–40 by mobilizations and conversions toward the Democrats in the lower reaches of society. On the other hand, even in its heyday the party of Franklin Roosevelt

**Regression estimation:* statistical method used to analyze the relationship between two or more variables.

FIGURE 1. ESTIMATES OF PERCENTAGE OF POTENTIAL ELECTORATE VOTING AND NOT VOTING, BY CLASS, IN PITTSBURGH, 1912–60[a]

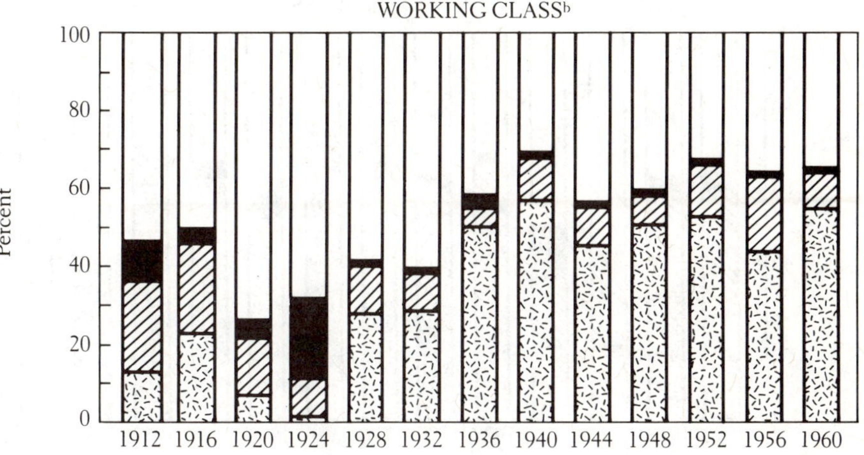

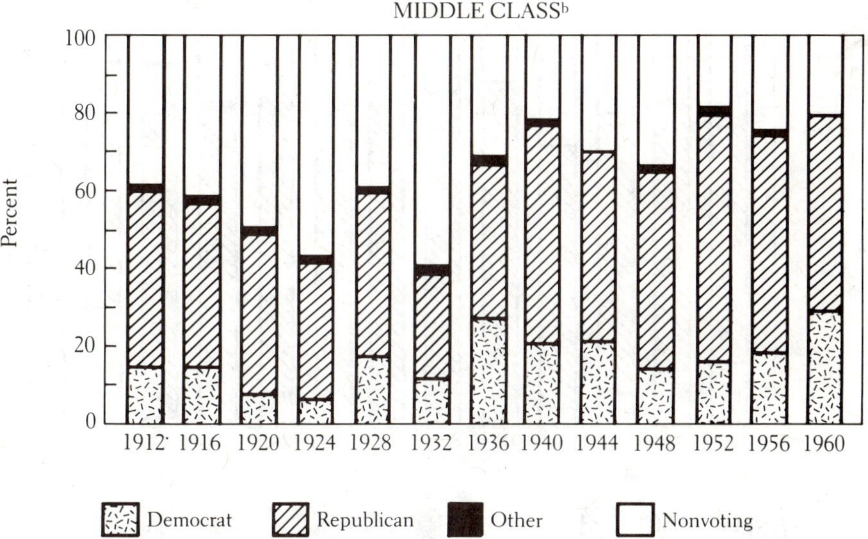

Sources: For election data, *Pennsylvania Manual*, various years; for occupational data, U.S. Census, 1940 and later years. From 1912 to 1940, the units are twenty-nine election wards; from 1940 to 1960, thirty-two wards. Ward boundaries have remained essentially unchanged, except for additions, since 1912; and each ward contains one or more census tracts that do not cut across ward boundaries. In 1912 the Republican and Progressive shares are summed as Republican.

[a] The procedures used are those of simple bivariate regression estimation. The dependent variable is the nonvoting, Democratic, Republican, or other share of the potential electorate. The regression used is based on a linear model of the form $Y = a + bX + e$, where Y is the value of the dependent variable, a is the intercept (the point at which the line derived from the equation crosses the vertical axis), bX is the slope, and e is the error term.

[b] As defined by occupational data in the census for 1940 and later years.

FIGURE 2. ESTIMATES OF PERCENTAGE OF POTENTIAL ELECTORATE VOTING AND NOT VOTING, BY CLASS, IN BOSTON AREA, 1912–60[a]

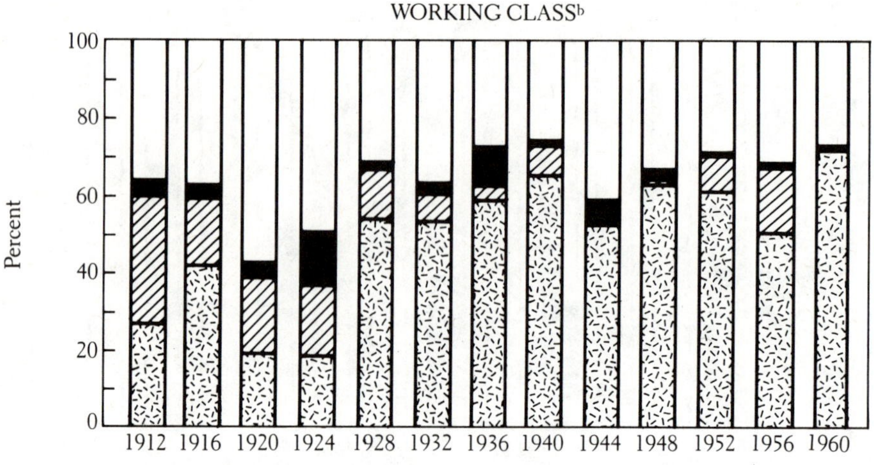

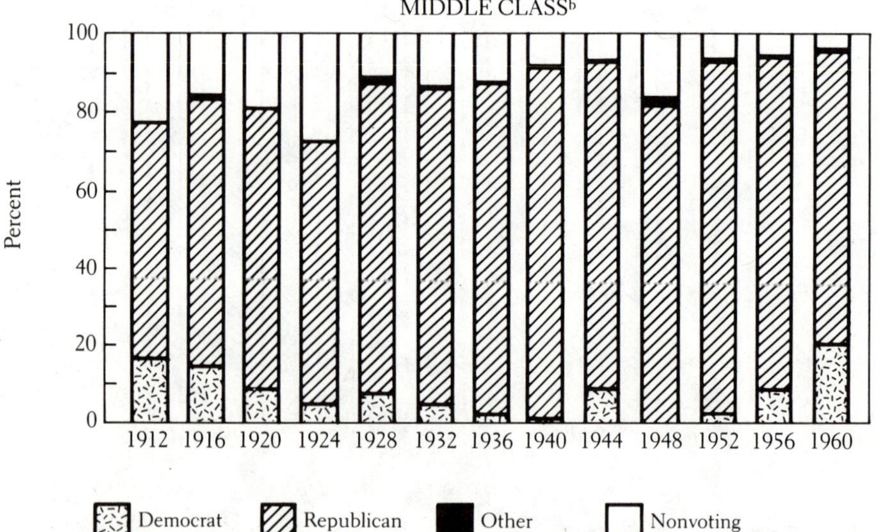

Sources: For election data, Commonwealth of Massachusetts, *Election Statistics*, Public Document 43, various years; for occupational data, U.S. Census, 1940 and later years. The units are forty-six towns comprising all cities in Massachusetts with a 1940 population of 100,000 and above and all towns and cities in the Boston metropolitan area with a 1940 population of 10,000 and above. In 1912 the Republican and Progressive shares are summed as Republican.

[a] See Figure 1 for explanation of procedures.

[b] As defined by occupational data in census for 1940 and later years.

was by no means a "Left" or "labor" party, although it was supported by both. It was and is a liberal substitute in a polity that does not admit alternatives of that sort. Persistence of the class gap in participation may provide a new reinforcement for this argument.

SELECTIVE DEMOBILIZATION: THE CONTEMPORARY SITUATION

American politics since 1960 has gone through changes that, cumulatively, are of almost revolutionary dimensions. These changes extend to all levels of action, from the policy initiatives of the 1980s to the altered foundations of electoral politics. To a striking extent, one can see contemporary parallels to the political situation of the 1920s: conservative and probusiness hegemony;* a Democratic opposition, representing the interests of many peripheries against a center and lacking common energizing perspectives and mobilizing capacities; and low, declining, and very skewed voting participation.

At the level of electoral entrepreneurship, the most decisive transformation has been the partial displacement of the parties as organizers of politics by the technologies, operatives, and candidates of what Sidney Blumenthal calls "the permanent campaign."[44] Blumenthal believes that the decisive moment of transition to the new order can be dated to 1968–72, and that this change is momentous enough to be described as a critical realignment in its own right, leading to the current "sixth electoral era." My own view is that he is almost certainly right in this intuitive judgment. The concept of the "permanent campaign" means partial or total dissolution of many of the features of party that are linked to the cognitive reactions of voters: collective identity, a kind of historical memory transmitted through party identification, and long-term collective commitments that permit relatively easy individual calculation of utilities at election time. What is substituted is personalism and a variety of imagistic appeals. "Party" coalitions tend increasingly to break down across the lines of constitutional separation between the executive and legislative branch[es]. This in turn leads to intractable problems of accountability and governability, as a whole chorus of writers has complained.[45]

Inchoate politics, fragmented electoral choices, and personalistic campaign images lead naturally to growth in the number of citizens who have a low sense of their external political efficacy; more citizens who find it difficult or impossible to make a utility calculation different from zero (or perhaps make one at all); and general erosion of the strength of party identification.[46] As politicians' incentives at elections shift more and more to considerations of "every person for himself," the notion of collective will tends to disappear; and so, in a highly selective way, does the active electorate.

Or, more precisely, one should say that "collective will" disappears not across the board, but in a differential way. Long ago, Maurice Duverger argued, "Parties are always more developed on the Left than on the Right, because they are always more necessary on the Left than on the Right."[47] This perfectly valid remark reflects realities of differentials in power and political consciousness in any class society between the better-educated, better-off owning classes on one side and the less-educated, propertyless, and poorer classes beneath them on the other. In modern American political conditions, the electoral vehicle for some of

**Hegemony*:the predominant influence of one state, group, or idea over other states, groups, or ideas.

the interests of the latter has been the Democratic party, just as the electoral vehicle for the former has been the Republican. While no one doubts that the Republican party suffers from some internal divisions and even occasional bouts of selective abstention among its supporters (as notably in the 1974 congressional election), the GOP remains much closer to being a true political party in the comparative sense than do today's Democrats. As the Democrats fall apart, and attempt continually to find a way to shift their appeals "upscale" in the information society's evolving structure of classes and strata, it should be no surprise that the post-1960 turnout decline has been concentrated among those who had already participated least in the 1940–60 period. Predominantly, these are people who, if they had any reason to vote at all, would vote mostly Democratic.

This assertion can be very straightforwardly documented, for the Census Bureau has provided since 1964 survey information that, because of the very large base of respondents, is the most accurate available.[48] Snapshots taken toward the beginning of this series and in 1980 suggest the direction of change in the electorate as measured by distribution among occupational categories of males in the labor force, the most stable long-term indicator of social stratification (see Table 19).

The *rate* of decline in participation revealed here is strongly differentiated along class lines. But the *fact* of decline is general. This means that increased nonvoting has also produced large numbers of middle-class nonvoters, even at the highest reaches of the reported occupational structure. It is not just working-class voters who, at the margins, seem to lack motivation to vote under the conditions created by the institutions and operations of the "permanent campaign." If one thinks about possibilities for party rebuilding or reforming the rules of the game in a society dominated by the middle classes, it is almost certainly going to be middle-class segments who are dissatisfied with the existing order who will lead the way if anyone does.

Yet granted all this, the overwhelming pattern that comes from these data is one of demobilization that, while general, is also strikingly selective. Relative to the mid-1960s (when decline had already begun), the attrition rate among various working-class categories is more than three times as high as in the professional and technical category and well over twice as high as for the middle classes as a whole, a relationship that is common both to presidential and off-year turnout dynamics.

The more recent surveys give considerably more information than the earlier ones. For example, they tell not only who votes but who registers, and among nonvoters the reasons they give for not voting or registering. Responses reflecting indifference to or dislike of politics as the chief reason for nonparticipation also climb systematically in both relative and absolute terms as one moves down the occupational structure. Many other attributes related to turnout and abstention are also now evident. Blacks typically vote less than whites, though if one allows for the great differences between black and white occupational structure, a large part of the difference disappears; and there are notable occasions (such as the 1983 and 1987 Chicago mayoral elections) in which black voting rates are at least the equal of white participation. Hispanics, on the other hand, are in a class by

TABLE 19. VOTER TURNOUT RATES IN PRESIDENTIAL AND OFF-YEAR ELECTIONS, BY OCCUPATION, MALE LABOR FORCE, 1964–80

	TURNOUT RATE, PRESIDENTIAL YEARS		PERCENT DECLINE,	TURNOUT RATE, OFF-YEARS		PERCENT DECLINE,
Occupational Category	1964	1980[a]	1964–80	1966	1978[b]	1966–78
MIDDLE-CLASS AND WHITE COLLAR	83.2	73.0	12.3	68.7	58.9	14.3
Professional and technical	84.7[c]	77.0	9.1	70.1	62.7	10.6
Managers (excluding farm)	82.8[c]	72.6	12.3	68.9	57.9	16.0
Farm owners and managers	84.7[c]	76.1	10.2	71.0	64.4	9.3
Sales and clerical	81.3[c]	67.8	16.6	66.3	54.3	18.1
SERVICE OCCUPATIONS	72.8	53.0	27.2	57.9	43.6	24.7
MANUAL (EXCLUDING SERVICE)	66.1	48.0	27.4	50.6	35.1	30.6
Craft and skilled workers	72.2[c]	53.6	25.8	56.7	40.6	28.4
Semiskilled operatives	63.5[c]	44.7	29.6	48.3	32.1	33.5
Laborers (excluding farm)	57.7[c]	41.4	28.2	41.1	28.1	31.6
Farm laborers	44.6[c]	35.0	21.5	32.7	24.4	25.4
UNEMPLOYED	56.9	38.1	33.0	42.7	25.9	39.3
Total	73.0	58.1	20.4	58.9	45.2	23.3

Sources: U.S. Bureau of the Census, *Current Population Reports*, series P-20, no. 143, "Voter Partitipation in the National Election: November 1964" (Government Printing Office, 1965); no. 174, "Voting and Registration in the Election of November 1966" (GPO, 1968); no. 344, "Voting and Registration in the Election of November 1978" (GPO, 1979); and no. 370, "Voting and Registration in the Election of November 1980" (GPO, 1982).

[a] The Census Bureau occupational classification scheme changed between the 1980 and 1982 reports on registration and voter participation. Particularly in view of the very small increase in presidential turnout between 1980 and 1984, it seemed best to use the 1980 data in order to maintain full time-series compatibility.

[b] I chose to use data for 1978 rather than 1982 because the latter year showed the only substantial turnout increase in the entire series to date, while in 1986 participation levels fell even below those of 1978. Since 1986 data are as yet unavailable, 1978 data appeared to be the closest approximation to the current situation.

[c] The 1964 survey, the first in the census series, gives occupation only by extremely broad categories (white-collar, manual, etc.). The 1980 survey gives the fuller picture. These turnouts by category are "retrodicted" estimates based on weighted figures derived from the immediate post-1964 surveys.

themselves, having much the lowest participation rate of any major "nonclass" group in the population.

Some analyses of the 1984 election pointed to the considerable differences in support for Ronald Reagan in terms not merely of social class but also of other measures of distance from or proximity to the various "cores" of American society. People with strong religious (especially Protestant and most especially evangelical) ties were much more solidly behind the president than those with weaker ties. Members of working nuclear families were more supportive than those living alone (as single heads of households, divorced, widowed) or in a collection of unrelated individuals sharing the same dwelling. By the same token, perhaps, recent census surveys show a huge participation differential along such lines as nuclear family versus other living arrangements and between homeowners and renters.[49] One senses the empirical existence of a kind of Norman Rockwell picture as part of a general cultural idea—a picture of a republic of property owners. The closer one is to this image—as well as to ownership of some of the productive assets of the political economy—the more likely one is to vote and participate in other ways, and the more likely that vote is to be Republican.

Viewing either the long run of American political evolution or the record of the most recent elections, one finds ample evidence for the existence of a center of the society and political economy competing with a periphery. More accurately, this could be said to include a number of "centers" and "peripheries" that over time seem to have an increasing tendency to converge around one or another of competing poles. For a considerable period after the smashup of the old laissez-faire political economy in 1929, the "periphery party," the Democrats, welded together a new majority coalition whose energizing center was not Wall Street or Main Street, but Washington, D.C. But its position as a combined Left and center in a political system that has no genuine Left but does have a genuine Right implied, as it still implies, that if anything should ever happen to dissolve this federal glue, the peripheries that the party largely represents will become dissociated and go their several ways. Such a case, which has of course duly materialized, is not far removed from a 1980s version of the Democrats' "politics of provincialism" of sixty and more years ago.[50] It is for some such reason that there was and is a systematic relationship at the margins between the party of nonvoters and the active Democratic electoral clientele. As the Democratic party dissociates and loses its common organizing institutions and principles, therefore, the ranks of the party of nonvoters are mightily swelled. So it was in the 1920s, so it is now. When the level of nonparticipation recorded in these two similar decades is reached, one could almost assert that so far as issues of social class are concerned, there are more significant differences between nonvoters and the active electorate than between voting Democrats and voting Republicans. One certainly can assert that the shift toward voting abstention since 1960 is by far the largest mass movement of our time, and that it is related, not coincidentally, to the rise of Ronald Reagan and his "new direction in American politics."

For understandable reasons, the census surveys do not report the partisan preferences of their respondents. It is thus necessary to turn again to some aggregate evidence that supports this partisan part of the discussion. Once again I will use the eastern Massachusetts conurbation, the only area for which at present I have data to spin out a forty-year time series. There are some noteworthy local peculiarities about the Bay State that have prompted President Reagan to call it the "people's republic of Massachusetts," despite the fact that he carried the state in both of his elections. In particular, there is vastly more support for the Democrats among the Boston area's upper strata than in most of the country, just as there was for John Anderson (for similar locally relevant reasons) in 1980. In this particular segment of the population, there is no doubt at all that Barry Goldwater's nomination and campaign in 1964 produced a genuine "critical realignment." The ascendancy of "upscale Democrats" in key leadership positions, and the extraordinary collapse of the Republican party at the state and local levels, are equally reflective of this phenomenon of a "middle class leading the way." To repeat, this is a specific local peculiarity. Nevertheless, the profiles of the top and bottom of the class structure (as based on simple regression estimation) are striking (see Figure 3).

FIGURE 3. ESTIMATES OF PERCENTAGE OF POTENTIAL ELECTORATE VOTING AND NOT VOTING, BY CLASS, IN BOSTON AREA, 1964–84[b]

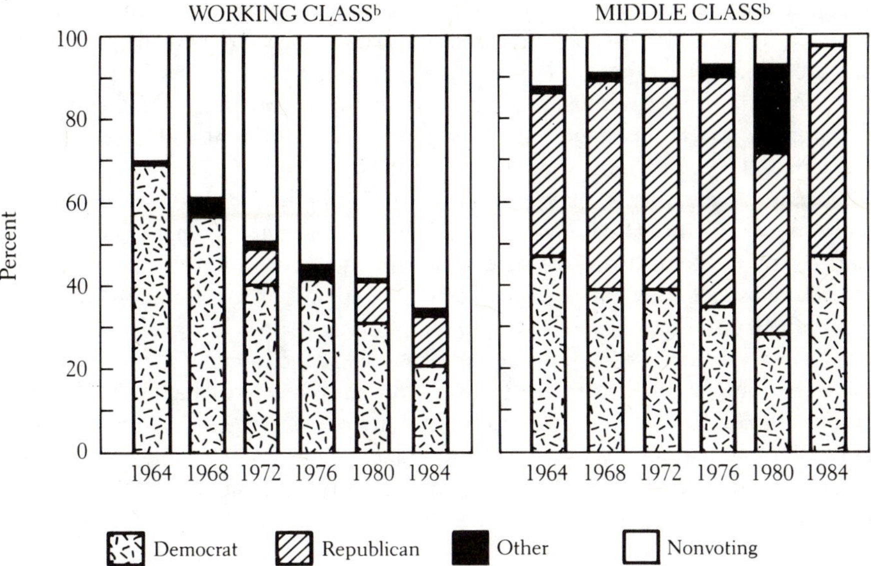

[a] See Figure 1 for explanation of procedures.
[b] As defined by occupational data in census for 1964 and later years.

One could almost say these figures portray electoral change in two different countries. While there has been some increase in working-class Republican support from the trace levels of the 1960s, the key change has been that turnout and the Democratic share of the potential working-class electorate have collapsed together.[51] In fact, if these estimates remotely correspond to reality, the abstention rate of two-thirds of working-class eligibles in 1984 considerably exceeds even those recorded in the 1920 and 1924 elections; it is by far the largest of all time. Assuming that Democratic party elites have realigned their interests and appeals toward high-tech and "yuppie" concerns (as clearly has happened under the leadership of Governor Michael Dukakis) and that the state Republican party has now been taken over by the Right, this enormous demobilization would make considerable sense from either of the analytic points of view here presented, especially from the utility-maximizing perspective. If poor or working-class voters feel abandoned by the Democrats, most would (as usual) have little incentive to vote for Republicans, since the latter have little but the politics of resentment to offer them. It might indeed be difficult for such people to feel connected, affectively or instrumentally, to choices and candidates hugely different from those presented in the age of James Michael Curley, Leverett Saltonstall, and John F. Kennedy.

For the top of the social array, on the other hand, there is profoundly different ordering. The pool of nonvoters in this environment is minuscule and has in fact declined over the years; at the top, fully nine-tenths or more of potential voters come to the polls. What they do when they get there differs extremely from the working-class profile; and in Massachusetts this is closely tied, even now, to major differences on matters of culture and history as well as economics between Irish Catholics and Yankee Protestants. The Yankees have remained participants but are strikingly politically divided—a division that clearly owes its origin and persistence to the local impact of the GOP's national realignment to the right in 1964 and to the choices and policies identified with national and state political elites over the twenty years since then.

In most environments, of course, no such division has occurred—just as there is today probably no state in the union in which the Republican party is organizationally or electorally in such bad shape as in Massachusetts. The evidence elsewhere is not only for a very wide class gap in participation, but also for Republican dominance toward the top, particularly in presidential elections, that almost reaches levels common before 1964 in Massachusetts. One very simple bivariate analysis* is illustrative: turnout and partisanship in the 1980 election among the seventy-two cities that make up most of Los Angeles County, California, using median family income as the independent variable. Since blacks and Hispanics constitute so large a share of the county's electorate, estimates are presented for cities whose 1980 population was at least two-thirds white and non-Hispanic, as well as all the cities (see Table 20).

Two features of this array should be noted: the powerful relationship between affluence and turnout, and the enormous bilateral asymmetry in the parties' mobilizing capacity at the highest and lowest points in the affluence continuum. The Democrat (Carter) was unable to win as much as one-fifth of the potential electorate in any category, and his share of eligibles dropped quite little from the poor to the rich ends of the spectrum. Republican (Reagan) support vaulted forward from very little at the bottom to three-quarters or more of the potential electorate at the top.

Major racial diversity is vastly more significant in Los Angeles County, with its large black and third world population, than in largely white Pittsburgh (as of 1960) and the even whiter Boston metropolitan area. The very crude "control" I have used—separately evaluating relationships in the cities that are predominantly white and non-Hispanic—is clear enough evidence that the relationship between nonvoting and poverty remains very strong even with minorities largely disregarded. Equally noteworthy is the considerable relative strength of Republican support not just at the top, but very far down toward the bottom of the income scale. Reagan in 1980 began moving into a lead when the median family income was no more than about $7,500. Of course, if the 57 percent abstention rate at that level were reduced to 25 percent and three-quarters of this difference voted Democratic, the results would probably look much more like 1940 or 1960 than 1980 or 1984.

**Bivariate analysis:* statistical analysis involving only two variables. The variable thought to cause (or be associated with) a change in the other variable is known as the "independent variable."

TABLE 20. ESTIMATES OF TURNOUT AND PRESIDENTIAL VOTE, AT SELECTED LEVELS IN MEDIAN FAMILY INCOME AND BY RACE, LOS ANGELES COUNTY, 1980

Percent								
Selected Level in Median Family Income (Dollars)[a]	*All Cities in Country (N = 72)*				*Cities with Population 66.7 Percent or More White, non-Hispanic (N = 35)*			
	NON-VOTING	*CARTER*	*REAGAN*	*OTHER*[b]	*NON-VOTING*	*CARTER*	*REAGAN*	*OTHER*[b]
0	84.3	19.7	4.5[c]	0.5	69.0	17.9	9.5	3.6
3,100	79.6	19.4	0.1	1.1	65.8	17.7	12.7	3.9
15,000	61.8	18.0	17.0	1.1	53.1	16.6	25.3	5.0
40,000	24.4	15.2	53.1	3.2	26.5	14.5	51.7	7.3
56,200	0.1	13.3	76.4	7.7	9.3	13.1	68.8[d]	8.8

Sources: Election data, Secretary of State of California, Supplement to Statement of Vote (1980 and 1984 elections); demographic data, data from American Civil Liberties Union of Southern California and 1980 U.S. Census.

[a] The selected median family income values correspond to points in the distribution where positive values of 0.1 or more in the estimated share of the electorate are recorded in at least one cell in one of the two arrays.

[b] Mostly for John Anderson.

[c] As not infrequently happens with linear regression estimation, "impossible" values (negative votes) can be produced, as here. The convention in such cases is to set the value at zero.

[d] As is well known from the survey literature, Reagan did not do less well among upper-status white than among upper-status blacks. Linear regression is very sensitive to extreme values in either of the two variables. Removal of most blacks and Hispanics has the effect, therefore, of reducing the steepness of the slope that defines the relationship, but only, as is clear, by a very limited amount.

A POLITICAL STATE OF NATURE

When nonvoting is examined across time, space, and political context, it emerges as an important indicator of the relative health of democracy in any political system based upon elections and the consent of the governed. In performing this examination, it is hardly possible to do full justice to the subject without some attempt to specify the relationship between turnout and partisanship.

In every political system that leaves it up to the individual to decide whether or not to vote, there is an irreducible minimum of adult citizens who are apolitical or disaffected or for other reasons abstain. But in most other democratic-capitalist polities, this minimum is relatively small. The body of nonvoters in these polities seems on the whole not to reflect systematic biases along sociological lines of obvious political importance, and tends to be highly stable, or at least has been so in the generation since the end of the Second World War.

In the United States, by contrast, there is overwhelming evidence of systematic participation biases along sociological lines of political importance. For my purposes here I have concentrated on only one but perhaps the most important of these, social class. Participation in the United States is also highly volatile by comparative standards. Since 1960, for example, about one-quarter of the active electorate as then defined has shifted into the party of nonvoters. There is a persistent, very strong, historical, and cross-sectional relationship at the margins between the Democratic voting streams and the party of nonvoters—a very dynamic relationship that has little counterpart on the Republican side. Marked social-structure bias in turnout and nonvoting is thus paralleled in politics by a no less striking asymmetry in the mobilizing capacities of the two rival parties. The two are indissolubly linked, appear to arise from the same systemic causes, and are becoming ever more manifest.

It is very hard to avoid the conclusion that the profound reorganization of the entrepreneurial foundations of the American electoral market in recent years is a vital causal agent in this swelling tide of nonvoting. The rise of the permanent campaign creates a network of conditions that could be predicted to contribute to the disconnection of voters—especially, but by no means exclusively, lower-status voters. Put another way, the relative disappearance of partisan teams in campaigns and their replacement by personalistic and imagistic appeals to voters creates conditons that make individual utility calculations difficult, if not impossible. If people are left to their own devices in a society with marked inequalities on all relevant dimensions of political consciousness, education, and information, some people will remain far better positioned to make accurate utility calculations than others. As the vast literature on the development of parties attests, it was the whole purpose of party-as-team and party-in-the-electorate to reduce this particular inequality as much as possible through organization, political education, and mass mobilization. The partial dissolution of those linkages in the permanent-campaign era inevitably means that this gradient will grow ever steeper until the situation approximates a political "state of nature"—a state that it was the entire purpose of party builders to end.

I sometimes think that, given the specific conditions and constraints surrounding democracy in America, a general political situation approximating that of the 1920s or the 1980s represents a kind of end point toward which we have been evolving. Such a view might be challenged as carrying determinism* and pessimism to excess. Whether it does or not, the ultimate key to the problem of mass abstention clearly lies in the broader problems of American electoral politics and its modern party system. New challenges may arise that create a new basis for serious contests among collective wills and for collective decisionmaking on some very powerful issue. If so, politicians will likely rediscover the need and thus the personal incentives for collective action. But this would require the elimination or at least the radical transformation of the existing permanent campaign structure. Obviously this would be a task of the most awesome magnitude. Yet there seems little reason to suppose that the general decomposition of the American political regime, of which growing voter abstention is only one of the more important components, can be arrested—much less reversed—unless that task is undertaken and successfully carried out.

**Determinism:* philosophical doctrine that states that all facts and events, including human decisions, are caused or determined by those that preceded them.

NOTES

[1]Most accounts give the total voting-age population as the denominator, although the census gives the noncitizen component and no state in the union has permitted aliens to vote since the election of 1920. Total voting-age population in the 1980s is about 104 percent of the citizen voting-age population, and the noncitizen trend has clearly been rising over the past twenty years. Using the citizen base, rather than the total, marginally increases the turnout estimate (in 1980, from 53 percent to 55.2 percent). In addition, the total participation rate (including "blank, void, and scattering," as New York calls it) is marginally higher than the vote cast for the highest office, that is, president, or in off-years governor or U.S. senator. In the 1980 Massachusetts election, for example, the total vote for all presidential candidates was 2,524,298, but an additional 42,509 blank votes were cast for this office, making a total participation of 2,566,807. The presidential vote cast was thus 98.3 percent of all ballots cast. Something like this is very probably the national average, and would mean that, while the turnout for president was 55.2 percent of potential voters in 1980, the whole vote cast would produce a participation rate of 56.1 percent. Even today, the conduct and reporting of elections is very largely the responsibility of each of the fifty states, and these differ considerably in both areas. Most of them do not report on the "blanks and voids," and therefore virtually all American election reporting gives only the valid vote. Comparatively, most continental European countries report both the total of all votes cast and the total of valid votes cast. The relationship between the two, except in countries that have compulsory voting, tends to be similar to the Massachusetts example.

[2]There was much unhappiness in ruling Christian Democratic party circles following the February 1987 election because many believed that the party's unexpectedly disappointing showing was partly caused by a slump in the participation rate—from nearly 90 percent in 1983 to about 85 percent in 1987.

[3]The evidence on this is by now overwhelming. For the most complete analysis, see Paul Kleppner, *Who Voted?: The Dynamics of Electoral Turnout, 1870–1980* (Praeger, 1982).

[4]This was very often associated with the presentation of German elections in the 1930–33 crisis period as a "horrible example" of voter mobilization. See, for example, Seymour Martin Lipset, *Political Man: The Social Bases of Politics* (Doubleday, 1960), especially pp. 140–52. It has become clear in recent years that such analyses, in additon to failing to incorporate the nearly half-century of electoral material that preceded the Weimar era, fundamentally misspecificed the relative importance of the mobilization of former nonvoters to the Nazi upsurge. The best technical discussion of the issues is Adam Przeworski, "Institutionalization of Voting Patterns, or Is Mobilization the Source of Decay?" *American Political Science Review*, vol. 69 (March 1975), pp. 49-67. See also Thomas Childers, *The Nazi Voter: The Social Foundations of Facism in Germany* (University of North Carolina Press, 1983).

[5]It is now a generation since Louis Hartz published his seminal work, *The Liberal Tradition in America: An Interpretation of American Political Thought since the Revolution* (Harcourt Brace, 1955); but time has not diminished its importance. For a more empirical but very convergent study, see Donald J. Devine, *The Political Culture of the United States: The Influence of Member Values on Regime Maintenance* (Little, Brown, 1972).

[6]Raymond E. Wolfinger and Steven J. Rosenstone, *Who Votes?* (Yale University Press, 1980), pp. 13–36.

[7]See the discussion in Sidney Verba and Norman H. Nie, *Participation in America: Political Democracy and Social Equality* (Harper and Row, 1972), especially pp. 125–37. This rich work represents the very best of the survey research tradition. However, it has become clearer since 1972 that there are significant differences between two types of political efficacy indices as constructed from sets of questions: *internal* ("Sometimes government and politics are so complicated . . . ") and *external* ("Officials don't care what people like me think . . ."). The former taps a sense of personal inadequacy; the latter, a sense of system unresponsiveness.

[8]Arthur T. Hadley, *The Empty Polling Booth* (Prentice-Hall, 1978).

[9]See the classic survey study, Angus Campbell and others, *The American Voter* (Wiley, 1960), especially pp. 475–81. Compare also Philip E. Converse's analysis, "The Nature of Belief Systems in Mass Publics," in David E. Apter, ed., *Ideology and Discontent* (Free Press, 1964).

[10]Samuel H. Barnes, *Representation in Italy: Institutionalized Tradition and Electoral Choice* (University of Chicago Press, 1977), especially pp. 97–115. For some similar findings about Spain's "new democracy," see Juan J. Linz, "The New Spanish Party System," in Richard Rose, ed., *Electoral Participation: A Comparative Analysis* (Beverly Hills: Sage, 1980), pp. 101–89.

[11]The classic expression of this is Donald E. Stokes, "Spatial Models of Party Competition," in Angus Campbell and others, *Elections and the Political Order* (Wiley, 1966), pp. 161–79.

[12]See David Butler and Donald E. Stokes, *Political Change in Britain* (London: Macmillan, 1969), pp. 23–43.

[13]Anthony Downs, *An Economic Theory of Democracy* (Harper, 1957); and V. O. Key, Jr., *The Responsible Electorate* (Harvard University Press, 1966).

[14]The most comprehensive and elegant statement thus far is Morris P. Fiorina, *Retrospective Voting in American National Elections* (Yale University Press, 1981).

[15]One can easily imagine a *U*-shaped distribution in a two-party system that would produce similar incentives for competitive mobilization rather than outreach to a (largely nonexistent) "swing vote." The Civil War party system seems to have produced a number of such cases—perhaps most notably in Indiana. See Melvyn Hammarberg, *The Indiana Voter: The Historical Dynamics of Party Allegiance during the 1870s* (University of Chicago Press, 1977), especially pp. 27–35; and also V. O. Key, Jr., and Frank Munger, "Social Determinism and Electoral Decision: The Case of Indiana," in Frank Munger and Douglas Price, eds., *Readings in Political Parties and Pressure Groups* (Crowell, 1964), pp. 366–84. Politics in this state between 1868 and 1900 or so had striking structural similarities to certain properties of contemporary multiparty systems. Electoral swings were usually tiny from year to year, and the state typically had presidential year turnouts well above 90 percent of the eligible electorate. Campaign styles sometimes in vogue at that time can be appreciated by a well-known comment by Republican Governor (and later U.S. Senator) Oliver P. Morton: "The Democratic party is the common sewer and loathesome receptacle of mankind. While it may be true that not every Democrat is a traitor, every traitor is a Democrat."

[16]Fiorina, *Retrospective Voting*, pp. 210–11.

[17]Downs, *Economic Theory of Democracy*, pp. 260–76.

[18]Edward R. Tufte, *Political Control of the Economy* (Princeton University Press, 1978). The "political business cycle" literature has grown to vast proportions since Tufte wrote. See, for example, David R. Cameron, "The Politics and Economics of the Business Cycle," in Thomas Ferguson and Joel D. Rogers, eds., *The Political Economy: Readings in the Politics and Economics of American Public Policy* (Armonk, N.Y.: M. E. Sharpe, 1984), pp. 237–62.

[19]Philip E. Converse, "The Nature of Belief Systems in Mass Publics," in David E. Apter, ed., *Ideology and Discontent* (Free Press, 1964).

[20]Two general accounts of realignment and party-system dynamics are Walter Dean Burnham, *Critical Elections and the Mainsprings of American Politics* (Norton, 1970); and James A. Sundquist, *Dynamics of the Party System: Alignment and Realignment of Political Parties in the United States*, rev. ed. (Brookings, 1983). With the exception of the New Deal realignment sequence, literature that specifically and empirically explores turnout dynamics in these crises is much less abundant than it should be. See Kristi Andersen, "Generation, Partisan Shift and Realignment: A Glance Back to the New Deal," in Norman Nie, Sidney Verba, and John R. Petrocik, *The Changing American Voter*, 2d ed. (Harvard University Press, 1979), pp. 74–95.

[21]A short but classic study is Douglas Rae, *The Political Consequences of Electoral Laws* (Yale University Press, 1967). The late Stein Rokkan produced a multitude of first-rate work on this topic and its relationship to the historical mobilization of social and geographical peripheries into the active electorate. See in particular his *Citizens, Elections, and Parties: Approaches to the Comparative Study of the Processes of Development* (David McKay, 1970), pp. 145–247.

[22]But specific historical context seems to be, if not all the story, then most of it. Although the basic electoral system in the United States has been one of its most stable political characteristics, presidential-year turnouts outside the South regularly exceeded 80 percent of the estimated potential electorate from 1876 through 1900 (see Table 3).

[23]Wolfinger and Rosenstone, *Who Votes?* pp. 61–88, provide an extensive discussion of the effect of registration laws on turnout. Their estimate is that if all states had registration laws as permissive as the most permissive states, turnout in 1972 would have been 9.1 percent higher than it actually was. I concluded in a 1978 study that the depressant impact of personal registration on turnout lay between 8 and 10 percent in 1960–76. See Walter Dean Burnham, "The Appearance and Disappearance of the American Voter," in Burnham, *The Current Cirsis in American Politics* (Oxford University Press, 1982), pp. 139–40.

[24]The classic statement of this point is Stanley Kelley, Jr., Richard E. Ayres, and William G. Bowen, "Registration and Voting: Putting First Things First," *American Political Science Review*, vol. 61 (June 1967), pp. 359–79. The 1966 Texas statute, properly labeled by critics as the old poll-tax law with the poll tax left out, occasioned litigation: *Beare* v. *Smith*, 32 F. Supp. 1100 (S.D. Tex. 1971). The case is discussed in Walter Dean Burnham, "A Political Scientist and Voting-Rights Litigation: The Case of the 1966 Texas Registration Statute," *Washington University Law Quarterly* (1971), pp. 335–58.

[25]In The *Beare* opinion, Judge Singleton summarized the position advanced by Texas's attorney general: "One such interest suggested by the state as compelling . . . is the purity of the ballot. In other words, the state contends that those who overcome the annual hurdle of registering at a time remote to the fall elections will more likely be better informed and have greater capabilities of making an intelligent choice than those who do not care enough to register." (321 F. Supp. at 1106.) This is, in a word, the old *melior pars* argument common to conservative thought in the seventeenth and eighteenth centuries. Elsewhere, such arguments and perspectives simply do not exist and have not for the past fifty to a hundred years. Here they persist, and the result is a remarkably opaque but very persistent struggle over the franchise—perhaps what one could expect from a political system in some ways so archaic and undeveloped that Samuel P. Huntington has aptly labeled it a "Tudor polity." Samuel P. Huntington, *Political Order in Changing Societies* (Yale University Press, 1968), chap. 2.

[26]The Civil Rights Act of 1965 lowered the minimum residence requirement for voting in presidential elections to thirty days, recognizing that this is a country whose population is very physically mobile. A number of states (for example, Minnesota and Maine) have adopted election-day registration, which practically abolishes the requirement and, for that matter, the electoral list. Others have drastically simplified the procedures, for example, by adopting drivers' license or postcard registration. As of this writing, a detailed analysis of reforms and their estimated consequences for the turnout rate is being generated by the Committee for the Study of the American Electorate. This document will provide a full survey of the diverse legal terrain affecting access to the ballot box in the fifty states.

[27]These figures are derived from U.S. Bureau of the Census, *Current Population Reports*, series P-20, no. 143, "Voter Participation in the National Election: November 1964" (Government Printing Office, 1965); and no. 405, "Voting and Registration in the Election of November 1984" (GPO, 1986).

[28]Walter Dean Burnham, "Theory and Voting Research: Some Relfections on Converse's 'Change in the American Electorate,' " *American Political Science Review*, vol. 68 (September 1974), pp. 1002–23. See also Kleppner, *Who Voted?* p. 62, where he concludes, "Personal-registration requirements accounted for between 30 and 40 percent of the turnout decrement in the counties in which they were in force." The other two-thirds, obviously, finds a much more directly political explanation.

[29]Ronald P. Formisano, "Deferential-Participant Politics: The Early Republic's Political Culture, 1789–1840," *American Political Science Review*, vol. 68 (June 1974), pp. 473–87. See also his "Federalists and Republicans: Parties, Yes—System, No" in Paul Kleppner and others, *The Evolution of American Electoral Systems* (Greenwood, 1981), pp. 113–46.

[30]In many respects, the first presidential election that the Inter-University Consortium for Political and Social Research archive and most others report, 1824, belong to the preceding political order and not to the Jacksonian period that followed. Not only did six states lack popular choice for presidential electors, but the election involved four individuals (J. Q. Adams, Jackson, Crawford, and Clay) who all at the time claimed allegiance to the same "party." It is thus hardly surprising that the turnout rate for this election in the states where there was popular election was only 26.7 percent, considerably below the 1812 figure.

[31]Eric L. McKitrick, "Party Politics and the Union and Confederate War Efforts," in William N.

Chambers and Walter Dean Burnham, eds., *The American Party Systems: Stages of Political Development*, 2d ed. (Oxford University Press, 1975), pp. 117–51.

[32]A discussion of these Confederate data is to be found in Walter Dean Burnham, "Elections as Democratic Institutions," in Kay L. Schlozman, ed., *Elections in America* (Allen and Unwin, 1987), pp. 37–43.

[33]See Kleppner, *Who Voted?* For an earlier discussion, see Walter Dean Burnham, "The Changing Shape of the American Political Universe," *American Political Science Review*, vol. 59 (March 1965), pp. 7–28. Kleppner has just published his comprehensive treatment of the "system of 1896": *Continuity and Change in Electoral Politics, 1893–1928* (Greenwood, 1987).

[34]See Burnham, "Theory and Voting Research," and the attendant discussion. A more recent and explicit explanation of the considerations that entered into my estimates is Walter Dean Burnham, "Those High Nineteenth-Century American Voting Turnouts: Fact or Fiction?" *Journal of Interdisciplinary History*, vol. 16 (Spring 1986), pp. 613–44.

[35]Sources previously cited strongly imply this, and some parts of the pattern are visible in Figures 1 and 2 below. A qualitative discussion of this era, heavily based on archival research, suggests some parallels and causes of this demobilization. See Michael E. McGerr, *The Decline of Popular Politics: The American North, 1865–1928* (Oxford University Press, 1986).

[36]See chap. 11. The classic discussion of these and other effects of direct primaries (and other state laws) on the integrity of party schedule and function is V. O. Key, Jr., *American State Politics* (Knopf, 1956).

[37]See the discussion of the transition to "advertised politics" in McGerr, *Decline of Popular Politics*, chap. 6.

[38]See Stephen Skowroneck, *Building a New American State: The Expansion of National Administrative Capacities, 1877–1920* (New York and Cambridge: Cambridge University Press, 1982).

[39]See Herbert L. A. Tingsten, *Political Behavior: Studies in Election Statistics* (London: P. S. King, 1937), pp. 156–58. In his analysis of the small city of Delaware, Ohio, in 1924, Tingsten found significantly lower participation rates among industrial workers and by similar socioeconomic differences.

[40]This was an issue of direct concern to reformist political scientists of an earlier generation such as Charles E. Merriam and Harold F. Gosnell (see their *Non-Voting, Causes and Methods of Control* [University of Chicago Press, 1924]). See also E. E. Schattschneider, *The Semisovereign People: A Realist's View of Democracy in America* (Holt, Rinehart and Winston, 1960); and his analysis, "United States: The Functional Approach to Party Government," in Sigmund Neumann, ed., *Modern Political Parties* (Univeristy of Chicago Press, 1956), pp. 194–215. In the South of this period and for long after, the term *oligarchy* is the only accurate characterization. See V. O. Key, Jr., *Southern Politics in State and Nation* (Knopf, 1949).

[41]Kristi Andersen, *The Creation of a Democratic Majority: 1928–1936* (Univeristy of Chicago Press, 1979). The problem with Andersen's analysis is that it is based upon assumptions that are partially false because they are anachronistic. The "Hoover surge" of 1928 that was so conspicuous in Protestant areas should have made it clear that in pre-New Deal conditions mobilizations among these "potential Democrats" could have led as easily to Republican as to Democratic voting among the new entrants.

[42]See the first modern survey of American voters, Paul Lazersfeld and others, *The People's Choice: How the Voter Makes Up His Mind in a Presidential Campaign* (New York: Duell Sloan Pearce, 1944). For further evidence on this point, see Robert R. Alford, *Party and Society: The Anglo-American Democracies* (Rand McNally, 1963), p. 152. It is now commonly understood that the success of the prescientific *Literary Digest* poll from 1908 through 1932 rested on the absence of any autonomous class cleavage in electoral politics, just as the poll's disastrous failure in 1936 reflected the emergence of this fatally decisive variable.

[43]Predominantly for ethnocultural reasons—the intense antagonism between a largely proletarian Irish Catholic community and a largely middle-class Yankee-Protestant counterpart—partisan competition in the Boston metropolitan area (and Massachusetts as a whole) remained much more robust there than in overwhelmingly Republican Pittsburgh (and Pennsylvania) during the tenure of the "system of 1896." Working-class participation rates tended over time, even in the trough of the 1920s, to be considerably higher in Eastern Massachusetts than in Pittsburgh.

[44]Sidney Blumenthal, *The Permanent Campaign*, rev. ed. (Simon and Schuster, 1983).

[45]Most recently James L. Sundquist.

[46]For a current survey-based analysis that stresses this point, see Martin P. Wattenberg, *The Decline of American Political Parties, 1952–1984* (Harvard University Press, 1985). The basic cognitive transformation has been away from a combined positive-negative response (that is, people who like Democrats tend to dislike Republicans and vice versa) to an affective neutral-neutral position. The latter implies that the parties are becoming more and more irrelevant at the level of popular politics. It is of course an open question as to whether the major changes in politics associated with the Reagan years have brought, or may bring, a reversal in these trends. At the moment, the more cautious view seems to be that they have considerably flattened out since 1980.

[47]Maurice Duverger, *Political Parties: Their Organization and Activity in the Modern State*, trans. Barbara and Robert North, 2d ed. rev. (Wiley, 1959), p. 426. Except in the United States, of course, where parties are more developed on the Right than on the Left.

[48]This has become part of the bureau's Current Population Surveys (Series P-20) with biennial reports of varying comprehensiveness. The most complete and informative was produced for the 1972 election. The 1984 report's comprehensiveness is considerably below that of 1980s, probably reflecting the Reagan administration's choices regarding the availability to the public of officially gathered information at reasonable cost, or sometimes at all. (One example is the unfortunate discontinuation in 1981–82 of Census Bureau election-year estimates of voting age population by congressional district.)

[49]In 1984, for example, the survey reports a turnout rate of 71.8 percent among homeowners (73 percent of the sample), compared with 43.7 percent among renters, a participation gap of nearly 30 points. For whites only, the rates are 72.5 percent and 42.8 respectively—an even larger gap than for the population as a whole.

[50]David Burner, *The Politics of Provincialism: The Democratic Party in Transition*, 1918–1932 (Knopf, 1968).

[51]As has also happened in New York State and especially in New York City. There are assembly districts in the city where fewer than one-fifth of the potential electorate voted in the 1984 presidential election. For the state as a whole, the turnout rate for governor in 1986 was 33.4 percent of the potential electorate—the lowest since the election of 1820 (32.7 percent). Indeed, before constitutional reform in 1821, New York allowed only freeholders with property worth $100 to vote, thus disfranchising about three-fifths of the adult white male population. During this period, there were six gubernatorial elections (1801–1816) that, despite this property qualification, showed higher voter participation than in 1986.

9

MORRIS P. FIORINA

THE DECLINE OF COLLECTIVE RESPONSIBILITY IN AMERICAN POLITICS

American national government suffers increasingly from single-issue politics, weak leadership in the face of important challenges, and a trend toward short-term approaches to long-term problems. In the past, the political parties helped clarify accountability for public policies. As the strength and coherence of political parties has declined in the United States, it has become more difficult to concert governmental action and assign responsibility clearly. Morris P. Fiorina, professor of government at Harvard, discusses these issues in the following piece, "The Decline of Collective Responsibility in American Politics" (1980). A scholar of American legislative and electoral processes, Fiorina is the author of Representatives, Roll Calls, and Constituencies *(1973),* Congress—Keystone of the Washington Establishment *(1977), and* Retrospective Voting in American National Elections *(1981) and coauthor with Bruce Cain and John Ferejohn of* The Personal Vote: Constituency Service and Electoral Independence *(1987).*

Though the Founding Fathers believed in the necessity of establishing a genuinely national government, they took great pains to design one that could not lightly do things *to* its citizens; what government might do *for* its citizens was to be limited to the functions of what we know now as the "watchman state." Thus the Founders composed the constitutional litany familiar to every schoolchild: they created a federal system, they distributed and blended powers within and across the federal levels, and they encouraged the occupants of the various positions to check and balance each other by structuring incentives so that one officeholder's ambitions would be likely to conflict with others'. The resulting system of institutional arrangements predictably hampers efforts to undertake major initiatives and favors maintenance of the status quo.

Given the historical record faced by the Founders, their emphasis on constraining government is understandable. But we face a later historical record, one that shows two hundred years of increasing demands for government to act positively. Moreover, developments unforeseen by the Founders increasingly raise the likelihood that the uncoordinated actions of individuals and groups will inflict serious damage on the nation as a whole. The by-products of the industrial and technological revolutions impose physical risks not only on us, but on future generations as well. Resource shortages and international cartels* raise the spectre of economic ruin. And the simple proliferation of special interests with their intense, particularistic demands threatens to render us politically incapable of

**Cartel:* see footnote on page 112.

taking actions that might either advance the state of society or prevent foreseeable deteriorations in that state. None of this is to suggest that we should forget about what government can do *to* us—the contemporary concern with the proper scope and methods of government intervention in the social and economic orders is long overdue. But the modern age demands as well that we worry about our ability to make government work *for* us. The problem is that we are gradually losing that ability, and a principal reason for this loss is the steady erosion of *responsibility* in American politics.

What do I mean by this important quality, responsibility? To say that some person or group is responsible for a state of affairs is to assert that he or they have the ability to take legitimate actions that have a major impact on that state of affairs. More colloquially, when someone is responsible, we know whom to blame. Human beings have asymmetric attitudes toward responsibility, as captured by the saying "Success has a thousand fathers, but failure is an orphan." This general observation applies very much to politicians, not surprisingly, and this creates a problem for democratic theory, because clear location or responsibility is vitally important to the operation of democratic governments. Without responsibility, citizens can only guess at who deserves their support; the act of voting loses much of its meaning. Moreover, the expectation of being held responsible provides representatives with a personal incentive to govern in their constituents' interest. As ordinary citizens we do not know the proper rate of growth of the money supply, the appropriate level of the federal deficit, the advantages of the MX over alternative missile systems, and so forth. We elect people to make those decisions. But only if those elected know they will be held accountable for the results of their decisions (or nondecisions, as the case may be), do they have a personal incentive to govern in our interest.[1]

Unfortunately, the importance of responsibility in a democracy is matched by the difficulty of attaining it. In an autocracy, individual responsibility suffices; the location of power in a single individual locates responsibility in that individual as well. But individual responsibility is insufficient whenever more than one person shares governmental authority. We can hold a particular congressman individually responsible for a personal transgression such as bribe-taking. We can even hold a president individually responsible for military moves where he presents Congress and the citizenry with a *fait accompli*. But on most national issues individual responsibility is difficult to assess. If one were to go to Washington, randomly accost a Democratic congressman, and berate him about a 20-percent rate of inflation, imagine the response. More than likely it would run, "Don't blame me. If 'they' had done what I've advocated for *x* years, things would be fine today." And if one were to walk over to the White House and similarly confront President Carter, he would respond as he already has, by blaming Arabs, free-spending congressmen, special interests, and, of course, us.

American institutional structure makes this kind of game-playing all too easy. In order to overcome it we must lay the credit or blame for national conditions on all those who had any hand in bringing them about: some form of *collective responsibility* is essential.

The only way collective responsibility has ever existed, and can exist given our institutions, is through the agency of the political party; in American politics, responsibility requires cohesive parties. This is an old claim to be sure, but its age does not detract from its present relevance.[2] In fact, the continuing decline in public esteem for the parties and continuing efforts to "reform" them out of the political process suggest that old arguments for party responsibility have not been made often enough or, at least, convincingly enough, so I will make these arguments once again in this essay.

A strong political party can generate collective responsibility by creating incentive for leaders, followers, and popular supporters to think and act in collective terms. First, by providing party leaders with the capability (e.g., control of institutional patronage, nominations, and so on) to discipline party members, genuine leadership becomes possible. Legislative output is less likely to be a least common denominator—a residue of myriad conflicting proposals—and more likely to consist of a program actually intended to solve a problem or move the nation in a particular direction. Second, the subordination of individual officeholders to the party lessens their ability to separate themselves from party actions. Like it or not, their performance becomes identified with the performance of the collectivity to which they belong. Third, with individual candidate variation greatly reduced, voters have less incentive to support individuals and more incentive to support or oppose the party as a whole. And fourth, the circle closes as party-line voting in the electorate provides party leaders with the incentive to propose policies that will earn the support of a national majority, and party backbenchers with the personal incentive to cooperate with leaders in the attempt to compile a good record for the party as a whole.

In the American context, strong parties have traditionally clarified politics in two ways. First, they allow citizens to assess responsibility easily, at least when the government is unified, which it more often was in earlier eras when party meant more than it does today.[3] Citizens need only evaluate the social, economic, and international conditions they observe and make a simple decision for or against change. They do not need to decide whether the energy, inflation, urban, and defense policies advocated by their congressman would be superior to those advocated by Carter—were any of them to be enacted!

The second way in which strong parties clarify American politics follows from the first. When citizens assess responsibility on the party as a whole, party members have personal incentives to see the party evaluated favorably. They have little to gain from gutting their president's program one day and attacking him for lack of leadership the next, since they share in the president's fate when voters do not differentiate within the party. Put simply, party responsibility provides party members with a personal stake in their collective performance.

Admittedly, party responsibility is a blunt instrument. The objection immediately arises that party responsibility condemns junior Democratic representatives to suffer electorally for an inflation they could do little to affect. An unhappy situation, true, but unless we accept it, Congress as a whole escapes electoral retribution for an inflation they *could* have done something to affect. Responsibility requires acceptance of both conditions. The choice is between a blunt instrument or none at all.

Of course, the United States is not Great Britain. We have neither the institutions nor the traditions to support a British brand of responsible party government, and I do not see either the possibility or the necessity for such a system in America. In the past the United States has enjoyed eras in which party was a much stronger force than today. And until recently—a generation, roughly—parties have provided an "adequate" degree of collective responsibility. They have done so by connecting the electoral fates of party members, via presidential coattails, for example, and by transforming elections into referenda on party performance, as with congressional off-year elections.

In earlier times, when citizens voted for the party, not the person, parties had incentives to nominate good candidates, because poor ones could have harmful fallout on the ticket as a whole.[4] In particular, the existence of presidential coattails (positive and negative) provided an inducement to avoid the nomination of narrowly based candidates, no matter how committed their supporters. And, once in office, the existence of party voting in the electorate provided party members with the incentive to compile a good *party* record. In particular, the tendency of national midterm elections to serve as referenda on the performance of the president provided a clear inducement for congressmen to do what they could to see that their president was perceived as a solid performer. By stimulating electoral phenomena such as coattail effects and mid-term referenda, party transformed some degree of personal ambition into concern with collective performance.

In the contemporary period, however, even the preceding tendencies toward collective responsibility have largely dissipated. As background for a discussion of this contemporary weakening of collective responsibility and its deleterious consequences, let us briefly review the evidence for the decline of party in America.

THE CONTINUING DECLINE OF PARTY IN THE UNITED STATES

Party is a simple term that covers a multitude of complicated organizations and processes. It manifests itself most concretely as the set of party organizations that exist principally at the state and local levels. It manifests itself most elusively as a psychological presence in the mind of the citizen. Somewhere in between, and partly a function of the first two, is the manifestation of party as a force in government. The discussion in this section will hold to this traditional schema, though it is clear that the three aspects of party have important interconnections.

Party Organizations

In the United States, party organization has traditionally meant state and local party organization. The national party generally has been a loose confederacy of subnational units that swings into action for a brief period every four years. This characterization remains true today, despite the somewhat greater influence and augmented functions of the national organizations.[5] Though such things are difficult to measure precisely, there is general agreement that the formal party organizations have undergone a secular decline since their peak at the end of the nineteenth century. The prototype of the old-style organization was the urban machine, a form approximated today only in Chicago.

Several long-term trends have served to undercut old-style party organizations. The patronage system has been steadily chopped back since passage of the Civil Service Act of 1883.* The social welfare functions of the parties have passed to the government as the modern welfare state developed. And, less concretely, the entire ethos of the old-style party organization is increasingly at odds with modern ideas of government based on rational expertise. These long-term trends spawned specific attacks on the old party organizations. In the late nineteenth and early twentieth centuries the Populists,† Progressives,‡ and assorted other reformers fought electoral corruption with the Australian Ballot§ and personal registration systems.‖ They attempted to break the hold of the party bosses over nominations by mandating the direct primary. They attacked the urban machines with drives for nonpartisan at-large elections and nonpartisan city managers. None of these reforms destroyed the parties; they managed to live with the reforms better than most reformers had hoped. But the reforms reflected changing popular attitudes toward the parties and accelerated the secular decline in the influence of the party organizations.

The New Deal** period temporarily arrested the deterioration of the party organizations, at least on the Democratic side. Unified party control under a "political" president provided favorable conditions for the state and local organizations.[6] But following the heyday of the New Deal (and ironically, in part, because of government assumption of subnational parties' functions) the decline continued.

In the 1970s two series of reforms further weakened the influence of organized parties in American national politics. The first was a series of legal changes deliberately intended to lessen organized party influence in the presidential nominating process. In the Democratic party, "New Politics" activists captured the national party apparatus and imposed a series of rules changes designed to "open up" the politics of presidential nominations. The Republican party—long more amateur and open than the Democratic party—adopted weaker versions of the Democratic rules changes. In addition, modifications of state electoral laws to conform to the Democratic rules changes (enforced by the federal courts) stimu-

**Civil Service Act of 1883:* law that created a merit system for federal civil servants and established a United States Civil Service Commission to develop and enforce the rules and regulations of the new personnel system. Also called the Pendleton Act of 1883.

†*Populists:* see footnote on page 138.

‡*Progressives:* see footnote on page 19.

§*Australian Ballot:* system by which the Australian government improved the electoral process in 1858 by printing and distributing the ballots and using government officials to collect them at polling places. For national elections, the United States adopted the concept in 1888 and later modified it by listing all candidates of one party in one column or all candidates for one office in one column. Prior to the use of the Australian Ballot in the U.S., ballots were printed by the political parties and voting was not secret.

‖*Personal registration systems:* means by which, prior to election day, citizens establish their eligibility to vote in a particular jurisdiction by filling out a form that establishes their identity and place of residence. The primary aim of the system is to prevent fraudulent voting.

***New Deal:* see footnote on page 17.

TABLE 21. RECENT CHANGES IN PRESIDENTIAL NOMINATION PROCESS

	Number of States Holding Primaries	PERCENTAGES OF DELEGATES SELECTED IN PRIMARIES	
		Democratic	*Republican*
1968	17	38	34
1972	23	61	53
1976	30	73	68
1980	36	76	76

Source: 1968–1976 figures from Austin Ranney, "The Political Parties: Reform and Decline," in *The New American Political System*, Anthony King (ed.) (Washington, D.C.: American Enterprise Institute, 1978), Table 6–1. Figures for 1980 are from *National Journal*, October 20, 1979: 1738–9.

lated Republican rules changes as well. Table 21 shows that the presidential nominating process has indeed been opened up. In little more than a decade after the disastrous 1968 Democratic conclave, the number of primary states has more than doubled, and the number of delegates chosen in primaries has increased from little more than a third to three-quarters. Moreover, the remaining delegates emerge from caucuses far more open to mass citizen participation, and the delegates themselves are more likely to be amateurs, than previously.[7] For example, in the four conventions from 1956 to 1968 more than 70 percent of the Democratic party's senators, 40 percent of their representatives, and 80 percent of their governors attended. In 1976 the figures were 18 percent, 15 percent, and 47 percent, respectively.[8] Today's youth can observe the back-room maneuvers of party bosses and favorite sons only by watching *The Best Man* on late night television.

A second series of 1970s reforms lessened the role of formal party organizations in the conduct of political campaigns. These are financing regulations growing out of the Federal Election Campaign Act of 1971 as amended in 1974 and 1976.* In this case the reforms were aimed at cleaning up corruption in the financing of campaigns; their effects on the parties were a by-product, though many individuals accurately predicted its nature. Serious presidential candidates are now publicly financed. Though the law permits the national party to spend two cents per eligible voter on behalf of the nominee, it also obliges the candidate to set up a finance committee separate from the national party. Between this legally mandated separation and fear of violating spending limits or accounting regulations, for example, the law has the effect of encouraging the candidate to keep his party at arm's length.[9]

At present only presidential candidates enjoy public financing, but a series of new limits on contributions and expenditures affects other national races. Prior to the implementation of the new law, data on congressional campaign financing

***Federal Election Campaign Act* (FECA): law enacted in 1971, and amended in 1974, 1976, and 1979, establishing the overarching rules of the national election process. It requires candidates, campaign organizations, and other contributors to report their financial records for review. FECA also provides public funding for major party nominating conventions and for their presidential candidates up to certain overall limits. Partial funding is available for minor party presidential candidates. Primary election campaigns that accept federal funding also must accept restrictions on their expenditures.

TABLE 22. RECENT SOURCES OF CONGRESSIONAL CAMPAIGN CONTRIBUTIONS (IN PERCENTAGES)

	Individual	*PACs*	*Parties*	*Personal*
		HOUSE		
1972	59	14	17	NA
1978	57	25	7	11
		SENATE		
1972	67	12	14	1
1978	70	13	6	11

Source: Michael Malbin, "Of Mountains and Molehills: PACs, Campaigns, and Public Policy," in Malbin (ed.), *Parties, Interest Groups, and Campaign Finance Laws* (Washington, D.C.: American Enterprise Institute, 1980), Table 1.

were highly unreliable, but consider some of the trends that have emerged in the short time the law has been in effect. Table 22 shows the diminished role of the parties in the financing of congressional races. In House races, the decline in the party proportion of funding has been made up by the generosity of political action committees* (also stimulated by the new law). In the Senate, wealthy candidates appear to have picked up the slack left by the diminished party role. The party funding contribution in congressional races has declined not only as a proportion of the total, but also in absolute dollars, and considerably in inflation-adjusted dollars. The limits in the new law restrict a House candidate to no more than $15,000 in funding from each of the national and relevant state parties (the average campaign expenditure of an incumbent in 1978 was about $121,000; of a challenger, about $54,000). A candidate for the Senate is permitted to receive a maximum of $17,500 from his senatorial campaign committee, plus two cents per eligible voter from the national committee and a like amount from the relevant state committee (twenty-one senatorial candidates spent over $1 million in 1978).

There is no detailed work on the precise effects of the contribution limits, but it appears doubtful that they are binding. If the national party were to contribute $15,000 to each of its congressional candidates, and a flat $17,500 to each of its senatorial candidates, that would be more than $8 million. *All* levels of the parties contributed only $10.5 million of the $157 million spent in 1978 congressional races.

Probably more constraining than limits on what the parties can contribute to the candidates are limits on what citizens and groups can contribute to the parties. Under current law, individual contributors may give $1,000 per election to a candidate (primary, runoff, general election), $5,000 per year to a political action committee, and $20,000 per year to a party. From the standpoint of the law, each of the two great national parties is the equivalent of four PACS. The

**Political action committees* (PACs): groups created primarily to raise and distribute campaign funds after federal law limited the amount of money individuals, unions, trade associations, and corporations can contribute to a candidate. PACs, first used by unions in the late 1940s, have rapidly increased in number; in 1975 there were approximately 608, but by 1987 there were over 4,000 contributing millions of dollars to national elections.

PACS themselves are limited to a $15,000 per year contribution to the national party. Thus financial angels are severely restricted. They must spread contributions around to individual candidates, each of whom is likely to regard the contribution as an expression of personal worthiness and, if anything, as less reason than ever to think in terms of the party.

The ultimate results of such reforms are easy to predict. A lesser party role in the nominating and financing of candidates encourages candidates to organize and conduct independent campaigns, which further weakens the role of parties. Of course, party is not the entire story in this regard. Other modern day changes contribute to the diminished party role in campaign politics. For one thing, party foot soldiers are no longer so important, given the existence of a large leisured middle class that participates out of duty or enjoyment, but that participates on behalf of particular candidates and issues rather than parties. Similarly, contemporary campaigns rely heavily on survey research, the mass media, and modern advertising methods—all provided by independent consultants outside the formal party apparatus. Although these developments are not directly related to the contemporary reforms, their effect is the same: the diminution of the role of parties in conducting political campaigns. And if parties do not grant nominations, fund their choices, and work for them, why should those choices feel any commitment to their party?

Party in the Electorate

In the citizenry at large, party takes the form of a psychological attachment. The typical American traditionally has been likely to identify with one or the other of the two major parties. Such identifications are transmitted across generations to some degree, and within the individual they tend to be fairly stable.[10] But there is mounting evidence that the basis of identification lies in the individual's experiences (direct and vicarious, through family and social groups) with the parties in the past.[11] Our current party system, of course, is based on the dislocations of the Depression period and the New Deal attempts to alleviate them. Though only a small proportion of those who experienced the Depression directly are active voters today, the general outlines of citizen party identifications much resemble those established at that time.

Again, there is reason to believe that the extent of citizen attachments to parties has undergone a long-term decline from a nineteenth century high.[12] And again, the New Deal appears to have been a period during which the decline was arrested, even temporarily reversed. But again, the decline of party has reasserted itself in the 1970s.

Since 1952 the Center for Political Studies at the University of Michigan has conducted regular national election surveys. The data elicited in such studies give us a graphic picture of the state of party in the electorate (Table 23). As the 1960s wore on, the heretofore stable distribution of citizen party identifications began to change in the general direction of weakened attachments to the parties. Between 1960 and 1976, independents, broadly defined, increased from less than a quarter to more than a third of the voting-age population. Strong

TABLE 23. SUBJECTIVE PARTY IDENTIFICATION, 1960–1976 (IN PERCENTAGES)

Party ID	*1960*	*1964*	*1968*	*1972*	*1976*
Strong Democrat	21	27	20	15	15
Weak Democrat	25	25	25	26	25
Independent Democrat	8	8	9	10	12
Independent	8	8	11	13	14
Independent Republican	7	6	9	11	10
Weak Republican	13	13	14	13	14
Strong Republican	14	11	10	10	9

Source: National Election Studies made available by The InterUniversity Consortium for Political and Social Research, University of Michigan.

identifiers declined from slightly more than a third to about a quarter of the population.

As the strength and extent of citizen attachments to the parties declined, the influence of party on the voting decisions of the citizenry similarly declined. The percentage of the voting-age population that reports consistent support of the same party's presidential candidate dropped from more than two-thirds in 1952 to less than half in 1976. As Table 24 shows, the percentage of voters who report a congressional vote consistent with their party identification has declined from over 80 percent in the late 1950s to under 70 percent today. And as Table 25 shows, ticket-splitting, both at the national and subnational levels, has probably doubled since the time of the first Eisenhower election.

Indisputably, party in the electorate has declined in recent years. Why? To some extent the electoral decline results from the organizational decline. Few party organizations any longer have the tangible incentives to turn out the faithful and assure their loyalty. Candidates run independent campaigns and deemphasize their partisan ties whenever they see any short-term electoral gain in doing so. If party is increasingly less important in the nomination and election of candidates, it is not surprising that such diminished importance is reflected in the attitudes and behavior of the voter.

Certain long-term sociological and technological trends also appear to work against party in the electorate. The population is younger, and younger citizens traditionally are less attached to the parties than their elders. The population is more highly educated; fewer voters need some means of simplifying the choices they face in the political arena, and party, of course, has been the principal means of simplification. And the media revolution has vastly expanded the amount of information easily available to the citizenry. Candidates would have little incentive to operate campaigns independent of the parties if there were no means to apprise the citizenry of their independence. The media provide the means.

Finally, our present party system is an old one. For increasing numbers of citizens, party attachments based on the Great Depression seem lacking in relevance to the problems of the late twentieth century. Beginning with the racial issue in the 1960s, proceeding to the social issue of the 1970s, and to the energy, environment, and inflation issues of today, the parties have been rent by internal

TABLE 24. PARTY-LINE VOTES IN HOUSE ELECTIONS

YEAR	1956	1958	1960	1962	1964	1966
PERCENTAGE	82	84	80	83	79	76
YEAR	1968	1970	1972	1974	1976	1978
PERCENTAGE	74	76	73	74	72	69

Source: National Election Studies made available by The InterUniversity Consortium for Political and Social Research, University of Michigan.

TABLE 25. TRENDS IN TICKET-SPLITTING, 1952–1976 (IN PERCENTAGES)

	President/House	*State/Local*
1952	12	34
1956	16	42
1960	14	46
1964	15	42
1968	18	48
1972	30	54
1976	25	—

Source: National Election Studies made available by The InterUniversity Consortium for Political and Social Research, University of Michigan.

dissension. Sometimes they failed to take stands, at other times they took the wrong ones from the standpoint of the rank and file, and at most times they have failed to solve the new problems in any genuine sense. Since 1965 the parties have done little or nothing to earn the loyalties of modern Americans.

Party in Government

If the organizational capabilities of the parties have weakened, and their psychological ties to the voters have loosened, one would expect predictable consequences for the party in government. In particular, one would expect to see an increasing degree of split party control within and across the levels of American government. The evidence on this point is overwhelming.

At the state level, twenty-seven of the fifty governments were under divided party control after the 1978 election. In seventeen states a governor of one party opposed a legislature controlled by the other, and in ten others a bicameral legislature was split between the parties. By way of contrast, twenty years ago the number of states with divided party control was sixteen.

At the federal level the trend is similar. In 1953 only twelve states sent a senator of each party to Washington. The number increased to sixteen by 1961, to twenty-one by 1972, and stands at twenty-seven today. Of course, the senators in each state are elected at different times. But the same patterns emerge when we examine simultaneous elections. There is an increasing tendency for congressional districts to support a congressman of one party and the presidential candidate of the other (Table 26). At the turn of the century it was extremely rare for a congressional district to report a split result. But since that time the trend has been steadily

TABLE 26. SPLIT RESULTS, CONGRESS AND PRESIDENT

YEAR	1900	1908	1916	1924	1932	1940
PERCENTAGE OF DISTRICTS	3	7	11	12	14	15
YEAR	1948	1956	1964	1972	1980	
PERCENTAGE OF DISTRICTS	23	30	33	42	?	

Source: The 1900–1964 figures are from Walter Dean Burham, *Critical Elections and the Mainspring of American Politics* (New York: Norton, 1970), p. 109. The 1972 figures are from *Congressional Quarterly's* compilation of official election returns.

upward. We may well be heading for a record in 1980 as a vulnerable Democratic president runs with 250-odd not-so-vulnerable Democratic congressmen.

Seemingly unsatisfied with the increasing tendencies of the voters to engage in ticket-splitting, we have added to the split of party in government by changing electoral rules in a manner that lessens the impact of national forces. For example, in 1920 thirty-five states elected their legislators, governors, and other state officials in presidential election years. In 1944 thirty-two states still did so. But in the past generation the trend has been toward isolation of state elections from national currents: as of 1970 only twenty states still held their elections concurrently with the national ones.[13] This legal separation of the state and national electoral arenas helps to separate the electoral fates of party officeholders at different levels of government, and thereby lessens their common interest in a good party record.

The increased fragmentation of the party in government makes it more difficult for government officeholders to work together than in times past (not that it has ever been terribly easy). Voters meanwhile have a more difficult time attributing responsibility for government performance, and this only further fragments party control. The result is lessened collective responsibility in the system.

In recent years it has become a commonplace to bemoan the decline of party in government. National commentators nostalgically contrast the Senate under Lyndon Johnson* with that under Robert Byrd.† They deplore the cowardice and paralysis of a House of Representatives, supposedly controlled by a two-thirds Democratic majority under the most activist, partisan speaker since Sam Rayburn.‡ And, of course, there are the unfavorable comparisons of Jimmy Carter to previous presidents—not only FDR and LBJ, but even Kennedy. Such observations may be descriptively accurate, but they are not very illuminating. It is not enough to call for more inspiring presidential leadership and to demand

**Lyndon B. Johnson* (1908–1973): United States senator from Texas from 1937 until 1961, who led the Democrats in the Senate from 1953 to 1961 and was Senate majority leader. Johnson was particularly effective at moving domestic legislation through the Congress. He served as vice-president to President John F. Kennedy and became president after Kennedy's assassination. He won the presidential election of 1964 by a landslide, but declined to run again in 1968.

†*Robert C. Byrd:* lawyer who became a Democratic senator from West Virginia in 1959 and leader of his party in the Senate through most of the 1980s.

‡*Samuel T. Rayburn* (1882–1961); eminent member of the U.S. House of Representatives from Texas from 1913 to 1961. He was the Speaker from 1940 to 1947, 1949 to 1953, and 1955 to 1961. From 1937 to 1961, whenever he was not serving as the Speaker, he was the leader of the Democratic party in the House.

that the majority party in Congress show more readiness to bite the bullet. Our present national problems should be recognized as the outgrowths of the increasing separation of the presidential and congressional electoral arenas.

By now it is widely understood that senatorial races are in a class by themselves. The visibility of the office attracts the attention of the media as well as that of organized interest groups. Celebrities and plutocrats* find the office attractive. Thus massive media campaigns and the politics of personality increasingly affect these races. Senate elections now are most notable for their idiosyncracy, and consequentially for their growing volatility; correspondingly, such general forces as the president and the party are less influential in senatorial voting today than previously.

What is less often recognized is that House elections have grown increasingly idiosyncratic as well. I have already discussed the declining importance of party identification in House voting and the increasing number of split results at the district level. These trends are both cause and consequence of incumbent efforts to insulate themselves from the electoral effects of national conditions. Figure 4 shows the distribution of the vote garnered by the Democratic candidate in incumbent-contested districts in 1948 and 1972.[14] Evidently, a massive change took place in the past generation. In 1948 most congressional districts were clustered around the 50-percent mark (an even split between the parties); most districts now are clustered away from the point of equal division. Two obvious questions arise: Why has the change occurred, and does it matter?

Taking the second question first, Figure 4 suggests a bleak future for such electoral phenomena as presidential coattails and midterm referenda on presidential performance. Consider a swing of 5 percent in the congressional vote owing to a particularly attractive (or repulsive) presidential candidate or an especially poor performance by a president. In the world represented by the 1948 diagram, such a swing has major consequences: it shifts a large proportion of districts across the 50-percent mark. The shift provides a new president with a "mandate" in an on-year election and constitutes a strong "message" to the president in an off-year election. In the world represented by the 1972 diagram, however, the hypothesized 5-percent shift has little effect: few seats are close enough to the tipping point to shift parties under the hypothesized swing. The president's victory is termed a "personal" victory by the media, or the midterm result is interpreted as a reflection of personal and local concerns rather than national ones.

Why has the distribution of the congressional voting results changed over time? Elsewhere I have argued that much of the transformation results from a temporal change in the basis of congressional voting.[15] We have seen that party influence in House voting has lessened. And, judging by the number of Democrats successfully hanging onto traditional Republican districts, programmatic and ideological influences on House voting probably have declined as well. What has taken up the slack left by the weakening of the traditional determinants of congressional voting? It appears that a variety of personal and local influences now play a major role in citizen evaluations of their representatives.[16] Along with

**Plutocrats:* members of a class or group that exert political power because of their wealth.

FIGURE 4. CONGRESSIONAL VOTE IN DISTRICTS WITH INCUMBENTS RUNNING

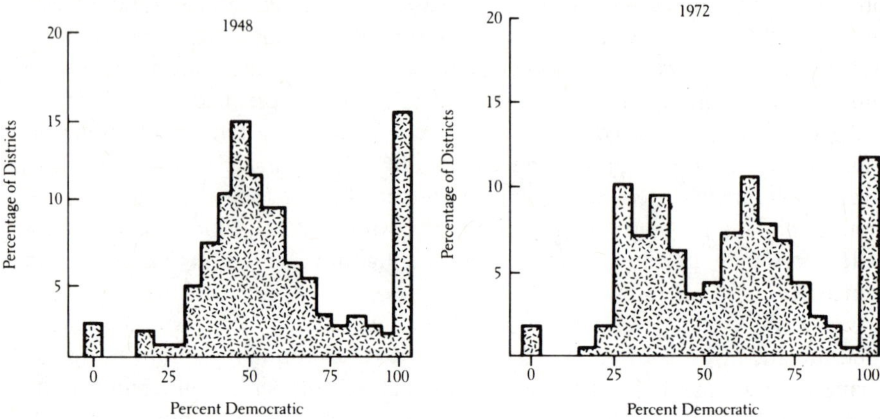

the expansion of the federal presence in American life, the traditional role of the congressman as an all-purpose ombudsman* has greatly expanded. Tens of millions of citizens now are directly affected by federal decisions. Myriad programs provide opportunities to profit from government largesse, and myriad regulations impose costs and/or constraints on citizen activities. And, whether seeking to gain profit or avoid costs, citizens seek the aid of their congressmen. When a court imposes a desegregation plan on an urban school board, the congressional offices immediately are contacted for aid in safeguarding existing sources of funding and in determining eligibility for new ones. When a major employer announces plans to quit an area, the congressional offices immediately are contacted to explore possibilities for using federal programs to persuade the employer to reconsider. Contractors appreciate a good congressional word with DOD† procurement officers. Local artistic groups cannot survive without NEA‡ funding. And, of course, there are the major individual programs such as social security and veterans' benefits that create a steady demand for congressional information and aid services. Such activities are nonpartisan, nonideological, and, most important, noncontroversial. Moreover, the contribution of the congressman in the realm of district service appears considerably greater than the impact of his or her single vote on major national issues. Constituents respond rationally to this modern state of affairs by weighing nonprogrammatic constituency service heavily when casting their congressional votes. And this emphasis on the part of constituents provides the means for incumbents to solidify their hold on the office. Even if elected by a narrow margin, diligent service activities

**Ombudsman:* official who hears and seeks to redress individuals' complaints about public administrative actions that affect them personally.

†*Department of Defense*, or *DOD:* created in 1949 by amendments to the National Security Act for the purpose of integrating military services. It includes the Departments of the Army, Navy, and Air Force.

‡*National Education Association*, or *NEA:* largest professional education organization in the United States, with approximately two million members. Its purpose is to improve American education and increase teachers' benefits. The organization was founded in 1857.

enable a congressman to neutralize or even convert a portion of those who would otherwise oppose him on policy or ideological grounds. Emphasis on local, nonpartisan factors in congressional voting enables the modern congressman to withstand national swings, whereas yesteryear's uninsulated congressmen were more dependent on preventing the occurrence of the swings.

Actually, the insulation of the modern congressman from national forces is even more complete than the preceding discussion suggests. Not only are few representatives so vulnerable that a reaction to a presidential candidate or his performance would turn them out of office, but such reactions themselves are less likely to find a reflection in the congressional voting. Several years ago Professor Edward Tufte formulated an elegant statistical model that predicts the magnitude of the in-party's losses in midterm elections as a function of two variables, the popularity of the incumbent president and the state of the national economy as measured by changes in real income.[17] For most of the post-World War II period the model predicts quite accurately. But in recent years the predictions have begun to go awry; specifically, in 1974 and 1978 the model significantly overpredicts the losses of the in-party.[18] The reason is quite apparent. As congressmen increasingly build personal organizations (largely with taxpayer-provided offices, staff, and communications resources) and base their campaigns on local issues and their personal record of service to the district, national conditions and the performance of the party leader have less and less of an impact on House races. In fact, analysis of the 1978 Center for Political Studies Congressional Election Study reveals that evaluations of President Carter's performance had no effect on the electoral fortunes of Democratic incumbents, and citizen evaluations of government's handling of the national economy had only the barest trace of an impact.[19]

The effects of the insulation of congressional incumbents have begun to show up in a systematic way in the governmental arena. Table 27 presents data on presidential success and presidential support in Congress for the first two years of the administrations of our last five elected presidents. As is evident, Carter ('77–78) was less successful than earlier presidents who enjoyed a Congress controlled by their own party; he was only as successful as Nixon, who faced an opposition Congress. Moreover, in the House, Carter has done relatively poorly in gaining the support of his own party. It is noteworthy that John F. Kennedy ('61–62) earned a significantly higher level of support from a congressional party that was nearly half Southern, whereas Carter enjoyed a majority in which the regional split was much less severe.[20]

Of course, it is possible to discount the preceding argument as an unjustified generalization of a unique situation—a particularly inept president, a Congress full of prima donnas still flexing their post-Watergate* muscles, and so on. But I

**Watergate*: hotel/office/apartment complex in Washington, D.C., in which the Democratic party housed its national headquarters during the 1972 presidential campaign. Acting under orders from senior aides in Republican President Richard Nixon's administration, burglars broke into the headquarters to obtain information about the Democratic campaign. Seven of Nixon's former aides were found guilty of conspiracy and participating in a cover-up and were sentenced to terms in prison. On August 8, 1974, Nixon resigned under the pressure of impending impeachment for his role in the affair. Immediately afterward Nixon was pardoned by his successor, Gerald Ford, for any crimes he may have committed even though Nixon had not been convicted of anything.

TABLE 27. RECENT TRENDS IN CONGRESSIONAL SUPPORT OF THE EXECUTIVE (IN PERCENTAGES)

			PRESIDENTIAL SUPPORT WITHIN HIS PARTY	
Congress	*Year*	*Presidential Success*	*House*	*Senate*
83rd	'53–54	83	72	72
87th	'61–62	83	73	64
89th	'65–66	87	69	61
91st	'69–70	76	62	63
95th	'77–78	77	61	67

Source: *Congressional Quarterly Almanacs.*

think not. The withering away of the party organizations and the weakening of party in the electorate have begun to show up as disarray in the party in government. As the electoral fates of congressmen and the president have diverged, their incentives to cooperate have diverged as well. Congressmen have little personal incentive to bear any risk in their president's behalf, since they no longer expect to gain much from his successes or suffer much from his failures. Only those who personally agree with the president's program and/or those who find that program well suited for their particular district support the president. And there are not enough of these to construct the coalitions necessary for action on the major issues now facing the country. By holding only the president responsible for national conditions, the electorate enables officialdom as a whole to escape responsibility. This situation lies at the root of many of the problems that now plague American public life.

SOME CONSEQUENCES OF THE DECLINE OF COLLECTIVE RESPONSIBILITY

The weakening of party has contributed directly to the severity of several of the important problems the nation faces. For some of these, such as the government's inability to deal with inflation and energy, the connections are obvious. But for other problems, such as the growing importance of single-issue politics and the growing alienation of the American citizenry, the connections are more subtle.

Immobilism

As the electoral interdependence of the party in government declines, its ability to act also declines. If responsibility can be shifted to another level or to another officeholder, there is less incentive to stick one's neck out in an attempt to solve a given problem. Leadership becomes more difficult, the ever-present bias toward the short-term solution becomes more pronounced, and the possibility of solving any given problem lessens.

Consider the two critical problems facing the country today, energy and inflation. Major energy problems were forecast years ago, the 1973 embargo underlined the dangers, and yet what passes for our national energy policy is still only a weak set of jerry-built compromises achieved at the expense of years of political infighting. The related inflation problem has festered for more than a decade, and our current president is on his fourth anti-inflation plan, a set of proposals widely regarded as yet another instance of two little, too late. The failures of policy-making in these areas are easy to identify and explain. A potential problem is identified, and actions that might head it off are proposed "for discussion." But the problem lies in the future, while the solutions impose costs in the present. So politicians dismiss the solutions as unfeasible and act as though the problem will go away. When it doesn't, popular concern increases. The president, in particular, feels compelled to act—he will be held responsible, both at election time and in the judgment of history. But congressmen expect to bear much less responsibility; moreover, the representatives face an election in less than two years, whereas the president can wait at least four (longer for the lame duck) for the results of his policy to become evident. Congressmen, logically enough, rebel. They denounce every proposed initiative as unfair, which simply means that it imposes costs on their constituents, whereas they prefer the costs to fall on everyone else's constituents. At first, no policy will be adopted; later, as pressure builds, Congress adopts a weak and ineffectual policy for symbolic purposes. Then, as the problem continues to worsen, congressmen join with the press and the public and attack the president for failures of leadership.

The preceding scenario is simplified, to be sure, but largely accurate, and in my opinion, rather disgusting. What makes it possible is the electoral fragmentation produced by the decline of party. Members of Congress are aware that national problems arising from inaction will have little political impact on them, and that the president's failures in dealing with those problems will have similarly little impact. Responsibility for inflation and energy problems? Don't look at congressmen.

In 1958 the Fourth Republic of France collapsed after years of immobilism. The features of congressional policy-making just discussed were carried to their logical extremes in that Parliamentary regime. According to contemporary observers, the basic principle of the French Deputy was to avoid responsibility.[21] To achieve that goal the deputies followed subsidiary rules, the most important of which was delay. Action would take place only when crisis removed any possible alternative to action (and most of the alternative actions as well). A slogan of the time was "Those who crawl do not fall."

No one seriously believes that the American constitutional order is in danger of collapse (and certainly we have no de Gaulle waiting in the wings). But political inability to take actions that entail short-run costs ordinarily will result in much higher costs in the long run—we cannot continually depend on the technological fix. So the present American immobilism cannot be dismissed lightly. The sad thing is that the American people appear to understand the depth of our present problems and, at least in principle, appear prepared to sacrifice in furtherance of the long-run good. But they will not have an opportunity to choose between two or more such long-term plans. Although both parties promise tough, equitable policies, in the present state of our politics, neither can deliver.

Single-Issue Politics

In recent years both political analysts and politicians have decried the increased importance of single-issue groups in American politics. Some in fact would claim that the present immobilism in our politics owes more to the rise of single-issue groups than to the decline of party. A little thought, however, should reveal that the two trends are connected. Is single-issue politics a recent phenomenon? The contention is doubtful; such groups have always been active participants in American politics. The gun lobby already was a classic example at the time of President Kennedy's assassination. And however impressive the antiabortionists appear today, remember the temperance movement, which succeeded in getting its constitutional amendment. American history contains numerous forerunners of today's groups, from anti-Masons to abolitionists to the Klan—singularity of purpose is by no means a modern phenomenon. Why, then, do we hear all the contemporary hoopla about single-issue groups? Probably because politicians fear them now more than before and thus allow them to play a larger role in our politics. Why should this be so? Simply because the parties are too weak to protect their members and thus to contain single-issue politics.

In earlier times single-issue groups were under greater pressures to reach accommodations with the parties. After all, the parties nominated candidates, financed candidates, worked for candidates, and, perhaps most important, party voting protected candidates. When a contemporary single-issue group threatens to "get" an officeholder, the threat must be taken seriously. The group can go into his district, recruit a primary or general election challenger, or both, and bankroll that candidate. Even if the sentiment espoused by the group is not the majority sentiment of the district, few officeholders relish the thought of a strong, well-financed opponent. Things were different when strong parties existed. Party leaders controlled the nomination process and would fight to maintain that control. An outside challenge would merely serve to galvanize the party into action to protect its prerogatives. Only if a single-issue group represented the dominant sentiment in a given area could it count on controlling the party organization itself, and therby electoral politics in that area.

Not only did the party organization have greater ability to resist single-issue pressures at the electoral level, but the party in government had greater ability to control the agenda, and thereby contain single-issue pressures at the policy-making level. Today we seem condemned to go through an annual agony over federal abortion funding. There is little doubt that politicians on both sides would prefer to reach some reasonable compromise at the committee level and settle the issue. But in today's decentralized Congress there is no way to put the lid on. In contrast, historians tell us that in the late nineteenth century a large portion of the Republican constituency was far less interested in the tariff and other questions of national economic development than in whether German immigrants should be permitted to teach their native language in their local schools, and whether Catholics and "liturgical Protestants" should be permitted to consume alcohol.[22] Interestingly, however, the national agenda of the period is devoid of such issues. And when they do show up on the state level, the exceptions prove the rule; they produce party splits and striking defeats for the party that allowed them to surface.[23]

One can cite more recent examples as well. Prior to 1970 popular commentators frequently criticized the autocratic antimajoritarian behavior of congressional committee chairmen in general, and of the entire Rules Committee in particular. It is certainly true that the seniority leadership killed many bills the rank and file might have passed if left to their own devices. But congressional scholars were always aware as well that the seniority leadership buried many bills that the rank and file wanted buried but lacked the political courage to bury themselves. In 1961, for example, the House Rules Committee was roundly condemned for killing a major federal aid to education bill over the question of extension of that aid to parochial schools. Contemporary accounts, however, suggest that congressmen regarded the action of the Rules Committee as a public service.[24] Of course, control of the agenda is a double-edged sword (a point we return to below), but today commentators on single-issue groups clearly are concerned with too little control rather than too much.

In sum, a strong party that is held accountable for the government of a nation-state has both the ability and the incentive to contain particularistic pressures. It controls nominations, elections, and the agenda, and it collectively realizes that small minorities are small minorities no matter how intense they are. But as the parties decline they lose control over nominations and campaigns, they lose the loyalty of the voters, and they lose control of the agenda. Party officeholders cease to be held collectively accountable for party performance, but they become individually exposed to the political pressure of myriad interest groups. The decline of party permits interest groups to wield greater influence, their success encourages the formation of still more interest groups, politics becomes increasingly fragmented, and collective responsibility becomes still more elusive.

Popular Alienation from Government

For at least a decade political analysts have pondered the significance of survey data indicative of a steady increase in the alienation of the American public from the political process. Table 28 presents some representative data: two-thirds of the American public feel the government is run for the benefit of big interests rather than for the people as a whole, three-quarters believe that government officials waste a lot of tax money and half flatly agree with the statement that government officials are basically incompetent. The American public is in a nasty mood, a cynical, distrusting, and resentful mood. The question is, Why?

Specific events and personalities clearly have some effect: we see pronounced "Watergate effects" between 1972 and 1976. But the trends clearly began much

TABLE 28. RECENT TRENDS IN POLITICAL ALIENATION AND DISTRUST (IN PERCENTAGES)

	Government Run for Few Big Interests	*Government Officials Waste "A Lot"*	*Government Officials Don't Know What They're Doing*
1964	29	46	27
1968	39	57	36
1972	45	56	34
1976	66	74	49
1978	68	77	50

Source: National Election Studies made available by The InterUniversity Consortium for Political and Social Research, University of Michigan.

earlier. Indeed, the first political science studies analyzing the trends were based on data no later than 1972.[25] At the other extreme it also appears that the American data are only the strongest manifestation of a pattern evident in many democracies, perhaps for reasons common to all countries in the present era, perhaps not. I do think it probable however, that the trends thus far discussed bear some relation to the popular mood in the United States.

If the same national problems not only persist but worsen while ever-greater amounts of revenue are directed at them, why shouldn't the typical citizen conclude that most of the money must be wasted by incompetent officials? If narrowly based interest groups increasingly affect our politics, why shouldn't citizens increasingly conclude that the interests run the government? For fifteen years the citizenry has listened to a steady stream of promises but has seen very little in the way of follow-through. An increasing proportion of the electorate does not believe that elections make a difference, a fact that largely explains the much-discussed post-1960 decline in voting turnout.[26]

Continued public disillusionment with the political process poses several real dangers. For one thing, disillusionment begets further disillusionment. Leadership becomes more difficult if citizens do not trust their leaders and will not give them the benefit of a doubt. Policy failure becomes more likely if citizens expect the policy to fail. Waste increases and government competence decreases as citizen disrespect for politics encourages a lesser breed of person to make careers in government. And "goverment by a few big interests" becomes more than a cliché if citizens increasingly decide the cliché is true and cease participating for that reason.

Finally, there is the real danger that continued disappointment with particular government officials ultimately metamorphoses into disillusionment with government per se. Increasing numbers of citizens believe that government is not simply overextended but perhaps incapable of any further bettering of the world. Yes, government is overextended, inefficiency is pervasive, and ineffectiveness is all too common. But government is one of the few instruments of collective action we have, and even those committed to selective pruning of government programs cannot blithely allow the concept of an activist government to fall into disrepute.

The concept of democracy does not submit to precise definition, a claim supported by the existence of numerous nonidentical definitions. To most people democracy embodies a number of valued qualities. Unfortunately, there is no reason to believe that all such valued qualities are mutually compatible. At the least, maximizing the attainment of one quality may require accepting middling levels of another.

Recent American political thought has emphasized government *of* the people and *by* the people. Attempts have been made to [ensure] that all preferences receive a hearing, especially through direct expression of those preferences, but if not, at least through faithful representation. Citizen *participation* is the reigning value, and arrangements that foster widespread participation are much in favor.

Of late, however, some political commentators have begun to wonder whether contemporary thought places sufficient emphasis on government *for* the people. In stressing participation have we lost sight of *accountability*? Surely, we should be as concerned with what government produces as with how many participate. What good is participation if the citizenry is unable to determine who merits their support?[27]

Participation and responsibility are not logically incompatible, but there is a degree of tension between the two, and the quest for either may be carried to extremes. Participation maximizers find themselves involved with quotas and virtual representation schemes, while responsibility maximizers can find themselves with a closed shop under boss rule.[28] Moreover, both qualities can weaken the democracy they supposedly underpin. Unfettered participation produces Hyde Amendments and immobilism. Responsible parties can use agenda power to thwart democratic decision—for more than a century the Democratic party used what control it had to suppress the racial issue. Neither participation nor responsibility should be pursued at the expense of all other values, but that is what has happened with participation over the course of the past two decades, and we now reap the consequences in our politics.

In 1970 journalist David Broder wrote:

> what we have is a society in which discontent, disbelief, cynicism and political inertia characterize the public mood; a country whose economy suffers from severe dislocations, whose currency is endangered, where unemployment and inflation coexist, where increasing numbers of people and even giant enterprises live on the public dole; a country whose two races continue to withdraw from each other in growing physical and social isolation; a country whose major public institutions command steadily less allegiance from its citizens; whose education, transportation, law enforcement, health and sanitation systems fall far short of filling their functions; a country whose largest city is close to being ungovernable and uninhabitable; and a country still far from reconciling its international responsibilities with its unmet domestic needs.

We are in trouble.[29]

Broder is not a Cassandra, and he was writing before FECA* before the OPEC† embargo, before Watergate, and before Jimmy Carter. If he was correct that we were in trouble then, what about now?

The depressing thing is that no rays of light shine through the dark clouds. The trends that underlie the decline of parties continue unabated, and the kinds of structural reforms that might override those trends are too sweeping and/or outlandish to stand any chance of adoption.[30] Through a complex mixture of accident and intention we have constructed for ourselves a system that articulates interests superbly but aggregates them poorly. We hold our politicians individually accountable for the proposals they advocate, but less so for the adoption of those proposals, and not at all for overseeing the implementation of those proposals and the evaluation of their results. In contemporary America officials do not govern, they merely posture.

NOTES

My thinking on the matters discussed in this essay has benefitted from the critical commentary of Lawrence Joseph and Robert Salisbury.

[1]This may sound cynical, but it is a standard assumption in American democratic theory. Certainly the Founders believed that the government should not depend on the nobility of heart of officialdom in order to operate properly.

[2]This argument was expounded at the turn of the century by writers such as Woodrow Wilson and A. Lawrence Lowell. It enjoyed a resurgence at mid-century in the thinking of scholars such as E. E. Schattschneider. For a thorough exegesis of the party responsibility argument, see Austin Ranney, *The Doctrine of Responsible Party Government* (Urbana: University of Illinois Press, 1962).

[3]During the postwar period the national government has experienced divided party control about half the time. In the preceding half century there were only six years of divided control.

[4]At this point skeptics invariably ask, "What about Warren G. Harding?" The statement in the text is meant to express a tendency. Certainly, in the first sixty years of this century we did not see a string of candidates comparable to the products of the amateur politics of the past fourteen years (Goldwater, McGovern, Carter, Reagan).

[5]See Gerald Pomper, "The Decline of the Party in American Elections," *Political Science Quarterly*, 92 (1977): 21–41; John Kessel, *Presidential Campaign Politics: Coalition Strategies and Citizen Responses* (Homewood, Illinois: Dorsey, 1980), ch. 10; Austin Ranney, "The Political Parties: Reform and Decline," in Anthony King (ed.), *The New American Political System* (Washington, D.C.: American Enterprise Institute, 1978), pp. 213–47. Both Kessel and Pomper have discussed the increased importance of the national party organizations in terms of maintenance of continuing operations, imposition of national rules and standards on the local parties, and so on. I believe with

*FECA: see footnote on page 161.

†*Organization of Petroleum Exporting Countries*, or OPEC: association founded in 1960 by Iran, Iraq, Kuwait, Saudi Arabia, and Venezuela in response to oil price cuts by American and European companies. Qatar, Indonesia, Libya, Abu Dhabi, Algeria, Nigeria, Ecuador, and Gabon subsequently joined OPEC to protect their oil interests. Though its initial purpose was only to support the world price of crude oil, OPEC managed to assert cartel power in the early 1970s by imposing dramatic price increases that strained the international economy. During the 1980s the cartel collapsed in the face of a world oil glut.

Ranney, however, that, considering all levels of the party together, there has been a decline in organizational strength even as the national party apparatuses have grown more influential.

[6]Though federal employment increased considerably during the New Deal era, the proportion covered by civil service declined. Thus the erosion of the patronage system was temporarily halted. In addition, scholars have documented the political basis of New Deal spending and program decisions. See Gavin Wright, "The Political Economy of New Deal Spending: An Econometric Analysis," *Review of Economics and Statistics*, 56 (1974): 30–38.

[7]Jeanne Kirkpatrick, *The New Presidential Elite* (New York: Russell Sage Foundation and Twentieth Century Fund, 1976).

[8]Ranney, "The Political Parties," p. 233.

[9]Michael Malbin (ed.), *Parties, Interest Groups, and Campaign Finance Laws* (Washington, D.C.: American Enterprise Institute, 1980), pt. 3.

[10]Angus Campbell, et al., *The American Voter* (New York: Wiley, 1960), chs. 6, 7.

[11]See Morris Fiorina, *Retrospective Voting in American National Elections* (New Haven: Yale University Press, forthcoming), ch. 5.

[12]For a discussion, see Walter Dean Burnham, *Critical Elections and the Mainsprings of American Politics* (New York: Norton, 1970).

[13]Ibid., p. 95.

[14]These diagrams are representative of the pre-1950 and post-1970 periods. To see how the earlier world gradually changed to the later, examine the series of diagrams in David Mayhew, "Congressional Elections: The Case of the Vanishing Marginals," *Polity*, 6 (1974): 295–317.

[15]See Morris Fiornia, *Congress—Keystone of the Washington Establishment* (New Haven: Yale University Press, 1977).

[16]Thomas Mann, *Unsafe at Any Margin* (Washington, D.C.: American Enterprise Institute, 1978).

[17]Edward Tufte, "Determinants of the Outcomes of Midterm Congressional Elections," *American Political Science Review*, 69 (1975): 812–26.

[18]Gary Jacobson and Samuel Kernell, *The Structure of Choice*, forthcoming, ch. 5.

[19]Fiorina, *Retrospective Voting*, ch. 10.

[20]This compositional change in the Democratic party has a lot to do with the recent increase in party cohesion in Congress, which some might regard as evidence inconsistent with the argument in the text. Kennedy faced a congressional party that was almost half Southern; Carter faces one only about a quarter Southern. *Ceteris paribus*, this fact should have produced significantly higher levels of party cohesion and presidential support. But party cohesion has only marginally increased, and, as shown in the text, party support for its nominal leader has declined. I suspect that the increase in party cohesion also stems partly from the explosion in roll-call votes. Under the electronic voting system it is now common to record votes on relatively minor legislation. If the Republicans perfunctorily object on a proportion of these, party votes would result, and the overall party cohesion figures would be inflated by such relatively unimportant votes.

[21]Nathan Leites, *On the Game of Politics in France* (Stanford: Stanford University Press, 1959).

[22]Paul Kleppner, *The Cross of Culture: A Social Analysis of Midwestern Politics, 1850–1900* (New York: Free Press, 1970), ch. 2.

[23]Ibid., chs. 3, 4.

[24]James Sundquist, *Politics and Policy* (Washington, D.C.: Brookings Institution, 1968).

[25]Arthur Miller, "Political Issues and Trust in Government: 1964–1970," *American Political Science Review*, 68 (1974): 951–72; Jack Citrin, "The Political Relevance of Trust in Government," *American Political Science Review*, 68 (1974): 973–88.

[26]John Ferejohn and Morris Fiorina, "The Decline in Turnout in Presidential Elections," paper presented at the Conference on Voter Turnout, San Diego, 1979.

[27]There is, of course, a school of thought, dating back at least to John Stuart Mill, that holds that participation is a good in itself. While I am prepared to conceded that self-expression is nice, I strongly object to making it the *raison d'être* of democratic politics.

[28]S. E. Finer, *The Changing British Party System, 1945–1979* (Washington, D.C.: American Enterprise Institute, 1980).

[29]*The Party's Over* (New York: Harper & Row, 1972), p. xxv.

[30]For example, party cohesion would no doubt be strengthened by revising existing statutes to prevent split-ticket voting and to permit campaign contributions only to parties. At the constitutional level, giving the president the power of dissolution and replacing the single-member district system with proportional representation would probably unify the party in government much more than at present. Obviously, changes such as these are not only highly improbable but also exceedingly risky, since we cannot accurately predict the unintended consequences that surely would accompany them.

10

JAMES L. SUNDQUIST

STRENGTHENING THE NATIONAL PARTIES

The prospects of adopting a "responsible party model" in American government are slim, according to James L. Sundquist. The separation of powers was designed, in large part, to prevent the dominance of political factions at the national level. Though political parties became important forces in national politics in the early 1800s, the separation of powers and independent election of the president remain serious impediments to the parties' ability to discipline their members in Congress. Sundquist discusses proposals for strengthening the parties, the obstacles to their implementation, and recent party reforms. Sundquist, a senior fellow emeritus at the Brookings Institution, is the author of Politics and Policy *(1968),* Making Federalism Work *(1969) with David W. Davis,* Dynamics of the Party System *(1973, 1983),* Dispersing Population: What Americans Can Learn from Europe *(1975),* The Decline and Resurgence of Congress *(1981), and* Constitutional Reform and Effective Government *(1986).*

Political parties have always occupied an ambiguous position in American public life. They are profoundly mistrusted—yet accepted. Their constant maneuvering for petty advantage is reviled and ridiculed, but millions of people call themselves either Democrats or Republicans and cherish the ideals of their party with a religious fervor. Parties have been credited with such supreme achievements as saving the Union and rescuing the country from the Great Depression.* But they have also been accused of placing partisan advantage ahead of the national good, of failing to conceive farsighted programs, of running away from problems and responsibilities, and sometimes of deep and pervasive corruption.

It was the last of these that led, during the Progressive era,† to a passionate reformist crusade to destroy the strength and influence of the party organizations that, at the end of the nineteenth century, had reached their zenith of power and plunder. Throughout this century the Progressive reforms have been serving that purpose, until by now the objective has been largely accomplished. Governmental administration has been cleansed of the grosser forms of corruption—in most places, anyway—but in the process the party organizations have been shorn of much of the patronage that had given them their armies of loyal workers. The direct primary gradually reduced, and by today has virtually eliminated, the organizations' control of, or even influence on, nominations for office, including the presidency itself. By law some states prohibit party organizations from making

**Great Depression*: see footnote on page 112.

†*Progressive era*: see footnote on page 19.

endorsements in primaries or from participating at all in nonpartisan general elections for mayors and city council members. With their organizations thus stripped of both nominating functions and active workers, political parties have in most places lost the motivation and the competence to organize, finance, and manage general election campaigns as well, and these responsibilities in contests for major offices have gravitated to a new and growing professional elite of private campaign management and consulting firms.

But as the traditional political party organizations die—whether victims of reformist zeal or of simple obsolescence—what becomes of the functions that political parties have performed well, at least at times, and that only the parties can perform? Are there, indeed, such functions? A new school of reformers is now answering that question emphatically in the affirmative, "Our political party system," proclaims the Committee for Party Renewal (CPR), ". . . is in serious danger of destruction. Without parties there can be no organized and coherent politics. When politics lacks coherence, there can be no accountable democracy. Parties are indispensable to the realization of democracy. The stakes are no less than that."[1] And the Committee on the Constitutional System (CCS), in its 1987 report, declares that "the weakening of parties in the electoral arena has contributed to the disintegration of party cohesion among the officials we elect to public office," and that "the decline of party loyalty and cohesion at all levels of the political system" is a principal cause of "the failures and weaknesses in governmental performance."[2]

Anyone who would renew or remold an institution must have a model. The ambiguity in the popular attitude toward political parties and the confusion as to the role they should play arise from a conflict between two models of the American governmental system that has been left unsettled throughout the whole two centuries of national life. The first model was embodied in the Constitution, with James Madison* its principal designer. It contemplated a national government without national political parties. But when the founding generation assumed responsibility for operating the new government, it discarded that model almost at once and embraced an alternative conception in which national parties occupied a central place. The nation's political leaders have ever since used parties as the means for gaining control of government and then for mobilizing the resources of the legislative and executive branches to enact and carry out programs. Yet the notion that organized parties, rather than unaffiliated and disconnected individuals, should take responsibility for the affairs of government—and be held accountable by the voters—has never been fully embraced in the country at large, and the Constitution has not been altered to accommodate it. Elements of both models are therefore reflected in America's institutional structures, political practices, and fundamental beliefs. And over the decades, the struggle to reconcile the models and achieve a workable blending of the two has come up against the hard fact that, in essential respects, the models are irreconcilable.

**James Madison:* see headnote on page 29.

THE MADISONIAN MODEL: A SYSTEM WITHOUT PARTIES

The Constitution that emerged from the Convention of 1787* made no place for parties. At that time, only the faint forerunners of modern political parties had appeared anywhere in the world. Factions had taken shape within legislative bodies in both the American states and in England, but they were not formally organized, and political organizations formed by citizens of the new states for purposes of particular elections were still local and rudimentary. Insofar as the Constitution's framers at Philadelphia referred to these groupings at all, they condemned them. They were usually termed factions or cabals rather than parties, and they were denounced as responsible for the "corruption" and "intrigue" of legislative bodies.

Accordingly, in designing the institutions of the new government, the men of 1787 deliberately sought to erect barriers against the development and influence of parties. Indeed, the basic tripartite structure of the government, as well as the division of the legislative branch into two houses, can be seen as having that essential purpose. The framers scattered power in order to forestall the evils of concentration in any individual or group, that is, in any one faction or party. They feared that a transient popular majority might be able to seize the House of Representatives and try to impose its will on the country, but they designed the Senate as a body of elder statesmen with long, overlapping terms who would rise above factionalism, and conceived the presidency, possessed of a veto in the legislative process, as the very embodiment of the nonpartisan ideal.

It was to ensure that kind of presidency that the framers, after extensive debate over the merits of the two obvious means of selecting a president—first, by the legislature, or second, by the people through direct election—ultimately rejected both. Either, they concluded, would encourage factionalism. "If the Legislature elect, it will be the work of intrigue, of cabal, and of faction," contended Gouverneur Morris of Pennsylvania at the midpoint of the Convention; ". . . real merit will rarely be the title to the appointment."[3] But others feared that factionalism and intrigue could come to dominate a direct national election. "The people are uninformed,"argued Elbridge Gerry of Massachusetts. Their "ignorance . . . would put it in the power of some one set of men dispersed through the Union and acting in Concert to delude them into any appointment."[4] To render the presidential election free of factions, the framers invented their alternative, the electoral college. The electors chosen in each state would be public-spirited and eminent citizens who would have no other duty, and officeholders would be ineligible to serve. They would not meet as a body but would cast their votes separately, in their own states. "As the electors would be chosen for the occasion, would meet at once, and proceed immediately to an appointment, there would be very little opportunity for cabal, or corruption," reasoned Madison.[5] The electoral college, then, would function as a more elaborate version of a civic club's nominating committee

Convention of 1787: meeting held in Philadelphia from May 25 to September 19. Although their original purpose was to revise the Articles of Confederation, after lengthy debates the 55 state delegates managed to design an entirely new constitution that they then took to their states for popular ratification. (See headnote on page 29.)

or an institution's search committee. Merit, achievement, and competence alone would be the touchstones. Parties or cabals would be excluded.

In *Federalist* number 10, Madison advanced as one of the Constitution's central merits that it would tend "to break and control the violence of faction," which he equated with party. No more powerful diatribe against the evils of parties has been penned in the United States or perhaps in any country than his famous essay. In it he denounces "the violence of faction" as "this dangerous vice" that introduces "the instability, injustice, and confusion" that have "been the mortal diseases under which popular governments have everywhere perished." In the new American states, public measures were "too often decided, not according to the rules of justice, and the rights of the minor party, but by the superior force of an interested and overbearing majority." All this was due "chiefly, if not wholly" to "the unsteadiness and injustice, with which a factious spirit has tainted our public administrations."

Creating the new union would help in "curing the mischiefs of faction" by raising decisions to the national level. There they would be more likely to be in the hands of representatives "whose enlightened views and virtuous sentiments render them superior to local prejudices and to schemes of injustice." A "greater variety of parties" would lessen the chance that any one party could "outnumber and oppress the rest." "Factious leaders" in individual states could not "spread a general conflagration through the other states." In later papers, particularly numberes 47, 48, and 62, Madison extols the separation of powers as the means to forestall the "tyranny" and "sinister combinations" that would follow if all elements of the government were to be controlled by any one individual or political faction.[6]

THE RESPONSIBLE-PARTY MODEL

The opposing model for organizing a government recognizes not only the inevitability but the necessity of parties and assigns them the role that they everywhere seek and come naturally to assume. This is the model that has been adopted in various forms by most of the other advanced democracies of the world, and it is the one that inspires the recommendations of such contemporary American reformist groups as the CPR and the CCS.

In this model, political parties are formed because groups of people, each sharing a philosophy and a set of goals, desire governmental power in order to carry out their programs. In competition with one another, they present their programs to the people in an open and free election. The party or coalition that wins the support of a majority of the people gains control of the government and enacts its programs. The minority party or parties form an opposition, with power to criticize, debate, and delay but not to block. After a few years the voters in another election render a verdict on the majority's stewardship. If they approve what has been done, they return the ruling party or coalition to office. If they disapprove, they turn the incumbents out and entrust power to an opposition party or combination of parties. At all times, one of the parties, or a combination, is responsible for the government, possesses authority commensurate with its responsibility (subject to check by the judiciary if it exceeds its constitutional powers), and is fully accountable for whatever the government (except for the judiciary) does. In the metaphors of political science textbook writers, the political party is the tie that binds, the glue that fastens, the bridge or the web that unites the disparate institutions that make up the government. Without parties, democracy on a national scale simply could not work.

Yet one can readily perceive why Madison and his colleagues saw such a model as dangerous. If a majority party can win the whole of governmental power, what is to prevent it from oppressing the minority? As Madison saw it in *Federalist* number 10, the natural party division would be between "those who hold, and those who are without property," between "those who are creditors, and those who are debtors." He feared that a majority party made up of the propertyless would exhibit "a rage for paper money, for an abolition of debts, for an equal division of property." He put his faith in the geographical scale of the country and in the division of powers among the branches of government. Others, however, demanded more ironclad guarantees against the tyranny of the majority, and those guarantees emerged from the First Congress, under Madison's own leadership, as the Constitution's Bill of Rights.

In the European countries, as monarchs either surrendered their power or were deposed, institutions evolved according to the responsible-party model. The executive authority was assumed by the legislative body in the fusion of power known as the parliamentary system. The larger, always popularly elected, legislative house achieved a dominant position. If a party won a majority of that house, it attained a virtual monopoly of governmental power—limited only by such restraints as might be embodied in a written constitution, and by whatever residual powers that were assigned to a smaller, and often indirectly elected, second chamber. Most continental European countries also adopted proportional representation, which fostered a multiplicity of parties and hence reduced the likelihood that any one party might obtain undivided control of the government. Yet, with these modifications the responsible-party model has prevailed throughout the democratic world save in America.[7]

Few would argue, surely, that the experience of Europe has borne out Madison's dread of party government. Tyrannies have appeared only when the forms of parliamentary government were abandoned or destroyed, not when they were sustained. The propertyless have used their majorities at times to redistribute to some degree the wealth of the properties by raising taxes for welfare programs. Whether the redistribution has been carried beyond the bounds of sound macroeconomic policy in some countries will always be debated, but the electorate can, and often does, reverse unwise policies by transferring power to the opposition party. In any case, no country has ever approached the "equal division" or "leveling" that arose so often as the specter haunting the 1787 Convention. Tradition, a sense of justice, and no doubt above all the compelling desire to sustain public confidence and democratic political support have been sufficient to restrain all-powerful majority parties from trampling on the rights of the propertied or wrecking market economies.

THE CLASH OF MODELS IN AMERICA

George Washington, who presided over both the Convention and the new government in its earliest years, tried to lead in the nonpartisan manner that the Constitution contemplated, only to observe the rise of factionalism not only in the Congress but also within his own cabinet. His dismay is expressed in the celebrated passage from his farewell address in which—echoing *Federalist* number 10—he warned his countrymen "in the most solemn manner against the baneful effects of the spirit of party generally." In popular governments that spirit serves to "distract the public councils" and "enfeeble the public administration." It "agitates the community with ill founded jealousies and false alarms . . . foments occasionally riot and insurrection . . . opens the door to foreign influence and corruption." Nearly two centuries later, ironically enough, deeply partisan senators and congressmen still gravely arise in an annual ritual on the observance of Washington's birthday to read that address, with its denunciations, to their colleagues, who have all been elected on party tickets, have organized their respective chambers through party caucuses and party-line votes, and have entrusted the conduct of legislative business to party organizations and leaders.

Within four years of the first president's retirement a two-party system, reflecting to a degree the propertied-landless and creditor-debtor cleavage that Madison had identified as fundamental, was in full operation, with two slates of candidates running nationally. The electoral college, conceived as a body of nonpartisan statesmen with complete discretion and independent judgment, was hardly formed when it was reduced to what it has since remained: a group of individuals performing a purely ministerial role, each casting his vote for a presidential and vice-presidential candidate nominated earlier by a national party. "The election of a President of the United States is no longer that process which the Constitution contemplated," one of the framers, Rufus King of New York, remarked in an 1816 Senate debate.[8] Parties, James Madison acknowledged in his retirement years, are "a natural offspring of Freedom."[9] By that time, of course, Madison had been elected and reelected president as a party nominee.

In organizing their parties the nation's political leaders then as now accepted the responsible-party concept. The parties have always asked for full control of both the legislative and executive branches. Since early in the nineteenth century they have presented their programs formally, in official party platforms. Asking for total control over the two elected branches, they have been eager to accept the total responsibility and accountability that would accompany it.

And the American people have seemed to accept the responsible-party model too. For the first century and a half under the Constitution, when the voters chose a president each four years they normally entrusted control of Congress to the same party, thus making it fully responsible. From the time the two-party system settled into place in Andrew Jackson's time until the second election of Dwight Eisenhower, only two presidents—Zachary Taylor, elected in 1848, and Rutherford B. Hayes, in 1876—had to contront immediately upon inauguration a House of Representatives organized by the opposition. Even the Senate, despite filling only one-third of its seats in any presidential election, had a majority of the opposition's party after only two quadrennial elections—those of 1848 and 1884.[10] In the nineteenth century these results might be discounted as largely an artifact of the election process itself. The parties printed separate ballots listing their slates, and the voter selected the ballot of the party he preferred and dropped it in the box. Yet after the government-printed secret ballot came into universal use early in this century, straight-ticket voting and the resultant single-party control of the government continued to prevail. A majority of the people clearly wanted the Republican party to be responsible for the entire government in the 1900s and the 1920s and the Democratic party in the 1930s and most of the 1940s. No president in the first half of this century had to confront upon inauguration a Congress of which either house was controlled by the opposing party, and few had the problem even after the normal setback to the president's party in the midterm election.

Meanwhile, the nation's leading students of government had rallied behind the idea of responsible parties. In 1950 the classic appeal for strengthening national parties as central instruments of government was issued by the sixteen-member Committee on Political Parties of the American Political Science Association under the title *Toward a More Responsible Two-Party System.*[11] To make a responsible-party system work as it should, said the committee, the parties needed stronger central institutional mechanisms—specifically, authoritative governing councils. Prefacing its recommendations for institutional change were some impassioned passages, the rhetoric that resonates today in the writings of the CPR and the CCS in defense of party government:

> Throughout this report political parties are treated as indispensable instruments of government. That is to say, we proceed on the proposition that *popular government in a nation of more than 150 million people requires political parties which provide the electorate with a proper range of choice between alternatives of action* (p. 15).
>
> In an era beset with problems of unprecedented magnitude at home and abroad, it is dangerous to drift without a party system that helps the nation to set a general course of policy for the government as a whole. . . . When the parties are unable to reach and pursue responsible decisions, difficulties accumulate and cynicism about all democratic institutions grows (p. 17).
>
> Historical and other factors have caused the American two-party system to operate as two loose associations of state and local governments, with very little national machinery and very little national cohesion. As a result, either major party, when in power, is ill-equipped to organize its members in the legislative and executive branches into a government held together and guided by the party program. Party responsibility at the polls thus tends to vanish. This . . . poses grave problems of domestic and foreign policy in an era when it is no longer safe for the nation to deal piecemeal with issues that can be disposed of only on the basis of coherent programs (p. v).
>
> An effective party system requires, first, that the parties are able to bring forth programs to which they commit themselves and, second, that the parties possess sufficient internal cohesion to carry out these programs (p. 1).

A generation later the reader is struck by how casually the committee took for granted that both the legislative and executive branches would be controlled by a single party. One of the major parties would be "in power," and if it possessed "sufficient internal cohesion" it could "organize its members" in the two branches to carry out the party program. In the lifetimes of the committee members, that had always been the case. But within a few years the U.S. government would pass through a momentous transition: from one of single-party government nearly all the time to one of divided government most of the time. In 1956, for the first time in more than seven decades, the people denied to a newly elected president a Congress controlled by his own party, and they repeated that decision in four of the next seven presidential elections. As in 1956, in 1968, 1972, 1980, and 1984 they placed Republican presidents in the White House but sent Democratic majorities to the House of Representatives, and in the first three of those elections to the Senate as well. Neither party was given full responsibility with corresponding accountability.

Does this mean, then, that beginning at mid-century the people came to reject the concept of responsible party government that until then they appeared to have accepted? By no means. In each of the five elections that produced divided outcomes, a large majority of individual voters continued to support the entire ticket of one or the other major party. In 1984, for instance, the Democrats won control of the House because their candidates ran about 9 percentage points ahead of their presidential candidate, Walter Mondale, in contested races. Even if one were to assume that the net differential of 9 points was the result of 5 percent of the voters splitting their tickets to support Mondale and the Republican House candidate—an assumption that would surely be too generous—and 14 percent splitting their tickets in the opposite direction, for Reagan and the Democratic congressional candidate, the proportion of all voters splitting their tickets between the two offices would still be only 19 percent. The other 81 percent, by their votes, would have sustained the concept of responsible party government.[12]

Yet if politicians and voters alike support that doctrine, one may ask why the Democratic and Republican parties have not developed the national machinery and the national cohesion that the Committee on Political Parties considered so essential. The committee did not identify the "historical and other factors" that left both parties "ill-equipped" to organize coherent government, but the basic cause is readily apparent: the scale of the country required a federal rather than a unitary government, and a federal structure of government was bound to be reflected in a corresponding party structure, each national party formed as a league of state parties. And the state units making up a national party would be as diverse as the states themselves—in the ethnic and religious backgrounds of members and leaders, in their interests and concerns, and in their ideologies and philosophies of government. Thus throughout its history the Democratic party has been deeply split between its northern liberals and its conservative southern elements, and the Republican party has had its northeastern industrial and its western agrarian wings. These schisms were so deep that at times the parties formally split, as when Theodore Roosevelt and his supporters left the Republicans in 1912 to form the Bull Moose party, and the States' Rights Democrats seceded from the national Democratic party in 1948.

Under these circumstances, a state governor or party chairman in either party could see the development of a strong, centralized national organization as portending only trouble. An authoritative national party would impose its policy positions on the entire party, even in states where they would be unpopular. It might try to influence the choice of party nominees within the state, which to the degree it was successful would lessen the power of state leaders. True, a state party might sometimes want to identify with an enormously popular president, but at other times it would wish to dissociate itself. To preserve its freedom to take either course, its leaders have had to insist on state party autonomy within a weak federal structure.

Those who advocate the responsible-party model have been, generally, those who want more from government. To move toward that model would enhance the possibility of a bolder and more vigorous government able to concert its powers to overcome the deadlock and indecisiveness conducted by the Madisonian structure. Those who want less government have been, on the whole, understandably happy with the Madisonian model as a barrier to governmental activism. Yet the Madisonian model stands impartially in the way of activists of every stripe. And now that conservatism has become, in the Reagan era, hardly less activist than liberalism—its statesmen as eager to dismantle the welfare state as the liberals were to build it, and anxious to write conservative social values into law and carry out a forceful foreign policy—the responsible-party model may have a new appeal over a broadened range of the political spectrum.[13]

The remainder of this chapter is addressed to those who, whether liberal or conservative and for whatever reason, would wish to nudge the nation's institutional system in the direction of the responsible-party model. Without arguing the case further, the discussion will pass from considering *whether* political parties should be strengthened to *how* that might be achieved.

RESPONSIBLE PARTIES IN A DIVIDED GOVERNMENT

The responsible-party model presupposes single-party control of the executive and legislative branches. By definition, if two parties divide control, neither can be responsible. Whatever happens is the result of conflict, negotiation, and compromise between political opponents, and each can point the finger at the other if things go wrong.

If divided government is to be the nation's destiny most of the time—as it will have been for twenty-two of the thirty-four years from the election of 1954 through 1988—strengthening the parties is in fact a dubious objective from the viewpoint of responsible-party advocates. Stronger parties confronting each other from their respective redoubts in the White House and on Capitol Hill would reduce rather than enhance the prospects for governmental unity. Conflict would intensify. In 1981 Ronald Reagan was able to redirect the course of government only because the Democratic majority in the House of Representatives split and enough Democrats followed the leadership of the Republican president to give him a working majority for the essential elements of his party's program. How would a united, disciplined Democratic majority in the House have conducted itself that year? We cannot deduce the answer from anyone's experience, of course, because the only times within memory that a Democratic House majority has approached anything that could be called unity and discipline has been when it has submitted to the leadership of a strong and popular fellow partisan in the White House, notably in the early years of Woodrow Wilson, Franklin D. Roosevelt, and Lyndon Johnson. But if the position favored by the majority of House Democrats in 1981 can be taken as the likely position of a united party, that party would have deadlocked the Reagan program and plunged the country into a long-drawn-out struggle. Negotiations would have ultimately taken place, presumably, but if the bargaining had extended into 1982, much of the Reagan program would surely have been lost, for by that date the economic slump had robbed the president of much of his popularity and even the Republican Senate had rebelled against his economic program. Beginning in 1982, even a disunited Democratic majority in the House was able to block further Reagan initiatives aimed at dismantling governmental programs, to curtail much of the expansion he sought in defense expenditures, and to limit his intervention in Nicaragua.

Those who advocate responsible-party government, then, must at the outset find a way to mitigate the three-decades-old phenomenon of divided government. And here they are sure to be frustrated. Changes in the electoral system to prevent the division of government can be conceived, but the prospect of their adoption is close to zero.

Two approaches are possible. Because divided government is the result of ticket-splitting, a requirement that voters choose between party slates, or "team tickets," consisting of a party's candidates for national office (presidency, vice-presidency, Senate, and House) would virtually assure the president's party control of the House and usually of the Senate also—as was the case in the nineteenth century when the ballot was printed in the form of party tickets. A second approach would be to award the party that won the presidency enough bonus seats in the Congress to assure a majority of both houses. Republicans might be expected to see some merit in devices such as these, for either would have converted them from the minority to the majority party in Congress during much of the past three decades. But Democrats would give no such proposal a second glance, for that very reason. Even Republican members of Congress could be expected to reject them. The team ticket would involve the risk that the individual member's fate would be tied to that of an unpopular presidential candidate (remembering Barry Goldwater*), while the addition of bonus members would reduce the status and influence of the members elected in their states and districts in the accustomed manner.[14]

Then what of the possibility that divided government might disappear through the normal course of events as suddenlly as it appeared? Until the 1970s that indeed appeared to be the prospect. As shown in Table 29, Democratic control of

**Barry Goldwater:* Republican senator from Arizona, first elected in 1952, after the state had 26 years of Democratic representation. He served as Arizona's senator from 1953 to 1965 and then from 1969 to 1989. Goldwater was overwhelmingly defeated by Lyndon B. Johnson in the 1964 presidential election largely because he was seen as an ultraconservative who might use nuclear weapons and who might dismantle the nation's social security system.

TABLE 29. THE FRAYING OF REPUBLICAN PRESIDENTIAL COATTAILS, 1952–84

	1952		1956		1968		1972		1980		1984	
	Republicans	*Democrats*	*Republicans*	*Democrats*	*Republicans*	*Democrats*	*Republicans*	*Democrats*	*Republicans*	*Democrats*	*Republicans*	*Democrats*
Presidential vote (percent)	55.1	44.4	57.4	42.0	43.4	42.7	60.7	37.5	50.7	41.0	58.8	40.6
HOUSE MEMBERS ELECTED												
Total	221	213	201	234	192	243	191	244	192	243	182	253
South[a]	6	99	7	99	26	80	34	74	39	69	43	73
Outside South	215	114	194	135	166	163	157	170	153	174	139	180
South plus border[b]	13	117	11	120	32	97	38	93	47	84	50	88
Outside South and border	208	96	190	114	160	146	153	151	145	159	132	165
Percent outside South and border	68.4	31.6	62.5	37.5	52.3	47.7	50.3	49.7	47.7	52.3	44.4	55.6

[a]The South is defined as consisting of the eleven states that made up the Confederacy: Virginia, North Carolina, South Carolina, Georgia, Florida, Alabama, Mississippi, Tennessee, Arkansas, Louisiana, and Texas.

[b]The border states included here are Kentucky, Missouri, and Oklahoma. All were carried by Republican presidential candidates in the six elections, with two exceptions. Kentucky went Democratic for president in 1952 by 700 votes and Missouri in 1958 by 3,984 votes, or 50.1 percent.

the House in the Eisenhower era and in the first Nixon term could be attributed directly to the historical accident of the Solid South. When in 1956 Dwight Eisenhower became the first winning presidential candidate in eighty years to fail to carry with him enough of his party's candidates to control the House, he did pull in a healthy plurality of 59 members from outside the South. But that was more than offset by the 92-seat margin that the Democrats maintained in that region—even though Eisenhower carried five southern states. When Richard Nixon won a much narrower presidential victory in 1968, his party's margin in the North and West was likewise narrower, 166 seats to 163, but it did exist. The 3-seat edge was, of course, overwhelmed by a Democratic majority of 54 from the South. In 1972 the Republican majority outside the South disappeared—despite the party's much more lopsided victory in the presidential race. Yet if one also excludes three border states—Kentucky, Missouri, and Oklahoma—that have been regularly carried by winning GOP* presidential candidates but whose rural areas had traditionally voted as solidly Democratic as the South itself, the rest of the country still gave Nixon a tiny Republican majority in the House.

The Senate reflected much the same pattern. In 1952 Eisenhower brought a Senate controlled by the GOP. After his even greater landslide in 1956, Eisenhower confronted a Senate in Democratic control by a 49–47 margin, but the Democrats' monopoly over Senate seats from the South accounted wholly for this result. After the 1968 election, in which the presidential votes were almost evenly divided, the Republicans held exactly half the seats outside the South. In winning the presidency in 1972 the Republicans also won 18 of the 34 Senate seats at stake, including 4 of 9 in the South.

Examining these figures, one could conclude that if the politics of the South and the border states ever came to resemble those of the rest of the country, the likelihood of divided government would be considerably reduced. The nation might not return to the pre-1954 decades, when the president's party invariably controlled Congress following each presidential election, but it would come close to that pattern. A Republican president could expect a Republican House of Representatives, if only by a small margin, and he would have a reasonable chance of a GOP Senate as well, depending on the party's share of the holdover members.

The South, moreover, appeared to be conforming its politics to the national pattern. Southern voters first found it acceptable to vote Republican for president in the 1950s, with Eisenhower; thirty years later voting Republican for other offices had become respectable, too. The GOP was still not organized in depth in much of the South, and the Democrats maintained their grip on the state legislatures and the rural courthouses. But the Republicans were able to bring their strength in the Senate to exactly half the region's members (11 of 22 after the 1982 election), increase their House representation from the South to 37 percent (43 of 116 in 1984), and elect governors in all but two southern states—Georgia and Mississippi.

Meanwhile, however, something else was happening in the rest of the country

*GOP: Grand Old Party, a nickname for the Republican party.

regarding the House of Representatives. While President Eisenhower had coattails strong enough to pull in a large majority of Republican representatives from the North and West, and Richard Nixon was still able to bring in bare Republican majorities outside the South and border states, in the 1980s that was not possible for Ronald Reagan. Table 29 shows that the loss of presidential coattail power apparent in the Nixon years continued at an astonishing pace in the 1980s. President Reagan won reelection in 1984 by an even larger margin than did Eisenhower in either 1952 or 1956, but the proportion of Republican House victories outside the South and border states fell by 24 percentage points compared with 1952. That translated into 76 fewer seats, or barely three-fifths of the number won in 1952. If the most popular Republican president in modern times could not even come close to breaking the Democratic lock on the House of Representatives that has held solid except for four years (1947–48 and 1953–54) since 1930, one may well ask what Republican leader possibly can.

GOP campaign committees place their faith in two possibilities. First, they attribute the continuing Democratic ascendancy in the House in large part to the power of incumbent members to win reelection for virtually as long as they desire, and they point out that sooner or later every incumbency must end.[15] How have the Republicans fared, then, in capturing seats that have become open through the retirement of incumbents? Not very well, obviously, for the period of continuous Democratic control since 1955 all but 9 Democratic House seats have been open at least once, and the party's margin is larger now than when the period began—even though the people have chosen Republican presidents during most of that time.

In the past four elections, when the most popular of all those presidents has been the party's leader, the Republicans did win a slight majority of the open seats, 78 to 72.[16] But the party had held 68 of the seats being vacated, leaving a net gain of 10. If the Republicans were able to maintain the relatively high rate of approval they enjoyed in the Reagan years, it would take more than three decades of picking up open seats at the rate of the 1980s for the party to gain the 40 seats it needs for a House majority. Even that projection assumes that the Republicans would remain as high in popular favor throughout that period as they have been in the 1980s, an assumption that defies both history and logic and ignores the recent drop in public confidence in the GOP.

Second, officials of the Republican National Committee place much of the blame for their minority position on the gerrymandering* of district boundaries by Democratic state legislatures. But the scholarly studies summarized by Thomas Mann do not confirm either that the redrawing of district boundaries after recent censuses has cost the GOP more than a few seats—mainly in California—or that even judicial intervention promises them much of a gain. The courts might prove reluctant to upset districting schemes that have become

**Gerrymandering:* process whereby those drawing geographical electoral districts do so in configurations that enhance their group's representation while dividing or weakening the opposition. The term was first used in 1811 when Massachusetts Governor Eldridge Gerry (1744–1814) approved a bill that created a district shaped like a salamander. In *Davis v. Bandemer* (1986) a plurality of the Supreme Court held unconstitutional any restriction that intentionally weakens a specific set of voters.

honored by tradition if they can be defended as having some measure of rationality—and most can, since there are various approaches to "objective" apportionment that produce different results but rest on equally defensible criteria. In the absence of court intervention, Republican hopes for significant gains through reapportionment are remote. Of the states that have more than one district, the GOP now controls both houses of the legislature and the governorship, which is necessary to give them complete control of the apportionment process, in only five, and those states have only eleven Democratic representatives. Ironically, seven of these are in Indiana, elected despite the fact that the Republican party had control of reapportionment after the 1980 census and drew a plan for the state's ten districts designed to give it maximum partisan advantage.

At bottom, the Democratic party's dominance of the House of Representatives for more than half a century reflects the fact that it has been the majority party in the country during the entire period. In 1984, after the second Reagan landslide, the Democrats held 58 percent of all state legislative seats, and that proportion was increased in 1986. The party is similarly preponderant in city halls and county courthouses, which along with the legislatures are the training ground for appealing candidates for Congress. Clearly, it will take another powerful swing of the pendulum to give the Republicans the strength in depth that would be necessary to produce a majority in the House of Representatives—and, if moving at all, the pendulum now is swinging toward the Democrats. One must reach the disappointing conclusion, then, that the responsible-party model is liable to be irrelevant for a long time as far as the Republican party is concerned. It may continue to elect its presidential candidate most of the time, but the consequence will be divided government, not government by a party able to enact its program and take responsibility for it. Strengthening the GOP as an organization is still a desirable goal, but only for the marginal improvements that it might bring in the capability of the candidates the party offers and the effectiveness of those it elects.

To strengthen the Democratic party, however, would contribute directly to the effectiveness of party government whenever the Democrats again elect a president, for they can expect at that time to control Congress also.

THE OBSTACLES TO STRENGTHENING PARTIES

The fundamental barrier to strengthening political parties is the survival in popular culture of the Madisonian model. Rejected almost unanimously by the country's political elite for two centuries, the Madisonian ideal of a factionless government has never lost its hold on the public. Factionalism is derived, and wherever possible averted, in the multitude of private organizations with which individual citizens are familiar. Why then, they ask, must politicians divide into factions that spend their energies in recrimination and petty squabbling rather than getting together to do what is best for the country?

The machines that were the target of antiparty legislation nearly a century ago have by now virtually disappeared, and the strongest political organizations in the country are those held together not by public jobs and other forms of patronage but by ideology and philosophy. Yet the antiparty rhetoric of the Progressive era still rings loudly in political campaigns. Both Jimmy Carter and Ronald Reagan trumpeted their antiestablishment sentiments, and candidates at every level still find their road to victory by running against a party organization wherever one exists—the "man against the machine." So advocates of stronger parties must struggle against the widespread and often prevailing view that powerful party organizations are more a menace than a boon.

A second obstacle, related to the first, is the self-interest of individual politicians. A stronger party is by definition one with a stronger center, possessing some institutional means of fostering unity and cohesion. But for reasons stated early in this chapter, the individual politician who does not aspire to national leadership usually finds more to lose than to gain by strengthening the center. With a loose, decentralized structure the state or local leader can follow the national party and its leaders when their policies are popular at home or defy them when they are not. The self-interest of thousands of politicians is a centrifugal force within the party structure that is operative constantly; centripetal political forces develop now and then, but most of the time they are overbalanced.

RECENT PROGRESS TOWARD STRONGER PARTIES

Yet advocates of stronger parties are the beneficiaries of one profound trend in American politics and one series of deliberate actions, and both of these give hope.

The promising trend is that the two major parties have both become, and are still becoming, more homogeneous ideologically. This trend is the simple consequence of the party realignment that began in the 1930s and has been working its way, gradually but inexorably, through the political system. Simply put, the minority wings, once strong enough to disrupt the internal unity of the two parties, have been dying out. The "four-party system" James MacGregor Burns condemned a generation ago for producing "the deadlock of democracy" is now much more nearly a genuine two-party system.[17]

First to fade were the progressive Republicans. The progressive wing of the GOP, which spanned the generations from Theodore Roosevelt through the La Follettes and George Norris to Nelson Rockefeller and George Romney, was powerful enough as recently as twenty years ago to contest seriously for the presidential nomination. But the progressive Republicans are now an ineffectual remnant. Their counterparts, the conservative Democrats, have been vanishing as well, although more slowly. Virtually confined to the South since the New Deal era, they have from the 1960s been gradually losing their base there to the burgeoning Republican party. As conservative Democrats have ended their careers one by one—usually through retirement rather than defeat—their successors have typically been either conservative Republicans or Democrats cut in the mold of their national party. Thus Republicans occupy the seats once held by such archconservative senators as Harry F. Byrd and A. Willis Robertson of Virginia and James O. Eastland of Mississippi, while new Democratic senators arriving from the South tend to be moderates, such as Terry Sanford of North Carolina and Bob Graham of Florida, or even bear the liberal label, like Wyche Fowler of Georgia. A corresponding transformation has taken place in both parties in the House.[18]

The deliberate actions are those taken by congressional Democrats over the past two decades to impose discipline on party dissenters. Any article on strengthening political parties written earlier than twenty years ago would have opened and closed with a call for destruction of the seniority system in the Congress. That has now been accomplished on the Democratic side. As long as seniority was automatically honored, any Democrat, no matter how out of step with the majority of the party in Congress, could acquire all the plenary power* of a committee chairmanship through mere longevity. Through that device some of the Senate and House committees most crucial to the enactment of the Democratic party's program were turned over to conservative Democrats who voted regularly with the Republicans against the majority of their own party. Sooner or later the situation was bound to prove intolerable. Finally the revolution occurred: liberals in the House forced through the party caucus a series of rules changes that not only scrapped seniority but reduced the arbitrary power of committee chairmen. The revolt was solidified in 1975 when the caucus deposed three chairmen. And it has continued to exercise disciplinary power. In 1987 the caucus voted to remove Les Aspin of Wisconsin from the chairmanship of the House Armed Services Committee, reversing itself only after Aspin humbly promised to accept its guidance on major questions of military policy.[19] The caucus has also assumed, and exercised, the power to instruct the Democratic committee majorities to bring specific measures to the House floor.

With this power of discipline, the caucus has been revived as an instrument for building policy consensus. In their drive to assert control over party policy, the liberals won a demand for regular monthly party caucuses plus additional meetings on petition of fifty members—a dramatic departure from the once-every-two-years tradition that had prevailed for a quarter of a century. The caucus has proved to be an effective consensus-building mechanism, particularly in the long and acrimonious debate over the Vietnam War† when the passion of the antiwar Democratic majority eventually persuaded some reluctant senior party figures to abandon their support. Since then it has expressed itself on a wide range of measures, including the issues of defense policy that led to Aspin's pledge of conformity. In early February 1987 the caucus denounced the Reagan adminis-

**Plenary power:* complete or absolute power. A plenary session is one attended by all qualified members.

†*Vietnam War:* American military involvement that dominated political life for over a decade and resulted in the death of over 58,000 Americans. President Dwight Eisenhower first committed the United States to maintaining South Vietnam as an independent nation in 1959. The number of military personnel assigned to Vietnam grew from 760 in 1959, to approximately 11,000 under Kennedy in 1962, escalated dramatically under Johnson to 536,000 in 1968, and peaked in 1969 at 543,000. Popular and congressional opposition to the war, as well as an inconclusive military position in Vietnam, led Nixon, in 1969, to order the gradual withdrawal of troops. Except for a few advisory personnel, the withdrawal was completed by March, 1973. The North Vietnamese and their allies in the south eventually prevailed and the Vietnam War ended in April, 1975.

tration's resumption of underground nuclear testing and urged the administration instead to begin negotiations with the Soviet Union for an agreement banning such tests.

Institutional change has occurred less formally in the clublike Senate, but the arbitrary power of Democratic committee chairmen has been effectively curtailed there as well. Within the committee structures in both houses, democratic norms now prevail.

Finally, the new Democratic party rule that guarantees seats in the quadrennial presidential nominating convention to 80 percent of the party's members of Congress may prove to be an important move in the direction of greater party cohesion. While most members will no doubt be guided by the sentiment of their states' voters as expressed in primaries and caucuses, and while they are unlikely to vote as a bloc in any case, their influence will be enhanced. In a close convention contest a determined network of House and Senate leaders could conceivably be decisive in selecting a nominee experienced in dealing with Congress, as opposed to an outsider like Jimmy Carter whose misfortunes in his relationships with the legislators and the rest of the party establishment spurred the rules revision.

So, whenever the next Democratic president is elected, advocates of responsible-party government may yet expect to see a close approximation to their model. Given reasonable luck in the presidential nominating lottery, today's homogeneous Democratic party should be able to attain a degree of cohesion under presidential leadership that observers of the party system have not seen—except for the honeymoon years of Lyndon Johnson—in half a century.

Perhaps that cohesion will provide a satisfactory enough version of responsible-party government. But if additional measures to strengthen parties could be taken, the possibilities are worth considering. Any such measures, however, are sure to be difficult. If they were easy, they would already have been adopted, for those who lead the two national parties would assuredly prefer to lead stronger organizations.

THE LIMITED OPPORTUNITIES FOR FURTHER ACTION

The first obvious possibility for further action is for the majorities in Congress to impose party discipline not merely to get measures out of committee but to get them passed. The means to that end is the binding caucus, which both houses last used with full effectiveness in the first Congress of the Wilson administration, in 1913–14. Through that device two-thirds of the Democratic caucus could bind the entire membership to vote with the majority.[20] When the rule was invoked, however, the Democrats laid themselves open to attack by the Republican opposition and its supporters in the media and elsewhere, as well as by independents revolted by the spectacle of coercion. Rule by "King Caucus" developed into a major political issue. Chastened by the public reaction and by intraparty opposition as well, Senate Democrats abandoned the device after the

Wilson era. The House party discarded it, too, after a brief revival in the early New Deal period. Any proposal for its reintroduction would undoubtedly arouse an even more adverse response in today's climate of political individualism, which makes the suggestion futile at the outset.

Another instrument employed by strong parties in other countries also appears beyond consideration in the United States. That is control by the national party, in one or another degree, over the selection of candidates for the national legislature. On reflection, it has to appear anomalous that anyone, no matter how ideologically opposed to the program and philosophy of the Democratic or Republican party, may run for Congress as the party's candidate, take his or her seat with the party upon election, and receive choice committee assignments as a matter of right from the party caucus. Yet neither party has ever developed mechanisms at any level for screening candidacies. Even to design such a mechanism would be difficult. Some have suggested that the copyright laws be made the vehicle, with only persons authorized by the national party allowed to use the party label. But the idea of national control of nominations has too antidemocratic a ring—smacking, like the binding caucus, of thought control—ever to acquire noticeable support. In emergencies, like the one that developed in Illinois in 1986 when two unacceptable candidates won Democratic nominations for state office, the party can devise extraordinary remedies, as the Democrats did in that case by organizing a temporary new party. Moreover, the principal reason for advocating control of candidacies disappeared on the Democratic side when the seniority system was scrapped, for while a dissenter can win committee assignments, he or she can now be denied on ideological grounds the power of a chairmanship. This, if the issue arises, would be the easier solution for the GOP as well.

In its 1950 report the American Political Science Association Committee on Political Parties proposed creation of a national council in each party to set party policy as a means for moving toward a more responsible two-party system. The council, to consist of about fifty members from both inside and outside government, would draft the preliminary party platform and, after its adoption by the convention, interpret it. The council would also make recommendations "in respect to congressional candidates," and perhaps presidential candidates as well. But any such proposal also founders on the rock of self-interest. Why would a president and leading legislators who had won governmental office through arduous election campaigns voluntarily share their policymaking power with outsiders and submit to their restraints? That was the experience when the Democratic National Committee, influenced by the APSA committee report, established its Democratic Advisory Council after the 1956 election. The party's congressional leaders simply declined to join.[21] The council issued well-considered policy pronouncements, but it spoke for only a segment of the party and could not serve its purpose as an institution to unify the party.

There remains one other instrument of discipline: money. Dependent as legislators are on campaign contributions, the power to grant or deny financial assistance can in theory be a powerful disciplinary tool. The national Republican party in recent years has demonstrated the capacity to raise and distribute an enormous treasury. The Democrats' capability is by no means comparable, but it has been improving. Is money a potential means, then, for tightening party discipline within Congress to achieve responsible-party government?

In theory, yes. In practice, probably not to a significant degree. Because discretionary power over congressional campaign funds would be a powerful device to achieve central control, the resistance that arises against central control of any aspect of party organization would in this case be commensurately potent. But even if discretion were granted to the national party committees, their self-interest would steer them away from exercising it as an instrument of party discipline. The overriding objective of the national party in congressional campaigns is to win a majority of seats. To this end, the party's self-interest is to support any candidate with a chance of victory, and to support most generously the candidates in the closest races, where additional spending is most likely to pay off in victories. In the heat of a campaign the national party officials making money decisions do not ask about the voting regularity of a party's incumbents or extract voting promises from nonincumbents. They ask only about election prospects. They take polls and are guided by the numbers.[22]

So it is that in these days of Republican opulence no complaints have been heard that the national party has been using its funds in a discriminatory fashion to penalize legislators who have deviated from the Reagan party line. After the 1986 election the party was proud to announce that it had "maxed out" on every candidate, that is, given the maximum amount permissible by law to its nominee in every race. No one was disciplined. Indeed, one true believer in party discipline, Patrick J. Buchanan, the White House director of communications, could complain after the election that President Reagan had been "travelling the nation as no other president before him, fighting to save the Senate for . . . Republicans, throwing his arm around men—some of whom had cut-and-run on him in every major engagement he has fought since he came to the White House."[23]

In any case, cash contributions to congressional campaigns by national party committees are now so tightly limited by law that the potential for monetary discipline is not great. In House campaigns a party committee is treated as just another political action committee limited to contributing the same $5,000 a race (in Senate contests the ceiling is $17,500). Compared with what the array of PACs can put into closely contested races, these sums are a pittance, particularly in the case of the senior members of key committees who—if any member needed discipline—might need it the most. Any major influence by party committees has to be exerted indirectly, through advice given by party officials to friendly PACs, rather than directly through the party's own funds.

The limits on party contributions could, of course, be raised by new legislation, but the Democrats are hardly likely to use their Senate and House majorities to enhance the advantage that the richer Republican party would get from freer spending. And if a large share of congressional campaign funds were to come from the public treasury, that would not change matters either. In the bill introduced in January 1987 as S. 2 by Democratic Senators David L. Boren of Oklahoma and Robert C. Byrd of West Virginia, the majority leader, the public funds would be distributed among candidates by formula, with the party not even serving as a channel.

Money, then, is not likely to become the powerful centralizing force within the parties that at first sight might appear possible. The handling of money has yielded to, and been conformed to, the prevailing pattern of decentralization in the party structure. And it is likely to remain that way, no matter how the sums at the disposal of the parties might be increased. The members of Congress who would write any public financing law and who already have the decisive voice in determining the national parties' policies for distributing congressional campaign funds will see to that.

Deliberate attempts, then, to strengthen political parties run counter to deep-seated public attitudes, to the self-interest of the politicians who would have to initiate change, and to the structure of governmental and political institutions, including the electoral system. The feasible actions have already been taken—notably the crucial decisions in the 1970s to assert majority rule within the congressional parties. There is a solid basis for hope, however, in political trends beyond the influence of even the political elite itself—the continuing realignment of the party system that is producing the homogeneity on which party cohesion and strength at the governmental level must rest.

If, when one party wins single-party control of the presidency and Congress, it succeeds in coping effectively with the problems of the country, the value of the responsible-party concept will have been demonstrated and the model will win a wider public acceptance. More people will then see the role of parties as those who believe in the responsible-party model see it—as institutions crucially necessary to formulate governmental programs, to enact and execute those programs, and to account for them to the electorate afterward.

Only such a period of success can provide the necessary popular support for institutional changes that will further the same ends. In the meantime, such changes of any consequence will simply have to wait.

NOTES

[1]Statement read by James MacGregor Burns, then chairman of the committee, at the Jefferson Memorial, Washington, D.C., September 2, 1977. The committee, formed in 1976, is composed of political scientists and Democratic and Republican party activists.

[2]Committee on the Constitutional System, A *Bicentennial Analysis of the American Political Structure* (January 1987), pp. 3, 5. The committee, organized in 1981, is made up of present and former members of Congress, former executive branch officials, academics, and others concerned with structural weaknesses in the government. Its cochairs are Lloyd N. Cutler, former White House counsel; C. Douglas Dillon, former cabinet member; and Senator Nancy Landon Kassebaum, Republican of Kansas.

[3]Max Farrand, ed., *The Records of the Federal Convention of 1787*, rev. ed., 4 vols. (Yale University Press, 1966), vol. 2, p. 29, proceedings of July 17, notes of James Madison.

[4]Ibid., p. 57, July 19, and p. 114, July 25, Madison notes. He even identified one existing national

organization that was "respectable, United, and influential" enough to have the power to elect the president—the Order of the Cincinnati.

[5]Ibid., pp. 110–11, July 25, Madison notes.

[6]The authorship of number 62 has been disputed, but the weight of scholarly opinion now appears to ascribe it to Madison rather than Hamilton.

[7]And, some would add, except in France under its current constitution. Executive powers are divided uneasily between the president and the premier, who may be of different parties.

[8]*Annals of Congress*, 14 Cong. 1 sess., p. 216, reprinted in Farrand, *Records*, vol. 3, p. 422. King was a delegate from Massachusetts to the Constitutional Convention, but moved to New York the following year.

[9]Note to his speech at the 1787 Convention on the right of suffrage, apparently written about 1821, when he was preparing his record of Convention proceedings for publication. Ibid., p. 452.

[10]After the 1880 election, the Senate was composed of 37 Republicans, 37 Democrats, and two minor-party senators.

[11]Supplement to *American Political Science Review*, vol. 44 (September 1950). The committee is known as the Schattschneider committee, after its chairman, E. E. Schattschneider.

[12]The figure of 9 percent (rounded up from 8.7 percent) is provided by Rhodes Cook of *Congressional Quarterly*. The estimate of 19 percent is supported by polling data. In the seven presidential elections from 1956 through 1980, the University of Michigan Center for Political Studies found that from 13.2 percent of the voters (in 1960) to 26.7 percent (in 1980) split their tickets between presidential and congressional candidates. John A. Ferejohn and Morris P. Fiorina, "Incumbency and Realignment in Congressional Elections," in John E. Chubb and Paul E. Peterson, eds., *The New Direction in American Politics* (Brookings, 1985), p. 100.

[13]See, for example, Paul M. Weyrich, "A Conservative's Lament," *Washington Post*, March 8, 1987. Weyrich, a leading organizer of New Right activism, cites the difficulty of making foreign policy decisions because of executive-legislative conflict and concludes, "As conservatives, we have to help the nation face a stark choice: either modify our institutions of government to play the game of great power, or move back toward our historic, less active foreign policy."

[14]These proposals as well as some less far-reaching measures to the same end are discussed in "Forestalling Divided Government," chap. 4 of my *Constitutional Reform and Effective Government* (Brookings, 1986).

[15]For analyses of the power of incumbency, see the chapter by Thomas E. Mann in this volume. Also see Ferejohn and Fiorina, "Incumbency and Realignment." More than 90 percent of House incumbents running for reelection are regularly returned to office. In 1986 the proportion was 98 percent, with only 8 incumbents suffering defeat out of 393 who sought reelection.

[16]Open seats are defined as those that are vacated by the incumbent for any reason—death, resignation, retirement, or defeat in a party primary. Technically, the Democrats won only 71. One of the seats vacated by a Democrat was won by an independent, but the seat reverted to the Democrats at the next election.

[17]Burns, *The Deadlock of Democracy* (Prentice-Hall, 1963).

[18]The homogeneity of the congressional Republicans has, of course, been demonstrated throughout the Reagan years. But Democratic unity has also improved; see A. James Reichley, "The Rise of National Parties," in Chubb and Peterson, eds., *New Direction*, p. 197.

[19]House and Senate Republicans also permit departures from seniority in selecting chairmen or ranking minority members of committees, but no member has yet been penalized. In a contested case in 1987, Senate Republicans upheld seniority in assigning Jesse Helms of North Carolina to the ranking minority post on the Foreign Relations Committee.

[20]Except for those who formally communicated their intention not to be bound, citing one or more of several permissible grounds. That privilege was, however, not often invoked.

[21]However, two members of the party's liberal wing in the Senate—Hubert Humphrey and Estes Kefauver—did join the Advisory Council at the outset. Senators John F. Kennedy and Stuart Symington joined late in 1959.

[22]A national party committee under presidential control might on occasion be tempted to intervene in a party primary against a recalcitrant member (despite the unhappy experience of President Franklin Roosevelt in his attempted "purge" of anti–New Deal Democrats in 1938). Early in 1986

President Reagan's political operatives were reportedly encouraging Governor Richard L. Thornburgh of Pennsylvania to challenge Senator Arlen Specter in that state's 1986 Republican primary. While the White House ultimately turned away from that course, it may have achieved a measure of discipline for a limited time through the threat to support Thornburgh. Significantly, the Senate Campaign Committee did not participate in threatening an incumbent senator.

[23]*Washington Post*, December 8, 1986.

PART FOUR

INTEREST GROUPS

Private groups such as trade associations, labor unions, farmers' lobbies, and civil rights organizations have long been recognized as important participants in American politics. Americans have a reputation for forming interest groups to promote their economic, political, and social objectives. As early as the 1830s, Alexis de Tocqueville observed that "Americans of all ages, all conditions, and all dispositions constantly form associations. They have not only commercial and manufacturing companies . . . but associations of a thousand other kinds, religious, moral, serious, futile, general or restricted, enormous or diminutive. . . . Wherever at the head of some new undertaking you see the government in France or a man of rank in England, in the United States you will be sure to find an association." What explains the American propensity to form groups? What are the effects of these groups on politics and public policy? These are questions that the classic literature on interest groups addresses.

In "American Hybrid," drawn from *A Preface to Democratic Theory* (1956), Robert A. Dahl analyzes the political and constitutional frameworks in which interest groups in the United States arise and operate. He argues that "neither elections nor interelection activity provide much insurance that decisions will accord with the preferences of a majority of adults or voters." Rather, "it is . . . apparent that the probable outcome of a policy decision is partly a function of the relative amount of political activity carried on for or against the alternatives. Hence: All other things being equal, the outcome of a policy decision will be determined by the relative intensity of preference among members in a group." Consequently, in Dahl's view, politically active groups are able to institute a kind of pluralistic rule by minorities. In such a system the formation of interest groups is a prerequisite to exercising significant influence on the making of public policy.

Mancur Olson's chapter on collective action from *The Rise and Decline of Nations* (1982) brings the analysis of group formation to the level of the individual. Olson seeks to explain why individuals join and work for groups by addressing a fundamental paradox: "The individual in any large group with a common interest will reap only a minute share of the gains from whatever sacrifices the individual makes to achieve this common interest. Since any gain goes to everyone in the group, those who contribute nothing to the effort will get just as much as those who made a contribution. It pays to 'let George do it,' but George has little or no incentive to do anything in the group interest either. . . . The paradox, then, is that . . . large groups, at least if they are composed of rational individuals, will *not* act in their group interest." However, as Olson argues, this paradox can be resolved in practice through the use of selective incentives, both positive and negative, to prompt individuals to contribute to group activities. Olson also notes that since small organizations may not be able to function without contributions from each of their few members, the logic of individual participation indicates that "smaller groups will have a greater likelihood of engaging in collective action than larger ones."

Finally, the impact of interest group politics on the political system as a whole is addressed by E. E. Schattschneider in "The Scope and Bias of the Pressure System" (1960). He warns that interest group politics exert a bias: "the notion that the pressure system is automatically representative of the whole community is a myth fostered by the universalizing tendency of modern group theories. Pressure politics is a selective process ill designed to serve diffuse interests. The system is skewed, loaded, and unbalanced in favor of a fraction of a minority."

11

ROBERT A. DAHL

AMERICAN HYBRID

Robert A. Dahl, formerly Sterling Professor of Political Science at Yale University, made substantial contributions to democratic theory throughout the second half of this century. His works include Politics, Economics, and Welfare *(1953), which he wrote with Charles E. Lindblom;* Who Governs? *(1961);* Democracy in the United States *(1972, 1973);* Dilemmas of Pluralist Democracy *(1982);* Controlling Nuclear Weapons: Democracy vs. Guardianship *(1985);* A Preface to Economic Democracy *(1985); and* Democracy, Liberty, and Equality *(1986). The selection that follows is the concluding chapter of his classic critique of Madisonian theory,* A Preface to Democratic Theory *(1956, 1967).*

Dahl argues that though the participants at the Constitutional Convention "were perhaps as brilliant an assembly as has ever gathered to devise a lasting constitution for a great nation . . . ," the system that evolved departed dramatically from the one they envisioned. As it turned out, majority tyranny, as discussed by Madison, has been only a minor threat to American democracy. Dahl makes a persuasive argument that more often than not "minorities rule." The fundamental distinction between democracy and dictatorship is that the former is government by minorities, *while the latter is government by a* minority. *The American system is unique for the "endless bargaining" it encourages, for its marked degree of decentralization, and for the access it provides to "active and legitimate" groups to participate in the decision-making process.*

Like a nagging tooth, Madison's* problem of majority tyranny has persistently troubled us throughout these essays. As we discovered at the outset, it is no simple matter even to define the terms satisfactorily. If momentarily it appeared that an examination of "intensity" might give us an answer, in the end our exploration of intensity turned up no clear solution.

Nevertheless, from what has gone before, seven important propositions bearing on this issue may, I think, be developed. If these propositions are somewhat speculative, they are not merely consistent with all that has been argued so far but to a substantial degree are implicit in the argument.

I

The first of these propositions is that on matters of specific policy the majority rarely rules.

**Madison:* see headnote, page 29.

In analyzing polyarchal democracy* we found it necessary to lay down seven separate conditions necessary to maximum attainment of the Rule during the election period, that is, we described seven continua against which the relative attainment of the Rule during the election period might be measured. This emphasis on the conditions of the election period is significant, for I think none of the developments in the past century and a half in understanding the operation of democratic societies, and certainly none of the recent developments in empirical political science should be interpreted as decreasing the critical role of elections in maximizing political equality and popular sovereignty. Although it is fashionable in some quarters to suggest that everything believed about democratic politics prior to World War I, and perhaps World War II, was nonsense, I am inclined to think that the radical democrats who, unlike Madison, insist upon the decisive importance of the elective process in the whole grand strategy of democracy are essentially correct. To be sure, if the social prerequisites of polyarchy do not exist, then the election process cannot mitigate, avoid, or displace hierarchical government. But if the social prerequisites of polyarchy do exist, then the election is the critical technique for insuring that governmental leaders will be relatively responsive to non-leaders; other techniques depend for their efficacy primarily upon the existence of elections and the social prerequisites.

Having said so much, it is important to notice how little a national election tells us about the preferences of majorities. Strictly speaking, all an election reveals is the first preferences of some citizens among the candidates standing for office. Let us see what it does not do.

Let us put to one side the fact that because of election machinery the outcome may actually run counter to the expressed preferences of a plurality of voters; for example, in three national elections in the United States, the candidate preferred by the most voters was not made President. Let us also put to one side the fact that when more than two candidates run for office, the winning candidate may have a plurality but not a majority of votes; and it is usually impossible to say what the outcome would have been if there had been a run-off election between the two candidates with the highest number of votes. Thus in nine American presidential elections the winning candidate has had a plurality but not a majority of popular votes. Hence in twelve cases, or more than one-third of the presidential elections since Jackson,[1] the winning candidate has not been the first choice of a majority of voters.

Far more significant is the fact that even when a candidate is evidently a first choice of a majority of voters, we cannot be sure in a national election that he is also a first choice of a majority of adults or eligible voters.[2] Although the American case is extreme, in every nation state where compulsory voting does not exist the basic proposition holds. In any given election we are almost never in a position to know for sure what the outcome would have been if some or all of the non-voters had actually voted. We have slight reason to suppose that the outcome would have been the same. In a close election a small last minute rise in

Polyarchal democracy: political system in which rulers are chosen in free and regularly held elections among competing elites.

the proportion of voters drawn from those favorable to one of the sides can change the outcome; something like this seems to have happened in the last two weeks of the 1948 campaign.[3] Moreover, one of the sides is often handicapped by non-voting more than the other; for example, when non-voting is inversely related to income, education, and other related factors, in a close division of opinion the candidate of the poor and uneducated is more likely to lose, even when he is the first preference of all the adults or eligible voters, than is the candidate of the educated and the well-to-do. In the 1952 presidential election, it appears that about 20 per cent of those who favored Eisenhower did not vote, whereas about 29 percent of those who favored Stevenson did not vote.[4] In a close division of opinion, the difference in the proportions of non-voters would have been crucial.[5]

Now if all the non-voters were indifferent as to the outcome, then . . . their preferences, or lack of them, could be ignored in determining what a majority of adults prefer. But unfortunately it is not true that all non-voters are indifferent; for example, in one national sample studied in 1952, out of 450 persons who said they cared very much which party won the presidential election, 76 (or 17 per cent) evidently did not vote. Of the Stevenson supporters who "cared very much" about the outcome, a much higher percentage (28 per cent) failed to vote than among highly concerned Eisenhower supporters (10 per cent).[6]

Finally, in appraising the significance of elections as an indication of first choices, it must be remembered that a great many voters do not really perceive a choice between candidate A and candidate B; for many people the only perceived alternatives are to vote for one of the candidates or not to vote at all.[7]

Even if we could rule out all these difficulties, it would still be true that we can rarely interpret a majority of first choices among candidates in a national election as being equivalent to a majority of first choices for a specific policy. Some people evidently vote for a candidate although they are quite indifferent about the issues. Others support a candidate who is opposed to them on some issues; in the 1952 sample already referred to, 29 percent of those who took a Democratic position on the Taft-Hartley Act* nonetheless supported Eisenhower. Furthermore, the supporters of a candidate often differ widely in their preferences on issues. In one sample of those who supported Eisenhower in 1952, about 64 per cent thought the United States had gone too far in concerning itself with problems in other parts of the world, about 27 per cent thought it had not, and about 9 per cent were neutral. Thus it becomes possible for a resounding majority of the voters to elect a candidate all of whose policies are the first choices of only a minority.

Imagine, for example, that voters must choose between two candidates who disagree on three policies as set forth in Table 1. Now let us suppose that each of these minorities is a distinct group, so that together the three minorities make up 75 per cent of the voters. Let us suppose that the first minority regards foreign policy as the crucial issue and ranks its choices: *u*, *x*, *z*, *w*, *y*, *v*. That is, these voters prefer candidate A because he offers them a foreign policy of which

*Taft-Hartley Act: see footnote on page 118.

TABLE 1

	Candidate A Prefers Alternative	*Supported by*	*Candidate B Prefers Alternative*	*Supported by*
Foreign policy	*u*	25 per cent of voters	*v*	75 per cent of voters
Farm policy	*w*	25 per cent of voters	*x*	75 per cent of voters
Fiscal policy	*y*	25 per cent of voters	*z*	75 per cent of voters

they approve, even though they dislike his farm and fiscal policies. Now suppose that the second minority of voters regards farm policy as crucial and ranks its choices: *w, z, v, u, y, x*. That is, these voters prefer candidate A because he offers them a farm policy they like, even though they disapprove of his stand on foreign and fiscal policy. Applying the same kind of reasoning to the third minority, it can be readily seen that candidate A might win 75 per cent of the votes, even though each of his policies is opposed by 75 per cent of the voters. This is an instance, not of majority or even of minority rule, but of *minorities* rule.

In addition, in so far as voters prefer a candidate because of his policies, frequently the support represents approval or disapproval of a policy already enacted, even if little or nothing can be done to change the consequences of the policy. No doubt many people voted against Stevenson in 1952 because Truman had not stopped the Chinese Communists in 1947.[8] The vote was more of a punishment for past action than a choice of future policy. Political leaders recognize this aspect of elections and frequently seek to avoid a decision until an election is over so that they may then act relatively free from campaign commitments. Thus paradoxically an election may actually prevent rather than facilitate policy choices by the electorate.

Now the unwary student of contemporary democracies may hastily conclude that the deficiencies in elections I have alluded to are characteristic only of the United States, but except for peculiarities that I agreed to put to one side as remediable in principle, what I have said applies with equal force, I believe, to the politics of any large nation state. Although political scientists sometimes appear to believe that many of the virtues and few of the vices of American politics are to be found in the English parliamentary system,* operating with two highly unified and disciplined parties, I am inclined to think that elections under that system are, if anything, even less controlling than our own.[9] The only important point to stress here is that in no large nation state can elections tell us much about the preferences of majorities and minorities, beyond the bare fact that among those who went to the polls a majority, plurality, or minority indicated their first choices for some particular candidate or group of candidates.

**Parliamentary system:* form of government, preferred by most of the world's democracies, in which an elected legislature selects from within its ranks both a prime minister or premier and the cabinet, who serve collectively as long as they enjoy the confidence of a majority of the legislature.

What the first choices of this electoral majority are, beyond that for the particular candidates, it is almost impossible to say with much confidence.

What is true of elections must be even more true of the interelection period. Our polyarchal model tried to account for the interelection period by means of its eighth condition:

> 8.1 Either all interelections decisions are subordinate or executory to those arrived at during the election stage
> 8.2 Or new decisions during the interelection period are governed by the preceding seven conditions, operating, however, under rather different institutional circumstances
> 8.3. Or both.

The reader may have felt at the time that this was a sorry way to bypass a formidable problem. I think so myself, but one cannot say everything at once.

We have just shown that condition 8.1 is, in practice, quite inadequately attained. The link between elections and policy choices is not feeble; but if an election rarely reveals the preferences of a majority on policy matters, there is no majority preference to which interelection decisions may be subordinate or executory. The other possible condition (8.2) meets with equally great difficulties, for most interelection policy seems to be determined by the efforts of relatively small but relatively active minorities. I believe there is no case in the whole history of American politics where interelection activity was at anything like the level of activity in an ordinary election. If you examine carefully any policy decision, even a very important one, you will always discover, I believe, that only a quite tiny proportion of the electorate is actively bringing its influence to bear upon politicians. In an area as critical as foreign policy, the evidence is conclusive that year in and year out the overwhelming proportion of American citizens makes its preferences effective, if at all, by no means other than going to the polls and casting a ballot. In a recent survey of American attitudes on world organization, the percentages of various opinion groups who reported that they had done nothing to spread their point of view, such as belonging to organizations, engaging in political activity, or even discussing their position with their friends, were as follows[10]:

Among "isolationists": 87 per cent
Among those favoring the United Nations as it is: 84 per cent
Among those favoring a stronger United Nations: 80 per cent
Among those supporting some kind of union among the democracies: 84 per cent

I am not suggesting that elections and interelection activity are of trivial importance in determining policy.[11] On the contrary, they are crucial processes for [e]nsuring that political leaders will be somewhat responsive to the preferences of some ordinary citizens. But neither elections nor interelection activity provide much insurance that decisions will accord with the preferences of a majority of adults or voters. Hence we cannot correctly describe the actual operations of democratic societies in terms of the contracts between majorities and minorities.

We can only distinguish groups of various types and sizes, all seeking in various ways to advance their goals, usually at the expense, at least in part, of others.[12]

II

I have shown both that elections are a crucial device for controlling leaders and that they are quite ineffective as indicators of majority preference. These statements are really not in contradiction. A good deal of traditional democratic theory leads us to expect more from national elections than they can possibly provide. We expect elections to reveal the "will" or the preferences of a majority on a set of issues. This is one thing elections rarely do, except in an almost trivial fashion. Despite this limitation the election process is one of two fundamental methods of social control which, operating together, make governmental leaders so responsive to non-leaders that the distinction between democracy and dictatorship still makes sense. The other method of social control is continuous political competition among individuals, parties, or both. Elections and political competition do not make for government by majorities in any very significant way, but they vastly increase the size, number, and variety of minorities whose preferences must be taken into account by leaders in making policy choices. I am inclined to think that it is in this characteristic of elections—not minority rule but minorities rule—that we must look for some of the essential differences between dictatorships and democracies.

III

But there is another characteristic of elections that is important for our inquiry. If the majority rarely rules on matters of specific policy, nevertheless the specific policies selected by a process of "minorities rule" probably lie most of the time within the bounds of consensus set by the important values of the politically active members of the society, of whom the voters are a key group. This, then, is our third proposition; and in this sense the majority (at least of the politically active) nearly always "rules" in a polyarchal system. For politicians subject to elections must operate within the limits set both by their own values, as indoctrinated members of the society, and by their expectations about what policies they can adopt and still be reelected.

In a sense, what we ordinarily describe as democratic "politics" is merely the chaff. It is the surface manifestation, representing superficial conflicts. Prior to politics, beneath it, enveloping it, restricting it, conditioning it, is the underlying consensus on policy that usually exists in the society among a predominant portion of the politically active members. Without such a consensus no democratic system would long survive the endless irritations and frustrations of elections and party competition. With such a consensus the disputes over policy alternatives are nearly always disputes over a set of alternatives that have already been winnowed down to those within the broad area of basic agreement.

Lest anyone conclude that these basic agreements are trivial: a century ago in the United States it was a subject of political debate whether the enslavement of human beings was or was not desirable. Today this question is not subject to political debate.

IV

If majorities in a democracy nearly always govern in the broad meaning of the term, they rarely rule in Madison's terms: for as we have seen, specific policies tend to be products of "minorities rule." In the sense in which Madison was concerned with the problem then, majority rule is mostly a myth. This leads to our fourth proposition: If majority rule is mostly a myth, then majority tyranny is mostly a myth. For if the majority cannot rule, surely it cannot be tyrannical.

The real world issue has not turned out to be whether a majority, much less "the" majority, will act in a tyrannical way through democratic procedures to impose its will on a (or the) minority. Instead, the more relevant question is the extent to which various minorities in a society will frustrate the ambitions of one another with the passive aquiescence or indifference of a majority of adults or voters.

That some minorities will frustrate and in that sense tyrannize over others is inherent in a society where people disagree, that is, in human society. But if frustration is inherent in human society, dictatorship is not. Howeever, if there is anything to be said for the processes that actually distinguish democracy (or polyarchy) from dictatorship, it is not discoverable in the clear-cut distinction between government by a majority and government by a minority. The distinction comes much closer to being one between government by a minority and government by *minorities*. As compared with the political processes of a dictatorship, the characteristics of polyarchy greatly extend the number, size, and diversity of the minorities whose preferences will influence the outcome of governmental decisions. Furthermore, these characteristics evidently have a reciprocal influence on a number of key aspects of politics: the kinds of leaders recruited, the legitimate and illegitimate types of political activity, the range and kinds of policies open to leaders, social processes for information and communication—indeed upon the whole ethos of the society. It is in these and other effects more than in the sovereignty of the majority that we find the values of a democratic process.

V

Our fifth proposition is that in so far as there is any general protection in human society against the deprivation by one group of the freedom desired by another, it is probably not to be found in constitutional forms. It is to be discovered, if at all, in extra-constitutional factors. Take the intensity problem, for example; our brief examination of American constitutional devices for protecting a relatively intense group from deprivation by a larger but relatively more apathetic group came to naught. Yet there may well be protections lying beyond constitutional forms. Without attempting to decide whether relative intensities can really be measured, we can say that if intensities can be measured at all, some kind of overt behavior must be taken as an index. If we accept as an index an individual's own statement about how he feels, then the following important hypothesis seems to be valid:

> Political activity is to a significant extent a function of relative intensity.[13]

Now it is also apparent that the probable outcome of a policy decision is partly a function of the relative amount of political activity carried on for or against the alternatives. Hence:

> All other things being equal, the outcome of a policy decision will be determined by the relative intensity of preference among the members of a group.

The main body of protections, however, is to be found in the preconditions and characteristics of polyarchy; the more fully the social prerequisites of polyarchy exist, the less probable it is that any given minority will have its most valued freedoms curtailed through governmental action. The extent of consensus on the polyarchal norms, social training in the norms, consensus on policy alternatives, and political activity: the extent to which these and other conditions are present determines the viability of a polyarchy itself and provides protections for minorities. The evidence seems to me overwhelming that in the various polyarchies of the contemporary world, the extent to which minorities are bedeviled by means of government action is dependent almost entirely upon non-constitutional factors; indeed, if constitutional factors are not entirely irrelevant, their significance is trivial as compared with the non-constitutional.

VI

What, then, is the significance of constitutional factors?

So far I have avoided a definition of "constitutional." As every political scientist knows, to specify the meaning of "constitutional" at all rigorously is difficult indeed. One is likely to start with a definition and end with a Weltanschauung.* Although I do not place much confidence in the utility of my definition, by "constitutional" I propose to mean determinants of governmental decisions (I leave these terms undefined) consisting of prescribed rules influencing the legitimate distribution, types, and methods of control among government officials. The rules may be prescribed by a variety of authorities accepted as legitimate among officials: the written Constitution, if there is one; decisions of a tribunal accepted as authoritative on constitutional interpretation; respected commentar-

**Weltanschauung:* German term that literally means "a manner of looking at the world." Weltanschauung refers to one's comprehensive world view and humankind's place in relation to it.

ies and the like. By non-constitutional factors, therefore, I mean all other determinants of governmental decisions.

In this sense, all contemporary polyarchies seem to possess such strikingly similar constitutions that the range of the constitutional variable is even more limited than might be thought at first glance. There are two causes for this similarity. In the first place, the characteristics and prerequisites of polyarchy impose a definite limitation on constitutional types available to any large polyarchal society. In the second place, given these characteristics and prerequisites, the efficiencies arising from division of labor impose an additional and highly significant limitation. There is need for a more or less representative body to legitimize basic decisions by some process of assent—however ritualized. Unless the process is entirely ritual, there is within this legislature at least some need for leaders, for committees, and for partisan organizations. There is a need for bureaucracies of permanent experts to formulate alternatives and to make most of the staggering number of decisions that a modern government must somehow make. These bureaucracies must be highly specialized among themselves since they perform highly differentiated tasks: they compete and conflict with one another and with other official groups in the system. Bureaucratic officials must, among other things, make decisions bearing directly upon the actions of particular individuals. Hence a specialized bureaucracy is necessary to pass upon appeals from these preliminary decisions; another specialized bureaucratic task is to adjudicate conflicts among individuals; both tasks are sometimes combined in the same specialized bureaucracy, namely, the judiciary. Bureaucratic, judicial, and legislative decisions must somehow be co-ordinated, and hence a specialized group of officials is needed as co-ordinators. Because the task of co-ordination is so often crucial, involving basic decisions among policy alternatives, it requires leaders of great status and power who can compete successfully at election time. The election process itself requires additional specialization; individuals dedicated mainly to the task of winning elections run nationwide party organizations.

In time, all these manifold specialized groups become vested interests with leaders and non-leaders dependent upon the permanence, the income, the prestige, and the legitimacy of their organizations. They become part of the fundamental warp and woof of society. In this sense, every polyarchal political system is marked by separation of powers: it has legislature, executive, administrative bureaucracy and judiciary, each of which is, in turn, divided and subdivided; in this sense, too, every polyarchal political system is a system of checks and balances, with numerous groups of officials in competition and conflict with one another.

Given these limits on the range of the constitutional variable, what is the significance of constitutional rules in the operation of democratic politics? So far we have shown that constitutional rules are not crucial, independent factors in maintaining democracy; rather, the rules themselves seem to be functions of underlying non-constitutional factors. We have also shown that the constitutional rules are not significant as guarantors either of government by majorities or of the liberty from majority tyranny.

Our sixth proposition is this: Constitutional rules are mainly significant because they help to determine what particular groups are to be given advantages or handicaps in the political struggle. In no society do people ever enter a political contest equally; the effect of the constitutional rules is to preserve, add to, or subtract from the advantages and handicaps with which they start the race. Hence, however trivial the accomplishments of the constitutional rules may be when measured against the limitless aspirations of traditional democratic thought, they are crucial to the status and power of the particular groups who gain or suffer by their operation. And for this reason, among others, the rules have often been the cause of bitter and even fratricidal struggle.

VII

Viewed in this perspective, we can see the American political system in the light of its special characteristics. Here we come to the seventh and last of the propositions bearing upon the problem of majority tyranny. A central guiding thread of American constitutional development has been the evolution of a political system in which all the active and legitimate groups in the population can make themselves heard at some crucial stage in the process of decision. The remainder of this chapter will be devoted to sketching out in broad strokes the development and character of this system, which I shall refer to as the "normal" American political process.

However, before turning to the way in which this normal system developed, it may be wise to specify what is meant by "active and legitimate." From all that has gone before, it is clear that the politically inactive members of a polyarchal organization cannot directly influence the outcome of decisions.[14] Hence if a group is inactive, whether by free choice, violence, intimidation, or law, the normal American system does not necessarily provide it with a checkpoint anywhere in the process. By "legitimate," I mean those whose activity is accepted as right and proper by a preponderant portion of the active. In the South, Negroes were not until recently an active group. Evidently, Communists are not now a legitimate group. As compared with what one would expect from the normal system, Negroes were relatively defenseless in the past, just as the Communists are now.

A group excluded from the normal political arena by prohibitions against normal activity may nevertheless often gain entry. It may do so (1) by engaging or threatening to engage in "abnormal" political activity—violence, for example; (2) by threatening to deprive groups already within the arena of their legitimacy; or (3) by acquiring legitimacy, and hence motivating the in-groups to incorporate the outgroup. The extension of voting privileges in the period from the American Revolution to Jackson is an example of all three. The belated protection of the lawful franchise of Negroes by the Supreme Court in the past two decades is an instance of the third method. However, as Negroes become a larger part of the active and legitimate electorate, the normal opportunities of the system become open to them and further protection of the franchise can then depend more and more upon use of checkpoints in the normal system. The full assimilation of Negroes into the normal system already has occurred in many northern states and now seems to be slowly taking place even in the South.

The "normal" system has developed through several stages. Except for Connecticut and Rhode Island, which continued their relatively democratic colonial charters, all of the states formed new written constitutions between 1776 and 1781. A number of factors—of which democratic ideas were only one—shaped these constitutions. In one respect, however, they tended to be similar: "under most of the Revolutionary constitutions, the legislature was truly omnipotent and the executive correspondingly weak."[15] In eight states, the executive was chosen by the legislature, and in one, New Hampshire, the legislature chose a council, which in turn chose a council president; except in three states, the executive was elected for a one-year term; in six southern states, he could not be re-elected; generally he could not prorogue,* adjourn, or dissolve the legislature; the power of appointment was for the most part lodged in the legislature; save for two states, the executive had no power to veto legislation; in every state there was an executive council to watch over him, and in ten states this council was elected by the legislature.

Because of the supremacy of the legislature, these state constitutions have sometimes been regarded as a triumph for populistic democracy,[16] but this is very far from the truth. For the flaw in the system was that the legislatures themselves were frequently highly unrepresentative; in many states legislative supremacy meant not so much the dominance of the people as it meant control over policy by the relatively small elites of wealth and status who were able to control one or both branches of the legislature. The rules, that is to say, were rigged in favor of some groups and against others. Generally speaking, they were rigged in favor of the old centers of population on the seaboard and against new settlers in the western portions of the states; and they were rigged in favor of the wealthy and against the poor.

Thus in Massachusetts, the Revolutionary constitution established the control of the commercial interests over state policy against the power of the farmers; by heavy property qualifications for both officeholding and voting, the wealthy gained power at the expense of the middling groups and the poor; the Senate, in which representation rested upon taxes paid, was a stronghold of the well-to-do; even the lower house was weighted in favor of the eastern mercantile towns. The legislature and the courts, as might be expected, operated in favor of owners of debt and against the debtors. Debt and poverty went too far; rebellion flared up; Daniel Shays† became a brief hero of the indebted and forever a symbol of the dangers of mass tyranny to the wellborn and the few; finally, ruthless repression was followed by mild reform. But the basic balance of benefits and handicaps imposed by the constitution remained unchanged.[17]

**Prorogue:* to discontinue a session of a legislative body.

†*Daniel Shays* (1747–1825): former Revolutionary War officer who led a popular insurrection by small farmers in western Massachusetts (1786–1787) to protest their mounting debts and high taxes. Shay's Rebellion exposed the weaknesses of the Articles of Confederation for managing internal social conflicts of this type.

First and last, the men at the Constitutional Convention in Philadelphia were realists; when they blundered it was not from lack of realism but from lack of knowledge. As realists they understood these things about the constitution they were designing: that constitutional rules must inevitably benefit some groups and penalize others; that the rules were therefore highly controversial and subject to bitter conflict; that the rules must operate within the limits set by the prevailing balance of social forces; that they would, in turn, have consequences for the social balance; and that to endure, a constitution would require the assent of more than the fifty-five distinguished gentlemen in Philadelphia but luckily much less than the whole adult population.

The men at the Convention were perhaps as brilliant an assembly as has ever gathered to devise a lasting constitution for a great nation. It is only an index to the pitiful limitations of human knowledge to note that, realistic and gifted as they were, many of their key assumptions proved to be false, and the constitution they created has survived not because of their predictions but in spite of them.

Madisonian theory provided a brilliant and enduring defense—one is tempted to say rationalization—of the rules they set up. We have seen in what respects the Madisonian approach is deficient. More relevant to our present purposes is the extent to which the members of this historic assemblage did not know what they were doing. They thought the popular House would be dynamic, populistic, egalitarian, levelling, and therefore a dangerous center of power that needed restraint; they thought the President would represent the wellborn and the few and that he would use his veto against popular majorities lodged in the House. They were wrong; for the dynamic center of power has proved to be the presidency, and after Jackson the President could claim, and frequently did claim, to be the only representative of a national majority in the whole constitutional system. Meanwhile, the House has scarcely revealed itself as the instrument of those impassioned majorities that the men at the Convention so desperately feared. Today the relationship they envisaged is, by and large, reversed. It is the President who is the policy-maker, the creator of legislation, the self-appointed spokesman for the national majority, whereas the power of Congress is more and more that of veto—a veto exercised, as often as not, on behalf of groups whose privileges are threatened by presidential policy.

Whether the men at the Convention anticipated judicial review is an issue that will probably never be settled; but there is not a single word in the records of the Convention or in the "Federalist Papers" to suggest that they foresaw the central role the court would from time to time assume as a policy-maker and legislator in its own right. They did not foresee clearly, if at all, the great organizing function political parties would perform, and the ways in which these instruments would transform the formal constitutional arrangements. The equal representation of states in the Senate, which has done so much to decentralize the parties, the executive, and, indeed, the entire policy-making process, was not a matter of high constitutional principle but a necessary bargain opposed by many of the best minds at the Convention, including Madison himself.

Most of all, however, the men at the Convention misunderstood the dynamics of their own society. They failed to predict correctly the social balance of power that was to prevail even in their own lifetime. They did not really understand that in an agrarian society lacking feudal institutions and possessing an open and expanding frontier, radical democracy was almost certain to become the dominant and conventional view, almost certain to prevail in politics, and almost certain to be conservative about property.

Despite their false predictions, however, the institutions their work helped to create have in large part survived. Three reasons may account for this: First, for a variety of reasons apotheosis of the Constitution began very early and in an astonishingly short time controversy over the basic constitutional framework was all but eliminated; even the constitutional debate preceding our Civil War was ostensibly concerned with the question of the real intentions of the Convention. Second, perhaps in no society have the conditions of polyarchy been so fully present as they were in the United States in the ante-bellum period (save, of course, for the position of Negroes). To assume that this country has remained democratic because of its Constitution seems to me an obvious reversal of the relation; it is much more plausible to suppose that the Constitution has remained because our society is essentially democratic. If the conditions necessary to polyarchy had not existed, no constitution intended to limit the power of leaders would have survived. Perhaps a variety of constitutional forms could easily have been adapted to the changing social balance of power. It is worth emphasizing again that the constitutional system did not work when it finally encountered, in slavery, an issue that temporarily undermined some of the main prerequisites for polyarchy.

In the third place, the Constitution survived only because it was frequently adapted to fit the changing social balance of power. Measured by the society that followed, the Constitution envisaged by the men at the Convention distributed its benefits and handicaps to the wrong groups. Fortunately, when the social balance of power they anticipated proved to be illusory, the constitutional system was altered to confer benefits and handicaps more in harmony with the social balance of power.

We see this strikingly both in the Jacksonian and in the Congressional phases of development. Had the state constitutions of the Revolutionary period conferred more benefits on the small farmers and artisans and fewer on commerce and tidewater, it is at least possible that when the almost inevitable spread of universal manhood suffrage gave representatives of the small farmers and artisans more control, they would have adapted the national constitutional system in a way quite different from the one which, in fact, they selected. Historical accident also helped to turn agrarian democracy away from legislative supremacy. In highly unified party government led by the President, Jefferson had invented a device that might just barely have permitted the myth of legislative supremacy to survive along with vigorous executive leadership. But Jefferson's system required control by the Congressional caucus over both nominations and policy, and leadership of the caucus by the President. After Jefferson, the caucus seems to have slipped gradually out of the orbit of presidential leadership. By 1824 the forces rallying behind Jackson were unable to make use of it and his election in 1828 spelled the end of the Jeffersonian system.

More than that, Jackson's presidency marks the effective end in this country of the classic identification of democratic rules with legislative supremacy. Radical democrats had feared executive power. Conservative interests in the states favored legislative supremacy because they could control the legislature. Their spokesmen at the Constitutional Convention had in turn feared a national legislature they could not be certain of controlling and looked for their own defense to an executive with veto powers. By working hand in glove with the Congressional caucus, Jefferson overcame the barrier between executive and legislature. Jackson, however, developed a new pattern of relationships, a new constitutional system, and since his day that system has largely prevailed, rather than the Jeffersonian, the Madisonian, or the Revolutionary. The Jacksonian system may be interpreted as asserting that[18]:

1. Groups not effectively represented in the legislature or judiciary may be effectively represented by the executive.
2. The election process confers at least as much legitimacy on the executive's representativeness as on that of the legislature.
3. The President has perhaps a better claim to represent a national majority.

It is the growth of the third principle that, I believe, sets off the period after Jackson from that preceding it, for the idea that the elected executive might be the true representative of the majority was revolutionary in import.

In the post-bellum period, Congress reasserted itself. It would be more accurate to say that highly powerful social groups, driving and ambitious, possessed of rising wealth and status, asserted themselves through Congress. But the power of the new commercial and industrial interests was by no means unlimited; the two political parties were inevitably a hodgepodge of delicate compromises: anything like a comprehensive and co-ordinated national policy was, as the fate of the radical Republicans revealed, impossible. Compromise was maintained, therefore, by a highly decentralized policy-making system that worked essentially by bargaining. Effective control of the political parties was decentralized to state and local machines; control in Congress was decentralized to the committees; and the executive was so decentralized that the President was hardly more than a member of the board of directors of a holding company.

The subsequent growth of bureaucratic organizations under the nominal control of the President or of President and Congress together has been powerfully shaped by the legacy of Congressional government and the political habits and outlooks it gave rise to. In the context of decentralized bargaining parties and a decentralized bargaining legislature, it was perhaps inevitable that despite the powerful efforts of many Presidents and the somewhat Utopian yearnings of many administrative reformers, the vast apparatus that grew up to administer the affairs of the American welfare state is a decentralized bargaining bureaucracy. This is merely another way of saying that the bureaucracy has become a part of what earlier I called the "normal" American political process.

VIII

I defined the "normal" American political process as one in which there is a high probability that an active and legitimate group in the population can make itself heard effectively at some crucial stage in the process of decision. To be "heard" covers a wide range of activities, and I do not intend to define the word rigorously. Clearly, it does not mean that every group has equal control over the outcome.

In American politics, as in all other societies, control over decisions is unevenly distributed; neither individuals nor groups are political equals. When I say that a group is heard "effectively" I mean more than the simple fact that it makes a noise; I mean that one or more officials are not only ready to listen to the noise, but expect to suffer in some significant way if they do not placate the group, its leaders, or its most vociferous members. To satisfy the group may require one or more of a great variety of actions by the responsive leader: pressure for substantive policies, appointments, graft, respect, expression of the appropriate emotions, or the right combination of reciprocal noises.

Thus the making of governmental decisions is not a majestic march of great majorities united upon certain matters of basic policy. It is the steady appeasement of relatively small groups. Even when these groups add up to a numerical majority at election time it is usually not useful to construe that majority as more than an arithmetic expression. For to an extent that would have pleased Madison enormously, the numerical majority is incapable of undertaking any co-ordinated action. It is the various components of the numerical majority that have the means for action.

As this is familiar ground, let me summarize briefly and dogmatically some well-known aspects of the constitutional rules: the groups they benefit, those they handicap, and the net result. When we examine Congress we find that certain groups are overrepresented, in the sense that they have more representatives (or more representatives at key places) and therefore more control over the outcome of Congressional decisions than they would have if the rules were designed to maximize formal political equality.[19] Equal representation in the Senate has led to overrepresentation of the less densely populated states. In practice this means that farmers and certain other groups—metal mining interests, for example—are overrepresented. State legislatures overrepresent agricultural and small-town areas and hence do not redistrict House seats in accordance with population changes; even the House significantly underrepresents urban populations. The operation of the seniority principle and the power of the committee chairman has led the voters in one-party or modified one-party states to be significantly overrepresented. According to one recent estimate, there are twenty-two such states.[20] Geographically these include the solid South, the border states, upper New England, four midwestern states, Oregon, and Pennsylvania. Of these only Pennsylvania is highly urban and industrial. Because of the operation of the single-member district system* in the House, on the average, a

***Single-member district system:* see footnote "single member constituencies" on page 130.*

net shift of 1 per cent of the electorate from one party to the other will result in a net gain of about 2.5 per cent of the House seats for the benefited party; and because of the operation of the two-member district* in the Senate, a shift of 1 per cent will result in a net gain for the benefited party of about 3 per cent of the Senate seats. Hence, when large heterogeneous groups, like the farmers, shift their party support the legislative effects are likely to be considerably exaggerated. (Cf. Figs. 1. and 2).

All those politicians and officials concerned with the election or re-election of a President, and hence with the vagaries of the electoral college, must necessarily be responsive to a somewhat different set of groups. Again, the general picture is so well known that I need only enumerate a few points. In general the presidential politicians must be responsive to populous states with large electoral votes; to states that are marginal between the parties, i.e., to the two-party states; to the "key" states, i.e., those both marginal and populous; to key groups in the key states—ethnic, religious, occupational; to relatively large nationwide groups; and to heavily populated urban and industrial areas. A careful examination of these will show, I think, that they are different from, and often have goals that run counter to, the groups that predominate in Congress.

The bureaucracies are much more complex. In varying degrees they must be responsive to both presidential and Congressional politicians. But the presidential and Congressional politicians to whom they must respond are themselves rather a narrow and specialized group. In Congress, typically, it is the chairmen of the House and Senate Appropriations Committees, of the relevant subcommittees, and of the relevant substantive committees. Among presidential politicians, administrators must usually be responsive to the Budget Bureau, to the departmental secretary, and, of course, to the President himself. They must also be responsive to their own specialized clienteles. The most effective clientele obviously is one like the farmers, that is also well represented in Congress and even in the executive branch; sometimes bureaucracy and clientele become so intertwined that one cannot easily determine who is responsive to whom.

IX

This is the normal system. I have not attempted to determine in these pages whether it is a desirable system of government nor shall I try to do so now. For appraisal of its merits and defects would require a subtle and extended discussion lying beyond the bounds of these essays.

This much may be said of the system. If it is not the very pinnacle of human achievement, a model for the rest of the world to copy or to modify at its peril, as our nationalistic and politically illiterate glorifiers so tiresomely insist, neither, I think, is it so obviously a defective system as some of its critics suggest.

To be sure, reformers with a tidy sense of order dislike it. Foreign observers,

**Two-member district system:* system in which each district selects two members of a legislative body in the same election.

FIGURE 1. POPULAR VOTES AND CONGRESSIONAL SEATS WON: DEMOCRATS IN THE HOUSE OF REPRESENTATIVES, 1928–54.

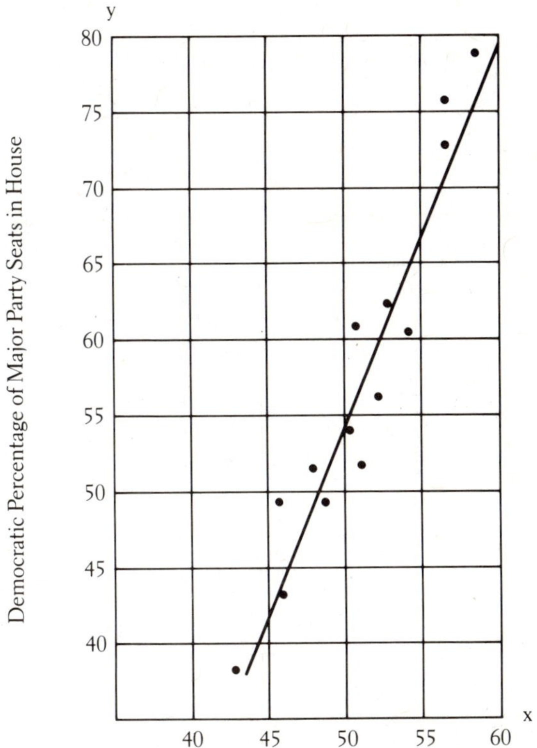

even sympathetic ones, are often astonished and confounded by it. Many Americans are frequently dismayed by its paradoxes; indeed, few Americans who look upon our political process attentively can fail, at times, to feel deep frustration and angry resentment with a system that on the surface has so little order and so much chaos.

For it is a markedly decentralized system. Decisions are made by endless bargaining; perhaps in no other national political system in the world is bargaining so basic a component of the political process. In an age when the efficiencies of hierarchy have been re-emphasized on every continent, no doubt the normal American political system is something of an anomaly, if not, indeed, at times an anachronism. For as a means to highly integrated, consistent decisions in some important areas—foreign policy, for example—it often appears to operate in a creaking fashion verging on total collapse.

Yet we should not be too quick in our appraisal, for where its vices stand out, its virtues are concealed to the hasty eye. Luckily the normal system has the virtues of its vices. With all its defects, it does nonetheless provide a high probability that any active and legitimate group will make itself heard effectively

FIGURE 2. POPULAR VOTES AND CONGRESSIONAL SEATS WON: DEMOCRATS IN THE SENATE, 1928–52.

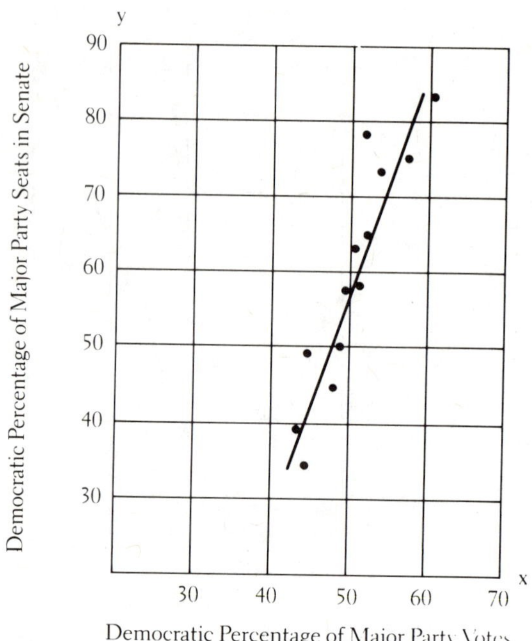

at some stage in the process of decision. This is no mean thing in a political system.

It is not a static system. The normal American system has evolved, and by evolving it has survived. It has evolved and survived from aristocracy to mass democracy, through slavery, civil war, the tentative uneasy reconciliation of North and South, the repression of Negroes and their halting liberation; through two great wars of world-wide scope, mobilization, far-flung miitary enterprise, and return to hazardous peace; through numerous periods of economic instability and one prolonged depression with mass unemployment, farm "holidays," veterans' marches, tear gas, and even bullets; through two periods of postwar cynicism, demagogic excesses, invasions of traditional liberties, and the groping, awkward, often savage, attempt to cope with problems of subversion, fear, and civil tension.

Probably this strange hybrid, the normal American political system, is not for export to others. But so long as the social prerequisites of democracy are substantially intact in this country, it appears to be a relatively efficient system for reinforcing agreement, encouraging moderation, and maintaining social peace in a restless and immoderate people operating a gigantic, powerful, diversified, and incredibly complex society.

This is no negligible contribution, then, that Americans have made to the arts of government—and to that branch, which of all the arts of politics is the most difficult, the art of democratic government.

NOTES

[1]Before Jackson, presidential electors were usually chosen by state legislatures. Consequently it is difficult to estimate the number of voters who supported a given candidate; compilations of popular votes in presidential elections usually begin with the election of 1828.

[2]However, modern sample surveys of public opinion are now helpful in this respect.

[3]See *The Pre-Election Polls of 1948* (New York: Social Science Research Council, 1949); Angus Campbell and R. L. Kahn, *The People Elect a President* (Ann Arbor: Institute for Social Research, 1952); Angus Campbell, Gerald Gurin, and Warren E. Miller, *The Voter Decides* (Evanston: Row, Peterson & Co., 1954).

[4]Campbell *et al.*, *op cit.*, p. 31, Table 3.2.

[5]It can easily be shown that in order for the winning candidate to be the first choice of a majority of all eligible voters, he must also be the first choice of a percentage of the nonvoters greater than: $(X - 2W)/2Z$, where X is the number of eligible voters, W is the number of votes obtained by the winning candidate, and Z is the number of non-voters. For example, in 1948, Mr. Truman was the first choice of a majority of all eligible voters only if he was also the first choice of more than 50.7 per cent of the non-voters; in 1952, on the other hand, Mr. Eisenhower would only have needed the support of more than 41.2 per cent of the non-voters. The estimates are based on data in tables in: *The Political Almanac of 1952* (New York: Forbes & Sons, 1952), p. 22; *Statistics of the Presidential and Congressional Elections of Nov. 4, 1952* (Washington: Government Printing Office, 1953), p. 52; and V. O. Key, A *Primer of Statistics for Political Scientists* (New York: Thomas Y. Crowell & Co., 1953), p. 197.

[6]My estimates are based on the data in Table 3.8, Campbell *et al.*, *op. cit.*, p. 37.

[7]In the 1948 election, in one sample of voters, 73 per cent said they had never thought of voting for the other candidate at any time during the campaign; in the 1952 election, in another sample of voters, the figure was 78 per cent, *ibid.*, p. 23, Table 2.7. This suggests the upper limit; the data do not indicate how many of these saw non-voting as an alternative to voting for their candidate.

[8]71 per cent of those who thought it "was our government's fault that China went Communistic" supported Eisenhower, *ibid.*

[9]Great Britain furnishes an interesting confirmation of the fact that electoral majorities rarely determine specific policy. The British political system has few of the constitutional and political barriers to majority rule characteristic of the American system. Nevertheless, it is comparatively rare for the party in power to have been the first preference of a majority of the voters—much less of the whole electorate—at the preceding election. Since 1923 there have been nine elections. Only two of these indicated a majority of first preferences for the ensuing government. Even the two exceptions are politically aberrant. In the election of 1931, candidates endorsing Ramsay MacDonald's national coalition won a majority of the votes, the Labor party having been badly hit by MacDonald's withdrawal. In 1935, the Conservative party candidates won only 47.7 per cent of the votes, but candidates endorsing the National government won 54.7 per cent of the votes. Not since 1945 has any government been the first preference of a majority of the voters. Indeed, in 1945, 10.4 million people eligible to vote either did not vote or voted for candidates other than Labor or Conservative compared with 9.6 million for the Conservatives and 12 million for the Labor candidates. In 1950, this group numbered 8.2 million, compared with 12.1 million Conservative voters and 13.2 million Labor voters. Cf. *The Constitutional Year Book, 1938* (London: Harrison, 1938), Vol. LII; D. E. Butler, *The Electoral System in Britain, 1918–1951* (Oxford: Clarendon Press, 1953), p. 173; John Bonham, *The Middle Class Vote* (London: Faber & Faber, 1955), p. 120.

[10]Elmo Roper, "American Attitudes on World Organization," *Public Opinion Quarterly*, XVII (winter, 1953–54), pp. 405–20.

[11]In this respect the otherwise excellent analysis of democracy in Joseph A. Schumpeter, *Capitalism, Socialism and Democracy* (2d ed.; New York: Harper & Bros., 1947), seems to me somewhat defective.

[12]Arthur F. Bentley, *The Process of Government* (Chicago: University of Chicago Press, 1908); David Truman, *The Governmental Process* (New York: A. A. Knopf, Inc., 1951); Earl Latham, *The Groups Basis of Politics: A Study in Basing Point Legislation* (Ithaca: Cornell University Press, 1952).

[13]For example, as might be expected, voting falls off rapidly from those who are "very much" interested in following a campaign to those who are "not much interested"; or from those who are "very much concerned about the outcome of the election" to those who are "not at all" concerned. Campbell *et al.*, *op. cit.*, Tables 3.6 and 3.8, pp. 35–37. On the other hand, gauged by opinion as to the importance of the outcome to the country, an interesting and unexplained difference is revealed in the sample. Among Eisenhower supporters considerably more of those who felt the outcome made much difference to the country voted than did those who felt the outcome made no difference. Among Stevenson supporters the differences were not statistically significant; actually, in the sample a slightly smaller percentage of those who thought the outcome of much importance to the country voted than among those who thought it of no importance to the country.

[14]Two seeming exceptions to this are: (1) If active members include among their own goals the protection or advancement of inactive members; (2) if presently active members expect that presently inactive members may become active in the future. Both are important cases in the real world. The first, however, can properly be called a case of indirect rather than direct influence on the outcome. The second merely requires that in principle the time dimension should somehow be specified. This, however, would become too complex for exposition and it is perhaps preferable to let our oversimple proposition stand as it is.

[15]H. G. Webster, "A Comparative Study of the State Constitutions of the American Revolution," *American Academy of Political and Social Science, Annals*, Vol. IX (1897).

[16]Cf. J. Allen Smith, *The Spirit of American Government* (New York: Macmillan Co., 1911), chaps. ii and ix.

[17]Cf. Oscar and Mary Flug Handlin, *Commonwealth: A Study of the Role of Government in the American Economy: Massachusetts, 1774–1861* (New York: New York University Press, 1947), pp. 26–27, 41, 44, 45, 49–52, and Appendix II, p. 267. In many respects the Massachusetts constitution was atypical, e.g., the governor had an absolute veto. "Although drafted by a convention elected by manhood suffrage, it was not only one of the most aristocratic of the Revolutionary period but also more thoroughly ensured government by the upper classes than the constitution of 1778 rejected by the same electorate." Elisha P. Douglas, *Rebels and Democrats: The Struggle for Equal Political Rights and Majority Rule during the American Revolution* (Chapel Hill: University of North Carolina Press, 1955), p. 211. In South Carolina, as might be expected, the constitution strengthened tidewater against piedmont. *Ibid.*, pp. 43–44. Cf. also Fletcher M. Green, *Constitutional Development in the South Atlantic States, 1776–1860* (Chapel Hill: University of North Carolina Press, 1930). In an unpublished doctoral dissertation, Norman Stamps has shown how the Connecticut constitution, which was the old colonial charter, was highly democratic in appearance and nicely designed to permit tight control by a tight oligarchy. Norman Stamps, "Political Parties in Connecticut, 1789–1819" (unpublished Ph.D. dissertation, Yale University, 1950). In Pennsylvania the pattern was unique. Universal suffrage was virtually a fact by 1790, forty years before it became general throughout the United States. Evidently because of this the balance remained more nearly favorable to the ordinary farmer and artisaan than in other states, even after the constitution adopted under the impetus of radical democracy during the Revolution was displaced in 1789. Douglas, *op. cit.*, chaps. xii–xiv; and Louis Hartz, *Economic Policy and Democratic Thought: Pennsylvania 1776–1860* (Cambridge: Harvard University Press, 1948), pp. 23 ff. In recent years the rise and decline of these state constitutions has lost the attention of political scientists. This is a pity. They provide a mine of information for the study of political institutions, and their decline has never been satisfactorily explained. However, for one aspect of the change, consult Leslie Lipson, *The American Governor: From Figurehead to Leader* (Chicago: University of Chicago Press, 1939).

[18]For example, see W. E. Binkley, *President and Congress* (New York: A. A. Knopf, Inc., 1947), chaps. iv and v.

[19]"Formal" because whether rules designed to maximize formal political equality would actually maximize political equality more than the present rules is a tough empirical question I wish to avoid.

[20]Austin Ranney and Willmoore Kendall, "The American Party Systems," *American Political Science Review*, XLVIII (June, 1954), p. 477.

12

MANCUR OLSON, JR.

COLLECTIVE ACTION: THE LOGIC

In his book The Logic of Collective Action: Public Goods and the Theory of Groups *(1965, 1971), Mancur Olson, Jr., prompted rethinking of conventional assumptions about political behavior and interest groups. The thrust of his reasoning is summarized in this excerpt from* The Rise and Decline of Nations; Economic Growth, Stagflation, and Social Rigidities *(1982). Olson, a professor of economics at the University of Maryland, discusses the relationship between the gain/loss calculations of rational individuals and incentives to act collectively in large and small groups. The maintenance of large voluntary associations is complicated by the "free rider" problem: a rational individual will calculate that his or her small contribution to a group will make little difference, and that if the group succeeds in its mission, collective benefits will be received whether or not he or she has contributed. Among Olson's other numerous works are:* The Economics of the Wartime Shortage *(1963); and* Beyond the Measuring Rod of Money *(forthcoming).*

I

. . . It has often been taken for granted that if everyone in a group of individuals or firms had some interest in common, then there would be a tendency for the group to seek to further this interest. Thus many students of politics in the United States for a long time supposed that citizens with a common political interest would organize and lobby to serve that interest. Each individual in the population would be in one or more groups and the vector of pressures of these competing groups explained the outcomes of the political process. Similarly, it was often supposed that if workers, farmers, or consumers faced monopolies harmful to their interests, they would eventually attain countervailing power through organizations such as labor unions or farm organizations that obtained market power and protective government action. On a larger scale, huge social classes are often expected to act in the interest of their members; the unalloyed form of this belief is, of course, the Marxian contention that in capitalist societies the bourgeois* class runs the government to serve its own interests, and that once the exploitation of the proletariat† goes far enough and "false consciousness"‡ has

**Bourgeois* see footnote on page 14.

†*Proletariat:* term popularized by Karl Marx (see footnote on page 13), who used it in reference to the industrial working class that sells its labor for a wage. According to Marx, the proletariat is exploited under capitalism because the owners of the means of production do not pay laborers for the true value of their work. Marx predicted that the proletariat would overthrow the capitalists and establish what he called a "dictatorship of the proletariat."

‡*False consciousness:* Marxian concept referring to the distortion of thought that arises from the concealment of the true nature of the relationships within and among the political, economic, and social systems.

disappeared, the working class will in its own interest revolt and establish a dictatorship of the proletariat. In general, if the individuals in some category or class had a sufficient degree of self-interest and if they all agreed on some common interest, then the group would to some extent also act in a self-interested or group-interested manner.

If we ponder the logic of the familiar assumption described in the preceding paragraph, we can see that it is fundamentally and indisputably faulty. Consider those consumers who agree that they pay higher prices for a product because of some objectionable monopoly or tariff, or those workers who agree that their skill deserves a higher wage. Let us now ask what would be the expedient course of action for an individual consumer who would like to see a boycott to combat a monopoly or a lobby to repeal the tariff, or for an individual worker who would like a strike threat or a minimum wage law that could bring higher wages. If the consumer or worker contributes a few days and a few dollars to organize a boycott or a union or to lobby for favorable legislation, he or she will have sacrificed time and money. What will this sacrifice obtain? The individual will at best succeed in advancing the cause to a small (often imperceptible) degree. In any case he will get only a minute share of the gain from his action. The very fact that the object or interest is common to or shared by the group entails that the gain from any sacrifice an individual makes to serve this common purpose is shared with everyone in the group. The successful boycott or strike or lobbying action will bring the better price or wage for everyone in the relevant category, so the individual in any large group with a common interest will reap only a minute share of the gains from whatever sacrifices the individual makes to achieve this common interest. Since any gain goes to everyone in the group, those who contribute nothing to the effort will get just as much as those who made a contribution. It pays to "let George do it," but George has little or no incentive to do anything in the group interest either, so (in the absence of factors that are completely left out of the conceptions mentioned in the first paragraph) there will be little, if any, group action. The paradox, then, is that (in the absence of special arrangements or circumstances to which we shall turn later) large groups, at least if they are composed of rational individuals, will *not* act in their group interest.

This paradox is elaborated and set out in a way that lets the reader check every step of the logic in a book I wrote entitled *The Logic of Collective Action*. . . .[1]

II

One finding in *The Logic* is that the services of associations like labor unions, professional associations, farm organizations, cartels,* lobbies (and even collusive group without formal organization) resemble the basic services of the state in one utterly fundamental respect. The services of such associations, like the

*Cartels: see footnote on page 112.

elemental services or "public goods"* provided by governments, if provided to anyone, go to everyone in some category or group. Just as the law and order, defense, or pollution abatement brought about by government accrue to everyone in some country or geographic area, so the tariff obtained by a farm organization's lobbying effort raises the price to all producers of the relevant commodity. Similarly, as I argued earlier, the higher wage won by a union applies to all employees in the pertinent category. More generally, every lobby obtaining a general change in legislation or regulation thereby obtains a public or collective good for everyone who benefits from that change, and every combination—that is, every "cartel"—using market or industrial action to get a higher price or wage must, when it restricts the quantity supplied, raise the price for every seller, thereby creating a collective good for all sellers.

If governments, on the one hand, and combinations exploiting their political or market power, on the other, produce public or collective goods that inevitably go to everyone in some group or category, then both are subject to the paradoxical logic set out above: that is, the individuals and firms they serve have in general no incentive voluntarily to contribute to their support.[2] It follows that if there is only voluntary and rational individual behavior,[3] then for the most part neither governments nor lobbies and cartels will exist, unless individuals support them for some reason *other* than the collective goods they provide. Of course, governments exist virtually everywhere and often there are lobbies and cartelistic organizations as well. If the argument so far is right, it follows that something *other* than the collective goods that governments and other organizations provide accounts for their existence.[4]

In the case of governments, the answer was explained before *The Logic of Collective Action* was written; governments are obviously supported by compulsory taxation. Sometimes there is little objection to this compulsion, presumably because many people intuitively understand that public goods cannot be sold in the marketplace or financed by any voluntary mechanism; as I have already argued, each individual would get only a minute share of any governmental services he or she paid for and would get whatever level of services was provided by others in any event.

In the case of organizations that provide collective goods to their client groups through political or market action, the answer has not been obvious, but it is no less clear-cut. Organizations of this kind, at least when they represent large groups, are again not supported because of the collective goods they provide, but rather because they have been fortunate enough to find what I have called *selective incentives*. A selective incentive is one that applies selectively to the individuals depending on whether they do or do not contribute to the provision of the collective good.

**Public goods:* goods, or services, such as defense or clean air, that cannot be provided to some persons within a geographic area without being provided to everyone. Since individuals cannot be excluded from their benefits, it is in each person's immediate economic interest to enjoy the good without paying for it. Consequently, the private sector cannot sell such nondivisible goods, whereas governments can supply them through revenues raised by involuntary taxation.

A selective incentive can be either negative or positive; it can, for example, be a loss or punishment imposed only on those who do *not* help provide the collective good. Tax payments are, of course, obtained with the help of negative selective incentives, since those who are found not to have paid their taxes must then suffer both taxes and penalties. The best-known type of organized interest group in modern democratic societies, the labor union, is also usually supported, in part, through negative selective incentives. Most of the dues in strong unions are obtained through union shop, closed shop, or agency shop arrangements which make dues paying more or less compulsory and automatic. There are often also informal arrangements with the same effect; David McDonald, former president of the United Steel Workers of America, describes one of these arrangements used in the early history of that union. It was, he writes, a technique

> which we called . . . visual education, which was a high-sounding label for a practice much more accurately described as dues picketing. It worked very simply. A group of dues-paying members, selected by the district director (usually more for their size than their tact) would stand at the plant gate with pick handles or baseball bats in hand and confront each worker as he arrived for his shift.[5]

As McDonald's "dues picketing" analogy suggets, picketing during strikes is another negative selective incentive that unions sometimes need; although picketing in industries with established and stable unions is usually peaceful, this is because the union's capacity to close down an enterprise against which it has called a strike is clear to all; the early phase of unionization often involves a great deal of violence on the part of both unions and anti-union employers and scabs.[6]

Some opponents of labor unions argue that, since many of the members of labor unions join only through the processes McDonald described or through legally enforced union-shop arrangements, most of the relevant workers do not want to be unionized. The Taft-Hartley Act* provided that impartial governmentally administered elections should be held to determine whether workers did in fact want to belong to unions. As the collective-good logic set out here suggests, the same workers who had to be coerced to pay union dues voted for the unions with compulsory dues (and normally by overwhelming margins), so that this feature of the Taft-Hartley Act was soon abandoned as pointless.[7] The workers who as individuals tried to avoid paying union dues at the same time that they voted to force themselves all to pay dues are no different from taxpayers who vote, in effect, for high levels of taxation, yet try to arrange their private affairs in ways that avoid taxes. Because of the same logic, many professional associations also get members through covert or overt coercion (for examples, lawyers in those states with a "closed bar"). So do lobbies and cartels of several other types; some of the contributions by corporate officials, for instance, to politicians useful to the corporation are also the result of subtle forms of coercion.[8]

Positive selective incentives, although easily overlooked, are also commonplace, as diverse examples in *The Logic* demonstrate.[9] American farm organizations offer prototypical examples. Many of the members of the stronger Ameri-

**Taft-Hartley Act:* see footnote on page 118.

can farm organizations are members because their dues are automatically deducted from the "patronage dividends" of farm cooperatives or are included in the insurance premiums paid to mutual insurance companies associated with the farm organizations. Any number of organizations with urban clients also provide similar positive selective incentives in the form of insurance policies, publications, group air fares, and other private goods made available only to members. The grievance procedures of labor unions usually also offer selective incentives, since the grievances of active members often get most of the attention. The symbiosis between the political power of a lobbying organization and the business institutions associated with it often yields tax or other advantages for the business institution, and the publicity and other information flowing out of the political arm of a movement often generates patterns of preference or trust that make the business activities of the movement more remunerative. The surpluses obtained in such ways in turn provide positive selective incentives that recruit participants for the lobbying efforts.

III

Small groups, or occasionally large "federal" groups that are made up of many small groups of socially interactive members, have an additional source of both negative and positive selective incentives. Clearly most people value the companionship and respect of those with whom they interact. In modern societies solitary confinement is, apart from the rare death penalty, the harshest legal punishment. The censure or even ostracism of those who fail to bear a share of the burdens of collective action can sometimes be an important selective incentive. An extreme example of this occurs when British unionists refuse to speak to uncooperative colleagues, that is, "send them to Coventry." Similarly, those in a socially interactive group seeking a collective good can give special respect or honor to those who distinguish themselves by their sacrifices in the interest of the group and thereby offer them a positive selective incentive. Since most people apparently prefer relatively like-minded or agreeable and respectable company, and often prefer to associate with those whom they especially admire, they may find it costless to shun those who shirk the collective action and to favor those who oversubscribe.

Social selective incentives can be powerful and inexpensive, but they are available only in certain situations. As I have already indicated, they have little applicability to large groups, except in those cases in which the large groups can be federations of small groups that are capable of social interaction. It also is not possible to organize most large groups in need of a collective good into small, socially interactive subgroups, since most individuals do not have the time needed to maintain a huge number of friends and acquaintances.

The availability of social selective incentives is also limited by the social heterogeneity of some of the groups or categories that would benefit from a collective good. Everyday observation reveals that most socially interactive groups are fairly homogeneous and that many people resist extensive social interaction with those they deem to have lower status or greatly different tastes. Even Bohemian or other nonconformist groups often are made up of individuals who are similar to one another, however much they differ from the rest of society. Since some of the categories of individuals who would benefit from a collective good are socially heterogeneous, the social interaction needed for selective incentives sometimes cannot be arranged even when the number of individuals involved is small.

Another problem in organizing and maintaining socially heterogeneous groups is that they are less likely to agree on the exact nature of whatever collective good is at issue or on how much of it is worth buying. All the arguments showing the difficulty of collective action mentioned so far in this chapter hold even when there is perfect consensus about the collective good that is desired, the amount that is wanted, and the best way to obtain the good. But if anything, such as social heterogeneity, reduces consensus, collective action can become still less likely. And if there is nonetheless collective action, it incurs the extra cost (especially for the leaders of whatever organization or collusion is at issue) of accommodating and compromising the different views. The situation is slightly different in the very small groups to which we shall turn shortly. In such groups differences of opinion can sometimes provide a bit of an incentive to join an organization seeking a collective good, since joining might give the individual a significant influence over the organization's policy and the nature of any collective good it would obtain. But this consideration is not relevant to any group that is large enough so that a single individual cannot expect to affect the outcome.

Consensus is especially difficult where collective goods are concerned because the defining characteristic of collective goods—that they go to everyone in some group or category if they are provided at all—also entails that everyone in the relevant group gets more or less of the collective good together, and that they all have to accept whatever level and type of public good is provided. A country can have only one foreign and defense policy, however diverse the preferences and incomes of its citizenry, and (except in the rarely attainable case of a "Lindahl equilibrium")[10] there will not be agreement within a country on how much should be spent to carry out the foreign and defense policy. This is a clear implication of the arguments for "fiscal equivalence"[11] and of the rigorous models of "optimal segregation"[12] and "fiscal federalism."[13] Heterogeneous clients with diverse demands for collective goods can pose an even greater problem for private associations, which not only must deal with the disagreements but also must find selective incentives strong enough to hold dissatisfied clients.

In short, the political entrepreneurs who attempt to organize collective action will accordingly be more likely to succeed if they strive to organize relatively homogeneous groups. The political managers whose task it is to maintain organized or collusive action similarly will be motivated to use indoctrination and selective recruitment to increase the homogeneity of their client groups. This is true in part because social selective incentives are more likely to be available to the more nearly homogeneous groups, and in part because homogeneity will help achieve consensus.

IV

Information and calculation about a collective good is often itself a collective good. Consider a typical member of a large organization who is deciding how much time to devote to studying the policies or leadership of the organization. The more time the member devotes to this matter, the greater the likelihood that his or her voting or advocacy will favor effective policies and leadership for the organization. This typical member will, however, get only a small share of the gain from the more effective policies and leadership: in the aggregate, the other members will get almost all the gains, so that the individual member does not have an incentive to devote nearly as much time to fact-finding and thinking about the organization as would be in the group interest. Each of the members of the group would be better off if they all could be coerced into spending more time finding out how to vote to make the organization best further their interests. This is dramatically evident in the case of the typical voter in a national election in a large country. The gain to such a voter from studying issues and candidates until it is clear what vote is truly in his or her interest is given by the difference in the value to the individual of the "right" election outcome as compared with the "wrong" outcome, *multiplied by the probability a change in the individual's vote will alter the outcome of the election*. Since the probability that a typical voter will change the outcome of the election is vanishingly small, the typical citizen is usually "rationally ignorant" about political affairs.[11] Often, information about public affairs is so interesting or entertaining that it pays to acquire it for these reasons alone—this appears to be the single most important source of exceptions to the generalization that *typical* citizens are rationally ignorant about public affairs.

Individuals in a few special vocations can receive considerable rewards in private goods if they acquire exceptional knowledge of public goods. Politicians, lobbyists, journalists, and social scientists, for example, may earn more money, power, or prestige from knowledge of this or that public business. Occasionally, exceptional knowledge of public policy can generate exceptional profits in stock exchanges or other markets. Withal, the typical citizen will find that his or her income and life chances will not be improved by zealous study of public affairs, or even of any single collective good.

The limited knowledge of public affairs is in turn necessary to explain the effectiveness of lobbying. If all citizens had obtained and digested all pertinent information, they could not then be swayed by advertising or other persuasion. With perfectly informed citizens, elected officials would not be subject to the blandishment of lobbyists, since the constituents would then know if their interests were betrayed and defeat the unfaithful representative at the next election. Just as lobbies provide collective goods to special-interest groups, so their effectiveness is explained by the imperfect knowledge of citizens, and this in turn is due mainly to the fact that information and calculation about collective goods is also a collective good.

This fact—that the benefits of individual enlightenment about public goods are usually dispersed through a group or nation, rather than concentrated upon the individual who bears the costs of becoming enlightened—explains many other phenomena as well. It explains, for example, the "man bites dog" criterion of what is newsworthy. If the television newscasts were watched or newspapers were read solely to obtain the most important information about public affairs, aberrant events of little public importance would be ignored and typical patterns of quantitative significance would be emphasized; when the news is, by contrast, for most people largely an alternative to other forms of diversion or entertainment, intriguing oddities and human-interest items are in demand. Similarly, events that unfold in a suspenseful way or sex scandals among public figures are fully covered by the media, whereas the complexities of economic policy or quantitative analyses of public problems receive only minimal attention. Public officials, often able to thrive without giving the citizens good value for their tax monies, may fall over an exceptional mistake striking enough to be newsworthy. Extravagant statements, picturesque protests, and unruly demonstrations that offend much of the public they are designed to influence are also explicable in this way: they make diverting news and thus call attention to interests and arguments that might otherwise be ignored. Even some isolated acts of terrorism that are described as "senseless" can, from this perspective, be explained as effective means of obtaining the riveted attention of a public that otherwise would remain rationally ignorant.

This argument also helps us to understand certain apparent inconsistencies in the behavior of modern democracies. The arrangement of the income-tax brackets in all the major developed democracies is distinctly progressive,* whereas the loopholes are more often tilted toward a minority of more prosperous taxpayers. Since both are the results of the same democratic institution, why do they not have the same incidence? As I see it, the progression of the income tax is a matter of such salience and political controversy that much of the electorate knows about it, so populist and majoritarian considerations dictate a considerable degree of progression. The details of tax laws are far less widely known, and they often reflect the interests of small numbers of organized and usually more prosperous taxpayers. Several of the developed democracies similarly have adopted programs such as Medicare† and Medicaid‡ that are obviously inspired by the concerns about the cost of medical care to those with low or middle incomes, yet implemented or administered these programs in ways that resulted in large increases in income for prosperous physicians and other providers of medical care. Again, these diverse consequences seem to be explained by the fact that conspicuous and controversial choices of overall policies become known to the majorities who consume health care, whereas the many smaller choices needed to implement these programs are influenced primarily by a minority of organized providers of health care.

**Progressive taxation policy:* policy in which those individuals or households in higher income brackets pay an increasingly higher rate of tax.

†*Medicare:* Federal program that provides hospital and medical insurance for people over 65, and for the disabled. Medicare was enacted through a 1965 amendment to the Social Security Act.

‡*Medicaid:* federally funded but state-administered health coverage for low income people that was authorized by a 1965 amendment to the Social Security Act.

The fact that the typical individual does not have an incentive to spend much time studying many of his choices concerning collective goods also helps to explain some otherwise inexplicable individual contributions toward the provision of collective goods. The logic of collective action that has been described in this chapter is not immediately apparent to those who have never studied it; if it were, there would be nothing paradoxical in the argument with which this chapter opened, and students to whom the argument is explained would not react with initial skepticism.[15] No doubt the practical implications of this logic for the individual's own choices were often discerned before the logic was ever set out in print, but this does not mean that they were always understood even at the intuitive and practical level. In particular, when the costs of individual contributions to collective action are very small, the individual has little incentive to investigate whether or not to make a contribution or even to exercise intuition. If the individual knows the costs of a contribution to collective action in the interest of a group of which he is a part are trivially small, he may rationally not take the trouble to consider whether the gains are smaller still. This is particularly the case since the size of these gains and the policies that would maximize them are matters about which it is usually not rational for him to investigate.

This consideration of the costs and benefits of calculation about public goods leads to the testable prediction that voluntary contributions toward the provision of collective goods for large groups without selective incentives will often occur when the costs of individual contributions are negligible, but that they will *not* often occur when the costs of the individual contributions are considerable. In other words, when the costs of individual action to help to obtain a desired collective good are small enough, the result is indeterminate and sometimes goes one way and sometimes the other, but when the costs get larger this indeterminacy disappears. We should accordingly find that more than a few people are willing to take the moment of time needed to sign petitions for causes they support, or to express their opinions in the course of discussion, or to vote for the candidate or party they prefer. Similarly, if the argument here is correct, we should not find many instances where individuals voluntarily contribute substantial sums of resources year after year for the purpose of obtaining some collective good for some large group of which they are a part. Before parting with a large amount of money or time, and particularly before doing so repeatedly, the rational individual will reflect on what this considerable sacrifice will accomplish. If the individual is a typical individual in a large group that would benefit from a collective good, his contribution will not make a perceptible difference in the amount that is provided. The theory here predicts that such contributions become less likely the larger the contribution at issue.[16]

V

Even when contributions are costly enough to elicit rational calculation, there is still only one set of circumstances in which collective action can occur without selective incentives. This set of circumstances becomes evident the moment we think of situations in which there are only a few individuals or firms that would benefit from collective action. Suppose there are two firms of equal size in an industry and no other firms can enter the industry. It still will be the case that a higher price for the industry's product will benefit both firms and that legislation favorable to the industry will help both firms. The higher price and the favorable legislation are then collective goods to this "oligopolistic"* industry, even though there are only two in the group that benefit from the collective goods. Obviously, each of the oligopolists is in a situation in which if it restricts output to raise the industry price, or lobbies for favorable legislation for the industry, it will tend to get half of the benefit. And the cost-benefit ratio of action in the common interest easily could be so favorable that, even though a firm bears the whole cost of its action and gets only half the benefit of this action, it could still profit from acting in the common interest. Thus if the group that would benefit from collective action is sufficiently small and the cost-benefit ratio of collective action for the group sufficiently favorable, there may well be calculated action in the collective interest even without selective incentives.

When there are only a few members in the group, there is also the possibility that they will bargain with one another and agree on collective action—then the action of each can have a perceptible effect on the interests and the expedient courses of actions of others, so that each has an incentive to act strategically, that is, in ways that take into account the effect of the individual's choices on the choices of others. This interdependence of individual firms or persons in the group can give them an incentive to bargain with one another for their mutual advantage. Indeed, if bargaining costs were negligible, they would have an incentive to continue bargaining with one another until group gains were maximized, that is, until what we shall term a *group-optimal outcome* (or what economists sometimes call a "Pareto-optimal" outcome for the group) is achieved. One way the two firms mentioned in the previous paragraph could obtain such an outcome is by agreeing that each will bear half the costs of any collective action; each firm would then bear half the cost of its action in the common interest and receive half the benefits. It therefore would have an incentive to continue action in the collective interest until the aggregate gains of collective action were maximized. In any bargaining, however, each party has an incentive to seek the largest possible share of the group gain for itself, and usually also an incentive to threaten to block or undermine the collective action—that is, to be a "holdout"—if it does not get its preferred share of the group gains. Thus the bargaining may very well not succeed in achieving a group-optimal outcome and may also fail to achieve agreement on any collective action at all. The upshot of all this, as I explain elsewhere,[17] is that "small" groups can often engage in collective action without selective incentives. In certain small groups ("privileged groups") there is actually a presumption that some of the collective good will be provided. Nonetheless, even in the best of circumstances collective action is problematic and the outcomes in particular cases are indeterminate.

Oligopolistic industry: an industry characterized by market concentration, with only few large suppliers of a good or service.

Although some aspects of the matter are complex and indeterminate, the essence of the relationship between the size of the group that would benefit from collective action and the extent of collective action is beautifully simple—yet somehow not widely understood. Consider again our two firms and suppose that they have *not* worked out any agreement to maximize their aggregate gains or to coordinate their actions in any way. Each firm will still get half the gains of any action it takes in the interest of the group, and thus it may have a substantial incentive to act in the group interest even when it is acting unilaterally. There is, of course, also a *group external economy,* or gain to the group for which the firm acting unilaterally is not compensated, of 50 percent, so unilateral behavior does not achieve a group-optimal outcome.[18] Now suppose there were a third firm of the same size—the group external economy would then be two thirds, and the individual firm would get only a third of the gain from any independent action it took in the group interest. Of course, if there were a hundred such firms, the group external economy would be 99 percent, and the individual firm would get only 1 percent of the gain from any action in the group interest. Obviously, when we get to large groups measured in millions or even thousands, the incentive for group-oriented behavior in the absence of selective incentives becomes insignificant and even imperceptible.

Untypical as my example of equal-sized firms may be, it makes the general point intuitively obvious: other things being equal, *the larger the number of individuals or firms that would benefit from a collective good, the smaller the share of the gains from action in the group interest that will accrue to the individual or firm that undertakes the action. Thus, in the absence of selective incentives, the incentive for group action diminishes as group size increases, so that large groups are less able to act in their common interest than small ones.* If an additional individual or firm that would value the collective good enters the scene, then the share of the gains from group-oriented action that anyone already in the group might take must diminish. This holds true whatever the relative sizes or valuations of the collective good in the group. . . .

The number of people who must bargain if a group-optimal amount of a collective good is to be obtained, and thus the costs of bargaining, must rise with the size of the group. This consideration reinforces the point just made. Indeed, both everyday observation and the logic of the matter suggest that for genuinely large groups, bargaining among all members to obtain agreement on the provision of a collective good is out of the question. The consideration mentioned earlier in this chapter, that social selective incentives are available only to small groups and (tenuously) to those larger groups that are federations of small groups, also suggests that small groups are more likely to organize than large ones.

The significance of the logic that has just been set out can best be seen by comparing groups that would have the same net gain from collective action, if they could engage in it, but that vary in size. Suppose there are a million individuals who would gain a thousand dollars each, or a billion in the aggregate, if they were to organize effectively and engage in collective action that had a total cost of a hundred million. If the logic set out above is right, they could not organize or engage in effective collective action without selective incentives.

Now suppose that, although the total gain of a billion dollars from collective action and the aggregate cost of a hundred million remain the same, the group is composed instead of five big corporations or five organized municipalities, each of which would gain two hundred million. Collective action is not an absolute certainty even in this case, since each of the five could conceivably expect others to put up the hundred million and hope to gain the collective good worth two hundred million at no cost at all. Yet collective action, perhaps after some delays due to bargaining, seems very likely indeed. In this case any one of the five would gain a hundred million from providing the collective good even if it had to pay the whole cost itself; and the costs of bargaining among five would not be great, so they would sooner or later probably work out an agreement providing for the collective action. The numbers in this example are arbitrary, but roughly similar situations occur often in reality, and the contrast between "small" and "large" groups could be illustrated with an infinite number of diverse examples.

The significance of this argument shows up in a second way if one compares the operations of lobbies or cartels within jurisdictions of vastly different scale, such as a modest municipality on the one hand and a big country on the other. Within the town, the mayor or city council may be influenced by, say, a score of petitioners or a lobbying budget of a thousand dollars. A particular line of business may be in the hands of only a few firms, and if the town is distant enough from other markets only these few would need to agree to create a cartel. In a big country, the resources needed to influence the national government are likely to be much more substantial, and unless the firms are (as they sometimes are) gigantic, many of them would have to cooperate to create an effective cartel. Now suppose that the million individuals in our large group in the previous paragraph were spread out over a hundred thousand towns or jurisdictions, so that each jurisdiction had ten of them, along with the same proportion of citizens in other categories as before. Suppose also that the cost-benefit ratios remained the same, so that there was still a billion dollars to gain across all jurisdictions or ten thousand in each, and that it would still cost a hundred million dollars across all jurisdictions or a thousand in each. It no longer seems out of the question that in many jurisdictions the groups of ten, or subsets of them, would put up the thousand-dollar total needed to get the thousand for each individual. Thus we see that, if all else were equal, small jurisdictions would have more collective action per capita than large ones.

Differences in intensities of preference generate a third type of illustration of the logic at issue. A small number of zealots anxious for a particular collective good are more likely to act collectively to obtain that good than a larger number with the same aggregate willingness to pay. Suppose there are twenty-five individuals, each of whom finds a given collective good worth a thousand dollars in one case, whereas in another there are five thousand, each of whom finds the collective good worth five dollars. Obviously, the argument indicates that there would be a greater likelihood of collective action in the former case than in the latter, even though the aggregate demand for the collective good is the same in both. The great historical significance of small groups of fanatics no doubt owes something to this consideration.

VI

The argument in this chapter predicts that those groups that have access to selective incentives will be more likely to act collectively to obtain collective goods than those that do not, and that smaller groups will have a greater likelihood of engaging in collective action than larger ones. The empirical portions of *The Logic* show that this prediction has been correct for the United States. More study will be needed before we can be utterly certain that the argument also holds for other countries, but the more prominent features of the organizational landscape of other countries certainly do fit the theory. In no major country are large groups without access to selective incentives generally organized—the masses of consumers are not in consumers' organizations, the millions of taxpayers are not in taxpayers' organizations, the vast number of those with relatively low incomes are not in organizations for the poor, and the sometimes substantial numbers of unemployed have no organized voice. These groups are so dispersed that it is not feasible for any nongovernmental organization to coerce them; in this they differ dramatically from those, like workers in large factories or mines, who are susceptible to coercion through picketing. Neither does there appear to be any source of the positive selective incentives that might give individuals in these categories an incentive to cooperate with the many others with whom they share common interests.[19] By contrast, almost everywhere the social prestige of the learned professions and the limited numbers of practitioners of each profession in each community has helped them to organize. The professions have also been helped to organize by the distinctive susceptibility of the public to the assertion that a professional organization, with the backing of government, ought to be able to determine who is "qualified" to practice the profession, and thereby to control a decisive selective incentive. The small groups of (often large) firms in industry after industry, in country after country, are similarly often organized in trade associations or organizations or collusions of one kind or another. So, frequently, are the small groups of (usually smaller) businesses in particular towns or communities.

Even though the groups that the theory says cannot be organized do not appear to be organized anywhere, there are still substantial differences across societies and historical periods in the extent to which the groups that our logic says *could* be organized *are* organized. . . .

NOTES

[1]Cambridge: Harvard University Press, 1965, 1971. The 1971 version differs from the first 1965 printing only in the addition of an appendix. Some readers may have access to the first paperback edition published by Schocken Books (New York: 1968), which is identical to the 1965 Harvard version. Readers whose first language is not English may prefer *Die Logik des Kollektiven Handelns* (Tübingen: J. C. B. Mohr [Paul Siebeck], 1968), or *Logique de l'Action Collective* (Paris: Presses

Universitaires de France, 1978). Translations in Japanese (from Minerva Shobo) and in Italian (from Feltrinelli) are forthcoming.

[2]There is a logically possible exception to this assertion, although not of wide practical importance, that is explained in footnote 68 of chapter 1 of *The Logic*, pp. 48–49.

[3]*Rational* need not imply *self-interested*. The argument in the text can hold even when there is altruistic behavior, although if particular types of altruistic behavior are strong enough it will not hold. Consider first altruistic attitudes about observable outcomes or results—suppose an individual would be willing to sacrifice some leisure or other personal consumption to obtain some amount of a collective good because of an altruistic concern that others should have this collective good. In other words, the individual's preference ordering takes account of the collective good obtained by others as well as personal consumption. This assumption of altruism does not imply irrationality, or a tendency to make choices that are inconsistent with the maximal satisfaction of the values or preferences the individual has. Altruism also does not call into question the normal diminishing marginal rates of substitution between any pair of goods or objectives; as more of any good or objective (selfish or altruistic) is attained, other things being equal, the extent to which other goods or objectives (selfish or altruistic) will be given up to attain more of that good or objective will diminish.

A typical altruistic and rational individual of the sort described will not make any substantial voluntary contributions to obtain a collective good for a large group. The reason is that in a sufficiently large group the individual's contribution will make only a small and perhaps imperceptible difference to the amount of collective good the group obtains, whereas at the same time every contribution reduces dollar-for-dollar the amount of personal consumption and private-good charity, and the diminishing marginal rates of substitution entail that these sacrifices become progressively more onerous. In equilibrium in large groups there is accordingly little or no voluntary contribution by the rational altruist to the provision of a collective good.

Jarring as it is to the common-sense notion of rationality, let us now make the special assumption that the altruist gets satisfaction not from observably better outcomes for others, but rather from his or her own sacrifices for them. On this assumption we can secure voluntary provision of collective goods even in the largest groups. Here each dollar of personal consumption that is sacrificed can bring a significant return in moral satisfaction, and the problem that substantial personal sacrifices bring little or no perceptible change in the level of public good provided is no longer relevant. Even though this latter participatory or "Kantian" altruism is presumably not the usual form of altruism, I think it does exist and helps to account for some observations of voluntary contributions to large groups. (Yet another possibility is that the altruist is result-oriented but neglects the observable levels of the public good, simply assuming that his or her sacrifices of personal consumption increase the utility of others enough to justify the personal sacrifice.) My own thinking on this issue has been clarified by reading Howard Margolis, *Selfishness, Altruism, and Rationality* (Cambridge: University Press, 1982).

[4]This argument need not apply to small groups, which are discussed later in the chapter.

[5]David J. McDonald, *Union Man* (New York: Dutton, 1969), p. 121, quoted in William A. Gamson, *The Strategy of Social Protest* (Homewood, Ill.: Dorsey Press, 1975), p. 68.

[6]The references to the often violent interaction between employers and employees in the early stages of unionization should not obscure the consensual and informal "unionization" that also sometimes occurs because of employers' initiatives. This sort of labor organization or collusion arises because some types of production require that workers collaborate effectively. When this is the case, the employer may find it profitable to encourage team spirit and social interaction among employees. Staff conferences and work-group meetings, newsletters for employees, firm-sponsored employee athletic teams, employer-financed office parties, and the like are partly explained by this consideration. In firms that have the same employment pattern for some time, the networks for employee interaction that the employer created to encourage effective cooperation at work may evolve into informal collusions, or occasionally even unions, of workers, and tacitly or openly force the employer to deal with his employees as a cartelized group. This evolution is unlikely when employees are, for example, day laborers or consultants, but when stable patterns of active cooperation are important to production, the employer may gain more from the extra production that this cooperation brings about than he loses from the informal or formal cartelization that he helps to create. The evolution of this type of informal unionization implies that there is more organization of labor than the statistics

imply, and that the differences between some ostensibly unorganized firms and unionized firms are not as great as might appear on the surface.

[7]*The Logic*, p. 85.

[8]This means in turn that sometimes individual corporations of substantial size can be political combinations with significant lobbying power. On less than voluntary corporate contributions, see J. Patrick Wright, *On a Clear Day You Can See General Motors* (Grosse Pointe, Mich.: Wright Enterprises, 1979), pp. 69–70.

[9]*The Logic*, pp. 132–67.

[10]Erik Lindahl, "Just Taxation—A Positive Solution," in Richard Musgrave and Alan T. Peacock, eds., *Classics in the Theory of Public Finance* (London: Macmillan, 1958), pp. 168–77 and 214–33. In a Lindahl equilibrium, the parties at issue are each charged a tax-price for marginal units of the public good that is equal to the value each places on a marginal unit of the good. When this condition holds, even parties that have vastly different evaluations of the collective good will want the same amount. It would take us far afield to discuss the huge literature on this matter now, but it may be helpful to nonspecialists to point out that in most circumstances in which the parties at issue expect Lindahl-type taxation, they would have an incentive to understate their true valuations of the collective good, since they would get whatever amount was provided however low their tax-price. There is an interesting literature on relatively subtle schemes that could give individuals an incentive to reveal their true valuations for public goods, thereby making Lindahl-equilibria attainable, but most of these schemes are a very long way indeed from practical application.

[11]See my primitive, early article, "The Principle of 'Fiscal Equivalence,' " *American Economic Review, Papers and Proceedings* 59 (May 1969):479–87.

[12]See, for a leading example, Martin C. McGuire, "Group Segregation and Optimal Jurisdictions," *Journal of Political Economy* 82 (1974):112–32.

[13]See most notably Wallace Oates, *Fiscal Federalism* (New York: Harcourt Brace Jovanovich, Inc., 1972).

[14]For very early work on the limited information voters may be expected to have, see Anthony Downs's classic *Economic Theory of Democracy* (New York: Harper, 1957).

[15]I am indebted to Russell Hardin for calling this point to my attention. For a superb and rigorous analysis of the whole issue of collective action, see Hardin's *Collective Action* (Baltimore: The Johns Hopkins University Press, 1982).

[16]There is another consideration that works in the same direction. Consider individuals who get pleasure from participating in efforts to obtain a collective good just as they would from ordinary consumption, and so are participation altruists (described in note 3). If the costs of collective action to the individual are slight, the costs of consuming the participation pleasure or satisfying the moral impulse to be a participant are unlikely to prevent collective action. With the diminishing marginal rates of substitution that are described in note 3, however, the extent of collective action out of these motives will decrease as its price rises.

[17]*The Logic*, pp. 5–65.

[18]The assumption that there are two firms that place an equal value on the collective good is expositionally useful but will not often be descriptively realistic. In the much more common case, where the parties place different valuations on the public good, the party that places the larger absolute valuation on the public good is at an immense disadvantage. When it provides the amount of the collective good that would be optimal for it alone, then the others have an incentive to enjoy this amount and provide none at all. But the reverse is not true. So the larger party bears the whole burden of the collective good. (The party that places the larger value on the collective good has the option of trying to force the others to share the cost by withholding provision, but it is also at a disadvantage in the bargaining because it will lose more from this action than those with whom it is bargaining.) Thus a complete analysis of the likelihood of collective action must consider the relative sizes or valuations of the collective good of the parties involved as well as the size of the group; see the references in the next note [not printed here] on "the exploitation of the great by the small" and other consequences of intragroup variations in valuations of collective goods.

If the corner solution with the larger party bearing all the burden does not occur, and both firms provide some amount of the collective good under Cournot assumptions, then the two firms will tend to be of exactly the same size, as in the example chosen for expositional convenience in the text.

Assume that each firm has to pay the same price for each unit of the collective good and that they have identical production functions for whatever private good they produce. Since they must, by the definition of a pure collective good, both receive the same amount of it, they can both be in equilibrium under Cournot assumptions only if their isoquants have the same slope at the relevant point. That is, the isoquants describing the output that results from each combination of the private good and public good inputs for each of the firms must have the same slope if the two firms enjoying the same amount of the collective good are each purchasing some of it at the same time. Under my identical production function and factor price assumptions, the two firms must then have exactly the same output or size.

Similarly remarkable results hold for consumers who share a collective good. Either the consumer that places the higher absolute valuation on the public good will bear the entire cost or else they will end up with equal incomes! When both consumers get the same amount of a collective good, they both can be continuing to purchase some under Cournot behavior only if they both have the same marginal rate of substitution between the public good and the private good, and thus (with identical utility functions and prices) identical incomes. Unless the two consumers have identical incomes *in the beginning*, there is inevitably exploitation of the great by the small. One possibility is that the richer consumer will bear the whole cost of the collective good. The only other possibility with independent adjustment is that the public good is so valuable that the richer consumer's initial purchases of it have such a large income effect on the poorer consumer that this poorer consumer ends up just as well off as the initially richer consumer, so both buy some amount of the collective good in equilibrium. I have profited from discussion of this point with my colleague Martin C. McGuire. For a stimulating and valuable, if partially incorrect, argument along related lines, see Ronald Jeremias and Asghar Zardkoohi, "Distributional Implications of Independent Adjustment in an Economy with Public Goods," *Economic Inquiry* 14 (June 1976):305–8.

[19]Even groups or causes that are so large or popular that they encompass almost everyone in the society cannot generate very substantial organizations. Consider those concerned about the quality of the environment. Although environmental extremists are a small minority, almost everyone is interested in a wholesome environment, and poll results suggest that in the United States, for example, there are tens of millions of citizens who think more ought to be done to protect the environment. In the late 1960s and early 1970s, certainly, environmentalism was faddish as well. Despite this, and despite subsidized postal rates for nonprofit organizations and reductions in the cost of direct mail solicitation due to computers, relatively few people pay dues each year to environmental organizations. The major environmental organizations in the United States have memberships measured in the tens or hundreds of thousands, with at least the larger (such as the Audubon Society, with its products for bird-watchers) plainly owing much of their membership to selective incentives. There are surely more than 50 million Americans who value a wholesome environment, but in a typical year probably fewer than one in a hundred pays dues to any organization whose main activity is lobbying for a better environment. The proportion of physicians in the American Medical Association, or automobile workers in the United Automobile Workers union, or farmers in the Farm Bureau, or manufacturers in trade associations is incomparably greater.

13

E. E. SCHATTSCHNEIDER

THE SCOPE AND BIAS OF THE PRESSURE SYSTEM

E. E. Schattschneider (1892–1971) developed a variety of highly sophisticated concepts and theories for understanding the role of political parties and pressure groups in American politics. He wrote Politics, Pressures and the Tariff *(1935),* Party Government *(1942),* The Struggle for Party Government *(1948),* The Semisovereign People: A Realist's View of Democracy in America *(1960), and* Two Hundred Million Americans in Search of a Government *(1969). In the following selection, an excerpt from his book,* The Semisovereign People, *Schattschneider methodically examines the meaning of such concepts as private and public interests and analyzes the distinction between organized and unorganized groups. The focus is on organized, special-interest groups, which Schattschneider finds are overwhelmingly business-oriented, and imbued with a strong class bias. The author argues that the strongest special interests are the least likely to seek political resolution of conflict and consequently it is "the losers of intrabusiness conflict who seek redress from public authority." The Republican party has played an important role in mediating intrabusiness conflicts and in aggregating business interests, which has beneficial effects for American society in the long run.*

. . . As a matter of fact, the distinction between *public* and *private* interests is a thoroughly respectable one; it is one of the oldest known to political theory. In the literature of the subject, the public interest refers to general or common interests shared by all or by substantially all members of the community.[1] Presumably no community exists unless there is some kind of community of interests, just as there is no nation without some notion of national interests. If it is really impossible to distinguish between private and public interests, the group theorists have produced a revolution in political thought so great that it is impossible to foresee its consequences. For this reason the distinction ought to be explored with great care.

At a time when nationalism is described as one of the most dynamic forces in the world, it should not be difficult to understand that national interests actually do exist.[2] It is necessary only to consider the proportion of the American budget devoted to national defense to realize that the common interest in national survival is a great one. Measured in dollars this interest is one of the biggest things in the world. Moreover, it is difficult to describe this interest as special. The diet on which the American leviathan feeds is something more than a jungle of disparate special interests. In the literature of democratic theory the body of common agreement found in the community is known as the "consensus," without which it is believed that no democratic system can survive.

The reality of the common interest is suggested by demonstrated capacity of the community to survive. There must be something that holds people together.

In contrast with the common interests are the special interests. The implication of this term is that these are interests shared by only a few people or a fraction of the community; they *exclude* others and may be *adverse* to them. A special interest is exclusive in about the same way as private property is exclusive. In a complex society it is not surprising that there are some interests that are shared by all or substantially all members of the community and some interests that are not shared so widely. The distinction is useful precisely because conflicting claims are made by people about the nature of their interests in controversial matters.

Perfect agreement within the community is not always possible, but an interest may be said to have become public when it is shared so widely as to be substantially universal. Thus, the difference between 99 percent agreement and perfect agreement is not so great that it becomes necessary to argue that all interests are special, that the interests of 99 percent are as special as the interests of the 1 percent. For example, the law is probably doing an adequate job of defining the public interest in domestic tranquility despite the fact that there is nearly always one dissenter at every hanging. That is, the law defines the public interest in spite of the fact that there may be some outlaws.

Since one function of theory is to explain reality, it is reasonable to add that it is a good deal easier to explain what is going on in politics by making a distinction between public and private interests than it is to attempt to explain *everything* in terms of special interests. The attempt to prove that all interests are special forces us into circumlocutions such as those involved in the argument that people have special interests in the common good. The argument can be made, but it seems a long way around to avoid a useful distinction.

What is to be said about the argument that the distinction between public and special interests is "subjective" and is therefore "unscientific"?

All discussion of interests, special as well as general, refers to the motives, desires, and intentions of people. In this sense the whole discussion of interests is subjective. We have made progress in the study of politics because people have observed some kind of relation between the political behavior of people and certain wholly impersonal data concerning their ownership of property, income, economic status, professions, and the like. All that we know about interests, private as well as public, is based on inferences of this sort. Whether the distinction in any given case is valid depends on the evidence and on the kinds of inferences drawn from the evidence.

The only meaningful way we can speak of the interests of an association like the National Association of Manufacturers is to draw inferences from the fact that the membership is a select group to which only manufacturers may belong and to try to relate that datum to what the association does. The implications, logic, and deductions are persuasive only if they furnish reasonable explanations of the facts. That is all that any theory about interests can do. It has seemed persuasive to students of politics to suppose that manufacturers do not join an association to which only manufacturers may belong merely to promote philanthropic or cultural or religious interests, for example. The basis of selection of the membership creates an inference about the organization's concerns. The conclusions drawn from this datum seem to fit what we know about the policies promoted by associations, i.e., the policies seem to reflect the exclusive interests of manufacturers. The method is not foolproof, but it works better than many other kinds of analysis and is useful precisely because special-interest groups often tend to rationalize their special interests as public interests.

Is it possible to distinguish between the "interests" of the members of the National Association of Manufacturers and the members of the American League to Abolish Capital Punishment? The facts in the two cases are not identical. First, *the members of the* A.L.A.C.P. *obviously do not expect to be hanged.* The membership of the A.L.A.C.P. is not restricted to persons under indictment for murder or in jeopardy of the extreme penalty. *Anybody* can join A.L.A.C.P. Its members oppose capital punishment, although they are not personally likely to benefit by the policy they advocate. The inference is therefore that the interest of the A.L.A.C.P. is not adverse, exclusive, or special. It is not like the interest of the Petroleum Institute in depletion allowances.

Take some other cases. The members of the National Child Labor Committee are not children in need of legislative protection against exploitation by employers. The members of the World Peace Foundation apparently want peace, but in the nature of things they must want peace for everyone because no group can be at peace while the rest of the community is at war. Similarly, even if the members of the National Defense League wanted defense only for themselves, they would necessarily have to work for defense for the whole country because national security is indivisible. Only a naive person is likely to imagine that the political involvements of the members of the American Bankers Association and members of the Foreign Policy Association are identical. In other words, we may draw inferences from the exclusive or the nonexclusive nature of benefits sought by organizations as well as we can from the composition of groups. The positions of these groups can be distinguished not on the basis of some subjective process, but by making reasonable inferences from verifiable facts.

On the other hand, because some special-interest groups attempt to identify themselves with the public interest it does not follow that the whole idea of the public interest is a fraud. Mr. Wilson's* famous remark that what is good for General Motors is good for the country assumes that people generally do in fact desire the common good. Presumably, Mr. Wilson attempted to explain the special interest of General Motors in terms of the common interest because that was the only way he could talk to people who do not belong to the General Motors organization. *Within* the General Motors organization, discussions might be carried on in terms of naked self-interest, but a *public discussion must be carried on in public terms.*

All public discussion is addressed to the general community. To describe the conflict of special-interest groups as a form of politics means that the conflict has become generalized, has become a matter involving the broader public. In the nature of things *a political conflict among special interests is never restricted to the*

**Woodrow Wilson:* see headnote on page 259.

group most immediately interested. Instead, it is an appeal (initiated by relatively small numbers of people) for the support of vast numbers of people who are sufficiently remote to have a somewhat different perspective on the controversy. It follows that Mr. Wilson's comment, far from demonstrating that the public interest is a fraud, proves that he thinks that the public interest is so important that even a great private corporation must make obeisance to it.

The distinction between public and special interests is an indispensable tool for the study of politics. To abolish the distinction is to make a shambles of political science by treating things that are different as if they were alike. The kind of distinction made here is a commonplace of all literature dealing with human society, but *if we accept it, we have established one of the outer limits of the subject;* we have split the world of interests in half and have taken one step toward defining the scope of this kind of political conflict.

We can now examine the second distinction, the distinction between organized and unorganized groups. The question here is not whether the distinction can be made but whether or not it is worth making. Organization has been described as "merely a stage or degree of interaction" in the development of a group.[3]

The proposition is a good one, but what conclusion do we draw from it? We do not dispose of the matter by calling the distinction between organized and unorganized groups a "mere" difference of degree because some of the greatest differences in the world are differences of degree. As far as special-interest politics is concerned the implication to be avoided is that a few workmen who habitually stop at a corner saloon for a glass of beer are essentially the same as the United States Army because the difference between them is merely one of degree. At this point we have distinction that makes a difference. The distinction between organized and unorganized groups is worth making because it ought to alert us against an analysis which begins as a general group theory of politics but ends with a defense of pressure politics as inherent, universal, permanent, and inevitable. This kind of confusion comes from the loosening of categories involved in the universalization of group concepts.

Since the beginning of intellectual history, scholars have sought to make progress in their work by distinguishing between things that are unlikely and by dividing their subject matter into categories to examine them more intelligently. It is something of a novelty, therefore, when group theorists reverse this process by discussing their subject in terms so universal that they wipe out all categories, because this is the dimension in which it is least possible to understand anything.

If we are able, therefore, to distinguish between public and private interests and between organized and unorganized groups we have marked out the major boundaries of the subject; *we have given the subject shape and scope*. We are now in a position to attempt to define the area we want to explore. Having cut the pie into four pieces, we can now appropriate the piece we want and leave the rest to someone else. For a multitude of reasons *the most likely field of study is that of the organized, special-interest groups*. The advantage of concentrating on organized groups is that they are known, identifiable, and recognizable. The advantage of concentrating on special-interest groups is that they have one important characteristic in common; they are all exclusive. This piece of the pie (the organized special-interest groups) we shall call the *pressure system*. The pressure system has boundaries we can define; we can fix its scope and make an attempt to estimate its bias.

It may be assumed at the outset that all organized special-interest groups have some kind of impact on politics. A sample survey of organizations made by the Trade Associations Division of the United States Department of Commerce in 1942 concluded that "From 70 to 100 percent (of these associations) are planning activities in the field of government relations, trade promotion, trade practices, public relations, annual conventions, cooperation with other organizations, and information services."[4]

The subject of our analysis can be reduced to manageable proportions and brought under control if we restrict ourselves to the groups whose interests in politics are sufficient to have led them to unite in formal organizations having memberships, bylaws, and officers. A further advantage of this kind of definition is, we may assume, that the organized special-interest groups are the most self-conscious, best developed, most intense and active groups. Whatever claims can be made for a group theory of politics ought to be sustained by the evidence concerning these groups, if the claims have any validity at all.

The organized groups listed in the various directories (such as *National Associations of the United States*, published at intervals by the United States Department of Commerce) and specialty yearbooks, registers, etc. and the *Lobby Index*, published by the United States House of Representatives, probably include the bulk of the organizations in the pressure system. All compilations are incomplete, but these are extensive enough to provide us with some basis for estimating the scope of the system.

By the time a group has developed the kind of interest that leads it to organize, it may be assumed that it has also developed some kind of political bias because *organization is itself a mobilization of bias in preparation for action*. Since these groups can be identified and since they have memberships (i.e., they include and exclude people), it is possible to think of the *scope* of the system.

When lists of these organizations are examined, the fact that strikes the student most forcibly is that *the system is very small*. The range of organized, identifiable, known groups is amazingly narrow; there is nothing remotely universal about it. There is a tendency on the part of publishers of directories of associations to place an undue emphasis on business organizations, an emphasis that is almost inevitable because the business community is by a wide margin the most highly organized segment of society. Publishers doubtless tend also to reflect public demand for information. Nevertheless, the dominance of business groups in the pressure system is so marked that it probably cannot be explained away as an accident of the publishing industry.

The business character of the pressure system is shown by almost every list available. *National Associations of the United States*[5] lists 1,860 business associations out of a total of 4,000 in the volume, though it refers without listing (p. VII) to 16,000 organizations of businessmen. One cannot be certain what the total content of the unknown associational universe may be, but, taken with the evidence found in other compilations, it is obvious that business is remarkably well represented. Some evidence of the over-all scope of the system is to be seen in the estimate that 15,000 national trade associations have a gross membership of about one million business firms.[6] The data are incomplete, but even if we do not have a detailed map this is the shore dimly seen.

Much more directly related to pressure politics is the *Lobby Index, 1946–1949* (an index of organizations and individuals registering or filing quarterly reports under the Federal Lobbying Act), published as a report of the House Select Committee on Lobbying Activities. In this compilation, 825 out of a total of 1,247 entities (exclusive of individuals and Indian tribes) represented business.[7] A selected list of the most important of the groups listed in the *Index* (the groups spending the largest sums of money on lobbying) published in the *Congressional Quarterly Log* shows 149 business organizations in a total of 265 listed.[8]

The business or upper-class bias of the pressure system shows up everywhere. Businessmen are four or five times as likely to write to their congressmen as manual laborers are. College graduates are far more apt to write to their congressmen than people in the lowest educational category are.[9]

The limited scope of the business pressure system is indicated by all available statistics. Among business organizations, the National Association of Manufacturers (with about 20,000 corporate members) and the Chamber of Commerce of the United States (about as large as the N.A.M.) are giants. Usually business associations are much smaller. Of 421 trade associations in the metal-products industry listed in *National Associations of the United States*, 153 have a membership of less than 20.[10] The median membership was somewhere between 24 and 50. Approximately the same scale of memberships is to be found in the lumber, furniture, and paper industries where 37.3 percent of the associations listed had a membership of less than 20 and the median membership was in the 25 to 50 range.[11]

The statistics in these cases are representative of nearly all other classifications of industry.

Data drawn from other sources support this thesis. Broadly, the pressure system has an upper-class bias. There is overwhelming evidence that participation in voluntary organizations is related to upper social and economic status; the rate of participation is much higher in the upper strata than it is elsewhere. The general proposition is well stated by Lazarsfeld:

> People on the lower SES levels are less likely to belong to any organizations than the people on high SES (Social and Economic Status) levels. (On an A and B level, we find 72 percent of these respondents who belong to one or more organizations. The proportion of respondents who are members of formal organizations decreases steadily as SES level descends until, on the D level only 35 percent of the respondents belong to any associations.)[12]

The bias of the system is shown by the fact that *even nonbusiness organizations reflect an upper-class tendency.*

Lazarsfeld's generalization seems to apply equally well to urban and rural populations. The obverse side of the coin is that large areas of the population appear to be wholly outside the system of private organization. A study made by Ira Reid of a Philadelphia area showed that in a sample of 963 persons, 85 percent belonged to no civic or charitable organization and 74 percent belonged to no occupational, business, or professional associations, while another Philadelphia study of 1,154 women showed that 55 percent belonged to no associations of any kind.[13]

A *Fortune* farm poll taken some years ago found that 70.5 percent of farmers belonged to no agricultural organizations. A similar conclusion was reached by two Gallup polls showing that perhaps no more than one third of the farmers of the country belonged to farm organizations,[14] while another *Fortune* poll showed that 86.8 percent of the low-income farmers belonged to no farm organizations.[15] All available data support the generalization that the farmers who do not participate in rural organizations are largely the poorer ones.

A substantial amount of research done by other rural sociologists points to the same conclusion. Mangus and Cottam say, on the basis of a study of 556 heads of Ohio farm families and their wives:

> The present study indicates that comparatively few of those who ranked low on the scale of living took any active part in community organizations as members, attendants, contributors, or leaders. On the other hand, those families that ranked high on the scale of living comprised the vast majority of the highly active participants in formal group activities. . . . Fully two-thirds of those in the lower class as defined in this study were non-participants as compared with only one-tenth of those in the upper class and one-fourth of those in the middle class. . . . When families were classified by the general level-of-living index, 16 times as large a proportion of those in the upper classes as of those in the lower class were active participants. . . .[16]

Along the same line Richardson and Bauder observe, "Socio-economic status was directly related to participation."[17] In still another study it was found that "a highly significant relationship existed between income and formal participation."[18] It was found that persons with more than four years of college education held twenty times as many memberships (per one hundred persons) as did those with less than a fourth-grade education and were forty times as likely to hold office in nonchurch organizations, while persons with an income over $5,000 hold ninety-four times as many offices as persons with incomes less than $250.[19]

D.E. Lindstrom found that 72 percent of farm laborers belonged to no organizations whatever.[20]

There is a great wealth of data supporting the proposition that participation in private associations exhibits a class bias.[21]

The class bias of associational activity gives meaning to the limited scope of the pressure system, because *scope and bias are aspects of the same tendency*. The data raise a serious question about the validity of the proposition that special-interest groups are a universal form of political organization reflecting *all* interests. As a matter of fact, to suppose that everyone participates in pressure-group activity and that all interests get themselves organized in the pressure system is to destroy the meaning of this form of politics. The pressure system makes sense only as the political instrument of a segment of the community. It gets results by being selective and biased; *if everybody got into the act, the unique advantages of this form of organization would be destroyed, for it is possible that if all interests could be mobilized the result would be a stalemate.*

Special-interest organizations are most easily formed when they deal with small numbers of individuals who are acutely aware of their exclusive interests. To describe the conditions of pressure-group organization in this way is, however, to say that it is primarily a business phenomenon. Aside from a few very large organizations (the churches, organized labor, farm organizations, and veterans' organizations) the residue is a small segment of the population. *Pressure politics is essentially the politics of small groups.*

The vice of the groupist theory is that it conceals the most significant aspects of the system. The flaw in the pluralist heaven is that the heavenly chorus sings with a strong upper-class accent. Probably about 90 percent of the people cannot get into the pressure system.

The notion that the pressure system is automatically representative of the whole community is a myth fostered by the universalizing tendency of modern group theories. *Pressure politics is a selective process* ill designed to serve diffuse interests. The system is skewed, loaded, and unbalanced in favor of a fraction of a minority.

On the other hand, pressure tactics are not remarkably successful in mobilizing general interests. When pressure-group organizations attempt to represent the interests of large numbers of people, they are usually able to reach only a small segment of their constituencies. Only a chemical trace of the fifteen million Negroes in the United States belong to the National Association for the Advancement of Colored People. Only one five hundredths of 1 percent of American women belong to the League of Women Voters, only one sixteen hundredths of 1 percent of the consumers belong to the National Consumers' League, and only 6 percent of American automobile drivers belong to the American Automobile Association, while about 15 percent of the veterans belong to the American Legion.

The competing claims of pressure groups and political parties for the loyalty of the American public revolve about the difference between the results likely to be achieved by small-scale and large-scale political organization. Inevitably, the outcome of pressure politics and party politics will be vastly different.

A CRITIQUE OF GROUP THEORIES OF POLITICS

It is extremely unlikely that the vogue of group theories of politics would have attained its present status if its basic assumptions had not been first established by some concept of economic determinism. The economic interpretation of politics has always appealed to those political philosophers who have sought a single prime mover, a sort of philosopher's stone of political science around which to organize their ideas. The search for a single, ultimate cause has something to do with the attempt to explain *everything* about politics in terms of group concepts. The logic of economic determinism is to *identify the origins of conflict and to assume the conclusion.* This kind of thought has some of the earmarks of an illusion. The somnambulatory quality of thinking in this field appears also in the tendency of research to deal only with successful pressure campaigns or the willingness of scholars to be satisfied with having placed pressure groups on the scene of the crime without following through to see if the effect can really be attributed to the cause. What makes this kind of thinking remarkable is the fact that in political contests there are as many failures as there are successes. Where in the literature of pressure politics are the failures?

Students of special-interest politics need a more sophisticated set of intellectual tools than they have developed thus far. The theoretical problem involved in the search for a single cause is that all power relations in a democracy are reciprocal. Trying to find the original cause is like trying to find the first wave of the ocean.

Can we really assume that we know all that is to be known about a conflict if we understand its *origins?* Everything we know about politics suggests that a conflict is likely to change profoundly as it becomes political. It is a rare individual who can confront his antagonists without changing his opinions to some degree. Everything changes once a conflict gets into the political arena—*who* is involved, *what* the conflict is about, the resources available, etc. It is extremely difficult to predict the outcome of a fight by watching its beginning because we do not even know who else is going to get into the conflict. The logical consequence of the exclusive emphasis on the determinism of the private origins of conflict is to assign zero value to the political process.

The very expression "pressure politics" invites us to misconceive the role of special-interest groups in politics. The word "pressure" implies the use of some kind of force, a form of intimidation, something other than reason and information, to induce public authorities to act against their own best judgment. In Latham's famous statement . . . the legislature is described as a "referee" who "ratifies" and "records" the "balance of power" among the contending groups.[22]

It is hard to imagine a more effective way of saying that Congress has no mind or force of its own or that Congress is unable to invoke new forces that might alter the equation.

Actually the outcome of political conflict is not like the "resultant" of opposing forces in physics. To assume that the forces in a political situation could be diagramed as a physicist might diagram the resultant of opposing physical forces is to wipe the slate clean of all remote, general, and public considerations for the protection of which civil societies have been instituted.

Moreover, the notion of "pressure" distorts the image of the power relations involved. *Private conflicts are taken into the public arena precisely because someone wants to make certain that the power ratio among the private interests most immediately involved shall not prevail.* To treat a conflict as a mere test of the strength of the private interests is to leave out the most significant factors. This is so true that it might indeed be said that the only way to preserve private power ratios is to keep conflicts out of the public arena.

The assumption that it is only the "interested" who count ought to be re-examined in view of the foregoing discussion. The tendency of the literature of pressure politics has been to neglect the low-tension force of large numbers because it *assumes that the equation of forces is fixed at the outset.*

Given the assumptions made by the group theorists, the attack on the idea of the majority is completely logical. The assumption is that conflict is monopolized narrowly by the parties immediately concerned. There is no room for a majority when conflict is defined so narrowly. It is a great deficiency of the group theory that it has found no place in the political system for the majority. The force of the majority is of an entirely different order of magnitude, something not to be measured by pressure-group standards.

Instead of attempting to exterminate all political forms, organizations, and alignments that do not qualify as pressure groups, would it not be better to attempt to make a synthesis, covering the whole political system and finding a place for all kinds of political life?

One possible synthesis of pressure politics and party politics might be produced by *describing politics as the socialization of conflict.* That is to say, the political process is a sequence: conflicts are initiated by highly motivated, high-tension groups so directly and immediately involved that it is difficult for them to see the justice of competing claims. As long as the conflicts of these groups remain *private* (carried on in terms of economic competition, reciprocal denial of goods and services, private negotiations and bargaining, struggles for corporate control or competition for membership), no political process is initiated. Conflicts become political only when an attempt is made to involve the wider public. Pressure politics might be described as a stage in the socialization of conflict. This analysis makes pressure politics an integral part of all politics, including party politics.

One of the characteristic points of origin of pressure politics is a breakdown of the discipline of the business community. The flight to government is perpetual. Something like this is likely to happen wherever there is a point of contact between competing power systems. It is the *losers in intrabusiness conflict who seek redress from public authority. The dominant business interests resist appeals to the government.* The role of the government as the patron of the defeated private interest sheds light on its function as the critic of private power relations.

Since the contestants in private conflicts are apt to be unequal in strength, it follows that *the most powerful special interests want private settlements* because they are able to dictate the outcome as long as the conflict remains private. If A is a hundred times as strong as B he does not welcome the intervention of a third party because he expects to impose his own terms on B; he wants to isolate B. He is especially opposed to the intervention of public authority, because public authority represents the most overwhelming form of outside intervention. Thus, if $A/B = 100/1$, it is obviously not to A's advantage to involve a third party a million times as strong as A and B combined. Therefore, it is the weak, not the strong, who appeal to public authority for relief. It is the weak who want to socialize conflict, i.e., to involve more and more people in the conflict until the balance of forces is changed. In the schoolyard it is not the bully but the defenseless smaller boys who "tell the teacher." When the teacher intervenes, the balance of

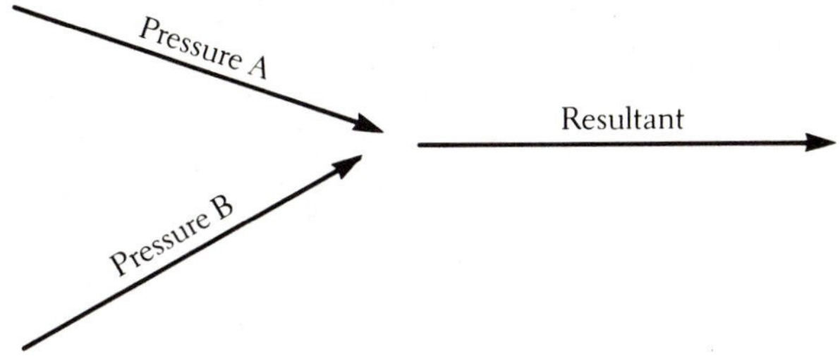

power in the schoolyard is apt to change drastically. It is the function of public authority to *modify private power relations by enlarging the scope of conflict.* Nothing could be more mistaken than to suppose that public authority merely registers the dominance of the strong over the weak. The mere existence of public order has already ruled out a great variety of forms of private pressure. Nothing could be more confusing than to suppose that the refugees from the business community who come to Congress for relief and protection *force* Congress to do their bidding.

Evidence of the truth of this analysis may be seen in the fact that the big private interests do not necessarily win if they are involved in public conflicts with petty interests. The image of the lobbyists as primarily the agents of big business is not easy to support on the face of the record of congressional hearings, for example. The biggest corporations in the country tend to avoid the arena in which pressure groups and lobbyists fight it out before the congressional committees. To describe this process exclusively in terms of an effort of business to intimidate congressmen is to misconceive what is actually going on.

It is probably a mistake to assume that pressure politics is the typical or even the most important relation between government and business. The pressure group is by no means the perfect instrument of the business community. What does big business want? The *winners* in intrabusiness strife want (1) to be let alone (they want autonomy) and (2) to preserve the solidarity of the business community. For these purposes pressure politics is not a wholly satisfactory device. The most elementary considerations of strategy call for the business community to develop some kind of common policy more broadly based than any special-interest group is likely to be.

The political influence of business depends on the kind of solidarity that, on the one hand, leads all business to rally to the support of *any* businessman in trouble with the government and, on the other hand, keeps internal business disputes out of the public arena. In this system businessmen resist the impulse to attack each other in public and discourage the efforts of individual members of the business community to take intrabusiness conflicts into politics.

The attempt to mobilize a united front of the whole business community does not resemble the classic concept of pressure politics. The logic of business politics is to keep peace within the business community by supporting as far as possible all claims that business groups make for themselves. The tendency is to support all businessmen who have conflicts with the government and support all businessmen in conflict with labor. In this way *special-interest politics can be converted into party policy*. The search is for a broad base of political mobilization grounded on the strategic need for political organization on a wider scale than is possible in the case of the historical pressure group. Once the business community begins to think in terms of a larger scale of political organization the Republican party looms large in business politics.

It is a great achievement of American democracy that business has been forced to form a political organization designed to win elections, i.e., has been forced to compete for power in the widest arena in the political system. On the other hand, *the power of the Republican party to make terms with business rests on the fact that business cannot afford to be isolated*.

The Republican party has played a major role in *the political organization of the business community*, a far greater role than many students of politics seem to have realized. The influence of business in the Republican party is great, but it is never absolute because business is remarkably dependent on the party. The business community is too small, it arouses too much antagonism, and its aims are too narrow to win the support of a popular majority. The political education of business is a function of the Republican party that can never be done so well by anyone else.

In the management of the political relations of the business community, the Republican party is much more important than any combination of pressure groups ever could be. The success of special interests in Congress is due less to the "pressure" exerted by these groups than it is due to the fact that Republican members of Congress are committed in advance to a general probusiness attitude. The notion that business groups coerce Republican congressmen into voting for their bills underestimates the whole Republican posture in American politics.[23]

It is not easy to manage the political interests of the business community because there is a perpetual stream of losers in intrabusiness conflicts who go to the government for relief and protection. It has not been possible therefore to maintain perfect solidarity, and when solidarity is breached the government is involved almost automatically. The fact that business has not become hopelessly divided and that it has retained great influence in American politics has been due chiefly to the over-all mediating role played by the Republican party. There has never been a pressure group or a combination of pressure groups capable of performing this function.

NOTES

[1]References to the public interest appear under a variety of headings in the literature of political theory.

See G. D. H. Cole's comment on "the will of all" and the "general will," pp. xxx and xxxi of his introduction to Everyman's edition of Rousseau's *Social Contract*, London, 1913.

See Ernst Cassirer, *The Myth of the State*, Garden City, 1955, pp. 88–93, for a discussion of Plato's concept of "justice" as the end of the state in his criticism of the sophists.

See S. D. Lindsay, *The Essentials of Democracy*, Philadelphia, 1929, p. 49, for a statement regarding consensus.

[2]It does not seem necessary to argue that nationalism and national interests are forces in the modern world. E. H. Carr writes about "the catastrophic growth of nationalism" in *Nationalism and After*, New York, 1945, p. 18. D. W. Brogan describes nations as "the only communities that now exist," *The American Character*, New York, 1944, p. 169. "The outstanding and distinctive characteristic of the people of the Western State System is their devotion and allegiance to the 'nations' into which they have got themselves divided," Frederick L. Schumann, *International Politics*, 3d ed., New York, 1941, p. 300. A. D. Lindsay in *The Essentials of Democracy*, Philadelphia, 1929, p. 49, has stated the doctrine of the democratic consensus as follows: "Nationality, however produced, is a sense of belonging together, involving a readiness on the part of the members of a state to subordinate their differences to it. It involves something more. It has a connection with the notion of a distinctive culture—some sort of rough ideal of the kind of common life for which the community stands, which always exists in people's minds as a rough criticism by which political proposals are to be judged. This at least is clear, that where such common understanding and sense of belonging together either does not exist or is overshadowed by other differences, successful democracy is not really possible."

[3]David Truman, *The Government Process*, New York, 1951, p. 51.

[4]*National Associations of the United States*, p. xi.

[5]Edited by Jay Judkins, Washington, 1949, p. viii.

[6]*National Associations of the United States*, p. viii.

[7]House Report No. 3197, 81st Congress, 2d Session, December 15, 1950, Washington.

[8]*Congressional Quarterly Log*, week ending February 24, 1950, pp. 217 ff. Another compilation, the list of approximately one thousand associations and societies published in the *World Almanac* for 1953, reflects to a very great extent the economic, professional and leisure interests and activities of the upper economic strata of the community. Scarcely more than a dozen or so of the associations listed in the *World Almanac* can be described as proletarian in their outlook or membership.

[9]*American Institute of Public Opinion*, May 29, 1946.

[10]Four hundred fifty associations are listed, but figures for membership are given for only 421.

[11]Membership statistics are given for only 177 of the 200 associations listed.

[12]Lazarsfeld and Associates, *The People's Choice*, p. 145.

[13]Reid and Ehle, "Leadership Selection in the Urban Locality Areas," *Public Opinion Quarterly* (1950), 14:262–284. See also Powell, *Anatomy of Public Opinion*, New York, 1951, pp. 180–181.

[14]See Carey McWilliams, *Small Farm and Big Farm*, Public Affairs Pamphlet, No. 100.

[15]*Fortune* poll, April, 1943.

[16]A. R. Mangus and H. R. Cottam, *Level of Living, Social Participation, and Adjustment of Ohio Farm People*, Ohio Agricultural Experiment Station, Wooster, Ohio, Bull. 624, September, 1941, pp. 51, 53.

Another study (of New York farmers) shows that there is a direct relation between organizational activity and the economic status of farmers. The author concludes that "the operators of farms of less than 55 acres in size are represented in only very small proportions in membership in the farm bureau and in the Dairymen's Leauge and other cooperatives." W. A. Anderson, *The Membership of Farmers in New York Organizations*, Cornell University Agricultural Experiment Station, Ithaca, N.Y., 1937, p. 20.

[17]P. D. Richardson and Ward W. Bauder, *Participation in Organized Activities in a Kentucky Rural Community*, Kentucky Agricultural Experimental Station, University of Kentucky, Bulletin 598, 1953, Lexington, Kentucky, pp. 26, 28. "The number of memberships varied directly with the socio-economic score."

[18]Harold F. Kaufman, *Participation in Organized Activities in Selected Kentucky Localities*, Bulletin 528, Kentucky Agricultural Experiment Station, University of Kentucky, Lexington, 1949, p. 19.

[19]*Ibid.*, pp. 11, 12, 13, 21.

See also Mirra Komorovsky, "The Voluntary Association of Urban Dwellers," *American Sociological Review*, 11:686–698, 1946.

[20]*Forces Affecting Participation of Farm People in Rural Organizations,* University of Illinois Agricultural Experiment Station, Bulletin 423, 1936, p. 103.

[21]"Associational participation is greatest at the top of Jonesville society and decreases on the way down the class hierarchy. The upper class belongs to the greatest number of associations, the upper-middle class next, and so on down to the lower-lower class which belongs to the least." Warner, *Democracy in Jonesville,* New York, 1949, p. 117. See also pp. 138, 140, 141, 143.

"A higher proportion of the members of the upper class belong to more associations than the members of any other class." Warner, *Jonesville,* p. 131.

"The upper and upper-middle classes are highly organized, well integrated social groups. The lower-middle and lower classes are more loosely organized and have fewer devices for maintaining their own distinctiveness in the community." Warner, *Jonesville,* p. 148. See also p. 153.

"Many organized groups touch only a few people in a community. Studies in cities reveal that 40 to 60 percent of adults are members of these organized groups if church membership is excluded. In rural communities the percentage is smaller. So when we bring in representatives from these organized groups, we should not pretend that we are getting a complete representation of the people of the community. The American practice of 'joining' is not as universal as popularly assumed." G. W. Blackwell, "Community Analysis," *Approaches to the Study of Politics,* Roland Young, ed., Northwestern University Press, 1958, p. 306.

"Aside from church participation, most urban individuals belong to one organization or none. Low socio-economic rank individuals and middle-rank individuals, usually belong to one organization at most, and it is usually work-connected for men, child-connected for women. Only in the upper socio-economc levels is the 'joiner' to be found with any frequency. When attendance at organizations is studied, some twenty per cent of the memberships are usually 'paper' memberships." Scott Greer, "Individual Participation in Mass Society," *Approaches to the Study of Politics,* p. 332.

[22]Earl Latham, *The Group Basis of Politics,* Ithaca, N.Y., 1952, pp. 35–36.

[23]See *Reporter,* November 25, 1958, for story of Senator Bricker and the Ohio Right-to-Work referendum.

PART FIVE

THE CONGRESS

Woodrow Wilson once described the Congress as "the predominant and controlling force" in the American government. "The legislature," he concluded, "is the aggressive spirit." Writing some eighty-five years later, Samuel P. Huntington struck a different chord. Modern critics, he noted, frequently say that "Congress either does not legislate or legislates too little and too late." "Today's 'aggressive spirit,' " Huntington claimed, "is clearly the executive branch."

So disparate are Wilson's and Huntington's views that one wonders whether they were talking about the same subject. To be sure, the Congress has changed importantly since Wilson's day. Virtually all congressional scholars agree that the organizational structure of the Congress is now much more fragmented, and power within it much more dispersed. In his treatise *Congressional Government* (1885), excerpted here, Wilson observed too that "Authority [in Congress] is perplexingly subdivided and distributed, and responsibility has to be hunted down in out-of-the-way corners." Yet the unmistakable impression one gets from his account is that legislative leadership was far stronger in Wilson's day, and the role of party organs much greater, than today. In the nineteenth century as at the present time, committees ruled Congress, but in the House of Representatives the Speaker held absolute discretion over committee appointments. Individual legislators then were often unruly and freewheeling; still, party caucuses imposed more discipline than they do nowadays: "Any individual, or any minority of weak numbers or small influence, who has the temerity to neglect the decisions of the caucus is sure, if the offense be often repeated, or even once committed upon an important issue, to be read out of the party, almost without chance of reinstatement."

The real debate, however, is not *whether* the institution has become more fractionated and decentralized, but rather *what differences* such developments have made for the status and performance of the institution. According to Huntington, the dispersion of power—due to the increasingly specialized and elaborate committee system, loss of leadership control, and so forth—has weakened Congress in relation to the presidency. Abetting the trend, Huntington argues in his 1973 article, is the growing insulation of Congress as a political institution. New blood no longer flows easily into it; incumbents reign too long; committee chairmanships continue to be distributed mostly by seniority; congressional leaders are older than were their predecessors; there is less lateral entry from other parts of the government, as congressional careers now typically follow a pattern of advancement within the institution itself. Additionally, Huntington finds, the strict territorial basis of congressional representation fails to reflect the increasingly national orientation of society's specialized economic and social interests.

Various facets of the issues raised in Huntington's article are explored in other essays that follow. The forces that in Huntington's opinion tend to insulate Congress from present-day political and social realities are revealed by Nelson W. Polsby as characteristics of a broader phenomenon: "institutionalization." Polsby, in his 1970 article reprinted here, observes:

> One major consequence of this process of institutionalization has been to shift the balance in the careers and life-styles of legislators from amateur to professional, from the status of a temporary ambassador from home to that of member of the legislative group. Where Congress used to embody a popular will in some formal sense by its collective representativeness, it now does so *de facto* through the piecemeal pressures of case work for constituents, legislative committee hearings, and the appropriations process. Where representation, emphasizing the ambassadorial function, was once the characteristic, conscious activity of Congressmen and Senators, today it is deliberation, emphasizing the increasing centrality to Congressmen of their lives as members of a legislative work group and status system.

Polsby explores the implications of this change for the legislative process. He concludes by suggesting that three reforms could enhance Congress's performance: (1) a mandatory retirement system, (2) the improvement of technical knowledge available to Congress, and (3) the election of House committee chairmen at the start of each Congress.

One feature of Congress that is central to almost all its functions is the standing committee system. Committees play a much more prominent role in the U.S. Congress than in [other] Western parliaments. Critics often stress this feature when lamenting the disaggregation of power in the American legislature. What the critics sometimes overlook, however, is that the roles of congressional committees differ widely. Some have much more power than others, and some, in fact, are such a potent force in the legislative process that, at least with respect to certain issues, they seem to steer the rest of the legislative body much as a group of party leaders might.

The definitive work on congressional committees remains Richard F. Fenno, Jr.'s *Congressmen in Committees*, published in 1973. Although Fenno's research predates the substantial changes in committee structure that took place in the ensuing years, most of his insights are still relevant. We have excerpted the key sections of three chapters providing a concise summary of his principal findings. Briefly, Fenno studied six important committees in the House of Representatives: Appropriations, Ways and Means, Interior, Post Office, Education and Labor, and Foreign Affairs. He discovered that they behaved differently according to the goals pursued by their members, the external political constraints placed upon them by other interested parties, and the "decision rules" adopted to accommodate these pressures and to conduct committee business. In some cases, committees developed a high degree of consensus on goals and the rules of decision making; in others, much less. For some (for example, Education and Labor), external clientele groups were an especially salient constraint, whereas in others (for example, Appropriations and Ways and Means), the dominant imperative was to wield influence *inside* Congress—that is, within the full House itself. The Appropriations Committee, for instance, functioned in such a fashion as to ensure that the parent chamber would acquiesce to its recommendations almost routinely.

14

WOODROW WILSON

CONGRESSIONAL GOVERNMENT

The following selection is the concluding chapter of Woodrow Wilson's (1856–1924) first and most widely read book, Congressional Government *(1885). Wilson analyzed the balance of power among the branches of the federal government during the post Civil War era and concluded that ". . . the central government is constantly becoming stronger and more active, and Congress is establishing itself as the one sovereign authority in that government." Wilson criticized Congress, arguing that it divided its powers dysfunctionally, and called for thoroughgoing reforms of congressional procedures. Dissatisfied with* Congressional Government, *Wilson rewrote it as* Constitutional Government in the United States *in 1908. Events between 1885 and 1908, particularly the war with Spain, had changed Wilson's view of the separation of powers and the system of checks and balances. By 1908 he concluded that the presidency had become dominant over Congress.*

After serving as the president of Princeton University (1902–1910) and the governor of New Jersey (1911–1913), Wilson became president of the United States and served two terms. Trained in history and political science, Wilson is often credited with launching the systematic study of public administration in the United States through his famous essay "The Study of Administration" (1887).

> Political philosophy must analyze political history; it must distinguish what is due to the excellence of the people, and what to the excellence of the laws; it must carefully calculate the exact effect of each part of the constitution, though thus it may destroy many an idol of the multitude, and detect the secret of utility where but few imagined it to lie.
>
> BAGEHOT*

Congress always makes what haste it can to legislate. It is the prime object of its rules to expedite law-making. Its customs are fruits of its characteristic diligence in enactment. Be the matters small or great, frivolous or grave, which busy it, its aim is to have laws always a-making. Its temper is strenuously legislative. That it cannot regulate all the questions to which its attention is weekly invited is its misfortune, not its fault; is due to the human limitation of its faculties, not to any narrow circumscription of its desires. If its committee machinery is inadequate to the task of bringing to action more than one out of every hundred of the bills

**Walter Bagehot* (1826–1877): English economist, essayist, and critic who is famous for his book *The English Constitution* (1867), in which he defended bicameralism, advocated a system of checks and balances, and argued for limitations on state power.

introduced, it is not because the quick clearance of the docket is not the motive of its organic life. If legislation, therefore, were the only or the chief object for which it should live, it would not be possible to withhold admiration from those clever hurrying rules and those inexorable customs which seek to facilitate it. Nothing but a doubt as to whether or not Congress should confine itself to law-making can challenge with a question the utility of its organization as a facile statute-devising machine.

The political philosopher of these days of self-government has, however, something more than a doubt with which to gainsay the usefulness of a sovereign representative body which confines itself to legislation to the exclusion of all other functions. Buckle* declared, indeed, that the chief use and value of legislation nowadays lay in its opportunity and power to remedy the mistakes of the legislation of the past; that it was beneficent only when it carried healing in its wings; that repeal was more blessed than enactment. And it is certainly true that the greater part of the labor of legislation consists in carrying the loads recklessly or bravely shouldered in times gone by, when the animal which is now a bull was only a calf, and in completing, if they may be completed, the tasks once undertaken in the shape of unambitious schemes which at the outset looked innocent enough. Having got his foot into it, the legislator finds it difficult, if not impossible, to get it out again. . . .

Legislation unquestionably generates legislation. Every statute may be said to have a long lineage of statutes behind it; and whether that lineage be honorable or of ill repute is as much a question as to each individual statute as it can be with regard to the ancestry of each individual legislator. Every statute in its turn has a numerous progeny, and only time and opportunity can decide whether its offspring will bring it honor or shame. Once begin the dance of legislation, and you must struggle through its mazes as best you can to its breathless end,—if any end there be.

It is not surprising, therefore, that the enacting, revising, tinkering, repealing of laws should engross the attention and engage the entire energy of such a body as Congress. It is, however, easy to see how it might be better employed; or, at least, how it might add others to this overshadowing function, to the infinite advantage of the government. Quite as important as legislation is vigilant oversight of administration; and even more important than legislation is the instruction and guidance in political affairs which the people might receive from a body which kept all national concerns suffused in a broad daylight of discussion. There is no similar legislature in existence which is so shut up to the one business of law-making as is our Congress. As I have said, it in a way superintends administration by the exercise of semi-judicial powers of investigation, whose limitations and insufficiency are manifest. But other national legislatures command administration and verify their name of "parliaments"† by talking official acts into notoriety. Our extra-constitutional party conventions, short-lived and poor in power as

George Earl Buckle (1854–1935): English journalist and author who wrote *The Life of Benjamin Disraeli* (1929) with William Flavelle Monypenny (1866–1912).

†*Parliament*: see footnote on page 208.

they are, constitute our only machinery for that sort of control of the executive which consists in the award of personal rewards and punishments. This is the cardinal fact which differentiates Congress from the Chamber of Deputies and from Parliament, and which puts it beyond the reach of those eminently useful functions whose exercise would so raise it in usefulness and in dignity.

An effective representative body, gifted with the power to rule, ought, it would seem, not only to speak the will of the nation, which Congress does, but also to lead it to its conclusions, to utter the voice of its opinions, and to serve as its eyes in superintending all matters of government—which Congress does not do. The discussions which take place in Congress are aimed at random. They now and again strike rather sharply the tender spots in this, that, or the other measure; but, as I have said, no two measures consciously join in purpose or agree in character, and so debate must wander as widely as the subjects of debate. Since there is little coherency about the legislation agreed upon, there can be no coherency about the debates. There is no one policy to be attacked or defended, but only a score or two of separate bills. To attend to such discussions is uninteresting; to be instructed by them is impossible. There is some scandal and discomfort, but infinite advantage, in having every affair of administration subjected to the test of constant examination on the part of the assembly which represents the nation. The chief use of such inquisition is, not the direction of those affairs in a way with which the country will be satisfied (though that itself is of course all-important), but the enlightenment of the people, which is always its sure consequence. Very few men are unequal to a danger which they see and understand; all men quail before a threatening which is dark and unintelligible, and suspect what is done behind a screen. If the people could have, through Congress, daily knowledge of all the more important transactions of the governmental offices, an insight into all that now seems withheld and private, their confidence in the executive, now so often shaken, would, I think, be very soon established. Because dishonesty *can* lurk under privacies now vouch-safed our administrative agents, much that is upright and pure suffers unjust suspicion. Discoveries of guilt in a bureau cloud with doubts the trustworthiness of a department. As nothing is open enough for the quick and easy detection of peculation or fraud, so nothing is open enough for the due vindication and acknowledgment of honesty. The isolation and privacy which shield the one from discovery cheat the other of reward.

Inquisitiveness is never so forward, enterprising, and irrepressible as in a popular assembly which is given leave to ask questions and is afforded ready and abundant means of getting its questions answered. No cross-examination is more searching than that to which a minister of the Crown is subjected by the all-curious Commons. "Sir Robert Peel once asked to have a number of questions carefully written down which they asked him one day in succession in the House of Commons. They seemed a list of everything that could occur in the British empire or to the brain of a member of parliament." If one considered only the wear and tear upon ministers of state, what the plague of constant interrogation must inflict, he could wish that their lives, if useful, might be spared this blight of unending explanation; but no one can overestimate the immense advantage of a facility so unlimited for knowing all that is going on in the places where authority lives. The conscience of every member of the representative body is at the service of the nation. All that he feels bound to know he can find out; and what he finds out goes to the ears of the country. The question is his, the answer the nation's. And the inquisitiveness of such bodies as Congress is the best conceivable source of information. Congress is the only body which has the proper motive for inquiry, and it is the only body which has the power to act effectively upon the knowledge which its inquiries secure. The Press is merely curious or merely partisan. The people are scattered and unorganized. But Congress is, as it were, the corporate people, the mouthpiece of its will. It is a sovereign delegation which could ask questions with dignity, because with authority and with power to act.

Congress is fast becoming the governing body of the nation, and yet the only power which it possesses in perfection is the power which is but a part of government, the power of legislation. Legislation is but the oil of government. It is that which lubricates its channels and speeds its wheels, that which lessens the friction and so eases the movement. Or perhaps I shall be admitted to have hit upon a closer and apter analogy if I say that legislation is like a foreman set over the forces of government. It issues the orders which others obey. It directs, it admonishes, but it does not do the actual heavy work of governing. A good foreman does, it is true, himself take a hand in the work which he guides; and so I suppose our legislation must be likened to a poor foreman, because it stands altogether apart from that work which it is set to see well done. Members of Congress ought not to be censured too severely, however, when they fail to check evil courses on the part of the executive. They have been denied the means of doing so promptly and with effect. Whatever intention may have controlled the compromises of constitution-making in 1787, their result was to give us, not government by discussion, which is the only tolerable sort of government for a people which tries to do its own governing, but only *legislation* by discussion, which is no more than a small part of government by discussion. What is quite as indispensable as the debate of problems of legislation is the debate of all matters of administration. It is even more important to know how the house is being built than to know how the plans of the architect were conceived and how his specifications were calculated. It is better to have skillful work—stout walls, reliable arches, unbending rafters, and windows sure to "expel the winter's flaw"—than a drawing on paper which is the admiration of all the practical artists in the country. The discipline of an army depends quite as much upon the temper of the troops as upon the orders of the day.

It is the proper duty of a representative body to look diligently into every affair of government and to talk much about what it sees. It is meant to be the eyes and the voice, and to embody the wisdom and will of its constituents. Unless Congress have and use every means of acquainting itself with the acts and the disposition of the administrative agents of the government, the country must be helpless to learn how it is being served; and unless Congress both scrutinize these things and sift them by every form of discussion, the country must remain in embarrassing, crippling ignorance of the very affairs which it is most important that it should understand and direct. The informing function of Congress should be preferred even to its legislative function. The argument is not only that discussed and interrogated administration is the only pure and efficient administration, but, more than that, that the only really self-governing people is that people which discusses and interrogates its administration. The talk on the part of Congress which we sometimes justly condemn is the profitless squabble of words over frivolous bills or selfish party issues. It would be hard to conceive of there being too much talk about the practical concerns and processes of government. Such talk it is which, when earnestly and purposefully conducted, clears the public mind and shapes the demands of public opinion.

Congress could not be too diligent about such talking; whereas it may easily be too diligent in legislation. It often overdoes that business. It already sends to its Committees bills too many by the thousand to be given even a hasty thought; but its immense committee facilities and the absence of all other duties but that of legislation make it omnivorous in its appetite for new subjects for consideration. It is greedy to have a taste of every possible dish that may be put upon its table, as an "extra" to the constitutional bill of fare. This disposition on its part is the more notable because there is certainly less need for it to hurry and overwork itself at law-making than exists in the case of most other great national legislatures. It is not state and national legislature combined, as are the Commons of England and the Chambers of France. Like the Reichstag of our cousin Germans, it is restricted to subjects of imperial scope. Its thoughts are meant to be kept for national interests. Its time is spared the waste of attention to local affairs. It is even forbidden the vast domain of the laws of property, of commercial dealing, and of ordinary crime. And even in the matter of caring for national interests the way has from the first been made plain and easy for it. There are no clogging feudal institutions to embarrass it. There is no long-continued practice of legal or of royal tyranny for it to cure—no clearing away of old débris of any sort to delay it in its exercise of a common-sense dominion over a thoroughly modern and progressive nation. It is easy to believe that its legislative purposes might be most fortunately clarified and simplified, were it to square them by a conscientious attention to the paramount and controlling duty of understanding, discussing, and directing administration.

If the people's authorized representatives do not take upon themselves this duty, and by identifying themselves with the actual work of government stand between it and irresponsible, half-informed criticism, to what harassments is the executive not exposed? Led and checked by Congress, the prurient and fearless, because anonymous, animadversions of the Press, now so often premature and inconsiderate, might be disciplined into serviceable capacity to interpret and judge. Its energy and sagacity might be tempered by discretion, and strengthened by knowledge. One of our chief constitutional difficulties is that, in opportunities for informing and guiding public opinion, the freedom of the Press is greater than the freedom of Congress. It is as if newspapers, instead of the board of directors, were the sources of information for the stockholders of a corporation. We look into correspondents' letters instead of into the Congressional Record to find out what is a-doing and a-planning in the departments. Congress is altogether excluded from the arrangement by which the Press declares what the executive is, and conventions of the national parties decide what the executive shall be. Editors are self-constituted our guides, and caucus delegates our government directors. . . .

The plain tendency is toward a centralization of all the greater powers of government in the hands of the federal authorities, and towards the practical confirmation of those prerogatives of supreme overlordship which Congress has been gradually arrogating to itself. The central government is constantly becoming stronger and more active, and Congress is establishing itself as the one sovereign authority in that government. In constitutional theory and in the broader features of past practice, ours has been what Mr. Bagehot has called a "composite" government. Besides state and federal authorities to dispute as to sovereignty, there have been within the federal system itself rival and irreconcilable powers. But gradually the strong are overcoming the weak. If the signs of the times are to be credited, we are fast approaching an adjustmment of sovereignty quite as "simple" as need be. Congress is not only to retain the authority it already possesses, but is to be brought again and again face to face with still greater demands upon its energy, its wisdom, and its conscience, is to have ever-widening duties and responsibilities thrust upon it without being granted a moment's opportunity to look back from the plough to which it has set its hands.

The sphere and influence of national administration and national legislation are widening rapidly. Our populations are growing at such a rate that one's reckoning staggers at counting the possible millions that may have a home and a work on this continent ere fifty more years shall have filled their short span. The East will not always be the centre of national life. The South is fast accumulating wealth, and will faster recover influence. The West has already achieved a greatness which no man can gainsay, and has in store a power of future growth which no man can estimate. Whether these sections are to be harmonious or dissentient depends almost entirely upon the methods and policy of the federal government. If that government be not careful to keep within its own proper sphere and prudent to square its policy by rules of national welfare, sectional lines must and will be known; citizens of one part of the country may look with jealousy and even with hatred upon their fellow-citizens of another part; and faction must tear and dissension distract a country which Providence would bless, but which man may curse. The government of a country so vast and various must be strong, prompt, wieldy, and efficient. Its strength must consist in the certainty and uniformity of its purposes, in its accord with national sentiment, in its unhesitating action, and in its honest aims. It must be steadied and approved by open administration diligently obedient to the more permanent judgments of public opinion; and its only active agency, its representative chambers, must be equipped with something besides abundant powers of legislation.

As at present constituted, the federal government lacks strength because its powers are divided, lacks promptness because its authorities are multiplied, lacks wieldiness because its processes are roundabout, lacks efficiency because its responsibility is indistinct and its action without competent direction. It is a government in which every officer may talk about every other officer's duty without having to render strict account for not doing his own, and in which the masters are held in check and offered contradiction by the servants. Mr. Lowell* has called it "government by declamation." Talk is not sobered by any necessity imposed upon those who utter it to suit their actions to their words. There is no day of reckoning for words spoken. The speakers of a congressional majority may, without risk of incurring ridicule or discredit, condemn what their own Committees are doing; and the spokesmen of a minority may urge what contrary courses they please with a well-grounded assurance that what they say will be forgotten before they can be called upon to put it into practice. Nobody stands sponsor for the policy of the government. A dozen men originate it; a dozen compromises twist and alter it; a dozen offices whose names are scarcely known outside of Washington put it into execution.

This is the defect to which, it will be observed, I am constantly recurring; to which I recur again and again because every examination of the system, at whatsoever point begun, leads inevitably to it as to a central secret. It is the defect which interprets all the rest, because it is their common product. It is exemplified in the extraordinary fact that the utterances of the Press have greater weight and are accorded greater credit, though the Press speaks entirely without authority, than the utterances of Congress, though Congress possesses all authority. The gossip of the street is listened to rather than the words of the law-makers. The editor directs public opinion, the congressman obeys it. When a presidential election is at hand, indeed, the words of the political orator gain temporary heed. He is recognized as an authority in the arena, as a professional critic competent to discuss the good and bad points, and to forecast the fortunes of the contestants. There is something definite in hand, and he is known to have studied all its bearings. He is one of the managers, or is thought to be well acquainted with the management. He speaks "from the card." But let him talk, not about candidates, but about measures or about the policy of the government, and his observations sink at once to the level of a mere individual expression of opinion, to which his political occupations seem to add very little weight. It is universally recognized that he speaks without authority, about things which his vote may help to settle, but about which several hundred other men have votes quite as influential as his own. Legislation is not a thing to be known beforehand. It depends upon the conclusions of sundry Standing Committees. It is an aggregate, not a simple, production. It is impossible to tell how many persons' opinions and influences have entered into its composition. It is even impracticable to determine from this year's law-making what next year's will be like.

Speaking, therefore, without authority, the political orator speaks to little purpose when he speaks about legislation. The papers do not report him carefully; and their editorials seldom take any color from his arguments. The Press, being anonymous and representing a large force of inquisitive newshunters, is much more powerful than he chiefly because it *is* impersonal and seems to represent a wider and more thorough range of information. At the worst, it can

**Joshua Adams Lowell* (1801–1874): Democrat from Maine who served as a member of the U.S. House of Representatives from 1839 to 1843.

easily compete with any ordinary individual. Its individual opinion is quite sure to be esteemed as worthy of attention as any other individual opinion. And, besides, it is almost everywhere strong enough to deny currency to the speeches of individuals whom it does not care to report. It goes to its audience; the orator must depend upon his audience coming to him. It can be heard at every fireside; the orator can be heard only on the platform or the hustings. There is no imperative demand on the part of the reading public in this country that the newspapers should report political speeches in full. On the contrary, most readers would be disgusted at finding their favorite columns so filled up. By giving even a notice of more than an item's length to such a speech, an editor runs the risk of being denounced as dull. And I believe that the position of the American Press is in this regard quite singular. . . . Since our politicians lack the credit of authority and responsibility, they must give place, except at election-time, to the Press, which is everywhere, generally well-informed, and always talking. It is necessarily "government by declamation" and editorial-writing.

It is probably also this lack of leadership which gives to our national parties their curious, conglomerate character. It would seem to be scarcely an exaggeration to say that they are homogeneous only in name. Neither of the two principle parties is of one mind with itself. Each tolerates all sorts of difference of creed and variety of aims within its own ranks. Each pretends to the same purposes and permits among its partisans the same contradictions to those purposes. They are grouped around no legislative leaders whose capacity has been tested and to whose opinions they loyally adhere. They are like armies without officers, engaged upon a campaign which has no great cause at its back. Their names and traditions, not their hopes and policy, keep them together.

It is to this fact, as well as to short terms which allow little time for differences to come to a head, that the easy agreement of congressional majorities should be attributed. In other like assemblies the harmony of majorities is constantly liable to disturbance. Ministers lose their following and find their friends falling away in the midst of a session. But not so in Congress. There, although the majority is frequently simply conglomerate, made up of factions not a few, and bearing in its elements every seed of discord, the harmony of party voting seldom, if ever, suffers an interruption. So far as outsiders can see, legislation generally flows placidly on, and the majority easily has its own way, acting with a sort of matter-of-course unanimity, with no suspicion of individual freedom of action. Whatever revolts may be threatened or accomplished in the ranks of the party outside the House at the polls, its power is never broken inside the House. This is doubtless due in part to the fact that there is no freedom of debate in the House; but there can be no question that it is principally due to the fact that debate is without aim, just because legislation is without consistency. Legislation is conglomerate. The absence of any concert of action amongst the Committees leaves legislation with scarcely any trace of determinate party courses. No two schemes pull together. If there is a coincidence of principle between several bills of the same session, it is generally accidental; and the confusion of policy which prevents intelligent cooperation also, of course, prevents intelligent differences and divisions. There is never a transfer of power from one party to the other during a session, because such a transfer would mean almost nothing. The majority remains of one mind so long as Congress lives, because its mind is more vaguely ascertained, and its power of planning a split consequently very limited. It has no common mind, and if it had, has not the machinery for changing it. It is led by a score or two of Committees whose composition must remain the same to the end; and who are too numerous, as well as too disconnected, to fight against. It stays on one side because it hardly knows where the boundaries of that side are or how to cross them.

Moreover, there is a certain well-known piece of congressional machinery long ago invented and applied for the special purpose of keeping both majority and minority compact. The legislative caucus has almost as important a part in our system as have the Standing Committees, and deserves as close study as they. Its functions are much more easily understood in all their bearings than those of the Committees, however, because they are much simpler. The caucus is meant as an antidote to the Committees. It is designed to supply the cohesive principle which the multiplicity and mutual independence of the Committees so powerfully tend to destroy. Having no Prime Minister to confer with about the policy of the government, as they see members of parliament doing, our congressmen confer with each other in caucus. Rather than imprudently expose to the world the differences of opinion threatened or developed among its members, each party hastens to remove disrupting debate from the floor of Congress, where the speakers might too hastily commit themselves to insubordination, to quiet conferences behind closed doors, where frightened scruples may be reassured and every disagreement healed with a salve of compromise or subdued with the whip of political expediency. The caucus is the drilling-ground of the party. There its discipline is renewed and strengthened, its uniformity of step and gesture regained. The voting and speaking in the House are generally merely the movements of a sort of dress parade, for which the exercises of the caucus are designed to prepare. It is easy to see how difficult it would be for the party to keep its head amidst the confused cross-movements of the Committees without thus now and again pulling itself together in caucus, where it can ask itself its own mind and pledge itself anew to eternal agreement.

The credit of inventing this device is probably due to the Democrats. They appear to have used it so early as the second session of the eighth Congress. Speaking of that session, a reliable authority says: "During this session of Congress there was far less of free and independent discussion on the measures proposed by the friends of the administration than had been previously practiced in both branches of the national legislature. It appeared that on the most important subjects, the course adopted by the majority was the effect of caucus arrangement or, in other words, had been previously agreed upon at meetings of the Democratic members held in private. Thus the legislation of Congress was constantly swayed by a party following feelings and pledges rather than according to sound reason or personal conviction." The censure implied in this last sentence may have seemed righteous at the time when such caucus pledges were in disfavor as new-fangled shackles, but it would hardly be accepted as just by the intensely practical politicians of to-day. They would probably prefer to put it thus: That the silvern speech spent in caucus secures the golden silence maintained on the floor of Congress, making each party rich in concord and happy in cooperation.

The fact that makes this defense of the caucus not altogether conclusive is that it is shielded from all responsibility by its sneaking privacy. It has great power without any balancing weight of accountability. Probably its debates would constitute interesting and instructive reading for the public, were they published; but they never get out except in rumors often rehearsed and as often amended. They are, one may take it for granted, much more candid and go much nearer the political heart of the questions discussed than anything that is ever said openly in Congress to the reporters' gallery. They approach matters without masks and handle them without gloves. It might hurt, but it would enlighten us to hear them. As it is, however, there is unhappily no ground for denying their power to override sound reason and personal conviction. The caucus cannot always silence or subdue a large and influential minority of dissentients, but its whip seldom fails to reduce individual malcontents and mutineers into submission. There is no place in congressional jousts for the free lance. The man who disobeys his party caucus is understood to disavow his party allegiance altogether, and to assume that dangerous neutrality which is so apt to degenerate into mere caprice, and which is almost sure to destroy his influence by bringing him under the suspicion of being unreliable—a suspicion always conclusively damning in practical life. Any individual, or a minority of weak numbers or small influence, who has the temerity to neglect the decisions of the caucus is sure, if the offense be often repeated, or even once committed upon an important issue, to be read out of the party, almost without chance of reinstatement. And every one knows that nothing can be accomplished in politics by mere disagreement. The only privilege such recalcitrants gain is the privilege of disagreement; they are forever shut out from the privilege of confidential cooperation. They have chosen the helplessness of a faction.

It must be admitted, however, that, unfortunate as the necessity is for the existence of such powers as those of the caucus, that necessity actually exists and cannot be neglected. Against the fatal action of so many elements of disintegration, it would seem to be imperatively needful that some energetic element of cohesion should be provided. It is doubtful whether in any other nation, with a shorter inheritance of political instinct, parties could long successfully resist the centrifugal forces of the committee system with only the varying attraction of the caucus to detain them. The wonder is that, despite the forcible and unnatural divorcement of legislation and administration and the consequent distraction of legislation from all attention to anything like an intelligent planning and superintendence of policy, we are not cursed with as many factions as now almost hopelessly confuse French politics. That we have had, and continue to have, only two national parties of national importance or real power is fortunate rather than natural. Their names stand for a fact, but scarcely for a reason.

An intelligent observer of our politics has declared that there is in the United States "a class, including thousands and tens of thousands of the best men in the country, who think it possible to enjoy the fruits of good government without working for them." Every one who has seen beyond the outside of our American life must recognize the truth of this; to explain it is to state the sum of all the most valid criticisms of congressional government. Public opinion has no easy vehicle for its judgments, no quick channels for its action. Nothing about the system is direct and simple. Authority is perplexingly subdivided and distributed, and responsibility has to be hunted down in out-of-the-way corners. So that the sum of the whole matter is that the means of working for the fruits of good government are not readily to be found. The average citizen may be excused for esteeming government at best but a haphazard affair, upon which his vote and all of his influence can have but little effect. How is his choice of a representative in Congress to affect the policy of the country as regards the questions in which he is most interested, if the man for whom he votes has no chance of getting on the Standing Committee which has virtual charge of those questions? How is it to make any difference who is chosen President? Has the President any very great authority in matters of vital policy? It seems almost a thing of despair to get any assurance that any vote he may cast will even in an infinitesimal degree affect the essential courses of administration. There are so many cooks mixing their ingredients in the national broth that it seems hopeless, this thing of changing one cook at a time.

The charm of our constitutional ideal has now been long enough wound up to enable sober men who do not believe in political witchcraft to judge what it has accomplished, and is likely still to accomplish, without further winding. The Constitution is not honored by blind worship. The more open-eyed we become, as a nation, to its defects, and the prompter we grow in applying with the unhesitating courage of conviction all thoroughly-tested or well-considered expedients necessary to make self-government among us a straightforward thing of simple method, single, unstinted power, and clear responsibility, the nearer we will approach to the sound sense and practical genius of the great and honorable statesmen of 1787. And the first step towards emancipation from the timidity and false pride which have led us to seek to thrive despite the defects of our national system rather than seem to deny its perfection is a fearless criticism of that system. When we shall have examined all its parts without sentiment, and gauged all its functions by the standards of practical common sense, we shall have established anew our right to the claim of political sagacity; and it will remain only to act intelligently upon what our opened eyes have seen in order to prove again the justice of our claim to political genius.

15

SAMUEL P. HUNTINGTON

CONGRESSIONAL RESPONSES TO THE TWENTIETH CENTURY

According to Samuel P. Huntington, the decline of congressional power in the twentieth century can be explained by the failure of Congress to adapt appropriately to external changes. Congress became insulated from other political institutions, leaders, and important social groups. Huntington, a professor of government at Harvard University, argues that while Congress has the need for specialization of functions through its elaborate system of committees and subcommittees, it has not been able to centralize its power adequately to make concerted policy leadership possible. The legislature is increasingly limited to the role of approving or delaying the president's initiatives and overseeing the bureaucracy. This article was published in 1973 in a book edited by David Truman, The Congress and America's Future. *Huntington also wrote* Political Order in Changing Societies *(1968) and* The Soldier and the State *(1957).*

Congress is a perennial source of anguish to both its friends and its foes. The critics point to its legislative failure. The function of a legislature, they argue, is to legislate and Congress either does not legislate or legislates too little and too late. The intensity of their criticism varies inversely with the degree and dispatch with which Congress approves the President's legislative proposals. When in 1963 the Eighty-eighth Congress seemed to stymie the Kennedy legislative program, criticism rapidly mounted. "What kind of legislative body is it," asked Walter Lippmann,* neatly summing up the prevailing exasperation, "that will not or cannot legislate?" When in 1964 the same Eighty-eighth Congress passed the civil rights, tax, and other bills, criticism of Congress correspondingly subsided. Reacting differently to this familiar pattern, the friends of Congress lamented its acquiescence to presidential dictate. Since 1933, they said, the authority of the executive branch—President, administation, and bureaucracy—has waxed, while that of Congress has waned. They warned of the constitutional perils stemming from the permanent subordination of one branch of government to another. In foreign and military policy, as well as domestic affairs, Congress is damned when it acquiesces in presidential leadership (Tonkin Gulf Resolution, 1964†) and also when it at-

**Walter Lippmann* (1889–1974): sagacious American journalist and author of numerous books including *Men of Destiny* (1927), *An Inquiry into the Principles of the Good Society* (1937), *Some Notes on War and Peace* (1940), *The Cold War* (1947), and *Essays in the Public Philosophy* (1955).

†*Tonkin Gulf Resolution* (1964): formal resolution by Congress approving President Lyndon B. Johnson's efforts to defend U.S. naval vessels from attacks in international waters. The resolution was later interpreted by the administration as legal affirmation by Congress of the chief executive's military campaign in Vietnam. The resolution was repealed in 1971.

tempts to seize the initiative (Mansfield Resolution, 1971*). At the same time that it is an obstructive ogre to its enemies, Congress is also the declining despair of its friends. Can both images be true? In large part, they are. The dilemma of Congress, indeed, can be measured by the extent to which congressional assertion coincides with congressional obstruction.

This paradox has been at the root of the "problem" of Congress since the early days of the New Deal.† Vis-à-vis the executive, Congress is an autonomous, legislative body. But apparently Congress can defend its autonomy only by refusing to legislate, and it can legislate only by surrendering its autonomy. In the past, there has been a familiar pattern: Congress balks, criticism, rises, the clamoring voices of reformers fill the air with demands for the "modernization" of the "antiquated procedures" of an "eighteenth century" Congress so it can deal with "twentieth century realities." The demands for reform serve as counters in the legislative game to get the President's measures through Congress. Independence thus provokes criticism; acquiescence brings approbation. If Congress legislates, it subordinates itself to the President; if it refuses to legislate, it alienates itself from public opinion. Congress can assert its power or it can pass laws, but it cannot do both.

LEGISLATIVE POWER AND INSTITUTIONAL CRISIS

The roots of this legislative dilemma lie in the changes in American society during the twentieth century. The twentieth centuy has seen: rapid urbanization and the beginnings of a postindustrial, technological society; the nationalization of social and economic problems and the concomitant growth of national organizations to deal with these problems; the increasing bureaucratization of social, economic, and governmental organizations; and the sustained high-level international involvement of the United States in world politics. These developments have generated new forces in American politics and initiated major changes in the distribution of power in American society. In particular, the twentieth century has witnessed the tremendous expansion of the responsibilities of the national government and the size of the national bureaucracy. In 1901, the national government had 351,798 employees or less than 1½ percent of the national labor force. In 1971 it had 5,637,000 employees, constituting almost 7 percent of the labor force. The expansion of the national government has been paralleled by the emergence of other large, national, bureaucratic organizations: manufacturing corporations, banks, insurance companies, labor unions, trade associations, farm organizations, newspaper chains, radio-TV networks. Each organization may have relatively specialized and concrete interests, but typically it functions on a national basis. Its headquarters are in New York or Washington;

**Mansfield Resolution* (1971): bill introduced by Michael J. Mansfield, a Democratic senator from Montana (1953–1977) and Senate majority leader (1961–1977), which would have required the United States to withdraw its troops from Vietnam and which requested that the president negotiate a cease-fire with North Vietnam. The bill passed the Senate but not the House of Representatives.

†*New Deal*: see footnote on page 17.

its operations are scattered across a dozen or more states. The emergence of these organizations truly constitutes, in Kenneth Boulding's* expressive phrase, an "organizational revolution." The existence of this private "Establishment," more than anything else, distinguishes twentieth-century America from nineteenth-century America. The leaders of these organizations are the notables of American society; they are the prime wielders of social and economic power.

Adaptation Crises

These momentous social changes have confronted Congress with an institutional "adaptation crisis." Such a crisis occurs when changes in the environment of a governmental institution force the institution either to alter its functions, affiliation, and modes of behavior, or to face decline, decay, and isolation. Crises usually occur when an institution loses its previous sources of support or fails to adapt itself to the rise of new social forces. Such a crisis, for instance, affected the Presidency in the second and third decades of the nineteenth century. Under the leadership of Henry Clay† the focal center of power in the national government was in the House of Representatives; the congressional caucus dictated presidential nominations; popular interest in and support for the Presidency were minimal. The "Executive," Justice Story‡ remarked in 1818, "has no longer a commanding influence. The House of Representatives has absorbed all the popular feelings and all the effective power of the country." The Presidency was on the verge of becoming a weak, secondary instrumental organ of government. It was rescued from this fate by the Jacksonian movement, which democratized the Presidency, broadened its base of popular support, and restored it as the center of vitality and leadership in the national government. The House of Commons was faced with a somewhat similar crisis during the agitation preceding the first Reform Bill of 1832. New social groups were developing in England which were demanding admission to the political arena and the opportunity to share in political leadership. Broadening the constituency of the House of Commons and reforming the system of elections enabled the House to revitalize itself and to continue as the principal locus of power in the British government.

In both these cases a governmental institution got a new lease on life, new vigor, new power, by embodying within itself dynamic, new social forces. When an institution fails to make such an alignment, it must either restrict its own authority or submit to limitations upon its authority imposed from outside. In 1910, when the House of Lords refused to approve Lloyd George's budget, it was

***Kenneth Boulding*: professor of economics, University of Colorado. His numerous books include *The Optimum Utilization of Knowledge* (1983), *The Economics of Human Betterment* (1984), and *Methodology in the Social Sciences* (1984).

†*Henry Clay* (1777–1852): U.S. senator from Kentucky (1806–1807, 1810–1811, 1831–1842, 1849–1852) and member of the U.S. House of Representatives (1811–1821, 1823–1825). He was Speaker of the House from 1811 to 1820 and from 1823 to 1825. Clay was unsuccessful in his two bids as the Whig presidential candidate in 1832 and in 1844.

‡*Joseph Story* (1779–1845): associate justice on the U.S. Supreme Court (1811–1845) who simultaneously held a chair at the Harvard Law School. He was a prodigious writer; among his numerous works are *Federal Constitution* (1833), *Equity Jurisprudence* (1836), *Bills of Exchange* (1843), and *Promissory Notes* (1845).

first compelled by governmental pressure, popular opinion, and the threat of the creation of new peers to acquiesce in the budget and then through a similar process to acquiesce in the curtailment of its own power to obstruct legislation approved by the Commons. In this case the effort to block legislation approved by the dominant forces in the political community resulted in a permanent diminution of the authority of the offending institution. A somewhat similar crisis developed with respect to the Supreme Court in the 1930s. Here again a less popular body attempted to veto the actions of more popular bodies. In three years the Court invalidated twelve acts of Congress. Inevitably this precipitated vigorous criticism and demands for reform, culminating in Roosevelt's court reorganization proposal in February of 1937. The alternatives confronting the Court were relatively clear-cut: it could "reform" or be "reformed." In "the switch in time that saved nine," it chose the former course, signaling its change by approving the National Labor Relations Act* in April 1935 and the Social Security Act† in May. With this switch, support for the reorganization of the Court drained away. The result was, in the words of Justice Jackson,‡ "a failure of the reform forces and a victory of the reform."

Congress's Response

Each of these four institutional crises arose from the failure of a governmental institution to adjust to social change and the rise of new viewpoints, new needs, and new political forces. Congress's legislative dilemma and loss of power stem from the nature of its overall institutional response to the changes in American society. This response involves three major aspects of Congress as an institution: its affiliations, its structure, and its functions. During the twentieth century Congress gradually insulated itself from the new political forces which social change had generated and which were, in turn, generating more change. Hence the leadership of Congress lacked the incentive to take the legislative initiative in handling emerging national problems. Within Congress power became dispersed among many officials, committees, and subcommittees. Hence the central leadership of Congress lacked the ability to establish national legislative priorities. As a result, the legislative function of Congress declined in importance, while the growth of the federal bureaucracy made the administrative overseeing function of Congress more important. These three tendencies—toward insulation, dispersion, and oversight—have dominated the evolution of Congress during the twentieth century.

***National Labor Relations Act*: see footnote on page 112.

†*Social Security Act of 1935*: law that, as part of Franklin D. Roosevelt's New Deal, established a contributory social insurance program for private sector employees. The act has been amended several times and now covers almost all occupations. Benefits are provided to retired workers, their survivors in the event of their death, certain dependents upon the worker's retirement, and the disabled. In addition, the present law requires the availability of Medicare. The system is administered by the Social Security Administration of the U.S. Department of Health and Human Services.

‡*Robert H. Jackson* (1892–1954): attorney general under President Franklin D. Roosevelt and then associate justice of the Supreme Court (1941–1954). Jackson is remembered for his erudite opinions and for his extraordinary role as chief Allied prosecutor at the Nuremburg Trials. Among his famous opinions are *West Virginia State Board of Education* v. *Barnette* (1943) and *Youngstown Sheet and Tube Co.* v. *Sawyer* (1952).

AFFILIATIONS: INSULATION FROM POWER

Congressional Evolution

Perhaps the single most important trend in congressional evolution for the bulk of this century was the growing insulation of Congress from other social groups and political institutions. In 1900 no gap existed between congressmen and the other leaders of American society and politics. Half a century later the changes in American society, on the one hand, and the institutional evolution of Congress, on the other, had produced a marked gap between congressional leaders and the bureaucratically oriented leadership of the executive branch and of the establishment. The growth of this gap can be seen in seven aspects of congressional evolution.

(1) Increasing Tenure of Office—In the nineteenth century few congressmen stayed in Congress very long. During the twentieth century the average tenure of congressmen has inexorably lengthened. In 1900 only 9 percent of the members of the House of Representatives had served five terms or more and less than 1 percent had served ten terms or more. In 1957, 45 percent of the House had served five terms or more and 14 percent ten terms or more. In 1897, for each representative who had served ten terms or more in the House, there were 34 representatives who had served two terms or less. In 1971 the ratio was down almost to equality, with 1.2 members who had served two terms or less for each ten-termer.[1] In the middle of the nineteenth century, only about half the representatives in any one Congress had served in a previous Congress, and only about one-third of the Senators had been elected to the Senate more than once. By the second half of the twentieth century, close to 90 percent of the House were veterans, and almost two-thirds of the senators were beyond their first term. The biennial infusion of new blood had reached an all-time low.

(2) The Increasingly Important Role of Seniority—Increasing tenure of congressmen is closely linked to increasingly rigid adherence to the practices of seniority. The longer men stay in Congress, the more likely they are to see virtue in seniority. Conversely, the more important seniority is, the greater is the constituent appeal of men who have been long in office. The rigid system of seniority in *both* houses of Congress is a product of the twentieth century.

In the nineteenth century seniority was far more significant in the Senate than in the House. Since the middle of that century apparently only in five instances—the last in 1925—has the chairmanship of a Senate committee been denied to the most senior member of the committee. In the House, on the other hand, the Speaker early received the power to appoint committees and to designate their chairmen. During the nineteenth century Speakers made much of this power. Committee appointment and the selection of chairmen were involved political processes, in which the Speaker carefully balanced factors of seniority, geography, expertise, and policy viewpoint in making his choices. Not infrequently prolonged bargaining would result as the Speaker traded committee positions for legislative commitments. Commenting on James G. Blaine's efforts at committee construction in the early 1870s, one member of his family wrote that Blaine "left for New York on

TABLE 1. VETERAN CONGRESSMEN IN CONGRESS

Congress	Date	Representatives Elected to House More than Once	Senators Elected to Senate More than Once
42nd	1871	53%	32%
50th	1887	63	45
64th	1915	74	47
74th	1935	77	54
87th	1961	87	66
92nd	1971	88	65

Source: Figures for representatives for 1871–1915 are from Robert Luce, *Legislative Assemblies* (Boston: Houghton Mifflin Company, 1924), p. 365. Other figures were calculated independently. I am indebted to Emily Lieberman for assistance in updating these and other statistics in this essay.

Wednesday. He had cotton and wool manufacturers to meet in Boston, and, over and above all, pressure to resist or permit. As fast as he gets his committees arranged, just so fast some after-consideration comes up which overtopples the whole list like a row of bricks."[2] Only with the drastic curtailment of the powers of the Speaker in 1910 and 1911 did the seniority system in the House assume the inflexible pattern which it has today. Only twice in the years after the 1910 revolt—once in 1915 and once in 1921—was seniority neglected in the choice of committee chairmen.

In the 1960s seniority came under increasing criticism within Congress and some small steps away from it were taken. In 1965 the House Democratic caucus stripped two southern congressmen of their committee seniority for supporting Barry Goldwater* in 1964. One of them, John Bell Williams of Mississippi, had been a member of the House since 1947 and was the second-ranking Democrat on the Committee on Interstate and Foreign Commerce. In 1967 a select House committee recommended punishing Representative Adam Clayton Powell by, among other things, taking away his seniority and hence his position as chairman of the Committee on Education and Labor. The House, however, instead voted to deny Mr. Powell a seat in the Ninetieth Congress. In 1971 the House Republican and Democratic caucuses decreed that the selection of committee chairmen should be subject to caucus approval; the Democratic caucus then approved as chairmen those who would have been chairmen by seniority. Nor was a serious effort made to change the seniority system in the Legislative Reorganization Act of 1970.† These events suggest that the system will remain but that deviations from it (at least in the House) will occasionally occur and will be accepted as legitimate.

(3) Extended Tenure: a Prerequisite for Leadership—Before 1896 Speakers, at the time of their first election, averaged only 7 years' tenure in the House. Since 1896 Speakers have averaged 23 years of House service at their first election. In 1811 and in 1859 Henry Clay and William Pennington were elected Speaker

**Barry Goldwater:* see footnote on page 188.

†Legislative Reorganization Act of 1970: law that required congressional votes to be recorded, congressional committees to be developed and follow written rules, the powers of committee chairpersons be decreased, and most committee votes be on public record.

when they first entered the House. In 1807 Thomas Jefferson arranged for the election of his friend, William C. Nicholas, to the House and then for his immediate selection by the party caucus as floor leader. Such an intrusion of leadership from the outside world would now be unthinkable. Today the Speaker and other leaders of the House and, to a lesser degree, the leaders of the Senate are legislative veterans of long standing. In 1971 46 House leaders averaged over 23 years' service in the House while 40 leading senators averaged 17 years of senatorial service. The top House leaders (Speaker, floor leaders, chairmen and ranking minority members of Ways and Means, Appropriations, and Rules Committees) averaged 26 years in the House and 8 in leadership positions in 1971. Top Senate leaders (President *pro tem.*, floor leaders, chairmen, and ranking minority members of Finance, Foreign Relations, and Appropriations Committees) averaged 23 years of service in the Senate and 11 in leadership positions. Increasing tenure means increasing age. In the nineteenth century the leaders of Congress were often in their thirties. Clay was 34 when he became Speaker in 1811; Hunter, 30 when he became Speaker in 1839; White, 36 at his accession to the Speakership in 1841; and Ore, 35 when he became Speaker in 1857. In contrast, Rayburn was 58 when he became Speaker, Martin 63, McCormack 71, and Albert 62. In 1971 the top leaders of the House averaged 63 years, those of the Senate 69 years.

(4) Leadership within Congress: a One-way Street—Normally in American life becoming a leader in one institution opens up leadership possibilities in other institutions: corporation presidents head civic agencies or become cabinet officers; foundation and university executives move into government; leading lawyers and bankers take over industrial corporations. The greater one's prestige, authority, and accomplishments within one organization, the easier it is to move to other and better posts in other organizations. Such, however, is not the case with Congress. Leadership in the House of Representatives leads nowhere except to leadership in the House of Representatives. To a lesser degree, the same has been true of the Senate. The successful House or Senate leader has to identify himself completely with his institution, its mores, traditions, and ways of behavior. "The very ingredients which make you a powerful House leader," one representative has commented, "are the ones which keep you from being a public leader."[3] Representatives typically confront a "fourth-term crisis": if they wish to run for higher office—for governor or senator—they must usually do so by the beginning of their fourth term in the House. If they stay in the House for four or more terms, they in effect choose to make a career in the House and to forswear the other electoral possibilities of American politics. Leadership in the Senate is not as exclusive a commitment as it is in the House. But despite such notable exceptions as Taft* and Johnson,† the most influential men in the Senate have

**Robert A. Taft* (1889–1953): U.S. senator from Ohio throughout the 1940s who led the conservative wing of the Republican party. He was a contender for the party's presidential nomination in 1948 and 1952, but lost out to Thomas Dewey and Dwight Eisenhower, respectively. Taft was co-sponsor of the Taft-Hartley Act of 1947 (see footnote on page 118). He was the author of *A Foreign Policy for Americans* (1951).

†*Lyndon Johnson:* see footnote on page 166.

typically been those who have looked with disdain upon the prospect of being anything but a United States Senator. Even someone with the high talent and broad ambition of Lyndon Johnson could not escape this exclusive embrace during his years as majority leader. In the words of Theodore H. White, the Senate, for Johnson, was "faith, calling, club, habit, relaxation, devotion, hobby, and love." Over the years it became "almost a monomania with him, his private life itself."[4] Such "monomania" is normally the prerequisite for Senate leadership. It is also normally an insurmountable barrier, psychologically and politically, to effective leadership outside the Senate.

(5) *The Decline of Personnel Interchange Between Congress and the Administration*—Movement of leaders in recent years between the great national institutions of the establishment and the top positions in the administration has been frequent, easy, and natural. This pattern of lateral entry distinguishes the American executive branch from the governments of most other modern societies. The circulation of individuals between leadership positions in governmental and private institutions eases the strains between political and private leadership and performs a unifying function comparable to that which common class origins perform in Great Britain or common membership in the Communist party does in the Soviet Union.

The frequent movement of individuals between administration and establishment contrasts sharply with the virtual absence of such movement between Congress and the administration or between Congress and the establishment. The gap between congressional leadership and administration leadership has increased sharply during this century. Seniority makes it virtually impossible for administration leaders to become leaders of Congress and makes it unlikely that leaders of Congress will want to become leaders of the administration. The separation of powers has become the insulation of leaders. Between 1861 and 1896, 37 percent of the people appointed to posts in the President's cabinet had served in the House or Senate. Between 1897 and 1940, 19 percent of the Cabinet positions were filled by former congressmen or senators. Between 1941 and 1963, only 15 percent of the cabinet posts were so filled. Former congressmen received only 4 percent of over 1,000 appointments of political executives made during the Roosevelt, Truman, Eisenhower, and Kennedy administrations.[5] In 1963, apart from the President and Vice-President, only one of the top 75 leaders of the Kennedy administration (Secretary of the Interior Udall) had served in Congress. The Nixon administration was somewhat more hospitable to legislators, but in 1971 only 4 of its top 75 leaders (apart from the President) had congressional experience.

Movement from the administration to leadership positions in Congress is almost equally rare. In 1971 only one of 84 congressional leaders (Senator Anderson) had previously served in the President's cabinet. Those members of the administration who do not move on to Congress are typically those who have come to the administration from state and local politics rather than from the great national institutions. Few congressmen and even fewer congressional leaders move from Congress to positions of leadership in national private organizations, and relatively few leaders of these organizations move on to Congress. Successful

TABLE 2. GEOGRAPHICAL MOBILITY OF NATIONAL LEADERS

	CONGRESSIONAL LEADERS		ADMINISTRATION LEADERS		POLITICAL EXECUTIVES	BUSINESS LEADERS
	(1963) N-*81*	*(1971)* N-*86*	*(1963)* N-*74*	*(1971)* N-*75*	*(1959)* N-*1865*	*(1952)* N-*8300*
None	37%	43%	11%	13%	} 14%	} 40%
Intrastate	40	35	19	25		
Interstate, intraregion	5	8	9	3	10	15
Interregion	19	14	61	52	73	45
International	0	0	0	7	3	0

Sources: "Political Executives," Warner et al. [see note 6], p. 332; business leaders, Warner and Abegglen [see note 6], p. 82; congressional and administration leaders, independent calculation. Geographical mobility is measured by comparing birthplace with current residence. For administration leaders, current residence was considered to be last residence before assuming administration position. The nine regions employed in this analysis are defined in Warner *et al.* [see note 6], pp. 42–43.

men who have come to the top in business, law, or education naturally hesitate to shift to another world in which they would have to start all over again at the bottom. In some cases, establishment leaders also consider legislative office simply beneath them.

(6) *The Social Origins and Careers of Congressmen*—Congressmen are much more likely to come from rural and small-town backgrounds than are administration and establishment leaders. A majority of the senators holding office between 1947 and 1957 were born in rural areas. Of the 1959 senators 64 percent were raised in rural areas or in small towns, and only 19 percent in metropolitan centers. In contrast, 52 percent of the presidents of the largest industrial corporations grew up in metropolitan centers, as did a large proportion of the political executives appointed during the Roosevelt, Truman, Eisenhower, and Kennedy administrations. The contrast in origins is reflected in fathers' occupations. In the 1950s, the proportion of farmer fathers among senators (32 percent) was more than twice as high as it was among administration leaders (13 percent) and business leaders (9 to 15 percent).[6]

Of perhaps greater significance is the difference in geographical mobility between congressmen and private and public executives. Forty-one percent of the 1959 senators, but only 12 percent of the 1959 corporation presidents, were currently residing in their original hometowns. Seventy percent of the presidents had moved 100 miles or more from their hometowns but only 29 percent of the senators had done so.[7] In 1971 over two-fifths of the leaders of Congress but only 13 percent of administration leaders were still living in their places of birth. Seventy-five percent of the congressional leaders were living in their states of birth, while 62 percent of the administration leaders had moved out of their states of birth. Fifty-nine percent of administration leaders had moved from one region of the country to another, but only 16 percent of congressional leaders had similar mobility.

During the course of this century the career patterns of congressmen and of executive leaders have diverged. At an earlier period both leaderships had exten-

TABLE 3. EXPERIENCE OF NATIONAL POLITICAL LEADERS IN STATE AND LOCAL GOVERNMENT

	CONGRESSIONAL LEADERS			ADMINISTRATION LEADERS		
Offices Held	*1903*	*1963*	*1971*	*1903*	*1963*	*1971*
Any state or local office	75%	64%	71%	49%	17%	31%
Elective local office	55	46	37	22	5	4
State legislature	47	30	42	17	3	9
Appointive state office	12	10	16	20	7	12
Governor	16	9	5	5	4	7

sive experience in local and state politics. In 1903 about one-half of executive leaders and three-quarters of congressional leaders had held office in state or local government. In 1971 the congressional pattern had not changed significantly, with 71 percent of the congressional leaders having held state or local office. The proportion of executive leaders with this experience, however, had dropped drastically. The proportion of administration leaders who had held state or local office was still less than half that of congressional leaders, although it had gone up to 31 percent from 17 percent in 1963. When coupled with the data presented earlier on the larger number of former congressmen in the Nixon administration than in the Kennedy administration, these figures suggest a slight shift in recruitment toward local politics and away from the national establishment for the former as compared to the latter.

In recent years, congressional leaders have also more often been professional politicians than they were earlier: in 1903 only 5 percent of the congressional leaders had no major occupation outside politics, while in 1963, 22 percent of the congressional leaders had spent almost all their lives in electoral politics. Roughly 90 percent of the members of Congress in recent years, it has been estimated, "have served apprenticeship in some segment of our political life."[8]

The typical congressman may have gone away to college, but he then returned to his home state to pursue an electoral career, working his way up through local office, the state legislature, and eventually to Congress. The typical political executive, on the other hand, like the typical corporation executive, went away to college and then did not return home but instead pursued a career in a metropolitan center or worked in one or more national organizations with frequent changes of residence. As a result, political executives have become divorced from state and local politics, just as the congressional leaders have become isolated from national organizations. Congressional leaders, in short, come up through a "local politics" line while executives move up through a "national organization" line.

The differences in geographical mobility and career patterns between congressional and administrative leaders reflect two different styles of life which cut across the usual occupational groupings. Businessmen, lawyers, and bankers are found in both Congress and the administration. But those in Congress are more likely to be small businessmen, small-town lawyers, and small-town bankers. Among the 66 lawyers in the Senate in 1963, for instance, only 2—Joseph Clark and Clifford Case—had been "prominent corporation counsel[s]" before going into politics.[9] Administration leaders, in contrast, are far more likely to be affiliated with large national industrial corporations, with Wall Street or State Street law firms, and with New York banks.

(7) The Provincialism of Congressmen—The absence of mobility between Congress and the executive branch and the differing backgrounds of the leaders of the two branches of government stimulate different policy attitudes. Congressmen have tended to be oriented toward local needs and small-town ways of thought. The leaders of the administration and of the great private national institutions are more likely to think in national terms. Analyzing consensus-building on foreign aid, James N. Rosenau concluded that congressmen typically had "segmental" orientations while other national leaders had "continental" orientations. The segmentally oriented leaders "give highest priority to the subnational units which they head or represent" and are "not prepared to admit a discrepancy between" the national welfare and "their subnational concerns." The congressman is part of a local consensus of local politicians, local businessmen, local bankers, local trade union leaders, and local newspaper editors who constitute the opinion-making elites of their districts. As Senator Richard Neuberger noted: "If there is one maxim which seems to prevail among many members of our national legislature, it is that local matters must come first and global problems a poor second—that is, if the member of Congress is to survive politically." As a result, the members of Congress are "isolated" from other national leaders. At gatherings of national leaders, "members of Congress seem more conspicuous by their absence than by their presence." One piece of evidence is fairly conclusive: of 623 national opinion-makers who attended ten American Assembly sessions between 1956 and 1960, only 9 (1.4 percent) were members of Congress![10]

The differences in attitude between segmentally oriented congressmen and the other, continentally oriented national leaders are particularly marked in those areas of foreign policy (such as foreign aid) which involve the commitment of tangible resources for intangible ends. But they have also existed in domestic policy. The approaches of senators and corporation presidents to economic issues, Andrew Hacker found, were rooted in "disparate images of society." Senators were provincially oriented; corporation presidents "metropolitan" in their thinking. Senators might be sympathetic to business, but they thought of business in small-town, small-business terms. They might attempt to accomodate themselves to the needs of the national corporations, but basically they were "faced with a power they do not really understand and with demands about whose legitimacy they are uneasy." As a result, Hacker suggests, "serious tensions exist between our major political and economic institutions. . . . There is, at base, a real lack of understanding and a failure of communication between the two elites."[11]

"Segmental" or "provincial" attitudes are undoubtedly stronger in the House than they are in the Senate. But they have also existed in the Senate. Despite the increased unity of the country caused by mass communications and the growth of "national as distinguished from local or sectional industry," the Senate in the 1950s was, according to an admiring portraitist, "if anything progressively less national in its approach to most affairs" and "increasingly engaged upon the protection of what is primarily local or sectional in economic life."[12]

For both House and Senate these local patterns are being challenged and in some degree undermined by the nationalizing impact of the media and the geographical extension of party competition.[13] Yet within Congress old ideas, old values, and old beliefs linger on. The structure of Congress encourages their perpetuation. The newcomer to Congress is repeatedly warned that "to get along he must go along." To go along means to adjust to the prevailing mores and attitudes. The more the young congressman desires a career in the House or Senate, the more readily he makes these adjustments. The country at large has become urban, suburban, and metropolitan. Its economic, social, educational, and technological activities are increasingly performed by huge national bureaucratic organizations. In the 1960s these developments were only beginning to make themselves felt in Congress, as gradually younger and more adventurous congressmen took the initiative in challenging the old ways. On Capitol Hill the nineteenth-century ethos of the small town, the independent farmer, and the small businessman slowly wanes behind the instituional defenses which developed in this century to insulate Congress from the new America.

Defects in Representation

In the twentieth century the executive branch grew in power vis-à-vis Congress for precisely the same reason that the House of Representatives grew in power vis-à-vis the executive in the second and third decades of the nineteenth century. It became more powerful because it had become more representative. Congress lost power because it had two defects as a representative body. One, relatively minor and in part easily remedied, dealt with the representation of people as individuals; the other, more serious and perhaps beyond remedy, concerned the representation of organized groups and interests.

Congress was originally designed to represent individuals in the House and governmental units—the states—in the Senate. In the course of time the significance of the states as organized interests declined, and popular election of senators was introduced. In effect, both senators and representatives now represent relatively arbitrarily defined territorial collections of individuals. This system of individual representation has suffered from two inequities. First, of course, is the constitutional equal representation of states in the Senate irrespective of population. Second, in the House, congressional districts have varied widely in size and may also be gerrymandered* to benefit one party or group of voters. For much of this century the net effect of these practices was to place the urban and suburban voter at a disadvantage vis-à-vis the rural and small-town voter. The correction of this imbalance moved rapidly ahead, however, following the Supreme Court decisions (*Baker* v. *Carr*, 1962; *Wesberry* v. *Sanders*, 1964) mandating equal size for districts. As a result of the Court action, there was a net shift of between 10 and 19 districts from predominantly rural to predominantly urban during the 1960s.[14] The application of the new standards to the 1970 census population, it

**Gerrymandered:* see footnote on page 191.

has been estimated, should result in 291 metropolitan districts in 1972 compared to 254 in 1962. Of these 129 would be suburban districts compared to 92 such districts in 1962. Central city representation, on the other hand, will drop to 100 congressmen from 106 in 1962 and a peak of 110 in 1966.[15] As Milton Cummings notes:

> In all this there is a very considerable irony. The battle for greater urban representation in the House in the 1950s and 1960s was often accompanied by rhetoric stressing the need to help the central cities, who, it was asserted, were penalized by rural overrepresentation. Now that the one-man/one-vote doctrine is being implemented, however, it is the suburbs, not the central cities, that stand to gain the most.[16]

The overall membership of the House will thus be increasingly metropolitan and suburban. Adherence to seniority, however, means that the leadership of the House will remain southern rural and northern urban for some years to come.

The second and more significant deficiency of Congress as a representative body concerns its insulation from the interests which have emerged in the twentieth century's "organizational revolution." How can national institutions be represented in a locally elected legislature? In the absence of any easy answer to this question, the administration has tended to emerge as the natural point of access to the government for these national organizations and the place where their interests and viewpoints are brought into the policy-making process. In effect, the American system of government is moving toward a three-way system of representation. Particular territorial interests are represented in Congress; particular functional interests are represented in the administration; and the national interest is represented territorially and functionally in the Presidency.

Every four years the American people choose a President, but they elect an administration. In this century the administration has acquired many of the traditional characteristics of a representative body that Congress has tended to lose. The Jacksonian principle of "rotation of office" and the classic concept of the Cincinnatus-like statesman are far more relevant now to the administration than they are to Congress. Administration officials, unlike congressmen, are more frequently mobile amateurs in government than career professionals in politics. The patterns of power in Congress are rigid. The patterns of power in the administration are flexible. The administration is thus a far more sensitive register of changing currents of opinion than is Congress. A continuous adjustment of power and authority takes place within each administration; major changes in the distribution of power take place at every change of administration. The Eisenhower administration represented one combination of men, interests, and experience, the Kennedy-Johnson administration another, and the Nixon administration yet a third. Each time a new President takes office, the executive branch is invigorated in the same way that the House of Representatives was invigorated by Henry Clay and his western congressmen in 1811. A thousand new officials descend on Washington, coming fresh from the people, representing the diverse forces behind the new President, and bringing with them new demands, new ideas, and new power. Here truly is representative government along classic lines and of a sort which Congress has not known for decades. One key to the "decline" of Congress lies in the defects of Congress as a representative body.

STRUCTURE: THE DISPERSION OF POWER IN CONGRESS

The influence of Congress in our political system thus varies directly with its ties to the more dynamic and dominant groups in society. The power of Congress also varies directly, however, with the centralization of power in Congress. The corollary of these propositions is likewise true: centralization of authority within Congress usually goes with close connections between congressional leadership and major external forces and groups. The power of the House of Representatives was at a peak in the second decade of the nineteenth century, when power was centralized in the Speaker and when Henry Clay and his associates represented the dynamic new forces of trans-Appalachian nationalism. Another peak in the power of the House came during Reconstruction,* when power was centralized in Speaker Colfax† and the Joint Committee on Reconstruction as spokesmen for triumphant northern radicalism. A third peak in the power of the House came between 1890 and 1910, when the authority of the Speaker reached its height and Speakers Reed‡ and Cannon§ reflected the newly established forces of nationalist conservatism. The peak in Senate power came during the post-Reconstruction period of the 1870s and 1880s. Within Congress, power was centralized in the senatorial leaders who represented the booming forces of the rising industrial capitalism and the new party machines. These were the years, as Wilfred Binkley‖ put it, of "the Hegemony of the Senate."

Specialization Without Centralization

Since its first years, the twentieth century has seen no comparable centralization of power in Congress. Instead, the dominant tendency has been toward the dispersion of power. This leaves Congress only partially equipped to deal with the problems of modern society. In general, the complex modern environment requires in social and political institutions *both* a high degree of specialization and a high degree of centralized authority to coordinate and to integrate the activities of the specialized units. Specialization of function and centralization of authority have been the dominant trends of twentieth-century institutional devel-

**Reconstruction:* era between 1865 and 1877 in which political efforts were made to reintegrate the former Confederate States into the Union after their defeat in the Civil War.

†*Schuyler Colfax* (1823–1885): Republican who represented Indiana in the U.S. House of Representatives (1855–1869), served as Speaker of the House (1863–1869), and was vice-president under Ulysses S. Grant (1869–1873). A political scandal ruined his career.

‡*Thomas B. Reed* (1839–1902): Republican from Maine and member of the U.S. House of Representatives (1877–1899). He served as Speaker for three terms (1889–1891, 1895–1899).

§*Joseph G. Cannon* (1836–1926): Republican from Illinois who served in the U.S. House of Representatives (1873–1891, 1893–1913, 1915–1923). Renowned Speaker of the House from 1903 until 1911, he is remembered for his strong—some might say arbitrary—rule.

‖*Wilfred E. Binkley* (1883–1965): historian, political scientist, and author of *American Political Parties* (1943).

opment. Congress, however, has adjusted only half-way. Through its committees and subcommittees it has provided effectively for specialization, much more effectively, indeed, than the national legislature of any other country. But it has failed to combine increasing specialization of function with increasing centralization of authority. Instead the central leadership in Congress has been weakened, and as a result Congress lacks the central authority to integrate its specialized bodies. In a "rational" bureaucracy authority varies inversely with specialization. Within Congress authority usually varies directly with specialization.

The authority of the specialist is a distinctive feature of congressional behavior. "Specialization" is a key norm in both House and Senate. The man who makes a career in the House, one congressman has observed, "is primarily a worker, a specialist, and a craftsman—someone who will concentrate his energies in a particular field and gain prestige and influence in that." "The members who are most successful," another congressman concurred, "are those who pick a specialty or an area and become real experts in it."[17] The emphasis on specialization as a norm, of course, complements the importance of the committee as an institution. It also leads to a great stress on reciprocity. In a bureaucracy, specialized units compete with each other for the support of less specialized officials. In Congress, however, reciprocity by specialists replaces coordination by generalists. When a committee bill comes to the floor, the non-specialists in that subject acquiesce in its passage with the unspoken but complete understanding that they will receive similar treatment. "The traditional deference to the authority of one of its committees overwhelms the main body," one congressman has observed. "The whole fabric of Congress is based on committee expertise. . . ." Similarly, in the Senate, "a large number of highly specialized experts generally accept each other's work without much criticism."[18] Reciprocity thus substitutes for centralization and confirms the diffusion of power among the committees.

History of Dispersion

The current phase of dispersed power in Congress dates from the second decade of this century. The turning point in the House came with the revolt against Speaker Cannon in 1910, the removal of the Speaker from the Rules Committee, and the loss by the Speaker of his power to appoint standing committees. For a brief period, from 1911 to 1915, much of the Speaker's former power was assumed by Oscar Underwood* in his capacities as majority floor leader and chairman of the Ways and Means Committee. In 1915, however, Underwood was elected to the Senate, and the dispersion of power which had begun with the overthrow of the Speaker rapidly accelerated.

During the first years of the Wilson administration, authority in the Senate was concentrated in the floor leader, John Worth Kern,† a junior senator first

**Oscar W. Underwood* (1862–1929): Democrat from Alabama who served in the U.S. House of Representatives (1895–1915) where he was Speaker from 1911 until 1915. Underwood was also a U.S. senator (1915–1927).

†*John Worth Kern* (1849–1917): Democrat from Indiana who served in the U.S. Senate (1911–1917). He was the majority leader from 1914 until 1915.

elected to the Senate in 1910. Under his leadership the seniority sytem was bypassed, and the Senate played an active and creative role in the remarkable legislative achievements of the Sixty-third Congress. Conceivably the long-entrenched position of seniority could have been broken at this pont. "If the rule of 'seniority' was not destroyed in 1913," says Claude G. Bowers, "it was so badly shattered that it easily could have been given the finishing stroke."[19] Kern, however, was defeated for re-election in 1916, seniority was restored to its earlier position of eminence, and the power which Kern had temporarily centralized was again dispersed. Except for a brief reversal in the 1930s, this process of dispersion has intensified over the years. This is, it has been argued, the natural tendency of the Senate, with centralizing moves usually requiring some outside stimulus. In the late 1960s "important institutional positions" were "being dispersed even more widely. . . ." As a result, "Virtually all senators acquire substantial legislative influence." The pattern is not even one of "decentralization"; it is one of "individualism."[20]

Thus since 1910 in the House and since 1915 in the Senate the overall tendency has been toward the weakening of central leadership and the strengthening of the committees. Most of the "reforms" which have been made in the procedures of Congress have contributed to this end. "Since 1910," observed the historian of the House in 1962, "the leadership of the House has been in commission. . . . The net effect of the various changes of the last 35 years in the power structure of the House of Representatives has been to diffuse the leadership, and to disperse its risks, among a numerous body of leaders."[21] The Budget and Accounting Act of 1921* strengthened the appropriations committees by giving them exclusive authority to report appropriations, but its primary effects were felt in the executive branch with the creation of the Bureau of the Budget. During the 1920s power was further dispersed among the Speaker, floor leaders, Rules, Appropriations, Ways and Means chairmen, and caucus chairman. In the following decade political development also contributed to the diffusion of influence when the conservative majority on the Rules Committee broke with the administration in 1937.

The dispersion of power to the committees of Congress was intensified by the Legislative Reorganization Act of 1946. In essence, this act was a "committee reorganization act" making the committees stronger and more effective. The reduction in the number of standing committees from 81 to 34 increased the importance of the committee chairmanships. Committee consolidation led to the proliferation of subcommittees, now estimated to number about 250. Thus the functions of integration and coordination which, if performed at all, would previously have been performed by the central leadership of the two houses, were now devolved on the leadership of the standing committees. Before the reorganization, for instance, committee jurisdictions frequently overlapped, and the

**Budget and Accounting Act of 1921*: law requiring the president to prepare and submit a budget for the federal government. It created a central budget agency, the Bureau of the Budget (which was replaced in 1970 by the Office of Management and Budget), to assist the president in this role. The act also created the General Accounting Office to audit financial records, to conduct program evaluations, and to strengthen the oversight functions of Congress.

presiding officers of the House and Senate could often influence the fate of a bill by exercising their discretion in referring it to committee. While jurisdictional uncertainties were not totally eliminated by the act, the discretion of the presiding officers was drastically curtailed. The committee chairman, on the other hand, could often influence the fate of legislation by manipulating the subcommittee structure of the committee and by exercising his discretion in referring bills to subcommittees. Similarly, the intention of the framers of the Reorganization Act to reduce, if not to eliminate, the use of special committees had the effect of restricting the freedom of action of the central leadership in the two houses at the same time that it confirmed the authority of the standing committees in their respective jurisdictions. The Reorganization Act also bolstered the committees by significantly expanding their staffs and by specifically authorizing them to exercise legislative overseeing functions with respect to the administrative agencies in their field of responsibility.

The act included few provisions strengthening the central leadership of Congress. Those which it did include in general did not operate successfully. A proposal for party policy committees in each house was defeated in the House of Representatives. The Senate subsequently authorized party policy committees in the Senate, but they did not become active or influential enough to affect the legislative process significantly. The act's provision for a Joint Committee on the Budget which would set an appropriation ceiling by February 15 of each year was implemented twice and then abandoned. In 1950 the appropriations committees reported a consolidated supply bill which cut the presidential estimates by $2 billion and was approved by Congress two months before the approval of the individual supply bills of 1949. Specialized interests within Congress, however, objected strenuously to this procedure, and it has not been attempted again. The net effect of the Reorganization Act was thus to further the dispersion of power, to strengthen and to institutionalize committee authority, and to circumscribe still more the influence of the central leadership. The Legislative Reorganization Act of 1970, a far more modest measure than that of 1946, reinforced these tendencies. It did not deal with seniority and none of its provisions was designed to strengthen central leadership. To the extent that it was implemented, its effects were, indeed, to disperse power still further within committees by reducing the prerogatives of the chairmen.

In the years after the 1946 reorganization, the issues which earlier had divided the central leadership and committee chairmen reappeared in each committee in struggles between committee chairmen and subcommittees. The chairmen attempted to maintain their own control and flexibility over the number, nature, staff, membership, and leadership of their subcommittees. Several of the most assertive chairmen either prevented the creation of subcommittees or created numbered subcommittees without distinct legislative jurisdictions, thereby reserving to themselves the assignment of legislation to the subcommittees. Those who wished to limit the power of the chairman, on the other hand, often invoked seniority as the rule to be followed in designating subcommittee chairmen. In 1961 31 of the 36 standing committees of the House and Senate had subcommittees and in 24 the subcommittees had fixed jurisdictions and significant autonomy, thus playing a major role in the legislative process. In many committees the subcommittees go their independent way, jealously guarding their autonomy and prerogatives against other subcommittees and their own committee chairman. "Given an active subcommittee chairman working in a specialized field with a staff of his own," one congressional staff member observes, "the parent committee can do no more than change the grammar of a subcommittee report."[22] In the Senate after World War II the predominant influence in legislation shifted from commitee chairmen to subcommittee chairmen and individual senators. Specialization of function and dispersion of power, which once worked to the benefit of the committee chairmen, now work against them.

Position of Central Leaders

The Speaker and the majority floor leaders are the most powerful men in Congress, but their power is not markedly greater than that of many other congressional leaders. In 1959, for instance, thirteen of nineteen committee chairmen broke with the Speaker to support the Landrum-Griffin bill.* "This graphically illustrated the locus of power in the House," one congressman commented. "The Speaker, unable to deliver votes, was revealed in outline against the chairmen. This fact was not lost on Democratic Members."[23] The power base of the central leaders has tended to atrophy, caught between the expansion of presidential authority and influence, on the one hand, and the institutionalization of committee authority, on the other.

At times individual central leaders have built up impressive networks of personal influence. These, however, have been individual, not institutional, phenomena. The ascendancy of Rayburn† and Johnson during the 1950s, for instance, tended to obscure the difference between personal influence and institutional authority. With the departure of the Texas coalition their personal networks collapsed. "Rayburn's personal power and prestige," observed Representative Richard Bolling, "made the institution *appear* to work. When Rayburn died, the thing just fell apart."[24] Similarly, Johnson's effectiveness as Senate leader, in the words of one of his assistants, was "overwhelmingly a matter of personal influence. By all accounts, Johnson was the most personal among recent leaders in his approach. For years it was said that he talked to every Democratic senator every day. Persuasion ranged from the awesome pyrotechnics known as 'Treatment A' to the apparently casual but always purposeful exchange as he roamed the floor and the cloakroom."[25] When Johnson's successor was accused of failing to provide the necessary leadership to the Senate, he defended himself on the grounds that he was Mansfield‡ and not Johnson. His definition of the leader's role was largely negative: "I am neither a circus ringmaster, the master of ceremonies of a Senate nightclub, a tamer of Senate lions, or a wheeler and dealer. . . ."[26] The majority leadership

**Landrum-Griffin Act*: popular name for the Labor-Management Reporting and Disclosure Act of 1959, which sought to eliminate corruption in the management of labor unions by requiring the disclosure of financial records and administrative practices. The act established procedures for the selection of union officials and listed a bill of rights for union members.

†*Sam Rayburn*: see footnote on page 166.

‡*Mike Mansfield*: see footnote "Mansfield Resolution" on page 271.

role was uninstitutionalized and the kindly, gentlemanly, easygoing qualities which Mansfield had had as Senator from Montana were not changed when he became majority leader. The power of the President had been institutionalized; the powers of the congressional committees and their chairmen have been institutionalized; but the power of the central leaders of Congress remains personal, *ad hoc*, and transitory.

In the House the dispersion of power has weakened the central leadership and strengthened committee and subcommittee chairmen. The latter, products of the seniority system, are normally legislative veterans of long standing. In the Senate, on the other hand, the more widespread dispersion of power within a smaller body has produced a more egalitarian situation in which freshman senators are often able to take the initiative on important issues of particular concern to them or on which they have developed special expertise. The dispersion of power in the Senate, in short, has tended to open up that body to new and outside influences while in the House it has had the reverse effect.

In both houses, however, the dispersion of power makes obstruction easy and the development of a coherent legislative program difficult. Congress cannot play a positive role in the legislative process so long as it lacks a structure of power which makes positive leadership possible. During the last decades of the nineteenth century, for instance, the Speakers of the House centralized power, exercised personal leadership, and played an innovative role in policy. In subsequent years, in contrast, the Speakers "lost or gave away powers" and what initiative there was in policy came from the executive branch.[27] So long as the Speaker remains, in Bolling's words, "a weak King surrounded by strong Dukes," the House cannot organize itself to lead: "A strong Speaker is crucial to the House. He is the indispensable man for its legislative and political health, education, and welfare."[28] The same is true of the majority leader in the Senate. Perpetuation there of the dispersion of power, on the other hand, means that there is "no general plan for bringing bills to the floor in a given order or at a given time"; the legislative process as a whole becomes "highly segmented"; and the prospects for organized institutional reform are very low.[29]

FUNCTION: THE SHIFT TO OVERSIGHT

Loss of Initiative

The insulation of Congress from external social forces and the dispersion of power within Congress have stimulated significant changes in the functions of Congress. The congressional role in legislation has largely been reduced to delay and amendment; congressional activity in overseeing administration has expanded and diversified. During the nineteenth century Congress frequently took the legislative initiative in dealing with major national problems. Even when the original proposal came from the President, Congress usually played an active and positive role in reshaping the proposal into law. "The predominant and controlling force, the centre and source of all motive and of all regulative power,"

Woodrow Wilson observed in 1885, "is Congress. . . . The legislature is the aggressive spirit."[30] Since 1933, however, the initiative in formulating legislation, in assigning legislative priorities, in arousing support for legislation, and in determining the final content of the legislation enacted has clearly shifted to the executive branch. All three elements of the executive branch—President, administration, and bureaucracy—have gained legislative functions at the expense of Congress. Today's "aggressive spirit" is clearly the executive branch.

In 1908, it is reported, the Senate, in high dudgeon at the effrontery of the Secretary of the Interior, returned to him the draft of a bill which he had proposed, resolving to refuse any further communications from executive officers unless they were transmitted by the President himself.[31] Now, however, congressmen expect the executive departments to present them with bills. Eighty percent of the bills enacted into law, one congressman has estimated, originate in the executive branch. Indeed, in most instances congressmen do not admit a responsibility to take legislative action except in response to executive requests. Congress, as one senator has complained, "has surrendered its rightful place in the leadership in the lawmaking process to the White House. No longer is Congress the source of major legislation. It now merely filters legislative proposals from the President, straining out some and reluctantly letting others pass through. These days no one expects Congress to devise the important bills."[32] The President now determines the legislative agenda of Congress almost as thoroughly as the British cabinet sets the legislative agenda for Parliament. The institutionalization of this role was one of the more significant developments in presidential-congressional relations after World War II.[33]

Loss of Policy Control

Congress has conceded not only the initiative in originating legislation but—and perhaps inevitably as the result of losing the initiative—it has also lost the dominant influence it once had in shaping the final content of legislation. Between 1882 and 1909 Congress had a preponderant influence in shaping the content of 16 (55 percent) out of 29 major laws enacted during those years. It had a preponderant influence over 17 (46 percent) of 37 major laws passed between 1910 and 1932. During the constitutional revolution of the New Deal, however, its influence declined markedly: only 2 (8 percent) of 24 major laws passed between 1933 and 1940 were primarily the work of Congress.[34] Certainly its record after World War II was little better.

The loss of congressional control over the substance of policy was most marked, of course, in the area of national defense and foreign policy. At one time Congress did not hesitate to legislate the size and weapons of the armed forces. During the 1940s and 1950s this power—to raise and support armies, to provide and maintain a navy—came to rest firmly in the hands of the executive. Is Congress, one congressional committee asked plaintively in 1962, to play simply "the passive role of supine acquiescence" in executive programs or is it to be "an active participant in the determination of the direction of our defense policy?" The committee, however, already knew the answer:

To any student of government, it is eminently clear that the role of the Congress in determining national policy, defense or otherwise, has deteriorated over the years. More and more the role of Congress has come to be that of a sometimes querulous but essentially kindly uncle who complains while furiously puffing on his pipe but who finally, as everyone expects, gives in and hands over the allowance, grants the permission, or raises his hand in blessing, and then returns to the rocking chair for another year of somnolence broken only by an occasional anxious glance down the avenue and a muttered doubt as to whether he had done the right thing.[35]

NOTES

[1]George B. Galloway, *History of the United States House of Representatives* (House Document 246, Eighty-seventh Congress, First Session, 1962), p. 31; T. Richard Witmer, "The Aging of the House," *Political Science Quarterly*, 79 (Dec. 1964), pp. 526–541. See Nelson Polsby, "The Institutionalization of the U.S. House of Representatives," *American Political Science Review*, 62 (March 1968), pp. 144–168, for documentation in historical detail for the House of Representatives of several of the trends posited here and analysis of them according to criteria of institutionalization (autonomy, coherence, complexity) which I elaborated in "Political Development and Political Decay," *World Politics*, 17 (April 1965), pp. 386–430.

[2]Gail Hamilton, *Life of James G. Blaine*, p. 263, quoted in DeAlva S. Alexander, *History and Procedure of the House of Representatives* (Boston: Houghton Mifflin, 1916), p. 69. On the development of the House seniority system, see Michael Abram and Joseph Cooper, "The Rise of Seniority in the House of Representatives," *Polity*, 1 (Fall 1968), pp. 52–85, and Nelson Polsby, Miriam Gallaher, and Barry Spencer Rundquist, "The Growth of the Seniority System in the U.S. House of Representatives," *American Political Science Review*, 63 (Sept. 1969), pp. 787–807. For the operation of the system, see, in general, Barbara Hinckley, *The Seniority System in Congress* (Bloomington: Ind. Univ. Press, 1971).

[3]Quoted in Charles L. Clapp, *The Congressman: His Work as He Sees It* (Washington: Brookings Institution, 1963), p. 21.

[4]Theodore H. White, *The Making of the President, 1960* (New York: Atheneum Press, 1961), p. 132.

[5]See Pendleton Herring, *Presidential Leadership* (New York: Farrar and Rinehart, 1940), pp. 164–165 for figures for 1861–1940; figures for 1940–1963 have been calculated on the same basis as Herring's figures; see Dean E. Mann, "The Selection of Federal Political Executives," *American Political Science Review*, 58 (March 1964), p. 97.

[6]See Andrew Hacker, "The Elected and the Anointed," *American Political Science Review*, 55 (Sept. 1961), pp. 540–541; Mann, *ibid.*, 58 (March 1964), pp. 92–93; Donald R. Matthews, *U.S. Senators and Their World* (Chapel Hill: Univ. of N.C. Press, 1960), pp. 14–17; W. Lloyd Warner *et al.*, *The American Federal Executive* (New Haven: Yale Univ. Press, 1963), pp. 11, 56–58, 333; W. Lloyd Warner and James C. Abegglen, *Occupational Mobility in American Business and Industry* (Minneapolis: Univ. of Minn. Press, 1955), p. 38; Suzanne Keller, "The Social Origins and Career Patterns of Three Generations of American Business Leaders" (Ph.D. dissertation, Columbia Univ., 1953), cited in Wendell Bell, Richard J. Hill, and Charles R. Wright, *Public Leadership* (San Francisco: Chandler Press, 1961), p. 106. Leroy N. Rieselbach has noted that congressmen in the 1950s and 1960s were not more rural or small-town in their birthplaces than the population of the country as a whole in 1900 and 1910. "Congressmen as 'Small Town Boys': A Research Note," *Midwest Journal of Political Science*, 14 (May 1970), pp. 321–330. His argument, however, involves a quite different question from that argued here which concerns not the representativeness of congress-

men compared to the general population, but rather the similarity or difference in background of congressional and other elites.

[7]Hacker, *op. cit.*, p. 544. For further analysis of the limited geographical mobility of representatives, see Roger H. Davidson, *The Role of the Congressman* (New York: Pegasus, 1969), pp. 54–59.

[8]Davidson, *Role of the Congressman*, p. 54.

[9]Andrew Hacker, "Are There Too Many Lawyers in Congress?" *New York Times Magazine*, January 5, 1964, p. 74.

[10]James N. Rosenau, *National Leadership and Foreign Policy* (Princeton: Princeton Univ. Press, 1963), pp. 30–31, 347–350.

[11]Hacker, *op. cit.*, pp. 547–549.

[12]William S. White, *Citadel* (New York: Harper & Bros., 1956), p. 136.

[13]See John S. Saloma III, *Congress and the New Politics* (Boston: Little, Brown, 1969), pp. 68–69.

[14]Authorities vary on the exact impact of the Court decisions on the rural-urban balance in Congress, but they generally agree that it was less than had been anticipated. See Saloma, *Congress and the New Politics*, pp. 77–87; Andrew Hacker, *Congressional Districting: The Issue of Equal Representation* (Washington: Brookings Institution, rev. ed., 1964).

[15]Richard Lehne, "Shape of the Future," *National Civic Review*, 58 (Sept. 1969), pp. 351–355.

[16]Milton C. Cummings, Jr., "Reapportionment in the 1970's: Its Effects on Congress," in Nelson W. Polsby, ed., *Reapportionment in the 1970's* (Berkeley: Univ. of Cal. Press, 1971), p. 222.

[17]Clapp, *op. cit.*, pp. 23–24.

[18]Clem Miller, *Member of the House* (New York: Scribner's, 1962), p. 51; Randall B. Ripley, *Power in the Senate* (New York: St. Martin's Press, 1969), p. 172.

[19]Claude G. Bowers, *The Life of John Worth Kern* (Indianapolis: Hollenback Press, 1918), p. 840.

[20]Ripley, *Power in the Senate*, pp. 15–16, 53, 77, 185.

[21]Galloway, *op. cit.*, pp. 95, 98, 128.

[22]George Goodwin, Jr., "Subcommittees: The Miniature Legislatures of Congress," *American Political Science Review*, 56 (Sept. 1962), pp. 596–601.

[23]Miller, *op. cit.*, p. 110.

[24]Quoted in Stewart Alsop, "The Failure of Congress," *Saturday Evening Post*, 236 (December 7, 1963), p. 24.

[25]Ralph K. Huitt, "Democratic Party Leadership in the Senate," *American Political Science Review*, 55 (June 1961), p. 338.

[26]*Congressional Record* (Nov. 27, 1963), pp. 21, 758 (daily ed.).

[27]Randall B. Ripley, *Party Leaders in the House of Representatives* (Washington: Brookings Institution, 1967), pp. 16–17.

[28]Richard Bolling, *Power in the House: A History of the Leadership of the House of Representatives* (New York: E. P. Dutton, 1968), p. 29.

[29]Ripley, *Power in the Senate*, pp. 13–14.

[30]Woodrow Wilson, *Congressional Government* (Boston: Houghton Mifflin, 1885), pp. 11, 36.

[31]George B. Galloway, *The Legislative Process in Congress* (New York: Crowell, 1955), p. 9.

[32]Abraham Ribicoff, "Doesn't Congress Have Ideas of Its Own?" *Saturday Evening Post*, 237 (March 21, 1964), p. 6.

[33]Richard E. Neustadt, "Presidency and Legislation: Planning the President's Program," *American Political Science Review*, 49 (Dec. 1955), pp. 980–1021.

[34]Lawrence H. Chamberlain, *The President, Congress, and Legislation* (New York: Columbia University Press, 1946), pp. 450–452.

[35]House Report 1406, Eighty-seventh Congress, Second Session (1962), p. 7.

16

NELSON W. POLSBY

STRENGTHENING CONGRESS IN NATIONAL POLICY-MAKING

In this article published in 1970, Nelson W. Polsby views Congress as an important incubator of policy innovations, but proposes three reforms to strengthen the institution: a system of mandatory retirement at age seventy for members; an improvement in the technical knowledge base available to the institution; and election of House committee chairpersons at the beginning of each new Congress. Polsby's other important works include: Congressional Behavior *(1971) and* Congress and the Presidency *(1976). He is also the author of* Presidential Elections: Strategies of American Electoral Politics *(1980) with Aaron Wildavsky;* Consequences of Party Reform *(1983); and* Political Innovation in America *(1984). Polsby is a professor of political science at the University of California, Berkeley.*

The word is out that the Congress of the United States may have had something to do with the alteration over the past year and a half of American policy toward Southeast Asia. On the domestic scene, Congressmen can be observed taking the lead in tax reform and increasing federal appropriations for education. Consequently, it may briefly be fashionable to take Congress seriously, and perhaps those few of us who all along have been arguing this view *sotto voce* ought to say a word or two before Congress resumes its accustomed role of thwarting the domestic programs of liberal Presidents, and is once more relegated to the dustbin of historians if not of history.

To be sure it is easy enough to see why that popular guide to Washington politics, Casual Observer, finds Congress hard to understand. It is organized quite differently from the conventional bureaucracy, which Casual Observer professes to despise, but which he and his friends comprehend. Instead of having a single head, Congress looks like the hydra of Greek mythology. Instead of neatly delegating work downward and responsibility upward. Congress is a complex, redundant, not always predictable, and purposely unwieldy network of crisscrossing and overlapping lines of authority and information.

The mere contemplation of this organizational design customarily leads Casual Observer to assert overhastily that Congressional decision-making is inefficient, cumbersome, and in need of instant reform. Consider, for example, the frequently regretted fact that Cabinet offices are asked to justify certain aspects of their programs in much the same language before authorization and appropriation committees in both houses—four presentations in all. Clearly an inefficient use of a busy executive's time, according to the busy executive and his friends. Yet this same busy executive as a matter of course insists that programs coming up the line to his office be justified repeatedly to program review committees, bureau chiefs, department level staff, and departmental budget officers, and he would think nothing of justifying the program again to other interested executive branch departments, to the President and the Budget Bureau. Cabinet-level officers quite commonly make presentations, formal and informal, justifying their programs to the general public, to interest groups, to newspapermen. Why, then, does the need for Congress to hear justifications as well constitute such an intolerable inconvenience? Why should this alleged inconvenience lead to recommendations that Congress revamp its structure?

Casual Observer also finds Congress hard to fathom because the political theories that are currently available do not help him resolve some basic choices that he generally has to make in order to defend his preferences with respect to the distribution of power within the national government. Does he want a strong Congress? A strong Congress means precisely one capable of asserting its will, even though Presidents, interest groups, courts, and ephemeral majorities of public opinion may find it inconvenient. A weak Congress means less effective oversight of executive policy-making and of the bureaucracies, and such weakness diminishes the capacity of Congressmen and Senators to play the roles of critic, goad, and ombudsman.* Further, he must decide whether to vest power in Congress or in the majority party within Congress. If the former, he must be prepared to tolerate coalitions which occasionally—and perhaps persistently—thwart the will of the majority of the majority party. Of such majorities are the conservative coalition—and the progressive one that unhorsed Joseph Cannon†—made. If he opts for stricter party responsibility, he must accept the weakening of Congress vis-à-vis national parties, and whoever controls them—presumably quite often the President. For a long time, there were modish and unequivocal answers to these structural dilemmas, just as in the 'thirties Casual Observer's father knew what he thought of an innately reactionary institution like the Supreme Court. Now, however, while the idea of Congressional checks and balances and initiatives seem to make a little sense, it is possible to give these choices more evenhanded consideration.

The reasons why Congress and Presidents generally get along rather badly are too well known to require much reiteration. Differing constituencies arising from, on the one hand, the unit of rule of the electoral college and, on the other, from the differential effects of party competition, the residuum of malapportionment, and the seniority system account for part of the conflict. So do purely institutional factors, the most important of which is the differing time scale of Presidential and Congressional careers.

President Kennedy understood this problem quite well, as the following quotation from Theodore Sorensen's‡ book suggests:

**Ombudsman:* see footnote on page 168.

†Joseph Cannon: see footnote on page 283.

‡Theodore Sorensen: lawyer who was an assistant to Senator John F. Kennedy (1953–1961), and Special Counsel to Presidents Kennedy and Johnson (1961–1964). He is the author of *Decision Making in the White House* (1963), *Kennedy* (1965), *The Kennedy Legacy* (1969), and *Watchmen in the Night: Presidential Accountability after Watergate* (1975).

> "Wilbur Mills," he said one day, "knows that he was chairman of Ways and Means before I got here and that he'll still be chairman after I've gone—and he knows I know it. I don't have any hold on him."

More generally, the argument is that the career expectations of political actors influence the rates at which they are willing to expend resources. By the standards of the operational leaders of Congress—Congressional party leaders, committee and subcommittee chairmen, their minority counterparts, and leading up-and-coming members in both parties—the career of any President is short. In the 91st Congress considerably more than a majority of both houses had already served with at least three Presidents of the United States. More to the point, the vast majority in both houses could plausibly entertain the prospect of continuing to serve on into the indefinite future. Thus, while Presidents are under a constitutional injunction to seize the day, the men of Capitol Hill—even supposing they agree with the President and his programs—must calculate the consequences of their support against future demands upon their own resources. This leads to strategic dilemmas and to disagreements between Congress and the Presidency that are scarcely touched by proposals such as the four-year Congressional term of office, which seeks to coordinate the time of election but not the terminal points of Presidential and Congressional careers.

There is no definitive, universally acceptable answer to the question of how strong Congress should be. On the whole, gains in institutional strength are likely to be had at costs in institutional responsiveness. But there are many possible mixtures of these two qualities. A legislature that is merely an arena for the registering of the policy preferences of groups organized in the society at large is obviously not the only alternative to a legislature that is totally impervious to external sentiment. There is at present no very satisfactory description of Congress which assesses the developing balance between these somewhat incompatible goals. Thus Casual Observer is also handicapped in his attempts to understand Congress because Congress itself has been changing over the years, while our descriptions and justifications for it have not kept pace.

The accepted view of what a legislature contributes to government is that it represents the people, and it is as a representative body that Congress finds its ultimate justification in our political system. The difficulty that all modern legislatures face, of course, is the tremendous increase in the scale of modern government that makes it almost impossible for individual legislators genuinely to represent the people back home in any simple or straightforward fashion. And most legislatures collectively have pretty much stopped doing so. In most parliamentary systems, they are now mindless creatures of the political parties that run them.

But Congress is an exception. Principally because of historical accidents that destroyed the temporary unity of both the national parties earlier in this century, Congress built on some nineteenth-century precedents in ways that have maintained and in some cases enhanced its independence in the political system. One major consequence of this process of institutionalization has been to shift the balance in the careers and life-styles of legislators from amateur to professional, from the status of temporary ambassador from home to that of member of the legislative group. Where Congress used to embody a popular will in some formal sense by its collective representativeness, it now does so *de facto* through the piecemeal pressures of case work for constituents, legislative committee hearings, and the appropriations process. Where representation, emphasizing the ambassadorial function, was once the characteristic, conscious activity of Congressmen and Senators, today it is deliberation, emphasizing the increasing centrality to Congressmen of their lives as members of a legislative work group and status system.

Thus in a sense Congress has been modernizing itself, through processes which have shifted the loyalties and the attention of Congressmen and Senators toward Washington and away from the grass roots, differentiated its internal functions, and professionalized legislative service.

However, we have not yet developed a fully articulate rationale for a legislature that takes this developmental path; instead we are still relying both descriptively and evaluatively on notions of representation that made more sense when Congressmen spent most of their time at home and came from relatively knowable communities.

Thus a discussion of the strength of Congress in the political system might profitably consider the ways in which the House and the Senate organize to do business, as a means of gaining insight into how a legislature can cope with the complex demands of a large heterogeneous society, including the rest of a big government. This may serve to throw some light on how or whether an effective legislature can contribute to democratic government.

As institutions, the House and the Senate differ markedly in their contemporary characters. The House is a highly specialized instrument for processing legislation. Its great strength is its firmly structured division of labor. This provides the House with a toehold in the policy-making process by virtue of its capacity to specialize and hence, in some collective sense, to provide for the mastery of technical details. House members are frequently better prepared than Senators in legislative conferences, and usually have the better grasp of the peculiarities of the executive agencies they supervise. This is a consequence of the strong division of labor that the House maintains: members are generally assigned to one or two committees only. Floor debate is normally limited to participation by committee members. There is an expectation that members will concentrate their energies rather than range widely over the full spectrum of public policy.

Patterns of news coverage encourage specialization. General pronouncements by House members are normally not widely reported. Senators, because they are fewer, more socially prominent, and serve longer terms (hence are around long enough for newsmen to cultivate) and allegedly serve "larger" districts, can draw attention to themselves by well-timed press releases almost regardless of their content. One result of all this publicity (among other things) is that the Senate is increasingly the home of presidential hopefuls, and this of course tends to generate still more Senate publicity. Some years ago I inquired of the chief of an important Washington new bureau if there was an imbalance between House and Senate news coverage. His response (bowdlerized) was: "The House! Look at them! There's no presidential timber there at all."

The maintenance of a perennially timberless ecology like the House is difficult because it cannot entail excessive centralization of power. Decentralization of power is necessary for the House to sustain its capacity to cope with the outside world through its complex and specialized division of labor. The House's major career incentive is the opportunity accorded a tenth to a fifth of its members to possess the substance of power in the form of a committee or subcommittee chairmanship or membership on a key committee. At present seniority acts as a bulwark of this incentive system by guaranteeing a form of job security at least within the division of labor of the organization. Without decentralization of power there would quite likely be no incentive for able men to stay in the House; without able men (there are few enough of these at any rate) there would be no expertise. Without mastery of subject matter, initiatives taken and modifications made in public policy are capricious, responsive largely to prejudice, or ineffective, or failing that, detrimental.

The essence of the Senate is that it is a great forum, an echo chamber, a publicity machine. Thus "passing bills," which is central to the life of the House, is peripheral to the Senate. In the Senate the three central activities are cultivating national constituencies; formulating questions for debate and discussion on a national scale (especially in opposition to the President); and incubating new policy proposals that may at some future time find their way into legislation.

Where the House of Representatives is a large, impersonal, and highly specialized machine for processing bills and overseeing the executive branch, the Senate is, in a way, a theatre where dramas—comedies and tragedies, soap operas and horse operas—are staged to enhance the careers of its members and to influence public policy by means of debate and public investigation.

In both the House and Senate the first commandment to newcomers is "specialize." But this means different things in each house. "Specialize" to a Representative means "tend to your knitting": work hard on the committee to which you are assigned, pursue the interests of your state and region. Consider, however, the consequences of these well-known features of Senate organization: Every Senator has several committee assignments. Boundaries between committees are not strictly observed. On the floor, quite unlike the House, virtually any Senator may speak for any length of time about anything. Thus the institution itself gives few cues and no compulsions to new Senators wondering what they should specialize in. For the Senate, specialization seems to mean finding a subject matter and a nationwide constituency interested in the subject that has not already been preempted by some more senior Senator.

It is a cliché of academic political science that, in legislative matters, it is the President who initiates policy, and Congress which responds, amplifying and modifying and rearranging elements that are essentially originated in the executive branch. Not much work has been done, however, on following this river of bills-becoming-and-not-becoming-laws back to its sources. Where do innovations in policy come from *before* the President "initiates" them?

It appears that a great many newly enacted policies have "been around," "in the air" for quite a while. In the heat of a presidential campaign or later, when a President wants a "new" program, desk drawers fly open all over Washington. Pet schemes are constantly being fished out, dusted off, and tried out on political leaders. There is often a hiatus of years, sometimes decades, between the first proposal of a policy innovation and its appearance as a presidential "initiative"—much less a law.

It is certainly not generally true that policy innovation begins with a presidential message to Congress. For behind each presidential message lurk months of man-hours of work and sometimes years of advocacy and controversy. The two great fountainheads of new policy seem to be, first, generally acknowledged "problems" producing the demands upon government that spur bureaucrats to ad hoc problem solving. This often later has to be codified or rationalized as "policy." Second, a longer range buildup in the society of something that is first not generally conceded to be a "problem." Those who see it that way may formulate demands upon the government in the guise of a "solution." This initiative may first be taken by a professor, or by staff professionals attached to an interest group, or by a government "expert." On rare occasions, experts attached to a Congressional committee will initiate a policy. More often, I think, Congress is in on the beginning of a policy innovation because it provides the first sympathy for an innovation concocted by outside experts.

Many of our most important policy innovations take years from initiation to enactment. Surely the idea of Medicare,* to take an obvious example, was not "initiated" by the Johnson administration in the 89th Congress. Proposals incorporating its main features had been part of the Washington landscape since the early Truman administration. Medicare, like other great policy innovations, required *incubation*, a process in which men of Congress often play very significant roles. Incubation entails keeping a proposal alive while it picks up support, or waits for a better climate, or while a consensus begins to form that the problem to which it is addressed exists. Senators and (to a lesser extent) Representatives contribute to incubation by proposing bills that they know will not pass, making speeches, making demands for data and for support from interest groups favoring the proposal. Sometimes a sympathetic committee chairman can be persuaded to allow hearings on such a proposal. This focuses public attention, mobilizes interest groups for and against, and provides an occasion for the airing of a proposal's technical justifications. Policy incubation is, of course, not exclusively a Congressional activity; lobbyists may plant stories in the press, organizations may pass resolutions, professors may write books and articles. Most major policy innovations have been incubated by methods such as these.

The net effect of the Congressional process of incubation in any event is to develop a sense of community among far-flung interest groups that favor the innovation by giving them occasional opportunities to come in and testify. It provides an incentive for persons favoring the innovation to maintain up-to-date information on its prospective benefits and technical feasibility. And it accustoms the uncommitted to a new idea.

**Medicare*: see footnote on page 232.

Thus the Senate is in some respects at a crucial nerve end of the polity. It articulates, formulates, shapes, and publicizes demands for significant policy innovation. Proposals to increase the structuredness of the Senate, to force germaneness in debates, to tighten committee assignment procedures, and reduce the number of assignments per Senator, misunderstand the nature of the Senate and the contribution it uniquely makes to the political system. What is needed in the Senate is as little structure as possible; its organizational flexibility enables it to incubate policy innovations, to advocate, to respond, to launch its great debates, in short, to pursue the continuous renovation of American public policy through the hidden self-promotion of its members.

I do not mean by this to suggest that Congress is entirely self-sufficient in the policy-making process, or that all demands on Congress are equally well treated. Far from it. In order finally to make new policy, Congress generally does need the power of the Presidency to set priorities and focus the energy sufficient to mobilize the successive majorities that law-making requires. A presidential priority is a tremendous advantage in clearing away obstacles, but the President's support is usually purchased at a price: the proposal becomes his. This is not merely a matter of credit, although who gets credit is no trivial matter. It also affects the substance of policy. The executive branch begins the process of bargaining by including some features of a proposal and dropping others, adding bait here and padding there. In some cases (e.g., foreign aid, civil rights) executive branch control over bargaining is tight and continues right through the legislative mill. In others (e.g., surtax, Medicare) influential members of Congress establish which provisions will survive and which will be sacrificed. Sometimes (e.g., the bill establishing a Department of Housing and Urban Development in the Kennedy administration) the most significant battle is precisely over who will control the bill.

But even with the President behind a bill, and despite years of Congressional incubation, the mortality rate for "new" proposals is high. Most Congressional policy-making takes place under adversary circumstances. Thus Congressional decision-makers ordinarily cannot enjoy the luxury of examining alternative means to stipulated ends. In an adversary process ends are not stipulated but contested. Agreement on means is often sought as a substitute for agreement on ends. Ends are often scaled down, pulled out of shape, or otherwise transformed. In short, from the standpoint of an outsider who cares about one or more pressing problems in society, the Congressional process of policy-making looks chaotic at best, perversely insensitive at worst.

If the perception of chaos is largely an optical illusion, the perception of insensitivity may not be. Insensitivity, slowness to register some kinds of new demands, exists in Congressional policy-making and is not altogether curable. It can come about because the strength of a demand in society as it is felt by an outsider has no counterpart equally strong within the Congressional process itself. Sometimes Congress does not reflect "needs" as defined in the society at large because Congress is malapportioned, or because the "wrong" sorts of people dominate the relevant committees. In this fashion a wave of short-run, intense demands might break futilely across the superstructure of any stable organization. Given the stately metabolism (fixed terms of office, staggered Senatorial elections) decreed for it by the founding fathers, Congress could hardly be expected to operate efficiently with respect to short-run demands in the best of circumstances.

A second source of Congressional insensitivity to innovation is of course the fact that many urgent demands are pressed upon Congress by groups with whom Congressmen—and quite often the bulk of their constituents—simply disagree. Not all righteous causes are popular. And, as a matter of fact, not all momentarily popular causes are necessarily righteous. Congressmen often have a keen appreciation of this.

It may be said that Congressmen are more concerned than they should be with popularity. But this constraint on their judgment is the result of the fact that they are popularly elected. They must ask who will get the credit or the blame for public policies. They must know who is for what and how strongly, because these matters affect not only their own future efficacy but also the present chances that a majority can be assembled.

Is there a practical alternative to a process of legislative policy-making in which alternative policies are put to stringent tests of internal political acceptability? If the internal politics of the institution did not matter, the legislature would be a mere arena, a place for forces as they exist in the outside society to contend. The group that captures such an organization may find it marginally useful in pressing claims upon leaders situated elsewhere since victory in some arenas can give legitimacy to a cause. But as an organization develops independent power and internal structure at the same time that it begins to devote a portion of its resources to self-maintenance, it also develops a measure of insensitivity. To require total responsiveness of a legislature is to require it to be powerless.

Although Congress has developed institutional strength within its political system to a degree unrivaled by most contemporary legislatures, it does not follow that nothing can be done to increase its sensitivity to social problems, or increase its effectiveness within the logic of its own developing character. To me the reason most reform proposals are uninteresting is not because reforms are necessarily less appealing than the status quo, but because they are usually addressed rather arbitrarily to "needs," and typically neither needs nor solutions are discussed within the context that includes the relevant features of the ongoing system.

A number of meritorious reforms have been suggested that do not bear on the operations of the Congressional collectivity except insofar as the general reputations of all members are affected by the transgressions of a few. Reforms bearing on conflict of interest, disclosure of income, and other such matters do not materially affect the strength of the institution except as the institution's strength is mirrored in its general reputation.

Problems of Congressional morality cannot really be addressed responsibly without considering comparable problems in the private sector. Even under the new tax law American taxpayers will be giving rather substantial subsidies, far exceeding in their magnitude salaries and perquisites furnished Congress, to certain privileged persons and industries—most conspicuously oil companies and banks. How relevant is it to condemn Congressmen for allegedly taking "junkets" at taxpayer expense while in the private sector all manner of extravagance is routinely charged off to "business expenses" as a tax dodge? When Congress recently voted to raise Congressional salaries the news media were generally outraged. The fact is, considering the weight of their responsibilities, even at the new rates, Congressmen are far from overcompensated. It is necessary for them to maintain out of pocket two bases of operation. Their campaign expenses are not deductible as business expenses. Consider, also, the compensation of men in positions of comparable responsibility in the private sector. I doubt that the top 535 men in the automotive industry, or on Wall Street, or in television make do with the equivalent of salaries of $42,500 plus small change in the way of stationery allowances, inexpensive haircuts, a few overseas junkets, and occasional trips home on military aircraft.

All this provides no excuse for Congressmen not to bring themselves within the scope of the conflict-of-interest laws as they presently apply to political executives. This may be more technically difficult than it sounds, since like the everyday activities of the Secretary of the Treasury, their votes touch everything, so no investment of capital is immune to a conflict-of-interest problem. There are, however, enough violations of propriety to make the problem worth thinking about.

Important as these matters are for public morality, they do not touch the institutional life of Congress. I want to list three suggestions that are pertinent to the functioning of the collectivity. They embody changes in present arrangements, but do not disturb most existing institutional values except in ways I shall describe.

First, a scheme for mandatory retirement. Mortality is a melancholy fact, which comes upon us in different ways, and at different rates of speed. Most modern organizations protect themselves against its creeping effects by requiring the retirement of members after a certain age is reached. Congress now has a generous pension plan that works no economic hardship upon most members forced into retirement by electoral defeat. Instead of relying wholly upon local party systems to replace ailing, failing, and senile members, Congress should protect the efficiency and integrity of its functioning by providing for mandatory retirement at a stated age. If on college campuses these days thirty years of age seems about right for this purpose, perhaps for Congress the age seventy is suitable.

It will be argued in opposition to this proposal that many valuable persons make Congress their second career, and Congress would be depriving itself of much-needed maturity and good judgment in legislative affairs; that no similar impositions are contemplated for other political officers, and thus that the proposal is inequitable; and that the proposal places an unnecessary requirement upon electors in states and districts.

All three objections lack weight. The first ignores the extent to which Congress is presently a young man's game though, to be sure, a young man's waiting game. Men who arrive in Congress past the age of fifty-five rarely have a chance to accumulate sufficient seniority to acquire institutionally based influence. This proposal would over the short run, in fact, give some older new arrivals more of a chance to shine, since it would clear the most senior men out of the way at a predictable rate. But it would not materially affect the incentive system as it currently applies differentially to men of different ages.

The second objection, that the proposal is inequitable, has no merit with respect to the executive branch, since the President's term of office is strictly limited by other means, and other political officials serve at his pleasure. As for the judicial branch, I have no desire to reopen the issue of court packing, but neither have I any objection in principle to the imposition of mandatory retirement upon all federal judges.

Finally, there is the matter of the protection of the interests of voters. Presumably, if they want to send elderly Representatives and Senators to Congress, they should be allowed to do so. I merely assert a competing interest, one that has grown in importance over the years, namely the interest that Congress has as an institution in maintaining a membership sufficiently vigorous to conduct its increasingly demanding business successfully. Surely each Congressional district and each state contains more than one potential Congressman or Senator, so the disability the requirement of mandatory retirement places on the voters of each district must be regarded as minimal. A more impressive objection is that the proposal is unconstitutional. This was not fully apparent until the Supreme Court decided Powell v. McCormack last year, holding that Congressmen could be excluded from sitting only if they failed to meet qualifications specified in the Constitution. It now appears that it will take remarkable agility at textual construction by future courts or two-thirds votes by each House of Congress respectively to expel in individual cases, or a Constitutional amendment, in order to give effect to a general retirement scheme.

The second suggestion has to do with the improvement of technical knowledge available to Congress. Congress gets technical knowledge principally from committee staff personnel who make themselves knowledgeable in the subject matter coming before them. But while the executive branch has systematically been engaged in professionalizing its means of technical understanding over the past decade or more, Congress on the whole has not done so. It is romantic for Congressmen to think of themselves as not in need of expert and detailed explicit analysis because they are "generalists." Generalism is too often a genteel name for ignorance. The professionalization of economic forecasting and defense procurement in the executive branch led to tremendous increases in the power of political decision-makers to identify options and choose among them. This is precisely the capacity many Congressmen feel they are losing. And, if they choose to do so, they can professionalize their own committee staffs, thereby increasing the efficiency of their explicit analytical activities and enhancing their own knowledge and power.

To "professionalize" entails continuous contact with a community outside the world of Capitol Hill. Professional men—economists, operations researchers, psychologists, and so on—maintain standards of performance by knowing and participating in their professional communities. Typically, nowadays, the top economists of the executive branch—the men who formulate fiscal policy, antitrust policy, international trade policy, and so forth—are first and foremost professional economists. Their loyalty to professional standards means (in general) that the options presented to political executives will be feasible and technically sound.

Typically, Congressional committees are staffed by means of an older, less effective process of patronage. This produces loyal service and, by the standards of an earlier day, highly competent service. But unswerving loyalty to the chairman is seldom enough to produce technically informed criticism of executive proposals, sophisticated insight into alternatives, or sensitive awareness of emerging problems in the world. Yet these are what Congress needs. Hence, two corrective proposals. Committees should be encouraged to constitute outside advisory groups to advise the chairman on the technical competence of the work the committee is receiving from its staff. Secondly, more extensive exchanges for one- or two-year hitches of service should be instituted between Congressional committee staffs and comparable staff in the executive branch, private business, labor unions, social service organizations, and universities.

The purpose of these proposals is to bring to bear upon explicit policy analysis on Capitol Hill the standards—and the considerations—that are commonly employed in policy analysis within the executive branch and elsewhere in society. Steps such as these will not necessarily bring Congress into harmony with the executive branch in areas where they now disagree, since there is no reason to suppose that a large number of disagreements over national policy are based on ignorance—though some may be. These disagreements should be resolved. Other disagreements may occur if Congress chooses to equip itself with more professional analytic personnel, since not all executive branch proposals are free from controversy even when they are grounded in thorough professional knowledge. Thus more professionalism in explicit analysis can assist Congress in finding disagreements and weak spots in executive branch recommendations and can increase the probability that Congress itself can initiate policy. These proposals, therefore, genuinely attempt to strengthen Congress rather than to weaken it.

My third suggestion is a simple endorsement of Representative Morris Udall's* proposal to elect House committee chairmen at the start of each Congress. Udall's plan is not a return to king caucus. Rather, it provides for the selection of committee chairmen from a slate of the three most senior members of the majority party to be elected by secret ballot by all majority caucus members, with the ranking member on the minority side to be picked by a similar process in his caucus. This provides an institutional hedge against a too-arbitrary chairman, or one who is incapacitated or hopelessly out of step with his colleagues, without wholly vitiating the advantages of seniority or placing chairmanships in the hands of some centralized authority.

I have mentioned that the great advantage of the seniority system is that it decentralizes power in the House of Representatives by creating multiple centers of policy influence and increasing the number of good Congressional jobs. This

**Morris K. Udall:* Democratic member of the U.S. House of Representatives from Arizona (1961–1987). He is the author of *Education of a Congressman* (1972) and coauthor of *The Job of the Congressman* (1966).

adds to the incentives of the Congressional career. Proposals to centralize power must always be weighed against the damage they may do to this incentive system. Effective legislatures in world history have been fragile and rare. In most places and at most times legislatures have been little more than arenas for the registering of organized group interests or electoral colleges for cabinets. The Udall plan has the advantage of even further decentralizing power—to Congressional party rank and file—rather than placing it in the hands of party leaders, and thus this plan increases the general level of incentives for House members to make careers in the House.

These proposals recognize that institutions must provide means by which they can respond to outside demands, yet at the same time retain the capacity to exercise independent choice. They recognize the peculiar contributions the House and the Senate make, individually and together, to American politics, and seek to enhance the participation of these institutions in the processes of policy-making by improving their capabilities rather than destroying their power.

17

RICHARD F. FENNO, JR.

CONGRESSMEN IN COMMITTEES

The following excerpt is drawn from several chapters of the book Congressmen in Committees *(1973) by Richard F. Fenno, Jr. In this pathbreaking study of a half-dozen standing committees of the House of Representatives, Fenno discovered that committees differ importantly in their organizational goals, institutional autonomy, responsiveness to external environments, and success rates on the House floor. Fenno's analysis offers behavioral profiles of the congressional committee structure that can help explain and predict key facets of legislative activity. Other books on congressional politics by the author are:* The Power of the Purse: Appropriations Politics in Congress *(1966),* Home Style: House Members in their Districts *(1978), and* The United States Senate: A Bicameral Perspective *(1982). Fenno is a professor of political science at the University of Rochester.*

. . . We have begun our committee analysis by trying to find out what the individual members of each committee want for themselves from their present committee service. And we have found three quite different patterns, each of which gives special prominence to one of the three basic goals of House members. Furthermore, we found a remarkable consensus on goals among each committee's membership, a discovery that has persuaded us to ground our analysis here. Moreover, each of the three goals (and this was more fortuitous than planned) is the consensual one for two of our six committees. Appropriations and Ways and Means are populated mostly by influence-oriented members; Interior and Post Office are populated mostly by re-election-oriented members; Education and Labor and Foreign Affairs are populated mostly by policy-oriented members. Such modal characterizations are admittedly oversimplifications. But they do have sufficient validity to serve as a basis for predicting gross similarities and differences in committee behavior. Assuming that members will work in committee to achieve their stated goals, committees with similar goal patterns should display important similarities in behavior, and committees with different goal patterns should display important differences in behavior. More specifically, these similarities and differences should appear with respect to decision-making processes and decisions. But even such rudimentary predictions as these will hold only when "all other things are equal." And we know enough about committees to know that such a condition does not obtain. Most important, perhaps, we know that each committee works in a somewhat different environment. We need, therefore, to add this key variable to the analysis.

. . . The question now arises: how far do committee patterns that are based on members' goals correspond to committee patterns based on environmental constraints? That is, do committees whose members have similar goals operate in similar environments? The answer to both questions, we would now have to conclude is: "a little, but not much."

The two committees with distinctively influence-oriented members are also the two committees with the parent chamber as the most prominent environmental element. Similarly, the two committees whose members are re-election-oriented are also the two committees for which clientele groups are the most prominent environmental element. This what we mean by "a little." On the other hand, for each of these two pairs of committees, there are some marked dissimilarities in environment. The policy coalitions facing Ways and Means are more complex and more partisan than those facing Appropriations. And the policy coalitions facing Interior are more complex and more pluralistic than those facing Post Office. In terms of their environments, the influence-oriented and re-election-oriented committees are as much unlike as they are like one another.

The environments of the two policy-oriented committees have almost nothing in common. The policy coalitions facing Education and Labor are more complex than those confronting Foreign Affairs. The environment of Foreign Affairs most closely resembles that of Post Office in its monolithic character. And the environment of Education and Labor most nearly resembles that of Ways and Means in its partisan character. Overall, within each pair of committees, one committee seems to confront a distinctly more complex, more pluralistic policy coalition than the other. The policy environment of the Ways and Means is more complex than that of Appropriations, that of Interior more complex than Post Office, and that of Education and Labor more complex than Foreign Affairs. As we move to describe committee behavior, we might expect it to be more difficult to predict the behavior of a committee operating in a complex environment than that of a committee, composed of members with the same goals, subject to a relatively simple set of constraints.

What seems most striking, in answering our earlier question, is the degree to which the environments of our pairs differ from one another. None of our three pairs, alike in member goals, is wholly alike with regard to the environment. We conclude, therefore, that the environmental variable is a largely *independent* one. It is not possible to predict the characteristics of a committee's environment by knowing only its members' goals. Nor is it possible to predict the goals simply by knowing the environment. Each variable can be expected to make an independent contribution in explaining a committee's behavior. And each must be investigated carefully. We do not mean there is no relationship between member goals and environmental constraints. The small degree of interconnection we have noted indicates that there are some linkages. And we would certainly expect that for any given committee, a change in one variable might produce a change in the other. But, clearly, each must be given independent weight throughout the analysis which follows.

. . . We have viewed the committee environment in terms of the influence outsiders have on committee members. But if one is searching for the antecedents of these external constraints, one finds that the subject of the policy and its associated characteristics must be given a central place. We have compared the relative prominence of four categories of interested outsiders. But we have found, again and again, that similarities and, more often, differences in their interest and prominence are related to the policy area itself. Our idea of "policy coalition" is intended to acknowledge the importance of policy subjects, without, at the same time, making them an independent variable of the analysis. Some readers will probably wish we had done just that—developed a classification of policy subjects and/or policy characteristics to serve as major independent variables. Those who feel this way should be encouraged to try. There is nothing in this study to challenge and much to confirm Capitol Hill wisdom that committee differences are related to policy differences. From the foregoing analysis, one might suggest that such policy characteristics as their importance to the parent institution, their salience, and their fragmentation would be useful categories. But we have chosen to compare committees at one level removed from their policy subjects because to do so helps us to advance the argument we have been making. We have given special emphasis to the goals of committee members; it is more in keeping with that emphasis to consider the environment in terms of people actively applying constraints to the members. From this perspective, policy subjects become important primarily because of the outsiders that take an interest in them and, hence, in the committee. It is obviously necessary to know about policy characteristics in order to locate the crucially important outsiders. But it is the outsiders that interest us most in this analysis . . .

On every committee the members try to accommodate their personal goals to important environmental expectations and to embody this accommodation in broad, underlying guidelines for decision making. No two committees, it appears, will produce the same set of guiding premises. One explanation is, of course, that no two committees share the same set of member goals and the same set of environmental constraints. Another explanation might be that no two committees deal with the same area of policy. For, once again, we find differences among our variables related to differences in policy subject. In this chapter as in the previous one, however, we have conducted our analysis at one level removed from policy subjects. We have been interested, here, in the *perceptions* that each committee's members have of their policy area—on the assumption that members' behavior is based on members' perceptions of policy subjects and not on the objective characteristics of the policies themselves. At least we would argue this way until such time as a satisfactory categorization of policy subjects could be made from which one could deduce members' perceptions. For now, we might simply underscore the value of knowing: that Appropriations members perceive their subject matter to be nonideological, while Education and Labor members perceive their subject matter to be ideological; that Ways and Means members think of their business as freighted with consequences, while Post Office members think of their business as inconsequential; that Interior members view their policy area as specific and detailed, while Foreign Affairs members see theirs as general and vague. These differences in perceptions of subject matter help to account for differences in the decision-making processes of the committees. For example, the perceptions of subject matter held by Appropriations, Ways and Means, and Interior are more conducive to developing and sustaining expertise as a basis for decision making than are the perceptions held by the other three committees.

Despite the uniqueness of each committee's decision rules, two interesting patterns did emerge—interesting because both of them distinguish Appropriations, Ways and Means, and Interior on the one hand from Education and Labor, Foreign Affairs, and Post Office on the other. Each of the first three committees has achieved a consensus on its decision rules; each of the latter three committees has not. Furthermore, the decision rules of the first three committees are all, in one way or another, oriented toward insuring success on the House floor; the decision rules of the latter three are not. By *floor success*, we mean to include *both* House members' reactions to the content of a committee's decisions and House members' reactions to the committee as a decision-making collectivity. Obviously, the explanation for the two patterns—in terms of members' goals, environmental constraints, and strategic problems—differs within and across the two clusters of committees. We have tried to supply committee-by-committee explanations as we went along.

It may be that the two patterns are related. The more a committee concerns itself about floor success, the more likely it is, perhaps, to come to agreement on an operative set of decision rules. Or, perhaps, the greater its agreement on decision rules, the more likely will a committee enjoy success on the floor. Or it may be that the two patterns are not connected at all. Starting with the observation, however, we can ask whether the three high-consensus, House-oriented committees will display different decision-making processes from those of the three low-consensus, non-House-oriented committees . . .

We have tried to demonstrate . . . that each committee's internal decision-making processes are shaped by its members' goals, by the constraints placed upon the members by interested outside groups, and by the strategic premises that members adopt in order to accommodate their personal goals to environmental constraints. One overall comparative dimension suggested by the independent variables of the analysis involves the relative impact of the members themselves and of external groups on decision-making processes. We might think of the dimension as *decision-making autonomy*. The greater the relative influence of the members, the more autonomous the committee; the greater the relative influence of outside groups, the less autonomous the committee. Making only the grossest kinds of distinctions, it appears that Ways and Means, Appropriations, and Interior are more autonomous decision makers than Foreign Affairs, Education and Labor, and Post Office. That is, members of the first three committees have a more independent influence on their own decision-making processes than do the members of the second three. For Ways and Means, we might mention the restraints on partisanship and the leadership of Wilbur Mills*; for Appropriations, there are the specialization and internal influence of its

**Wilbur D. Mills:* Democrat from Arkansas and member of the U.S. House of Representatives (1939–1977). As Chairman of the Ways and Means Committee, the House's tax-writing committee, Mills became one of the most powerful politicians on Capitol Hill. His career ended after a spectacular episode in which Mills was discovered cavorting with an exotic dancer into the Tidal Basin adjacent to the Jefferson Memorial in Washington, D.C.

subcommittees; for Interior, there are its participatory democracy and the leadership of Wayne Aspinall.* The sources of committee autonomy are not always the same, but the result—a marked degree of internal, member control of decision making—is the same. With the other three committees, it is the environmental impact on decision making that seems most noteworthy. For Foreign Affairs, it is executive domination; for Education and Labor, it is the permeation of partisan policy coalitions; for Post Office, it is clientele domination. The three more autonomous committees emphasize expertise in decision making more than the three less autonomous ones, suggesting that perception of subject matter is related to decision-making processes.

The clustering of committees with regard to decision-making autonomy parallels the clustering noted in the last chapter, based on some similarities and differences in the committees' decision rules. Appropriations, Ways and Means, and Interior have, in common, and consensus on decision rules, a House-oriented set of decision rules, and decision-making autonomy. The three characteristics are probably closely interrelated. But the main thrust of our argument would be that the first two contribute to the third. When a committee's members agree on what they should do, they are more likely to be able to control their own decision making than when they cannot agree on what to do. When a committee's decision rules are oriented toward success (i.e., winning plus respect and confidence) on the House floor, the committe will have a greater desire to establish its operating independence than when its strategies are not especially concerned with floor success. House members, we recall, *want* their committees to be relatively autonomous, relatively expert decision makers. They are more likely, therefore, to follow and to respect committees that can demonstrate some political and intellectual independence of outside, non-House groups. Whether or not distinguishing the two clusters of committees will, in turn, help us to differentiate and explain committee decisions is a question we will keep in mind as we turn to a discussion of that subject . . .

We have presented evidence to demonstrate that committee decisions do, indeed, follow those decision rules that each committee's members have devised to accommodate their personal goals to the constraints of their environment. That is, a committee's decisions are explainable in terms of its members' goals, the constraints of its environment, its decision strategies, and—to a lesser, refining degree, perhaps—by its decision-making processes. Enough evidence has been mustered, we hope, to lend strength to the line of argument we have pursued. We have not, of course, *proven* anything, for we have not tried very determinedly to muster a contrary body of evidence. Those who find themselves resisting our selective use of evidence are invited to provide counterexamples and to fashion another line of argument. We hope that what we have presented will seem worth that kind of further development and testing.

To the degree that a committee's decisions follow its decision rules, committee members and the most interested outside groups should be reasonably satisfied

**Wayne N. Aspinall:* Democrat from Colorado, member of the U.S. House of Representatives (1949–1973).

with committee performance. For those rules are, after all, an effort to accommodate the views of each. We have not found a measure of satisfaction that would allow us to describe and compare amounts of internal and/or external satisfaction. But we have detected varying degrees of it. For member satisfaction, a necessary condition would seem to be committee *activity*. No member goal can be achieved without some minimal level of activity. Post Office members' dissatisfaction arose because that Committee slipped below an acceptable level of activity; it "wasn't doing anything." Foreign Affairs has simmered with dissatisfaction because its members have felt they "weren't doing enough." Both would have been satisfied with increased activity. The other committees have been active. For Education and Labor members, indeed, their increased activity was the basis for their newly found satisfaction in the Powell* years.

Members of our other three committees require an additional condition for their satisfaction. They feel the need to make an *independent* contribution to decision making. Especially, they want to feel a measure of independence relative to the executive branch—in both an institutional and a policy sense. They want to preserve autonomous decision-making processes and they want to develop substantive expertise. When they do achieve such independence, they develop a psychological feeling of group identity, which further strengthens their independence. Ways and Means, Appropriations, and Interior members' satisfaction, then, seems to be based on both their *activity* and their *independence*. During the period studied, these three committees maintained a higher and steadier level of satisfaction with their own performance than did the three other committees.

It is hard to generalize about the conditions of satisfaction for the groups comprising the environment. Perhaps it is enough to remind ourselves, again, that individual committees face quite varied sets of environmental constraints. For two of our committees, the institutional constraints of the parent chamber are most important. House expectations call for a balance between autonomous and responsive decision making. And, so far, Ways and Means and Appropriations seem to have maintained a balance satisfactory to House leaders and House majorities. For the other four, the policy coalitions of their environments are more important. But dominance in those policy coalitions varies, so that the expectations confronting the four committees also vary. The executive-led coalition confronting Foreign Affairs wants legitimation plus assessments of political feasibility. The clientele-led coalitions facing Interior and Post Office want access to members plus sympathetic committee member spokesmen. The party-led coalitions facing Education and Labor want all these things plus a partisanship that will abet victory at the polls. How can we compare levels of satisfaction across such diverse expectations? Is the executive branch more satisfied with the legitimation it gets than clientele groups are with the spokesmanship they get? All we can say is that the leaders of each coalition do seem pretty well satisfied with the committees that interest them—the executive with Foreign Affairs, the postal

**Adam Clayton Powell* (1908–1972): Democrat from New York City, member of the U.S. House of Representatives (1945–1971). During the 1960s Powell was one of the nation's most powerful black politicians.

employees with Post Office, all but the preservationist groups with Interior, the Democrats and Republicans with Education and Labor.

Looking across the six committees, some of the gross similarities and difference noted earlier do appear to carry through to their decisions. That is, Ways and Means, Appropriations, and Interior remain strikingly similar to one another and strikingly different from Education and Labor, Foreign Affairs, and Post Office. The three committees with a consensus on House-oriented decision rules do seem to be more successful on the House floor than the three committees whose decision rules are not House-oriented. Members of the same three, more autonomous committees express a greater overall satisfaction with their committee's decision processes and decisions than do the members of the three less autonomous committees with theirs. And from the autonomy and satisfaction of the first three flows a sense of corporate identity and corporate pride that is missing in the three less autonomous, less satisfied committees. On the other hand, the decisions of our three less autonomous committees seem to bring relatively greater satisfaction to interested and influential environmental groups than do the decisions of our three more autonomous committees. Education and Labor, Foreign Affairs, and Post Office are more permeable and, hence, relatively more responsive to the wishes of people outside the Congress than are Ways and Means, Appropriations, and Interior.

Utilizing these *relative* distinctions, we find two types of House committees. One type is identified by the House orientation of its decision rules, the autonomy of its decision-making processes, its emphasis on committee expertise, its success on the House floor, its members' sense of group identity, and the relatively higher ratio of member to nonmember satisfaction with its performance. The other type is identified by its extra-House-oriented decision rules, the permeability of its decision-making processes, the de-emphasis on committee expertise, its lack of success on the House floor, the absence of any feeling of group identification, and the relatively higher ratio of nonmember to member satisfaction with its performance.

Since no committee falls completely into one category or the other, we probably should think of these as "ideal types" toward which committees tend—a *corporate* type, on the one hand, and a *permeable* type, on the other. Committees of the corporate type tend to be more influential but less responsive than permeable committees. Permeable committees tend to be more responsive but less influential than corporate committees. Ways and Means, Appropriations and Interior come closest to the corporate type of committee. Education and Labor, Foreign Affairs, and Post Office come closest to the permeable type of committee. And, we might add, all Senate committees tend toward the permeable category. There are no corporate committees in the Senate.

PART SIX

THE PRESIDENCY

With the advent of President Franklin D. Roosevelt's New Deal in the 1930s, the presidency emerged as the focal point of American government. Whereas in the nineteenth century it was possible to think in terms of "Congressional Government," today it is far more common to come across books with titles such as *A Presidential Nation* [1] and *The Imperial Presidency*. [2] Not only has the president taken on greater and more complex roles and the executive office expanded dramatically in conjunction with this development, but popular expectations of the president have also risen disproportionately to the president's ability to fulfill them. Thomas Cronin laments, the president is now considered almost synonymous with American government itself: "The President's values, his qualities of character and intellect, his capacity for leadership, his political skills, his definition of his own role, and the way he performs it— *these* are fundamental determinants of the working of the American government and of American politics."[3] However, as popular attention focused on the presidential office, the paradoxical nature of the presidency became more evident. According to several contemporary political scientists the office is currently at once too powerful and too weak, too large and yet inadequately staffed, too political and not political enough. In part these paradoxes are due to the Founders' inability to develop a clear theory of the presidency. Indeed, they voted twelve times on how to choose a president and five on the term of office. To the extent that the Founders had a general approach to the office, it was to create a presidency that was independent and strong enough to resist the legislature, but also too limited to take far-reaching independent action. Yet our difficulty in understanding the presidency is not due just to the absence of a comprehensive constitutional or political theory of that office. It results also from the contemporary complexity of the presidency and the fact that presidential power depends on both idiosyncratic personal factors and institutional features.

Each of the essays in this section offers an invaluable and different perspective on the presidency. Although each represents a distinct approach to analyzing the presidency, the essays complement one another, and taken together provide a comprehensive discussion of the kinds of questions and concerns that must be addressed when contemplating this institution.

The first of these essays is Aaron Wildavsky's "The Two Presidencies," originally published in 1966. Wildavsky argues that the presidency operates in two realms—domestic affairs on the one hand and defense and foreign policy on the other. The president is far more powerful in the defense and foreign policy arena than in the domestic sphere. But the nature of politics and policy-making in the two arenas also differs. In Wildavsky's words, "The President's normal problem

[1]Joseph Califano, Jr., *A Presidential Nation* (New York: W. W. Norton, 1975).
[2]Arthur Schlesinger, Jr., *The Imperial Presidency* (Boston: Houghton Mifflin, 1973).
[3]Quoted by Thomas E. Cronin, *The State of the Presidency* (Boston: Little, Brown, 1975), p. 30.

with domestic policy is to get congressional support for the programs he prefers. In foreign affairs, in contrast, he can almost always get support for policies that he believes will protect the nation—but his problem is to find a viable policy." The stakes, too, vary greatly: "Few failures in domestic policy, presidents soon realize, could have as disastrous consequences as any one of dozens of mistakes in the international arena." As a result, "foreign policy concerns tend to drive out domestic policy."

But what is the essence of presidential power? Richard Neustadt in "The Power to Persuade" from *Presidential Power* (1960, 1976), argues that formal powers are insufficient for effective presidential performance. Ultimately, presidential power is the power to persuade. As the author states it, "Presidential 'powers' may be inconclusive when a president commands, but always remain relevant as he persuades." For Neustadt, "The power to persuade is the power to bargain." His analysis explores the advantages and limitations of the presidential bargaining position. Neustadt emphasizes that the vantage points available to the presidency are of particular importance in enhancing the president's persuasive abilities.

A president's persuasive abilities can be enhanced by many factors and events. James David Barber looks to "presidential character" as a resource for presidential performance and power. In "Adding It Up" (1985) from the third edition of his famous book *The Presidential Character* Barber provides a summary statement of his theory regarding the psychological underpinnings of presidential behavior. He employs a four-category typology of presidential personality to explain how and why presidents respond as they do to the challenges, pressures, and events they confront in office. He also notes that the American people have psychological needs that focus on the presidency and that the manner in which presidential candidates and presidents respond to them is of critical importance to American politics. Barber's essay is wide-ranging, but at its core is the belief that we must:

> Look to character first. At least by the time the man emerges as an adult, he has displayed a stance toward his experience, a proto-political orientation. The first clues are simple: by and large, does he actively make his environment, or is he passively made by it? And how does he feel about his experience—is his effort in life a burden to be endured or an opportunity for personal enjoyment? From those two starting points, we can move to a richer, more dynamic understanding of the four types [of presidential character]*. . . . Character is the force, the motive power, around which the person gathers his view of the world and from which his style receives its impetus. The issues will change, the character of the president will last.

In the final essay, Thomas Cronin considers a different aspect of the presidency. His analysis is strictly institutional. It focuses on the president's White House staff and the officials in the executive departments and agencies as a group "upon whom presidents are exceptionally dependent." In " 'Everybody Believes in Democracy until He Gets to the White House' " (1970), Cronin explores the tensions between the White House Office and the executive bureaucracy. He notes that the perspectives of the White House and the bureaucracy differ and

*That is, active-positive, active-negative, passive-positive, and passive-negative.

that presidents cannot assume that the latter will be responsive to their initiatives. Cronin concludes that the organizational fragmentation of the executive branch is itself a serious limitation on presidential power: "We come back, inevitably, to a realization that the presidents are limited in the degree to which they can eliminate executive branch conflicts, and alternatively try to strengthen White House–department ties." Thus, a culminating paradox of the presidency is that the executive branch is both a major resource and a check on the exercise of presidential power.

18

AARON WILDAVSKY

THE TWO PRESIDENCIES

Presidents play different roles as they manage domestic affairs, on the one hand, and make defense and foreign policy on the other. The distinction between these two domains is so great, according to Aaron Wildavsky, there are really "two presidencies." The following article was first published in 1966 before the Nixon presidency, the Watergate scandal, and the withdrawal of troops from Vietnam. Although events since that time have altered the president's political environment, Wildavsky's analysis remains relevant to the contemporary presidency. Presidents probably still have more power in the defense and foreign policy arena than in the domestic policy arena for many of the reasons discussed here.

Wildavsky is the editor of two collections on the presidency, The Presidency *(1969) and* Perspectives on the Presidency *(1975), and the coaouthor with Nelson W. Polsby of* Presidential Elections *(1964, 1976). A political scientist with many fields of specialization, Wildavsky has written numerous works, including* The Politics of the Budgetary Process *(1964),*The New Politics of the Budgetary Process *(1988),* Implementation *(1973, 1979), with Jeffrey Pressman,* Speaking Truth to Power: The Art and Craft of Policy Analysis *(1979), and* Budgeting: A Comparative Theory of Budgetary Processes *(1975, 1986).*

The United States has one President, but it has two presidencies; one presidency is for domestic affairs, and the other is concerned with defense and foreign policy. Since World War II, Presidents have had much greater success in controlling the nation's defense and foreign policies than in dominating its domestic policies. Even Lyndon Johnson has seen his early record of victories in domestic legislation diminish as his concern with foreign affairs grows.

What powers does the President have to control defense and foreign policies and so completely overwhelm those who might wish to thwart him?

The President's normal problem with domestic policy is to get congressional support for the programs he prefers. In foreign affairs, in contrast, he can almost always get support for policies that he believes will protect the nation—but his problem is to find a viable policy.

Whoever they are, whether they begin by caring about foreign policy like Eisenhower and Kennedy or about domestic policies like Truman and Johnson, Presidents soon discover they have more policy preferences in domestic matters than in foreign policy. The Republican and Democratic parties possess a traditional roster of policies, which can easily be adopted by a new President—for example, he can be either for or against Medicare* and aid to education. Since

**Medicare:* see footnote on page 232.

existing domestic policy usually changes in only small steps, Presidents find it relatively simple to make minor adjustments. However, although any President knows he supports foreign aid and NATO,* the world outside changes much more rapidly than the nation inside—Presidents and their parties have no prior policies on Argentina and the Congo. The world has become a highly intractable place with a wirl of forces we cannot or do not know how to alter.

THE RECORD OF PRESIDENTIAL CONTROL

It takes great crises, such as Roosevelt's hundred days† in the midst of the depression, or the extraordinary majorities that Barry Goldwater's‡ candidacy willed to Lyndon Johnson, for Presidents to succeed in controlling domestic policy. From the end of the 1930's to the present (what may roughly be called the modern era), Presidents have often been frustrated in their domestic programs. From 1938, when conservatives regrouped their forces, to the time of his death, Franklin Roosevelt did not get a single piece of significant domestic legislation passed. Truman lost out on most of his intense domestic preferences, except perhaps for housing. Since Eisenhower did not ask for much domestic legislation, he did not meet consistent defeat, yet he failed in his general policy of curtailing governmental commitments. Kennedy, of course, faced great difficulties with domestic legislation.

In the realm of foreign policy there has not been a single major issue on which Presidents, when they were serious and determined, have failed. The list of their victories is impressive: entry into the United Nations, the Marshall Plan,§ NATO, the Truman Doctrine,‖ the decisions to stay out of Indochina in 1954 and to intervene in Vietnam in the 1960's, aid to Poland and Yugoslavia, the test-ban treaty, and many more. Serious setbacks to the President in controlling foreign policy are extraordinary and unusual.

Table 1, compiled from the Congressional Quarterly Service tabulation of presidential initiative and congressional response from 1948 through 1964, shows that Presidents have significantly better records in foreign and defense matters than in domestic policies. When refugees and immigration—which Congress considers primarily a domestic concern—are removed from the general

North Atlantic Treaty Organization, or NATO: alliance uniting North America and Western Europe in a commitment to collective defense aimed primarily at preventing Soviet expansion in Europe.

†*Roosevelt's hundred days:* see footnote on page 68.

‡*Barry Goldwater:* see footnote on page 188.

§*Marshall Plan:* common name for the European Recovery Program proposed by George C. Marshall, President Harry S Truman's secretary of state. Implemented in 1948 under the Economic Cooperation Administration, the plan provided funds to European nations to aid in reconstructing their economies and bolster their resistance to communism.

‖*Truman Doctrine:* a 1947 "containment" policy of President Truman's that provided aid to countries trying to resist Communist takeover. Truman lobbied Congress to provide $400 million to support Greece and Turkey in their struggles against leftist movements when Great Britain ended its aid program after World War II.

TABLE 1 CONGRESSIONAL ACTION ON PRESIDENTIAL PROPOSALS FROM 1948–1964

	CONGRESSIONAL ACTION		
Policy Area	*% Pass*	*% Fail*	*Number of Proposals*
Domestic policy (natural resources, labor, agriculture, taxes, etc.)	40.2	59.8	2499
Defense policy (defense, disarmament, manpower, misc.)	73.3	26.7	90
Foreign policy	58.5	41.5	655
Immigration, refugees	13.2	86.0	129
Treaties, general foreign relations, State Department, foreign aid	70.8	29.2	445

Source: Congressional Quarterly Service, *Congress and the Nation,* 1945–1964 (Washington, 1965).

foreign policy area, it is clear that Presidents prevail about 70 per cent of the time in defense and foreign policy, compared with 40 per cent in the domestic sphere.

WORLD EVENTS AND PRESIDENTIAL RESOURCES

Power in politics is control over governmental decisions. How does the President manage his control of foreign and defense policy? The answer does not reside in the greater constitutional power in foreign affairs that Presidents have possessed since the founding of the Republic. The answer lies in the changes that have taken place since 1945.

The number of nations with which the United States has diplomatic relations has increased from 53 in 1939 to 113 in 1966. But sheer numbers do not tell enough; the world has also become a much more dangerous place. However remote it may seem at times, our government must always be aware of the possibility of nuclear war.

Yet the mere existence of great powers with effective thermonuclear weapons would not, in and of itself, vastly increase our rate of interaction with most other nations. We see events in Assam or Burundi as important because they are also part of a larger worldwide contest, called the cold war, in which great powers are rivals for the control or support of other nations. Moreover, the reaction against the blatant isolationism of the 1930's has led to a concern with foreign policy that is worldwide in scope. We are interested in what happens everywhere because we see these events as connected with larger interests involving, at the worst, the possibility of ultimate destruction.

Given the overriding fact that the world is dangerous and that small causes are perceived to have potentially great effects in an unstable world, it follows that Presidents must be interested in relatively "small" matters. So they give Azerbaijan or Lebanon or Vietnam huge amounts of their time. Arthur Schlesinger, Jr., wrote of Kennedy that "in the first two months of his administration he probably spent more time on Laos than on anything else." Few failures in domestic policy, Presidents soon realize, could have as disastrous consequences as any one of dozens of mistakes in the international arena.

The result is that foreign policy concerns tend to drive out domestic policy. Except for occasional questions of domestic prosperity and for civil rights, foreign affairs have consistently higher priority for Presidents. Once, when trying to talk to President Kennedy about natural resources, Secretary of the Interior Stewart Udall remarked, "He's imprisoned by Berlin."

The importance of foreign affairs to Presidents is intensified by the increasing speed of events in the international arena. The event and its consequences follow closely on top of one another. The blunder at the Bay of Pigs* is swiftly followed by the near catastrophe of the Cuban missile crisis.† Presidents can no longer count on passing along their most difficult problems to their successors. They must expect to face the consequences of their actions—or failure to act—while still in office.

Domestic policy-making is usually based on experimental adjustments to an existing situation. Only a few decisions, such as those involving large dams, irretrievably commit future generations. Decisions in foreign affairs, however, are often perceived to be irreversible. This is expressed, for example, in the fear of escalation or the various "spiral" or "domino" theories‡ of international conflict.

If decisions are perceived to be both important and irreversible, there is every reason for Presidents to devote a great deal of resources to them. Presidents have to be oriented toward the future in the use of their resources. They serve a fixed term in office, and they cannot automatically count on support from the populace, Congress, or the administrative apparatus. They have to be careful, therefore, to husband their resources for pressing future needs. But because the consequences of events in foreign affairs are potentially more grave, faster to manifest themselves, and less easily reversible than in domestic affairs, Presidents are more willing to use up their resources.

THE POWER TO ACT

Their formal powers to commit resources in foreign affairs and defense are vast. Particularly important is their power as Commander-in-Chief to move troops. Faced with situations like the invasion of South Korea or the emplacement of missiles in Cuba, fast action is required. Presidents possess both the formal power to act and the knowledge that elites and the general public expect them to act. Once they have committed American forces, it is difficult for Congress or anyone else to alter the course of events. The Dominican venture is a recent case in point.

Presidential discretion in foreign affairs also makes it difficult (though not impossible) for Congress to restrict their actions. Presidents can use executive

**Bay of Pigs:* see footnote on page 355.

†*Cuban missile crisis:* incident in 1962 during which President Kennedy ordered a naval quarantine of Cuba until the Soviet Union dismantled long-range nuclear missile launch it was building there. The Soviets soon complied on condition that the United States pledge not to invade Cuba.

‡*Domino theory:* concept, first popularized by President Eisenhower in 1954, that if one country became Communist, neighboring countries would also fall in an inevitable chain reaction. The metaphor was used to gain support for U.S. military policy in Indochina, especially during the Vietnam War.

agreements instead of treaties, enter into tacit agreements instead of written ones, and otherwise help create *de facto* situations not easily reversed. Presidents also have far greater ability than anyone else to obtain information on developments abroad through the Departments of State and Defense. The need for secrecy in some aspects of foreign and defense policy further restricts the ability of others to compete with Presidents. These things are all well known. What is not so generally appreciated is the growing presidential ability to *use* information to achieve goals.

In the past Presidents were amateurs in military strategy. They could not even get much useful advice outside of the military. As late as the 1930's the number of people outside the military establishment who were professionally engaged in the study of defense policy could be numbered on fingers. Today there are hundreds of such men. The rise of the defense intellectuals has given the President of the United States enhanced ability to control defense policy. He is no longer dependent on the military for advice. He can choose among defense intellectuals from the research corporations and the academies for alternative sources of advice. He can install these men in his own office. He can play them off against each other or use them to extend spheres of coordination.

Even with these advisers, however, Presidents and Secretaries of Defense might still be too bewildered by the complexity of nuclear situations to take action—unless they had an understanding of the doctrine and concept of deterrence.* But knowledge of doctrine about deterrence has been widely diffused; it can be picked up by any intelligent person who will read books or listen to enough hours of conversation. Whether or not the doctrine is good is a separate question; the point is that civilians can feel they understand what is going on in defense policy. Perhaps the most extraordinary feature of presidential action during the Cuban missile crisis was the degree to which the Commander-in-Chief of the Armed Forces insisted on controlling even the smallest moves. From the positioning of ships to the methods of boarding, to the precise words and actions to be taken by individual soldiers and sailors, the President and his civilian advisers were in control.

Although Presidents have rivals for power in foreign affairs, the rivals do not usually succeed. Presidents prevail not only because they may have superior resources but because their potential opponents are weak, divided, or believe that they should not control foreign policy. Let us consider the potential rivals—the general citizenry, special interest groups, the Congress, the military, the so-called military-industrial complex, and the State Department.

COMPETITORS FOR CONTROL OF POLICY

The Public The general public is much more dependent on Presidents in foreign affairs than in domestic matters. While many people know about the impact of social security and Medicare, few know about politics in Malawi. So it

**Deterrence:* prevention of military agression by persuading enemies that the price of aggression would be unacceptably high. American defense policy is based on the idea that an unsurpassed military capacity is the best guarantor of national security because the consequences of engaging the United States in hostilities would be too great.

is not surprising that people expect the President to act in foreign affairs and reward him with their confidence. Gallup Polls consistently show that presidential popularity rises after he takes action in a crisis—whether the action is disastrous as in the Bay of Pigs or successful as in the Cuban missile crisis. Decisive action, such as the bombing of oil fields near Haiphong, resulted in a sharp (though temporary) increase in Johnson's popularity.

The Vietnam* situation illustrates another problem of public opinion in foreign affairs: it is extremely difficult to get operational policy directions from the general public. It took a long time before any sizable public interest in the subject developed. Nothing short of the large scale involvement of American troops under fire probably could have brought about the current high level of concern. Yet this relatively well developed popular opinion is difficult to interpret. While a majority appear to support President Johnson's policy, it appears that they could easily be persuaded to withdraw from Vietnam if the administration changed its line. Although a sizable majority would support various initiatives to end the war, they would seemingly be appalled if this action led to Communist† encroachments elsewhere in Southeast Asia. (See "The President, the Polls, and Vietnam" by Seymour Martin Lipset, *Trans-Action*, Sept/Oct 1966.)

Although Presidents lead opinion in foreign affairs, they know they will be held accountable for the consequences of their actions. President Johnson has maintained a large commitment in Vietnam. His popularity shoots up now and again in the midst of some imposing action. But the fact that a body of citizens do not like the war comes back to damage his overall popularity. We will support your initiatives, the people seem to say, but we will reserve the right to punish you (or your party) if we do not like the results.

SPECIAL INTEREST GROUPS Opinions are easier to gauge in domestic affairs because, for one thing, there is a stable structure of interest groups that covers virtually all matters of concern. The farm, labor, business, conservation, veteran, civil rights, and other interest groups provide cues when a proposed policy affects them. Thus people who identify with these groups may adopt their views. But in foreign policy matters the interest group structure is weak, unstable, and thin rather than dense. In many matters affecting Africa and Asia, for example, it is hard to think of well-known interest groups. While ephemeral groups arise from time to time to support or protest particular policies, they usually disappear when the immediate problem is resolved. In contrast, longer-lasting elite groups like the Foreign Policy Association and Council on Foreign Relations are composed of people of diverse views; refusal to take strong positions on controversial matters is a condition of their continued viability.

The strongest interest groups are probably the ethnic associations whose members have strong ties with a homeland, as in Poland or Cuba, so they are rarely activated simultaneously on any specific issue. They are most effective when

**Vietnam:* see footnote on page 194.

†*Communist:* In the modern context, as discussed by Marx and Engels, a communist is one who supports a society characterized by the absence of private property, distribution of goods and services based on individuals' needs, and the withering away of the state.

most narrowly and intensely focused—as in the fierce pressure from Jews to recognize the state of Israel. But their relatively small numbers limit their significance to Presidents in the vastly more important general foreign policy picture—as continued aid to the Arab countries shows. Moreover, some ethnic groups may conflict on significant issues such as American acceptance of the Oder-Neisse line separating Poland from what is now East Germany.

THE CONGRESS Congressmen also exercise power in foreign affairs. Yet they are ordinarily not serious competitors with the President because they follow a self-denying ordinance. They do not think it is their job to determine the nation's defense policies. Lewis A. Dexter's extensive interviews with members of the Senate Armed Services Committee, who might be expected to want a voice in defense policy, reveal that they do not desire for men like themselves to run the nation's defense establishment. Aside from a few specific conflicts among the armed services which allow both the possibility and desirability of direct intervention, the Armed Services Committee constitutes a sort of real estate committee dealing with the regional economic consequences of the location of military facilities.

The congressional appropriations power is potentially a significant resource, but circumstances since the end of World War II have tended to reduce its effectiveness. The appropriations committees and Congress itself might make their will felt by refusing to allot funds unless basic policies were altered. But this has not happened. While Congress makes its traditional small cuts in the military budget, Presidents have mostly found themselves warding off congressional attempts to increase specific items still further.

Most of the time, the administration's refusal to spend has not been seriously challenged. However, there have been occasions when individual legislators or committees have been influential. Senator Henry Jackson in his campaign (with the aid of colleagues on the Joint Committee on Atomic Energy) was able to gain acceptance for the Polaris weapons system and Senator Arthur H. Vandenberg played a part in determining the shape of the Marshall Plan and so on. The few congressmen who are expert in defense policy act, as Samuel P. Huntington* says, largely as lobbyists with the executive branch. It is apparently more fruitful for these congressional experts to use their resources in order to get a hearing from the executive than to work on other congressmen.

When an issue involves the actual use or threat of violence, it takes a great deal to convince congressmen not to follow the President's lead. James Robinson's tabulation of foreign and defense policy issues from the late 1930's to 1961 (Table 2) shows dominant influence by Congress in only one case out of seven—the 1954 decision not to intervene with armed force in Indochina. In that instance President Eisenhower deliberately sounded out congressional opinion and, finding it negative, decided not to intervene—against the advice of Admiral Radford, chairman of the Joint Chiefs of Staff. This attempt to abandon responsibility did not succeed, as the years of American involvement demonstrate.

**Samuel P. Huntington*: see headnote on page 270.

TABLE 2 CONGRESSIONAL INVOLVEMENT IN FOREIGN AND DEFENSE POLICY DECISIONS

Issue	*Congressional Involvement (High, Low, None)*	*Initiator (Congress or Executive)*	*Predominat Influence (Congress or Executive)*	*Legislation or Resolution (Yes or No)*	*Violence at Stake (Yes or No)*	*Decision Time (Long or Short)*
Neutrality Legislation, the 1930's	High	Exec	Cong	Yes	No	Long
Lend-Lease, 1941	High	Exec	Exec	Yes	Yes	Long
Aid to Russia, 1941	Low	Exec	Exec	No	No	Long
Repeal of Chinese Exclusion, 1943	High	Cong	Cong	Yes	No	Long
Fullbright Resolution, 1943	High	Cong	Cong	Yes	No	Long
Building the Atomic Bomb, 1944	Low	Exec	Exec	Yes	Yes	Long
Foreign Services Act of 1946	High	Exec	Exec	Yes	No	Long
Truman Doctrine, 1947	High	Exec	Exec	Yes	No	Long
The Marshall Plan, 1947–48	High	Exec	Exec	Yes	No	Long
Berlin Airlift, 1948	None	Exec	Exec	No	Yes	Long
Vandenberg Resolution, 1948	High	Exec	Cong	Yes	No	Long
North Atlantic Treaty, 1947–49	High	Exec	Exec	Yes	No	Long
Korean Decision, 1950	None	Exec	Exec	No	Yes	Short
Japanese Peace Treaty, 1952	High	Exec	Exec	Yes	No	Long
Bohlen Nomination, 1953	High	Exec	Exec	Yes	No	Long
Indo-China, 1954	High	Exec	Cong	No	Yes	Short
Formosan Resolution, 1955	High	Exec	Exec	Yes	Yes	Long
International Finance Corporation, 1956	Low	Exec	Exec	Yes	No	Long
Foreign Aid, 1957	High	Exec	Exec	Yes	No	Long
Reciprocal Trade Agreements, 1958	High	Exec	Exec	Yes	No	Long
Monroney Resolution, 1958	High	Cong	Cong	Yes	No	Long
Cuban Decision, 1961	Low	Exec	Exec	No	Yes	Long

Source: James A. Robinson, *Congress and Foreign Policymaking* (Homewood, Illinois, 1962).

THE MILITARY The outstanding feature of the military's participation in making defense policy is their amazing weakness. Whether the policy decisions involve the size of the armed forces, the choice of weapons systems, the total defense budget, or its division into components, the military have not prevailed. Let us take budgetary decisions as representative of the key choices to be made in defense policy. Since the end of World War II the military has not been able to achieve significant (billion dollar) increases in appropriations by their own efforts. Under Truman and Eisenhower defense budgets were determined by what Huntington calls the remainder method: the two Presidents estimated revenues, decided what they could spend on domestic matters, and the remainder was assigned to defense. The usual controversy was between some military and congressional groups supporting much larger expenditures while the President and his executive allies refused. A typical case, involving the desire of the Air Force to increase the number of groups of planes is described by Huntington in the *The Common Defense:*

> The FY [fiscal year] 1949 budget provided 48 groups. After the Czech coup, the Administration yielded and backed an Air Force of 55 groups in its spring rearmament program. Congress added additional funds to aid Air Force expansion to 70 groups. The Administration refused to utilize them, however, and in the gathering economy wave of the summer and fall of 1948, the Air Force goal was cut back again to 48 groups. In 1949 the House of Representatives picked up the challenge and appropriated funds for 58 groups. The President impounded* the money. In June, 1950, the Air Force had 48 groups.

The great increases in the defense budget were due far more to Stalin and modern technology than to the military. The Korean War resulted in an increase from 12 to 44 billions and much of the rest followed Sputnik and the huge costs of missile programs. Thus modern technology and international conflict put an end to the one major effort to subordinate foreign affairs to domestic policies through the budget.

It could be argued that the President merely ratifies the decisions made by the military and their allies. If the military and/or Congress were united and insistent on defense policy, it would certainly be difficult for Presidents to resist these forces. But it is precisely the disunity of the military that has characterized the entire postwar period. Indeed, the military have not been united on any major matter of defense policy. The apparent unity of the Joint Chiefs of Staff turns out to be illusory. The vast majority of their recommendations appear to be unanimous and are accepted by the Secretary of Defense and the President. But this facade of unity can only be achieved by methods that vitiate the impact of the recommendations. Genuine disagreements are hidden by vague language that commits no one to anything. Mutually contradictory plans are strung together so everyone appears to get something, but nothing is decided. Since it is impossible to agree on really important matters, all sorts of trivia are brought in to make a

**Impounded:* a tactic used by the executive branch that prevents the disbursement of funds already authorized and appropriated by the legislature.

record of agreement. While it may be true, as Admiral Denfield, a former Chief of Naval Operations, said, that "On nine-tenths of the matters that come before them the Joint Chiefs of Staff reach agreement themselves," the vastly more important truth is that "normally the *only* disputes are on strategic concepts, the size and composition of forces, and budget matters."

MILITARY-INDUSTRIAL But what about the fabled military-industrial complex? If the military alone is divided and weak, perhaps the giant industrial firms that are so dependent on defense contracts play a large part in making policy.

First, there is an important distinction between the questions "Who will get a given contract?" and "What will our defense policy be?" It is apparent that different answers may be given to these quite different questions. There are literally tens of thousands of defense contractors. They may compete vigorously for business. In the course of this competition, they may wine and dine military officers, use retired generals, seek intervention by their congressmen, place ads in trade journals, and even contribute to political campaigns. The famous TFX controversy—should General Dynamics or Boeing get the expensive contract?—is a larger than life example of the pressures brought to bear in search of lucrative contracts.

But neither the TFX case nor the usual vigorous competition for contracts is involved with the making of substantive defense policy. Vital questions like the size of the defense budget, the choice of strategic programs, massive retaliation vs. a counter-city strategy, and the like were far beyond the policy aims of any company. Industrial firms, then, do not control such decisions, nor is there much evidence that they actually try. No doubt a precipitous and drastic rush to disarmament would meet with opposition from industrial firms among other interests. However, there has never been a time when any significant element in the government considered a disarmament policy to be feasible.

It may appear that industrial firms had no special reason to concern themselves with the government's stance on defense because they agree with the national consensus on resisting communism, maintaining a large defense establishment, and rejecting isolationism. However, this hypothesis about the climate of opinion explains everything and nothing. For every policy that is adopted or rejected can be explained away on the grounds that the cold war climate of opinion dictated what happened. Did the United States fail to intervene with armed force in Vietnam in 1954? That must be because the climate of opinion was against it. Did the United States send troops to Vietnam in the 1960's? That must be because the cold war climate demanded it. If the United States builds more missiles, negotiates a testban treaty, intervenes in the Dominican Republic, fails to intervene in a dozen other situations, all these actions fit the hypothesis by definition. The argument is reminiscent of those who defined the Soviet Union as permanently hostile and therefore interpreted increases of Soviet troops as menacing and decreases of troop strength as equally sinister.

If the growth of the military establishment is not directly equated with increasing military control of defense policy, the extraordinary weakness of the professional soldier still requires explanation. Huntington has written about how major military leaders were seduced in the Truman and Eisenhower years into believing that they should bow to the judgment of civilians that the economy could not stand much larger military expenditures. Once the size of the military pie was accepted as a fixed constraint, the military services were compelled to put their major energies into quarreling with one another over who should get the larger share. Given the natural rivalries of the military and their traditional acceptance of civilian rule, the President and his advisers—who could claim responsibility for the broader picture of reconciling defense and domestic policies—had the upper hand. There are, however, additional explanations to be considered.

The dominant role of the congressional appropriations committee is to be guardian of the treasury. This is manifested in the pride of its members in cutting the President's budget. Thus it was difficult to get this crucial committee to recommend even a few hundred million increase in defense; it was practically impossible to get them to consider the several billion jump that might really have made a difference. A related budgetary matter concerned the planning, programming, and budgeting system introduced by Secretary of Defense McNamara. For if the defense budget contained major categories that crisscrossed the services, only the Secretary of Defense could put it together. Whatever the other debatable consequences of program budgeting, its major consequence was to grant power to the secretary and his civilian advisers.

The subordination of the military through program budgeting is just one symptom of a more general weakness of the military. In the past decade the military has suffered a lack of intellectual skills appropriate to the nuclear age. For no one has (and no one wants) direct experience with nuclear war. So the usual military talk about being the only people to have combat experience is not very impressive. Instead, the imaginative creation of possible future wars—in order to avoid them—requires people with a high capacity for abstract thought combined with the ability to manipulate symbols using quantitative methods. West Point has not produced many such men.

THE STATE DEPARTMENT Modern Presidents expect the State Department to carry out their policies. John F. Kennedy felt that State was "in some particular sense 'his' department." If a Secretary of States forgets this, as was apparently the case with James Byrnes under Truman, a President may find another man. But the State Department, especially the Foreign Service, is also a highly professional organization with a life and momentum of its own. If a President does not push hard, he may find his preferences somehow dissipated in time. Arthur Schlesinger fills his book on Kennedy with laments about the bureaucratic inertia and recalcitrance of the State Department.

Yet Schlesinger's own account suggests that State could not ordinarily resist the President. At one point, he writes of "the President, himself, increasingly the day-to-day director of American foreign policy." On the next page, we learn that "Kennedy dealt personally with almost every aspect of policy around the globe. He knew more about certain areas than the senior officials at State and probably called as many issues to their attention as they did to his." The President insisted on his way in Laos. He pushed through his policy on the Congo against strong opposition with the State Department. Had Kennedy wanted to get a great deal more initiative out of the State Department, as Schlesinger insists, he could have replaced the Secretary of State, a man who did not command special support in the Democratic party or in Congress. It may be that Kennedy wanted too strongly to run his own foreign policy. Dean Rusk* may have known far better than Schlesinger that the one thing Kennedy did not want was a man who might rival him in the field of foreign affairs.

Schlesinger comes closest to the truth when he writes that "the White House could always win any battle it chose over the [Foreign] Service; but the prestige and proficiency of the Service limited the number of battles any White House would find it profitable to fight." When the President knew what he wanted, he got it. When he was doubtful and perplexed, he sought good advice and frequently did not get that. But there is no evidence that the people on his staff came up with better ideas. The real problem may have been a lack of good ideas anywhere. Kennedy undoubtedly encouraged his staff to prod the State Department. But the President was sufficiently cautious not to push so hard that he got his way when he was not certain what that way should be. In this context Kennedy appears to have played his staff off against elements in the State Department.

The growth of a special White House staff to help Presidents in foreign affairs expresses their need for assistance, their refusal to rely completely on the regular executive agencies, and their ability to find competent men. The deployment of this staff must remain a presidential prerogative, however, if its members are to serve Presidents and not their opponents. Whenever critics do not like the existing foreign and defense policies, they are likely to complain that the White House staff is screening out divergent views from the President's attention. Naturally, the critics recommend introducing many more different viewpoints. If the critics could maneuver the President into counting hands all day ("on the one hand and on the other"), they would make it impossible for him to act. Such a viewpoint is also congenial to those who believe that action rather than inaction is the greatest present danger in foreign policy. But Presidents resolutely refuse to become prisoners of their advisers by using them as other people would like. Presidents remain in control of their staff as well as of major foreign policy decisions.

HOW COMPLETE IS THE CONTROL?

Some analysts say that the success of Presidents in controlling foreign policy decisions is largely illusory. It is achieved, they say, by anticipating the reactions of others, and eliminating proposals that would run into severe opposition. There is some truth in this objection. In politics, where transactions are based on a high degree of mutual interdependence, what others may do has to be taken into account. But basing presidential success in foreign and defense policy on anticipated reactions suggests a static situation which does not exist. For if Presidents

Dean Rusk: Secretary of state (1961–1969) under Presidents Kennedy and Johnson.

propose only those policies that would get support in Congress, and Congress opposes them only when it knows that it can muster overwhelming strength, there would never be any conflict. Indeed, there might never by any action.

How can "anticipated reaction" explain the conflict over the policies like the Marshall Plan* and the test-ban treaty in which severe opposition was overcome only by strenuous efforts? Furthermore, why doesn't "anticipated reaction" work in domestic affairs? One would have to argue that for some reason presidential perception of what would be successful is consistently confused on domestic issues and most always accurate on major foreign policy issues. But the role of "anticipated reactions" should be greater in the more familiar domestic situations, which provide a backlog of experience for forecasting, than in foreign policy with many novel situations such as the Suez crisis or the Rhodesian affair.

Are there significant historical examples which might refute the thesis of presidential control of foreign policy? Foreign aid may be a case in point. For many years, Presidents have struggled to get foreign aid appropriations because of hostility from public and congressional opinion. Yet several billion dollars a year are appropriated regularly despite the evident unpopularity of the program. In the aid programs to Communist countries like Poland and Yugoslavia, the Congress attaches all sorts of restrictions to the aid, but Presidents find ways of getting around them.

What about the example of recognition of Communist China? The sentiment of the country always has been against recognizing Red China or admitting it to the United Nations. But have Presidents wanted to recognize Red China and been hamstrung by opposition? The answer, I suggest, is a qualified "no." By the time recognition of Red China might have become a serious issue for the Truman administration, the war in Korea effectively precluded its consideration. There is no evidence that President Eisenhower or Secretary Dulles ever thought it wise to recognize Red China or help admit her to the United Nations. The Kennedy administration viewed the matter as not of major importance and, considering the opposition, moved cautiously in suggesting change. Then came the war in Vietnam. If the advantages for foreign policy had been perceived to be much higher, then Kennedy or Johnson might have proposed changing American policy toward recognition of Red China.

One possible exception, in the case of Red China, however, does not seem sufficient to invalidate the general thesis that Presidents do considerably better in getting their way in foreign and defense policy than in domestic policies.

THE WORLD INFLUENCE

The forces impelling Presidents to be concerned with the widest range of foreign and defense policies also affect the ways in which they calculate their power stakes. As Kennedy used to say, "Domestic policy . . . can only defeat us; foreign policy can kill us."

**Marshall Plan:* see footnote on page 318.

It no longer makes sense for Presidents to "play politics" with foreign and defense policies. In the past, Presidents might have thought that they could gain by prolonged delay or by not acting at all. The problem might disappear or be passed on to their successors. Presidents must now expect to pay the high costs themselves if the world situation deteriorates. The advantages of pursuing a policy that is viable in the world, that will not blow up on Presidents or their fellow citizens, far outweigh any temporary political disadvantages accrued in supporting an initially unpopular policy. Compared with domestic affairs, Presidents engaged in world politics are immensely more concerned with meeting problems on their own terms. Who supports and opposes a policy, though a matter of considerable interest, does not assume the crucial importance that it does in domestic affairs. The best policy Presidents can find is also the best politics.

The fact that there are numerous foreign and defense policy situations competing for a President's attention means that it is worthwhile to organize political activity in order to affect his agenda. For if a President pays more attention to certain problems he may develop different preferences; he may seek and receive different advice; his new calculations may lead him to devote greater resources to seeking a solution. Interested congressmen may exert influence not by directly determining a presidential decision, but indirectly by making it costly for a President to avoid reconsidering the basis for his action. For example, citizen groups, such as those concerned with a change in China policy, may have an impact simply by keeping their proposals on the public agenda. A president may be compelled to reconsider a problem even though he could not overtly be forced to alter the prevailing policy.

In foreign affairs we may be approaching the stage where knowledge is power. There is a tremendous receptivity to good ideas in Washington. Most anyone who can present a convincing rationale for dealing with a hard world finds a ready audience. The best way to convince Presidents to follow a desired policy is to show that it might work. A man like McNamara thrives because he performs; he comes up with answers he can defend. It is, to be sure, extremely difficult to devise good policies or to predict their consequences accurately. Nor is it easy to convince others that a given policy is superior to other alternatives. But it is the way to influence with Presidents. For if they are convinced that the current policy is best, the likelihood of gaining sufficient force to compel a change is quite small. The man who can build better foreign policies will find Presidents beating a path to his door.

FURTHER READING SUGGESTED BY THE AUTHOR

The Common Defense, by Samuel P. Huntington. New York: Columbia University Press, 1963. The best study of presidential participation in the making of defense policy.

Congress and the Presidency, by Nelson W. Polsby. Englewood Cliffs, New Jersey: Prentice-Hall, 1965. A fine short study of executive-legislative relationships.

19

RICHARD E. NEUSTADT

THE POWER TO PERSUADE

The first edition of Presidential Power *(1960), a study of the Truman and Eisenhower administrations, received national attention and served to alert the incoming president, John F. Kennedy, of the limitations of power. In subsequent editions, Richard E. Neustadt updated and expanded the original analysis to cover Presidents Rosevelt, Kennedy, Johnson, Nixon, and Carter. His analysis of presidential power shows that presidents cannot simply rely on the formal authority of their office and on partisan loyalties for effective leadership. They must know how to persuade and cajole other government actors, interest groups, and the public to support presidential initiatives. The following excerpt of* Presidential Power *is from the 1976 edition. Neustadt's other works include:* Alliance Politics *(1970);* The Epidemic that Never Was: Policymaking and the Swine Flu Affair *(1982) written with Harvey Fineberg; and* Thinking in Time: The Uses of History for Decision-Makers *(1986) written with Ernest R. May.*

The limits on command suggest the structure of our goverment. The constitutional convention of 1787 is supposed to have created a government of "separated powers." It did nothing of the sort. Rather, it created a goverment of separated institutions *sharing* powers.[1] "I am part of the legislative process," Eisenhower often said in 1959 as a reminder of his veto.[2] Congress, the dispenser of authority and funds, is no less part of the administrative process. Federalism adds another set of separated institutions. The Bill of Rights adds others. Many public purposes can only be achieved by voluntary acts of private institutions; the press, for one, in Douglass Cater's phrase, is a "fourth branch of government."[3] And with the coming of alliances abroad, the separate institutions of a London,[3] or a Bonn, share in the making of American policy.

What the Constitution separates our political parties do not combine. The parties are themselves composed of separated organizations sharing public authority. The authority consists of nominating powers. Our national parties are confederations of state and local party institutions, with a headquarters that represents the White House, more or less, if the party has a president in office. These confederacies manage presidential nominations. All other public offices depend upon electorates confined with the states.[4] All other nominations are controlled within the states. The president and congressmen who bear one party's label are divided by dependence upon different sets of voters. The differences are sharpest at the stage of nomination. The White House has too small a share in nominating congressmen, and Congress has too little weight in nominating presidents for party to erase their constitutional separation. Party links are stronger than is frequently supposed, but nominating processes assure the separation.[5]

The separateness of institutions and the sharing of authority prescribe the terms on which a president persuades. When one man shares authority with another, but does not gain or lose his job upon the other's whim, his willingness to act upon the urging of the other turns on whether he conceives the action right for him. The essence of a president's persuasive task is to convince such men that what the White House wants of them is what they ought to do for their sake and on their authority.

Persuasive power, thus defined, amounts to more than charm or reasoned argument. These have their uses for a president, but these are not the whole of his resources. For the men he would induce to do what he wants done on their own responsibility will need or fear some acts by him on his responsibility. If they share his authority, he has some share in theirs. Presidential "powers" may be inconclusive when a president commands, but always remain relevant as he persuades. The status and authority inherent in his office reinforce his logic and his charm.

Status adds something to persuasiveness; authority adds still more. When Truman urged wage changes on his secretary of commerce while the latter was administering the steel mills, he and Secretary Sawyer were not just two men reasoning with one another. Had they been so, Sawyer probably would never have agreed to act. Truman's status gave him special claims to Sawyer's loyalty, or at least attention. In Walter Bagehot's* charming phrase "no man can *argue* on his knees." Although there is no kneeling in this country, few men—and exceedingly few cabinet officers—are immune to the impulse to say "yes" to the president of the United States. It grows harder to say "no" when they are seated in his oval office at the White House, or in his study on the second floor, where almost tangibly he partakes of the aura of his physical surroundings. In Sawyer's case, moreover, the president possessed formal authority to intervene in many matters of concern to the secretary of commerce. These matters ranged from jurisdictional disputes among the defense agencies to legislation pending before Congress and, ultimately, to the tenure of the secretary, himself. There is nothing in the record to suggest that Truman voiced specific threats when they negotiated over wage increases. But given his *formal* powers and their relevance to Sawyer's other interests, it is safe to assume that Truman's very advocacy of wage action conveyed an implicit threat.

A president's authority and status give him great advantages in dealing with the men he would persuade. Each "power" is a vantage point for him in the degree that other men have use for his authority. From the veto to appointments, from publicity to budgeting, and so down a long list, the White House now controls the most encompassing array of vantage points in the American political system. With hardly an exception, the men who share in governing this country are aware that at some time, in some degree, the doing of *their* jobs, the furthering of *their* ambitions, may depend upon the president of the United States. Their need for presidential action, or their fear of it, is bound to be recurrent if not actually continuous. Their need or fear is his advantage.

**Walter Bagehot:* see footnote on page 259.

A president's advantages are greater than mere listing of his "powers" might suggest. The men with whom he deals must deal with him until the last day of his term. Because they have continuing relationships with him, his future, while it lasts, supports his present influence. Even though there is no need or fear of him today, what he could do tomorrow may supply today's advantage. Continuing relationships may convert any "power," any aspect of his status, into vantage points in almost any case. When he induces other men to do what he wants done, a president can trade on their dependence now *and* later.

The president's advantages are checked by the advantages of others. Continuing relationships will pull in both directions. These are relationships of mutual dependence. A president depends upon the men he would persuade; he has to reckon with his need or fear of them. They too will possess status, or authority, or both, else they would be of little use to him. Their vantage points confront his own; their power tempers his.

Persuasion is a two-way street. Sawyer, it will be recalled, did not respond at once to Truman's plan for wage increases at the steel mills. On the contrary, the secretary hesitated and delayed and only acquiesced when he was satisfied that publicly he would not bear the onus of decision. Sawyer had some points of vantage all his own from which to resist presidential pressure. If he had to reckon with coercive implications in the president's "situations of strength," so had Truman to be mindful of the implications underlying Sawyer's place as a department head, as steel administrator, and as a cabinet spokesman for business. Loyalty is reciprocal. Having taken on a dirty job in the steel crisis, Sawyer had strong claims to loyal support. Besides, he had authority to do some things that the White House could ill afford. Emulating Wilson, he might have resigned in a huff (the removal power also works two ways). Or emulating Ellis Arnall, he might have declined to sign necessary orders. Or, he might have let it be known publicly that he deplored what he was told to do and protested its doing. By following any of these courses Sawyer almost surely would have strengthened the position of management, weakened the position of the White House, and embittered the union. But the whole purpose of a wage increase was to enhance White House persuasiveness in urging settlement upon union and companies alike. Although Sawyer's status and authority did not give him the power to prevent an increase outright, they gave him capability to undermine its purpose. If his authority over wage rates had been vested by a statute, not by revocable presidential order, his power of prevention might have been complete. So Harold Ickes dimonstrated in the famous case of helium sales to Germany before the Second World War.[6]

The power to persuade is the power to bargain. Status and authority yield bargaining advantages. But in a government of "separated institutions sharing powers," they yield them to all sides. With the array of vantage points at his disposal, a president may be far more persuasive than his logic or his charm could make him. But outcomes are not guaranteed by his advantages. There remain the counter pressures those whom he would influence can bring to bear on him from vantage points at their disposal. Command has limited utility; persuasion becomes give-and-take. It is well that the White House holds the vantage points it does. In such a business any president may need them all—and more.

This view of power as akin to bargaining is one we commonly accept in the sphere of congressional relations. Every textbook states and every legislative session demonstrates that save in times like the extraordinary Hundred Days of 1933*—times virtually ruled out by definition at mid-century—a president will often be unable to obtain congressional action on his terms or even to halt action he opposes. The reverse is equally accepted: Congress often is frustrated by the president. Their formal powers are so intertwined that neither will accomplish very much, for very long, without the acquiescence of the other. By the same token, though, what one demands, the other can resist. The stage is set for that great game, much like collective bargaining,† in which each seeks to profit from the other's needs and fears. It is a game played catch-as-catch-can, case by case. And everybody knows the game, observers and participants alike.

The concept of real power as a give-and-take is equally familiar when applied to presidential influence outside the formal structure of the federal government. The Little Rock affair‡ may be extreme, but Eisenhower's dealings with the governor—and with the citizens—become a case in point. Less extreme but no less pertinent is the steel seizure case with respect to union leaders, and to workers, and to company executives as well. When he deals with such people a president draws bargaining advantage from his status or authority. By virtue of the public places or their private rights they have some capability to reply in kind.

In spheres of party politics the same thing follows, necessarily, from the confederal nature of our party organizations. Even in the case of national nominations a president's advantages are checked by those of others. In 1944 it is by no means clear that Roosevelt got his first choice as his running mate. In 1948 Truman, then the president, faced serious revolts against his nomination. In 1952 his intervention from the White House helped assure the choice of Adlai Stevenson, but it is far from clear that Truman could have done as much for any other candidate acceptable to him.[7] In 1956 when Eisenhower was president, the record leaves obscure just who backed Harold Stassen's§ effort to block Richard Nixon's renomination as vice-president. But evidently everything did not go quite as Eisenhower wanted, whatever his intentions may have been.[8] The outcomes in these instances bear all the marks of limits on command and of

*_Hundred Days of 1933:_ see footnote on page 68.

†_Collective bargaining:_ (see footnote page 112.

‡_Little Rock affair:_ confrontation between Arkansas Governor Orville Faubus and the federal government regarding desegregation. In defiance of the U.S. Supreme Court's instruction to desegregate public schools, Faubus temporarily closed all the state's public schools in 1958. Later they were reopened as private, segregated institutions. President Dwight Eisenhower reluctantly dispatched the National Guard to Little Rock, the state capital, to end the crisis.

§_Harold Stassen:_ Director of the Mutual Security Administration from January to August 1953, director of Foreign Operations Administration from August 1953 to March 1955, and special assistant to the president for disarmament from March 1955 to February 1958. Stassen began his political career brilliantly as a progressive Republican governor of Minnesota. But he was unable to attract a national following and since 1948 became the symbol of a perennial loser in his numerous bids to become president.

power checked by power that characterize congressional relations. Both in and out of politics these checks and limits seem to be quite widely understood.

Influence becomes still more a matter of give-and-take when presidents attempt to deal with allied governments. A classic illustration is the long unhappy wrangle over Suez policy in 1956. In dealing with the British and the French before their military intervention, Eisenhower had his share of bargaining advantages but no effective power of command. His allies had their share of counter pressures, and they finally tried the most extreme of all: action despite him. His pressure then was instrumental in reversing them. But had the British government been on safe ground *at home*, Eisenhower's wishes might have made as little difference after intervention as before. Behind the decorum of diplomacy—which was not very decorous in the Suez affair—relationships among allies are not unlike relationships among state delegations at a national convention. Power is persuasion and persuasion becomes bargaining. The concept is familiar to everyone who watches foreign policy.

In only one sphere is the concept unfamiliar: the sphere of executive relations. Perhaps because of civics textbooks and teaching in our schools, Americans instinctively resist the view that power in this sphere resembles power in all others. Even Washington reporters, White House aides, and congressmen are not immune to the illusion that administrative agencies comprise a single structure, "the" executive branch, where presidential word is law, or ought to be. Yet we have seen . . . that when a president seeks something from executive officials his persuasiveness is subject to the same sorts of limitations as in the case of congressmen, or governors, or national committeemen, or private citizens, or foreign governments. There are no generic differences, no differences in kind and only sometimes in degree. The incidents preceding the dismissal of MacArthur* and the incidents surrounding seizure of the steel mills make it plain that here as elsewhere influence derives from bargaining advantages; power is a give-and-take.

Like our governmental structure as a whole, the executive establishment consists of separated institutions sharing powers. The president heads one of these; cabinet officers, agency administrators, and military commanders head others. Below the departmental level, virtually independent bureau chiefs head many more. Under mid-century conditions, federal operations spill across dividing lines on organization charts; almost every policy entangles many agencies; almost every program calls for interagency collaboration. Everything somehow involves the president. But operating agencies owe their existence least of all to one another—and only in some part to him. Each has a separate statutory base; each has its statutes to administer; each deals with a different set of subcommittees at the Capitol. Each has its own peculiar set of clients, friends, and enemies outside the formal government. Each has a different set of specialized careerists inside its own bailiwick. Our Constitution gives the president the "take-care" clause and the appointive power. Our statutes give him central budgeting and a degree of personnel control. All agency administrators are responsible to him. But they *also* are responsible to Congress, to their clients, to their staffs, and to them-

**Douglas MacArthur*: see footnote on page 349.

selves. In short, they have five masters. Only after all of those do they owe any loyalty to each other.

"The members of the cabinet," Charles G. Dawes used to remark, "are a president's natural enemies." Dawes had been Harding's budget director, Coolidge's vice-president, and Hoover's ambassador to London; he also had been General Pershing's chief assistant for supply in the First World War. The words are highly colored, but Dawes knew whereof he spoke. The men who have to serve so many masters cannot help but be somewhat the "enemy" of any one of them. By the same token, any master wanting service is in some degree the "enemy" of such a servant. A president is likely to want loyal support but not to relish trouble on his doorstep. Yet the more his cabinet members cleave to him, the more they may need help from him in fending off the wrath of rival masters. Help, though, is synonymous with trouble. Many a cabinet officer with loyalty ill-rewarded by his lights and help withheld, has come to view the White House as innately hostile to department heads. Dawes' dictum can be turned around.

A senior presidential aide remarked to me in Eisenhower's time: "If some of these cabinet members would just take time out to stop and ask themselves 'What would I want if I were president?' they wouldn't give him all the trouble he's been having." But even if they asked themselves the question, such officials often could not act upon the answer. Their personal attachment to the president is all too often overwhelmed by duty to their other masters.

Executive officials are not equally advantaged in their dealings with a president. Nor are the same officials equally advantaged all the time. Not every officeholder can resist like a MacArthur, or like Arnall, Sawyer, Wilson, in a rough descending order of effective counter pressure. The vantage points conferred upon officials by their own authority and status vary enormously. The vaiance is heightened by particulars of time and circumstance. In mid-October 1950, Truman, at a press conference, remarked of the man he had considered firing in August and would fire the next April for intolerable insubordination:

> Let me tell you something that will be good for your souls. It's a pity that you . . . can't understand the ideas of two intellectually honest men when they meet. General MacArthur . . . is a member of the Government of the United States. He is loyal to that Government. He is loyal to the President. He is loyal to the President in his foreign policy. . . . There is no disagreement between General MacAurthur and myself. . . .[9]

MacArthur's status in and out of government was never higher than when Truman spoke those words. The words, once spoken, added to the general's credibility thereafter when he sought to use the press in his campaign against the president. And what had happened between August and October? Near-victory had happened, together with that premature conference on *post*-war plans, the meeting at Wake Island.*

**Wake Island:* South Pacific location of a meeting between President Harry S Truman and General Douglas MacArthur held in October 1950. An overconfident MacArthur predicted the Chinese Communists would not enter the Korean War and the war would be over by the year's end. He was wrong on both counts. The Truman administration's rejection of MacArthur's subsequent plans to end the war set off a public controversy that resulted in MacArthur's United Nations being relieved of his command.

If the bargaining advantages of a MacArthur fluctuate with changing circumstances, this is bound to be so with subordinates who have at their disposal fewer "powers," lesser status, to fall back on. And when officials have no "powers" in their own right, or depend upon the president for status, their counter pressure may be limited indeed. White House aides, who fit both categories, are among the most responsive men of all, and for good reason. As a director of the budget once remarked to me,

> Thank God I'm here and not across the street. If the President doesn't call me, I've got plenty I can do right here and plenty coming up to me, by rights, to justify my calling him. But those poor fellows over there, if the boss doesn't call them, doesn't ask them to do something, what *can* they do but sit?

Authority and status so conditional are frail reliances in resisting a president's own wants. Within the White House precincts, lifted eyebrows may suffice to set an aide in motion; command, coercion, even charm aside. But even in the White House a president does not monopolize effective power. Even there persuasion is akin to bargaining. A former Roosevelt aide once wrote of cabinet officers:

> Half of a President's suggestions, which theoretically carry the weight of orders, can be safely forgotten by a Cabinet member. And if the President asks about a suggestion a second time, he can be told that it is being investigated. If he asks a third time, a wise Cabinet officer will give him at least part of what he suggests. But only occasionally, except about the most important matters, do Presidents ever get around to asking three times.[10]

The rule applies to staff as well as to the cabinet, and certainly has been applied *by* staff in Truman's time and Eisenhower's.

Some aides will have more vantage points than a selective memory. Sherman Adams, for example, as the assistant to the president under Eisenhower, scarcely deserved the appellation "White House aide" in the meaning of the term before his time or as applied to other members of the Eisenhower entourage. Although Adams was by no means "chief of staff" in any sense so sweeping—or so simple—as press commentaries often took for granted, he apparently became no more dependent on the president than Eisenhower on him. "I need him," said the president when Adams turned out to have been remarkably imprudent in the Goldfine case,* and delegated to him even the decision on his own departure.[11] This instance is extreme, but the tendency it illustrates is common enough. Any aide who demonstrates to others that he has the president's consistent confidence and a consistent part in presidential business will acquire so much business on his

**Goldfine case:* Political scandal involving Sherman Adams, President Eisenhower's presidential assistant and campaign manager. Adams resigned under pressure for allegedly intervening on behalf of Bernard Goldfine with the Federal Trade Commission and the Securities Exchange Commission. Goldfine, a Boston textile magnate and friend of Adams, allegedly paid over $3,000 in hotel bills for Adams between 1953 and 1958. In addition, Goldfine gave Adams an expensive vicuna coat, two suits, and a $2,400 Oriental rug. Although Adams claimed these contributions were gifts between old friends, this defense fell apart when it was revealed that Goldfine had claimed the hotel bills and the rug as business expenses.

own account that he becomes in some sense independent of his chief. Nothing in the Constitution keeps a well-placed aide from converting status into power of his own, usable in some degree even against the president—an outcome not unknown in Truman's regime or, by all accounts, in Eisenhower's.

The more an officeholder's status and his "powers" stem from sources independent of the president, the stronger will be his potential pressure *on* the president. Department heads in general have more bargaining power than do most members of the White House staff; but bureau chiefs may have still more, and specialists at upper levels of established career services may have almost unlimited reserves of the enormous power which consists of sitting still. As Franklin Roosevelt once remarked:

> The Treasury is so large and far-flung and ingrained in its practices that I find it is almost impossible to get the action and results I want—even with Henry [Morgenthau]* there. But the Treasury is not to be compared with the State Department. You should go through the experience of trying to get any changes in the thinking, policy, and action of the career diplomats and then you'd know what a real problem was. But the Treasury and the State Department put together are nothing compared with the Na-a-vy. The admirals are really something to cope with—and I should know. To change anything in the Na-a-vy is like punching a feather bed. You punch it with your right and you punch it with your left until you are finally exhausted, and then you find the damn bed just as it was before you started punching.[12]

[Three pages of original text omitted at this point.]

The essence of a president's persuasive task with congressmen and everybody else, *is to induce them to believe that what he wants of them is what their own appraisal of their own responsibilities requires them to do in their interest, not his.* Because men may differ in their views on public policy, because differences in outlook stem from differences in duty—duty to one's office, one's constituents, oneself—that task is bound to be more like collective bargaining than like a reasoned argument among philosopher kings. Overtly or implicitly, hard bargaining has characterized all illustrations offered up to now. This is the reason why: persuasion deals in the coin of self-interest with men who have some freedom to reject what they find counterfeit.

NOTES

[1]The reader will want to keep in mind the distinction between two senses in which the word *power* is employed. When I have used the word (or its plural) to refer to formal constitutional, statutory, or customary authority, it is either qualified by the adjective "formal" or placed in quotation marks as "power(s)." Where I have used it in the sense of effective influence upon the conduct of others, it

**Henry Morgenthau* (1856–1946): secretary of the treasury under President Franklin D. Roosevelt. Earlier he was ambassador to Turkey (1913–1916) under President Woodrow Wilson.

appears without quotation marks (and always in the singular). Where clarity and convenience permit, *authority* is substituted for "power" in the first sense and *influence* for power in the second sense.

[2]See, for example, his press conference of July 22, 1959, as reported in the *New York Times* for July 23, 1959.

[3]See Douglass Cater, *The Fourth Branch of Government* (Boston: Houghton Mifflin, 1959).

[4]With the exception of the vice-presidency, of course.

[5]See David B. Truman's illuminating study of party relationships in the 81st Congress, *The Congressional Party* (New York: Wiley, 1959), especially chaps. 4, 6, and 8.

[6]As secretary of the interior in 1939, Harold Ickes refused to approve the sale of helium to Germany despite the insistence of the State Department and the urging of President Roosevelt. Without the secretary's approval, such sales were forbidden by statute. See *The Secret Diaries of Harold L. Ickes*, vol. 2 (New York: Simon and Schuster, 1954), especially pp. 391–393, 396–399. See also Michael J. Reagan, "The Helium Controversy" in the forthcoming case book on civil-military relations prepared for the Twentieth Century Fund under the editorial direction of Harold Stein.

In this instance the statutory authority ran to the secretary as a matter of *his* discretion. A president is unlikely to fire cabinet officers for the conscientious exercise of such authority. If the president did so, their successors might well be embarrassed both publicly and at the Capitol were they to reverse decisions previously taken. As for a president's authority to set aside discretionary determinations of this sort, it rests, if it exists at all, on shaky legal ground not likely to be trod save in the gravest of situations.

[7]Truman's *Memoirs* indicate that having tried and failed to make Stevenson an avowed candidate in the spring of 1952, the president decided to support the candidacy of Vice President Barkley. But Barkely withdrew early in the convention for lack of key northern support. Though Truman is silent on the matter, Barkley's active candidacy nearly was revived during the balloting, but the forces then aligning to revive it were led by opponents of Truman's Fair Deal, principally southerners. As a practical matter, the president could not have lent his weight to *their* endeavors and could back no one but Stevenson to counter them. The latter's strength could not be shifted, then, to Harriman or Kefauver. Instead the other northerners had to be withdrawn. Truman helped withdraw them. But he had no other option. See Memoirs by Harry S. Truman, vol. 2, *Years of Trial and Hope* (Garden City: Doubleday, 1956, copr. 1956 Time Inc.), pp. 495–496.

[8]The reference is to Stassen's public statement of July 23, 1956, calling for Nixon's replacement on the Republican ticket by Governor Herter of Massachusetts, the later secretary of state. Stassen's statement was issued after a conference with the president. Eisenhower's public statements on the vice-presidential nomination, both before and after Stassen's call, permit of alternative inferences: either that the president would have preferred another candidate, provided this could be arranged without a showing of White House dictation, or that he wanted Nixon on condition that the latter could show popular appeal. In the event, neither result was achieved. Eisenhower's own remarks lent strength to rapid party moves which smothered Stassen's effort. Nixon's nomination thus was guaranteed too quickly to appear the consequence of popular demand. For the public record on this matter see reported statements by Eisenhower, Nixon, Stassen, Herter, and Leonard Hall (the Republican National Chairman) in the *New York Times* for March 1, 8, 15, 16; April 27; July 15, 16, 25–31; August 3, 4, 17, 23, 1956. See also the account from private sources by Earl Mazo in *Richard Nixon: A Personal and Political Portrait* (New York: Harper, 1959), pp. 158–187.

[9]Stenographic transcript of presidential press conference, October 19, 1950, on file in the Truman Library at Independence, Missouri.

[10]Jonathan Daniels, *Frontier on the Potomac* (New York: Macmillan, 1946), pp. 31–32.

[11]Transcript of presidential press conference, June 18, 1958, in *Public Papers of the Presidents: Dwight D. Eisenhower*, 1958 (Washington: The National Archives, 1959), p. 479. In the summer of 1958, a congressional investigation into the affairs of a New England textile manufacturer, Bernard Goldfine, revealed that Sherman Adams had accepted various gifts and favors from him (the most notoriety attached to a vicuña coat). Adams also had made inquiries about the status of a Federal Communications Commisssion proceeding in which Goldfine was involved. In September 1958, Adams was allowed to resign. The episode was highly publicized and much discussed in that year's congressional campaigns.

[12]As reported in Marriner S. Eccles, *Beckoning Frontiers* (New York: Knopf, 1951), p. 336.

20

James David Barber

ADDING IT UP FROM THE PRESIDENTIAL CHARACTER

Over a period of twenty years, James David Barber, the James B. Duke Professor of Political Science and Policy Studies at Duke University, developed a psychological interpretation of presidential behavior. His book on the subject, The Presidential Character: Predicting Performance in the White House *(1985), includes an explanation of his method and theory as well as detailed accounts of the Nixon, Ford, Carter, and Reagan presidencies. Barber's model focuses on how early environment shapes personality, character, world view, and political style. He then looks at the "psychology of adaptation" through which a personality adjusts to the national political environment. Barber's work is important for its substance as well as for its ability to integrate psychological analysis with political analysis.*

The American public expects from presidents reassurance, a sense of progress and action, and a sense of legitimacy. According to Barber, the country goes through cycles during which one or another need becomes prominent. These cycles may predispose voters to select a president whose psychological profile best matches the public's dominant need of the time.

Barber has also written The Lawmakers: Recruitment and Adaptation to Legislative Life *(1965),* Citizen Politics: An Introduction to Political Behavior *(1972),* The Pulse of Politics: Electing Presidents in the Media Age *(1980),* Politics by Humans: Research on American Leadership *(1988), and a drama,* Erasmus: A Play on Words *(1981).*

This strange book, written in chunks over a period of twenty years, is addressed to the future. It is both less and more than history: less, in that it makes no claim to be the whole story of the Presidential past; more, in that it dares to draw from what has been a picture of what yet may be. It is meant to help the thoughtful and sensible citizen sort out the significant particulars of the next Presidential choice, but also to help us hear, despite the cackle of daily events, the fundamental cultural themes that echo through the White House time and time again. With luck and determination, we can use what we know to build the conditions for survival—even progress.

CHARACTER AND CULTURE

Before a President is elected, debate centers on his stands on particular issues, his regional and group connections, his place in the left-right array of ideologies. *After* a President has left office and there has been time to see his rulership in perspective, the connection between his character and his Presidential actions emerges as paramount. Then it becomes clear that the kind of man he was stamped out the shape of his performance. Recognizing this, we ought to be able to find a way to a better prescience, a way to see in potential Presidents the factors which have turned out to be critical for actual Presidents.

Look to character first. At least by the time the man emerges as an adult, he has displayed a stance toward his experience, a proto-political orientation. The first clues are simple: by and large, does he actively make his environment, or is he passively made by it? And how does he feel about his experience—is his effort in life a burden to be endured or an opportunity for personal enjoyment? From those two starting points, we can move to a richer, more dynamic understanding of the four types. The lives of Presidents past and of the one still with us show, I think, how a start from character makes possible a realistic estimate of what will endure into a man's White House years. Character is the force, the motive power, around which the person gathers his view of the world and from which his style receives its impetus. The issues will change, the character of the President will last.

The swirl of emotions which will surround the next President—and the one after that and the one after that—cannot be wished away. For better or for worse, the Presidency remains the prime focus for our political sentiments and the prime source of guidance and inspiration for national politics. The next and future Presidents will each inherit a climate of expectations not of his making. If he is lucky and effective, he can call forth from that climate new energies, a new vision, a new way of working to suit a perennially new age. Or he can help us drift into lassitude or tragedy. Much of what he is remembered for will depend on the fit between the dominant forces in his character and the dominant feelings in his constituency.

Deep in the political culture with which the President must deal are four themes, old in the American spirit, new in contemporary content. A President to suit the age must find in these themes a resonance with his own political being. The dangers of discord in that resonance are severe.

POLITICS AND THE DRIVE FOR POWER

Americans vastly overrate the President's power—and they are likely to continue to do so. The logic of that feeling is clear enough: the President is at the top and therefore he must be able to dominate those below him. The psychology is more complicated. The whole popular ethic of struggle, the onward-and-upward, fight-today-to-win-tomorrow spirit gets played out vicariously as people watch their President. The President should be working, trying, striving forward—living out in his life what makes life meaningful for the citizen at work. Life is tough, life is earnest. A tough, earnest President symbolizes and represents that theme, shows by the thrust of his deeds that the fight is worth it after all. Will he stand up to his—and our—enemies, or will he collapse? Has he the guts to endure the heat in the kitchen? Will he (will he please) play out for us the drama that leads through suffering to salvation?

To a character attuned to power, this popular theme can convey a heady message. It comes through loudest to the active-negative type, whose inner struggle between aggression and control resonates with the popular plea for toughness. For Wilson, Hoover, Johnson, and Nixon, and for active-negative Presidents in the future, the temptation to stand and fight receives wide support from the culture. The most dangerous confusion in that connection is the equating of political power—essentially the power to persuade—with force. Such a President, frustrated in efforts at persuasion, may turn to those aspects of his role least constrained by the chains of compromise—from domestic to foreign policy, from foreign policy to military policy, for instance, where the tradition of obedience holds. Then we may see a President, doubtful within but seemingly certain without, huffing and puffing with *machismo* as he bravely orders other men to die.

Short of that, the active-negative character may show his colors not in some aggressive crusade but in a defensive refusal—as Hoover did in his adamant stand toward direct relief. Although such a stand may undermine his immediate popularity, it too resonates with the culture's piety of effort. Paradoxically, the same public which may turn against a President's policy may respect him for resisting their demands. The President shares with them the awareness of an historical tradition of the lone hero bucking the tide of his times in favor of some eternal purpose. Particularly now that the President is restricted to two terms, in that second term the temptation to clean up one's integrity and long-term reputation with some unpopular heroism may be very strong indeed. This may not require an active-negative President to feel he must follow the martial model. What he may well feel impelled to do is to rigidly defend some position previously occupied, to translate some experiment into a commitment.

For a long time, potential Presidents attuned to the ethic of struggle will continue to appear in the candidate lists. For the child is father to the man, and they received their basic cast of mind a long time ago—as did many of their constituents.

POLITICS AND THE SEARCH FOR AFFECTION

Betimes the people want a hero, betimes they want a friend. The people's desire for community in an age of fragmentation, their need to sense themselves as members sharing in the national doings, strikes a chord within the passive-positive President. From his youth he has personified the politician as giver and taker of affection. There he found reward for his air of hopefulness in the scads of friends he attracted and the smiles he helped bring to their faces. Raised in a highly indulgent setting, he came to expect that almost everyone would like him and that those who did not could be placated by considerateness and compromise. He needed that. For behind the surface of his smile he sensed how fragile the supply of love could be, how much in need of protection was the impression he had that he was lovable.

The affectionate side of politics (much neglected in research) appeals to a people broken apart less by conflict and rivalry than by isolation and anxiety. Most men and women lead lives of *quiet* desperation; the scattering families, the anonymity of work life, the sudden shifts between generations and neighborhoods, the accidents a wavering economy delivers, all contribute to the lonesome vulnerability people feel and hide, supposing they are exceptions to the general rule of serenity. Politics offers some opportunities for expressing that directly, as when brokenhearted people line up to tell their Congressman whatever it is they have to tell. But for many who never tell anybody, politics offers a scene for reassurance, a medium for the vicarious experience of fellowship.

This can affect a President or Presidential candidate. He can come to symbolize in his manner the friendliness people miss. Whatever he is to himself, his look-on-the-bright-side optimism conveys a sense that things cannot be all that bad—and God knows he has more to worry about than I do. So there can develop between a President's cheerfulness and his people's need for reassurance a mutually reinforcing, symbiotic ding-dong.

Every President is somewhat passive-positive (and partly each of the other types); all have drawn a sustenance of sorts from the cheering crowds and flattering mail. At the extreme this sentiment can lapse over into sentimentality or hysteria, as with the "jumpers" for Kennedy screaming "I seen him, I seen him." Then the show business dimension of politics comes to the fore. The President as star brings his audience together in their admiration of him, lets their glamorization of him flow freely around the hall, where, for a moment at least, all experience simultaneously the common joy of his presence. The transformation of a middle-aged politician into a glamorous star is a mysterious process, one perhaps understood best by the managers of rock groups. A most unlikely case would be the political beatification of Eugene McCarthy. Somehow the man catches on, becomes an "in" thing; he ceases to be a curiosity and becomes a charismatic figure. What is important in that, besides the gratifications it supplies the public, is what it can do to the star himself. For a Lyndon Johnson it meant a confirmation of power. But for a passive-positive type, a modern-day inheritor of the Taft-Harding-Reagan character, such adulation touches deeper. The resonance is with his inner sense that such fleeting expressions of allegiance are the reality of affection.

These themes reinforce the obsession with technique that affects so much of contemporary political rhetoric. Political cosmetology becomes a fine art, despite the lack of evidence that it changes votes or polls. The money floods into the hands of those who know how to make a silk purse statesman out of a sow's ear politico. Politics is sexualized; the glance and the stance are carefully coached; the cruciality of just the right rhetorical flair is vastly exaggerated; the political club becomes a fan club. Ultimately the technique itself becomes an object of evaluation: people admire the man who does the most artful job of conning them. There are present-day equivalents aplenty of whom Harry Daugherty could say, as he said of Harding, "Gee, what a great-looking President he'd make!"

All of this can make an incompetent like Harding think he is not only qualified for high office but also personally attractive. That is the dividing line for the individual comparable to the transition to charismatic followership in the audience. The personal need for such pseudo-love is fundamentally insatiable—the applause pours into a bottomless pit. The larger political danger is that such a man will convince himself and others that he has untapped talents, only to discover later that he does not, and to reveal that to all who inquire.

The affection problem of a realistic politics is to help us love one another without lapsing into sentimentality or hero-worship. The passive-positive character feels the problem, but is too easily diverted by the sham and sentimentality of politics to do much about it.

POLITICS AND THE QUEST FOR LEGITIMACY

The Presidency exists solely in the minds of men. The White House is not the Presidency any more than the flag is the nation. This "institution" is nothing more than images, habits, and intentions shared by the humans who make it up and by those who react to them. There is not even, as in a church, a clearly sanctified place for it; the Oval Office is no altar—it is an office. The reverence people pay the President, the awe his visitors experience in his presence—all that is in their heads—and his. A fragile base for Presidential stability? Only to those who see in the tangible appurtenances of life a foundation more secure than man's sense of life's continuities.

In our culture the religious-monarchical focus of the Presidency—the tendency to see the office as a sort of divine-right kingship—gets emphasized less in chiliastic, evangelical, or even ecumenical ways than in a quest for legitimacy. The essential legitimating quality is trust. The problem is not in the succession—the transfer of power from one rightful ruler to the next; even after assassinations Americans do not hesitate to accord authority to the new President. Rather, it resides in a fear that the men entrusted to rule are proving all too human, are politicking away the high dignity and ancient honor of the Republic for hidden reasons of their own.

The dangers people seem to fear are two, pride and perfidy. Mechanically these come down to too little and too much compromise, but it is not a mechanical matter. Pride is feared when a President seems to be pushing harder and faster than the issues call for—and doing that more and more on his own, without proper consultation. FDR's attack on the Supreme Court is an example. The primal version is the fear of tyranny growing out of hubris. The response is to wish for a return to the Constitutional restraints, a reassertion of the basic system Americans have elevated to an article of political faith.

Perfidy stands for characterological betrayal, subtler than the constitutional form. Legitmacy is threatened not so much by one who would break the rules as by one who seems to break trust in the image of the President as dignified, episcopal, plain, and clean in character. Part of the public mind always realizes that the President is only a man, with all man's vulnerability to moral error; part wants to deny that, to foist on the President a priestliness setting him above the congregation. There is a real ambivalence here, one that makes it all the more necessary to reassert legitimacy in the Presidency when the pendulum swings too far. Presidents realize this. They try to be careful not to "demean the office." But especially after a time when the feeling has been growing that the Presidency is getting too "political" and that evil persons (Communists, grafters) are crawling too close to the throne, the call for a man of unquestionable honor will go out.

The appeal for a moral cleansing of the Presidency resonates with the passive-negative character in its emphasis on *not doing* certain things. It also reinforces the character attuned to moral appeals to duty. A man who cares little for the roils of politics or the purposes of policy may respond much more strongly to the appeal: save the nation, keep the faith, bring back the oldtime way of our forefathers. Such a man is eminently draftable. In the end he has no answer to the question, if not you, who? So he serves. In serving, the moral themes push his mind upward, stimulate whatever pontifical propensities he has. Especially if he is basically an apolitical man, unused to the issues and the informal processes of negotiation, he will find ways to rise above all that. For Coolidge the tendency was toward a proverbial, increasingly abstract rhetoric, for Eisenhower the drift was toward a Mosaic role—final arbiter of otherwise unresolvable conflicts. The effect is to unbuckle the President from politics, leaving the forces at hand free to charge off in their own directions.

CREATIVE POLITICS

But in the culture also is an awareness of these ills and dangers. The sham of the typical Presidential campaign has not gone unnoticed. The militant tough guys, the technocrats* who counsel so coolly about kill-ratios and free-fire zones, the puffed-up claims for low-budget programs, the violations of Constitutional rights rationalized as protections of Constitutional order, the substitution of abstract moralisms for substance—I am not the first to point out these pathologies. Amidst much confusion, the public, especially in an election year when attention is paid, sees with a slow but stubborn vision the very distortions its own needs have helped to create. The press and television help with that; a President or candidate who knows how to say simply what many feel deeply can make an even greater contribution to cutting away the underbrush of lies and bluster.

Nor does the people's disillusionment easily sour into despair. Kennedy's call for vigor stopped short with his murder; Johnson's initial politico-religiosity fell apart; Nixon pleaded for national reconciliation and then polarized opinion; Carter called for competence and seemed to practice its opposite. Yet aside from a few pathetic Weathermen and their Birchite conterparts, most Americans want to make the system work and are capable of doing so. The generation which went through the Wilson-Harding-Hoover disillusionments did recover. The cultural memory of that recovery has not disappeared, even in this age of the momentary. Beyond the candid confession of failure, the task of Presidential leadership these

**Technocrats:* individuals trained in a technical field, such as science or computer technology, who hold influential positions in a government agency with a technical or scientific mission. Their influence or power is based on technical expertise.

days is to remind the people that their past was not without achievement and that their future is not yet spoiled.

That is in the active-positive spirit. Those themes resonate with a character confident enough to see its weaknesses and the potentialities it might yet grow into. The active-positive Presidents did not invent the sentiments they called forth. They gave expressin in a believable way to convictions momentarily buried in fear and mistrust. From their perception of a basically capable public they drew strength for their own sense of capability. For like everyone else, active-positive Presidents feed on reinforcements from the environment. What is different about them is their ability to see the strengths hidden in public confusion and to connect with those strengths.

A goodly part of the contemporary disillusionment is the gap between what people see governments doing and what they hear politicians telling them. The rule is policy-making by-guess-and-by-God, always in a hurry. The odds of success—that is, actual, significant improvements in the lives of citizens—are reduced by the general lack of attention to the real results of policy. When people see the contrast between headline Washington "victories" and how it is to get to work in the morning, they wonder.

The active-positive Presidents help get past that gap by focusing on results beyond Washington. FDR's insistent curiosity about how life was going for people, Truman's hunger for "the facts," Kennedy's probing questions in the Cuban missile crisis illustrate how a character in concord with itself can reach for reality. Active-positive Presidents are more open to evidence because they have less need to deny and distort their perceptions for protective purposes. Their approach is experimental rather than deductive, which allows them to try something else when an experiment fails to pan out, rather than escalate the rhetoric or pursue the villians responsible. Flexibility in style and a world view containing a variety of probabilities are congruent with a character ready for a trial and error and furnish the imagination with a wide range of alternatives. A people doubtful about government programs as the final answer to anything might well respond to a candid admission of uncertainty, a determination to try anyway, and a demonstration of attention of results. The need for energetic, optimistic realism in the Presidency will be with us as long as that office endures. If we but pay attention to the characters who can offer that, we may yet move on to the future our children deserve.

LOOKING BACKWARD

Since 1972, when the first edition of *The Presidential Character* appeared, the political world has evolved almost as fast as did the writings about it. It is time to look back over those years—at the new biographies of the old characters, and at the important questions critics have raised about this study. In the Appendix, I lay out evidence that the book's basic typology may reflect real types of people rather than merely the population of my own imagination.

It would be surprising indeed if newfound revelations about twentieth-century

Presidents laid bare wholly new personalities. After all, the characters and styles and worldviews of Presidents have been scrutinized constantly from the time they first acquired plausible candidature until the present moment. The relevant power situations and climates of expectation are perpetually reappraised and reinterpreted, but the basic facts hold fairly constant. In a good many cases, though, new biographies light up new facets of a familiar President, clarifying obscurities and illuminating neglected paths of exploration.

William Howard Taft keeps his character in Judith Icke Anderson's substantial biography. In a rare psychological comment, she takes note of Taft the passive-positive: "To the person who feels insecure, inadequate, and exceedingly vulnerable in a potentially hostile and threatening world, love and admiration appear to be the only means of securing safety."[1] Taft got away from Washington at every opportunity, running away from conflict and critics, into the arms of adoring crowds. "I am mighty glad to see you," he told them in Montana, "And the reason why I am glad to see you is . . . that you are glad to see me."[2] Then after his Presidency, Taft expressed precisely the passive-positive's enthusiasm for the role of spectator: "You don't know how much fun it is to sit back . . . and watch the playing of the game down there in Washington, without any responsibility of my own." Taft's character persisted, but Anderson's biography makes clear that it was specifically his *Presidential* character, his stance toward *that* life, that brought Taft his terrible troubles. Once he made it to the Supreme Court bench, where conflict could be masked and muted in a way it could never be in the White House, then Taft could perform much more effectively. The Court's close collegial life suited his style, and his conventional worldview found congenial reinforcement.

As for *Woodrow Wilson,* the basic patterns hold up well through a flood of new writing. Wilson the active-negative whose ultimate rigidification burnt down his dream of world peace, Wilson the political orator, Wilson whose worldview was built around God's marching history—these findings persist. But new work, particularly Edward A. Weinstein's biography,[3] suggest clarifications of several Wilson mysteries. Nearly invisible in previous biographies, Wilson's mother Jessie turns out to have been a very strong influence. Her Scots ancestry dominated Wilson's family identification, not her husband's Irish heritage. Her relatives visited frequently through the boy's childhood. Jessie's attitude toward little Tommy was "wholly approving and uncritical," in contrast to his father's continual correction. And Jessie Wilson hovered over the boy, as her letters show, long after he needed her nurturing. Weinstein's description paints her as an unusually reserved person: intensely involved with her family, "she was often unhappy in her relationships outside the home. She had a great sense of status and personal dignity, and some of Dr. Wilson's parishioners thought that she felt superior and was cold and stand-offish."[4] That at least suggests a mother not fundamentally different from the mothers of Johnson and Nixon, a mother working out her status-loss problem—consciously or not—through her son.[5]

Weinstein also finds evidence that Wilson the child suffered from dyslexia. If true, that would go a long way to explain why he could not read well for so long a time and why his father found his inability inexplicable, frustrating, and in need of moral correction. Whether the reading disability or the paternal admonishments came first is trivial for our purposes—probably they grew together. An intelligent and diligent boy, he simply could not get his words right for years on end. All the more important to his self-esteem to gain control and keep it, whatever the cost.

It is clearer now how little is known about Wilson's childhood years, how speculative the hypothesized acounts are. Clearly Father Wilson was not the one-dimensional tyrant previous biographers portrayed. And curiously, and incident which might well have stamped Woodrow Wilson's soul when he was still a little boy has been largely neglected by his psychiatrically oriented biographers. War suddenly came home to him when Union prisoners and Confederate casualties were brought to his father's church in Augusta, Georgia, and little Tommy, with "his thin pale face," watched the defiant bluecoats billeted in the elm grove and heard and perhaps saw the agonies of the greycoats carried inside for emergency treatment. Might not those images—and the attendant terror and pity—have come back to him in powerful form much later, when war and peace became his own responsibilities? But whatever the exact configuration of origins, Wilson in the Presidency played out his tragedy in classic active-negative form.

Warren G. Harding, it is revealed, had one blue eye and one brown eye, a marvelous symbol of his characteristic ambivalence. A spoiled boy like Taft, Harding as an adult rewarded his indulgent mother by sending her flowers every Sunday morning for the rest of her life.[6] He himself blossomed into a bloviating political indulger. The rise of this unlikely sap to the Presidency is clarified in Robert K. Murray's book, *The Politics of Normalcy: Governmental Theory and Practive in the Harding-Coolidge Era*.[7] In 1920, anxiety was loose in the land. Postwar demobilization plunged the nation into economic chaos: surging unemployment, soaring inflation, then sudden price collapses, bankruptcies, bank failures, strikes, bombings, and rural riots. Theodore Roosevelt died. News of President Wilson's incapacity spread throughout the land. True, Harding offered certain oratorical skills, but what Murray describes as "The Great Mandate of 1920" owed a great deal to the public's readiness for a surcease of anxiety—to a massive shift in the national climate of expectations. People not only wanted a change, they wanted the particular kind of change Harding suggested: not challenge, but a "return to normalcy." 1920, it seems probable, represented a powerful reaction against the conditions of life Wilson and Wilsonism had come to represent. As in 1932, the public probably would have voted for nearly any more or less plausible alternative to what they had been suffering through. The electoral scrutinizing of Warren G. Harding, therefore, stressed not what he was, but what he wasn't—not Wilson. And of course, as ever, he and his pals read the result as a "mandate." Economic recovery followed. It is not at all out of the question that Harding, had he not died beforehand, could have been reelected in 1924 on a wave of prosperity, despite the emerging scandals.

Calvin Coolidge once welcomed reporter H. V. Kaltenborn to the Oval Office this way: "Sit down (pause) for a minute." Enough said.

A new biography by George N. Nash presents direct evidence on what was before mostly conjecture: that *Herbert Hoover* experienced his growing-up years as a long period of unhappiness. When his parents died and eight-year-old Herbert went to live with his stern Quaker uncle, his "sensitive nature" was "jarred" by the harshness of his new life, according to his brother Theodore. "I do not think he was very happy," the uncle wrote. "He always seemed to me to resent even being told to do anything by us although he did what he was told to do." Herbert poured out his continuing resentment in letters to his cousin Henrietta.[8] Idyllic accounts of Hoover's childhood love of the solitude of the woods and the stream need adjustment when it comes to social life: from age eight to age seventeen, when he went to Stanford, the boy knew mainly the pains of dependency on a dominating taskmaster.

Another evidential blank in the Hoover story was his role in the armed attack on the unarmed Bonus Marchers* in Washington in the summer of 1932. Was it fair to say they had been "gassed by order of President Hoover," as was alleged at the time? Apparently not. Donald J. Lisio writes that Hoover "did not authorize the rout, but tried to stop it."[9] Hoover "rejected issuing the insurrection proclamation." The military, particularly Douglas MacArthur† dashed off and did their dirty work, burning the Marchers' camp. On July 28, 1932, the officers came to the White House and "presented Hoover with a *fait accompli*, then triumphantly met the press."[10] Hoover shut up about his resistance and publicly supported his soldiers. He seemed an ogre. But in fact he served not as a commander in this political crime, but as an endorser, and a reluctant on at that. He was in process of rigidification—busily backing himself into a losing corner. The simple notion that he was a Nero, chuckling over the flames of his capital city, cannot be sustained. Like the other active-negatives, Hoover meant well.

Strange as it may seem, *Franklin Delano Roosevelt* continues to escape the psychobiographers. That historical hiatus stands as a symptom of psychology's focus on pathology, its difficulty in grappling with the dynamics of a creative personality. The result is to leave the twentieth-century's most significant politician virtually unanalyzed, except in the comparative style of books like this one. Recent attention seems to have been arrested by FDR's sex life which, were we to believe the more prurient accounts, would put him in line for the wheelchair Olympics. His son Elliott Roosevelt hints that FDR had long-term romantic attachments to both Lucy Mercer and Missy LeHand.[11] The rough side of FDR—the cruel side—comes out in Elliott's account of the deal he struck with Eleanor, who, having found his letters to Lucy, asked for a divorce, which in those days would have ruined him politically. They agreed to a divorce within

***Bonus Marchers*, or *Bonus Army*, or *Bonus Expeditionary Force*: over 12,000 World War I veterans who marched on Wahington during the summer of 1932, amid the Great Depression, demanding bonus payments for their wartime services. Half of the veterans returned home after the government claimed it could not fulfill their request and the rest, incredibly, were driven out by the U.S. Army using tanks and tear gas.

†*General Douglas MacArthur* (1880–1964): Supreme Commander of Allied Powers in the Pacific from 1945 to 1951. He also was Commander of the United Nations Forces in Korea from 1950 to 1951. As chief of staff of the United States Army (1930—1935), his leadership of the Army against the Bonus Marchers was widely criticized. MacArthur's public statements criticizing President Harry Truman's policies in the Korean War strained his relationship with Truman, who dismissed him in April 1951.

the marriage: no more intimate relations, but no public break. That resolution seems to have freed her for her own line of achievement and satisfaction and to have freed him for such comforts as he could find elsewhere.

William E. Leuchtenburg's superb study of Roosevelt's impact on his Presidential successors also shows how FDR could be cruel, as when he called General Marshall,* who desperately wanted the job, and dictated to him a telegram announcing that Eisenhower would run the invasion of Europe.[12] At the same time, characterologists such as Joseph Kennedy, father of John F., thought they discerned in the Roosevelt of 1932 "immaturity, vacillation, and general weak-kneed character," Leuchtenburg reports. Roosevelt's mysteriousness remains, despite his long years in the Presidential limelight. His kaleidoscopic image helps explain why the Presidents who came after him—including Ronald Reagan the "conservative"—could pluck from the repertoire of his personality those qualities most like their own, making of FDR, like Lincoln, an inkblot test of the observers' own projections. Contemporaries, too, we are reminded, could feed on that multifaceted persona. And Roosevelt himself could play all the Presidential parts; on election day in 1936 he put on a good luck charm—Andy Jackson's big gold watch chain.[13]

Harry S. Truman is rescued for the human race—from the clutches of his latter-day idolators—by the publication of letters, especially those to Bess, his wife, to Margaret, his daughter, and to himself, that is, the letters he wrote but never mailed, some because they were too sentimental, most because they were too angry to be politically effective. Harry Truman's struggle, a successful one I think, to overcome the active-negative trends in his character are illuminated in some of this correspondence. On a dark day in September 1946, for instance, he wrote, Dear Bess, "It seems that no one can be trusted any more to deal squarely with facts as they are."[14] But ten years later he straightened out his daughter Margie on the subject of trust:

> There's one thing that worried me in our phone conversation last night. You said no one is to be trusted. Maybe your dad, who has had more contacts and experiences with people than anyone alive, [can] tell you that more than 95% of all people can be trusted.
>
> If you don't trust the people you love and those who work for you in all capacities, you'll be the unhappiest and [most] frustrated person alive.
>
> Think of the immense number of people I've had under me—County Court, Senate, V.P. and President of the United States. I had two no-goods in the county setup, one in the Senate, and only two in the Cabinet, only two on the staff. Now the good ones added up to several hundred.
>
> . . . Well. Think about it, Baby.
>
> Your dad loves you and wants you to be happy—you can't be unless you trust and have faith in people.
>
> Dad[15]

Light is shed in the correspondence on Truman's difficulties in dealing with insubordinates like Francis Biddle, Henry Wallace, James Byrnes, and Douglas

**George C. Marshall* (1880–1959): U.S. general and statesman. Marshall served as the U.S. army chief of staff (1939–1945) and was appointed secretary of state (1947–1949) by Harry S Truman.

MacArthur—difficulties so great that they seem to have warped his memory of his own conversations.[16] As President, Truman felt he had to straighten out top policy makers who were mucking up his main lines of action. But he hated doing it. Such experiences tapped, I think, a long-time stress between his toughness and his softness as a superior. In the midst of Truman's first independent political success, his emergence as a capable officer in World War I, Truman was wrestling with this very problem. He rallied his fleeing troopers in "the Battle of Who Run." The fleers included the first sergeant. "I made some corporals and first-class privates out of those who stayed with me and busted the sergeant."[17] He wrote to Bess about that on November 23, 1918; on January 11, 1919, camped near Verdun in the rain, he wrote her again:

> The better I like 'em, the meaner I have to be to them just to show 'em that I'm impartial. You've no idea how I hate to call a man down. I'd almost rather take a beating than tell a man how good-for-nothing he is when he's done something he shouldn't. Two of my men overstayed a pass I gave them to Verdun the other day and I talked so mean to them when they came back that one of 'em cried and I almost let him off without any punishment. If we stay in this place much longer, I'll either have a disposition like a hyena or be the dippy one. If there's one thing I've always hated in a man it is to see him take his spite out on someone who couldn't talk back to him. I've done my very best not to jump on someone under me when someone higher up jumps on me, because I hate the higher-up when he does it and I'm sure the next fellow will hate me if I treat him the same way. Anyway I can't jump all over a man for doing something that I'm sure I'd have done myself if I'd had the opportunity and been in his place. Justice is an awful tyrant . . . [18]

Truman the active-positive worked his way through that problem—that is, he learned to recognize it in himself and to deal with it directly and effectively, if not completely, as his later troubles show. Truman could handle the weight of it. After he died, they found this little note in his desk drawer:

October 2, 1960

> Bess: I have decided to walk to the station. It will be my morning walk both ways. The grip isn't heavy.
>
> Harry S Truman[19]

Three new books on *Dwight D. Eisenhower* help considerably in clarifying a Presidential character still relatively obscure in 1972, before his letters and papers were fully available. The most interesting is by political scientist Fred I. Greenstein, who mines the new material to assess the hypothesis that Eisenhower, dismissed as a weak leader largely on the basis of his public performance, was really a highly effective "hidden-hand" President, working behind the scenes.[20] Biographer William Bragg Ewald, Jr. had noted Ike's use of "arm's-length strategies," but had concluded that the important Eisenhower legacy would be "the legacy not of what he *did*, but of what he himself *was*. And this is the most notable bequest that Dwight Eisenhower—and indeed George Washington—has left us."[21] Stephen E. Ambrose shares the others' admiration of Eisenhower—"a great and good man," says his first sentence; Ambrose's new volume traces Ike's history up to his Presidency.[22] For our purposes the excitement of these new studies is not so much their relevance to some global, great-or-not-great assessment of the Eisenhower Presidency as it is their provision of a second chance to figure out the Eisenhower character. History will, no doubt, continue in its up-and-down evaluations of this as well as all the other Presidents. What counts for prediction is estimating the nature and degree of risk entailed in the choice of a particular President.

Eisenhower the passive-negative comes through more clearly than before. The relative passivity (compared to the active Presidents) is clearer than it was in 1972[23] in his daily work schedule[24] and in the time he spent recreating—playing golf, for instance, about twice a week. Though he was an "activist" (as was Coolidge) in the sense of believing that people should be more active, he himself did not approach a Roosevelt or a Lyndon Johnson in the exertion of Presidential energy. His fidgeting and doodling and pacing at meetings, far from showing Presidential energy, show how impatient he was to get out of that business, particularly after his heart attack; Ike wrote in January 1956 that his doctor told him "to avoid all situations that tend to bring about such reactions as irritation, frustration, anxiety, fear, and above all, anger. When doctors give me such instructions, I say to them, 'Just what do you think the Presidency is?' "[25] But from the start Ike's behind-the-scenes activities were mild, to say the least, compared to the work of the active Presidents. He is continually discovered adopting strategies or conducting assaults which consist of little more than asking someone else to write a letter or make a phone call. "Well, all right, you see him and talk to him, but be very, very gentle," he tells Leonard Hall, who thinks Nixon can easily be bumped from the ticket in 1956.[26] He pursues a "strategy of remaining silent,"[27] maneuvers "to sidestep a potentially divisive encounter,"[28] is found "asserting his strategy of not criticizing others personally,"[29] and in myriad varieties of circumstances avoiding, reserving, refusing, shunning, submitting, and—in characteristic passive-negative fashion—feeling bothered by the necessary action of choosing inaction, of having to decide to step back from the brink of energetic commitment.

Eisenhower's stance toward his own Presidential experience is nowhere clearer than in newly revealed personal letters describing his decision to run again in 1956. "I suppose there are no two people in the world who have more than Mamie and I earnestly wanted, for a number of years, to retire to their home, a home which we did not even have until a year or so ago," he wrote his old pal Swede Hazlett on March 2, 1956.[30] "When I first rallied from my attack of September 24th, I recall that almost my first conscious thought was 'Well, at least this settles one problem for me for good and all. . . . ' As I look back, I truly believe that could I have anticipated in early October what later public reaction was going to be, I would have probably issued a short statement to the effect that I would determine as soon as possible whether it was physically possible for me to finish out this term, but that I would thereafter retire from public life." His first reason for nevertheless deciding to run (a reason that "has been mentioned to no one else") "had to do with a guilty feeling on my own part that I had failed to bring forward and establish a logical successor for myself," and thus that duty once again demanded he let himself be drafted. That sort of thing was always happening to him, he wrote: "When I consider how many times I have been driven away from personal plans, I sometimes think that I must be a very weak character." He marks as "defeats" his failure to stay out of politics after 1948 and his allowing "myself to be talked out of my purposes of announcing, in my Inaugural Address, that I was a one-term President only."[31] All that fits the passive-negative pattern to a T: the sense of reluctant and self-sacrificial service and the consequent air of suppressed anger, leaking out on rare occasion in outbursts of irritation, which must be quickly contained.

The reality behind Eisenhower's public grin—registered in hundreds of photographs—is interestingly generalized in a document Greenstein quotes, a draft introduction Eisenhower did not publish in his book *Crusade in Europe*. That his political campaign smile was a facade had been known, but so was his military campaign smile. Like President Ike, General Ike grinned to keep from weeping: in warfare "strain and tension wear away at a leader's endurance, his judgment and his confidence. . . . [T]he commander inherits an additional load in preserving optimism in himself and in his command. Without confidence, enthusiasm and optimism in in the command, victory is scarely obtainable." The commander's public optimism "has the most extraordinary effect upon all with whom he comes in contact. With this clear realization, I firmly determined that my mannerisms and speech in public would always reflect the cheerful certainty of victory—that any pessimism and discouragement I might ever feel would be reserved for my pillow. . . . I did my best to meet everyone from general to private with a smile, a pat on the back and a definite interest in his problems." Similarly his 1952 campaign featured "the candidate's stepping blithely out to face the crowd, doing his best to conceal with a big grin the ache in his bones and the exhaustion in his mind."[32]

The combat with depression consumes a good deal of the passive-negative's psychic evergy. The roots of the struggle in Eisenhower's case are helpfully traced in Ambrose's study. His smiling mother (in contrast to his sour father) believed in a certain kind of noninterference: "You can't keep healthy boys from scrapping," she said. "It isn't good to interfere too much." And she practiced what she preached. Once when bigger brother Edgar grabbed little Dwight's hair and began "to thump his head against the floor," other brother "Earl rushed in to help Dwight. Ida, without turning away from the stove, said sharply to Earl, 'Let them alone.' " Thus Ike learned "let them alone" at home, early.[33]

Ambrose confirms that "Sports remained the center of his life" right on into West Point.[34] When he injured his knee and had to quit football, he wrote his girlfriend Ruby, "Seems like I'm never cheerful any more," and "The fellows that used to call me 'Sunny Jim' call me 'Gloomy Face' now. The chief cause is this game pin of mine—I sure hate to be so helpless and worthless. Anyway I'm getting to be such a confirmed grouch you'd hardly know me."[35] But even after his benching, they joy of the team's victory could lift his heart: he wrote Ruby when Army beat Navy. "Back from N.Y.! and we surely turned the trick—22–9. Oh you beautiful doll! Some game, some game! Just a small crowd saw us do it, you know. Just 45,000 people. Sure was sad! . . . You should have seen us after the game. Oh! Oh! Oh! Believe me, girl, I *enjoyed* myself. Course I couldn't raise a riot for I was in uniform—but I went down to Murray's in a crowd of four—and we danced and ate—and oh say—the joy of the thing is too much—I feel my reason toppling."[36]

By contrast, when news of Ike's victorious election to his first political office came over the television in 1952, Mamie wept and, after a brief speech, Eisenhower threw himself down on a bed, exhausted." Claire Booth Luce* told him he would have to call Hoover. "Groaning, he went to the phone and put through a call to the last Republican President."[37]

What was tentative in 1972, Eisenhower's placement as a passive-negative, is buttressed by stronger and more complete evidence a dozen years later. The historical significance of that is considerable; the significance for the future more so. For it is not at all unlikely that another of these dutiful heroes will come along. The results may be dangerous to the national health.

The idea that Eisenhower achieved in private what other major Presidents achieved through public leadership is a hard case to prove. Newly revealed letters show a good deal of Eisenhower savvy about such matters as the East-West nuclear confrontation and a good deal of sound moral judgment about domestic threats to democracy. But the most important lines in these letters are the words across the top: "personal and confidential." Eisenhower's way left the public in the dark, again and again, as he pulled back from exploiting his popular strength for progressive purposes. That is clear in the matter of Senator Joseph R. McCarthy. Greenstein tackles that knotty business head-on, arraying lots of relevant evidence in a manner directly to the point. The description is convincing: Ike hid his hand and it was not a totally inactive one. He did in fact encourage others to go after McCarthy, and he wrote some forceful memos on the subject. But the large facts are unaffected. Ike stood aside while McCarthy ran rampant, ripping to shreds the careers and the civil liberties of innocent people. His excuse—that opposing McCarthy publicly would have enhanced the Senator's publicity—is simply implausible. McCarthy got enormous publicity with no help from the President. Indeed, every day that the nation sat in puzzlement waiting for the President to tell them whether McCarthy's charges were true or false, McCarthy's stock rose. Eisenhower's private huffing and puffing lacked public impact, while, for example, Dulles's† urgent cooperation in weeding from the State Department's overseas libraries works by Tom Paine and Dashiell Hammett sent a very loud message. So did Eisenhower's own political endorsement of McCarthy and the President's apparent indifference to McCarthy's slander of General George C. Marshall. And it was Eisenhower who went far beyond Truman's "loyalty" concept, beyond weeding out communist sympathizers in government

**Claire Booth Luce* (1903—1987): Republican member of the U.S. House of Representatives from Connecticut (1943–1947) and the U.S. ambassador to Italy (1953–1957). She was also the author of numerous plays.

†*Allen W. Dulles* (1893–1969): officer in the Diplomatic Service (1916–1926), deputy director of the Central Intelligence Agency (CIA) (1951–1953), and director of the CIA (1953–1961). He wrote *Germany's Underground* (1947), *The Craft of Intelligence* (1963), and *The Secret Surrender* (1966).

to going after "security risks"—innocents who might have something to hide and thus be subject to communist blackmail. The President left civil liberties far weaker than he found them. As for McCarthy, he was brought down when he attacked the Army, exposed his drunken demagoguery* to millions of television viewers, and caught hell from a tough little Yankee lawyer named Joe Welch. It was the Senate that condemned McCarthy. The President may have been tweaking around in private but he held back from spending his great popularity to secure the rights of citizens when the chips were down. In private, Ike likened McCarthy to Hitler. In public, he treated McCarthy as a respectable fellow Republican. On state together in Wisconsin, Ike let Joe shake his hand.

Eisenhower's failure in public leadership left other harmful legacies. That he bought a period of tranquility by postponing to the next decade action on a wide range of domestic problems still rings true. Shortly after taking office, he did bring the Korean conflict to a stop, perhaps by threatening to use nuclear weapons. South Korea subsequently installed a brutally repressive government. Eisenhower's indirection and delegation let the CIA knock over relatively progressive governments in Iran and Guatemala, without Congressional approval and with results the United States still, at this writing, has to struggle with, as our democracy is linked with some of the world's most vicious tyrants. Near the end of Eisenhower's reign, in 1960, Allen Dulles and some aides brought the President a plan for sabotaging a sugar refinery in Cuba. Eisenhower said, "Instead of this one-shot action, Allen, why don't you come back with a complete program?"[38] That question opened the way to the Bay of Pigs† disaster and to the confirmation of Castro's Cuban dictatorship.

But perhaps the most pervasive of Eisenhower's legacies swamped forward in his own party. Credited with establishing a responsible and pragmatic version of modern Republicanism, Eisenhower might have passed his torch to men of his own stripe. Instead, he lent his enormous prestige to the candidacy of Richard Nixon, whom he despised, and later to Barry Goldwater,‡ whose views were far afield from his. The opportunity to shape a real world party of the right in America slipped by.

The biographical rhythmics currently boosting Eisenhower are currently dipping *John F. Kennedy*, in a clutch of impassioned damnations from an interesting variety of perspectives. The Kennedy who mocked his own overhyped "charisma" must be chuckling up his ghostly sleeve at the overhyped yelps critics now produce. Each adds usefully to the store of information, but the analyses and interpretations too often waft away on the wings of this or that unanchored theory. *The Kennedy Neurosis*,[39] for example, comes at Kennedy from a psychoanalytic perspective. The few new details are lost in a sea of pejoratives, whereby nearly every act or thought or expression is given a pathological turn. Lacking

**Demagoguery*: practice of using emotional rhetoric to reinforce mass prejudices for the purpose of obtaining or holding political power.

†*Bay of Pigs*: site where exiled Cuban rebels, trained and supplied by the U.S. government, attempted an unsuccessful invasion of Cuba in 1961. President John F. Kennedy acknowledged his responsibility for the fiasco one week later.

‡*Barry Goldwater*: see footnote on page 188.

comparison with other Presidents, the book makes Kennedy sound too sick in the head to get through the day. *Pragmatic Illusions*,[40] on the other hand, sees Kennedy not as neurotically macho but as ideologically tepid: a President who, like the other liberals, is unwilling or unable to upset "the prevailing social or economic order,"[41] especially the dominance of big corporations. Kennedy policies are helpfully reviewed; how Kennedy should have attacked the foundations of American capitalism is not set forth. *The Kennedy Imprisonment*[42] offers little in the way of new facts and less in the way of balanced interpretation. The author's furious envy of Kennedy and all things Kennedyite finds vivid expression. A much more interesting (because politically real) interpretation is Lewis Paper's *The Promise and the Performance*,[43] although holding Presidents up against their pre-Presidential promises is unlikely to cast any of them in favorable light.

On the interesting, if speculative, question of whether or not Kennedy would have pulled back from a commitment in Vietnam* of Johnsonian proportions, Paper points out that in September 1963, Kennedy was saying on talk shows that it would be "a great mistake" to withdraw from Vietnam. As of them, Kennedy clearly stood among the hawks. But more convincing, and of opposite import, is the evidence Paper presents—not always in admiration—of Kennedy's flexibility, curiosity, and pragmatism. What the President would have done can never be known. But his brother Robert, according to Doris Kearns, was arguing for a softer line on Vietnam as early as 1963, and of course Robert Kennedy eventually became a leading opponent of the war.[44] That John F. Kennedy would have done the same is plausible; that he would have dug his own grave on the issue, as Johnson did, still strikes me as quite out of character.

Two obscurities about Kennedy's actual history are clarified in Herbert S. Parmet's 1980 biography.[45] Was his run and win for Congress in 1946 really a style-setting first *independent* political success?[46] His father virtually dictated some passages in young Jack's *Why England Slept* and in 1946 poured money and advice into his son's Congressional campaign. But it was Jack's campaign: he "made literally hundreds of speeches, not only in the district he eventually sought to represent but throughout the state,"[47] even though speechmaking was awkward for him at first, a trying ordeal. His father's biographer David E. Koskoff notes that "By the time he got very far into the 1946 campaign, Jack Kennedy began speaking more like a New Dealer and less like his father," and that after his victory in the primary Jack gave a paternity-free explanation: "The fact that I was the only veteran running is what did it."[48] Not long after he got to Washington, John and his father and a friend, Kay Halle, were talking at a cocktail party:

> "Kay," she remembered the father saying, "I wish you would tell Jack that he's going to vote the wrong way. . . . I think Jack is making a terrible mistake." At which the congressman turned to his father and said: "Now, look here, Dad, you have your political views and I have mine. I'm going to vote exactly the way I feel I must vote on this. I've got great respect for you but when it comes to voting, I'm voting my way."
>
> The Ambassador then turned to Halle, smiled, and said "Well, Kay, that's why I settled a million dollars on each of them, so they could spit in my eye if they wished."[49]

**Vietnam*: see footnote on page 194.

Kennedy's subsequent voting record confirms the many cases in which father and son diverged, especially on foreign policy. "We don't even discuss it any more," said Congressman Kennedy. "I've given up arguing with him."[50] Father was there, at the other end of the telephone line, but it was the son who decided when to call, when to listen, and when to go his own way.

His way in the House of Representatives lacked Kennedy vigor; it was puzzling, to me in 1972, why he had not done more, even as a freshman. Parmet has a strong explanation: Kennedy was sick. Representative Richard Bolling said, "He was a frail, sick hollow man when I saw him in 1947." and "people with knowledge of his physical pain," Parmet explains, "regarded him as shy, even somewhat of a loner."[51] On the way to a visit to the Soviet Union, he suddenly fell ill in London. A British doctor said he would be dead in less than a year. He was rushed back to a hospital in New York. He himself told Joseph Alsop he expected to die in his early forties. Kennedy had Addison's disease, a "marked adrenocortical insufficiency," which would have killed or incapacitated him had not cortisone saved him.[52] Kennedy's performance as a freshman Congressman thus owed much less to his psychological than to his physical condition. He was not particularly shy, not a loner in a withdrawn sense; he *hurt*, badly, and that tied him down. Never completely freed of that burden, Kennedy over the ensuing years improved markedly and learned to manage his illness (including concealing it) so as to reveal his characteristic vigor and elan.

If Robert A. Caro is right, much of the *Lyndon Johnson* story as recounted by Lyndon Johnson has to be taken with a large grain of salt.[53] For example, his supposed genius as a Congressional coalition-builder owed a good deal to his persuasive skills, but he was also the man with big Texas money to pass out for Congressmen hungrily in need of campaign funds. This was "the basic source of Johnson's power on Capitol Hill," in Caro's judgment; the Johnson Treatment razzle-dazzle pawings and starings and rantings "were only tassels on the bludgeon of power."[54]

And the San Marcos *College Star* editorials appearing over the name of "Editorial Writer Lyndon B. Johnson"—and analyzed up, down, and sideways in subsequent biographies—were written by a quiet little fellow named Wilton Woods, pretty much on his own. "Lyndon was always loading me down with work," Woods reported. "He'd say, 'Write an editorial on Thanksgiving.' I'd say, 'Where am I going to get the dope?' He'd say, 'Go to the encyclopedia.' "[55] Thus the passages quoted above on page 119 may possibly express the emerging Johnson worldview, but only as filtered through language Mr. Wilton Woods thought Lyndon would like. On the other hand, Caro confirms that "All the traits of personality which the nation would witness decades later—all the traits which affected the course of history—can be seen at San Marcos naked and glaring and raw. The Lyndon Johnson of college years was the Lyndon Johnson who would become President."[56]

Then there is the Johnson adolescent hegira to California, where, as a teenage runaway, "Up and down the coast I tramped, washing dishes, waiting on tables, doing farm work when it was available, and always growing thinner," said Johnson,[57] describing what could be taken as a lenten interlude in an otherwise id-dominated period. Not so, says Caro. The real story, if Caro has it, is a good deal more consonant with Johnson's typical mode of operation. "What Johnson actually did, from beginning to end of his fabled stay in California," Caro writes, was to "work in his cousin's paneled office and live in his cousin's comfortable home." As soon as he got to California, Johnson phoned the cousin, lawyer Tom Martin, and asked for a job; Martin phoned the Johnsons in Texas, got their consent, picked up Lyndon and bought him two new suits on the way home to Martin's four-bedroom ranch house. The lawyer was glad to take the boy on as clerk—to cover up for him during his long and frequent absences from the office with his actress girlfriend and extensive supply of bottled gin. Seventeen-year-old Lyndon plunged in; soon he was virtually practicing law on the telephone. Realizing that that could get him into big trouble, Lyndon went home quick—not two years later, but less than a year after the "runaway," and not as a hungry hitchhiker but as a well-fed boy driven to his own front door by Tom Martin's father in a big Buick.[58] In *The Politician: The Life and Times of Lyndon Johnson*, biographer Ronnie Dugger presents a similar account, adding the story Lyndon told his Aunt Jessie as to why he had quit cousin Tom's job: "Well, I'll just tell you right now, he charged them actresses from two to five thousand dollars to get them a divorce. Aunt Jessie, you know that wasn't right. I knew that wasn't right, quickly I got enough money to come home and I come home. I just went off and left him."[59]

In *Lyndon Johnson and the American Dream*,[60] Doris Kearns may be too quick to take aging Johnson's word for what youthful Johnson had done and been, but she succeeds better than any in depicting the Johnson worldview in its perfected form, especially the mythic Western and Southern themes swirling through his imagaic history. Thus tough Johnson could draw on the frontier heritage; speaking of Vietnam in 1965, he said, "We have kept our guns over the mantel and our shells in the cupboard for a long time now. And what was the result? They are killing our men while they sleep in the night. I can't ask our American soldiers out there to continue to fight with one hand tied behind their backs."[61] In contrast, kind Johnson could draw on the charitable Southern way: speaking that same year, 1965, to Congress, he remembered his days as a teacher in Cotulla, saying "Somehow you never forget what poverty and hatred can do when you see its scars on the hopeful face of a young child. . . . It never occurred to me in my fondest dreams that I might have the chance to help the sons and daughters of those students and to help people like them all over the country. But now I do have that chance—I'll let you in on a secret—I mean to use it."[62] As the war crisis deepened, Johnson's internal crisis intensified. In the end, "I was bound to be crucified either way I moved," he said.[63] Kearns pierces to the childhood root of that conflict. "From his earliest days," she writes, "he had learned that if he chose his father, he might jeopardize the love and respect of his mother; if he chose his mother, his identity as a man would be in danger."[64] Rarely has the fundamental active-negative dilemma been more concisely defined.

Lyndon Johnson's ultimate political ambition was fulfilled on Election Night 1964, when his Presidential power was blessed in a massive popular victory. Did that make him happy? That night and the next morning he grouched around, wondering whether he had beaten FDR's 1936 vote record.[65]

The idea that *Richard M. Nixon* would retire to quiet contemplation never made sense and has not held up. He keeps working on a comeback, counting on some combination of public amnesia and forgiveness. An interesting feature of that effort has been his attempt to associate himself with power and prominence. His 1982 book *Leaders*[66] might have been predicted; in prose and pictures, Nixon puts himself up there with *Churchill, de Gaulle, MacArthur,* and *Adenauer*—indeed above them, as he reaches for a status from which to condescend. It is a far reach. Churchill, we learn, shook Nixon's hand and "said he was very happy to meet me for the first time."[67] Nixon tells Churchill he suffers from seasickness. Churchill says, by Nixon's report, "Young man, don't worry. As you get older, you'll outgrow it." These historic moments recorded, Nixon goes on to help Churchill with his oratory: "In his first speech to the House of Commons as Prime Minister, Churchill said, 'I have nothing to offer but blood, toil, tears, and sweat.' He could well have added *leadership* to the list."[68] Nixon's post-Presidential recreations included visitations (there is no other word) with two old leaders in New York's Waldorf Towers, Herbert Hoover (31A) and Douglas MacArthur (37A), who no doubt welcomed the chance to share their disdain for Eisenhower, Kennedy, Truman, and the like with a fellow disdainer. Nixon's first meeting with MacArthur got off to a good start: "MacArthur walked toward me as I entered the room and took both of my hands in his. He said, "How good of you to come" and introduced me to Mrs. MacArthur. . . ."[69]

It is plausible that Nixon has read of—maybe even read in—*The Presidential Character;* as early as the spring of 1972 someone in the Nixon White House issued the opinion that the book amounted to "psychobaloney." Whether Nixon was responding to the book or to other stimuli at large in the culture, it is interesting that he dwells so much on the problem of his negativity. According to Fawn M. Brodie, in a 1981 biography stressing the psychological Nixon,[70] the President spent Christmas Eve, 1972, with a strange concern. He was at Key Biscayne. He had called a 24-hour halt in his notorious "Christmas bombing" in Southeast Asia. Unable to sleep, he wrote this in his diary at a recorded 4:00 a.m.: "The main thought that occurred to me at this early hour of the morning the day before Christmas, in addition to the overriding concern with regard to bringing the war to an end, is that I must get away from the thought of considering the office at any time a burden. I actually do not consider it a burden, an agony, etc., as Eisenhower and also to a certain extent Johnson. As a matter of fact, I think the term glorious burden is the best description."[71] A decade later, in the last chapter of *Leaders*, the same problem persists. Titled "In the Arena," the chapter has nothing in particular to do with leaders other than Nixon himself and his task of making sure he has the right feelings.

"Power is not for the nice guy down the street or for the man next door." Nixon writes. As President, he found "most irritating" the "gushing query: 'Isn't it fun to be President?' " To speak of the exercise of power "as 'fun' trivializes and demeans it. One who believes that his own judgment is best, even though fallible, and who chafes at seeing lesser men mishandle the reins of power yearns, even aches, to hold those reins himself. Watching another bungle and blunder can be almost physically painful. Once he has the reins, he relishes their use." And on and on: "To enjoy power, he has to recognize that mistakes are inevitable and be able to live with them. . . . Unless a leader cares so strongly about the issues he must deal with that things like 'fun' become simply irrelevant, he ought not to be a leader and will probably be an unsuccessful, maybe even a dangerous, one. He should carve out time for recreation, and this can include 'fun', however he defines it, but he must keep the separation between this and his work. . . . I do not mean to suggest that I regarded the presidency as a 'splendid agony' or in any of those other self-pitying terms sometimes applied to it. I wanted the presidency. I struggled to get it and I fought to keep it. I enjoyed it, most of the time—but, as with most leaders, not in the sense of fun. . . . There are few satisfactions to match it for those who care about such things. But it is not happiness. Those who seek happiness will not acquire power and would not use it well if they did acquire it."[72]

Nixon the negative thus is to be found perpetually turning over the rock of his affections, perpetually rediscovering that no merry moss is growing there. It is impossible to imagine any of the positive Presidents, from Teddy Roosevelt to Reagan, picking so compulsively at a little word like "fun." They felt it; they did not need to define it.

Nixon presumes to reappear in a forgetful world, offering advice on the proper uses of power. In an interview, biographer Seymour Hersh offers a reminding account of what Nixon had done before and immediately after this book got printed and sold:

> My version of it is the guy gets in office in January, within two months he starts secretly bombing Cambodia, he's got a secret policy to end the war in Vietnam, he's making secret threats; by May, four months into his administration, he begins the wiretapping that lasts 21 months, the secret bombing that lasts 14 months. He took 110,000 tons of bombs out on Cambodia without anybody knowing about it. In '70, he can operate with impunity against Allende in Chile and also against the American anti-war movement through domestic spying by the CIA, he's got the CIA working at home and abroad. In '71, if he wants to, and he does, he sets up an internal police force and they go after Dan Ellsberg, they break into his psychiatrist's office in Beverly Hills and they get away with that.
>
> Somebody comes to him in June '72 and says they had trouble with a wiretap in Larry O'Brien's office in the Democratic headquarters, should we reinstall it. Is this man going to think twice before saying sure? This man's been able to drop 110,000 tons of bombs on Cambodia without being nailed? Who's he afraid of?[73]

No doubt Nixon's biographical day will come, and he will be revealed in new, more favorable light. So the scythe of history swings, harvesting for authors the fruits of their novel plantings and prunings. Biographies cycle in and out of evaluative light and shadow. Yesterday's villain, the hero of today. What wise citizens will attend to is not the is-he-great dimension, but the what-was-he dimension, which opens the way to an understanding of what-will-he-be the next time a Nixon comes around.

As for the post-Nixon Presidents—Ford, Carter, Reagan—no doubt new studies will shed new light on their achievements and debasements. The biographical imagination will combine with paper revelations to produce new insights which, however, I predict will leave the basics of this book intact.

ANSWERING THE CRITICS

A critic, they say, is the fellow who goes out on the battlefield after the battle and shoots the wounded. *The Presidential Character* has not been without its critics, some of whom show so little interest in the problem the book addresses that it would take a whole course in American politics to straighten them out. Those who deny that who the President is can make a mighty difference in public policy, for example, ought to read other books before they take on this one. Those who think social science is poised at the brink of perfection—almost ready to explore and prescribe with scientific precision—surely should not take time from their own production of such works to study this one. Those whose taste is for political entertainment (wondering what the king is doing tonight) can find much zippier stories in the grocery store press. But not all the critics drop into these dustbins of inquiry. Responding to serious concerns about how to improve our chances for better Presidential choice can at least help clarify what I have meant to do in these pages, even if the achievement still falls short.

1. *Bias*. The easiest criticism is to assert that I have cooked my facts to suit my theory or my own political philosophy or partisan purpose. If examples are offered, the criticism can be dealt with and perhaps profited from: history corrects history. Lacking examples of supposed bias, my interest in the criticism flags. The saving fact is this: the information this book relies on is not my secret preserve. It is public knowledge. And it is, for Presidents, quite extensive. Progress in this field will happen, if at all, by *testing alternative theories against the facts*. The information is there waiting for the critic who wants to demonstrate that his theory fits the empirical reality better than mine does, that I have ignored or slighted or hyped data which support a more useful pattern of prediction.

2. *Personalism*. Does *The Presidential Character* put too much stress on the psychology of an individual? What about the institution of the Presidency? What about the situation a President is trying to deal with—does not that shape action importantly? What about the impact of events—unpredictable lightning bolts which transform the political landscape? Can you really boil it all down to the psyche of one middle-aged man?

Not all, I'd say, but a lot. Please notice that the book includes, for every President, an account of the power situation and the climate of expectations extant at the time. The world beyond the President's nose is not ignored. But the stress is on the person; in the study of the Presidency, that is realism. For in fact—however much we might wish it otherwise—the Presidency remains an extraordinarily personalized office. It has grown its own bureaucracy (the White House staff, the Executive Office of the Presidency), but the bureaucrats, like the press, concentrate enormous curiosity and the most arcane calculations on the Presidential state of mind. They understand that, insofar as the Presidency is concerned, situations and events take their political coloration and direction from the ways the President and the intimate aides he has selected interpret them. In short, personalism in the Presidency is an existential reality, not the product of some exotic psychological theory. The way to reform that, if it needs reform, is not to deny it, but to confront and correct it.

3. *Citizen shrinks?* A comic criticism is that the book is written in ordinary English and therefore cannot be serious social science. On the contrary, the discipline of writing for the public rather than for specialists only is more, not less, rigorous. Put into American, a significant proportion of social science reveals itself as fantastic or banal. Writing for the culture at large opens the theory and data to a much wider arena of competition, including, but reaching far beyond the obscure little circles in which technicians discuss the public business in a private language. Still, are citizens capable of making these difficult character judgments? Shouldn't the public debate stick to the issues rather than getting involved in personal psychology? I think the first answer is that the choice is a false one: the public not only can make character judgments, they *must* make them, and thus they *do* make them. A person must be picked for President, a person judged better for that job than alternative persons. From day one of the Presidency right down to the present day, public discussion has centered on the qualities of those particular human beings—including, but far from confined to, what they hoped to do if elected. The question is not whether citizens should get into the act of psyching out Presidents, but how they can do that better.

There is room for a great deal of improvement in public deliberation on the choice of a President. The key to that improvement is the progress of journalism, for the public at large is almost totally dependent on journalism to tell us what we need to know about potential Presidents. While they are still few and far between, certain highly professional journalists have taken to generating data on candidates' backgrounds, practices, and perceptions in interesting and informative style. Much of it comes too late: after the conventions, the candidate biographies appear. Deeper, longer stories may be postponed to inauguration day. But the experience of repeated Presidential failure has aroused public demand for, and thus the journalistic supply of, analyses of character, style, and worldview, along with all the horserace hoopla, campaign travelogues, and utopian issue pieces. In another book, *The Pulse of Politics,* I explore how journalists could enhance, at one and the same time, their popular appeal and their contribution to public judgment on these matters. Nothing less than the reshaping of the democratic dialogue will address this fundamental problem, and the journalists who ask the questions and report the answers will shape that conversation for good or ill.

4. *Psychoanalytic mumbo jumbo?* Unless the historians have missed him completely, the United States does not seem to have had a psychotic President—that is, a President suffering from such terrible mental illness that he cast himself adrift from the real world. There ought to be a psychiatrist in the White House, as part of the President's medical team, in case that comes along, especially in this nuclear age in which even a temporary lapse into insanity could be fatal for us all. But that horror is likely to develop, if it ever does, after a President is ensconced in the Oval Office. In the selection phase, with its continuous public

scrutiny, Presidential psychosis would stand out like a sore thumb and relegate the candidate quickly to the political outer darkness. It would take a psychotic genius to wend his way through the multifarious jumps and dives the system sets for him without revealing his broken personality.

This book addresses a different problem: short of psychoses, how can we identify patterns of likely Presidential performance before the election? Psychoanalysis, which is essentially a personal therapy, can help and harm that effort. The harm is the wildly speculative overinterpretation of blips of behavior indicative of deep-running currents of the unconscious. Freud's interest in errors as one clue (among many) to underlying personality patterns finds in the campaign gaffe story its mocking imitation. An isolated little verbal mistake is snatched from the flow of experience and turned into an icon of neurosis. It may take weeks for the candidate and his media managers to get it back into context, twisting and turning through various apologetic, explanatory, and expiational rituals. That is a silly business. Its predictive batting average is approximately zero. Anyone who thinks this is that kind of book ought to see his or her psychiatrist.

The helpful link between psychoanalytic literature and what goes on in these pages is a shared interest in pattern discernment. Year after year, patients have been bringing to the mind-doctors their individual terrors and worries. Each is unique, like a fingerprint. But like fingerprints, the "presenting symptoms" patients display are patterned. The same basic bundles of trouble show up again and again, enabling the psychiatrist to diagnose before he prescribes. Which therapy works best is far more controversial than which familiar pattern is present. Like many other observers, then, psychoanalytic ones aid in the work of President-picking by systematically telling what they see, in the light of what main similarities among cases their colleagues have noticed through the years.

5. *The Iron Box.* Before one takes comfort in the fact that his critics contradict one another, he should entertain the possibility that both sides are right. On the one hand, the book jams together such strange combinations as Wilson and Nixon, Taft and Reagan, Coolidge and Eisenhower, Ford and Roosevelt—obviously very different folks. On the other hand, it details the peculiarities of individual lives, thus obviously sacrificing pattern for the variety of cases. The problem with such criticisms is in the word "obviously." For what is similar and what different is only superficially obvious. Newton's various laws hold for big rocks and little rocks, round ones and square ones, blue ones and brown ones. Presidents different in many ways may be similar in crucial ways. The similarities are very important, because it is only by the discernment of similarity that generalization and, consequently, prediction can be made. Science—including social science—progresses by the extension of webs of similarity? The real question is, how far can we go with how few character similarities The answer is empirical, but we cannot get to the answer until the question is posed in meaningful—not obvious—terms.

To proceed to the next question, namely what more can we learn by reviewing the uniqueness of the case, in no way contradicts the first question. The one adds to the other. Placing an individual in a category is an act of abstraction, not an assertion of identity. The concrete, individual life history details fill in the broadbrush sketch. Indeed, in the very process of categorical placement, one brings up evidence pointing in other directions, so that, for example, one notes Kennedy's tendency to withdraw (passive-negative), Truman's compulsive tendencies (active-negative), and Roosevelt's bent for compliance (passive-positive), though on balance all three are active-positives. It is a matter of dominance, of regnancy of certain qualities over others, rather than "pure" types unsullied by variation. The advance over uniformity or randomness in such a scheme is what makes it worth the trouble.

6. *Fake active-positives?* Did I teach Jimmy Carter how to smile? Did Ronald Reagan ride his horse to make me think him active? Aside from fleeting megalomaniacal moments, I doubt it. Neither needed my book to motivate him to seem to be what our culture wants him to be: energetic and optimistic. Thus Eisenhower, even without the benefit of *The Presidential Character*, pasted his campaign smile over his bored brain and gave up his twice-a-week golf for the rigors of the campaign trail. Even Herbert Hoover was known to grin while campaigning. How then can we make reasonable assessments of and predictions about candidates who are acting in such uncharacteristic ways? Even the campaign biographies and, later, heavily partisan first-term accounts are notably distorted in their reporting. Therefore, are not the data themselves far too shaky to sustain the theory?

As for the performance during the campaign, I agree. the *average* candidate for President is not a practiced professional actor: he will have a hard time keeping up a character-contradicting act over a period of months. But some can come close and a few, like Reagan, have the dramatic talent to play Henry V while feeling like Polonius, for weeks on end. Furthermore, the role of campaigner contrasts markedly with the role of President, so that reactions to the one may be significantly different from reactions to the other. The campaign worldview, for example, is hypothetical and subjunctive—what he would do—as distinct from the visions upon which a President has to act. The campaign tests style differently from the Presidential tests; Presidential negotiating skill, for instance, gets little examination in the rush of campaigning. Running for President is part of being President, typically, as a race for a second term looms ahead. But the regular Washington work is so different from campaigning in critical ways that it would be folly to read the campaign to find the President.

The corrective is to survey the candidate's *past:* how, over a long period of years, has he behaved and expressed himself on the key questions? That does mean reliance on biographies or journalism, with their partisan biases. But for the particular purpose of predicting performance in the White House, we are in the first place not particularly interested in the biographer's evaluations. What we are after are reports of experiences, not attributions of virtue or vice. Quite often even a quite biased account will furnish *information* of value and interest for testing categorical hypotheses. Of course, politicans and writers have been known to make up stories. There the best corrective is another biography or deep profile, preferably written from a different perspective, against which to check the facts. Not even that process eliminates error, as the revelations about Lyndon Johnson's history, recounted above, make clear. But by concentrating on the time before the Presidential bug bit the man and by drawing on as wide a variety of sources as practical, the researcher can usually move a quantum leap beyond the casual impressions of the campaign. There the truth will out. Jimmy Carter's mother taught him to smile. Ronald Reagan was riding horses back when he was still an FDR Democrat.

7. *The Mechanists.* A "model"—squares and circles connected by lines and arrows—is not to be found in *The Presidential Character.* Neither is a kind of chemistry manual where another researcher can pop together ingredients in given proportions and automatically produce a character analysis. There are still in social science some incredible optimists who really believe we are on the verge of breaking through into a wonderful land of mechanical research, in which highly significant findings are ground out of little whirring models set in motion by precise instructions. That has been about to happen for far too many years now. In fact, the results to date have been less than inspiring. In real politics, strictly structural-mechanical reforms have been noted for "unanticipated consequences." In political science, the mechanists' awesome techniques typically turn out eminently neglectible results. The attempt to squeeze the blood of culture and history out of the research enterprise has not, so far, done much to strengthen knowledge.

The findings in this book do not depend upon the author's authority or insight, if any, because the evidence and inference are right out there in the open for all to see and test as they see fit. But this work does depend on a degree of common sense. The "instruments" and "operations" involved are simple: you read biographies and take notes when you find material relevant (pro or con) to the various hypothesized key concepts, such as first independent political success. Not claiming to be Freud, my approach is like his, as expressed in the first sentence of *The Defense of Neuro-Psychoses:* "After a close study of several patients suffering from phobias and obsessions a tentative explanation of these symptoms forced itself upon me; and as it later enabled me successfully to divine the origin of similar pathological ideas in other cases, I consider it worthy of publication and of further tests." It is important to keep awake while reading, to notice all the appropriate incidents, to hold in mind the comparative context, to prefer the specific to the global statement, to move toward a judgment of the balance among competing interpretations—in other words, to use one's head and keep at it.

8. *Change in adulthood.* It seems unfair to the middle-aged to suggest that character, worldview, and style are pretty well set by the time young adulthood is over. Our culture has always valued change, has often confused it with progress. Ours is the land of beginning again. The dominant religion preaches the possibility of late-life salvation. In recent years, many have switched careers and spouses well after thirty, and many have shifted "life styles" as they move into the "golden years." New research has also charted interesting patterns of development in adulthood that should contribute significantly to our understanding of political leadership.

My reading of the biographies and psychological studies still leaves me thinking that the weight of the evidence is for continuity over change. Every character elaborates itself throughout life, but after thirty or forty years character is rarely transformed. Styles and worldviews are more malleable, but there too the continuities are more impressive than the changes. In short, given the present state of knowledge of the subject, I would advise the citizen choosing a President not to count on major changes in basic personality, basic beliefs, or basic political skills as that creature of habit moves into White House. The scientific question remains an empirical one: the mere assertion that change is possible is trivial. What is needed is research to test the significance and explanatory and predictive power of theories of mildlife change applied to real life politicians.

9. *Downplaying worlview.* Worldview is not neglected in any case depicted in *The Presidential Character.* But it clearly gets short shrift compared with character and style. Again, this becomes an empirical question; we need studies of the hypothesis that the worldview of a President-to-be is a valuable (i.e., prediction-improving) clue to the performance of a President-as-is. My reading is that not even Herbert Hoover carried through consistently on his pre-Presidential beliefs and that not even Reagan, that supposedly ultimate ideologue, can be scored high on worldview carrythrough. But the material is there, waiting for the research which will demonstrate the power of belief as predictor.

It is natural for scholars, whose own world is a world of ideas, to make more of political belief systems than the facts warrant. In public opinion research, it came as shocking news when the early voting studies showed how little attention people paid to "ideology" in the Eisenhower years. We tend to forget that the dominant American political belief has been pragmatism, an anti-ideology, a philosophy of not putting too much weight on philosophy. Politicians in particular, perhaps even more than their counterparts in business, tend to run with their fingers in the air, testing the popular breeze to find the currently compelling concepts. Sorting back through Presidency after Presidency, one encounters instance after instance of principle adjustment, so that a behaviorally meaningful concept of worldview has to be pitched at a relatively high level of abstraction. Certainly "conservative" and "liberal" do not go far as explainers of what happens.

Perhaps one day we will get a President whose character and style lend great force to a mistaken worldview—say, an active-positive fascist rhetorician. Such a President could, I suppose, do considerable harm. But in the historical cases reviewed in this book, no active-positive character—of whatever worldview—did, or was likely to, let an ideological commitment carry him over the brink into political disaster. Given time to see harmful consequences actually developing into tragic ones, the active-positive turns aside from the path of rigidification. In economic policy, environmental matters, the maneuvering of alliances, and other familiar lines of policy, in which disaster can be avoided by learning, by the observation of the actual course of events, there should be time for a reasoning and life-loving leader to see, think, and dodge.

Given time . . . but there is one decision-area in which time is disappearing: nuclear attack, by accident or design. Our survival may depend on the emergence of a new dimension of political imagination, the capacity of leaders to project from the realities of the day into the probabilities of the future. This capacity acquires an urgent relevance in the picking of a President.

10. *Inside my head.* The funniest critics are those who focus on where I got

the book's basic typology. A very wide selection of original thinkers have been suggested, ranging from Karen Horney and Harold Lasswell to Eric Berne and Norman Vincent Peale. Surely I stole it somewhere, the thesis seems to be, and once we find out where, we will be in a position to assess its validity. At least one critic has suggested I got it from him, but then, alas, ruined it. These originologists suppose a predestined course once the intellectual ball starts rolling.

The truth is simpler. Having been committed to institutions of higher education since age sixteen, I had read a fair amount when I wrote my doctoral dissertation, pushing age thirty. At least some residue of that reading was in my mind as I tried to make sense of responses some state legislators had given to my inquiries, responses which seemed strangely inconsistent in that they showed virtually no relationship between measures of satisfaction and measures of activity. By a twist of the mental dial, I entertained the conjecture that the data might be right—and if so, how could that be? It could be if there were legislators who enjoyed passivity and others who were disappointed with activity. And so there were, in significant numbers and (when one went into their interviews) displaying common patterns of adaptation. The crucial step was the question, not the answer. And that was, of course, but the first step in a long process of detailed studying, checking and cross-checking, reading and elaborating and extending, which eventually gave shape to the present effort.

It is impossible for me to sort out which of my teachers in their classrooms and in their books may be guilty or innocent of what degree of influence. I take up the question last, among criticisms, as it is doubtless the silliest. Newton may or may not have been beaned by someone else's apple, but what is interesting is what, in a lifetime of labor, he made of the event.

It may be that someday down through the years the United States will develop a political system in which the Presidency is but one of several major forces. Certainly it seems likely that the Congress will eventually reconvert itself from a fragmented collection of little specialized heirarchies into a single deliberative body in which equal representatives debate and decide the major political questions of the day. It is at least possible that the steady preachment of one scholar after another urging the revitalization of political parties will take hold and come to pass. No other political mechanism ever invented has approximated the party's success in building a common front linking the leaders and the led in a common purpose. It is even conceivable that the Supreme Court, and the whole legal structure it stands atop, will learn how to break through the toils of complexity that now threaten the very legitimacy of the idea of law itself and stand as the trusted ultimate guardians of American justice.

If any of that ever happens, I am willing to predict, a President will be in the middle of the fight. The era this side of the great horizon is and will be a Presidential era. It will be up to Presidents, more than any other force of government, to grapple with the terrors and the possibilities of a new age, a new world, a new generation of vicious and worthy Americans.

That age will throw at Presidents-to-be two overarching challenges. Will we find ways to harness the enormous new powers of technology and organization to the ancient task of building a humane and life-sustaining polity? Will we find ways, in time, to turn aside from the escalating probability that our world and all that is in it to pass into oblivion because humans could not control their explosives? Presidents who know how the world works and how Washington works in it, Presidents who have mastered the skills it takes to make the White House an efficent machine for social progress, Presidents who can call up from their own characters the steady, hopeful, insistent reason to shape a good life from a mixed society—such we yet may find before the great American adventure stops.

NOTES

[1]Judith Icke Anderson, *William Howard Taft: An Intimate History* (New York: Norton 1981), p. 45.

[2]*Ibid.*, p.35.

[3]Edward A. Weinstein, *Woodrow Wilson: A Medical and Psychological Biography* (Princeton, N.J.: Princeton University Press, 1983), p. 14.

[4]*Ibid.*, p. 11.

[5]Bragdon had pointed out that Wilson's very handwriting imitated that of his mother, and he quotes a former family butler as saying, "Outside Mr. Tommy was his father's boy. But inside it was his mother all over." Henry Wilkinson Bragdon, *Woodrow Wilson: The Academic Years*, p. 7. Wilson's relationships with women in his adulthood are consistent with this image. And he did, after all, choose to make his mother's family name his own first name.

[6]Charles L. Mee, Jr., *The Ohio Gang: The World of Warren G. Harding* (New York: M. Evans and Company, Inc., 1981), pp. 34, 43.

[7]Robert K. Murray, *The Politics of Normalcy: Governmental Theory and Practice in the Harding-Coolidge Era*. (New York: Norton, 1973), chapter 1.

[8]George N. Nash, *The Life of Herbert Hoover: The Engineer, 1874–1914* (New York: Norton, 1983), p. 17.

[9]Donald J. Lisio, *The President and Protest: Hoover, Conspiracy, and the Bonus Riot* (Columbia, Missouri: University of Missouri Press, 1974), p. 316.

[10]*Ibid.*, p. 315.

[11]Elliott Roosevelt and James Brough, *An Untold Story: The Roosevelts of Hyde Park* (New York: Dell, 1973).

[12]Williamk E. Leuchtenberg, *In the Shadow of FDR: From Harry Truman to Ronald Reagan* (Ithaca and London: Cornell University Press, 1983), p. 41.

[13]*Ibid.*, p. 241.

[14]Robert H. Ferrell, ed., *Dear Bess: The Letters From Harry to Bess Truman, 1910–1959* (New York: Norton, 1983), p. 537.

[15]Margaret Truman, ed., *Letters from Father: The Truman Family's Personal Correspondence* (New York: Pinnacle Books, 1982), pp. 123–4.

[16]*Ibid.*, pp. 288–89.

[17]Ferrell, *Dear Bess*, p. 269.

[18]*Ibid.*, p. 291.

[19]Monte M. Poen, ed., *Strictly Personal and Confidential: The Letters Harry Truman Never Mailed* (Boston: Little, Brown, 1982), p. 186.

[20]Fred I. Greenstein, *The Hidden-Hand Presidency: Eisenhower as Leader* (New York: Basic Books, 1982).

[21]William B. Ewald, Jr., *Eisenhower the President: Crucial Days, 1951–60* (Englewood Cliffs, N.J.: Prentice-Hall, 1981), pp. 264, 318.
[22]Stephen E. Ambrose, *Eisenhower, Volume One: Soldier, General of the Army, President-Elect, 1890–1952* (New York, Simon and Schuster, 1983), p. 9.
[23]*Ibid.*, p. 157.
[24]Greenstein, *The Hidden-Hand Presidency*, pp. 41–42.
[25]Ewald, *Eisenhower the President*, p. 182.
[26]Greenstein, *The Hidden-Hand President*, p. 63.
[27]*Ibid.*, p. 68.
[28]*Ibid.*, p. 69.
[29]*Ibid.*, p. 73.
[30]Ewald, *Eisenhower the President*, p. 183.
[31]Ewald, *Eisenhower the President*, pp. 183–4.
[32]Greenstein, *The Hidden-Hand President*, p. 37.
[33]Ambrose, *Eisenhower*, p. 22.
[34]Ambrose, *Eisenhower*, p. 48.
[35]Ambrose, *Eisenhower*, p. 49.
[36]Ambrose, *Eisenhower*, p. 50.
[37]Ambrose, *Eisenhower*, p. 571.
[38]Ewald, *Eisenhower the President*, p. 270. Eisehower's record in civil rights also shows his characteristic reluctance to take public action, despite the repeated pleas of Martin Luther King, Jr., and others. See Stephen B. Oates, *Let the Trumpet Sound: The Life of Martin Luther King, Jr.* (New York: Harper and Row, 1982).
[39]Nancy Gager Clinch, *The Kennedy Neurosis* (New York: Grosset & Dunlap, 1973).
[40]Bruce Miroff, *Pragmatic Illusions: The Presidential Politics of John F. Kennedy* (New York: D. McKay, 1976).
[41]*Ibid.* p. 276.
[42]Garry Wills, *The Kennedy Imprisonment: A Meditation on Power* (Boston: Little, Brown, 1981).
[43]Lewis J. Paper, *The Promise and the Performance: The Leadership of John F. Kennedy* (New York: Crown Publishers Inc., 1975).
[44]Doris Kearns, *Lyndon Johnson and the American Dream* (New York: Harper and Row, 1976), p. 259.
[45]Herbert S. Parmet, *Jack: The Struggles of John F. Kennedy* (New York: Dial Press, 1980).
[46]*Ibid.*, pp. 310ff.
[47]*Ibid.*, p. 149.
[48]David E. Koskoff, *Joseph P. Kennedy: A Life and Times* (Englewood Cliffs, N.J.: Prentice-Hall, Inc., 1974), pp. 408–9.
[49]Parmet, *Jack*, p. 207.
[50]*Ibid.*
[51]*Ibid.*, pp. 165, 170.
[52]*Ibid.*, pp. 189–92.
[53]Robert A. Caro, *The Years of Lyndon Johnson: The Path to Power* (New York: Knopf, 1982).
[54]*Ibid.*, p. xxi.
[55]*Ibid.*, p. 195.
[56]*Ibid.*, p. 201.
[57]*Ibid.*, p. 134.
[58]*Ibid.*, pp. 127–19.
[59]Ronnie Dugger, *The Politician: The Life and Times of Lyndon Johnson* (New York: Norton, 1982), p. 103.
[60]Doris Kearns, *Lyndon Johnson and the American Dream* (New York: Harper and Row, 1976).
[61]*Ibid.*, p. 261.
[62]*Ibid.*, p. 230.
[63]*Ibid.*, p. 253.
[64]*Ibid.*, p. 373.

[65]Leuchtenburg, *In the Shadow of FDR*, p. 145.

[66]Richard M. Nixon, *Leaders* (New York: Warner Books, 1982).

[67]*Ibid.*, p. 8.

[68]*Ibid.*, p. 29, italics in the original.

[69]*Ibid.*, p. 91.

[70]Fawn M. Brodie, *Richard Nixon: The Shaping of His Character* (New York: Norton, 1981).

[71]*Ibid.*, p. 510.

[72]*Ibid.*, pp. 321–24.

[73]James Graff, "Seymour Hersh and *The Price of Power*," *University of Chicago Magazine*, Winter 1984, p. 13.

21

THOMAS E. CRONIN

EVERYBODY BELIEVES IN DEMOCRACY UNTIL HE GETS TO THE WHITE HOUSE

Thomas E. Cronin's interest in the American presidency began when he served as a White House Fellow in the mid-1960s. Since then he has acquired an insider's perspective on the presidency by interviewing White House aides, cabinet officials, and top advisers, as well as by using oral histories in presidential libraries. Cronin, a professor of political science at Colorado College, has focused attention on the institutionalization of the presidency and the problems it presents in terms of presidential power and responsibility and the vast growth in the size of the Executive Office. He is the author of The State of the Presidency *(1975, 1980),* Rethinking the Presidency *(1982), and* Direct Democracy: The Politics of Initiative, Referenda, and Recall *(1989), and the coauthor of* The Presidency Reappraised *(1974) with Rexford Guy Tugwell, and* Government by the People *(1975, 1987) and* State and Local Politics *(1978) both with James MacGregor Burns and Jack Walter Peltason. The following article, first published in 1970, examines the complex relationship between White House staff and executive department officials. Cronin notes that since both staffs are needed to accomplish the functions of the executive branch, an informal "executive branch exchange system" develops to increase cooperation and a sense of united purpose.*

ON DIRECTING THE FEDERAL ESTABLISHMENT FROM THE WHITE HOUSE

A President is expected to perform three overriding functions: to recast the nation's policy agenda in line with contemporary needs, to provide symbolic affirmation of the nation's basic values, and to galvanize the vast machinery of government to carry out his programs and those he has inherited. The slippage and gap between the first and third functions is the primary concern of this discussion. The annual unveiling of a President's legislative program now has much in common with Madison Avenue's broadsides advertising each year's "spectacular new line" of Detroit-made combustion engine automobiles: the perceptive citizenry is increasingly sensitive to performance standards of both.

And so it is that the recently arrived President, aspiring to "unite the nation" and "get the country moving again," expecting that he and his lieutenants will succeed where previous administrations faltered, customarily feels he must order first his own executive branch "household." Recent Presidents often have gone out of their way to solicit the loyalty and support of senior civil servants.* President Nixon, for example, immediately after his inauguration, personally traveled to each executive department and met with and addressed thousands of these senior officials. Presidents and their inner circle of aides continuously strive to secure greater internal managerial control over the executive departments. They even learn (after awhile) that one way to do this is to forge a unity on policy priorities among the general American public *outside* of the executive branch.

But, as Bailey has pointed out, the executive branch of the federal government is a many-splintered thing.[1] The President is soon acquainted with the considerable difficulty of promoting unity in the face of the basic pluralism of the American political system.[2] Presidents Kennedy, Johnson, and Nixon have each complained bitterly about the recalcitrance of the federal bureaucracy, and seemingly turned more and more to their personal White House staffs for help in gaining control of their own executive establishment. And the collective record of Kennedy, Johnson, and Nixon as chief executive, especially with respect to the achievement of their domestic policy goals, has raised considerable questioning and criticism. As Rexford Tugwell concluded:

> The truth is that Kennedy did not function as an executive. He had only the most meager contacts with the secretaries of the domestic departments, largely because he had no interest in their operations.[3] This inability of a president—who must be political leader and chief legislator and who is sole custodian of the national security—to direct the domestic establishment has become almost total.[4]

Kennedy, after being in office two years, publicly complained that the nation's problems "are more difficult than I imagined" and "there are greater limitations upon our ability to bring about a favorable result than I had imagined."[5]

One Kennedy White House aide put the frustration more bluntly: "Everybody believes in democracy until he gets to the White House and then you begin to believe in dictatorship, because it's so hard to get things done. Everytime you turn around, people just resist you, and even resist their own job." Again, the same John Kennedy who in many ways inspired the country, was moved to quip about a relatively low priority project, the architectural remodeling of Lafayette Square across from the White House, "let's stay with it. Hell, this may be the only thing I'll ever really get done."[6] President Johnson also expressed disappointment over seemingly slow and uncooperative departmental responses. He attempted to "ride herd" on a multitude of programs by insisting on getting up-to-date figures on varied federal and international grant programs and routinely required departmental written reports. But he eventually resorted to vesting more and more authority for departmental coordination in the White House domestic policy aides and his Budget Bureau director. It was a no doubt disillusioned President Johnson, tired with continually battling the bureaucracy, who solemnly warned the incoming Nixon Administration that they should spare no effort in selecting thoroughly loyal people to man key departmental positions. It

**Civil servants:* all nonmilitary employees of a government. In the United States, the term "civil service" generally denotes a body of civilian public employees who are not appointed on the basis of patronage and who cannot be dismissed for political reasons.

is as though Johnson believed that a significant portion of the Great Society* programs, for which he had fought so hard, had been sabotaged by indifferent federal officials. And, in the wake of the Great Society legislative victories, both Presidents Johnson and Nixon held that the scaffolding of the federal government and the federal system needed extensive revamping, if not major surgery. Said Nixon: ". . . I have concluded that a sweeping reorganization of the Executive Branch is needed if the government is to keep up with the times and with the needs of the people."[7]

The thesis running implicitly if not explicitly through this paper is that White House staffs and executive department officials, upon whom contemporary Presidents are exceptionally dependent, are more specialized, professionalized, and differentiated than has been generally acknowledged. Presidents find themselves continuously surrounded—some would say afflicted—by problems of complexity, diversity, and a seemingly endless series of jurisdictional and territorial disputes. Presidential staffs, cabinet members, and advisors are invariably associated with, if not captured by, professionally, politically, or personally skewed sets of policy preferences. No cabinet officer or White House adviser consistently and singularly acts for "Everyman" or "the public interest." Priority setting, budget cutting, and preferred procedural strategies necessarily promote selective interests at the expense of others. Hence, Presidents are constantly, and rightfully, faced with conflicting claims; calibration and management of conflict is the core of presidential leadership. Those who would somehow reorganize the federal government so as to remove or elevate the American presidency away from bureaucratic or societal conflicts should be fully aware that they may at the same time be stripping the presidency of the strategic occasions for exercising essential leadership skills.

To the extent that White House staff and senior department officials maintain close communications and negotiations—or exchanges—we can speak of the existence of an executive branch exchange system.[8] Both sides are needed to perform the functions of the executive branch; each wants certain types of help from the other, and each seeks to avoid overt antagonism toward the other. White House staff members can be viewed as performing important linkage roles in this exchange system, connecting a President with a vast network of administrative officials. Presidents and most of their staff grow well aware that cooperation from the permanent federal departments is earned rather than taken for granted. Loyalty and support as well as crucially needed expertise are eagerly sought, for a basic premise in the exchange system is that departmental officials, especially civil servants, play, or can play, a strategic role in administering federal government activities.

Some of the relationships within this exchange system can be briefly suggested here. Richard Neustadt has commented:

> Agencies need decisions, delegations, and support, along with bargaining arenas and a court of last resort, so organized as to assure that their advice is always heard and often

**Great Society*: see footnote on page 78.

> taken. A President needs timely information, early warning, close surveillance, organized to yield him the controlling judgment, with his options open, his intent enforced. In practice these two sets of needs have proved quite incompatible; presidential organizations rarely serve one well without disservice to the other.[9]

And Bill Moyers adds:

> The job of the White House assistant is to help the President impress his priorities on the Administration. This may throw him into a sharp adversary role between two Cabinet members who are also competing with the President for their views of what the priorities should be. . . . Their [White House assistants] job is to make sure that decisions get implemented; it is not to manage the implementations. The follow-through aspect of it is very, very important. In recent years, the White House staff may have tended to become far too much of a managerial operation and less an overseer.[10]

The general White House view reflects a concern for teamwork, cohesiveness, interdepartmental coordination, follow-through on the President's program, and protection of the President's reputation. White House aides generally spend a sizeable portion of their time engaged in intra-executive branch alliance building. How best to communicate what the President wants done? How to give the departmental leaders a sense of involvement in presidential decisions? How politely but firmly to tell "them" of the President's dissatisfaction with department performance? How to motivate them to give added energy to get "our" programs moving? Should we promote an inside man into that new vacancy or bring in someone from the outside? How can we extricate this program operation from that nearly impossible group of people over there? A standard joke during the 1960's had White House staff members trying to figure out how to contract out to private enterprise or foundations the work that the State Department was assigned to perform. A standard exercise during the late 1960's, especially within the Nixon Administration, was the design of programs that might shortcircuit the federal bureaucracy with the hope of getting federal monies and programs more swiftly into the hands of state and local officials. In short, the problem becomes how to employ the resources and sanctions of the presidency to make the machinery of government act in accord with the administration's overriding goals.

Senior departmental officials are no less involved in exchanges with the presidential staff. Some of them are temporary political appointees, most are career civil servants with a long legacy of dealing with the presidency, especially with the budget officials attached to the Executive Office of the President.* Their concern is often a blend of wishing to satisfy and cooperate with the objectives of the current presidential team, but at the same time attending to departmental

Executive Office of the President (EOP): created in 1939 under Franklin D. Roosevelt to improve the president's effectiveness and to facilitate communication between the president, Congress, cabinet departments, and the public. The office has grown and changed considerably over time and currently employs approximately 1,500 individuals as counselors to the president, assistants to the president, and special consultants to the president. Each president organizes the EOP as he sees fit. In 1986 the EOP included the White House Office, Office of Management and Budget, Council of Economic Advisers, National Security Council, Office of Policy Development, Office of the U.S. Trade Representative, Council on Environmental Quality, Office of Science and Technology, and Office of the Vice-President.

priorities and the always present need for maintaining departmental integrity. White House requests for the most part are honored; pressure and arrogant communications are resented. But the day-to-day concerns are reflected in the following types of questions: How can we get White House endorsement and increased budget approvals for this new department initiative? How can we get the White House to side with us in this jurisdictional matter? How can we make an end run around that unsympathetic and amateur White House aide and make sure the President hears about this new idea? When should we supply a potentially great news announcement to the White House and risk not being able to use it here to gain publicity for "our" cabinet officer and departmental programs? In short, how do we deal with the White House when necessary, or when it can help us, but otherwise preserve our autonomy?

There are a variety of "rules of the game" governing White House departmental exchanges. Some are easy to define, most are elusive and variable.

The focus of analysis in the following discussions is on the exchange relationships between White House staff and departmental executives, especially on the "middleman" role of the White House staff. These alliances, often uneasy and almost always fragile, are difficult to comprehend without examining the observations and perceptions of centrally involved participants. With this in mind, I interviewed forty-three members of the Kennedy, Johnson, and Nixon presidential staffs. Of these, twenty-four served under Kennedy, thirty-four under Johnson, and six under Nixon (many staff members served under more than one administration).[11] Additionally, more than twenty-five cabinet and sub-cabinet members from these administrations were interviewed or consulted.

The 1960's and the presidential administrations of John Kennedy and Lyndon Johnson present a fascinating laboratory for examining White House–departmental relations. It seems fair to assume that cooperative and responsive relationships are particularly tested during and immediately after periods of sustained presidential activism, that is, when major new programs are being launched and old ones being discarded or revitalized. That the sixties were a major period for such change is well-documented and need not be retold here.[12]

Simple but previously neglected questions such as the following need to be asked: How much tension and strain exist between White House staff and departmental executives? Why do some White House staffers see considerable conflict whereas others view departmental relations as essentially harmonious? What variance exists over time or among the departments? What are the major sources of perceived conflicts? To what extent should and can conflict be resolved? . . .

A. *The Presidential Perspective*

This perspective, popular among most presidential advisors, university liberals (at least during the 1950's and 1960's), and probably a majority of the Washington press corps, holds that the presidency should be a strong and visible force in making sure that presidential policy objectives get effectively translated into desired policy performance. "This is the great office, the only truly national office in the whole system." The basic premise corresponds with Alexander Hamilton's point of view—that the requisite unity and drive for our political system would only come from a strong executive.[13] Only the presidency should retain discretion over budget choices and over the way federal policies are administered. And only the presidency can provide the needed direction and orchestration of complex, functionally interdependent federal programs. Presidents and their staffs, if properly organized, can assure that the laws of the land not only will be administered faithfully, but also imaginatively. There is an explicit assumption that a strong presidency can make a major difference in the way government works and that this difference will be in the direction of a more constructive (desirable) set of policy outcomes.

Presidentialists invariably also argue that the presidency is not properly organized, staffed, or funded. The presidency needs not just "more help" but a major infusion of skills, talent, tools, and loyalty if it is to gain control over the permanent federal departments. Implicitly, if not explicitly, "More Power To The White House!" is the slogan. Partly because so many previous Presidents have bypassed existing departments and set up their own new independent agencies, and partly because of the sheer size and diversity of the executive establishment, the White House too often serves at the pleasure of the bureaucracy, rather than vice versa. McGeorge Bundy speaks for many believers of the presidential persuasion when he observes that the executive branch in many areas "more nearly resembles a collection of badly separated principalities than a single instrument of executive action."[14]

The presidential camp never completely trusts civil servants, and frequently mistrusts political appointees as well. Whatever of importance needs doing either ought to be done directly from the White House, or should be done with expectation that the departmental people will temper or undermine the desired policy intentions. As former Kennedy staffer, Arthur Schlesinger, explains:

> At the start we all felt free to "meddle" when we thought we had a good idea or someone else a poor one. But, as the ice began to form again over the government, freewheeling became increasingly difficult and dangerous . . . [and] our real trouble was that we had capitulated too much to the existing bureaucracy. Wherever we have gone wrong . . . has been because we have not had sufficient confidence in the New Frontier* approach to impose it on the government. Every important mistake has been the consequence of excessive deference to the permanent government. . . . The problem of moving forward seemed in great part the problem of making the permanent government responsive to the policies of the presidential government.[15]

The goal of the presidentialists in its crudest form is "to presidentialize" the executive branch. Toward that end there are catalogues of reform proposals, a few of which can be mentioned as examples:

> The strong Presidency will depend upon the Chief Executive's capacity to control and direct the vast bureaucracy of national administration. Ideally, the President should

*New Frontier: collective policies and programs of President Kennedy.

> possess administrative powers comparable to those of business executives. . . . What the President needs most can be simply formulated: a power over personnel policy, planning, accounting, and the administration of the executive branch that approaches his power over the executive budget.[16]

Other variations on this theme call for better policy evaluation and program management staffs within the Executive Office. Presidentialists with narrow policy interests are always asking that the formulation and administration of their particular policy concerns be brought closer within the presidential orbit "much along the lines of the Council of Economic Advisers." Another suggestion would give the presidency some field agents or "expediters" (federal domestic program "czars") located in federal regional offices or large metropolitan areas to insure that presidential priorities are being properly effected at the grass roots level.

B. Departmental Perspective

This perspective holds that the success or failure of the federal government's efforts to manage federal programs rests almost entirely on the quality and competence of the executive departments. An assumption here is that all programs at the federal level possess considerable discretionary aspects. Those holding a departmental perspective say that for programs to be effectively administered, discretion and authority must (at least to a large extent) be vested in departmental and bureau leaders. The sentiment here is that the role of the White House, particularly in regard to the administration of domestic programs, should be a highly selective one, and one that is tremendously and rightfully dependent on career civil servants and professional departmental expertise. Certain department officials, for example, deplored the amount of White House involvement in AID* grant clearances, HUD† model city selections, and HEW‡ desegregation proceedings. To be sure, even the most extreme departmentalist would agree that crisis situations and various types of national security matters necessarily should be subject to substantial presidential discretion.

The departmentalist view has varying support among professional civil servants, among some former cabinet officers, and even among some former White House staff assistants. Moreover, there are increasing numbers of skeptics who are persuaded that a larger and more "resourceful" presidency (or more "institutionalization" of the presidency) is not a realistic answer to the problem of managing a responsive federal government. There are even those who argue that it probably does not make much difference which of the various presidential candidates gets elected. "You can elect your favorite presidential hopeful at the

**Agency for International Development*, or *AID*: federal agency charged with assisting less-developed countries to build economic and social systems that will improve the quality of life of their people. AID was created by the Foreign Assistance Act of 1961 and is currently a unit of the U.S. International Development Cooperation Agency.

†*United States Department of Housing and Urban Development*, or *HUD*: cabinet-level department created in 1965 to consolidate housing and urban economic development programs.

‡*United States Department of Health, Education, and Welfare*, or *HEW*: cabinet-level department created in 1953 and reorganized into two departments in 1979—the Department of Health and Human Services and the Department of Education.

next election but the basic problems of government non-responsiveness will still be with us!"[17]

Some advocates of the departmental perspective come to their position because of a recognition that the political facts of life just do not permit intensive or extensive presidential involvement in most matters of federal policy administration. The limits of the presidency are cited, such as in David Truman's appropriate cautions:

> [the President] cannot take a position on every major controversy over administrative policy, not merely because his time and energies are limited, but equally because of the positive requirements of his position. He cannot take sides in any dispute without giving offense in some quarters. He may intervene where the unity of his supporters will be threatened by inaction; he may even, by full use of the resources of his office, so dramatize his action as to augment the influence he commands. But he cannot "go to the country" too often, lest the tactic become familiar and his public jaded. Rather than force an administrative issue, he may choose to have his resources for a legislative effort . . . [For effectiveness he] must preserve some of the detachment of a constitutional monarch.[18]

And while the President remains detached or "above" the day-to-day operations of the federal government, cabinet members and their staffs want both a relative independence and a vote of confidence with which to carry on their work. As one prerequisite, they insist that White House staff members should not have authority independent from the President to issue directives to cabinet and agency leaders. And when they need it cabinet members and agency heads should have the right to direct access to the President. It follows too that Presidents should get involved only in broad policy questions, not in the nuts and bolts concerns of program execution and application. White House people are viewed as "amateurs and terribly ill-informed nuisances" who are seen as "breathing down our necks."

The more the White House usurps functional responsibilities from their "proper" home in the departments, the more the White House may undermine the goal of competent departmental management of presidentially sponsored programs. A cabinet member who is made to look weak within his department will be treated with less respect by his subordinates as well as by relevant congressional and client support groups. Department officials who must fight strenuously to maintain access and rapport with the White House have correspondingly less energy left over for their internal department management concerns. When the White House staff or other presidential advisers step in and temporarily take over certain departmental functions, the action may further diminish the capacity of the department to streamline or revitalize its capability for managing these functions in the future. Too frequent intervention from the White House creates morale problems within the departments. Resentment and hostility are likely to impede subsequent cooperation. Imaginative professional people will not long remain in their departmental posts if they are frequently underused or misused.

Departmentalists, charging that White House aides get rewarded for "meddling" in department affairs, note that on closer inspection it is frequently a disadvantageous strategy for everyone involved, excepting perhaps the White House aide who has to look "busy." George Reedy, a former Johnson aide, notes that "there is, on the part of the White House assistants, a tendency to bring to the White House problems which should not properly be there, frequently to the disadvantage of the president."[19]

If these arguments appear overdrawn and unrealistic, listen to President Johnson's former Housing and Urban Development Secretary, Robert Wood, as he decidedly posits the departmentalist over the presidentialist persuasion:

> The longer one examines the awesome burdens and limited resources of those who help the president from within his immediate circle, the more skeptical one becomes of a strategy for overseeing government by "running" it from 1600 Pennsylvania Avenue. The semiheroic, semihopeless picture has been captured many times in several administrations: dedicated men, of great intelligence and energy, working selflessly through weekends and holidays to master an endlessly increasing array of detail on complex subjects beyond their understanding on which decisions must be made "*here*" because a resolution elsewhere is not to be trusted. They persevere, taking their stand against "the bureaucrats," pushing programs through against sullen, hidden resistance from the departments. Committees are abolished, agencies rejuggled, staff reviews simplified, new reporting forms introduced, all in the effort to assure that more and more decisions are, or can be, presidential. Yet, in the end, after thirty years, the effort to help the president in making government work has not succeeded.[20]

III

A. *Amount of Conflict Perceived by White House Staffers*

Conflicts in the executive branch exchange system are widely acknowledged by most recent White House staff members. The forty-three aides interviewed for this study were asked whether they experienced major difficulties in working with the federal executive departments: "can you give your view of this; is this really a problem?" As shown in Table 1, approximately two-thirds answered that there were extensive and considerable troubles in dealing with the departments. Some talked of this as the single greatest problem in contemporary government. One man who has worked for both Presidents Kennedy and Johnson said that "it was an absolutely terrible problem. . . . There are major problems with cabinet members and civil servants alike. Even the great cabinet members like McNamara* and Freeman† were terrible in evading their share of many of our efforts." A senior Johnson Administration counselor observed that the "separation of governments is not so great between Congress and the President as between a President and those people like sub-cabinet and bureau officials, who become locked into their own special subsystems of self-interested policy concerns." Others talked about the increasing defiance of department people toward the White House:

**Robert S. McNamara:* secretary of defense (1961–1968) for Presidents Kennedy and Johnson.
†Orville Freeman: secretary of agriculture (1961–1969) for Presidents Kennedy and Johnson.

TABLE 1 WHITE HOUSE STAFF PERCEPTION OF CONFLICT WITH DEPARTMENTS

Problem of Tensions and Conflict in These Exchanges Was:	*Percentages* N = 43
Considerable	65%
Moderate	25
Insignificant	10
Total	100

Source: Personal interviews with forty-three White House staff members serving between 1961 and 1970.

> It's a terrible problem and it's getting worse, particularly with the State Department. The major problem is the lack of any identification [on their part] with the president's program priorities. At State they try to humor the president but hope he will not interfere in their complex matters and responsibilities. It is equally a problem with civil servants and cabinet types. It is amazing how soon the cabinet people get captured by the permanent staffs. Secretary [David] Kennedy [of Treasury] under Nixon, for example, was captured within days . . . and Nixon's staff didn't even try to improve things. They just assumed there was a great problem. Personally, I think you can't expect too much from the bureaucracy. It is too much to expect that they will see things the president's way.

Some aides were more inclined to note that conflicts varied with different departments and with different cabinet members. For example: "yes there are certainly many problems, but it differs from area to area and from President to President. I think the amount of friction is related to the role of the White House staff and what they undertake and what presidents let them do." Another example of a more tempered assessment of the existence of conflict comes from a Congressional relations aide to the Kennedy-Johnson White House:

> Oh, yes—there are problems to an extent. There is deep suspicion around the whole government toward the new president when he comes into power. . . . But the fights you get in are different all around town. . . . We had some excellent men around town, and some bombs. The important thing for a president to do is to get good men and then decentralize the responsibility. Let the department people do their job and don't let your [White House] staff interfere too much. . . .

Some White House staff who had less involvement with departments were the most likely to acknowledge little if any serious conflict.

On balance, a substantial majority of recent presidential staffers complain of considerable difficulty and conflict in their work with the federal executive departments. To a man, all these aides were proud of having worked for recent Presidents and quite obviously enjoyed the ambiance of White House political life (said one: "It is the ice cream parlor of American politics!"). Most of them, however, left frustrated with the task of making the permanent government responsive to the White House. The modal if not the consensus view was "the greatest difficulty we had was getting things out of the executive agencies. The magnitude of change and effort that is needed to get things back into shape . . .

and how futile it all seems to be . . . [as] requests get lost among the bureaucracy and it is so tough to penetrate all their crap."

B. What White House Staffers See as Sources of Conflict

Conflicts in the executive branch exchange system can be attributed to both subjective and objective factors. The difference in allegiance to the presidential or departmental perspectives illustrate[s] a major subjective factor. Some other subjective factors include differing definitions of priorities and roles, personality clashes, and personal ambitions. Objective factors would include such things as sheer size of the federal effort (and the time and communications restrictions that stem from that size), restrictive budget limitations (Presidents and cabinet heads find they have little control over ninety per cent or more of "their" budgets[21]), centrifugal pulls inherent in federalism and in the functionally independent departments, and various knowledge gaps (for example, "we don't have all the answers!"). Presidential staff members seem to be well aware of most of these sources, but seem to stress the subjective differences and the ill effects of the divorce between presidential and departmental perspectives.

Extended interviews with White House staff yield the persuasive impression that no one set of difficulties lies at the root of executive branch conflict. Their discussions often moved back and forth from noting causes to complaining about symptoms. But their multiple citations here (see Table 2) are instructive both for their diversity and for unexpectedly candid criticism of the way the White House itself contributed to these difficulties.[22]

1. ON WHITE HOUSE "SOURCES" OF CONFLICT White House staffers suggest that their own definition of their roles, and the pressures they had to work under frequently exacerbate relations with cabinet and department officials. Presidents and their staffs arrive at the White House charged up to get things done, to produce results, to make good on the pledges of their campaign. The frenzy and simplification of problems and issues generated in the campaign, coupled with the post election victory euphoria result in strategies of over-extension and insensitivity:

> Well, a Kennedy staff hallmark was to seize power from around town. In retrospect I think they often were insensitive to the channels of the existing government. They came in after the campaign with a pretentious "know it all" attitude and they hurt their case by this stance. For example, I think the White House staffers often called people low in the departments and deliberately undercut cabinet people too much in the early years. . . . In retrospect I don't think you can coordinate much from the White House. You just don't have the people and the numbers . . . [and] you can't evaluate all that much [not to mention managing it]. . . .

No Emily Post manual is available for White House aides to learn about the numerous nuances and diverse expectations that come with their staff roles. At best, it is a learning by doing, and a learning from your mistakes type of experience. The goldfish bowl and pressure cooker atmosphere is an invitation to problems, and the opportunities for mishaps and mistakes abound. Hatchet men

TABLE 2 PRESIDENCY STAFF PERSPECTIVES ON THE SOURCES OF CONFLICT AND STRAIN IN WHITE HOUSE-EXECUTIVE DEPARTMENT RELATIONSHIPS

Types and Sources of Conflict	*Percentages* N = 41
WHITE HOUSE "SOURCES":	
WH staff insensitivity toward department officials	51%
WH staff and President communications failures	44
WH staff usurpation of department roles and/or excessive interference in department affairs	37
WH "tried to do too much too quickly"	29
DEPARTMENTAL "SOURCES":	
Civil servant and bureaucratic parochialism	49
Cabinet "leadership" too weak or unimaginative	46
Departmental leaders captured by narrow special interests	46
Red tape, and inept staff work	37
Departments unable to work together	24
COMPLEXITY/DIVERSITY FACTORS:	
Sheer size and complexity of federal efforts	37
Lack of time for the needed follow-through/coordination/implementation	27
Substantive and ideological differences about policy choices within the federal system	27

Source: Personal interviews conducted by the author with forty-one presidential staff members who served at the White House during 1961–70. Respondents could give more than one reply. *See* n. 22 *supra*.

for the opposition party and aggressive columnists in search of scandal and conflicts of interest are ever-present with their predatory instincts. There frequently arise situations in which White House aides try desperately to get faster results for "their President" from securely tenured officials in the various governmental departments. But the White House aides are damned if they become overly arrogant with department people on the one hand, and on the other hand become superfluous or irrelevant men if they grow afraid to use the available resources of their positions. Eager for fast results, there were many staffers who, according to a former White House aide, "if they had the option between (1) giving an order to the bureaucracy, or (2) trying to win their cooperation, would always settle quickly for issuing orders."

Staff insensitivity to cabinet and department executives occurs for a variety of reasons. Presidents often want to "put the heat on" some cabinet member or bureau chief, but prefer not to take the blame for being tough. Presidents understandably eschew the "bad guy" role, hence the bearing of unpleasant news befalls various staff members.

Discussions about the problem of staff insensitivity were often ambiguous. On the one hand, aides somewhat contemptuously talked of the need for more "care and feeding" of cabinet members (as though some of the cabinet were kept symbols for window dressing alone). But they would also insist that one just has to be aggressive and "hard-nosed" in order to get anything accomplished. For example:

> I think most of the problem lies in the disregard of some White House aides of the rank, and age, and positional dignity or status of cabinet members and agency heads. Three little words can give a White House aide a lot of power, "the President wants. . . ." You need to combine a proper sense of firmness with deference . . . but you have to know the danger traps and the mine fields and always have to keep in mind the question: "How can I serve the president?" I'll tell you exactly how to deal with this problem: you can use two plans. Plan A: get in touch with the cabinet or department head and say "the President is anxious to have your judgment on X matter." If they squirm or delay or fail to comply then you use Plan B: "Damn it Mr. Secretary, the President wants it by 3:00 this afternoon!" You have to be tough in this business.

Some aides stressed that the always delicate distinction between *staff* or advisory roles at the White House, and operational administrative *line* responsibilities in the cabinet departments became overly blurred during the Kennedy and Johnson years. Too many of the staff tried to do more than they were supposed to be doing and gradually came "to give orders" rather than transmit requests. But as mentioned earlier, Presidents frequently encouraged this development and some cabinet members respect decisive and competent White House aides, brusk though they may be. Impatient or disillusioned with some of their cabinet, Kennedy, Johnson and Nixon turned more and more to their White House staff for advice, coordination, and particularly for help in resolving jurisdictional disputes between executive agencies. One result, in the words of one top Johnson aide, was that "after awhile he [Johnson] never even bothered to sit down with most of the cabinet members (domestic cabinet) even to discuss their major problems and program possibilities." Partly because of the war, and partly because he had grown used to leaning on his own staff so heavily, "Johnson became lazy and wound up using some of the staff as both line managers as well as staff and, I think in retrospect, it *frequently* didn't work out!"

Some of the most instructive commentary was devoted to the problem of intraexecutive branch communications. Numerous aides mentioned that a "basic reason for conflict is the lack of communications." Fault in this regard is generally placed upon White House staff and sometimes on the President. Often it is not that cabinet and departmental officials fail to respond to White House policy directives, but rather that those directives are too hazy or inadequately communicated. Sometimes it is because Presidents and their aides just have not made up their minds.[23] Occasionally, different White House aides send out contradictory messages to the departments. For example, the domestic program and legislative development staff might be pressing a department for new program ideas while the budget director and his staff are warning department officials of the need to reduce their activities, especially their more costly programs. Often the President has not made his view known forcefully enough to overcome uncertainty and confusion. Presidents are handicapped in this sense because they often have multiple audiences in mind when preparing their remarks. The capacity of the departments to understand what the President means and to believe that he really means it should never be taken for granted. In his farewell pep talk to the Nixon cabinet, Daniel Moynihan posed the problem as follows:

> [I]t is necessary for members of the administration . . . to be far more attentive to what it is the President has said, and proposed. Time and again, the President has said things of startling insight, taken positions of great political courage and intellectual daring, only to be greeted with silence or incomprehension.
>
> . . . But his [Nixon's] initial thrusts were rarely followed up with a sustained, reasoned, reliable second and third order of advocacy.
>
> Deliberately or no, the impression was allowed to arise with respect to the widest range of Presidential initiatives that the President wasn't really behind them.[24]

Another aspect of the communications problem is rooted in the sheer size of the federal enterprise. One story was mentioned by a former Johnson aide as a lesson relevant to understanding the communications responsibilities of the presidency. He suggested that the dinosaur probably became extinct not because it was too big or too clumsy, but rather because it suffered a failure of communication. Signals were not transmitted from brain to foot, or from foot to brain rapidly or accurately enough to create a picture of reality on which the dinosaur could act. A few weeks after hearing this story, I was intrigued by the seemingly quite analogous but more specific account of another Johnson aide, who trenchantly summed up many of Lyndon Johnson's troubles in directing the war in Vietnam as follows:

> Even if the Vietnam problem could have been managed by the President of the United States acting as the Vietnam Desk Officer, the system would soon have broken down from sheer lack of communication. It is one thing for Great Men to make policy, it is another to implement it, monitor it, coordinate it with existing policies and programs, and undertake the advance planning to meet foreseeable problems and possible contingencies.[25]

One other problem discussed by close to a third of the White House aides (again, see Table 2) was that their Administration tried to do too much too fast. Even President Johnson was quoted to this effect in the last days of his presidential term.[26] It was not that Great Society programs were ill-intentioned or misplaced, but rather that not enough planning had preceded implementation. One veteran budget counselor to Presidents explained his view of the conflict this way:

> Too much was attempted under LBJ. We didn't ask ourselves enough questions about whether we could do these things. Expectations outran the capability to work things out. There were too many other demands or problems in the mid and late 60's. Vietnam, inadequately trained manpower at all levels of government, and the structure of intergovernmental relations was inadequate. The space and missile programs had the backing of the people, but public support was terribly splintered over the War on Poverty* etc. . . . It was like a Tower of Babel with no one interested in the other people's programs.

***War on Poverty:* collection of social programs launched by Lydon B. Johnson to ameliorate conditions of poverty and urban unrest in the 1960s.

If the departments are, in fact occasionally "parochial" in their behavior, Presidents and presidential staff can often be overly "political" in their behavior. For example, Nixon's vetoes of various health and education bills—for balancing his political budget—incurred the hostility of several HEW officials. Likewise President Kennedy's highly political decision to support federal subsidies for the construction of the Cross-Florida Barge Canal angered many budget and conservation counselors within his own administration. Likewise the typical Executive office attitude toward the Agricultural Department—"keep prices down and the farmers off our back!"—annoyed many department officials who held expansionary hopes for turning their department into a rural development and a major conservation agency. The point to be appreciated in several of these illustrations is that the political perspectives and substantive preferences of Presidents and their staffs produce their share of executive branch conflicts.

2. ON DEPARTMENTAL "SOURCES" OF CONFLICT There is an increasingly popular view that much of the conflict in the federal executive branch can be explained by the fact that the departments are "specialized, parochial, self-interested," while the President and his advisers have "a government-wide point of view."[27] The extent to which this is the overriding explanation is easily overestimated. While House staff members (whom we would expect to be prime enthusiasts for this interpretation) fault the White House and its operations about as often as they fault the cabinet and the departments. The battlefield depiction of the departments rapacious challengers of the presidential prerogative, as illustrated by the Schlesinger quote below, is, at least in the context of my series of interviews, an overdrawn or embellished position:

> Kennedy . . . was determined to restore the personal character of the office and recover presidential control over the sprawling feudalism of government. This became the central theme of his administration and, in some respects, a central frustration. The presidential government, coming to Washington aglow with new ideas and a euphoric sense that it could do no wrong, promptly collided with the feudal barons of the permanent government, entrenched in their domains and fortified by their sense of proprietorship; and the permanent government, confronted by this invasion, began almost to function (with, of course, many notable individual exceptions) as a resistance movement. . . .[28]

Approximately half of the White House aides mentioned a seeming inability of many government workers to adopt "the presidential perspective." This latter commodity, always ill-defined, seems capaciously to include "the public interest," responsiveness to the electorate, maturity of judgment, virtue, and wisdom.[29] Whatever all this is, quite a number of the White House policy staff assistants are convinced that department people either do not understand it or just stubbornly resist it. "Mostly the bureaucrats are unresponsive, they view themselves as the professionals and see your [White House] impact as purely political. They don't fight you openly, but they don't cooperate if they can help it!"

Another way for White House aides to explain departmental sources of conflict is to question the competence or loyalty of the cabinet member. Cabinet members get faulted for being "too much of an individualist," "too aloof," "too stubborn" and sometimes for not being "a take charge type." In any event, the traditional complaint that cabinet members get captured by narrow special interests was a frequent response; to some it was the number one problem:

> —Often times we appointed weak cabinet people to start with. Luther Hodges* at Commerce was very weak. And Ribicoff† [HEW] chickened out after he came aboard and saw the mess which he was supposed to administer—so he merely presided over it temporarily while he began making plans to leave and run for a Connecticut U.S. Senate seat.

> —It all comes down to people, some people do a great job like McNamara. They really run their show and get great people to help them and don't need White House interference. Rusk‡ and McNamara were talented and loyal, but Weaver§ [HUD] was very weak and had loyalties mainly to his department's interests. Even John Gardner‖ [HEW] became seduced [by special interests] much faster than anyone predicted. And Willard Wirtz** [Labor] was terrible. . . . He saw himself as Labor's representative to the president rather than as part of the president's cabinet. He even out-Meanyed George Meany a few times!

One of the most significant factors promoting conflict between the departments and the White House staffs is their different time perspectives. This same variable is also at play in White House–congressional relations.[30] A President and his staff think in terms of two and four year time frames—at the most. They strive to fulfill campaign pledges, convention platforms, and earlier announced priorities as soon as possible, seeking always to build a respectable record for forthcoming election campaigns. The haste with which the White House rushed the announcements of the Model Cities†† and the Teacher Corps‡‡ programs may well have damaged the chances for effective design and launching of these programs.[31] Career civil servants, on the other hand, will be around after the elections regardless of outcomes, and more importantly, they are held accountable to the General Accounting Office, the Office of Management and Budget,

Luther Hodges, Sr.: Secretary of Commerce, Kennedy Administration.

†*Abraham A. Ribicoff*: secretary of the U.S. Department of Health, Education, and Welfare (1961–1962). He then served as a Democratic senator from Connecticut (1963–1981).

‡*Rusk:* see footnote on page 328.

§*Robert C. Weaver:* secretary of the U.S. Department of Housing from 1966 to 1968.

‖John W. Gardner: secretary of the U.S. Department of Health, Education, and Welfare from 1965 until 1968.

***Willard Wirtz:* undersecretary of Labor from January 1961 until September 1962, when he became secretary. He served in this capacity until January 1969.

††*Model Cities:* pertained to the Demonstration Cities and Metropolitan Development Act of 1966. The act provided coordinated housing and development programs for designated low-income neighborhoods in select cities. The effort was discontinued under President Nixon.

‡‡*Teacher Corps:* program created by the Elementary and Secondary Education Act of 1965, to increase the supply of teachers in low income districts by training and supporting volunteers to teach in the designated areas.

or to congressional investigation committees for the way federal programs are administered (and for any mistakes that might be made). The work incentives for most careerists are stacked in the direction of doing a thorough, consistent, and even cautious job, rather than any hurried dancing to the current tunes of the White House staff.

C. Conflict as a Result of Complexity

Nearly all of the White House aide commentary on executive branch conflict can be traced back to problems of government size and problem complexity. White House aides become arrogant and insensitive because they are often asked to do too much in too short a time. White House aides "breathe down the necks" of cabinet and department leaders because Presidents become impatient and restless for results. Departments appear inert or unresponsive because they are having difficulty pulling together diverse specialists to work on complex questions. Cabinet members give the impression of being "weak" (and sometimes are) because they must preside over huge holding companies of diverse, functionally specialized enterprises. White House aides are continuously disillusioned and disappointed by the lack of coordination both within and among departments; but the White House vision of coordination unrealistically presupposes that department people share an understanding of complex problems, and a sophisticated appreciation of the realtedness of one problem to another, of one agency to another. Communications problems exist because large numbers of people are involved in administering programs all over the country and are confronted by constantly changing and shifting circumstances. Legislative or executive intent, or the GAO* and Civil Service Commission "rulebooks and regulations," even if they could be memorized, do not have all the answers for all seasons. Uncertainties, changing environment, and shifting priorities all make policy implementation harder (and pleasing the White House near impossible). One White House counselor to President Eisenhower summed up what he refers to as the pervasive fact of political life that continually affected the Eisenhower Administration:

> the sheer size and intricacy of government conspire to taunt and to thwart all brisk pretensions to set sensationally new directions. The vast machinery of national leadership—the tens of thousands of levers and switches and gears—simply do not respond to the impatient jab of a finger or the angry pounding of a fist.[32]

There is, finally, the constantly faced dilemma of choosing between competing values. Ideological preferences enter here. That not many White House aides mention ideological factors as a source of conflict may imply that a relatively common political culture unites executive department officialdom with recent members of the presidential government. But there are differences of view, sometimes reflecting political party points of view, but more often reflecting

***General Accounting Office*, or GAO: agency created by the Budget and Accounting Act of 1921. The GAO audits financial records of federal government bureaus and assists Congress in the evaluation of federal programs.

differences about the role of the federal government in solving local or international problems. There is always the problem of making the critical distinction between what the federal government can do and what it cannot do. The occasional quest to push the governmental system to great levels of commitment and compassion gets generated in presidential elections and later by major presidential policy addresses (*e.g.*, the quest *to end* poverty, *to achieve* equality of opportunity, *to renew* our cities, *to help develop* Latin America, *to return power* to the people, and so forth). However, even the "best laid plans" of Presidents or Congress often get rescinded because of the "bottlenecks" of problem complexity and jurisdictional interdependency. As White House aides well know, however, "you have to start somewhere"—despite manifest opposition and complexity. One aide explained the fate of many Great Society programs as follows:

> . . . complexity of problems and complexity of the executive establishment [those were the chief problems]. . . . A program today often needs three or four departments and an equal number of Congressional committees and sub-committees to even get things started. It is the interdependency of policy and responsibilities that slows things down. There are just more and more people and more institutional drags involved. It takes a lot of time and testing to get things to work. For example, in the fields of job training and civil rights—LBJ knew he had to start things even though he couldn't be sure everything would work out well. He was terribly aware that there were so many bottlenecks. . . .

Listening to White House aides' views of those conflicts heightens one's appreciation for the responsibilities of the chief executive. The President has to act, even in the face of uncertainties, complexity, and opposition; eventually the consequences of inaction may outweigh the results of an ill-fated action. The President can ask the right questions, can act as educator, can preside over appropriate compromises, and can do much to shape and sharpen new policy directions, but the constraints on directing an effective application of those policies to problems are enormous. As the general public expects more and more of the presidency, and as its responsibilities for performance become greater and greater, the President is often thrust in the middle of a disillusioning squeeze play. . . .

D. White House Congressional Relations Staff

White House congressional relations aides differ from their fellow staff having substantive policy responsibilities in several ways. Their concern is less with policy formulation than it is with policy promotion. While the program and policy staff are busy trying to win support and cooperation for White House policy interests within the departments, congressional relations aides spend their time seeking political support from within congressional committees and among diverse factions on Capitol Hill. Not surprisingly, program and congressional liaison aides sometimes differ over the relative merits and feasibility of newly suggested program ideas. And at least under the recent Democratic administrations, the congressional relations aides have frequently mirrored the more conservative views of congressional chairmen in internal White House staff deliberations. Congressional relations aides only infrequently pay attention to policy implementation activities and on those occasions, more often than not, they argue the case as viewed on Capitol Hill to their White House colleagues.

Several factors help explain the congressional relations staff's more moderate estimates of contention between White House and departments. First, the White House congressional relations staff by vocation are far more geared to political accommodation and compromise than others on the White House staff. Consensus-building rather than policy incubation and program generation is their life style and preoccupation. They define their task as helping the President get his program passed by Congress. They consciously work for the reelections of the President (or his party) and the President's supporters within the Congress. To these ends they necessarily seek to minimize conflict and maximize cohesion. A reasonably unified executive branch is an added advantage for successful enactment of major legislation. Division and dissension within or among these departments will usually hurt a bill's chances for passage. Because they, more than any other staff at the White House, are conscious of the ingredients (*i.e.*, new proposals) that go into the making of the box scores of wins and losses that (albeit simplistically) characterize presidential-congressional relations, the legislative liaison aides favor "practical" proposals. While domestic and budget White House staff often remain disappointed by the dearth of new ideas or the hesitancy of the President to back a controversial proposal, the congressional relations officers are more easily satisfied by modest accomplishments and are also less inclined to encourage new or complicated legislative initiatives that might be difficult to pass—"we obviously don't want to be put in the position of having to sell programs that don't have a reasonable chance of passing."

Second, at least during the 1960's, the congressional relations officials had explicitly designated lieutenants in all major departments.[33] For the most part these department officers were loyal partisans who owe allegiance almost equally to their cabinet members *and* to the White House congressional relations office, for the White House legislative liaison team had authority to remove or fire departmental legislative relations aides. These department contacts frequently had "graduated" to their posts from campaign or Capitol Hill staff work. In general, the White House staff enjoyed cordial and close (often with weekly meetings) relations with these "compatible" counterparts in the departments. In marked contrast with the White House domestic and budget aides it was quite rare for the White House congressional relations aides to have much if any contact with non-partisan civil servants or "bureaucrats." To some extent, their departmental lieutenants took the brunt of and absorbed department conflicts, thereby leaving the White House congressional relations aides relatively free to deal with senior congressional officials and preside over White House–congressional relations strategies.

Finally, the primary preoccupation of White House congressional relations aides is dealing with the leadership and committee chairmen in Congress. Since congressional aides are employed first and foremost to help forge viable coalitions of congressional support from bill to bill and from one legislative season to the next, their chief opposition consists of dissident members of their own party or influential opponents on the other side of the congressional aisle. Departmental concerns, especially departmental debates about alternative programs, are less appreciated and probably less well understood by congressional relations White House aides; these latter concerns necessarily take a back seat to their principal attention which is devoted to congressional and partisan strategy and tactics. In sum, then, both the fact that congressional relations aides have less actual contact with cabinet members and civil servants and the fact that they have distinctively different functional responsibilities account for less perceived conflict with departments. . . .

E. On the Modern Presidential Cabinet

An apparent pattern characterizes White House–cabinet relations over time. Just as there is a distinctive presidential "honeymoon" with the press and with partisan critics, so also White House–department ties usually are the closest and most cooperative during the first year of an administration. The first six months of the relationship is usually cordial, "healthy," and often bordering on the euphoric. The election victory is still being celebrated. A new team of "leaders" has arrived in Washington. New faces provide for extensive new copy. A new federal policy agenda is being recast. The newly staffed executive branch gives everyone an impression of bubbling over with new ideas, new possibilities, and imminent breakthroughs. In contrast to the much publicized arrival of the cabinet members, White House staff receive less publicity at this time. White House ceremonies feature the announcement, installation, and self-congratulatory rituals of welcoming in the recently anointed cabinet chieftains who, at least in the Nixon version, are men possessed of special "extra dimensions." The Washington political community, the executive branch in particular, is a veritable merry-go-round of good will and cheerful open doors. One Kennedy cabinet member, remembering those early days, noted that Kennedy told his cabinet that there would be frequent cabinet meetings and that individual cabinet officers should telephone him or Vice President Lyndon Johnson on anything of importance; when in doubt they should "err on the side of referring too much" on policy matters.[34] Even the egregiously silly or blandest of proposals coming from cabinet members at this time are tolerated and entertained by a deferential White House staff and a happily elected President.

But as policy formulation is accentuated in the early years of a presidential term, program management and implementation receive increasing attention in the later period (especially if a President has been successful in passing a fair amount of new legislation by then). Critical domestic developments and international crises begin to monopolize the presidential schedule. Presidents gradually find that they have much less time for personally dealing with cabinet members as they had in the administration's early months. Cabinet members become less inclined to refer "too much" to the President, knowing full well that they may prematurely exhaust their personal political credit with him. Additionally, the President's program becomes somewhat fixed; priorities get set and budget ceilings produce some new rules of the game. Ambitious, expansionist cabinet officers become painfully familiar with various Executive Office staff refrains, usually to the effect that "there just isn't any more money available for programs of that magnitude," "budget projections for the next two or three years just can't absorb that type of increment," and perhaps harshest of all—"yes, I agree that this is an excellent proposal, but excellent though it may be, it will just have to wait until the next term."

When, in the course of an administration, cabinet members grow bitter about the way they are treated and increasingly left out of White House affairs, they seldom make their opinions public. There are, of course, some exceptions and privately a good number of cabinet officers will talk about the problem. The case of Interior Secretary Walter Hickel is perhaps an extreme case; the fact that he had only two or three private meetings with his President during a two year period seems an unusually restrictive arrangement. Most recent cabinet officers have had more frequent relations with their White House superiors, but few of the domestic cabinet members have been wholly pleased by the quantity or quality of these meetings. Said one Johnson cabinetman, "I just don't know what you can do—you just have to realize that his day is the same length as yours and become resigned to the reality that he just can't afford to spend much time with most of us—especially with that war going on."

A cabinet member who served both Presidents Kennedy and Johnson stated that there should unquestionably have been more cabinet meetings:

> there are two important things that should be done through the use of the cabinet meetings. First, meetings should be held to inform the cabinet members about major developments or new priorities. Secondly, the president should occasionally bring some major policy issue before the cabinet and open it up for detailed discussion. He should take advantage of the broad gauged abilities of these very able men. For example, never once was there any discussion of whether we should send more troops to Vietnam. This type of policy matter was always confined to the national security council group—but they could have benefitted from our views and ideas on this type of matter, for we had less personal involvement in the earlier decisions and might have been able to give valuable added perspective or fresh appraisals.

An insightful commentary is provided by John Kennedy's Postmaster General in his witty but somewhat bitter memoir-recollections. J. Edward Day suggests that Kennedy had neither the time nor the inclination to utilize the collective judgment of his cabinet; Day also hints that Kennedy hardly made use of several of the cabinet members even in their individualized department leadership roles. It is worth citing three of his observations at length, not so much because he is one of the few cabinet members to express his views openly, as because his views are similar to the private complaints of several other cabinet officers:

> . . . President Kennedy had never had the experience of being an executive among lesser but by no means subservient executives; he had been served by a fanatically devoted band of men of his own creation. His Cabinet was a different run of shad. Each member was independent and quick to express his views, perhaps too much so for the President's taste. . . .

> The impression was created . . . that the President preferred smaller meetings with those Cabinet members concerned with a specific problem. *But his absorption with politics, publicity, and foreign policy allowed him little time to be concerned about the domestic departments*, unless they had an immediate political aspect. For the domestic Cabinet, *personal meetings with the President became fewer and farther between*, and more than one member grew increasingly unhappy because it was so difficult to see the President.
>
> The atmosphere at Cabinet meetings should have been right for free-and-easy, frank discussion. At the outset it had been only natural to assume that such discussion would be encouraged. . . .
>
> The setting may have been right, but after the first two or three meetings one had the distinct impression that the President felt that decisions on major matters were not made—or even influenced—at Cabinet sessions, and what discussion there was a waste of time. . . . When members spoke up to suggest or to discuss major Administration policy, the President would listen with thinly disguised impatience and then postpone or otherwise bypass the question. . . .[35]

A senior Kennedy staff member tells of the occasion when one cabinet officer had repeatedly requested him to make an appointment with the President. "He kept calling and calling, and so finally about the forty-third time—after I had told him over and over again that this wasn't the type of problem the President wanted to discuss with cabinet members—I finally relented and scheduled an appointment. Immediately after Secretary X completed his appointment and had left, Kennedy stormed into my office and [in emphatically strong language] chewed me out for letting the cabinet member in!"

Cabinet members who went to President Johnson with requests were often faced with a *quid pro quo** situation, and at least for some cabinet members, presidential requests were an added factor in keeping them at a distance. One cabinet officer noted that most of the domestic department heads tried as much as possible to leave the President alone because of the enormous Vietnam war burdens the President was carrying. "But even at that, it was known that the President would welcome visits by domestic cabinet members on Saturday mornings. In retrospect, several of us regret that we did not make greater and better use of those opportunities. But part of the reason we didn't was because Johnson had an uncanny way of asking favors of you or giving you a number of political chores to do that you knew you didn't want and often couldn't carry out."

By mid-term election time, the White House also expects cabinet members to campaign for the administration and to celebrate the administrative and legislative record of the past two years. Like it or not, cabinet members become judged on their capacity to generate favorable publicity, and to proclaim the virtues of the recent "White House" achievements and, above all, to exclaim the performance of the sitting President. . . .

**Quid pro quo:* Latin term that translates as "something for something." The expression is used commonly in law to describe the exchange of one thing or favor for another.

In recent years several members of the White House staff have performed cabinet-level counselor roles. Eisenhower, for example, explicitly designated Sherman Adams* as a protocol member of his cabinet. Kennedy clearly looked upon Theodore Sorenson,† McGeorge Bundy,‡ and some of his economic advisors as co-equals if not more vital to his work than most of his cabinet members. Johnson and Nixon have likewise assigned many of their "staff" men to cabinet-type counseling responsibilities. Indeed, President Nixon, quite reasonably, has appropriated this term—cabinet counselor—for several of his personal staff, including Messrs. Burns,§ Moynihan,‖ Harlow,** and Finch.†† These counselors, whether in department posts or on the White House staff, are expected to rise above the narrowing frame of reference of the conventional advocate and, in Moynihan's view "It is not enough [that they] know one subject, one department. The President's men must know them all, must understand how one thing relates to another, must find in the words the spirit that animates them. . . .[36] The people to whom Presidents turn for White House overview presentations to congressmen and cabinet gatherings provide another indicator of inner "cabinet" status. When Kennedy wanted to have his cabinet briefed on his major priorities, he would typically ask Secretary of State Dean Rusk to review foreign affairs considerations, Chairman of the Council of Economic Advisers Walter Heller would review major questions about the economy, and Ted Sorensen might sum up and give a status report on the domestic legislative program. In like manner, when Lyndon Johnson would hold special "seminars" for large gatherings of congressmen and their staffs, he would invariably call up the Secretaries of State and Defense to explain national security matters, and then ask his Budget Director and his Chairman of The Council of Economic Advisers to comment upon economic, budgetary, and domestic program considerations. More recently, President Nixon would typically call upon his Secretary of State, his director of the Office of Management and Budget, and one of his chief White House domestic policy counselors to inform and instruct members of his assembled cabinet and sub-cabinet. These illustrations indicate that recent Presidents often believe that members of their own Executive Office are better equipped to talk about and counsel "significant others" regarding the "President's" program rather

***Sherman Adams*: see footnote "Goldfine case" on page 337.

†*Theodore Sorensen*: see footnote on page 293.

‡*McGeorge Bundy*: special White House assistant for national security (1961–1966).

§*Arthur F. Burns*: economist who was a counselor with cabinet status (1969–1970) to President Nixon until his appointment as chairman of the Federal Reserve Board, where he served from 1970 until 1978.

‖*Daniel P. Moynihan*: urban affairs advisor (1969–1973) to President Nixon. He later served as ambassador to India (1973–1975), and ambassador to the United Nations (1975–1976). He has been a Democratic senator from New York since 1976.

***Bryce N. Harlow*: President Nixon's assistant for legislative affairs during 1969 and a counselor with cabinet rank in charge of national affairs in 1970. Harlow resigned from his post in 1970 to work in the private sector, but returned in 1973 to assist Nixon during the Watergate investigation.

††*Robert Finch*: President Nixon's secretary of Health, Education, and Welfare from January 1969 through June 1970. Amid declining support for his initiatives, Nixon moved him to the White House as counsel to the president in 1970, where he was kept on the periphery until his resignation in 1972.

than let most cabinet members attempt to do the same. Kallenbach's reasoning in this regard seems appropriate:

> [A]s the departments have grown and supervision of their operations has become more burdensome, the heads have less opportunity to concern themselves with questions of general policy outside their own spheres of interest. Another factor is the steady enlargement of the Cabinet group itself. . . . This creates a condition which tends to induce the President to rely more heavily upon one or more individuals in the group for general advice, rather than upon all equally.[37]

What has generally happened in recent years is that the Secretaries of State and Defense still remain as prominent national security advisors though the National Security Assistant to the President has joined them as an inner-circle counselor. In domestic and economic matters Treasury Secretaries and most Attorney Generals still play a major role in rendering advice and broad-ranging policy counsel, but they have been joined in the inner "cabinet" by the Budget Director, and variously prominent White House and staff economists and domestic policy coordinators. President Nixon's 1971 cabinet reform proposal is an apparent recognition of the problem of the outer cabinet's "distance" from the presidency. His proposals would abolish some of the outer cabinet departments and attempt to bring four newly packaged or consolidated "outer" departments into closer proximity if not full-fledged status with his inner cabinet. It is impossible to tell whether his recommendations will make any significant difference in this regard, although his motives for proposing this change are no doubt related to the seemingly estranged relationships between the outer departments and the White House. . . .

VI. STRENGTHENING WHITE HOUSE–DEPARTMENT RELATIONS?

There is little difficulty in establishing the existence of considerable White House frustration with department "unresponsiveness" or parochialism and the existence of cabinet and department distress at the sometimes unnecessary political and abrasive behavior of the White House staff. But it is much less easy to evaluate the varied prescriptions that are put forth as a means toward improving White House–department relations. This last section discusses some proposals suggested by former White House staff and concludes with some general observations about strengthening White House relations with the cabinet departments.

We have seen in preceding sections that there is no one single cause of White House–department conflicts; moreover there is no one simple solution. Indeed, it would seem reasonable that the appropriate reforms will vary not only with the type of problem but also according to staff functions at the White House and the differentiated departments involved. Most of the White House aides at least implicitly acknowledge that numerous remedial or regenerating efforts are needed within the White House as well as between the White House and departments.

Many former presidential aides began their discussion of reforms by pointing out the obvious: no two Presidents are exactly alike; styles differ as well as policy preferences. Hence, "each president should organize his office more or less as he sees fit." And not a few aides recalled instances of intentions for remedying bad habits at the White House which quickly evaporated:

> Johnson would occasionally try to organize us into some better relationship to the cabinet and agencies. He would get memos on a certain day from two different White House people with two differing views or competing thoughts. He must have told me several times [after such occasions] and I know he told some of the others on the White House staff to "ORGANIZE THIS PLACE!!—organize it along more coherent lines so there won't be so much overlap." But this, [when tried], wouldn't last for more than a few days, because the President himself wouldn't stick to it or honor it. In practice the White House just does not lend itself very easily to that type of straight line or box-like organization.

As seen in Table 3, rather than uniformly calling for the presidential or "more power to the White House" perspective, these aides support what might be called an integration model just as much, and many of them support a department/cabinet approach as well. Almost eighty per cent of the domestic and budget policy aides offered suggestions that would strengthen the White House policy planning and management capabilities. Even those who complained about White House staff arrogance often concluded that Presidents must have tough and aggressive staff help. The following responses provide some flavor of the strong presidentialist beliefs of many of the aides. (One could conclude about the first response that it is less a solution than a source of conflict itself).

> The presidency has to be the activist within the very conservative federal bureaucracy. The bureaucracy is the conservative agent or the custodian of old laws and old policies. They fight against anything new suggested by the White House, hence a president has to be the destabilizing factor in the system. The inability of department institutions to be creative or to take on new responsibilities is fantastic! In my view, the most important thing for a president is to know how to *shake* up the bureaucracy! My own law is that for every new major priority you need to create a new agency—never give it to the existing department. You need a new agency to get the resources and the leadership to pull off anything that is a major departure—like getting a man to the moon.

> I think it is impossible to run the White House staff without having tough men to do the work of the president. Sorensen, Feldman* and Dungan† (Kennedy aides) were of this type. They could be very tough, abrasive, and uncompromising. But they had to be tough because if they were not the people in the agencies and departments just wouldn't respect the communications that came from the White House. I think it is a

***Myer Feldman:* legislative assistant to Senator John F. Kennedy (1958–1961), deputy special counsel to Presidents Kennedy and Johnson (1961–1964), and counsel to Johnson (1964–1965)

†*Ralph A. Dungan:* assistant and later an advisor on labor legislation and politics to President John F. Kennedy. He was a speech writer during the 1960 presidential campaign, a talent scout for political appointees. From 1964–1967, he served as U.S. ambassador to Chile under President Lyndon B. Johnson.

TABLE 3 PRESIDENCY STAFF PERSPECTIVES ON THE QUESTION OF IMPROVING COOPERATION AND REDUCING CONFLICT BETWEEN WHITE HOUSE AND THE EXECUTIVE DEPARTMENTS

Strategy Perspectives[b]	*Percentages*[a] N = 43
I. PRESIDENTIAL PERSPECTIVE:	
—Stronger WH Management-Monitoring System	45%
—More Aggressive WH Sanctions and Controls over Executive Departments	41
—Stronger WH Policy Determinating Capability	33
II. INTEGRATIVE PERSPECTIVE:	
—Make It More of a "Two-Way Street"	45
—More Collaboration and Departmental Involvement in Policy Setting	40
—More WH Staff Sensitivity and Homework Re: Intra-Departmental Concern	36
III. DEPARTMENTAL—CABINET PERSPECTIVE:	
—Strengthen Cabinet Secretaries and Cabinet-President Linkage	26
—Delegate More to Departments—Less WH Interference and Primacy; More Trust and Better Communications	24

Source: Personal Interviews of White House Staff Members Who Served During 1961–1970 period.
[a]Percentages here reflect multiple responses.
[b]Aggregate responses to the three perspectives were as follows: 69% of the respondents recommended the presidential perspective, 69% recommended the integrative perspective, and 40% recommended the departmental/cabinet perspective.

> fundamental dilemma that people working for a president have to be arrogant, and almost be bastards in order to get White House work done with the departments.

Although there is a good deal of overlap between those supporting the presidential and integrative perspectives, the integration approach was relatively more supported among the administrative and public relations assistants and among the national security policy aides than among the domestic and budget policy advisers. Integrative recommendations are seemingly based on the assumption that the White House is not likely to have much of an effect on federal program implementation unless it can win supportive cooperation from among the middle and higher echelons of the executive branch departments. For example:

> I think the basic solution to the problem of dealing with the departments is to get one or two top staff people in the office of a cabinet member or department head and have these people work closely with the White House team. This helps a lot. It has to be a two-way street between the White House and the Cabinet members. It is very important for White House aides to do favors for Cabinet members when they really want to get a promotion for somebody, or get some projects done. If you don't go along with them occasionally, and do this type of thing for them, they in turn are going to be difficult to deal with for yourself. It should be a bargaining, give and take, two-way relationship.

Some forty per cent of the former White House staff aides noted that a strong presidency could only succeed in an executive branch which also was characterized by the existence of strong cabinet and departmental leadership. Many of these aides felt that Kennedy, and Johnson, and their senior staff had neglected the cabinet members and underestimated their importance in making the government work. One aide insisted that it was a major mistake to let the domestic cabinet departments become so divorced from the White House:

> One way to improve things is to have the president and the cabinet members, particularly in domestic areas, meet at least six or seven times a year and talk in great detail, and in highly substantive terms, about the major priorities of the administration. You have to have better communication. Basically you have to make the cabinet less insecure.

Other aides criticized certain of their colleagues for having taken over operational responsibilities of the regular agencies, adding that too often these aides neither expedited program implementation nor accomplished anything else except possibly enlarging their own importance. Other aides aren't so sure of remedies as they are convinced that past behavior by the White House is no longer adequate:

> I think one major problem is the care and feeding of cabinet members. Most of these guys are people too, and the White House staff must be sensitive to that. Luther Hodges spent four miserable years there [as Secretary of Commerce] and Ed Day [Postmaster General] was also very discontented. They got the feeling that they were left out. As the White House gets more of the action and much larger—the cabinet people will resent it even more. Even if and when you are able to recruit good people to the cabinet, they are likely to let their jobs go and be less excited about the challenges of their work if they are continually kept at a distance from the White House. . . .

Those aides who held sub-cabinet positions in one of the departments or agencies (either before or immediately after they worked on the White House staff) were significantly more sympathetic to the departmental/cabinet perspective than most of their White House colleagues who had not served "in the other fellow's shoes."

VII. CONCLUSION

A democracy must serve as a forum or arena for the practical and just mediation of conflicts. If our elected chief executive and his lieutenants were not constantly surrounded, or "afflicted," by a wide diversity of conflicts, they would probably be avoiding their legitimate public responsibilities. The conflicts discussed in this paper are those that exist within the executive branch, but it seems fair to assume that executive branch conflicts in large part mirror the existing and potential conflicts of society at large and as such they deserve far more detailed scrutiny. In general, however, we can conclude with Lewis Coser* that such conflicts as exist are multilateral rather than unilateral, multidimensional rather than unidimensional, and occasioned by mixed rather than single motives. This

***Lewis A. Coser:* Distinguished Professor of Sociology at the State University of New York. Among his numerous works are: *Political Sociology* (1967), *Continuities in the Study of Social Conflict* (1967), and *Masters of Sociological Thought* (1971, enlarged edition, 1977).

paper suggests, if anything, that the conflicts which abound in the executive branch admit no single source, nor are they generated by any one set of political actors or agents. Size, complexity, specialization, and differing policy preferences are but a few of the factors contributing to that richness of contention that often exists within the American executive establishment. . . .

The way in which our elections and campaign systems are run makes it easy to accentuate discussions about policy issues rather than policy strategies, and this emphasis seemed overextended during the 1960's. At the beginning of a presidential term White House staffs are initially comprised of policy-generating and policy-distillating activists who attempt to make good on the sweeping proposals that were vaguely articulated in previous campaigns. The emphasis is on policy change and the development of brand new sets of policies rather than the adaptation or improvement of existing policy. It may well be that the initial investment in a staff gathered for the purpose of developing and selling new policies skews the White House counseling resources in such a way that the White House is less effective in managerial and implementation aspects of policy leadership. Since it appears that White House work emphases are somewhat subject to cycles of accentuated policy formulation or accentuated policy implementation, it may be that staffing patterns should similarly be subject to shifting composition. During the Kennedy-Johnson presidencies, however, the internal composition of the staff did not noticeably change. The domestic policy staff, for example, continued to be comprised of youthful Washington lawyers who were geared to putting together new programs for the next State of the Union. But during periods when program implementation and interdepartmental jurisdictional disputes become the overriding concerns of a presidential administration it may not be enough to rely solely upon this type of staff. And to overcome some of the operational deficiencies of major new programs such as those making up the core of the War on Poverty, Alliance for Progress,* and Great Society it may not be enough to have White House lawyers and economists occasionally seek the advice of management consultants or appoint managerial project directors to secondary departmental posts.

Even if Presidents reshuffle their executive branch departments, even if Presidents could redesign the congressional committee structure to their own preference and banish lobbyists from the metropolitan Washington community—conflicts would still exist and flourish within the executive establishment. Therefore, no matter what other reforms are attempted, Presidents and their senior-most advisers ought to give far more consideration to the need for skilled management mediators, who will not be afraid occasionally to widen the scope of conflict, who can selectively step in and divide up controversial pieces of the action. By custom if not by preparation, White House aides have increasingly been forced to serve as arbitrators among competing agencies, competing policies, and competing priorities. Indeed, the increasing prominence and importance of domestic, budget, and national security policy aides at the White

Alliance for Progress: President Kennedy's program to promote economic cooperation between the United States and Latin America.

House derive from their sitting as judges on the high court of executive branch jurisdictional claims. But ironically many of these people were recruited to the White House not because of their special talents in this area, but because of their help on the campaign trail or as an academic adviser to a presidential candidate or a President-elect in search of a legislative program. It is an understatement to suggest that the White House is in great need of decisive executive branch mediators who can, with the full confidence of the President, preside over the thorniest of complicated claims and counter-claims by competing cabinet members and know when worthy and important elements of a debate are being seriously neglected or misrepresented within these cabinet level negotiations. . . .

. . . A distinction between an inner and outer clustering of the cabinet can be inferred. Inner cabinet members (Defense, State, Treasury and Justice) seem to enjoy closer and more collaborative ties with the White House; outer departments are more characterized by centrifugal pulls that dissipate close counseling relationships with the White House. But there are some implications of this dichotomy which are not entirely clear at first glance; the problem for the White House may not be to try to make the outer cabinet precisely like the inner cabinet, but to consider whether the inner cabinet might not benefit from some aspects of the way in which the White House relates to the outer cabinet. That is, the cordial and frequent contact between White House and Defense, Justice, Treasury, and the Secretary of State may actually camouflage substantive problems that should be contended, and issues that should be subject to the clashing of adversary viewpoints. United States policy in Vietnam, the Bay of Pigs* episode, inadequate tax reform, and too casual a concern for civil liberties are general illustrations that come most readily to mind as by-products of the inner cabinet in the 1960's. It may be . . . because White House relationships with the counseling departments seem so close, comfortable, and professional in comparison with White House relationships with the overt advocate departments, that the White House too readily accepts the judgments of these departments, overlooks potentially divisive issues, and neglects the creation of an effective system of multiple and critical advocacy for the substantive and operational aspects of these departments. Too often in the 1960's the debates and adversary proceedings came too late or were procedurally foreclosed with reference to inner cabinet policy choices. If this be so, then many of the more conventional structural reforms (including some of those which President Nixon proposed in his 1971 State of the Union address) misunderstand an important aspect of White House–department relationships. Efforts must be made to increase certain types of conflicts and advocacy proceedings to ferret out differences of views, to generate alternative policy choices (and their rationale), and to estimate the likely consequences of diverse policies. . . .

No one should dispute that our modern presidency is charged with enormous new obligations to act as an overseer of executive branch *responsiveness* and

**Bay of Pigs:* see footnote on page 355.

integrity. Who else can recruit talented departmental leadership? Who else can better motivate, educate, and inspire federal officials to higher levels of public commitment? And who else can both authoritatively mediate interdepartmental squabbles and wage vigilant pressure campaigns against those within the federal governments who see themselves as the chief constituency of their own federal departments? All this and more is expected of the modern presidency and the expanded super staffs at the White House. But notions of government integrity and responsiveness are always slippery and should necessarily be subject to continuous definitional disputes. Responsiveness to whom? Is the presidentialists' perspective really free of special interests, or does this depend almost entirely on whether one happens to like the sitting President?

We come back, invariably to a realization that Presidents are limited in the degree to which they can eliminate executive branch conflicts, and alternatively try to strengthen White House–department ties. Presidents have been and will continue to be frustrated by the sluggishness of the federal executive branch's response to new priorities. And increasingly, Presidents are disillusioned by the seeming incapacity to inspire and recharge the batteries of the sprawling federal government. But there are occasions, I think, when Presidents and their staff are justifiably thwarted from any easy resolution of substantive and procedural conflicts. We must be careful to maintain a political climate in which uncomfortable questions can be asked of a President from within—or without—the White House. Sometimes an issue is of sufficient divisiveness that it is not then amenable to any majoritarian point of view, and displacement or avoidance of conflict may be the best approach. Moreover, certain types of conflict-resolution or coordination are essentially forms of coercion that might threaten the rightfully independent bases of influence and opposing viewpoints in Congress or society.[38]

We might measurably contribute to the health of our presidency by examining and ultimately appreciating those conflicts that are avoidable or unavoidable, appropriate or inappropriate, and by trying to understand how these conflicts can limit as well as strengthen the presidency. Properly conceived and carried through, such analyses will undoubtedly help to limit and refine our expectations and assessments of democratic presidential leadership.

NOTES

[1]Bailey, *The President and His Political Executives*, ANNALS, Sept. 1956, at 24.

[2]*See* R. FENNO, THE PREESIDENT'S CABINET 271 (1959).

[3]Tugwell, *The President and His Helpers: A Review Article*, 82 POL. SCI. Q. 253, 262 (1967).

[4]*Id.* at 265.

[5]Interview with President John F. Kennedy televised December 16, 1962.

[6]Quoted in Rovere, *Letter from Washington*, THE NEW YORKER, Nov. 30, 1963.

[7]Nixon, State of the Union address, Jan. 22, 1971, in 117 CONG. REC. H92, H94 (daily ed. Jan. 22, 1971).

[8]For more theoretical treatments of the exchange system notion, see G. HOMANS, SOCIAL BEHAVIOUR (1961); P. BLAU, EXCHANGE AND POWER IN SOCIAL LIFE (1964). *Cf.* Heath, *Review Article: Exchange Theory*, 1 B. J. POL. SCI. 91 (1971).

[9]Neustadt, *Politicians and Bureaucrats, in* THE CONGRESS AND AMERICA'S FUTURE 102, 113 (D. Truman ed. 1965).

[10]Quoted in an interview by Sidey, *The White House Staff vs. the Cabinet*, THE WASHINGTON MONTHLY, Feb. 1969, at 4.

[11]Since the period under study here is 1961 through 1970, the bulk of these interviews were with Kennedy and Johnson staff aides. These interview/informants serve as substitutes for direct participant observation by the author. From the various "informants," through a careful process of filling in parts of the complex mosaic, we can construct a richer descriptive-analytical account of the exchange relationships.

[12]*See, e.g.*, A. SCHLESINGER, A THOUSAND DAYS (1965); J. SUNDQUIST, POLITICS AND POLICY: THE EISENHOWER, KENNEDY, AND JOHNSON YEARS (1968).

[13]*See* THE FEDERALIST NO. 70 (Hamilton).

[14]M. BUNDY, THE STRENGTH OF GOVERNMENT 37 (1968). *See also id.* ch. 2.

[15]SCHLESINGER, *supra* note 12, at 683.

[16]L. KOENIG, THE CHIEF EXECUTIVE 417 (rev. ed. 1968).

[17]This view was expressed by one former cabinet member interviewed for this study.

[18]D. TRUMAN, THE GOVERNMENTAL PROCESS 407–08 (1951).

[19]REEDY, *supra* note 17, at 94.

[20]WOOD, *When Government Works*, THE PUBLIC INTEREST, Winter, 1970, at 39, 45.

[21]*See* C. SCHULTZE, ET AL., SETTING NATIONAL PRIORITIES (1970); Weidenbaum, *Budget "Uncontrollability" as an Obstacle to Improving the Allocation of Government Resources*, in I THE ANALYSIS AND EVALUATION OF PUBLIC EXPENDITURES: THE PPB SYSTEM 353–68 (Compendium of papers presented to the Joint Economic Committee of the United States Congress, 1969).

[22]The staff perceptions of the sources of conflict shown in Table 2 do not adequately reflect the intensity of the respondents' views. Although they blamed White House staff operations approximately as often as they faulted the departments, the author feels their criticisms of department officials and civil servants were more intense than their criticisms of their White House colleagues.

[23]For a discussion of indecisiveness and ambiguity during the Eisenhower years, see N. POLSBY, CONGRESS AND THE PRESIDENCY 19–22 (1964).

[24]Farewell comments to the Nixon cabinet and subcabinet delivered by Daniel P. Moynihan in the East Room of the White House, Washington, D.C., Dec. 21, 1970, reprinted in 6 WEEKLY COMP. PRES. DOC. 1729, 1731 (1970).

[25]C. COOPER, THE LOST CRUSADE 414 (1970).

[26]*See* H. GRAFF, THE TUESDAY CABINET 172 (1970).

[27]*See, e.g.*, J. DAVIS, THE NATIONAL EXECUTIVE BRANCH 146 (1970).

[28]SCHLESINGER, *supra* note 12, at 681.

[29]An attempt to explicate the "presidential perspective" is made in T. SORENSEN, DECISION-MAKING IN THE WHITE HOUSE 78–86 (1963).

[30]*See* POLSBY, *supra* note 23, at 102–03, for a discussion of this same variable in executive-legislative relations.

[31]*See* H. SEIDMAN, POLITICS, POSITION, AND POWER 76 (1970); Kempton, *Proclaim and Abandon: The Life and Hard Times of the Teacher Corps*, THE WASHINGTON MONTHLY, Feb. 1969, 10–19.

[32]E. HUGHES, THE ORDEAL OF POWER 59 (1963).

[33]*See* A. HOLTZMAN, LEGISLATIVE LIAISON: EXECUTIVE LEADERSHIP IN CONGRESS 263 & ch. 9 (1970).

[34]J. DAY, MY APPOINTED ROUND: 929 DAYS AS POSTMASTER GENERAL 97 (1965).

[35]*Id.* at 96–98.

[36]Moynihan comments, *supra* note 24, at 1731.

[37]J. KALLENBACH, THE AMERICAN CHIEF EXECUTIVE 439–40 (1966).

[38]This point is made in Wildavsky, *Salvation by Staff: Reform of the Presidential Office*, in THE PRESIDENCY 700 (1969).

PART SEVEN

THE BUREAUCRACY

Government at all levels in the United States is bureaucratized. Today there are close to 3 million federal civil servants and about 12 million state and local public employees. Many of them are engaged in setting the public policy agenda as well as formulating, implementing, evaluating, and revising public policy. Their jobs combine aspects of management, politics, and law. They have discretionary authority over large sums of money, and they promulgate rules that have the force of law and adjudicate cases arising under the statutes and regulations that their agencies execute. Power over public bureaucracies is generally divided primarily between the elected executive and the legislature, though in recent years the courts have also played a large part in public administration. The bureaucratic form of organization relies on specialization for efficiency; hierarchy for coordination and accountability; formalization for precision; impersonality for the rapid processing of cases and for treating like cases alike; and recruitment and promotion on the basis of some conception of merit to assure that civil servants are qualified for their jobs and insulated from partisan manipulation. The development of large-scale and politically powerful bureaucracies was not envisioned by the framers; nor does the constitutional framework provide for it in any comprehensive fashion. Not surprisingly, therefore, managing and controlling the bureaucracy have been a constant struggle in American government.

No one has explored questions of bureaucracy more thoughtfully than James Q. Wilson. In an essay reprinted here, Wilson stresses that "the bureaucracy problem" is really several problems—efficiency, equity, fiscal integrity, responsiveness, accountability, and control—many of which require solutions that may be mutually incompatible. Thus, administrative reorganizations, budgetary adjustments, or better congressional oversight are unlikely to improve bureaucratic performance. Rather, government must clarify the programmatic goals of its bureaucratic agencies, come to terms with limits of administrative feasibility, and recognize that no bureaucracy can perform satisfactorily if it is expected to serve inconsistent social objectives.

Contrary to much wishful thinking about how public administration *ought* to be depoliticized, the fact is that public bureaucracies are essentially political organizations, and must be understood as such by students of the administrative process. Among the first to emphasize this simple, but oft neglected observation was Norton E. Long. In his famous essay, "Power and Administration" (1949), Long writes that "the lifeblood of administration is power." As a result of the fragmentation found in the American political system, public bureaucrats "must supplement the resources available through the hierarchy with those they can muster on their own." Unlike Wilson, however, Long argues that bureaucratic power can be harmonized with democratic government if administrative decisions are responsive to organized interest groups. "The bureaucracy is recognized by all interested groups as a major channel of representation to such an extent that Congress rightly feels the competition of a rival."

22

JAMES Q. WILSON

THE BUREAUCRACY PROBLEM

Regardless of one's position on the political spectrum, the federal bureaucracy is problematic. The "bureaucracy problem" means different things to different people: accountability, equity, efficiency, political responsiveness, and fiscal integrity. Unfortunately, the solutions to these problems are often mutually inconsistent. James Q. Wilson, the Collins Professor of Management and Public Policy at UCLA, and one of the nation's foremost political scientists, suggests we address the problems of bureaucracy by first reexamining fundamental public goals and clarifying programmatic objectives. Wilson has been a major contributor to policy studies in several areas: urban politics, public administration and bureaucracy, regulatory administration, organization theory and behavior, and criminal justice. Among his books are: The Politics of Regulation *(1980),* Thinking about Crime *(1975, 1983),* American Government: Institutions and Policies *(1983), and with Richard J. Herrnstein,* Crime and Human Nature *(1985). His latest book on the subject,* Bureaucracy, *will be published by Basic Books in 1989. "The Bureaucracy Problem" was published in* The Public Interest *in 1967.*

The federal bureaucracy, whose growth and problems were once only the concern of the Right, has now become a major concern of the Left, the Center, and almost all points in between. Conservatives once feared that a powerful bureaucracy would work a social revolution. The Left now fears that this same bureaucracy is working a conservative reaction. And the Center fears that the bureaucracy isn't working at all.

Increasing federal power has always been seen by conservatives in terms of increasing *bureaucratic* power. If greater federal power merely meant, say, greater uniformity in government regulations—standardized trucking regulations, for example, or uniform professional licensing practices—a substantial segment of American businessmen would probably be pleased. But growing federal power means increased discretion vested in appointive officials whose behavior can neither be anticipated nor controlled. The behavior of state and local bureaucrats, by contrast, can often be anticipated *because* it can be controlled by businessmen and others.

Knowing this, liberals have always resolved most questions in favor of enhancing federal power. The "hacks" running local administrative agencies were too often, in liberal eyes, the agents of local political and economic forces—businessmen, party bosses, organized professions, and the like. A federal bureaucrat, because he was responsible to a national power center and to a single President elected by a nationwide constituency, could not so easily be bought off by local vested interests; in addition, he would take his policy guidance from a President elected by a process that gave heavy weight to the votes of urban, labor, and minority groups. The New Deal* bureaucrats, especially those appointed to the new, "emergency" agencies, were expected by liberals to be free to chart a radically new program and to be competent to direct its implementation.

It was an understandable illusion. It frequently appears in history in the hopes of otherwise intelligent and far-sighted men. Henry II thought his clerks and scribes would help him subdue England's feudal barons; how was he to know that in time they would become the agents of Parliamentary authority directed at stripping the king of his prerogatives? And how were Parliament and its Cabinet ministers, in turn, to know that eventually these permanent undersecretaries would become an almost self-governing class whose day-to-day behavior would become virtually immune to scrutiny or control? Marxists thought that Soviet bureaucrats would work for the people, despite the fact that Max Weber† had pointed out why one could be almost certain they would work mostly for themselves. It is ironic that among today's members of the "New Left," the "Leninist problem"—i.e., the problem of over-organization and of self-perpetuating administrative power—should become a major preoccupation.

This apparent agreement among polemicists of the Right and Left that there is a bureaucracy problem accounts, one suspects, for the fact that non-bureaucratic solutions to contemporary problems seem to command support from both groups. The negative income tax as a strategy for dealing with poverty is endorsed by economists of such different persuasions as Milton Friedman‡ and James Tobin,§ and has received favorable consideration among members of both the Goldwater‖ brain trust and the Students for Democratic Society.** Though the interests of the two groups are somewhat divergent, one common element is a desire to scuttle the social workers and the public welfare bureaucracy, who are usually portrayed as prying busybodies with pursed lips and steel-rimmed glasses ordering midnight bedchecks in public housing projects. (Police officers who complain that television makes them look like fools in the eyes of their children will know just what the social workers are going through.)

Now that everybody seems to agree that we ought to do something about the problem of bureaucracy, one might suppose that something would get done. Perhaps a grand reorganization, accompanied by lots of "systems analysis," "citi-

*New Deal: see footnote on page 17.

†Max Weber: see footnote on page 24.

‡*Milton Friedman:* Winner of the 1976 Nobel Prize for Economics, and a leading advocate of government deregulation and laissez-faire economics. Friedman has written numerous books including: *A Theory of the Consumption Function* (1957), *Dollars and Deficits* (1968), *Price Theory* (1971, 1976), and *Capitalism and Freedom* (1974).

§*James Tobin:* Sterling Professor of Economics at Yale University, who won the Nobel Prize for Economics in 1981. His numerous books include *Asset Accumulation and Economic Activity* (1980), *Essays in Economics* (1987), and *Policies for Prosperity* (1987) with Peter McLeod Jackson.

‖*Barry Goldwater:* see footnote on page 188.

***Students for a Democratic Society* (SDS): radical political organization in the United States from 1962 until internal dispute led to its dissolution in the late 1960's. SDS opposed United States participation in the Vietnam War, sought an end to racial discrimination and poverty, and argued that colleges and universities should be more responsive to the political, intellectual, social, and cultural agendas of their students.

zen participation," "creative federalism," and "interdepartmental co-ordination." Merely to state this prospect is to deny it.

There is not one bureaucracy problem, there are several, and the solution to each is in some degree incompatible with the solution to every other. First, there is the problem of accountability or control—getting the bureaucracy to serve agreed-on national goals. Second is the problem of equity—getting bureaucrats to treat like cases alike and on the basis of clear rules, known in advance. Third is the problem of efficiency—maximizing output for a given expenditure, or minimizing expenditures for a given output. Fourth is the problem of responsiveness—inducing bureaucrats to meet, with alacrity and compassion, those cases which can never be brought under a single national rule and which, by common human standards of justice or benevolence, seem to require that an exception be made or a rule stretched. Fifth is the problem of fiscal integrity—properly spending and accounting for public money.

Each of these problems mobilizes a somewhat different segment of the public. The problem of power is the unending preoccupation of the President and his staff, especially during the first years of an administration. Equity concerns the lawyers and the courts, though increasingly the Supreme Court seems to act as if it thinks its job is to help set national goals as a kind of auxiliary White House. Efficiency has traditionally been the concern of businessmen who thought, mistakenly, that an efficient government was one that didn't spend very much money. (Of late, efficiency has come to have a broader and more accurate meaning as an optimal relationship between objectives and resources: Robert McNamara* has shown that an "efficient" Department of Defense costs a lot more money than an "inefficient" one; his disciples are now carrying the message to all parts of a skeptical federal establishment.) Responsiveness has been the concern of individual citizens and of their political representatives, usually out of wholly proper motives, but sometimes out of corrupt ones. Congress, especially, has tried to retain some power over the bureaucracy by intervening on behalf of tens of thousands of immigrants, widows, businessmen, and mothers-of-soldiers, hoping that the collective effect of many individual interventions would be a bureaucracy that, on large matters as well as small, would do Congress's will. (Since Congress only occasionally has a clear will, this strategy only works occasionally.) Finally, fiscal integrity—especially its absence—is the concern of the political "outs" who want to get in and thus it becomes the concern of "ins" who want to keep them out.

Obviously the more a bureaucracy is responsive to its clients—whether those clients are organized by radicals into Mothers for Adequate Welfare or represented by Congressmen anxious to please constituents—the less it can be accountable to presidential directives. Similarly, the more equity, the less responsiveness. And a preoccupation with fiscal integrity can make the kind of program budgeting required by enthusiasts of efficiency difficult, if not impossible.

Indeed, of all the groups interested in bureaucracy, those concerned with fiscal integrity usually play the winning hand. To be efficient, one must have clearly

***Robert McNamara:* see footnote on page 379.

stated goals, but goals are often hard to state at all, much less clearly. To be responsive, one must be willing to run risks, and the career civil service is not ordinarily attractive to people with a taste for risk. Equity is an abstraction, of concern for the most part only to people who haven't been given any. Accountability is "politics," and the bureaucracy itself is the first to resist that (unless, of course, it is the kind of politics that produces pay raises and greater job security.) But an absence of fiscal integrity is welfare chiseling, sweetheart deals, windfall profits, conflict of interest, malfeasance in high places—in short, corruption. Everybody recognizes *that* when he sees it, and none but a few misguided academics have anything good to say about it. As a result, fiscal scandal typically becomes the standard by which a bureaucracy is judged (the FBI is good because it hasn't had any, the Internal Revenue Service is bad because it has) and thus the all-consuming fear of responsible executives.

If it is this hard to make up one's mind about how one wants the bureaucracy to behave, one might be forgiven if one threw up one's hands and let nature take its course. Though it may come to that in the end, it is possible—and important—to begin with a resolution to face the issue squarely and try to think through the choices. Facing the issue means admitting what, in our zeal for new programs, we usually ignore: *There are inherent limits to what can be accomplished by large hierarchical organizations.*

The opposite view is more often in vogue. If enough people don't like something, it becomes a problem; if the intellectuals agree with them, it becomes a crisis; any crisis must be solved; it it must be solved, then it can be solved—and creating a new organization is the way to do it. If the organization fails to solve the problem (and when the problem is a fundamental one, it will almost surely fail), then the reason is "politics," or "mismanagement," or "incompetent people," or "meddling," or "socialism," or "inertia."

Some problems cannot be solved and some government functions cannot, in principle, be done well. Notwithstanding, the effort must often be made. The rule of reason should be to try to do as few undoable things as possible. It is regrettable, for example, that any country must have a foreign office, since none can have a good one. The reason is simple: it is literally impossible to have a "policy" with respect to *all* relevant matters concerning *all* foreign countries, much less a consistent and reasonable policy. And the difficulty increases with the square of the number of countries, and probably with the cube of the speed of communications. The problem long ago became insoluble and any sensible Secretary of State will cease trying to solve it. He will divide his time instead between *ad hoc* responses to the crisis of the moment and appearances on Meet the Press.

The answer is not, it must be emphasized, one of simply finding good people, though it is at least that. Most professors don't think much of the State Department, but it is by no means clear that a department made up only of professors would be any better, and some reason to believe that it would be worse. One reason is that bringing in "good outsiders," especially good outsiders from universities, means bringing in men with little experience in dealing with the substantive problem but many large ideas about how to approach problems "in general." General ideas, no matter how soundly based in history or social science, rarely tell one what to do tomorrow about the visit from the foreign trade mission from Ruritania or the questions from the Congressional appropriations subcommittee.

Another reason is that good people are in very short supply, even assuming we knew how to recognize them. Some things literally cannot be done—or cannot be done well—because there is no one available to do them who knows how. *The supply of able, experienced executives is not increasing nearly as fast as the number of problems being addressed by public policy.* All the fellowships, internships, and "mid-career training programs" in the world aren't likely to increase that supply very much, simply because the essential qualities for an executive—judgment about men and events, a facility for making good guesses, a sensitivity to political realities, and an ability to motivate others—are things which, if they can be taught at all, cannot be taught systematically or to more than a handful of apprentices at one time.

This constraint deserves emphasis, for it is rarely recognized as a constraint at all. Anyone who opposed a bold new program on the grounds that there was nobody around able to run it would be accused of being a pettifogger at best and a reactionary do-nothing at worst. Everywhere except in government, it seems, the scarcity of talent is accepted as a fact of life. Nobody (or almost nobody) thinks seriously of setting up a great new university overnight, because anybody familiar with the university business knows that, for almost any professorship one would want to fill, there are rarely more than five (if that) really top-flight people in the country, and they are all quite happy—and certainly well-paid—right where they are. Lots of new business ideas don't become profit-making realities because good business executives are both hard to find and expensive to hire. The government—at least publicly—seems to act as if the supply of able political executives were infinitely elastic, though people setting up new agencies will often admit privately that they are so frustrated and appalled by the shortage of talent that the only wonder is why disaster is so long in coming. Much would be gained if this constraint were mentioned to Congress *before* the bill is passed and the hopes aroused, instead of being mentioned afterward as an excuse for failure or as a reason why higher pay scales for public servants are an urgent necessity. "Talent is Scarcer Than Money" should be the motto of the Budget Bureau.

If administrative feasibility is such a critical issue, what can be done about it? Not a great deal. If the bureaucracy problem is a major reason why so many programs are in trouble, it is also a reason why the problem itself cannot be "solved." But it can be mitigated—though not usually through the kinds of expedients we are fond of trying: Hoover Commissions,* management studies,

***Hoover Commissions:* two commissions chaired by Herbert Hoover (1874–1964), former president of the United States (1929–1933). They were formally titled Commissions on the Organization of the Executive Branch of Government. Several recommendations of the first commission (1947–1949) calling for increased managerial capacity in the executive branch were adopted. The second commission (1953–1955) was unable to win substantial support for its recommendations to limit federal activities that competed with business.

expensive consultants, co-ordinating committees, "czars," and the like. The only point at which very much leverage can be gained on the problem *is when we decide what it is we are trying to accomplish*. When we define our goals, we are implicitly deciding how much, or how little, of a bureaucracy problem we are going to have. A program with clear objectives, clearly stated, is a program with a fighting chance of coping with each of the many aspects of the bureaucracy problem. Controlling an agency is easier when you know what you want. Equity is more likely to be assured when over-all objectives can be stated, at least in part, in general rules to which people in and out of the agency are asked to conform. Efficiency is made possible when you know what you are buying with your money. Responsiveness is never easy or wholly desirable; if every person were treated in accordance with his special needs, there would be no program at all. (The only system that meets the responsiveness problem squarely is the free market.) But at least with clear objectives we would know what we are giving up in those cases when responsiveness seems necessary, and thus we would be able to decide how much we are willing to tolerate. And fiscal integrity is just as easy to insure in a system with clear objectives as in one with fuzzy ones; in the former case, moreover, we are less likely to judge success simply in terms of avoiding scandal. We might even be willing to accept a little looseness if we knew what we were getting for it.

The rejoinder to this argument is that there are many government functions which, by their nature, can never have clear objectives. I hope I have made it obvious by now that I am aware of that. We can't stop dealing with foreign nations just because we don't know what we want; after all, they may know what *they* want, and we had better find out. My argument is advanced, not as a panacea—there is no way to avoid the problem of administration—but as a guide to choice in those cases where choice is open to us, and as a criterion by which to evaluate proposals for coping with the bureaucracy problem.

Dealing with poverty—at least in part—by giving people money seems like an obvious strategy. Governments are very good at taking money from one person and giving it to another; the goals are not particularly difficult to state; measures are available to evaluate how well we are doing in achieving a predetermined income distribution. There may be many things wrong with this approach, but administrative difficulty is not one of them. And yet, paradoxically, it is the last approach we will probably try. We will try everything else first—case work, counseling, remedial education, community action, federally-financed mass protests to end "alienation," etc. And whatever else might be said in their favor, the likelihood of smooth administration and ample talent can hardly be included.

Both the White House and the Congress seem eager to do something about the bureaucracy problem. All too often, however, the problem is described in terms of "digesting" the "glut" of new federal programs—as if solving administrative difficulties had something in common with treating heartburn. Perhaps those seriously concerned with this issue will put themselves on notice that they ought not to begin with the pain and reach for some administrative bicarbonate of soda; they ought instead to begin with what was swallowed and ask whether an emetic is necessary. *Coping with the bureaucracy problem is inseparable from rethinking the objectives of the programs in question.* Administrative reshuffling, budgetary cuts (or budgetary increases), and congressional investigation of lower-level boondoggling will not suffice and are likely, unless there are some happy accidents, to make matters worse. Thinking clearly about goals is a tough assignment for a political system that has been held together in great part by compromise, ambiguity, and contradiction. And if a choice must be made, any reasonable person would, I think, prefer the system to the clarity. But now that we have decided to intervene in such a wide range of human affairs, perhaps we ought to reassess that particular trade-off.

23

NORTON E. LONG

POWER AND ADMINISTRATION

Norton E. Long challenged the idea, entrenched in orthodox public administration theory, that public bureaucracy could divorce its administrative functions from politics. His essay, "Power and Administration," published in the Autumn 1949 issue of Public Administration Review *was pathbreaking. It argued convincingly that public administrators must engage in politics and power-seeking to accomplish their objectives. Certain characteristics of the American polity, such as the absence of a strong party system and the rivalry between the presidency and the Congress, block the flow of power from elected officials to career civil servants. American public administrators have adapted to those conditions by developing their own power base through alliances with interest groups and key members of Congress. Long, the Curators Professor of Political Science and Director of the Center for Community and Metropolitan Studies at the University of Missouri—St. Louis, has also written such influential essays as "The Local Community as an Ecology of Games,"* American Journal of Sociology *(1958),* The Polity *(1962),* The Unwalled City *(1972), and "Public Administration: Ethics and Epistemology"* (American Review of Public Administration, *June 1988).*

I

There is no more forlorn spectacle in the administrative world than an agency and a program possessed of statutory life, armed with executive orders,* sustained in the courts, yet stricken with paralysis and deprived of power. An object of contempt to its enemies and of despair to its friends.

The lifeblood of administration is power. Its attainment, maintenance, increase, dissipation, and loss are subjects the practitioner and student can ill afford to neglect. Loss of realism and failure are almost certain consequences. This is not to deny that important parts of public administration are so deeply entrenched in the habits of the community, so firmly supported by the public, or so clearly necessary as to be able to take their power base for granted and concentrate on the purely professional side of their problems. But even these islands of the blessed are not immune from the plague of politics, as witness the fate of the hapless Bureau of Labor Statistics and the perennial menace of the blind 5 per cent across-the-board budget cut. Perhaps Carlyle's aphorism holds here, "The healthy know not of their health but only the sick." To stay healthy one needs to recognize that health is a fruit, not a birthright. Power is only one of the considerations that must be weighed in administration, but of all it is the most overlooked in theory and the most dangerous to overlook in practice.

**Executive orders:* rules, proclamations, or regulations issued by the president or other chief executive.

The power resources of an administrator or an agency are not disclosed by a legal search of titles and court decisions or by examining appropriations or budgetary allotments. Legal authority and a treasury balance are necessary but politically insufficient bases of administration. Administrative rationality requires a critical evaluation of the whole range of complex and shifting forces on whose support, acquiescence, or temporary impotence the power to act depends.

Analysis of the sources from which power is derived and the limitations they impose is as much a dictate of prudent administration as sound budgetary procedure. The bankruptcy that comes from an unbalanced power budget has consequences far more disastrous than the necessity of seeking a deficiency appropriation. The budgeting of power is a basic subject matter of a realistic science of administration.

It may be urged that for all but the top hierarchy of the administrative structure the question of power is irrelevant. Legislative authority and administrative orders suffice. Power adequate to the function to be performed flows down the chain of command. Neither statute nor executive order, however, confers more than legal authority to act. Whether Congress or President can impart the substance of power as well as the form depends upon the line-up of forces in the particular case. A price control law wrung from a reluctant Congress by an amorphous and unstable combination of consumer and labor groups is formally the same as a law enacting a support price program for agriculture backed by the disciplined organizations of farmers and their congressmen. The differences for the scope and effectiveness of administration are obvious. The Presidency, like Congress, responds to and translates the pressures that play upon it. The real mandate contained in an Executive order varies with the political strength of the group demand embodied in it, and in the context of other group demands.

Both Congress and President do focus the general political energies of the community and so are considerably more than mere means for transmitting organized pressures. Yet power is not concentrated by the structure of government or politics into the hands of a leadership with a capacity to budget it among a diverse set of administrative activities. A picture of the Presidency as a reservoir of authority from which the lower echelons of administration draw life and vigor is an idealized distortion of reality.

A similar criticism applies to any like claim for an agency head in his agency. Only in varying degrees can the powers of subordinate officials be explained as resulting from the chain of command. Rarely is such an explanation a satisfactory account of the sources of power.

To deny that power is derived exclusively from superiors in the hierarchy is to assert that surbordinates stand in a feudal relation in which to a degree they fend for themselves and acquire support peculiarly their own. A structure of interests friendly or hostile, vague and general or compact and well-defined, encloses each significant center of administrative discretion. This structure is an important determinant of the scope of possible action. As a source of power and authority it is a competitor of the formal hierarchy.

Not only does political power flow in from the sides of an organization, as it were; it also flows up the organization to the center from the constituent parts.

When the staff of the Office of War Mobilization and Reconversion advised a hard-pressed agency to go out and get itself some popular support so that the President could afford to support it, their action reflected the realities of power rather than political cynicism.

It is clear that the American system of politics does not generate enough power at any focal point of leadership to provide the conditions for an even partially successful divorce of politics from administration. Subordinates cannot depend on the formal chain of command to deliver enough political power to permit them to do their jobs. Accordingly they must supplement the resources available through the hierarchy with those they can muster on their own, or accept the consequences in frustration—a course itself not without danger. Administrative rationality demands that objectives be determined and sights set in conformity with a realistic appraisal of power position and potential.

II

The theory of administration has neglected the problem of the sources and adequacy of power, in all probability because of a distaste for the disorderliness of American political life and a belief that this disorderliness is transitory. An idealized picture of the British parliamentary system as a Platonic form to be realized or approximated has exerted a baneful fascination in the field. The majority party with a mandate at the polls and a firmly seated leadership in the Cabinet seems to solve adequately the problem of the supply of power necessary to permit administration to concentrate on the fulfillment of accepted objectives. It is a commonplace that the American party system provides neither a mandate for a platform nor a mandate for a leadership.

Accordingly, the election over, its political meaning must be explored by the diverse leaders in the executive and legislative branches. Since the parties have failed to discuss issues, mobilize majorities in their terms, and create a working political consensus on measures to be carried out, the task is left for others—most prominently the agencies concerned. Legislation passed and powers granted are frequently politically premature. Thus the Council of Economic Advicers was given legislative birth before political acceptance of its functions existed. The agencies to which tasks are assigned must devote themselves to the creation of an adequate consensus to permit administration. The mandate that the parties do not supply must be attained through public relations and the mobilization of group support. Pendleton Herring* and others have shown just how vital this support is for agency action.

The theory that agencies should not confine themselves to communicating policy suggestions to executive and legislature, and refrain from appealing to their clientele and the public, neglects the failure of the parties to provide either a clear-cut decision as to what they should do or an adequately mobilized political

E. Pendleton Herring: influential public administration scholar, and the author of *Public Administration and the Public Interest* (1936), *Presidential Leadership* (1940), and *Some Perspectives on Political Science and Science* (1959–1961).

support for a course of action. The bureaucracy under the American political system has a large share of responsibility for the public promotion of policy and even more in organizing the political basis for its survival and growth. It is generally recognized that the agencies have a special competence in the technical aspects of their fields which of necessity gives them a rightful policy initiative. In addition, they have or develop a shrewd understanding of the politically feasible in the group structure within which they work. Above all, in the eyes of their supporters and their enemies they represent the institutionalized embodiment of policy, an enduring organization actually or potentially capable of mobilizing power behind policy. The survival interests and creative drives of administrative organizations combine with clientele pressures to compel such mobilization. The party system provides no enduring institutional representation for group interest at all comparable to that of the bureaus of the Department of Agriculture. Even the subject matter committees of Congress function in the shadow of agency permanency.

The bureaucracy is recognized by all interested groups as a major channel of representation to such an extent that Congress rightly feels the competition of a rival. The weakness in party structure both permits and makes necessary the present dimensions of the political activities of the administrative branch—permits because it fails to protect administration from pressures and fails to provide adequate direction and support, makes necessary because it fails to develop a consensus on a leadership and a program that makes possible administration on the basis of accepted decisional premises.

Agencies and bureaus more or less perforce are in the business of building, maintaining, and increasing their political support. They lead and in large part are led by the diverse groups whose influence sustains them. Frequently they lead and are themselves led in conflicting directions. This is not due to a dull-witted incapacity to see the contradictions in their behavior but is an almost inevitable result of the contradictory nature of their support.

Herbert Simon* has shown that administrative rationality depends on the establishment of uniform value premises in the decisional centers of organization. Unfortunately, the value premises of those forming vital elements of political support are often far from uniform. These elements are in Barnard's† and Simon's sense "customers" of the organization and therefore parts of the organization whose wishes are clothed with a very real authority. A major and most time-consuming aspect of administration consists of the wide range of activities de-

**Herbert Simon:* administrative theorist and economist who holds the Richard King Mellon Chair in Computer Science and Psychology at Carnegie-Mellon University. Simon won the Nobel Prize for Economics in 1987 for his work in managerial decision making. He is the author of numerous books including *Administrative Behavior* (1945), *Models of Man: Social and Rational* (1958), *The New Science of Management Decision* (1960), *The Shape of Automation for Men and Management* (1965), and *Human Problem Solving* (1972).

†*Chester I. Barnard* (1886–1961): former president of New Jersey Bell Telephone (1927–1948) and the Rockefeller Foundation (1952–1954). He is well known for his book *The Functions of the Executive* (1938), which focused attention on the relationship between formal and informal groups in organizations. He noted that successful executives demonstrate a willingness to communicate and learn the needs of their employees, as well to as preserve and advance the purposes of the organization. He also wrote *Organization and Management* (1948).

signed to secure enough "customer" acceptance to survive and, if fortunate, develop a consensus adequate to program formulation and execution.

To varying degrees, dependent on the breadth of acceptance of their programs, officials at every level of significant discretion must make their estimates of the situation, take stock of their resources, and plan accordingly. A keen appreciation of the real components of their organization is the beginning of wisdom. These components will be found to stretch far beyond the government payroll. Within the government they will encompass Congress, congressmen, committees, courts, other agencies, presidential advisers, and the President. The Aristotelian analysis of constitutions is equally applicable and equally necessary to an understanding of administrative organization.

The broad alliance of conflicting groups that makes up presidential majorities scarcely coheres about any definite pattern of objectives, nor has it by the alchemy of the party system had its collective power concentrated in an accepted leadership with a personal mandate. The conciliation and maintenance of this support is a necessary condition of the attainment and retention of office involving, as Madison so well saw, "the spirit of party and faction in the necessary and ordinary operations of government." The President must in large part be, if not all things to all men, at least many things to many men. As a consequence, the contradictions in his power base invade administration. The often criticized apparent cross-purposes of the Roosevelt regime cannot be put down to inept administration until the political facts are weighed. Were these apparently self-defeating measures reasonably related to the general maintenance of the composite majority of the Administration? The first objective—ultimate patriotism apart—of the administrator is the attainment and retention of the power on which his tenure of office depends. This is the necessary pre-condition for the accomplishment of all other objectives.

The same ambiguities that arouse the scorn of the naive in the electoral campaigns of the parties are equally inevitable in administration and for the same reasons. Victory at the polls does not yield either a clear-cut grant of power or a unified majority support for a coherent program. The task of the Presidency lies in feeling out the alternatives of policy which are consistent with the retention and increase of the group support on which the Administration rests. The lack of a budgetary theory (so frequently deplored) is not due to any incapacity to apply rational analysis in the comparative contribution of the various activities of government to a determinate hierarchy of purposes. It more probably stems from a fastidious distaste for the frank recognition of the budget as a politically expedient allocation of resources. Appraisal in terms of their political contribution to the Administration provides almost a sole common denominator between the Forest Service and the Bureau of Engraving.

Integration of the administrative structure through an over-all purpose in terms of which tasks and priorities can be established is an emergency phenomenon. Its realization, only partial at best, has been limited to war and the extremity of depression. Even in wartime the Farm Bureau Federation, the American Federation of Labor, the Congress of Industrial Organizations, the National Association of Manufacturers, the Chamber of Commerce, and a host of lesser interests resisted coordination of themselves and the agencies concerned with their interests. A Presidency temporarily empowered by intense mass popular support acting in behalf of a generally accepted and simplified purpose can, with great difficulty, bribe, cajole, and coerce a real measure of joint action. The long-drawn-out battle for conversion and the debacle of orderly reconversion underline the difficulty of attaining, and the transitory nature of, popularly based emergency power. Only in crises are the powers of the Executive nearly adequate to impose a common plan of action on the executive branch, let alone the economy.

In ordinary times the manifold pressures of our pluralistic society work themselves out in accordance with the balance of forces prevailing in Congress and the agencies. Only to a limited degree is the process subject to responsible direction or review by President or party leadership.

The program of the President cannot be a Gosplan* for the government precisely because the nature of his institutional and group support gives him insufficient power. The personal unity of the Presidency cannot perform the function of Hobbes' sovereign since his office lacks the authority of Hobbes' contract.† Single headedness in the executive gives no assurance of singleness of purpose. It only insures that the significant pressures in a society will be brought to bear on one office. Monarchy solves the problem of giving one plan to a multitude only when the plenitude of its authority approaches dictatorship.‡ Impatient social theorists in all ages have turned to the philosopher king as a substitute for consensus. Whatever else he may become, it is difficult to conceive of the American president ruling as a philosopher king,§ even with the advice of the Executive Office. The monarchical solution to the administrative problems posed by the lack of a disciplined party system capable of giving firm leadership and a program to the legislature is a modern variant of the dreams of the eighteenth century savants‖ and well nigh equally divorced from a realistic appraisal of social realities.

Much of administrative thought, when it does not assume the value of coordination for coordination's sake, operates on the assumption that there must be something akin to Rousseau's** *volonté générale*†† in administration to which the errant *volonté de tous*‡‡ of the bureaus can and should be made to conform. This

**Gosplan:* central planning organization of the Soviet Union responsible for directing economic and social development. Its comprehensive plans, once approved by the Supreme Soviet, or legislature, are legally binding.

†*Thomas Hobbes* (1588–1679): English political theorist and philosopher, and the author of *Leviathan* (1651), a systematic analysis of human nature, political authority, and law. Hobbes argued that governments are formed to protect individuals from each other as well as from external threats. His work influenced that of Locke, Rousseau, and the framers of the U.S. Constitution.

‡*Dictatorship:* form of government in which one person or group assumes absolute political control, often without consent of the governed.

§*Philosopher king:* as conceived by Plato, one who legitimately holds and wields power because he has sought and found the truth. Plato developed this concept as an *ideal*, rather than a practical model.

‖*Savant:* French term for a person of considerable wisdom and education.

***Rousseau:* see footnote on page 16.

††*Volonté generale:* French term meaning "general will."

‡‡*Volonté de tous:* French term meaning the "will of all."

will-o'-the-wisp was made the object of an illuminating search by Pendleton Herring in his *Public Administration and the Public Interest*. The answer for Rousseau was enlightened dictatorship or counting the votes. The administrative equivalent to the latter is the resultant of the relevant pressures, as Herring shows. The first alternative seems to require at least the potency of the British Labour party and elsewhere has needed the disciplined organization of a fascist, nazi, or communist party to provide the power and consensus necessary to coordinate the manifold activities of government to a common plan.

Dictatorship, as Sigmund Neumann* has observed, is a substitute for institutions which is required to fill the vacuum when traditional institutions break down. Force supplies the compulsion and guide to action in place of the normal routines of unconscious habit. Administrative organizations, however much they may appear the creations of art, are institutions produced in history and woven in the web of social relationships that gives them life and being. They present the same refractory material to the hand of the political artist as the rest of society of which they form a part.

Just as the economists have attempted to escape the complexities of institutional reality by taking refuge in the frictionless realm of theory, so some students of administration, following their lead, have seen in the application of the doctrine of opportunity costs† a clue to a science of administration. Valuable as this may be in a restricted way, Marx‡ has more light to throw on the study of institutions. It is in the dynamics and interrelations of institutions that we have most hope of describing and therefore learning to control administrative behavior.

III

The difficulty of coordinating government agencies lies not only in the fact that bureaucratic organizations are institutions having survival interests which may conflict with their rational adaptation to over-all purpose, but even more in their having roots in society. Coordination of the varied activities of a modern government almost of necessity involves a substantial degree of coordination of the economy. Coordination of government agencies involves far more than changing the behavior and offices of officials in Washington and the field. It involves the publics that are implicated in their normal functioning. To coordinate fiscal policy, agricultural policy, labor policy, foreign policy, and military policy, to name a few major areas, moves beyond the range of government charts and the habitat of the bureaucrats to the market place and to where the people live and work. This suggests that the reason why government reorganization is so difficult is that far more than government in the formal sense is involved in reorganization. One could overlook this in the limited government of the nine-

**Sigmund Neumann* (1904–1962): social scientist who coauthored *Dictatorship in the Modern World* (1939). He also wrote *Makers of Modern Strategy* (1949) and *European Political Systems* (1953).

†*Opportunity cost:* in social science, the price, in the form of alternative opportunities foregone, of choosing one course of action instead of another.

‡*Karl Marx:* see footnote on page 13.

teenth century but the multi-billion dollar government of the mid-twentieth permits no facile dichotomy between government and economy. Economy and efficiency are the two objectives a laissez faire society can prescribe in peacetime as over-all government objectives. Their inadequacy either as motivation or standards has long been obvious. A planned economy clearly requires a planned government. But, if one can afford an unplanned economy, apart from gross extravagance, there seems no compelling and therefore, perhaps, no sufficiently powerful reason for a planned government.

Basic to the problem of administrative rationality is that of organizational identification and point of view. To whom is one loyal—unit, section, branch, division, bureau, department, administration, government, country, people, world history, or what? Administrative analysis frequently assumes that organizational identification should occur in such a way as to merge primary organization loyalty in a larger synthesis. The good of the part is to give way to the reasoned good of the whole. This is most frequently illustrated in the rationalizations used to counter self-centered demands of primary groups for funds and personnel. Actually the competition between governmental power centers, rather than the rationalizations, is the effective instrument of coordination.

Where there is a clear common product on whose successful production the sub-groups depend for the attainment of their own satisfaction, it is possible to demonstrate to almost all participants the desirability of cooperation. The shoe factory produces shoes, or else, for all concerned. But the government as a whole and many of its component parts have no such identifiable common product on which all depend. Like the proverbial Heinz, there are fifty-seven or more varieties unified, if at all, by a common political profit and loss account.

Administration is faced by somewhat the same dilemma as economies. There are propositions about the behavior patterns conducive to full employment—welfare economics. On the other hand, there are propositions about the economics of the individual firm—the counsel of the business schools. It is possible to show with considerable persuasiveness that sound considerations for the individual firm may lead to a depression if generally adopted, a result desired by none of the participants. However, no single firm can afford by itself to adopt the course of collective wisdom; in the absence of a common power capable of enforcing decisions premised on the supremacy of the collective interest, *sauve qui peut** is common sense.

The position of administrative organizations is not unlike the position of particular firms. Just as the decisions of the firms could be coordinated by the imposition of a planned economy so could those of the component parts of the government. But just as it is possible to operate a formally unplanned economy by the loose coordination of the market, in the same fashion it is possible to operate a government by the loose coordination of the play of political forces through its institutions.

**Sauve qui peut:* French term that literally translates as "let him save himself who can." The more commonly used translation is "every man for himself."

The unseen hand of Adam Smith* may be little in evidence in either case. One need not believe in a doctrine of social or administrative harmony to believe that formal centralized planning—while perhaps desirable and in some cases necessary—is not a must. The complicated logistics of supplying the city of New York runs smoothly down the grooves of millions of well adapted habits projected from a distant past. It seems naive on the one hand to believe in the possibility of a vast, intricate, and delicate economy operating with a minimum of formal over-all direction, and on the other to doubt that a relatively simple mechanism such as the government can be controlled largely by the same play of forces.

Doubtless the real reasons for seeking coordination in the government are the same that prompt a desire for economic planning. In fact, apart from waging war with its demand for rapid change, economic planning would seem to be the only objective sufficiently compelling and extensive to require a drastic change in our system of political laissez faire. Harold Smith,† testifying before the Senate Banking and Currency Committee on the Employment Act of 1946, showed how extensive a range of hitherto unrelated activities could be brought to bear on a common purpose—the maintenance of maximum employment and purchasing power. In the flush of the war experience and with prophecies of reconversion unemployment, a reluctant Congress passed a pious declaration of policy. Senator Flanders‡ has recorded the meager showing to date.

Nevertheless, war and depression apart, the Employment Act of 1946 for the first time provides an inclusive common purpose in terms of which administrative activities can be evaluated and integrated. While still deficient in depth and content, it provides at least a partial basis for the rational budgeting of government activities. The older concept of economy and efficiency as autonomous standards still lingers in Congress, but elsewhere their validity as ends in themselves is treated with skepticism.

If the advent of Keynesian economics§ and the erosion of laissez faire have created the intellectual conditions requisite for the formulation of over-all government policy, they do not by any means guarantee the political conditions necessary for its implementation. We can see quite clearly that the development of an integrated administration requires an integrating purpose. The ideals of Locke,‖

**Adam Smith* (1723–1790): Scottish philosopher and classical political economist who is often called the father of classical economics. His most influential work, *The Wealth of Nations* (1776), conceived of laissez-faire capitalism as the best means to improve social welfare. Smith believed that rational individuals, in pursuit of their self interests, would be guided by the "invisible hand" of the market to promote the common good. He also argued that production would increase by a division of labor based on specialization.

†*Howard R. Smith:* economist and author of many books including *Government and Business* (1958), *Democracy and Public Interest* (1960), *The Capitalist Imperative* (1975), and *Management* (1980).

‡*Ralph E. Flanders* (1880–1970): Republican senator from Vermont (1946–1958).

§*Keynesian economics:* economic theory developed by Lord John Maynard Keynes (1883–1946), a British economist. Keynes's macroeconomic theory was exposited in his widely read book *The General Theory of Employment, Interest, and Money* (1936). Keynes proposed a theoretical foundation for a mixed economy and for government intervention by fiscal and monetary instruments to counteract business cycles.

‖*John Locke:* see footnote on page 12.

Smith, Spencer,* and their American disciples deny the need for such a purpose save for economy and efficiency's sake. Marx, Keynes, and their followers by denying the validity of the self-regulating economy have endowed the state with an over-arching responsibility in terms of which broad coordination of activities is not only intellectually possible but theoretically, at least, necessary. Intellectual perception of the need for this coordination, however, has run well ahead of the public's perception of it and of the development of a political channeling of power adequate to its administrative implementation.

Most students of administration are planners of some sort. Most congressmen would fly the label like the plague. Most bureaucrats, whatever their private faith, live under two jealous gods, their particular clientele and the loyalty check. Such a condition might, if it exists as described, cast doubt on whether even the intellectual conditions for rational administrative coordination exist. Be that as it may, the transition from a government organized in clientele departments and bureaus, each responding to the massive feudal power of organized business, organized agriculture, and organized labor, to a government integrated about a paramount national purpose will require a political power at least as great as that which tamed the earlier feudalism. It takes a sharp eye or a tinted glass to see such an organized power on the American scene. Without it, administrative organization for over-all coordination has the academic air of South American constitution making. One is reminded of the remark attributed to the Austrian economist Mises;† on being told that the facts did not agree with his theory, he replied "*desto schlechter für die Tatsache.*"‡

IV

It is highly appropriate to consider how administrators should behave to meet the test of efficiency in a planned polity; but in the absence of such a polity and while, if we like, struggling to get it, a realistic science of administration will teach administrative behavior appropriate to the existing political system.

A close examination of the presidential system may well bring one to conclude that administrative rationality in it is a different matter from that applicable to the British ideal. The American Presidency is an office that has significant monarchical characteristics despite its limited term and elective nature. The literature on court and palace has many an insight applicable to the White House. Access to the President, reigning favorites, even the court jester, are topics that show the

**Herbert Spencer* (1820–1903): British social theorist who argued in *Principles of Sociology* (vols. I, II, III) that social organizations and society have a tendency to develop from simple to complex forms over time. He was associated with social Darwinism in the United States.

†*Ludwig von Mises* (1881–1973): Austrian-born economist and social philosopher. He was an uncompromising defender of laissez-faire capitalism and critic of government intervention in the economy. He is the author of numerous books including *Socialism* (1922, 1981), *Bureaucracy* (1944), *Omnipotent Government* (1944), *On the Manipulation of Dollars and Credit* (1978) with Percy L. Greaves, and *Nation, State, and Economy* (1983).

‡*Desto schlechter für die Tatsache*": German expression that means ". . . so much worse for the fact!"

continuity of institutions. The maxims of LaRochefoucauld* and the memoirs of the Duc de Saint Simon† have a refreshing realism for the operator on the Potomac.

The problem of rival factions in the President's family is as old as the famous struggle between Jefferson and Hamilton, as fresh and modern as the latest cabal against John Snyder.‡ Experience seems to show that this personal and factional struggle for the President's favor is a vital part of the process of representation. The vanity, personal ambition, or patriotism of the contestants soon clothes itself in the generalities of principle and the clique aligns itself with groups beyond the capital. Subordinate rivalry is tolerated if not encouraged by so many able executives that it can scarcely be attributed to administrative ineptitude. The wrangling tests opinion, uncovers information that would otherwise never rise to the top, and provides effective opportunity for decision rather than mere ratification of prearranged plans. Like most judges, the Executive needs to hear argument for his own instruction. The alternatives presented by subordinates in large part determine the freedom and the creative opportunity of their superiors. The danger of becoming a Merovingian§ is a powerful incentive to the maintenance of fluidity in the structure of power.

The fixed character of presidential tenure makes it necessary that subordinates be politically expendable. The President's men must be willing to accept the blame for failures not their own. Machiavelli's‖ teaching on how princes must keep the faith bears re-reading. Collective responsibility is incompatible with a fixed term of office. As it tests the currents of public opinion, the situation on the Hill, and the varying strength of the organized pressures, the White House alters and adapts the complexion of the Administration. Loyalties to programs or to groups and personal pride and interest frequently conflict with whole-souled devotion to the Presidency. In fact, since such devotion is not made mandatory by custom, institutions, or the facts of power, the problem is perpetually perplexing to those who must choose.

The balance of power between executive and legislature is constantly subject to the shifts of public and group support. The latent tendency of the American Congress is to follow the age-old parliamentary precedents and to try to reduce the President to the role of constitutional monarch. Against this threat and to secure his own initiative, the President's resources are primarily demagogic,**

**François, Duc de La Rochefoucauld* (1613–1680): French classical writer who is noted for his numerous volumes of maxims, or statements of general principle.

†*Louis de Rouvroy, Duc de Saint Simon* (1675–1755): French nobleman who wrote *Memoires* (1829–1830), a voluminous record of life in the court of Louis XIV.

‡*John Snyder:* acting undersecretary at the U.S. Department of Commerce from 1983 until 1985, after serving in various positions in the department.

§*Merovingians:* dynasty who ruled from about 500 A.D. to 751 in what is today France and parts of Western Germany. After several generations of fighting their enemies and struggling among themselves they were overthrown by the Carolingians, who then established their own dynasty (751–987 in France, 751–911 in Germany).

‖*Niccolo de Bernardo Machiavelli* (1469–1527): Italian statesman and political philosopher who wrote *The Prince* (1532), an examination of the means of acquiring and maintaining power that has become a classic in political science.

***Demagogic:* see footnote on page 355.

with the weaknesses and strengths that dependence on mass popular appeal implies. The unanswered question of American government—"who is boss?"—constantly plagues administration. The disruption of unity of command is not just the problem of Taylor's* functional foreman, but goes to the stability and uniformity of basic decisional premises essential to consequent administration.

It is interesting to speculate on the consequences for administration of the full development of congressional or presidential government. A leadership in Congress that could control the timetable of the House and Senate would scarcely content itself short of reducing the President's Cabinet to what in all probability it was first intended to be, a modified version of the present Swiss executive. Such leadership could scarcely arise without centrally organized, disciplined, national parties far different from our present shambling alliances of state and local machines.

A Presidency backed by a disciplined party controlling a majority in Congress would probably assimilate itself to a premiership by association of legislative leadership in the formualtion of policy and administration. In either line of development the crucial matter is party organization. For the spirit of the party system determines the character of the government.

That the American party system will develop toward the British ideal is by no means a foregone conclusion. The present oscillation between a strong demagogic Presidency and a defensively powerful congressional oligarchy may well prove a continuing pattern of American politics, as it was of Roman. In the absence of a party system providing an institutionalized centripetal force in our affairs, it is natural to look to the Presidency as Goldsmith's weary traveler† looked to the throne.

The Presidency of the United States, however, is no such throne as the pre-World War I *Kaiserreich*‡ that provided the moral and political basis for the Prussian bureaucracy.§ Lacking neutrality and mystique, it does not even perform the function of the British monarchy in providing a psychological foundation for the permanent civil service. A leaderless and irresponsible Congress frequently makes it appear the strong point of the republic. The Bonapartist‖ experience in

**Frederick W. Taylor* (1856–1915): American mechanical engineer who founded scientific management, the science of discovering and utilizing the most efficient way to perform a job. Through time and motion studies Taylor established that efficiency could be enhanced by grouping similar activities together and using a division of labor to sort activities. Scientific management views workers as part of the industrial machinery, an approach that workers may resist despite promises of increased wages. Taylor wrote *Shop Management* (1903) and *The Principles of Scientific Management* (1911).

†*Goldsmith's weary traveler:* wanderer depicted by Oliver Goldsmith (1728–1774), famous Irish poet, novelist, dramatist, and historian, in his epic poem "The Traveler" (1765). The poem was based on his own wanderings through Europe as a young man.

‡*Kaiserreich:* German term referring to the empire ruled by the *caesar*, a Latin word for emperor. Wilhelm II was the last German kaiser; he ruled from 1888 until 1918.

§*Prussian bureaucracy:* hierarchically organized, authoritarian government built by the Prussian monarchy to establish Prussian military dominance in Northern Europe. The Prussian empire reached the height of its powers in the mid-1800s becoming the largest state of the German Empire.

‖*Bonapartist:* advocate of the policies of Napoleon Bonaparte (1769–1821), revolutionary French general who declared himself the emperor of France (see footnote on page 14), and later of his nephew's regime (Louis Napoleon, who ruled France during the so-called Second Empire, 1848–1870).

France, the Weimar Republic, and South American examples nearer home, despite important social differences, are relevant to any thoughtful consideration of building a solution to legislative anarchy on the unity of the executive.

The present course of American party development gives little ground for optimism that a responsible two party system capable of uniting Congress and Executive in a coherent program will emerge. The increasingly critical importance of the federal budget for the national economy and the inevitable impact of world power status on the conduct of foreign affairs make inescapable the problem of stable leadership in the American system. Unfortunately they by no means insure a happy or indeed any solution.

Attempts to solve administrative problems in isolation from the structure of power and purpose in the polity are bound to prove illusory. The reorganization of Congress to create responsibility in advance of the development of party responsibility was an act of piety to principle, of educational value; but as a practical matter it raised a structure without foundation. In the same way, reorganization of the executive branch to centralize administrative power in the Presidency while political power remains dispersed and divided may effect improvement, but in a large sense it must fail. The basic prerequisite to the administration of the textbooks is a responsible two party system. The means to its attainment are a number one problem for students of administration. What Schattschneider* calls the struggle for party government may sometime yield us the responsible parliamentary two party system needed to underpin our present administrative theory. Until that happy time, exploration of the needs and necessities of our present system is a high priority task of responsible scholarship.

*E. E. *Schattschneider:* see headnote on page 241.

PART EIGHT

THE JUDICIARY

When we addressed the uniqueness of the American political culture in the first section, we pointed out that some classic interpretations attribute much of American political development to "constitutionalism." The place of the Constitution in American life is clearly unique among the world's democratic political systems. The document is used not only as a guide in public policymaking, but also as a restraint upon the exercise of political power. It even provides moral and ethical guidance in the implementation of policy. Ever since Tocqueville's time, political observers have noted the American tendency to discuss policy issues in terms of their constitutionality. Today, issues such as abortion, affirmative action, drug testing in the government service, and religious displays on public property are examples.

A major consequence of American constitutionalism is that it bestows great power on the judiciary, especially on the Supreme Court. The Court has long since established the power of judicial review—that is, the power to declare the acts of other units of government, both federal and state, unconstitutional. There is no true equivalent to this judicial power in other nations. As "keeper" of the Constitution, the Supreme Court is, as Alexander Bickel points out, "the most extraordinarily powerful court of law the world has ever known." Paradoxically, though, even the world's most powerful court is weak in comparison to the presidency and to Congress. Its size, budget, and much of its jurisdiction are established by legislation, not by the Constitution itself. The judiciary also must rely on the executive branch to carry out its decisions. The judiciary's overriding political task is to secure its power through its judgment; to do so it must maintain and constantly strive to strengthen its legitimacy. It is around these themes that all the classic works on the American judiciary revolve.

Edward S. Corwin's "The 'Higher Law' Background of American Constitutional Law" (1928, 1955) reaches back into the history of Western jurisprudence to explain American constitutionalism. Corwin concludes that the supremacy of the Constitution in American politics cannot be attributed solely to that document's origins and ratification. Rather, he suggests, the Constitution's place in American political life is due to its content, its "embodiment of an essential and unchanging justice"; it is to these elemental principles that American public officials must be faithful.

Alexander M. Bickel's discussion of the "Establishment and General Justification of Judicial Review" (1962) is complex and subtle. Bickel comes to grips with "the essential reality that judicial review is a deviant institution in the American democracy." Yet he also considers judicial review to be a crucial aspect of the American political system and its culture. The institution is deviant because it does not rest on popular election; it is crucial because it enables the Constitution to be adapted to changing conditions. In roughly the same vein as Corwin, he addresses the symbolic, or even "mystic," functions of the Supreme Court: "But the Supreme Court as a legitimating force in society also casts a less palpable yet larger spell. With us the symbol of nationhood, of continuity, of unity and common purpose, is, of course, the Constitution, without particular reference to what exactly it means in this or that application. . . . [A]nd . . . it has in large part been left to the Supreme Court to concretize the symbol of the Constitution."

Martin Shapiro's "The Presidency and the Federal Courts" (1981) considers the contemporary role of the federal judiciary in the public policy process from the perspective of the presidency. Shapiro concludes that as a result of statutes that create rights for individuals and decades of judicial activism, ". . . the president now faces a Supreme Court which rivals his authority in formulating public goals and values and in agenda setting." Furthermore, ". . . the federal judiciary plays a substantial role in the fragmentation of political authority . . . ," confronting the president—and the political system for that matter. Like Bickel, Shapiro is concerned about "the power of the nonelected branch to interfere in our individuals lives and to set our national priorities. . . ."

To complete this section we have included, in abridged form, two Supreme Court decisions of fundamental importance.[1] They were delivered by Chief Justice John Marshall, a major architect of American constitutionalism: *Marbury v. Madison* (1803), in which judicial review was established, and *McCulloch v. Maryland* (1819), in which a broad view of national power was asserted with the words "Let the end be legitimate, let it be within the scope of the Constitution, and all means which are appropriate, which are plainly adapted to that end, which are not prohibited, but consistent with the letter and spirit of the Constitution, are constitutional."

[1]In the text of these cases, abbreviations and capitalization have been modernized, citations have been omitted, and second references to cases mentioned by the Supreme Court have been shortened to include the name of the first party only.

24

EDWARD S. CORWIN

THE "HIGHER LAW" BACKGROUND OF AMERICAN CONSTITUTIONAL LAW

Edward S. Corwin (1878–1963) was a prolific scholar who published eighteen books, coauthored two more, and wrote over eighty articles. The following selection is the introduction to "The 'Higher Law' Background of American Constitutional Law," one of his most famous pieces. Originally published in the 1928–1929 Harvard Law Review, *the article probes why Americans revere the Constitution and accept its supremacy. Central to the explanation is that American political culture has traditionally regarded the Supreme Court as the custodian, not merely of legislated law, but of a higher code. Several additional essays by Corwin can be found in* Corwin on the Constitution *(Volume I:1981, and II:1987), and* Presidential Power and the Constitution (1976), *compiled and edited by Richard Loss. Among his numerous other works are* The Constitution and What It Means Today *(1920);* The President, Office and Powers, 1787–1957 *(1957),* The President's Control of Foreign Relations *(1970).*

> Theory is the most important part of the dogma of the law, as the architect is the most important man who takes part in the building of a house.
>
> *Collected Legal Papers*, HOLMES*

The Reformation† superseded an infallible Pope with an infallible Bible; the American Revolution replaced the sway of a king with that of a document. That such would be the outcome was not unforeseen from the first. In the same number of *Common Sense* which contained his electrifying proposal that America should declare her independence from Great Britain, [Thomas] Paine‡ urged also a "Continental Conference," whose task he described as follows:

> The conferring members being met, let their business be to frame a Continental Charter, or Charter of the United Colonies; (answering to what is called the Magna Charta of England) fixing the number and manner of choosing members of congress and members of assembly . . . and drawing the line of business and jurisdiction

**Oliver Wendell Holmes:* see footnote page 19.

†*Reformation:* religious movement that was associated with sweeping changes in Europe during the sixteenth century and that led to splits in the Christian church between Catholics and Protestants. (See footnotes "Catholicism" and "Protestantism" on pages 25, 24.

‡*Thomas Paine:* (1737–1809): author of the pamphlets *Common Sense* (1776) and *The American Crisis* (1776), which provided a philosophical rationale for severing ties with England and inspired support for the Revolutionary War.

> between them: (always remembering, that our strength is continental, not provincial) securing freedom and property to all men . . . with such other matter as it is necessary for a charter to contain. . . . But where, say some, is the King of America? Yet that we may not appear to be defective even in earthly honors, let a day be solemnly set apart for proclaiming the charter; let it be brought forth placed in the divine law, the word of God; let a crown be placed thereon, by which the world may know, that so far as we approve of monarchy, that in America the law is King.[1]

This suggestion, which was to eventuate more than a decade later in the Philadelphia Convention, is not less interesting for its retrospection than it is for its prophecy.

In the words of the younger Adams, "the Constitution itself had been extorted from the grinding necessity of a reluctant nation"[2]; yet hardly had it gone into operation than hostile criticism of its provisions not merely ceased but gave place to "an undiscriminating and almost blind worship of its principles"[3]—a worship which continued essentially unchallenged till the other day. Other creeds have waxed and waned, but "worship of the Constitution" has proceeded unabated.[4] It is true that the Abolitionists* were accustomed to stigmatize the Constitution as "an agreement with Hell," but their shrill heresy only stirred the mass of Americans to renewed assertion of the national faith. Even Secession† posed as loyalty to the *principles* of the Constitution and a protest against their violation, and in form at least the constitution of the Southern Confederacy was, with a few minor departures, a studied reproduction of the instrument of 1787. For by far the greater reach of its history, Bagehot's‡ appraisal of the British monarchy is directly applicable to the Constitution: "The English Monarchy strengthens our government with the strength of religion."[5]

The fact that its adoption was followed by a wave of prosperity no doubt accounts for the initial launching of the Constitution upon the affections of the American people. Travelling through various parts of the United States at this time, Richard Bland Lee§ found "fields a few years ago waste and uncultivated filled with inhabitants and covered with harvests, new habitations reared, contentment in every face, plenty on every board. . . ." "To produce this effect," he continued, "was the intention of the Constitution, and it has succeeded." Indeed it is possible that rather too much praise was lavished upon the Constitution on this score: "It has been usual with declamatory gentlemen," complained the astringent Maclay,‖ "in their praises of the present government, by way of con-

**Abolitionists:* vociferous antislavery activists. From 1820 until the end of the Civil War in 1865 they kept the slavery issue on the political agenda by writing and publishing books, periodicals, newspapers, and pamphlets aimed at building support for the abolition of slavery. They also assisted runaway slaves making their way through the Underground Railroad to Canada.

†*Secession:* Several southern states tried to secede from the union in 1861, asserting that their state governments were sovereign. The Civil War ensued.

‡*Walter Bagehot:* see footnote on page 259.

§*Richard Bland Lee* (1761–1827): congressman from Virginia to the U.S. House of Representatives (1789–1795).

‖*William Maclay* (1734–1804): senator from Pennsylvania to the first Congress (1789–1791). *Sketches of Debates in the First Senate of the United States* (1880), a journal he kept, is the best continuous report of the period.

trast, to paint the state of the country under the old (Continental) congress, as if neither wood grew nor water ran in America before the happy adoption of the new Constitution"; and a few years later, when the European turmoil at once assisted, and by contrast advertised, our own blissful state, Josiah Quincy* voiced a fear that "we have grown giddy with good fortune, attributing the greatness of our prosperity to our own wisdom, rather than to a course of events, and a guidance over which we had no influence."[6]

But while the belief that it drew prosperity in its wake may explain the beginning of the worship of the Constitution, it leaves a deeper question unanswered. It affords no explanation why this worship came to ascribe to the Constitution the precise virtues it did as an efficient cause of prosperity. To answer this question we must first of all project the Constitution against a background of doctrinal tradition which, widespread as European culture, was at the time of the founding of the English colonies especially strong in the mother country, though by the irony of history it had become a century and a half later the chief source of division between mother country and colonies.

It is customary nowadays to ascribe the *legality* as well as the *supremacy* of the Constitution—the one is, in truth, but the obverse of the other—exclusively to the fact that, in its own phraseology, it was "ordained" by "the people of the United States." Two ideas are thus brought into play. One is the so-called "positive" conception of law as a general expression merely for the particular commands of a human lawgiver, as a series of acts of human will[7]; the other is that the highest possible source of such commands, because the highest possible embodiment of human will, is "the people." The same two ideas occur in conjunction in the oft-quoted text of Justinian's *Institutes:*† "Whatever has pleased the prince has the force of law, since the Roman people by the *lex regia*‡ enacted concerning his *imperium,*§ have yielded up to him all their power and authority."[8] The sole difference between the Constitution of the United States and the imperial legislation justified in this famous text is that the former is assumed to have proceeded immediately from the people, while the latter proceeded from a like source only mediately.

The attribution of supremacy to the Constitution on the ground solely of its rootage in popular will represents, however, a comparatively late outgrowth of American constitutional theory. Earlier the supremacy accorded to constitutions was ascribed less to their putative source than to their supposed content, to their

***Josiah Quincy* (1772–1864): congressman from Massachusetts to the U.S. House of Representatives (1805–1813), a state senator (1804–1805, 1813–1820), and a member of the Massachusetts legislature (1821–1822). In addition, Quincy was mayor of Boston (1823–1829) and president of Harvard (1829–1845). He wrote *The History of Harvard University* (1840) and *A Municipal History of the Town and City of Boston* (1852).

†*Justinian's "Institutes":* handbook for law students and a part of the Corpus Juris Civilis (corpus of civil law), a remarkable legacy left by the Byzantine Emperor Justinian I (483), ruler of the Eastern Roman Empire (527–565). The four parts of the Corpus Juris Civilis were compiled by ten experts commissioned by Justinian.

‡*Lex regia:* Latin term for "imperial law"—edicts issued by the Roman emperor that had the force of law.

§*Imperium:* Latin term for the right to command, including the right to use force.

embodiment of an essential and unchanging justice. The theory of law thus invoked stands in direct contrast to the one just reviewed. *There are,* it is predicated, *certain principles of right and justice which are entitled to prevail of their own intrinsic excellence, altogether regardless of the attitude of those who wield the physical resources of the community. Such principles were made by no human hands; indeed, if they did not antedate deity itself, they still so express its nature as to bind and control it. They are external to all Will as such and interpenetrate all Reason as such. They are eternal and immutable. In relation to such principles, human laws are, when entitled to obedience save as to matters indifferent, merely a record or transcript, and their enactment and act not of will or power but one of discovery and declaration.*[9] The Ninth Amendment of the Constitution of the United States, in stipulating that "the enumeration of certain rights in this Constitution shall not prejudice other rights not so enumerated," illustrates this theory perfectly except that the principles of transcendental justice have been here translated into terms of personal and private rights. The relation of such rights, nevertheless, to governmental power is the same as that of the principles from which they spring and which they reflect. They owe nothing to their recognition in the Constitution—such recognition was necessary if the Constitution was to be regarded as complete.

Thus the *legality* of the Constitution, its *supremacy,* and its claim to be worshipped, alike find common standing ground on the belief in a law superior to the will of human governors. Certain questions arise: Whence came this idea of a "higher law?" How has it been enabled to survive, and in what transformations? What special forms of it are of particular interest for the history of American constitutional law and theory? By what agencies and as a result of what causes was it brought to America and wrought into the American system of government? . . .

NOTES

[1]Paine, *Political Writings* (1837) 45–46.

[2]Adams, *Jubilee Discourse on the Constitution* (1839) 55.

[3]Woodrow Wilson, *Congressional Government* (13th ed. 1898) 4.

[4]On the whole subject, see 1 Von Holst, *Constitutional History* (1877) c. 2; Schechter, *Early History of the Tradition of the Constitution* (1915) 9 *Am. Pol. Sci. Rev.* 707 *et seq.*

[5]Bagehot, *English Constitution* (2d ed. 1952) 39. "The monarchy by its religious sanction now confirms all our political order. . . . It gives . . . a vast strength to the entire constitution, by enlisting on its behalf the credulous obedience of enormous masses." *Ibid.* 43–44.

[6]Schechter, *supra* note 4, at 720–21.

[7]Bentham, as quoted in Holland, *Elements of Jurisprudence* (12th ed. 1916) 14. For further definitions of "positive law," see *ibid.* 22–23; Willoughby, *Fundamental Concepts of Public Law* (1924) c. 10.

[8]*Inst.* 1, 2, 6: "Quod principi placuit, legis habet vigorem, cum lege regia quae de ejus imperio lata est, populus ei et in eum, omne imperium suum et potestatem concessit." The source is Ulpian, *Dig.*

I, 4, 1. The Romans always regarded the people as the source of the legislative power. "Lex est, quod populus Romanus senatorie magistratu interrogante, veluti Consule, constituebat." *Inst.* 1, 2, 4. During the Middle Ages the question was much debated whether the *lex regia* effected an absolute alienation (*translatio*) of the legislative power to the Emperor, or was a revocable delegation (*cessio*). The champions of popular sovereignty at the end of this period, like Marsiglio of Padua in his *Defensor Pacis,* took the latter view. See Gierke, *Political Theories of the Middle Ages* (Maitland's tr. 1922) 150, notes 158, 159.

[9]For definitions of law incorporating this point of view, see Holland, *op. cit. supra* note 7, at 19–20, 32–36. *Cf.* 1 Blackstone, *Commentaries*, Intro.

25

ALEXANDER M. BICKEL

ESTABLISHMENT AND GENERAL JUSTIFICATION OF JUDICIAL REVIEW

The Supreme Court has the power of judicial review, that is, the authority to decide the constitutionality of the actions of every level and branch of government in the United States. Through the exercise of judicial review, the Supreme Court at once interprets and symbolizes the Constitution. However, this role raises questions for democratic theory: judicial review is, in principle, counter-majoritarian. Alexander M. Bickel (1924–1974) analyzes the dilemma carefully in this selection, an excerpt from the first chapter of his book The Least Dangerous Branch: The Supreme Court at the Bar of Politics *(1962, 1986). Bickel also wrote* Reform and Continuity *(1971),* Caseload of the Supreme Court *(1973),* Politics and the Warren Court *(1973),* The Morality of Consent *(1975),* The Supreme Court and the Idea of Progress *(1970, 1978), and* The Judiciary and Responsible Government, 1910–1921 *(1984) with Benno C. Schmidt.*

The least dangerous branch of the American government is the most extraordinarily powerful court of law the world has ever known. The power which distinguishes the Supreme Court of the United States is that of constitutional review of actions of the other branches of government, federal and state. Curiously enough, this power of judicial review, as it is called, does not derive from any explicit constitutional command. The authority to determine the meaning and application of a written constitution is nowhere defined or even mentioned in the document itself. This is not to say that the power of judicial review cannot be placed in the Constitution; merely that it cannot be found there. . . .

THE MORAL APPROVAL OF THE LINES: HISTORY

[W]e come to examine foundations for the doctrine of judicial review other than textual exegesis. *Marbury* v. *Madison,** relating to the power to hold federal statutes unconstitutional, and *Martin* v. *Hunter's Lessee*† and *Cohens* v. *Virginia,*‡

**Marbury v. Madison*, 1 Cranch 137 (1803) (excerpted on page 463): landmark U.S. Supreme Court case that established the authority of the Court to determine the constitutionality of laws, thus establishing the court's power of judicial review.

†*Martin v. Hunter's Lessee*, 1 Wheaton 304 (1816): case in which the Supreme Court ruled that it had the right to hear appeals of state court decisions in suits between individuals in which a federal issue was involved.

‡*Cohens v. Virginia*, 6 Wheaton 264 (1821): case establishing the supremacy of the national over the state judiciary. The Supreme Court held that it had the right to review state court decisions that involved constitutional and national issues, even when the state itself was a party to the suit.

which assumed the power of judicial review of state actions, were decided, respectively, in 1803, 1816, and 1821. They met with controversy, to be sure, which has also recurred sporadically since. But their doctrines have held sway for roughly a century and a half. So long have they been among the realities of our national existence. Settled expectations have formed around them. The life of a nation that now encompasses 185 million people spread over a continent and more depends upon them in a hundred different aspects of its organization and coherence. It is late for radical changes. Perhaps *Marbury* v. *Madison* is a historical accident attributable to the political configuration of the earliest years, to Marshall's* political antecedents, and to the force and statesmanlike deviousness of his personality. It was a half century before the power to strike down an act of Congress was again exercised, and at that time, in the *Dred Scott Case*† of exceedingly bad odor, it was asserted in a fashion that would have assured its evanescence rather than permanence. But *Marbury* v. *Madison* did occur, and if it was an accident, it was not the first to play an important role in the permanent shaping of a government. One of the reasons that the "accident" has endured is that Marshall's own view of the scope of legislative power had grandeur. He undertook to expound the Constitution with finality, but it was Marshall himself who enjoined his posterity never to forget "that it is a *constitution* we are expounding," a living charter, embodying implied as well as expressed powers, "adapted to the various *crises* of human affairs," open to change, capable of growth. This was the Marshall of *McCulloch* v. *Maryland*,‡ decided in 1819. If assumption of the power was accident, the vision and wisdom with which it was exercised in the early years cannot have been. And if it was accident, it had nevertheless been somewhat arranged; if *Marbury* v. *Madison* was *ex tempore*,§ it had nonetheless been well prepared. For, although the Framers of the Constitution had failed to be explicit about the function of judicial review, the evidence of their deliberations demonstrates that they foresaw—indeed, invited—it.

This has frequently been denied, whenever the impulse to radical change has come upon people. And *Marbury* v. *Madison* has been attacked, not merely for its apparent frailties, but as an act of "usurpation." Yet, as Professor Felix Frankfurter wrote in 1924: "Lack of historical scholarship, combined with fierce prepossessions, can alone account for the persistence of this talk. One would suppose that, at least, after the publication of Beard, *The Supreme Court and the Constitution*, there would be an end to this empty controversy." Beard wrote in 1912; Farrand published *The Records of the Federal Convention* in 1911 and *The Framing of the Constitution* in 1913. There have been further accessions to our knowledge since, to be sure, and the books of history are never closed. Nor are

**John Marshall:* see footnote on page 17.

†*Dred Scott* v. *Sanford*, 60 U.S. 393 (1857): case decided by the Supreme Court that maintained Congress, in the Missouri Compromise of 1820, had violated the Constitution, and did not have the authority to prohibit slavery in the territories of the Louisiana Purchase.

‡*McCulloch* v. *Maryland*, 4 Wheaton 316 (1819): landmark Supreme Court decision that viewed the federal government's power broadly and asserted federal supremacy over state legislatures by holding that states could not tax federal entities. (Excerpted on page 472.)

§*Ex tempore:* Latin term that means "as a consequence of the passage of time."

historical hypotheses provable with mathematical precision. But it is as clear as such matters can be that the Framers of the Constitution specifically, if tacitly, expected that the federal courts would assume a power—of whatever exact dimensions—to pass on the constitutionality of actions of the Congress and the President, as well as of the several states. Moreover, not even a colorable showing of decisive historical evidence to the contrary can be made. Nor can it be maintained that the language of the Constitution is compellingly the other way. At worst it may be said that the intentions of the Framers cannot be ascertained with finality; that there were some who thought this and some that, and that it will never be entirely clear just exactly where the collective judgment—which alone is decisive—came to rest. In any debate over the force of the tradition, such is the most that can be said against the claims of judicial review.

Continuity with the past, said Holmes, is not a duty; it is merely a necessity. But Holmes also told us that it is "revolting to have no better reason for a rule of law than that so it was laid down in the time of Henry IV. It is still more revolting if the grounds upon which it was laid down have vanished long since, and the rule simply persists from blind imitation of the past." Judicial review is a present instrument of government. It represents a choice that men have made, and ultimately we must justify it as a choice in our own time. What are the elements of choice?

THE COUNTER-MAJORITARIAN DIFFICULTY

The root difficulty is that judicial review is a counter-majoritarian force in our system. There are various ways of sliding over this ineluctable reality. Marshall did so when he spoke of enforcing, in behalf of "the people," the limits that they have ordained for the institutions of a limited government. And it has been done ever since in much the same fashion by all too many commentators. Marshall himself followed Hamilton, who in the 78th *Federalist* denied that judicial review implied a superiority of the judicial over the legislative power—denied, in other words, that judicial review constituted control by an unrepresentative minority of an elected majority. "It only supposes," Hamilton went on, "that the power of the people is superior to both; and that where the will of the legislature, declared in its statutes, stands in opposition to that of the people, declared in the Constitution, the judges ought to be governed by the latter rather than the former." But the word "people" so used is an abstraction. Not necessarily a meaningless or a pernicious one by any means; always charged with emotion, but nonrepresentational—an abstraction obscuring the reality that when the Supreme Court declares unconstitutional a legislative act or the action of an elected executive, it thwarts the will of representatives of the actual people of the here and now; it exercises control, not in behalf of the prevailing majority, but against it. That, without mystic overtones, is what actually happens. It is an altogether different kettle of fish, and it is the reason the charge can be made that judicial review is undemocratic.

Most assuredly, no democracy operates by taking continuous nose counts on the broad range of daily governmental activities. Representative democracies—that is to say, all working democracies—function by electing certain men for certain periods of time, then passing judgment periodically on their conduct of public office. It is a matter of a laying on of hands, followed in time by a process of holding to account—all through the exercise of the franchise. The elected officials, however, are expected to delegate some of their tasks to men of their own appointment, who are not directly accountable at the polls. The whole operates under public scrutiny and criticism—but not at all times or in all parts. What we mean by democracy, therefore, is much more sophisticated and complex than the making of decisions in town meeting by a show of hands. It is true also that even decisions that have been submitted to the electoral process in some fashion are not continually resubmitted, and they are certainly not continually unmade. Once run through the process, once rendered by "the people" (using the term now in its mystic sense, because the reference is to the people in the past), myriad decisions remain to govern the present and the future despite what may well be fluctuating majorities against them at any given time. A high value is put on stability, and that is also a counter-majoritarian factor. Nevertheless, although democracy does not mean constant reconsideration of decisions once made, it does mean that a representative majority has the power to accomplish a reversal. This power is of the essence, and no less so because it is often merely held in reserve.

I am aware that this timid assault on the complexities of the American democratic system has yet left us with a highly simplistic statement, and I shall briefly rehearse some of the reasons. But nothing in the further complexities and perplexities of the system, which modern political science has explored with admirable and ingenious industry, and some of which it has tended to multiply with a fertility that passes the mere zeal of the discoverer—nothing in these complexities can alter the essential reality that judicial review is a deviant institution in the American democracy.

It is true, of course, that the process of reflecting the will of a popular majority in the legislature is deflected by various inequalities of representation and by all sorts of institutional habits and characteristics, which perhaps tend most often in favor of inertia. Yet it must be remembered that statutes are the product of the legislature and the executive acting in concert, and that the executive represents a very different constituency and thus tends to cure inequities of over- and underrepresentation. Reflecting a balance of forces in society for purposes of stable and effective government is more intricate and less certain than merely assuring each citizen his equal vote. Moreover, impurities and imperfections, if such they be, in one part of the system are no argument for total departure from the desired norm in another part. A much more important complicating factor—first adumbrated by Madison in the 10th *Federalist* and lately emphasized by Professor David B. Truman and others—is the proliferation and power of what Madison foresaw as "faction," what Mr. Truman calls "groups," and what in popular parlance has always been deprecated as the "interests" or the "pressure groups."

No doubt groups operate forcefully on the electoral process, and no doubt they seek and gain access to and an effective share in the legislative and executive decisional process. Perhaps they constitute also, in some measure, an impurity or imperfection. But no one has claimed that they have been able to capture the governmental process except by combining in some fashion, and thus capturing or constituting (are not the two verbs synonymous?) a majority. They often tend themselves to be majoritarian in composition and to be subject to broader majoritarian influences. And the price of what they sell or buy in the legislature is determined in the biennial or quadrennial electoral marketplace. It may be, as Professor Robert A. Dahl has written, that elections themselves, and the political competition that renders them meaningful, "do not make for government by majorities in any very significant way," for they do not establish a great many policy preferences. However, "they are a crucial device for controlling leaders." And if the control is exercised by "groups of various types and sizes, all seeking in various ways to advance their goals," so that we have "minorities rule" rather than majority rule, it remains true nevertheless that only those minorities rule which can command the votes of a majority of individuals in the electorate. In one fashion or another, both in the legislative process and at elections, the minorities must coalesce into a majority. Although, as Mr. Dahl says, "it is fashionable in some quarters to suggest that everything believed about democratic politics prior to World War I, and perhaps World War II, was nonsense," he makes no bones about his own belief that "the radical democrats who, unlike Madison, insist upon the decisive importance of the election process in the whole grand strategy of democracy are essentially correct."

The insights of Professor Truman and other writers into the role that groups play in our society and our politics have a bearing on judicial review. They indicate that there are other means than the electoral process, though subordinate and subsidiary ones, of making institutions of government responsive to the needs and wishes of the governed. Hence one may infer that judicial review, although not responsible, may have ways of being responsive. But nothing can finally depreciate the central function that is assigned in democratic theory and practice to the electoral process; nor can it be denied that the policy-making power of representative institutions, born of the electoral process, is the distinguishing characteristic of the system. Judicial review works counter to this characteristic.

It therefore does not follow from the complex nature of a democratic system that, because admirals and generals and the members, say, of the Federal Reserve Board or of this or that administrative agency are not electorally responsible, judges who exercise the power of judicial review need not be responsible either, and in neither case is there a serious conflict with democratic theory. For admirals and generals and the like are most often responsible to officials who are themselves elected and through whom the line runs directly to a majority. What is more significant, the policies they make are or should be interstitial or technical only and are reversible by legislative majorities. Thus, so long as there has been a meaningful delegation by the legislature to administrators, which is kept within proper bounds, the essential majority power is there, and it is felt to be there—a fact of great consequence. Nor will it do to liken judicial review to the general lawmaking function of judges. In the latter aspect, judges are indeed something like administrative officials, for their decisions are also reversible by any legislative majority—and not infrequently they are reversed. Judicial review, however, is the power to apply and construe the Constitution, in matters of the greatest moment, against the wishes of a legislative majority, which is, in turn, powerless to affect the judicial decision.

"For myself," said the late Judge Learned Hand,*

> it would be most irksome to be ruled by a bevy of Platonic Guardians, even if I knew how to choose them, which I assuredly do not. If they were in charge, I should miss the stimulus of living in a society where I have, at least theoretically, some part in the direction of public affairs. Of course I know how illusory would be the belief that my vote determined anything; but nevertheless when I go to the polls I have a satisfaction in the sense that we are all engaged in a common venture. If you retort that a sheep in the flock may feel something like it; I reply, following Saint Francis, "My brother, the Sheep."

This suggests not only the democratic value that inheres in obtaining the broad judgment of a majority of the people in the community and thus tending to produce better decisions. Judge Hand, if anything, rather deprecated the notion that the decisions will be better, or are affected at all. Some might think that he deprecated it beyond what is either just or realistic when he said that the belief that his vote determined anything was illusory. Hardly altogether. But the strong emphasis on the related idea that coherent, stable—and *morally supportable*—government is possible only on the basis of consent; and that the secret of consent is the sense of common venture fostered by institutions that reflect and represent us and that we can call to account.

It has been suggested that the Congress, the President, the states, and the people (in the sense of current majorities) have from the beginning and in each generation acquiesced in, and thus consented to, the exercise of judicial review by the Supreme Court. In the first place, it is said that the Amending Clause of the Constitution has been employed to reverse the work of the Court only twice, perhaps three times; and it has never been used to take away or diminish the Court's power. But the Amending Clause itself incorporates an extreme minority veto. The argument then proceeds to draw on the first Judiciary Act,† whose provisions regarding the jurisdiction of the federal courts have been continued in effect to this day. Yet we have seen that the Judiciary Act can be read as a grant of the power to declare federal statutes unconstitutional only on the basis of a previously and independently reached conclusion that such a power must exist. And even if the Judiciary Act did grant this power, as it surely granted the power to declare state actions unconstitutional, it amounted to an expression of the opinion of the first Congress that the Constitution implies judicial review. It is, in fact, extremely likely that the first Congress thought so. That is important; but it merely adds to the historical evidence on the point, which, as we have seen, is in any event quite strong. Future Congresses and future generations can only be

**Learned Hand:* see footnote on page 19.

†*Judiciary Act of 1789:* first bill of the first session of the first Congress, signed into law by President George Washington. The act provided for the initial organization of the federal judiciary.

said to have acquiesced in the belief of the first Congress that the Constitution implies this power. And they can be said to have become resigned to what follows, which is that the power can be taken away only by constitutional amendment. That is a very far cry from consent to the power on its merits, as a power freely continued by the decision or acquiescence of a majority in each generation. The argument advances not a step toward justification of the power on other than historical grounds.

A further, crucial difficulty must also be faced. Besides being a counter-majoritarian check on the legislature and the executive, judicial review may, in a larger sense, have a tendency over time seriously to weaken the democratic process. Judicial review expresses, of course, a form of distrust of the legislature. "The legislatures," wrote James Bradley Thayer* at the turn of the century,

> are growing accustomed to this distrust and more and more readily inclined to justify it, and to shed the considerations of constitutional restraints,—certainly as concerning the exact extent of these restrictions,—turning that subject over to the courts; and what is worse, they insensibly fall into a habit of assuming that whatever they could constitutionally do they may do,—as if honor and fair dealing and common honesty were not relevant to their inquiries. The people, all this while, become careless as to whom they send to the legislature; too often they cheerfully vote for men whom they would not trust with an important private affair, and when these unfit persons are found to pass foolish and bad laws, and the courts step in and disregard them, the people are glad that these few wiser gentlemen on the bench are so ready to protect them against their more immediate representatives. . . . [I]t should be remembered that the exercise of it [the power of judicial review], even when unavoidable, is always attended with a serious evil, namely, that the correction of legislative mistakes comes from the outside, and the people thus lose the political experience, and the moral education and stimulus that comes from fighting the question out in the ordinary way, and correcting their own errors. The tendency of a common and easy resort to this great function, now lamentably too common, is to dwarf the political capacity of the people, and to deaden its sense of moral responsibility. It is no light thing to do that.

To this day, in how many hundreds of occasions does Congress enact a measure that it deems expedient, having essayed consideration of its constitutionality (that is to say, of its acceptability on principle), only to abandon the attempt in the declared confidence that the Court will correct errors of principle, if any? It may well be, as has been suggested, that any lowering of the level of legislative performance is attributable to many factors other than judicial review. Yet there is no doubt that what Thayer observed remains observable. It seemed rather a puzzle, for example, to a scholar who recently compared British and American practices of legislative investigation. Professor Herman Finer wrote, with what might have seemed to Thayer charming ingenuousness:

> Is it not a truly extraordinary phenomenon that in the United States, where Congress is not a sovereign body, but subordinate to a constitution, there appear to be less re-

**James Bradley Thayer:* professor at Harvard Law School (1831–1902) who helped create the case method approach to the teaching of law. His expertise was constitutional law and the law of evidence. He wrote *A Preliminary Treatise on Evidence of Common Law* (1898).

> straints upon the arbitrary behavior of members in their . . . rough handling of the civil rights of the citizen during investigations . . . ? Though Parliament is sovereign and can legally do anything it likes, its practices are kinder, more restrained, and less invasive of the rights of those who come under its investigative attention. The student is forced to pause and reflect upon this remarkable reversal of demeanor and status.

Finally, another, though related, contention has been put forward. It is that judicial review runs so fundamentally counter to democratic theory that in a society which in all other respects rests on that theory, judicial review cannot ultimately be effective. We pay the price of a grave inner contradiction in the basic principle of our government, which is an inconvenience and a dangerous one; and in the end to no good purpose, for when the great test comes, judicial review will be unequal to it. The most arresting expression of this thought is in a famous passage from a speech of Judge Learned Hand, a passage, Dean Eugene V. Rostow* has written, "of Browningesque passion and obscurity," voicing a "gloomy and apocalyptic view." Absent the institution of judicial review, Judge Hand said:

> I do not think that anyone can say what will be left of those [fundamental principles of equity and fair play which our constitutions enshrine]; I do not know whether they will serve only as counsels; but this much I think I do know—that a society so riven that the spirit of moderation is gone, no court *can* save; that a society where that spirit flourishes, no court *need* save; that in a society which evades its responsibility by thrusting upon the courts the nurture of that spirit, that spirit in the end will perish.

Over a century before Judge Hand spoke, Judge Gibson of Pennsylvania, in his day perhaps the ablest opponent of the establishment of judicial review, wrote: "Once let public opinion be so corrupt as to sanction every misconstruction of the Constitution and abuse of power which the temptation of the moment may dictate, and the party which may happen to be predominant will laugh at the puny efforts of a dependent power to arrest it in its course." And Thayer also believed that "under no system can the power of courts go far to save a people from ruin; our chief protection lies elsewhere."

THE MORAL APPROVAL OF THE LINES: PRINCIPLE

Such, in outline, are the chief doubts that must be met if the doctrine of judicial review is to be justified on principle. Of course, these doubts will apply with lesser or greater force to various forms of the exercise of the power. For the moment the discussion is at wholesale, and we are seeking a justification on principle, quite aside from supports in history and the continuity of practice. The search must be for a function which might (indeed, must) involve the making of policy, yet which differs from the legislative and executive functions; which is

**Eugene V. Rostow:* law professor emeritus of Yale and author of numerous books including *Law, Power, and the Pursuit of Peace* (1968), *Peace in the Balance* (1972), and *The Ideal in Law* (1978). He was the dean of Yale's Law School from 1955 to 1965.

peculiarly suited to the capabilities of the courts; which will not likely be performed elsewhere if the courts do not assume it; which can be so exercised as to be acceptable in a society that generally shares Judge Hand's satisfaction in a "sense of common venture"; which will be effective when needed; and whose discharge by the courts will not lower the quality of the other departments' performance by denuding them of the dignity and burden of their own responsibility. It will not be possible fully to meet all that is said against judicial review. Such is not the way with questions of government. We can only fill the other side of the scales with countervailing judgments on the real needs and the actual workings of our society and, of course, with our own portions of faith and hope. Then we may estimate how far the needle has moved.

The point of departure is a truism; perhaps it even rises to the unassailability of a platitude. It is that many actions of government have two aspects: their immediate, necessarily intended, practical effects, and their perhaps unintended or unappreciated bearing on values we hold to have more general and permanent interest. It is a premise we deduce not merely from the fact of a written constitution but from the history of the race, and ultimately as a moral judgment of the good society, that government should serve not only what we conceive from time to time to be our immediate material needs but also certain enduring values. This in part is what is meant by government under law. But such values do not present themselves ready-made. They have a past always, to be sure, but they must be continually derived, enunciated, and seen in relevant application. And it remains to ask which institution of our government—if any single one in particular—should be the pronouncer and guardian of such values.

Men in all walks of public life are able occasionally to perceive this second aspect of public questions. Sometimes they are also able to base their decisions on it; that is one of the things we like to call acting on principle. Often they do not do so, however, particularly when they sit in legislative assemblies. There, when the pressure for immediate results is strong enough and emotions ride high enough, men will ordinarily prefer to act on expediency rather than take the long view. Possibly legislators—everything else being equal—are as capable as other men of following the path of principle, where the path is clear or at any rate discernible. Our system, however, like all secular systems, calls for the evolution of principle in novel circumstances, rather than only for its mechanical application. Not merely respect for the rule of established principles but the creative establishment and renewal of a coherent body of principled rules—that is what our legislatures have proven themselves ill equipped to give us.

Initially, great reliance for principled decision was placed in the Senators and the President, who have more extended terms of office and were meant to be elected only indirectly. Yet the Senate and the President were conceived of as less closely tied to, not as divorced from, electoral responsibility and the political marketplace. And so even then the need might have been felt for an institution which stands altogether aside from the current clash of interests, and which, insofar as is humanly possible, is concerned only with principle. We cannot know whether, as Thayer believed, our legislatures are what they are because we have judicial review, or whether we have judicial review and consider it necessary because legislatures are what they are. Yet it is arguable also that the partial separation of the legislative and judicial functions—and it is not meant to be absolute—is beneficial in any event, because it makes it possible for the desires of various groups and interests concerning immediate results to be heard clearly and unrestrainedly in one place. It may be thought fitting that somewhere in government, at some stage in the process of law-making, such felt needs should find unambiguous expression. Moreover, and more importantly, courts have certain capacities for dealing with matters of principle that legislatures and executives do not possess. Judges have, or should have, the leisure, the training, and the insulation to follow the ways of the scholar in pursuing the ends of government. This is crucial in sorting out the enduring values of a society, and it is not something that institutions can do well occasionally, while operating for the most part with a different set of gears. It calls for a habit of mind, and for undeviating institutional customs. Another advantage that courts have is that questions of prinicple never carry the same aspect for them as they did for the legislature or the executive. Statutes, after all, deal typically with abstract or dimly foreseen problems. The courts are concerned with the flesh and blood of an actual case. This tends to modify, perhaps to lengthen, everyone's view. It also provides an extremely salutary proving ground for all abstractions; it is conducive, in a phrase of Holmes, to thinking things, not words, and thus to the evolution of principle by a process that tests as it creates.

Their insulation and the marvelous mystery of time gives courts the capacity to appeal to men's better natures, to call forth their aspirations, which may have been forgotten in the moment's hue and cry. This is what Justice Stone* called the opportunity for "the sober second thought." Hence it is that the courts, although they may somewhat dampen the people's and the legislatures' efforts to educate themselves, are also a great and highly effective educational institution. Judge Gibson,† . . . highly critical as he was, took account of this. "In the business of government," he wrote, "a recurrence to first principles answers the end of an observation at sea with a view to correct the dead reckoning; and, for this purpose, a written constitution is an instrument of inestimable value. It is of inestimable value also, in rendering its principles familiar to the mass of the people. . . ." The educational institution that both takes the observation to correct the dead reckoning and makes it known is the voice of the Constitution: the Supreme Court exercising judicial review. The Justices, in Dean Rostow's phrase, "are inevitably teachers in a vital national seminar." No other branch of the American government is nearly so well equipped to conduct one. And such a seminar can do a great deal to keep our society from becoming so riven that no court will be able to save it. Of course, we have never quite been that society in which the spirit of moderation is so richly in flower that no court need save it.

Thus, as Professor Henry M. Hart, Jr., has written, and as surely most of the

***Harlan Fiske Stone* (1872–1946): associate justice of the Supreme Court (1925–1941) before serving as chief justice (1941–1946).

†*John Bannister Gibson* (1780–1853): associate justice on the Pennsylvania Supreme Court (1816–1827, 1851–1853) and chief justice of that court for twenty-four years (1827–1851). He was instrumental in the development of Pennsylvania law.

profession and of informed laity believe; for if not this, what and why?—thus the Court appears "predestined in the long run, not only by the thrilling tradition of Anglo-American law but also by the hard facts of its position in the structure of American institutions, to be a voice of reason, charged with the creative function of discerning afresh and of articulating and developing impersonal and durable principles. . . ." This line of thought may perhaps blunt, if it does not meet, the force of all the arguments on the other side. No doubt full consistency with democratic theory has not been established. The heart of the democratic faith is government by the consent of the governed. The further premise is not incompatible that the good society not only will want to satisfy the immediate needs of the greatest number but also will strive to support and maintain enduring general values. I have followed the view that the elected institutions are ill fitted, or not so well fitted as the courts, to perform the latter task. This rests on the assumption that the people themselves, by direct action at the ballot box, are surely incapable of sustaining a working system of general values specifically applied. But that much we assume throughout, being a representative, deliberative democracy. Matters of expediency are not generally submitted to direct referendum. Nor should matters of principle, which require even more intensive deliberation, be so submitted. Reference of specific policies to the people for initial decision is, with few exceptions, the fallacy of the misplaced mystics, or the way of those who would use the forms of democracy to undemocratic ends. It is not the way in which working democracies live. But democracies do live by the idea, central to the process of gaining the consent of the governed, that the majority has the ultimate power to displace the decision-makers and to reject any part of their policy. With that idea, judicial review must achieve some measure of consonance.

Democratic government under law—the slogan pulls in two opposed directions, but that does not keep it from being applicable to an operative policy. If it carries the elements of explosion, it doesn't contain a critical mass of them. Yet if the critical mass is not to be reached, there must be an accommodation, a degree of concord between the diverging elements. Having been checked, should the people persist; having been educated, should the people insist, must they not win over [every] fundamental principle save one—which is the principle that they must win? Are we sufficiently certain of the permanent validity of any other principle to be ready to impose it against a consistent and determined majority, and could we do so for long? Have not the people the right of peaceable revolution, as assuredly, over time, they possess the capacity for a bloody one?

The premise of democracy is egalitarian, and, as Professor Herbert J. Muller has written, every bright sophomore knows how to punch holes in it. Yet, as Mr. Muller goes on to say, there is "no universal standard of superiority," there are no sure scales in which to weigh all the relevant virtues and capacities of men, and many a little man may rightly claim to be a better citizen than the expert or the genius. Moreover, and most significantly, "all men are in fact equal in respect of their common structure and their common destiny." Hence, to repeat the insight of Judge Hand, government must be their common venture. Who will think it moral ultimately to direct the lives of men against the will of the great number of them? Or wise? "Man's historical experience should sober the revolutionaries who know the certain solution to our problems, and sober as well the traditionalists whose solution is a return to the ancient faiths, which have always failed in the past."

To bring judicial review into concord with such presuppositions requires a closer analysis of the actual operation of the process in various circumstances. The preliminary suggestions may be advanced that the rule of principle imposed by the Court is seldom rigid, that the Court has ways of persuading before it attempts to coerce, and that, over time, sustained opinion running counter to the Court's constitutional law can achieve its nullification, directly or by desuetude.* It may further be that if the process is properly carried out, an aspect of the current—not only the timeless, mystic—popular will finds expression in constitutional adjudication. The result may be a tolerable accommodation with the theory and practice of democracy.

THE MYSTIC FUNCTION

This inquiry into a general justification of judicial review cannot end without taking account of a most suggestive and perceptive argument recently advanced by Professor Charles L. Black, Jr. It begins by emphasizing that the court performs not only a checking function but also a legitimating one, as Mr. Black well calls it. Judicial review means not only that the Court may strike down a legislative action as unconstitutional but also that it may validate it as within constitutionally granted powers and as not violating constitutional limitations. Mr. Black contends, further, that the legitimating function would be impossible of performance if the checking function did not exist as well: what is the good of a declaration of validity from an institution which is by hypothesis required to validate everything that is brought before it? This is plainly so, though it is oddly stated. The picture is accurate, but it is stood on its head. The truth is that the legitimating function is an inescapable, even if unintended, by-product of the checking power. But what follows? What is the nature of this legitimating function, and what the need for it?

With a relish one can readily share, Mr. Black cites the story of the French intellectual who, upon arrival in New York harbor, exclaims: "It is wonderful to breathe the sweet air of legitimacy!" He contends essentially that what filled the Frenchman's lungs, what smelled to him so different from the succession of short-lived empires and republics endemic to his homeland, was the sweet odor of the Supreme Court of the United States. But I think it much simpler and nearer the reality of both the American and the French experience to begin with the proposition that legitimacy comes to a regime that is felt to be good and to have proven itself as such to generations past as well as in the present. Such a government must be principled as well as responsible, but it must be felt to be the one without having ceased to be the other, and unless it is responsible it cannot

**Desuetude*: term, often applied to obsolete statutes and other legalities, that refers to their nullification through disuse.

in fact be stable, and is not in my view morally supportable. Quite possibly, there have been governments that were electorally responsible and yet failed to attain stability. But that is not to say that they would have attained it by rendering themselves less responsible—that is, by divorcing the keepers of their principles from the electoral process. Legitimacy, being the stability of a good government over time, is the fruit of consent to specific actions or to the authority to act; the consent to the exercise of authority, whether or not approved in each instance, of as unified a population as possible, but most importantly, of a present majority.

Very probably, the stability of the American Republic is due in large part, as Professor Louis Hartz has eloquently argued, to the remarkable Lockeian* consensus of a society that has never known a feudal regime; to a "moral unity" that was seriously broken only once, over the extension of slavery. This unity makes possible a society that accepts its principles from on high, without fighting about them. But the Lockeian consensus is also a limitation on the sort of principles that will be accepted. It is putting the cart before the horse to attribute the American sense of legitimacy to the institution of judicial review. The latter is more nearly the fruit of the former, although the "moral unity" must be made manifest, it must be renewed and sharpened and brought to bear—and this is an office that judicial review can discharge.

No doubt it is in the interest of the majority to obtain the acquiescence of the minority as often and in as great a degree as possible. And no doubt the Court can help bring about acquiescence by assuring those who have lost a political fight that merely momentary interest, not fundamental principle, was in play. Yet it is reasonable to assume that the majority would wish to see itself checked from time to time just to have an institution which, when it chooses to go along with the majority's will, is capable of helping to assuage the defeated minority? That is too much of an indirection. The checking power must find its own justification, particularly in a system which, in a number of important ways (e.g., the Senate's reflection of the federal structure, practices of legislative apportionment), offers prodigious political safeguards to the minority.

Thus the legitimating function of judicial review cannot be accepted as an independent justification for it. Yet it exists. Not only is the Supreme Court capable of generating consent for hotly controverted legislative or executive measures; it has the subtler power of adding a certain impetus to measures that the majority enacts rather tentatively. There are times when the majority might, because of strong minority feelings, be inclined in the end to deny itself, but when it comes to embrace a measure more firmly, and the minority comes to accept it, because the Court—intending perhaps no such consequence—has declared it consistent with constitutional principle. This tendency touches on Thayer's anxiety that judicial review will "dwarf the political capacity of the people" and "deaden its sense of moral responsibility." We shall return to it as a consideration that should cause the Court to stay its hand from time to time.

But the Supreme Court as a legitimating force in society also casts a less

*John Locke: see footnote on page 12.

palpable yet larger spell. With us the symbol of nationhood, of continuity, of unity and common purpose, is, of course, the Constitution, without particular reference to what exactly it means in this or that application. The utility of such a symbol is a commonplace. Britain—the United Kingdom, and perhaps even the Commonwealth—is the most potent historical demonstration of the efficaciousness of a symbol, made concrete in the person of the Crown. The President in our system serves the function somewhat, but only very marginally, because the personification of unity must be above the political battle, and no President can fulfill his office while remaining above the battle. The effective Presidents have of necessity been men of power, and so it has in large part been left to the Supreme Court to concretize the symbol of the Constitution. Keeping in mind that this is offered as an observation, not as justification, it is surely true that the Court has been able to play the role partly—but only partly—by virtue of its power of judicial review.

The Court is seen as a continuum. It is never, like other institutions, renewed at a single stroke. No one or two changes on the Court, not even if they include the advent of a new Chief Justice, are apt to be as immediately momentous as a turnover in the presidency. To the extent that they are instruments of decisive change, Justices are time bombs, not warheads that explode on impact. There are exceptions, to be sure. In 1870, President Grant made two appointments that promptly resulted in the reversal of a quite crucial recent decision concerning the monetary powers of the federal government. And it may seem that strong new doctrine became ascendant soon after the first of President Roosevelt's appointees, Mr. Justice Black, came on the Bench in 1937. But on the whole, the movements of the Court are not sudden and not suddenly affected by new appointments. Continuity is a chief concern of the Court, as it is the main reason for the Court's place in the hearts of its countrymen.

No doubt, the Court's symbolic—or, if you will, mystic—function would not have been possible, would not have reached the stage at which we now see it, if the Court did not exercise the power of judicial review. It could scarcely personify the Constitution unless it had the authority finally to speak of it. But as the symbol manifests itself today, it seems not always to depend on judicial review. It seems at times to have as much to do with the life tenure of the Court's members and with the fact of the long government service of some of them, not only on the Court, in short, with the total impression of continuity personified. Here the human chain goes back unbroken in a small, intimate group to the earliest beginnings. Take two recent retirements. Mr. Justice Minton, who left in October 1956, was a fire-eating New Deal Senator, and when he retired from the Court men no doubt remembered his stance in the 'thirties and thought, perhaps a little self-deprecatingly, of the emotions it had aroused. Mr. Justice Reed, who retired in early 1957, had, some twenty years earlier, when he was Solicitor General, argued a number of celebrated New Deal cases. His was the second of President Franklin Roosevelt's appointments, and he sat with Hughes and Brandeis and McReynolds. When McReynolds went, in 1941, a remembrance of the Wilson era and of trust-busting in the early 1900's went with him. Justice Van Devanter, a contemporary of McReynolds who retired in 1937, had been appointed by Taft, had held office under McKinley, and had sat with appointees of Cleveland and of Hayes. And so on back.

Senior members of the Court are witnesses to the reality and validity of our present—distracted, improbable, illegitimate as it often appears—because in their persons they assure us of its link to the past which they also witnessed and in which they were themselves once the harbingers of something outrageously new. This is true not only of those who are constructive and creative; it is true of Justices who oppose all that is not as they knew it. Say what they will, their very existence among us reassures us. When the great Holmes, who was wounded at Ball's Bluff and at Antietam, retired in 1932, being past ninety, the emotional public response was not due wholly to his undoubted greatness. It was also that his years, his years alone, fulfilled one of the functions of the Supreme Court.

26

MARTIN M. SHAPIRO

THE PRESIDENCY AND THE FEDERAL COURTS

The following article was included in a book edited by Arnold J. Meltsner, Politics and the Oval Office *(1981). The volume sought to inform President Reagan about the challenges of the contemporary presidency and to suggest ways to approach the implementation of his major objectives, directing his staff and the bureaucracy, and restoring the public's confidence in government. Martin M. Shapiro, a professor at the University of California–Berkeley is an expert on the judiciary, public administration, and public policy. His works include* The Supreme Court and Administrative Agencies *(1968),* The Pentagon Papers and the Courts *(1972),* Courts: A Comparative and Political Analysis *(1981), and* Who Guards the Guardians? *(1988). Shapiro provides a brief overview of the transition from the theory of judicial restraint in policy-making to the acceptance of judicial activism in the 1960s and 1970s. Judicial activism has created a problem for presidential governance because the court is now heavily involved in setting the national agenda, reviewing executive agency rule-making, distributing resources, and protecting legal rights. Shapiro argues that presidents need to be especially cautious in making appointments to the federal judiciary.*

Political scientists generally accept that recent presidents have been losing control over executive agencies and budget decisions. The current wisdom is that presidential power—certainly in the domestic arena—is seriously constrained by the existence of "*iron triangles*,"* or alliances between Congress, an agency, and an interest group. This may be so. But an equally important development has been less widely recognized, and that is the increasingly active participation of the courts in policymaking since the early 1960s.

The courts have been steadily reducing the discretionary power of executive agencies and rewriting their regulations. At the same time, a new iron triangle has appeared consisting of agency, court, and interest group. Congress initiates the triangle by creating a statutory right, but then it withdraws. The triangle perpetuates itself. The president is effectively excluded from its policy actions, since he has almost no influence over judges (once appointed) as contrasted with his power over members of congressional subcommittees. Just as a president faces a mass of past spending commitments that obligate much of his budgetary resources, he now faces an increasing number of statutorily created rights which arm the courts to obligate even more commitments and to mandate that the executive branch pursue implementation policies that run counter to those it favors.

*"*Iron triangle*": concept describing the almost impenetrable alliance between three sets of actors in a specific policy field. Lobbying organizations, administrative agencies, and congressional subcommittees—through the exchange of information and support—develop dominance over the course of policy development and can resist control from political appointees and other outsiders.

The president now faces courts which are his rival in agenda setting and in the formulation of public goals and values. How did this happen, and what can he do to protect his authority?

POLITICAL SUASION AND JUDICIAL POWER

A new president faces not only political institutions but also contemporary attitudes about those institutions. This is nowhere more important than for the Supreme Court. Deprived of direct control over both the purse and the sword, the Court's political effectiveness depends largely on voluntary compliance with its commands by other political institutions and by the people. Historically, the Supreme Court has suffered more than the other two branches from problems of legitimacy. If the meaning of our Constitution were absolutely clear and the Court simply acted to enforce it, then the Court's actions would be perfectly legitimate. If the Constitution had no fixed meanings, so that the Supreme Court simply wrote its own policy preferences into the Constitution as it went along, then its actions would be perfectly illegitimate. But because the Constitution has some fixity and some flexibility, and because actions of the justices mix law and policy, the Supreme Court has always lived in a state of uncertain legitimacy. Americans have always asked how much the president and Congress should govern, but they have not questioned their right to govern. There is no more characteristic question of American political discourse, however, than the question of whether the Court should govern at all.

There is a New Deal* theory of the Supreme Court just as there are New Deal theories of the presidency and Congress, and like those theories it has honorable roots. The three theories are, of course, interdependent. New Deal proponents of the strong presidency argued that the president, rather than Congress, should act as chief lawmaker because the presidency was more unified and because it more truly represented the national majority will. At the same time, a New Deal school of judicial self-restraint was busy subordinating the Supreme Court to Congress. If the Court's judgments on the constitutionality of federal legislation merely substituted judicial policy preferences for legislative ones, then the Court ought to stop reviewing and to leave policy decision to Congress . . .

While New Deal commentators never openly put the two streams of thought together, the political arithmetic was clear. Congress ought to defer to the lawmaking of the president. The Supreme Court ought to defer to the lawmaking of Congress. Therefore, the Supreme Court ought to defer to the president. QED.† The only legitimate role for the Supreme Court was that of whipping the state legal systems into line with the Constitution and federal statutes . . .

This attitude predominated during the presidencies of Roosevelt, Truman, and Eisenhower. A chink in the New Deal theory, however, allowed the Su-

**New Deal:* see footnote on page 17.

†*QED:* letters standing for the Latin phrase *quod erat demonstrandum*, which means "that which was to be shown or proven."

preme Court to reemerge as a rival to and manipulator of the presidency. For if the Court were still free to whip the states into line, it might whip them into a different line or require different modes of whipping than the president would have chosen.

Eisenhower's experience with Little Rock* is instructive. Clearly, at the time of *Brown* v. *Board of Education*† (347 U.S. 483 [1954]) there was a national majority against Jim Crow laws,‡ but it was a marginal majority both in breadth and depth of sentiment—not the kind of majority that would find expression through Congress or the presidency. Once the Supreme Court had put the new anti–Jim Crow policy in place, however, the president's power stakes changed rapidly. Because his military background had led to "man on horseback" fears, Eisenhower was particularly reluctant to use the military to enforce the law. Yet he found himself using the army to do the Supreme Court's bidding—a bidding for which he had no great personal enthusiasm. He did so because the Court had built a coalition that he could not resist. It had added the constituency which believed that the law must be obeyed to the constituency which believed that Jim Crow was a national disgrace. He need not have sent troops to end Jim Crow. He had no choice but to send troops to enforce the Constitution as interpreted by the Court (see Wilkinson 1978).

The New Deal theory of judicial restraint did not die with *Brown* v. *Board of Education* and Little Rock. Indeed, it continued to flourish in the academy long after the Warren Court§ had passed it by. Nevertheless, it became increasingly difficult to insist that the Court could and should do nothing when it was doing a great deal and when much of what it was doing seemed good. President Nixon could still seize upon judicial self-restraint as a campaign issue—both intellectually alive and emotionally appealing—but it is unlikely that any president or presidential candidate will be able to do so in the near future.

JUDICIAL ACTIVISM

In part, of course, the decline of judicial self-restraint as a political slogan results from the change from the Warren to the Burger Court.‖ The Burger Court is less given to dramatic gestures. Yet this is not the whole story. Even in the bitter controversy over the Burger Court's abortion decisions, the "pro-life"

**Little Rock:* see footnote on page 334.

†*Brown v. Board of Education:* landmark Supreme Court decision ruling that racial segregation in public schools based on law is unconstitutional, in violation of the equal protection clause of the Fourteenth Amendment.

‡*Jim Crow Laws:* practices or policies aimed at segregating and discriminating against black Americans.

§*Warren Court,* (1953–1969): the Supreme Court under the leadership of the fourteenth chief justice of the United States, Earl Warren (1891–1974). An activist court, the Warren Court promoted civil rights and liberties.

‖*Burger Court:* Supreme Court under Chief Justice Warren Earl Burger, 1969 to 1986. He was appointed by President Nixon, who expected Burger to lead the court away from the "loose construction" and activism that had been the hallmark of the Warren Court. Overall, however, the Burger Court did not practice significantly greater "strict construction" or judicial restraint.

forces have never asserted that the Court had no right to make public policy, only that the Court made an immoral policy.

The major new fact about the Supreme Court is that there has been a fundamental change in the predominant conception of its appropriate role. While some remnants of New Deal theory remain, there is now a strong consensus that the Court should *either* support minority interests not adequately represented elsewhere in the political process *or* defend fundamental public values (Choper 1980; Fiss 1979, pp. 1–58; Ely 1980). Whichever way judicial activism is justified, it reduces the New Deal role of the president. It was Roosevelt who was supposed to protect minorities; Roosevelt, not his Court, who announced the Four Freedoms.*

Today's most fashionable school of constitutional thought argues that one great purpose of government is to provide an arena in which men and women can come together to debate and thus create public values. The courts are ideal for this, every bit as good as Congress and the presidency. Indeed, they are better, because the reasoned argument and elaboration of litigational procedures are particularly good vehicles for ethical/political discourse . . .

This new school of thought may be seen as part of the comtemporary revolt of the intellectuals against popular majorities. For it asserts that public values are best discovered, not by the messy processes of politics, but by a group of Harvard and Yale lawyers arguing with one another according to a ritual that only they understand in front of a judge drawn from their own ranks.

From a slightly different perspective, the new movement can be seen as part of the rights fetishism that has become a principal tool of the left for extracting what it wants from the political system no matter what the majority or its elected representatives want (see, e.g., Michelman 1969, pp. 7–56). When an interest—what somebody wants—is transformed into a right, it goes to the head of the line. The normal political process by which legislatures and agencies establish priorities among competing interests are set aside (Shapiro 1979, pp. 126–31). Thus if a court decides that mental patients in state hospitals have a right to treatment, more state money must be spent on psychiatrists even if the state legislature would have preferred to spend the money on fire inspectors. The principal problem that judges pose for other politicians is that recently they have been using their rights-declaring powers liberally and thus asserting ultimate, even if only sporadically exercised, control over the distributional politics that are the focus of the legislative process.

Political executives confronted with their own unpopularity often take comfort in the widespread disparagement of legislatures. It has become a commonplace that many congressmen seek reelection by campaigning against Congress . . . The creation of judicial rights is another form of that disdain. For when a court converts an interest into a right, it is declaring that it does not trust the legislature to be fair. The ultimate defense of judicial rights creation is the belief that if some people in a society are being badly treated, someone must step in if the legislature

**Four Freedoms:* freedom of speech and expression, freedom of religion, freedom from poverty, and freedom from fear. President Roosevelt proclaimed, in a speech to the U.S. Congress in January 1941, that the government should protect these four freedoms.

fails to do so. While forty years ago the someone was typically thought to be the president, today the most frequently nominated someone is the judge . . .

It would be excessive to suggest that judges have replaced elected officials as our dominant political leaders or that presidential leadership has been replaced by Supreme Court leadership. The president's problem is that the courts may create rights which bring issues to the fore that he might prefer not to confront—desegregation, school busing, abortion. By creating rights, the courts set themselves up as rivals with the president in national agenda setting. Moreover, the particular charm of rights creation is that it can ignore the relational aspects of politics and treat each right as totally independent. As a result, the ability to create rights encourages the single-issue politics that are so troublesome to presidents who are necessarily concerned with coalition building. The Supreme Court can and does promote single-issue movements, leaving the president to deal with them.

STATUTORY RIGHTS

Courts today participate vigorously in announcing values, establishing priorities, and setting agendas, all of which in the days of the Imperial Presidency seemed to be increasingly the preserve of the executive branch. But to appreciate the dynamics of executive/judicial interaction, we must go beyond judicial rights creation to the legislative process. While the Supreme Court has dramatically announced new constitutional rights like the "right" to abortion, Congress has also added to our law an amazing new assortment of statutory rights.

During the Roosevelt administration it became the habit of Congress to pass very broadly worded statutes delegating large chunks of its lawmaking power either directly to the president, to exercise by executive order, or to the federal agencies, to be exercised by administrative regulations. Many of these regulations amounted to major pieces of legislation. The Supreme Court has long since approved such delegations to the executive branch[1] and has held that its regulations have the same force of law as statutes enacted by Congress itself.[2]

In New Deal days such delegation followed the New Deal theory of separation of powers. Congress was deferring to the executive branch, and the Supreme Court was nominally deferring to Congress but was actually deferring to the presidency. Delegation was an unmixed blessing to the president, however, only for so long as certain conditions were met. First, the president had to control the bureaucracy. Second, the delegations had to create wide-ranging administrative discretion rather than vesting legal rights in individuals. A statute that says agency X may do whatever it pleases to alleviate problem Y strengthens the president if he controls agency X. A statute that says agency X is entitled to enforce the right Y of citizen Z may delegate wide rule-making power to the agency. It also enables citizen Z to make demands upon the agency, no matter what the president wants. Third, the delegation had to be unreviewable by the courts. Where delegation is accompanied by active judicial review, then, even if he controls the agency the president must share the lawmaking power with the courts that do the reviewing. For whatever the pretense, judicial review of agency lawmaking amounts to judicial participation in lawmaking.

All three conditions for presidential control have been eroded. President Roosevelt enjoyed a suddenly enormously expanded bureaucracy staffed largely by people attracted to Washington by the promise of the New Deal. Presidents since Eisenhower have faced an entrenched New Deal bureaucracy. Thus, delegation of lawmaking power to the agencies has strengthened another rival to presidential authority.

At the same time, Congress and the courts have interacted to produce a shift from administrative discretion to statutory rights. A 1940 statute called the "National Transportation Policy" may provide the ultimate New Deal model of administrative discretion. This act simply empowered the Interstate Commerce Commission to regulate modes of transportation "so . . . as to . . . preserve the inherent advantages of each; to promote . . . efficient service and foster sound economic conditions." In more recent years, however, Congress has tended to conceive the task of solving massive social and economic problems in terms of creating statutory rights vested in individuals, with broad delegations to administrative agencies to implement those rights. For instance, the Education for Handicapped Children Act invests handicapped children with a right to an adequate education and their parents with a right to participate in determining their education. It goes on to delegate to the agency broad discretion to write regulations defining standards of adequacy as well as processes necessary to ensure participation.

Rights are not negotiable. Faced with a handicapped child who has a right to an adequate education, we are unlikely to say that any education that the president says is adequate is adequate or that some bureaucrat should have the discretion to decide that injured athletes rather than handicapped children should have first crack at the hydrotherapy equipment. Rights—whether statutory or constitutional—are assertions of absolute entitlement.

A mere change in statutory rhetoric from agency discretion to citizens' rights would not, in itself, greatly limit the discretion of the executive branch. But the change in rhetoric *plus* the growth of judicial review has done so. In the late 1930s and 1940s the Supreme Court was not only busy providing constitutional legitimacy for vast delegations of congressional lawmaking power to the executive branch, but was also working hard to construct a theory under which administrators wielding that power would be insulated from judicial review. The Court argued that the executive branch constituted a reservoir of technical expertise upon which most administrative decisions depended. It followed that judges, who were not experts, should defer to the decisions of administrators, who were. This general doctrine was supplemented by a special doctrine which called for judicial deference to administrators even in the one area in which it might be argued that judges were the most expert: questions of the meaning of the delegating statute. Even though freeing agencies to interpret these statutes as they pleased would enable them to expand their powers indefinitely, the Supreme Court held that such regulations had the same force of law as if Congress itself had enacted them. The courts would not review them, and the agencies became the final authority on questions of the legal meaning of the statutory provisions under which they operated.[3]

During the 1960s and 1970s, however, their insulation from judicial review broke down. Led by the District of Columbia and 2nd Circuits, judges began to challenge the expertise of the agencies, sometimes directly, but mostly by procedural indirection. The courts came to hold that the agencies must listen to all sides of questions and that failure to do so, and to provide a record proving that they had done so, would lead to judicial invalidation of their regulations.[4] Under the guise of inspecting whether the agency had followed consultative procedures, judges came more and more to second-guess agency policy decisions and to at least delay those they didn't like. At the same time, standing doctrines were liberalized so that not only were courts more willing to review, but also more people were enabled to ask for review. Despite some unease,[5] the Supreme Court has basically accepted this trend. So while the doctrine that agency regulations have the force of law has not changed, courts have again set themselves up as rival interpreters of the congressional language under which the agencies' delegated lawmaking powers are exercised . . .

This change in the courts' behavior has been seconded by Congress. Many recent statutes delegating lawmaking authority require agencies to engage in the kinds of elaborate consultative procedures that the courts have been requiring. And many of those same statutes give rights to individuals and allow them to vindicate those rights in court.

THE NEW IRON TRIANGLE

What does all this mean for the president? The original New Deal delegations increased his power because they gave full policy discretion to agencies that he controlled. Today the president exercises less control over the federal agencies; the agencies have less discretion in that they cannot refuse to implement statutorily created rights, and the courts have triumphantly reentered the policy arena.

Congressionally created individual rights have been rigidified through agency regulations and judicial review to the point of constraining the president's discretion in vast areas of federal regulation. In addition, networks—"iron triangles"—of congressional subcommittee, executive bureau, and interest group alliances make their own public policy and resist outside control. Now there is the new triangle, consisting of agency, court, and interest group, which is bringing about a new diminution of presidential authority.

Congress or the courts or both give the interest group standing to lobby the agency and the courts. The agency knows that, unless it satisfies the group, the group will sue, thus increasing the cost and delaying the implementation of the proposed policy. The agency also knows that unless it anticipates the policy views of the courts, the judges will find some way to reverse or at least delay the proposed policy if a suit takes place. The interest group knows that the cheapest thing to do is to persuade the agency. It also knows that, if properly approached, courts may strengthen its statutory entitlements, thus providing a stronger base for negotiation with the agency. And the courts know that all they can do is to increase the time and money costs to the agency, which can eventually win if it is willing to pay those costs. The courts also know that if they attempt to build a barrier to some agency policy by announcing a statutory right debarring it, Congress may reverse them. It follows that the agencies, interest groups, and courts live by mutual accommodation over relatively long periods of time, effectively excluding the president.

The new triangle is worse for the president than the old. An alert president might discover ways to reward or punish individual members of the congressional subcommittee involved. He could reward or punish the agency at budget time. And most interest groups would prefer presidential patronage to presidential animosity. But there is little he can do for—or to—the federal judges who now participate in the "administration" of statutes.

A brief example will illustrate these points. In the Age Discrimination Act of 1975 Congress prohibited discrimination on the basis of age in all federally assisted programs. It also provided several broadly worded exceptions to the prohibition which allow "reasonable" use of age as a criterion in assigning jobs and benefits. As Peter Schuck . . . has pointed out in his illuminating case study of the statute, it looks toward two policy goals: bettering the social and economic status of the aged and improving economic efficiency. It creates specific statutory rights for the aged and delegates lawmaking power to the Department of Labor to effectuate them. Because the two goals conflict, and the trade-offs between them are not clearly specified in the statute, the Department of Labor has enormous discretion in writing the real law—its own detailed regulations. In doing so, however, it must follow the protracted procedures required by the courts. Moreover, once the regulations are enacted, aged people who feel they do not adequately protect their rights as established by the statute will challenge them in court. Courts may or may not be tempted into writing their own version of the statute. Congress having acted, the law on age discrimination is now being written. It will take a long time to write, and it will be the product of a great deal of discretion. But almost none of that discretion will be wielded by the president.

THE PRESIDENT'S RESOURCES

In summary, the president now faces a Supreme Court which rivals his authority in formulating public goals and values and in agenda setting. And in formulating values, the Court often contributes to the single-issue politics that make it difficult for the president to form and lead a winning national coalition. Furthermore, the Court has the power to implicate the president in the achievement of the goals *it* chooses, thus diverting presidential energies and creating expectations about presidential performance that the president may be unable to satisfy. The Supreme Court and the other federal courts have also returned to a major role in day to day, detailed lawmaking. That return has helped to create an agency/interest group/court triangle which dominates much of the routine decision-making of government and is largely impervious to presidential intervention.

What resources does the president command to meet his judicial rivals? Unfortunately for him, the answer is more than enough resources to meet the micro problems and almost none to meet the macro developments I have just outlined. Compared to these macro phenomena, the various points of microtension between president and Supreme Court which appear so dramatically to threaten his power are really trivial.

The microlevel problems are "point" problems that tend to come to a head in a single case or a short series of cases which bring to constitutional issue the legitimacy of some particular claim of presidential authority. The batting average of the presidency in such disputes is high. The president's massive constitutional authority has been increased rather than decreased by successive Supreme Court decisions, even those of the Nixon years. In these areas, the president is fully armed with the executive mystique and has the power both to fine-tune his claims to the political exigencies and to adopt alternative means of achieving his goals (Scigliano 1972).

It is one of the small ironies of history that a Republican president, Nixon, was smashed in the process of attempting to push the New Deal theory of the presidency to its logical extreme. His insistence on the absolute power to impound funds appropriated by Congress and to be the sole judge of when the exigencies of national security required him to exercise an executive privilege* to withhold whatever information he pleased from Congress, the courts, and the people was met by an alliance of Congress and the courts. Nevertheless, the presidency emerged with legal recognition of both the impoundment power and executive privilege, recognition that had not existed before. Similarly, President Nixon suffered congressional refusal to accept two consecutive presidential nominations to the Supreme Court, but the appointment power remained firmly in his hands. The Nixon administration was repulsed in an attempt to restrain publication of the Pentagon Papers† in the name of national security, but the security classification system is still with us . . .

At the macro level, the causes of the president's problems are beyond his control. The increase in judicial willingness to intervene in administrative lawmaking was caused by a basic increase in judicial self-confidence resulting from changing public attitudes toward technocratic government. As Americans lost faith in the technocrat,‡ the judge emerged as the lay hero riding forth to curb his arbitrary power. Because American attitudes toward technocracy are funda-

***Executive privilege:* the power, claimed by presidents since George Washington, to withhold documents or information from Congress or the courts, a right that, the executive has argued, is based on the need to maintain the autonomy of each branch within the separation of powers. A test of the executive privilege principle came during the Watergate investigation and the subsequent Nixon cases (*U.S. v. Nixon*, 418 U.S. 683 [1974], and *Nixon v. Administrator of General Services*, 433 U.S. 425 [1977]). President Nixon used executive privilege as a rationale to support his assertion that he did not have to provide documents or information requested as evidence in a criminal prosecution. The court acknowledged that executive privilege might sometimes be appropriate, but not in all cases.

†*Pentagon Papers:* 47 volumes of unedited documents leaked to the *New York Times* in 1971 by former Defense Department employee Daniel Ellsberg. The documents detailed decisions made regarding the Vietnam War. President Nixon tried to prevent their publication, but the Supreme Court determined they should not be suppressed.

‡*Technocrat:* see footnote on page 345.

mentally ambivalent, we may shortly experience another swing in favor of the expert and a consequent decline in judicial activity. But there is little that any given president can do to bring this about except, perhaps, to learn that denouncing the bureaucracy strengthens the hands of judges.

On another front, however, each new president can contribute something to an increase in presidential discretion. Presidents have probably already learned that massive congressional delegations of lawmaking power to the bureaucracy are not necessarily delegations to them. They must also recognize that massive congressional creations of new statutory rights obligate administrative resources just as massive spending programs obligate financial resources. And along with the obligation come higher levels of judicial intervention. To counter this, the president can be careful about the kinds of legislation he proposes. A bill authorizing the federal government to spend X billion to improve education for the handicapped has far different consequences for presidential authority than one that gives the handicapped a right to adequate education and requires the Department of Education to write regulations sustaining that right. Presidents can control spending far more readily than rights once they have been let loose in the rights triangle. Presidents must learn to draft their statutes so as to promise government programs, not to guarantee legal rights. The movement toward rights legislation has been so strong, however, that any given president seems likely to make only limited headway against it.

What about the power of appointment? This is a very weak resource. As recent history shows, the voting of justices on matters of immediate constitutional concern to the president does not depend on who appointed them. No president is likely to be so insightful about the two mysteries of human personality and future events as to appoint just the right person for just those constitutional issues of presidential power that will arise during his term . . .

Nor is a president likely to find appointees who exactly share his value preferences. Justices appointed because they are tough on crime or pro-busing will turn out to have values different from his in other areas such as welfare or presidential power or economic regulation.

Even more important, the new iron triangle does not depend on the Supreme Court alone, but also on certain key courts of appeal and district courts. In many areas of law, appointments to the District of Columbia and 2nd Circuits are as crucial as those to the Supreme Court. Nevertheless, when so many judges sitting for life share judicial power, no single president's appointments make much immediate difference. There is no doubt that the five Democratic terms after 1932 filled the federal bench with judges whose ideology made the judicial activism of the 1960s and 1970s possible, but no single president could have achieved that result, nor did presidents Roosevelt and Truman intend the results they achieved.

Presidents ought to take their judicial appointments seriously as an opportunity to influence long-range policy directions and perhaps to have a more immediate impact on one or two areas of policymaking with which they are particularly concerned. The appointment power can do little, however, to bring the judicial rivals of the president to heel.

We must conclude that the federal judiciary plays a substantial role in the fragmentation of political authority that confronts the president. From time to time it can and does seize the initiative from him in setting the issue agenda and proclaiming dominant values. And it can and does participate in the mass of low-level incremental decision-making that fixes most of the policies of government in channels that the president can do little about. Should we continue to pile up statutes that mandate legal duties to public and private authorities and assign rights to individuals and groups to obtain judicial enforcement of those mandates, we will not only greatly increase the power of the nonelected branch to interfere in our individual lives and set our national priorities, but we will arrive at a stage of legal overkill that will reduce the president's options in a domestic policy to the vanishing point. The president's best defense is to seize the initiative in proclaiming values, but to avoid the rhetoric of rights that invites both judicial intervention and policy rigidity.

Notes

[1]*Amalgamated Meat Cutters* v. *Connally*, 337 F. Supp. 737 (D.D.C. 1971).

[2]*Mourning* v. *Family Publications Services, Inc.*, 411 U.S. 356 (1973).

[3]Idem.

[4]This development is traced in detail in Davis 1976.

[5]See *Vermont Yankee Nuclear Power Corp.* v. *Natural Resources Defense Council*, 435 U.S. 519 (1978).

Sources

Abraham, Henry. *Justices and Presidents* (New York: Oxford Press, 1974).

Choper, Jesse H. "The Alienated Voter," *Taxing and Spending* (Volume 1, Oct./Nov., 1980).

Ely, John Hart. *Democracy and Distrust: A Theory of Judicial Review* (Cambridge, MA: Harvard University Press, 1980).

Fenno, Richard F., Jr. *Homestyle: House Members in Their Districts* (Boston: Little Brown, 1978).

Fisher, Louis, *The Constitution between Friends: Congress, the President, and the Law* (New York: St. Martin's, 1978).

Fiss, Owen. "The Forms of Justice," *Harvard Law Review* (Volume 93, 1979).

Freedman, James O. *Crisis and Legitimacy: The Administrative Process and American Government* (Cambridge: Cambridge University Press, 1978).

Hand, Learned. *The Bill of Rights* (Cambridge, MA: Harvard University Press, 1958).

Horowitz, Donald. *Courts and Social Policy* (Washington, D.C.: The Brookings Institution, 1977).

Mendelson, Wallace. *Justices Black and Frankfurter: Conflict on the Court* (Chicago: University of Chicago Press, 1961).

Michelman, Frank. "On Protecting the Poor through the Fourteenth Amendment," *Harvard Law Review* (Volume 83, 1969).

Schmidhauser, John. *Supreme Court as Final Arbiter in Federal State Relations* (Chapel Hill, N.C.: University of North Carolina Press, 1958).

Schuck, Peter. "The Graying of Civil Rights Law: The Age Discrimination Act of 1975," *Yale Law Journal* (Volume 89, 1979).

Scigliano, Robert. *The Supreme Court and the Presidency* (New York: Free Press, 1972).

Stewart, Richard. "The Reformation of American Administrative Law," *Harvard Law Review* (Volume 88, 1975).

Tribe, Lawrence. "Puzzling Persistence of Progress-Based Constitutional Theories," *Yale Law Journal* (Volume 89, 1980).

Wilkinson, J. Harvie. *From Brown to Bakke: The Supreme Court and School Integration, 1954–1978* (New York: Oxford Press, 1978).

27

MARBURY V. MADISON (1803)

Just before leaving office, President John Adams appointed William Marbury to the post of justice of the peace in Washington, D.C. However, in the presidential transition, Marbury failed to receive his commission—a legal document enabling him to exercise the authority of that position. After taking office, the new secretary of state, James Madison, refused to deliver the commission and was sued by Marbury. The technical issue before the Supreme Court involved section 13 of the Judiciary Act of 1789. The act gave the Supreme Court original jurisdiction and authority to issue writs of mandamus in such cases. The political problem facing the Court was the very real prospect that for partisan reasons Madison would ignore such a writ, if issued. The Court's decision was to declare section 13 unconstitutional because it expanded the Court's original jurisdiction, which was established by the Constitution. Thus, the Court asserted the power of judicial review and avoided confrontation with the executive branch, but left Marbury without his commission.

Mr. Chief Justice Marshall* delivered the opinion of the Court:

At the last term on the affidavits then read and filed with the clerk, a rule was granted in this case, requiring the secretary of state to show cause why a *mandamus*† should not issue, directing him to deliver to William Marbury his commission as a justice of the peace for the county of Washington, in the District of Columbia.

No cause has been shown, and the present motion is for a *mandamus*. The peculiar delicacy of this case, the novelty of some of its circumstances, and the real difficulty attending the points which occur in it, require a complete exposition of the principles on which the opinion to be given by the Court is founded.

These principles have been, on the side of the applicant, very ably argued by the bar. In rendering the opinion of the Court, there will be some departure in form, though not in substance, from the points stated in that argument.

In the order in which the Court has viewed this subject, the following questions have been considered and decided.

1st. Has the applicant a right to the commission he demands?

2d. If he has a right, and that right has been violated, do the laws of his country afford him a remedy?

3d. If they do afford him a remedy, is it a *mandamus* issuing from this Court?

The first object of inquiry is,

Has the applicant a right to the commission he demands? . . .

It is . . . decidedly the opinion of the Court, that when a commission has been signed by the president, the appointment is made; and that the commission

**John Marshall:* see footnote on page 17.

†*Mandamus:* ability of a court of superior jurisdiction to order an inferior court, corporation, or person to perform an act owed to a complainant by right or privilege.

is complete when the seal of the United States has been affixed to it by the secretary of state.

Where an officer is removable at the will of the executive, the circumstance which completes his appointment is of no concern; because the act is at any time revocable; and the commission may be arrested, if still in the office. But when the officer is not removable at the will of the executive, the appointment is not revocable, and cannot be annulled. It has conferred legal rights which cannot be resumed.

The discretion of the executive is to be exercised, until the appointment has been made. But having once made the appointment, his power over the office is terminated, in all cases where, by law, the officer is not removable by him. The right to the office is then in the person appointed, and he has the absolute unconditional power of accepting or rejecting it.

Mr. Marbury, then, since his commission was signed by the president, and sealed by the secretary of state, was appointed; and as the law creating the office, gave the officer a right to hold for five years, independent of the executive, the appointment was not revocable, but vested in the officer legal rights, which are protected by the laws of his country.

To withhold his commission, therefore, is an act deemed by the Court not warranted by law, but violative of a vested legal right.

This brings us to the second inquiry; which is,

If he has a right, and that right has been violated, do the laws of this country afford him a remedy?

The very essence of civil liberty certainly consists in the right of every individual to claim the protection of the laws, whenever he receives an inquiry. One of the first duties of government is to afford that protection. . . .

The government of the United States has been emphatically termed a government of laws, and not of men. It will certainly cease to deserve this high appellation if the laws furnish no remedy for the violation of a vested legal right.

If this obloquy* is to be cast on the jurisprudence of our country, it must arise from the peculiar character of the case.

It behooves us, then, to inquire whether there be in its composition any ingredient which shall exempt it from legal investigation, or exclude the injured party from legal redress. . . .

Is it in the nature of the transaction? Is the act of delivering or withholding a commission to be considered as a mere political act, belonging to the executive department alone, for the performance of which entire confidence is placed by our Constitution in the supreme executive; and for any misconduct respecting which, the injured individual has no remedy? That there may be such cases is not to be questioned; but that every act of duty, to be performed in any of the great departments of government, constitutes such a case, is not to be admitted. . . .

It follows, then, that the question, whether the legality of an act of the head of a department be examinable in a court of justice or not, must always depend on the nature of that act.

*_Obloquy_: censure or reproach.

If some acts be examinable, and others not, there must be some rule of law to guide the court in the exercise of its jurisdiction.

In some instances, there may be difficulty in applying the rule to particular cases; but there cannot, it is believed, be much difficulty in laying down the rule.

By the Constitution of the United States, the president is invested with certain important political powers, in the exercise of which he is to use his own discretion, and is accountable only to his country in his political character and to his own conscience. To aid him in the performance of these duties, he is authorized to appoint certain officers, who act by his authority, and in conformity with his orders.

In such cases, their acts are his acts; and whatever opinion may be entertained of the manner in which executive discretion may be used, still there exists, and can exist, no power to control that discretion. The subjects are political. They respect the nation, not individual rights, and being intrusted to the executive, the decision of the executive is conclusive. The application of this remark will be perceived by adverting to the act of Congress for establishing the department of foreign affairs. This officer, as his duties were prescribed by that act, is to conform precisely to the will of the president. He is the mere organ by whom that will is communicated. The acts of such an officer, as an officer, can never be examinable by the courts.

But when the legislature proceeds to impose on that officer other duties; when he is directed peremptorily to perform certain acts; when the rights of individuals are dependent on the performance of those acts; he is so far the officer of the law; is amenable to the laws for his conduct; and cannot at his discretion sport away the vested rights of others.

The conclusion from this reasoning is, that where the heads of departments are the political or confidential agents of the executive, merely to execute the will of the president, or rather to act in cases in which the executive possesses a constitutional or legal discretion, nothing can be more perfectly clear than that their acts are only politically examinable. But where a specific duty is assigned by law, and individual rights depend upon the performance of that duty, it seems equally clear that the individual who considers himself injured, has a right to resort to the laws of his country for a remedy. . . .

It is, then, the opinion of the Court,

1st. That by signing the commission of Mr. Marbury, the president of the United States appointed him a justice of peace for the county of Washington, in the District of Columbia; and that the seal of the United States, affixed thereto by the secretary of state, is conclusive testimony of the verity of the signature, and of the completion of the appointment, and that the appointment conferred on him a legal right to the office for the space of five years.

2dly. That, having this legal title to the office, he has a consequent right to the commission; a refusal to deliver which is a plain violation of that right, for which the laws of his country afford him a remedy.

It remains to be inquired whether,

3dly. Is he entitled to the remedy for which he applies?

This depends on—1st. The nature of the writ applied for; and 2dly. The power of this court.

The nature of the writ. . . .

This writ, if awarded, would be directed to an officer of government, and its mandate to him would be, to use the words of Blackstone, "to do a particular thing therein specified, which appertains to his office and duty, and which the court has previously determined, or at least supposes, to be consonant to right and justice." Or, in the words of Lord Mansfield,* the applicant, in this case, has a right to execute an office of public concern, and is kept out of possession of that right.

These circumstances certainly concur in this case.

Still, to render the *mandamus* a proper remedy, the officer to whom it is to be directed, must be one to whom, on legal principles, such writ may be directed; and the person applying for it must be without any other specific and legal remedy.

With respect to the officer to whom it would be directed.

The intimate political relation subsisting between the president of the United States and the heads of departments, necessarily renders any legal investigation of the acts of one of those high officers peculiarly irksome, as well as delicate; and excites some hesitation with respect to the propriety of entering into such investigation. Impressions are often received without much reflection or examination, and it is not wonderful that in such a case as this the assertion, by an individual, of his legal claims in a court of justice, to which claims it is the duty of that court to attend, should at first view be considered by some, as an attempt to intrude into the cabinet, and to intermeddle with the prerogatives of the executive.

It is scarcely necessary for the court to disclaim all pretentions to such jurisdiction. An extravangance, so absurd and excessive, could not have been entertained for a moment. The province of the court is, solely, to decide on the rights of individuals, not to inquire how the executive, or executive officers, perform duties in which they have a discretion. Questions in their nature political, or which are, by the Constitution and laws, submitted to the executive, can never be made in this Court.

But, if this be not such a question; if, so far from being an intrusion into the secrets of the cabinet, it respects a paper which, according to law, is upon record, and to a copy of which the law gives a right, on the payment of ten cents; if it be no intermeddling with a subject over which the executive can be considered as having exercised any control; what is there in the exalted station of the officer, which shall bar a citizen from asserting, in a court of justice, his legal rights, or shall forbid a court to listen to the claim, or to issue a *mandamus* directing the performance of a duty, not depending on executive discretion, but on particular acts of Congress, and the general principles of law?

. . . [W]here [the head of a department] is directed by law to do a certain act affecting the absolute rights of individuals, in the performance of which he is not

**Lord Mansfield* (1705–1793): William Murray, First Earl of Mansfield, who was known as the "founder of English commercial law." He revised medieval law and formulated the principles of contracts.

placed under the particular direction of the president, and the performance of which the president cannot lawfully forbid, and therefore is never presumed to have forbidden; as for example to record a commission, or a patent for land, which has received all the legal solemnities; or to give a copy of such record; in such cases, it is not perceived on what ground the courts of the country are further excused from the duty of giving judgment that right be done to an injured individual, than if the same services were to be performed by a person not the head of a department. . . .

This, then, is a plain case for a *mandamus*, either to deliver the commission, or a copy of it from the record; and it only remains to be inquired,

Whether it can issue from this Court.

The act to establish the judicial courts of the United States authorized the Supreme Court "to issue writs of *mandamus* in cases warranted by the principles and usages of law, to any courts appointed, or persons holding office, under the authority of the United States."

The secretary of state, being a person holding an office under the authority of the United States, is precisely within the letter of the description, and if this court is not authorized to issue a writ of *mandamus* to such an officer, it must be because the law is unconstitutional, and therefore absolutely incapable of conferring the authority, and assigning the duties which its words purport to confer and assign.

The Constitution vests the whole judicial power of the United States in one Supreme Court, and such inferior courts as Congress shall, from time to time, ordain and establish. This power is expressly extended to all cases arising under the laws of the United States; and, consequently, in some form, may be exercised over the present case; because the right claimed is given by a law of the United States.

In the distribution of this power it is declared that "the Supreme Court shall have original jurisdiction in all cases affecting ambassadors, other public ministers and consuls, and those in which a state shall be a party. In all other cases, the Supreme Court shall have appellate jurisdiction."

It has been insisted, at the bar, that as the original grant of jurisdiction, to the Supreme and inferior courts, is general, and the clause, assigning original jurisdiction to the Supreme Court, contains no negative or restrictive words, the power remains to the legislature, to assign original jurisdiction to that Court in other cases than those specified in the article which has been recited; provided those cases belong to the judicial power of the United States.

If it had been intended to leave it in the discretion of the legislature to apportion the judicial power between the supreme and inferior courts according to the will of that body, it would certainly have been useless to have proceeded further than to have defined the judicial power, and the tribunals in which it should be vested. The subsequent part of the section is mere surplusage, is entirely without meaning, if such is to be the construction. If Congress remains at liberty to give this Court appellate jurisdiction, where the Constitution has declared their jurisdiction shall be original; and original jurisdiction where the Constitution has declared it shall be appellate; the distribution of jurisdiction, made in the Constitution, is form without substance.

Affirmative words are often, in their operation, negative of other objects than those affirmed; and in this case, a negative or exclusive sense must be given to them, or they have no operation at all.

It cannot be presumed that any clause in the Constitution is intended to be without effect; and, therefore, such a construction is inadmissible, unless the words require it.

If the solicitude of the convention, respecting our peace with foreign powers, induced a provision that the Supreme Court should take original jurisdiction in cases which might be supposed to affect them; yet the clause would have proceeded no further than to provide for such cases, if no further restriction on the powers of Congress had been intended. That they should have appellate jurisdiction in all other cases, with such exceptions as Congress might make, is no restriction; unless the words be deemed exclusive of original jurisdiction. . . .

To enable this court, then, to issue a *mandamus*, it must be shown to be an exercise of appellate jurisdiction, or to be necessary to enable them to exercise appellate jurisdiction. . . .

It is the essential criterion of appellate jurisdiction, that it revises and corrects the proceedings in a cause already instituted, and does not create that cause. Although, therefore, a *mandamus* may be directed to courts, yet to issue such a writ to an officer for the delivery of a paper, is in effect the same as to sustain an original action for that paper, and, therefore, seems not to belong to appellate but to original jurisdiction. Neither is it necessary in such a case as this, to enable the Court to exercise its appellate jurisdiction.

The authority, therefore, given to the Supreme Court, by the act establishing the judicial courts of the United States, to issue writs of *mandamus* to public officers, appears not to be warranted by the Constitution; and it becomes necessary to inquire whether a jurisdiction so conferred can be exercised.

The question, whether an act, repugnant to the Constitution, can become the law of the land, is a question deeply interesting to the United States; but happily, not of an intricacy proportioned to its interest. It seems only necessary to recognize certain principles, supposed to have been long and well established, to decide it.

That the people have an original right to establish, for their future government, such principles, as, in their opinion, shall most conduce to their own happiness is the basis on which the whole American fabric has been erected. The exercise of this original right is a very great exertion; nor can it, or ought it, to be frequently repeated. The principles, therefore, so established, are deemed fundamental. And as the authority from which they proceed is supreme, and can seldom act, they are designed to be permanent.

This original and supreme will organizes the government, and assigns to different departments their respective powers. It may either stop here, or establish certain limits not to be transcended by those departments.

The government of the United States is of the latter description. The powers of the legislature are defined and limited; and that those limits may not be mistaken, or forgotten, the Constitution is written. To what purpose are powers limited, and to what purpose is that limitation committed to writing, if these limits may, at any time, be passed by those intended to be restrained? The distinction between a government with limited and unlimited powers is abolished, if those limits do not confine the persons on whom they are imposed, and if acts prohibited and acts allowed, are of equal obligation. It is a proposition too plain to be contested, that the Constitution controls any legislative act repugnant to it; or, that the legislature may alter the Constitution by an ordinary act.

Between these alternatives there is no middle ground. The Constitution is either a superior paramount law, unchangeable by ordinary means, or it is on a level with ordinary legislative acts, and, like other acts, is alterable when the legislature shall please to alter it.

If the former part of the alternative be true, then a legislative act contrary to the Constitution is not law: if the latter part be true, then written constitutions are absurd attempts, on the part of the people, to limit a power in its own nature illimitable.

Certainly all those who have framed written constitutions comtemplate them as forming the fundamental and paramount law of the nation, and, consequently, the theory of every such government must be, that an act of the legislature, repugnant to the Constitution, is void.

This theory is essentially attached to a written Constitution, and is, consequently, to be considered, by this Court, as one of the fundamental principles of our society. It is not therefore to be lost sight of in the further consideration of this subject.

If an act of the legislature, repugnant to the Constitution, is void, does it, notwithstanding its invalidity, bind the courts, and oblige them to give it effect? Or, in other words, though it be not law, does it constitute a rule as operative as if it was a law? This would be to overthrow in fact what was established in theory; and would seem, at first view, an absurdity too gross to be insisted on. It shall, however, receive a more attentive consideration.

It is emphatically the province and duty of the judicial department to say what the law is. Those who apply the rule to particular cases, must of necessity expound and interpret that rule. If two laws conflict with each other, the courts must decide on the operation of each.

So if a law be in opposition to the Constitution; if both the law and the Constitution apply to a particular case, so that the court must either decide that case conformably to the law, disregarding the Constitution; or conformably to the Constitution, disregarding the law; the court must determine which of these conflicting rules governs the case. This is of the very essence of the judicial duty.

If, then, the courts are to regard the Constitution, and the Constitution is superior to any ordinary act of the legislature, the Constitution, and not such ordinary act, must govern the case to which they both apply.

Those, then, who controvert the principle that the Constitution is to be considered, in court, as a paramount law, are reduced to the necessity of maintaining that courts must close their eyes on the Constitution, and see only the law.

This doctrine would subvert the very foundation of all written constitutions. It would declare that an act which, according to the principles and theory of our government, is entirely void, is yet, in practice, completely obligatory. It would declare that if the legislatures shall do what is expressly forbidden, such act, notwithstanding the express prohibition, is in reality effectual. It would be giving to the legislature a practical and real omnipotence, with the same breath which professes to restrict their powers within narrow limits. It is prescribing limits, and declaring that those limits may be passed at pleasure.

That it thus reduces to nothing what we have deemed the greatest improvement on political institutions, a written constitution, would of itself be sufficient, in America, where written constitutions have been viewed with so much reverence, for rejecting the construction. But the peculiar expressions of the Constitution of the United States furnish additional arguments in favour of its rejection.

The judicial power of the United States is extended to all cases arising under the Constitution.

Could it be the intention of those who gave this power, to say that in using it the Constitution should not be looked into? That a case arising under the Constitution should be decided without examining the instrument under which it arises?

This is too extravagant to be maintained.

In some cases, then, the Constitution must be looked into by the judges. And if they can open it at all, what part of it are they forbidden to read or to obey?

There are many other parts of the Constitution which serve to illustrate this subject.

It is declared that "no tax or duty shall be laid on articles exported from any state." Suppose a duty on the export of cotton, of tobacco, or of flour; and a suit instituted to recover it. Ought judgment to be rendered in such a case? Ought the judges to close their eyes on the Constitution, and only see the law?

The Constitution declares "that no bill of attainder or *ex post facto* law shall be passed."

If, however, such a bill should be passed, and a person should be prosecuted under it; must the Court condemn to death those victims whom the Constitution endeavors to preserve?

"No person," says the Constitution, "shall be convicted of treason unless on the testimony of two witnesses to the same overt act, or on confession in open court."

Here the language of the Constitution is addressed especially to the courts. It prescribes, directly for them, a rule of evidence not to be departed from. If the legislature should change that rule, and declare *one* witness, or a confession *out* of court, sufficient for conviction, must the constitutional principle yield to the legislative act?

From these, and many other selections which might be made, it is apparent, that the framers of the Constitution contemplated that instrument as a rule for the government of courts, as well as of the legislature.

Why otherwise does it direct judges to take an oath to support it? This oath certainly applies in an especial manner, to their conduct in their official character. How immoral to impose it on them, if they were to be used as the instruments, and the knowing instruments, for violating what they swear to support! . . .

It is also not entirely unworthy of observation, that in declaring what shall be the *supreme* law of the land, the *Constitution* itself is first mentioned; and not the laws of the United States generally, but those only which shall be made in *pursuance* of the Constitution, have that rank.

Thus, the particular phraseology of the Constitution of the United States confirms and strengthens the principle, supposed to be essential to all written constitutions, that a law repugnant to the Constitution is void; and that courts, as well as other departments, are bound by the instrument.

The rule must be

Discharged.

28

MCCULLOUCH V. MARYLAND (1819)

The question whether in the absence of specific constitutional authorization the federal government could establish a national bank had been an issue since the 1790s. In 1818 Maryland directly confronted the Bank of the United States, established by Congress in 1816, by requiring that all banks not chartered in that state pay a fee or tax for the issuance of bank notes. The cashier of the Baltimore branch of the Bank of the United States, James McCulloch, refused to pay the required tax and was convicted of violating the law by the Maryland courts. His case was appealed to the U.S. Supreme Court, where Chief Justice Marshall delivered a wide-ranging discourse on the nature of Congress's constitutional powers and the states' limited sovereignty.

Mr. Chief Justice Marshall* delivered the opinion of the Court:

The first question . . . is: Has Congress power to incorporate a bank?

It has been truly said, that this can scarcely be considered as an open question, entirely unprejudiced by the former proceedings of the nation respecting it. The principle now contested was introduced at a very early period of our history, has been recognized by many successive legislatures, and has been acted upon by the judicial department, in cases of peculiar delicacy, as a law of undoubted obligation. . . .

The power now contested was exercised by the first Congress elected under the present Constitution. The bill for incorporating the Bank of the United States did not steal upon an unsuspecting legislature, and pass unobserved. Its principle was completely understood, and was opposed with equal zeal and ability. After being resisted, first in the fair and open field of debate, and afterwards in the executive cabinet, with as much persevering talent as any measure has ever experienced, and being supported by arguments which convinced minds as pure and as intelligent as this country can boast, it became a law. The original act was permitted to expire; but a short experience of the embarrassments to which the refusal to revive it exposed the government, convinced those who were most prejudiced against the measure of its necessity, and induced the passage of the present law. It would require no ordinary share of intrepidity to assert, that a measure adopted under these circumstances, was a bold and plain usurpation, to which the Constitution gave no countenance. . . .

In discussing this question, the counsel for the state of Maryland have deemed it of some importance, in the construction of the Constitution, to consider that instrument not as emanating from the people, but as the act of sovereign and independent states. The powers of the general government, it has been said, are delegated by the states, who alone are truly sovereign; and must be exercised in subordination to the states, who alone possess supreme dominion.

**John Marshall:* see footnote on page 17.

. . . It would be difficult to sustain this proposition. The convention which framed the Constitution was, indeed, elected by the state legislatures. But the instrument, when it came from their hands, was a mere proposal, without obligation, or pretensions to it. It was reported to the then existing Congress of the United States, with a request that it might "be submitted to a convention of delegates, chosen in each state by the people thereof, under the recommendation of its legislature, for their assent and ratification." This mode of proceeding was adopted; and by the convention, by Congress, and by the state legislatures, the instrument was submitted to the *people*. They acted upon it, in the only manner in which they can act safely, effectively, and wisely, on such a subject by assembling in convention. It is true, they assembled in their several states; and where else should they have assembled? No political dreamer was ever wild enough to think of breaking down the lines which separate the states, and of compounding the American people into one common mass. Of consequence, when they act, they act in their states. But the measures they adopt do not, on that account, cease to be the measures of the people themselves, or become the measures of the state governments. . . .

It has been said that the people had already surrendered all their powers to the state sovereignties, and had nothing more to give. But, surely, the question whether they may resume and modify the powers granted to government, does not remain to be settled in this country. Much more might the legitimacy of the general government be doubted, had it been created by the states. The powers delegated to the state sovereignties were to be exercised by themselves, not by a distinct and independent sovereignty, created by themselves. To the formation of a league, such as was the confederation, the state sovereignties were certainly competent. But when, "in order to form a more perfect union," it was deemed necessary to change this alliance into an effective government, possessing great and sovereign powers, and acting directly on the people, the necessity of referring it to the people, and of deriving its powers directly from them, was felt and acknowledged by all.

The government of the Union, then (whatever may be the influence of this fact on the case), is emphatically and truly a government of the people. In form and in substance it emanates from them, its powers are granted by them, and are to be exercised directly on them, and for their benefit.

This government is acknowledged by all to be one of the enumerated powers. . . . But the question respecting the extent of the powers actually granted, is perpetually arising, and will probably continue to rise, as long as our system shall exist. In discussing these questions, the conflicting powers of the general and state governments must be brought into view, and the supremacy of their respective laws, when they are in opposition, must be settled.

If any one proposition could command the universal assent of mankind, we might expect that it would be this—that the government of the Union, though limited in its powers, is supreme within its sphere of action. This would seem to result, necessarily, from its nature. It is the government of all; its powers are delegated by all; it represents all, and acts for all. Though any one state may be willing to control its operations, no state is willing to allow others to control them. The nation, on those subjects on which it can act, must necessarily bind its component parts. But this question is not left to mere reason: the people have, in express terms, decided it, by saying, "this Constitution, and the laws of the United States, which shall be made in pursuance thereof," "shall be the supreme law of the land," and by requiring that the members of the state legislatures, and the officers of the executive and judicial departments of the states, shall take the oath of fidelity to it.

The government of the United States, then, though limited in its powers, is supreme; and its laws, when made in pursuance of the Constitution, form the supreme law of the land, "anything in the constitution or laws of any state, to the contrary notwithstanding."

Among the enumerated powers, we do not find that of establishing a bank or creating a corporation. But there is no phrase in the instrument which, like the Articles of Confederation, excludes incidental or implied powers; and which requires that everything granted shall be expressly and minutely described. Even the Tenth Amendment, which was framed for the purpose of quieting the excessive jealousies which had been excited, omits the word "expressly," and declares only that the powers "not delegated to the United States, nor prohibited to the states, are reserved to the states or to the people"; thus leaving the question, whether the particular power which may become the subject of contest, has been delegated to the one government, or prohibited to the other, to depend on a fair construction of the whole instrument. The men who drew and adopted this amendment had experienced the embarrassments resulting from the insertion of this word in the Articles of Confederation, and probably omitted it, to avoid those embarrassments. A constitution, to contain an accurate detail of all the subdivisions of which its great powers will admit, and of all the means by which they may be carried into execution, would partake of the prolixity of a legal code, and could scarcely be embraced by the human mind. It would, probably, never be understood by the public. Its nature, therefore, requires, that only its great outlines should be marked, its important objects designated, and the minor ingredients which compose those objects, be deduced from the nature of the objects themselves. That this idea was entertained by the framers of the American Constitution, is not only to be inferred from the nature of the instrument, but from the language. Why else were some of the limitations, found in the ninth section of Article I, introduced? It is also, in some degree, warranted, by their having omitted to use any restrictive term which might prevent its receiving a fair and just interpretation. In considering this question, then, we must never forget, that it is a *constitution* we are expounding.

Although, among the enumerated powers of government, we do not find the work "bank," or "incorporation," we find the great powers, to lay and collect taxes; to borrow money; to regulate commerce; to declare and conduct war; and to raise and support armies and navies. The sword and the purse, all the external relations, and no inconsiderable portion of the industry of the nation, are intrusted to its government. It can never be pretended, that these vast powers draw after them others of inferior importance, merely because they are inferior. Such an idea can never be advanced. But it may with great reason be contended, that a government, intrusted with such ample powers, on the due execution of which the happiness and prosperity of the nation so vitally depends, must also be intrusted with ample means for their execution. The power being given, it is the interest of the nation to facilitate its execution. It can never be their interest, and cannot be presumed to have been their intention, to clog and embarrass its execution, by withholding the most appropriate means. Throughout this vast republic . . . , from the Atlantic to the Pacific, revenue is to be collected and expended, armies are to be marched and supported. The exigencies of the nation may require, that the treasure raised in the north should be transported to the south, that raised in the east, conveyed to the west, or that this order should be reversed. Is that construction of the Constitution to be preferred, which would render these operations difficult, hazardous, and expensive? Can we adopt that construction (unless the words imperiously require it), which would impute to the framers of that instrument, when granting these powers for the public good, the intention of impeding their exercise by withholding a choice of means? If, indeed, such be the mandate of the Constitution, we have only to obey; but that instrument does not profess to enumerate the means by which the powers it confers may be executed; nor does it prohibit the creation of a corporation, if the existence of such a being be essential to the beneficial exercise of those powers. It is, then, the subject of fair inquiry, how far such means may be employed. . . .

The creation of a corporation, it is said, appertains to sovereignty. This is admitted. But to what portion of sovereignty does it appertain? Does it belong to one more than to another? . . . The power of creating a corporation, though appertaining to sovereignty, is not, like the power of making war, or levying taxes, or of regulating commerce, a great substantive and independent power, which cannot be implied as incidental to other powers, or used as a means of executing them. It is never the end for which other powers are exercised, but a means by which other objects are accomplished. No contributions are made to charity for the sake of an incorporation, but a corporation is created to administer the charity; no seminary of learning is instituted in order to be incorporated, but the corporate character is conferred to subserve the purposes of education. . . . The power of creating a corporation is never used for its own sake, but for the purpose of effecting something else. No sufficient reason is, therefore, perceived, why it may not pass as incidental to those powers which are expressly given, if it be a direct mode of executing them.

But the Constitution of the United States has not left the right of Congress to employ the necessary means for the execution of the powers conferred on the government to general reasoning. To its enumeration of powers is added that of making "all laws which shall be necessary and proper, for carrying into execution the foregoing powers, and all other powers vested by this Constitution, in the government of the United States, or in any department thereof."

The counsel for the state of Maryland have urged . . . that this clause, though in terms a grant of power, is not so in effect; but is really restrictive of the general right, which might otherwise be implied, of selecting means for executing the enumerated powers. . . .

. . . [T]he argument on which most reliance is placed, is drawn from the peculiar language of this clause. Congress is not empowered by it to make all laws, which may have relation to the powers conferred on the government, but such only as may be "necessary and proper" for carrying them into execution. The word "necessary" is considered as controlling the whole sentence, and as limiting the right to pass laws for the execution of the granted powers, to such as are indispensable, and without which the power would be nugatory. That it excludes the choice of means, and leaves to Congress, in each case, that only which is most direct and simple.

Is it true, that this is the sense in which the world "necessary" is always used? Does it always import an absolute physical necessity, so strong, that one thing, to which another may be termed necessary, cannot exist without that other? We think it does not. If reference be had to its use, in the common affairs of the world, or in approved authors, we find that it frequently imports no more than that one thing is convenient, or useful, or essential to another. To employ the means necessary to an end, is generally understood as employing any means calculated to produce the end, and not as being confined to those single means, without which the end would be entirely unattainable. . . . A thing may be necessary, very necessary, absolutely or indispensably necessary. To no mind would the same idea be conveyed by these several phrases. This comment on the word is well illustrated by the passage cited at the bar, from the tenth section of Article I of the Constitution. It is, we think, impossible to compare the sentence which prohibits a state from laying "imposts, or duties on imports or exports, except what may be *absolutely* necessary for executing its inspection laws," with that which authorizes Congress "to make all laws which shall be necessary and proper for carrying into execution" the powers of the general government, without feeling a conviction, that the convention understood itself to change materially the meaning of the word "necessary" by prefixing the word "absolutely." This word, then, like others, is used in various senses; and, in its construction, the subject, the context, the intention of the person using them, are all to be taken into view.

Let this be done in the case under consideration. The subject is the execution of those great powers on which the welfare of a nation essentially depends. It must have been the intention of those who gave these powers, to insure, as far as human prudence could insure, their beneficial execution. This could not be done, by confining the choice of means to such narrow limits as not to leave it in the power of Congress to adopt any which might be appropriate, and which were conducive to the end. This provision is made in a constitution, intended to endure for ages to come, and consequently, to be adapted to the various *crises* of human affairs. To have prescribed the means by which government should, in all future time, execute its powers, would have been to change, entirely, the character of the instrument, and give it the properties of a legal code. It would have been an unwise attempt to provide, by immutable rules, for exigencies which, if foreseen at all, must have been seen dimly, and which can be best provided for as they occur. To have declared, that the best means shall not be used, but those alone, without which the power given would be nugatory, which have been to deprive the legislature of the capacity to avail itself of experience, to exercise its reason, and to accommodate its legislation to circumstances. . . .

Take, for example, the power "to establish post offices and post roads." This power is executed by the single act of making the establishment. But, from this has been inferred the power and duty of carrying the mail along the post road, from one post office to another. And, from this implied power, has again been inferred the right to punish those who steal letters from the post office, or rob the mail. It may be said, with some plausibility, that the right to carry the mail, and to punish those who rob it, is not indispensably necessary to the establishment of a post office and post road. This right is indeed essential to the beneficial exercise of the power, but not indispensably necessary to its existence. So, of the punishment of the crimes of stealing or falsifying a record or process of a court of the United States, or of perjury in such court. To punish these offences is certainly conducive to the due administration of justice. But courts may exist, and may decide the causes brought before them, though such crimes escape punishment. . . .

If this limited construction of the word "necessary" must be abandoned, in order to punish, whence is derived the rule which would reinstate it, when the government would carry its powers into execution, by means not vindictive in their nature? If the word "necessary" means "needful," "requisite," "essential," "conducive to," in order to let in the power of punishment for the infraction of law; why is it not equally comprehensive, when required to authorize the use of means which facilitate the execution of the powers of government, without the infliction of punishment?

In ascertaining the sense in which the word "necessary" is used in this clause of the Constitution, we may derive some aid from that with which it is associated. Congress shall have power "to make all laws which shall be necessary and proper to carry into execution" the powers of the government. If the word "necessary" was used in that strict and rigorous sense for which the counsel for the state of Maryland contend, it would be an extraordinary departure from the usual course of the human mind, as exhibited in composition, to add a word, the only possible effect of which is, to qualify that strict and rigorous meaning; to present to the mind the idea of some choice of means of legislation, not strained and compressed within the narrow limits for which gentlemen contend.

But the argument which most conclusively demonstrates the error of the construction contended for by the counsel for the state of Maryland, is founded on the intention of the convention, as manifested in the whole clause. . . .

We think so for the following reasons:

1st. The clause is placed among the powers of Congress, not among the limitations on those powers.

2d. Its terms purport to enlarge, not to diminish the powers vested in the government. It purports to be an additional power, not a restriction on those already granted. . . . The framers of the Constitution wished its adoption, and well knew that it would be endangered by its strength, not by its weakness. Had they been capable of using language which would convey to the eye one idea, and, after deep reflection, impress on the mind, another, they would rather have disguised the grant of power, than its limitation. If then, their intention had been, by this clause, to restrain the free use of means which might otherwise have been implied, that intention would have been inserted in another place, and would have been expressed in terms resembling these. "In carrying into execution the foregoing powers and all others," &c., "no laws shall be passed but such as are necessary and proper." Had the intention been to make this clause restrictive, it would unquestionably have been so in form as well as in effect.

The result of the most careful and attentive consideration bestowed upon this clause is, that if it does not enlarge, it cannot be construed to restrain the powers of Congress, or to impair the right of the legislature to exercise its best judgment in the selection of measures, to carry into execution the constitutional powers of the government. If no other motive for its insertion can be suggested, a sufficient one is found in the desire to remove all doubts respecting the right to legislate on that vast mass of incidental powers which must be involved in the Constitution, if that instrument be not a splendid bauble.

We admit, as all must admit, that the powers of the government are limited, and that its limits are not to be transcended. But we think the sound construction of the Constitution must allow to the national legislature that discretion, with respect to the means by which the powers it confers are to be carried into execution, which will enable that body to perform the high duties assigned to it, in the manner most beneficial to the people. Let the end be legitimate, let it be within the scope of the Constitution, and all means which are appropriate, which are plainly adapted to that end, which are not prohibited, but consistent with the letter and spirit of the Constitution, are constitutional. . . .

It being the opinion of the Court, that the act incorporating the bank is constitutional; and that the power of establishing a branch in the state of Maryland might be properly exercised by the bank itself, we proceed to inquire—

Whether the state of Maryland may, without violating the Constitution, tax that branch? . . .

The power of Congress to create, and of course, to continue, the bank, was the subject of the preceding part of this opinion; and is no longer to be considered as questionable.

That the power of taxing it by the states may be exercised so as to destroy it, is too obvious to be denied. But taxation is said to be an absolute power, which acknowledges no other limits than those expressly prescribed in the Constitution, and like sovereign power of every other description, is trusted to the discretion of those who use it. But the very terms of this argument admit, that the sovereignty of the state, in the article of taxation itself, is subordinate to, and may be controlled by, the Constitution of the United States. How far it has been controlled by that instrument must be a question of construction. In making this construction, no principle not declared, can be admissible, which would defeat the legitimate operations of a supreme government. It is of the very essence of supremacy, to remove all obstacles to its action within its own sphere, and so to modify every power vested in subordinate governments, as to exempt its own operations from their own influence. This effect need not be stated in terms. It is so involved in the declaration of supremacy, so necessarily implied in it, that the expression of it could not make it more certain. We must, therefore, keep it in view, while construing the Constitution. . . .

The sovereignty of a state extends to everything which exists by its own authority, or is introduced by its permission; but does it extend to those means which are employed by Congress to carry into execution—powers conferred on that body by the people of the United States? We think it demonstrable that it does not. Those powers are not given by the people of a single state. They are given by the people of the United States, to a government whose laws, made in pursuance of the Constitution, are declared to be supreme. Consequently, the people of a single state cannot confer a sovereignty which will extend over them.

If we measure the power of taxation residing in a state, by the extent of sovereignty which the people of a single state possess, and can confer on its government, we have an intelligible standard, applicable to every case to which the power may be applied. We have a principle which leaves the power of taxing the people and property of a state unimpaired; which leaves to a state the command of all its resources, and which places beyond its reach, all those powers which are conferred by the people of the United States on the government of the Union, and all those means which are given for the purpose of carrying those powers into execution. We have a principle which is safe for the states, and safe for the Union. We are relieved, as we ought to be, from clashing sovereignty; from interfering powers; from a repugnancy between a right in one government to pull down, what there is an acknowledged right in another to build up; from the incompatibility of a right in one government to destroy, what there is a right in another to preserve. We are not driven to the perplexing inquiry, so unfit for the judicial department, what degree of taxation is the legitimate use, and what degree may amount to the abuse of the power. . . .

. . . That the power to tax involves the power to destroy; that the power to destroy may defeat and render useless the power to create; that there is a plain repugnancy in conferring on one government a power to control the constitutional measures of another, which other, with respect to those very measures, is declared to be supreme over that which exerts the control, are propositions not to be denied. But all inconsistencies are to be reconciled by the magic of the word *confidence*. Taxation, it is said, does not necessarily and unavoidably destroy. To carry it to the excess of destruction, would be an abuse, to presume which, would banish that confidence which is essential to all government.

But is this a case of confidence? Would the people of any state trust those of another with a power to control the most significant operations of their state government? We know they would not. Why, then, should we suppose, that the people of any one state should be willing to trust those of another with a power to control the operations of a government to which they have confided their most important and valuable interests? In the legislature of the Union alone, are all represented. The legislature of the Union alone, therefore, can be trusted by the people with the power of controlling measures which concern all, in the confidence that it will not be abused. . . .

If we apply the principle for which the state of Maryland contends, to the Constitution generally, we shall find it capable of changing totally the character of that instrument. We shall find it capable of arresting all the measures of the government, and of prostrating it at the foot of the states. The American people have declared their Constitution and the laws made in pursuance thereof, to be supreme; but this principle would transfer the supremacy, in fact, to the states.

If the states may tax one instrument, employed by the government in the execution of its powers, they may tax any and every other instrument. They may tax the mail; they may tax the mint; they may tax patent rights; they may tax the papers of the custom-house; they may tax judicial process; they may tax all the means employed by the government, to an excess which would defeat all the ends of government. This was not intended by the American people. . . .

It has also been insisted, that, as the power of taxation in the general and state governments is acknowledged to be concurrent, every argument which would sustain the right of the general government to tax banks chartered by the states, will equally sustain the rights of the states to tax banks chartered by the general government.

But the two cases are not on the same reason. The people of all the states have created the general government, and have conferred upon it the general power of taxation. The people of all the states, and the states themselves, are represented in Congress, and, by their representatives, exercise this power. When they tax the chartered institutions of the states, they tax their constituents; and these taxes must be uniform. But when a state taxes the operations of the government of the United States, it acts upon institutions created, not by their own constituents, but by people over whom they claim no control. It acts upon the measures of a government created by others as well as themselves, for the benefit of others in common with themselves. The difference is that which always exists, and always must exist, between the action of the whole on a part, and the action of a part on the whole—between the laws of a government declared which, when in opposition to those laws, is not supreme.

But if the full application of this argument could be admitted, it might bring into question the right of Congress to tax the state banks, and could not prove the right of the states to tax the Bank of the United States.

The Court has bestowed on this subject its most deliberate consideration. The results is a conviction that the states have no power, by taxation or otherwise, to retard, impede, burden, or in any manner control, the operations of the constitutional laws enacted by Congress to carry into execution the powers vested in the general government. This is, we think, the unavoidable consequence of that supremacy which the Constitution had declared.

We are unanimously of opinion, that the law passed by the legislature of Maryland, imposing a tax on the Bank of the United States, is unconstitutional and void.

This opinion does not deprive the states of any resources which they originally possessed. It does not extend to a tax paid by the real property of the bank, in common with the other real property within the state, nor to a tax imposed on the interest which the citizens of Maryland may hold in this institution, in common with other property of the same description throughout the state. But this is a tax on the operations of the bank, and is, consequently, a tax on the operation of an instrument employed by the government of the Union to carry its powers into execution. Such a tax must be unconstitutional.

Reversed.

PART NINE

THE POLICY PROCESS

For decades critics have lamented the fact that government often seems unable to manage major policy problems *comprehensively*. In recent years, the critical outcry has become particularly shrill, as the political system struggles with complex new issues, such as environmental crises, drug wars, educational reform, trade imbalances, and a stubborn budgetary deficit. These and other complicated issues would seem to require integrated, long-term answers, instead of piecemeal and short-term adjustments.

Many reformers, often trained in private-sector management, have advocated a policy-making approach that would better approximate the following procedure: First, clear objectives would be set out; next all possible techniques for achieving the objectives would be presented; then, an optimal course of action would be selected, after examining systematically all the possible results of each approach; finally, throughout the entire exercise, extant policies and precedents would not constrain the choice among alternatives (in other words, if necessary, even radical departures from past practices would be open for consideration).

In actuality, most public policy decisions are not formulated in anything like this fashion. At best, policymakers become adept at "muddling through," as Charles E. Lindblom put it in his 1959 essay. Past decisions usually restrict present choices. No one has the capability and few have the inclination to consider carefully *all* possible means of attaining desired ends, much less to evaluate all their ramifications. In fact, the search for an optimal solution is quickly abandoned, once it becomes obvious that there is frequent disagreement about basic goals, or even about the existence of the problem to be solved. In short, policy is rarely informed by comprehensive analysis. Rather, it evolves through a series of incremental modifications (or, to use Lindblom's terminology, a succession of drastically limited comparisons among available alternatives).

Is disjointed incrementalism necessarily undesirable? The essay by Edward C. Banfield (1961) suggests the answer is more complicated than is generally understood. When policy seems to comprise little more than an assemblage of segmental decisions and marginal adjustments, it is because the actions of government in a pluralistic polity are seldom prescribed by a central decision maker with an explicit goal (or set of goals), but rather by the continual pulling and hauling of competing interests whose diverse preferences must be reconciled. In the final chapter of his fascinating book on policy decisions in the Chicago city government, Banfield emphasizes that legitimate public policy must weigh sensitively the disparate values of a variety of interested parties. Comprehensive planners—even enlightened and scrupulous ones, supported by the most elaborate cost-benefit studies—risk weighting the competing values arbitrarily when they impose their own judgment. Policies shaped not through "central decisions" but by spontaneous mutual accommodations among the affected interests are more likely to reflect just "social choices." As in an adversary proceeding, the process of negotiation and debate elicits the participation (and thus presumably takes into account the claims) of those groups in society whose stakes are greatest with respect to the issue at hand, while discounting the claims of indifferent, irrelevant, or frivolous groups. True, coherent policies often fail to emerge from pluralistic bargaining. But sometimes incoherent "resultants" are actually in the public interest.

To say that the policy process in the United States seldom resembles the rational-comprehensive model is not to say that it is *uniformly* incremental, haphazard, and given to interest-group haggling. Much seems to depend on the nature of the issue in question. In an influential paper that appeared in 1964, Theodore J. Lowi made one of the first serious attempts to classify the styles of politics related to differing types of policy issues. Lowi suggests that "distributive" policies (wherein the government is extending highly particularized benefits to specific groups) are characterized by the most intensely pluralistic pattern, as a multitude of small organized interests press for a share of the government pork barrel. "Regulatory" decisions (aimed at restricting or promoting interests within broader sectors, such as entire industries or occupations) also evoke pluralist politics, but of a higher order: coalitions are formed on the basis of shared desires to adopt, modify, or defeat governmental initiatives. Finally, "redistributive" programs (taking from some broad groups or classes and giving to others) tend to involve a contest between the broadest associations, often divided along class lines. Distributive and regulatory policies tend to be the more disaggregated and heavily bartered; redistributive schemes, which by definition necessitate a fairly clear-cut victory by one side over the other, are naturally less so.

29

CHARLES E. LINDBLOM

THE SCIENCE OF "MUDDLING THROUGH"

How are public policy decisions made? Charles E. Lindblom argues that public administrators tend to use the method of "successive limited comparisons" so that policy change is incremental. Administrative theorists, on the other hand, often advocate a rational-comprehensive approach (or the root method) in which all plausible policy alternatives are comprehensively analyzed before any choices are made. Lindblom systematically compared the two methods in his article, "The Science of 'Muddling Through,' " which was originally published in the Spring 1959 edition of the Public Administration Review. *His formulation of the incremental model has vastly enriched our understanding of policy-making in practice by examining how administrators actually arrive at policy. Lindblom, Sterling Professor of Economics and Political Science and Director of the Institute for Social and Policy Studies at Yale University, is the author of* Politics, Economics, and Welfare *(1953) with Robert Dahl;* The Intelligence of Democracy *(1965);* A Strategy of Decision *(1963) with David Braybrooke;* Politics and Markets *(1977);* Useable Knowledge *(1979) with David K. Cohen; and* The Policy Making Process *(1968, 1980).*

Suppose an administrator is given responsibility for formulating policy with respect to inflation. He might start by trying to list all related values in order of importance, e.g., full employment, reasonable business profit, protection of small savings, prevention of a stock market crash. Then all possible policy outcomes could be rated as more or less efficient in attaining a maximum of these values. This would of course require a prodigious inquiry into values held by members of society and an equally prodigious set of calculations on how much each value is equal to how much of each other value. He could then proceed to outline all possible policy alternatives. In a third step, he could undertake systematic comparison of his multitude of alternatives to determine which attains the greatest amount of values.

In comparing policies, he would take advantage of any theory available that generalized about classes of policies. In considering inflation, for example, he would compare all policies in the light of the theory of prices. Since no alternatives are beyond his investigation, he would consider strict central control and the abolition of all prices and markets on the one hand and elimination of all public controls with reliance completely on the free market on the other, both in the light of whatever theoretical generalizations he could find on such hypothetical economies.

Finally, he would try to make the choice that would in fact maximize his values.

An alternative line of attack would be to set as his principal objective, either explicitly or without conscious thought, the relatively simple goal of keeping prices level. This objective might be compromised or complicated by only a few other goals, such as full employment. He would in fact disregard most other social values as beyond his present interest, and he would for the moment not even attempt to rank the few values that he regarded as immediately relevant. Were he pressed, he would quickly admit that he was ignoring many related values and many possible important consequences of his policies.

As a second step, he would outline those relatively few policy alternatives that occurred to him. He would then compare them. In comparing his limited number of alternatives, most of them familiar from past controversies, he would not ordinarily find a body of theory precise enough to carry him through a comparison of their respective consequences. Instead he would rely heavily on the record of past experience with small policy steps to predict the consequences of similar steps extended into the future.

Moreover, he would find that the policy alternatives combined objectives or values in different ways. For example, one policy might offer price level stability at the cost of some risk of unemployment; another might offer less price stability but also less risk of unemployment. Hence, the next step in his approach—the final selection—would combine into one the choice among values and the choice among instruments for reaching values. It would not, as in the first method of policy-making, approximate a more mechanical process of choosing the means that best satisfied goals that were previously clarified and ranked. Because practitioners of the second approach expect to achieve their goals only partially, they would expect to repeat endlessly the sequence just described, as conditions and aspirations changed and as accuracy of prediction improved.

BY ROOT OR BY BRANCH

For complex problems, the first of these two approaches is of course impossible. Although such an approach can be described, it cannot be practiced except for relatively simple problems and even then only in a somewhat modified form. It assumes intellectual capacities and sources of information that men simply do not possess, and it is even more absurd as an approach to policy when the time and money that can be allocated to a policy problem is limited, as is always the case. Of particular importance to public administrators is the fact that public agencies are in effect usually instructed not to practice the first method. That is to say, their prescribed functions and constraints—the politically or legally possible—restrict their attention to relatively few values and relatively few alternative policies among the countless alternatives that might be imagined. It is the second method that is practiced.

Curiously, however, the literatures of decision-making, policy formulation, planning, and public administration formalize the first approach rather than the second, leaving public administrators who handle complex decisions in the position of practicing what few preach. For emphasis I run some risk of overstatement. True enough, the literature is well aware of limits on man's capacities and of the inevitability that policies will be approached in some such style as the second. But attempts to formalize rational policy formulation—to lay out explicitly the necessary steps in the process—usually describe the first approach and not the second.[1]

The common tendency to describe policy formulation even for complex problems as though it followed the first approach has been strengthened by the attention given to, and success enjoyed by, operations research,* statistical decision theory,† and systems analysis.‡ The hallmarks of these procedures, typical of the first approach, are clarity of objective, explicitness of evaluation, a high degree of comprehensiveness of overview, and, wherever possible, quantification of values for mathematical analysis. But these advanced procedures remain largely the appropriate techniques of relatively small-scale problem-solving where the total number of variables to be considered is small and value problems restricted. Charles Hitch, head of the Economics Division of RAND Corporation, one of the leading centers for application of these techniques, has written:

> I would make the empirical generalization from my experience at RAND and elsewhere that operations research is the art of sub-optimizing, i.e., of solving some lower-level problems, and that difficulties increase and our special competence diminishes by an order of magnitude with every level of decision making we attempt to ascend. The sort of simple explicit model which operations researchers are so proficient in using can certainly reflect most of the significant factors influencing traffic control on the George Washington Bridge, but the proportion of the relevant reality which we can represent by any such model or models in studying, say, a major foreign-policy decision, appears to be almost trivial.[2]

Accordingly, I propose in this paper to clarify and formalize the second method, much neglected in the literature. This might be described as the method of *successive limited comparisons*. I will contrast it with the first approach, which might be called the rational-comprehensive method.[3] More impressionistically and briefly—and therefore generally used in this article—they could be characterized as the branch method and root method, the former continually building out from the current situation, step-by-step and by small degrees; the latter starting from fundamentals anew each time, building on the past only as experience is embodied in a theory, and always prepared to start completely from the ground up.

Let us put the characteristics of the two methods side by side in simplest terms.

Rational-Comprehensive (Root)

1. Clarification of values or objectives distinct from and usually prerequisite to empirical analysis of alternative policies.

**Operations research:* type of analysis, based on mathematical models, used to determine the most efficient use of resources for a set of goals.

†*Statistical decision theory:* theory that allows one to make choices between alternatives by objectifying problems and analyzing them quantitatively. Also called Bayesian decision theory after Thomas Bayes (1702–1761), who developed the mathematical foundation of inference, the method of using information on a sample to infer characteristics about a population.

‡*Systems analysis:* analysis of systemic data by means of advanced quantitative techniques to aid in selecting the most appropriate course of action among a series of alternatives.

2a. Policy-formulation is therefore approached through means-end analysis: First the ends are isolated, then the means to achieve them are sought.
3a. The test of a "good" policy is that it can be shown to be the most appropriate means to desired ends.
4a. Analysis is comprehensive; every important relevant factor is taken into account.
5a. Theory is often heavily relied upon.

Assuming that the root method is familiar and understandable, we proceed directly to clarification of its alternative by contrast. In explaining the second, we shall be describing how most administrators do in fact approach complex questions, for the root method, the "best" way as a blueprint or model, is in fact not workable for complex policy questions, and administrators are forced to use the method of successive limited comparisons.

INTERTWINING EVALUATION AND EMPIRICAL ANALYSIS (1B)

The quickest way to understand how values are handled in the method of successive limited comparisions is to see how the root method often breaks down in *its* handling of values or objectives. The idea that values should be clarified, and in advance of the examination of alternative policies, is appealing. But what happens when we attempt it for complex social problems? The first difficulty is that on many critical values or objectives, citizens disagree, congressmen disagree, and public administrators disagree. Even where a fairly specific objective is prescribed for the administrator, there remains considerable room for disagreement on sub-objectives. Consider, for example, the conflict with respect to locating public housing, described in Meyerson and Banfield's study of the Chicago Housing Authority[4]—disagreement which occurred despite the clear objective of providing a certain number of public housing units in the city. Similarly conflicting are objectives in highway location, traffic control, minimum wage administration, development of tourist facilities in national parks, or insect control.

Successive Limited Comparisons (Branch)

1b. Selection of value goals and empirical analysis of the needed action are not distinct from one another but are closely intertwined.
2b. Since means and ends are not distinct, means-end analysis is often inappropriate or limited.
3b. The test of a "good" policy is typically that various analysts find themselves directly agreeing on a policy (without their agreeing that it is the most appropriate means to an agreed objective).
4b. Analysis is drastically limited: i) Important possible outcomes are neglected. ii) Important alternative potential policies are neglected. iii) Important affected values are neglected.
5b. A succession of comparison greatly reduces or eliminates reliance on theory.

Administrators cannot escape these conflicts by ascertaining the majority's preference, for preferences have not been registered on most issues; indeed, there often *are* no preferences in the absence of public discussion sufficient to bring an issue to the attention of the electorate. Furthermore, there is a question of whether intensity of feeling should be considered as well as the number of persons preferring each alternative. By the impossibility of doing otherwise, administrators often are reduced to deciding policy without clarifying objectives first.

Even when an administrator resolves to follow his own values as a criterion for decisions, he often will not know how to rank them when they conflict with one another, as they usually do. Suppose, for example, that an administrator must relocate tenants living in tenements scheduled for destruction. One objective is to empty the buildings fairly promptly, another is to find suitable accommodation for persons displaced, another is to avoid friction with residents in other areas in which a large influx would be unwelcome, another is to deal with all concerned through persuasion if possible, and so on.

How does one state even to himself the relative importance of these partially conflicting values? A simple ranking of them is not enough; one needs ideally to know how much of one value is worth sacrificing for some of another value. The answer is that typically the administrator chooses—and must choose—directly among policies in which these values are combined in different ways. He cannot first clarify his values and then choose among policies.

A more subtle third point underlies both the first two. Social objectives do not always have the same relative values. One objective may be highly prized in one circumstance, another in another circumstance. If, for example, an administrator values highly both the dispatch with which his agency can carry through its projects *and* good public relations, it matters little which of the two possibly conflicting values he favors in some abstract or general sense. Policy questions arise in forms which put to administrators such a question as: Given the degree to which we are or are not already achieving the values of dispatch and the values of good public relations, is it worth sacrificing a little speed for a happier clientele, or is it better to risk offending the clientele so that we can get on with our work? The answer to such a question varies with circumstances.

The value problem is, as the example shows, always a problem of adjustments at a margin. But there is no practicable way to state marginal objectives or values except in terms of particular policies. That one value is preferred to another in one decision situation does not mean that it will be preferred in another decision situation in which it can be had only at great sacrifice of another value. Attempts to rank or order values in general and abstract terms so that they do not shift from decision to decision end up by ignoring the relevant marginal preferences. The significance of this third point thus goes very far. Even if all administrators had at hand an agreed set of values, objectives, and constraints, and an agreed ranking of these values, objectives, and constraints, their marginal values in actual choice situations would be impossible to formulate.

Unable consequently to formulate the relevant values first and then choose among policies to achieve them, administrators must choose directly among alternative policies that offer different marginal combinations of values. Somewhat paradoxically, the only practicable way to disclose one's relevant marginal values even to oneself is to describe the policy one chooses to achieve them. Except roughly and vaguely, I know of no way to describe—or even to understand—what my relative evaluations are for, say, freedom and security, speed and accuracy in governmental decisions, or low taxes and better schools than to describe my preferences among specific policy choices that might be made between the alternatives in each of the pairs,

In summary, two aspects of the process by which values are actually handled can be distinguished. The first is clear: evaluation and empirical analysis are intertwined; that is, one chooses among values and among policies at one and the same time. Put a little more elaborately, one simultaneously chooses a policy to attain certain objectives and chooses the objectives themselves. The second aspect is related but distinct: the administrator focuses his attention on marginal or incremental values. Whether he is aware of it or not, he does not find general formulations of objectives very helpful and in fact makes specific marginal or incremental comparisons. Two policies, X and Y, confront him. Both promise the same degree of attainment of objectives *a*, *b*, *c*, *d*, and *e*. But X promises him somewhat more of *f* than does Y, while Y promises him somewhat more of *g* than does X. In choosing between them, he is in fact offered the alternative of a marginal or incremental amount of *f* at the expense of a marginal or incremental amount of *g*. The only values that are relevant to his choice are these increments by which the two policies differ; and, when he finally chooses between the two marginal values, he does so by making a choice between policies.[5]

As to whether the attempt to clarify objectives in advance of policy selection is more or less rational than the close intertwining of marginal evaluation and empirical analysis, the principal difference established is that for complex problems the first is impossible and irrelevant, and the second is both possible and relevant. The second is possible because the administrator need not try to analyze any values except the values by which alternative policies differ and need not be concerned with them except as they differ marginally. His need for information on values or objectives is drastically reduced as compared with the root method; and his capacity for grasping, comprehending, and relating values to one another is not strained beyond the breaking point.

RELATIONS BETWEEN MEANS AND ENDS (2B)

Decision-making is ordinarily formalized as a means-ends relationship: means are conceived to be evaluated and chosen in the light of ends finally selected independently of and prior to the choice of means. This is the means-ends relationship of the root method. But it follows from all that has just been said that such a means-ends relationship is possible only to the extent that values are agreed upon, are reconcilable, and are stable at the margin. Typically, therefore, such a means-ends relationship is absent from the branch method, where means and ends are simultaneously chosen.

Yet any departure from the means-ends relationship of the root method will strike some readers as inconceivable. For it will appear to them that only in such a relationship is it possible to determine whether one policy choice is better or worse than another. How can an administrator know whether he has made a wise or foolish decision if he is without prior values or objectives by which to judge his decisions? The answer to this question calls up the third distinctive difference between root and branch methods: how to decide the best policy.

THE TEST OF "GOOD" POLICY (3B)

In the root method, a decision is "correct," "good," or "rational" if it can be shown to attain some specified objective, where the objective can be specified without simply describing the decision itself. Where objectives are defined only through the marginal or incremental approach to values described above, it is still sometimes possible to test whether a policy does in fact attain the desired objectives; but a precise statement of the objectives takes the form of a description of the policy chosen or some alternative to it. To show that a policy is mistaken one cannot offer an abstract argument that important objectives are not achieved; one must instead argue that another policy is more to be preferred.

So far, the departure from customary ways of looking at problem-solving is not troublesome, for many administrators will be quick to agree that the most effective discussion of the correctness of policy does take the form of comparison with other policies that might have been chosen. But what of the situation in which administrators cannot agree on values or objectives, either abstractly or in marginal terms? What then is the test of "good" policy? For the root method, there is no test. Agreement on objectives failing, there is no standard of "correctness." For the method of successive limited comparisons, the test is agreement on policy itself, which remains possible even when agreement on values is not.

It has been suggested that continuing agreement in Congress on the desirability of extending old age insurance stems from liberal desires to strengthen the welfare programs of the federal government and from conservative desires to reduce union demands for private pension plans. If so, this is an excellent demonstration of the ease with which individuals of different ideologies often can agree on concrete policy. Labor mediators report a similar phenomenon: the contestants cannot agree on criteria for settling their disputes but can agree on specific proposals. Similarly, when one administrator's objective turns out to be another's means, they often can agree on policy.

Agreement on policy thus becomes the only practicable test of the policy's correctness. And for one administrator to seek to win the other over to agreement on ends as well would accomplish nothing and create quite unnecessary controversy.

If agreement directly on policy as a test for "best" policy seems a poor substitute for testing the policy against its objectives, it ought to be remembered that objectives themselves have no ultimate validity other than they are agreed upon. Hence agreement is the test of "best" policy in both methods. But where the root method requires agreement on what elements in the decision constitute objectives and on which of these objectives should be sought, the branch method falls back on agreement wherever it can be found.

In an important sense, therefore, it is not irrational for an administrator to defend a policy as good without being able to specify what it is good for.

NON-COMPREHENSIVE ANALYSIS (4B)

Ideally, rational-comprehensive analysis leaves out nothing important. But it is impossible to take everything important into consideration unless "important" is so narrowly defined that analysis is in fact quite limited. Limits on human intellectual capacities and on available information set definite limits to man's capacity to be comprehensive. In actual fact, therefore, no one can practice the rational-comprehensive method for really complex problems, and every administrator faced with a sufficiently complex problem must find ways drastically to simplify.

An administrator assisting in the formulation of agricultural economic policy cannot in the first place be competent on all possible policies. He cannot even comprehend one policy entirely. In planning a soil bank program, he cannot successfully anticipate the impact of higher or lower farm income on, say, urbanization—the possible consequent loosening of family ties, possible consequent eventual need for revisions in social security and further implications for tax problems arising out of new federal responsibilities for social security and municipal responsibilities for urban services. Nor, to follow another line of repercussions, can he work through the soil bank program's effects on prices for agricultural products in foreign markets and consequent implications for foreign relations, including those arising out of economic rivalry between the United States and the U.S.S.R.

In the method of successive limited comparisons, simplification is systematically achieved in two principal ways. First, it is achieved through limitation of policy comparisons to those policies that differ in relatively small degree from policies presently in effect. Such a limitation immediately reduces the number of alternatives to be investigated and also drastically simplifies the character of the investigation of each. For it is not necessary to undertake fundamental inquiry into an alternative and its consequences; it is necessary only to study those respects in which the proposed alternative and its consequences differ from the status quo. The empirical comparison of marginal differences among alternative policies that differ only marginally is, of course, a counterpart to the incremental or marginal comparison of values discussed above.[6]

RELEVANCE AS WELL AS REALISM

It is a matter of common observation that in Western democracies public administrators and policy analysts in general do largely limit their analyses to incremental or marginal differences in policies that are chosen to differ only incrementally. They do not do so, however, solely because they desperately need some way to simplify their problems; they also do so in order to be relevant. Democracies change their policies almost entirely through incremental adjustments. Policy does not move in leaps and bounds.

The incremental character of political change in the United States has often been remarked. The two major political parties agree on fundamentals; they offer alternative policies to the voters only on relatively small points of difference. Both parties favor full employment, but they define it somewhat differently; both favor the development of water power resources, but in slightly different ways; and both favor unemployment compensation, but not the same level of benefits. Similarly, shifts of policy within a party take place largely through a series of relatively small changes, as can be seen in their only gradual acceptance of the idea of government responsibility for support of the unemployed, a change in party positions beginning in the early 30's and culminating in a sense in the Employment Act of 1946.*

Party behavior is in turn rooted in public attitudes, and political theorists cannot conceive of democracy's surviving in the United States in the absence of fundamental agreement on potentially disruptive issues, with consequent limitation of policy debates to relatively small differences in policy.

Since the policies ignored by the administrator are politically impossible and so irrelevant, the simplification of analysis achieved by concentrating on policies that differ only incrementally is not a capricious kind of simplification. In addition, it can be argued that, given the limits on knowledge within which policy-makers are confined, simplifying by limiting the focus to small variations from present policy makes the most of available knowledge. Because policies being considered are like present and past policies, the administrator can obtain information and claim some insight. Non-incremental policy proposals are therefore typically not only politically irrelevant but also unpredictable in their consequences.

The second method of simplification of analysis is the practice of ignoring important possible consequences of possible policies, as well as the values attached to the neglected consequences. If this appears to disclose a shocking shortcoming of successive limited comparisons, it can be replied that, even if the exclusions are random, policies may nevertheless be more intelligently formulated than through futile attempts to achieve a comprehensiveness beyond human capacity. Actually, however, the exclusions, seeming arbitrary or random from one point of view, need be neither.

Achieving a Degree of Comprehensiveness

Suppose that each value neglected by one policy-making agency were a major concern of at least one other agency. In that case, a helpful division of labor would be achieved, and no agency need find its task beyond its capacities. The shortcomings of such a system would be that one agency might destroy a value

**Employment Act of 1946:* act mandating federal responsibility for promoting full employment and for stabilizing the economy. The act created the Council of Economic Advisers, a unit of the Executive Office of the President.

either before another agency could be activated to safeguard it or in spite of another agency's efforts. But the possibility that important values may be lost is present in any form of organization, even where agencies attempt to comprehend in planning more than is humanly possible.

The virtue of such a hypothetical division of labor is that every important interest or value has its watchdog. And these watchdogs can protect the interests in their jurisdiction in two quite different ways: first, by redressing damages done by other agencies; and second, by anticipating and heading off injury before it occurs.

In a society like that of the United States in which individuals are free to combine to pursue almost any possible common interest they might have and in which government agencies are sensitive to the pressures of these groups, the system described is approximated. Almost every interest has its watchdog. Without claiming that every interest has a sufficiently powerful watchdog, it can be argued that our system often can assure a more comprehensive regard for the values of the whole society than any attempt at intellectual comprehensiveness.

In the United States, for example, no part of government attempts a comprehensive overview of policy on income distribution. A policy nevertheless evolves, and one responding to a wide variety of interests. A process of mutual adjustment among farm groups, labor unions, municipalities and school boards, tax authorities, and government agencies with responsibilities in the fields of housing, health, highways, national parks, fire, and police accomplishes a distribution of income in which particular income problems neglected at one point in the decision process become central at another point.

Mutual adjustment is more pervasive than the explicit forms it takes in negotiation between groups; it persists through the mutual impacts of groups upon each other even where they are not in communication. For all the imperfections and latent dangers in this ubiquitous process of mutual adjustment, it will often accomplish an adaptation of policies to a wider range of interests than could be done by one group centrally.

Note, too, how the incremental pattern of policy-making fits with the multiple pressure pattern. For when decisions are only incremental—closely related to known policies—it is easier for one group to anticipate the kind of moves another might make and easier for it to make correction for injury already accomplished.[7]

Even partisanship and narrowness, to use pejorative terms, will sometimes be assets to rational decision-making, for they can doubly insure that what one agency neglects, another will not; they specialize personnel to distinct points of view. The clain is valid that effective rational coordination of the federal administrator, if possible to achieve at all, would require an agreed set of values[8]—if "rational" is defined as the practice of the root method of decision-making. But a high degree of administrative coordination occurs as each agency adjusts its policies to the concerns of the other agencies in the process of fragmented decision-making I have just described.

For all the apparent shortcomings of the incremental approach to policy alternatives with its arbitrary exclusion coupled with fragmentation, when compared to the root method, the branch method often looks far superior. In the root method, the inevitable exclusion of factors is accidental, unsystematic, and not defensible by any agrument so far developed, while in the branch method the exclusions are deliberate, systematic, and defensible. Ideally, of course, the root method does not exclude; in practice it must.

Nor does the branch method necessarily neglect long-run considerations and objectives. It is clear that important values must be omitted in considering policy, and sometimes the only way long-run objectives can be given adequate attention is through the neglect of short-run considerations. But the values omitted can be either long-run or short-run.

SUCCESSION OF COMPARISONS (5B)

The final distinctive element in the branch method is that the comparisons, together with the policy choice, proceed in a chronological series. Policy is not made once and for all; it is made and re-made endlessly. Policy-making is a process of successive approximation to some desired objectives in which what is desired itself continues to change under reconsideration.

Making policy is at best a very rough process. Neither social scientists, nor politicians, nor public administrators yet know enough about the social world to avoid repeated error in predicting the consequences of policy moves. A wise policy-maker consequently expects that his policies will achieve only part of what he hopes and at the same time will produce unanticipated consequences he would have preferred to avoid. If he proceeds through a *succession* of incremental changes, he avoids serious lasting mistakes in several ways.

In the first place, past sequences of policy steps have given him knowledge about the probable consequences of further similar steps. Second, he need not attempt big jumps toward his goals that would require predictions beyond his or anyone else's knowledge, because he never expects his policy to be a final resolution of a problem. His decision is only one step, one that if successful can quickly be followed by another. Third, he is in effect able to test his previous predictions as he moves on to each further step. Lastly, he often can remedy a past error fairly quickly—more quickly than if policy proceeded through more distinct steps widely spaced in time.

Compare this comparative analysis of incremental changes with the aspiration to employ theory in the root method. Man cannot think without classifying, without subsuming one experience under a more general category of experiences. The attempt to push categorization as far as possible and to find general propositions which can be applied to specific situations is what I refer to with the word "theory." Where root analysis often leans heavily on theory in this sense, the branch method does not.

The assumption of root analysis is that theory is the most systematic and economical way to bring relevant knowledge to bear on a specific problem. Granting the assumption, an unhappy fact is that we do not have adequate theory to apply to problems in any policy area, although theory is more adequate in some areas—monetary policy, for example—than in others. Comparative analysis, as in the branch method, is sometimes a systematic alternative to theory.

Suppose an administrator must choose among a small group of policies that differ only incrementally from each other and from present policy. He might aspire to "understand" each of the alternatives—for example, to know all the consequences of each aspect of each policy. If so, he would indeed require theory. In fact, however, he would usually decide that, *for policy-making purposes*, he need know, as explained above, only the consequences of each of those aspects of the policies in which they differed from one another. For this much more modest aspiration, he requires no theory (although it might be helpful, if available), for he can proceed to isolate probable differences by examining the differences in consequences associated with past differences in policies, a feasible program because he can take his observations from a long sequence of incremental changes.

For example, without a more comprehensive social theory about juvenile delinquency than scholars have yet produced, one cannot possibly understand the ways in which a variety of public policies—say on education, housing, recreation, employment, race relations, and policing—might encourage or discourage delinquency. And one needs such an understanding if he undertakes the comprehensive overview of the problem prescribed in the models of the root method. If, however, one merely wants to mobilize knowledge sufficient to assist in a choice among a small group of similar policies—alternative policies on juvenile court procedures, for example—he can do so by comparative analysis of the results of similar past policy moves.

THEORISTS AND PRACTITIONERS

This difference explains—in some cases at least—why the administrator often feels that the outside expert or academic problem-solver is sometimes not helpful and why they in turn often urge more theory on him. And it explains why an administrator often feels more confident when "flying by the seat of his pants" than when following the advice of theorists. Theorists often ask the administrator to go the long way round to the solution of his problems, in effect ask him to follow the best canons of the scientific method, when the administrator knows that the best available theory will work less well than more modest incremental comparisons. Theorists do not realize that the administrator is often in fact practicing a systematic method. It would be foolish to push this explanation too far, for sometimes practical decision-makers are pursuing neither a theoretical approach nor successive comparisons, not any other systematic method.

It may be worth emphasizing that theory is sometimes of extremely limited helpfulness in policy-making for at least two rather different reasons. It is greedy for facts; it can be constructed only through a great collection of observations. And it is typically insufficiently precise for application to a policy process that moves through small changes. In contrast, the comparative method both economizes on the need for facts and directs the analyst's attention to just those facts that are relevant to the fine choices faced by the decision-maker.

With respect to precision of theory, economic theory serves as an example. It predicts that an economy without money or prices would in certain specified ways misallocate resources, but this finding pertains to an alternative far removed from the kind of policies on which administrators need help. On the other hand, it is not precise enough to predict the consequences of policies restricting business mergers, and this is the kind of issue on which the administrators need help. Only in relatively restricted areas does economic theory achieve sufficient precision to go far in resolving policy questions; its helpfulness in policy-making is always so limited that it requires supplementation through comparative analysis.

SUCCESSIVE COMPARISON AS A SYSTEM

Successive limited comparisons is, then, indeed a method or system; it is not a failure of method for which administrators ought to apologize. None the less, its imperfections, which have not been explored in this paper, are many. For example, the method is without a built-in safeguard for all relevant values, and it also may lead the decision-maker to overlook excellent policies for no other reason than that they are not suggested by the chain of successive policy steps leading up to the present. Hence, it ought to be said that under this method, as well as under some of the most sophisticated variants of the root method—operations research, for example—policies will continue to be as foolish as they are wise.

Why then bother to describe the method in all the above detail? Because it is in fact a common method of policy formulation, and is, for complex problems, the principal reliance of administrators as well as of other policy analysts.[9] And because it will be superior to any other decision-making method available for complex problems in many circumstances, certainly superior to a futile attempt at superhuman comprehensiveness. The reaction of the public administrator to the exposition of method doubtless will be less a discovery of a new method than a better acquaintance with an old. But by becoming more conscious of their practice of this method, administrators might practice it with more skill and know when to extend or constrict its use. (That they sometimes practice it effectively and sometimes not may explain the extremes of opinion on "muddling through," which is both praised as a highly sophisticated form of problem-solving and denounced as no method at all. For I suspect that in so far as there is a system in what is known as "muddling through," this method is it).

One of the noteworthy incidental consequences of clarification of the method is the light it throws on the suspicion an administrator sometimes entertains that a consultant or adviser is not speaking relevantly and responsibly when in fact by all ordinary objective evidence he is. The trouble lies in the fact that most of us approach policy problems within a framework given by our view of a chain of successive policy choices made up to the present. One's thinking about appropriate policies with respect, say, to urban traffic control is greatly influenced by one's knowledge of the incremental steps taken up the the present. An administrator enjoys an intimate knowledge of his past sequences that "outsiders" do not share, and his thinking and that of the "outsider" will consequently be different in ways that may puzzle both. Both may appear to be talking intelligently, yet each may find the other unsatisfactory. The relevance of the policy chain of succession is even more clear when an American tries to discuss, say, antitrust policy with a Swiss, for the chains of policy in the two countries are strikingly different and the two individuals consequently have organized their knowledge in quite different ways.

If this phenomenon is a barrier to communication, an understanding of it promises an enrichment of intellectual interaction in policy formulation. Once the source of difference is understood, it will sometimes be stimulating for an administrator to seek out a policy analyst whose recent experience is with a policy chain different from his own.

This raises again a question only briefly discussed above on the merits of like-mindedness among government administrators. While much of organization theory argues the virtues of common values and agreed organizational objectives, for complex problems in which the root method is inapplicable, agencies will want among their own personnel two types of diversification: administrators whose thinking is organized by reference to policy chains other than those familiar to most members of the organization and, even more commonly, administrators whose professional or personal values or interests create diversity of view (perhaps coming from different specialties, social classes, geographical areas) so that, even within a single agency, decision-making can be fragmented and parts of the agency can serve as watchdogs for other parts.

NOTES

[1]James G. March and Herbert A. Simon similarly characterize the literature. They also take some important steps, as have Simon's recent articles, to describe a less heroic model of policy-making. See *Organizations* (John Wiley and Sons, 1958), p. 137.

[2]Operations Research and National Planning—A Dissent," 5 *Operations Research* 718 (October, 1957). Hitch's dissent is from particular points made in the article to which his paper is a reply; his claim that operations research is for low-level problems is widely accepted.

For examples of the kind of problems to which operations research is applied, see C. W. Churchman, R. L. Ackoff and E. L. Arnoff, *Introduction to Operations Research* (John Wiley and Sons, 1957); and J. F. McCloskey and J. M. Coppinger (eds.), *Operations Research for Management*, Vol. II (The Johns Hopkins Press, 1956).

[3]I am assuming that administrators often make policy and advise in the making of policy and am treating decision-making and policy-making as synonymous for purposes of this paper.

[4]Martin Meyerson and Edward C. Banfield, *Politics, Planning and the Public Interest* (The Free Press, 1955).

[5]The line of argument is, of course, an extension of the theory of market choice, especially the theory of consumer choice, to public policy choices.

[6]A more precise definition of incremental policies and a discussion of whether a change that

appears "small" to one observer might be seen differently by another is to be found in my "Policy Analysis," 48 *American Ecnomic Review* 298 (June, 1958).

[7]The link between the practice of the method of successive limited comparisons and mutual adjustment of interests in a highly fragmented decision-making process adds a new facet to pluralist theories of government and administration.

[8]Herbert Simon, Donald W. Smithburg, and Victor A. Thompson, *Public Administration* (Alfred A. Knopf, 1950), p. 434.

[9]Elsewhere I have explored this same method of policy formulation as practiced by academic analysts of policy ("Policy Analysis," 48 *American Economic Review* 298 [June 1958]). Although it has been here presented as a method for public administrators, it is no less necessary to analysts more removed from immediate policy questions, despite their tendencies to describe their own analytical efforts as though they were the rational-comprehensive method with an especially heavy use of theory. Similarly, this same method is inevitably resorted to in personal problem-solving, where means and ends are sometimes impossible to separate, where aspirations or objectives undergo constant development, and where drastic simplification of the complexity of the real world is urgent if problems are to be solved in the time that can be given to them. To an economist accustomed to dealing with the marginal or incremental concept in market processes, the central idea in the method is that both evaluation and empirical analysis are incremental. Accordingly, I have referred to the method elsewhere as "the incremental method."

30

EDWARD C. BANFIELD

INFLUENCE AND THE PUBLIC INTEREST

The following selection is from Edward C. Banfield's Political Influence *(1961), a study of policy-making in Chicago. Based on observations in six case studies, Banfield found that decision making on salient community issues often resembled what he calls "social choices," more than "central decisions" made by a solitary public manager acting independently of other interested parties. In "social choices"—or "mixed" decisions in which a central actor plays some role—competing groups participate in a pluralist bargaining process, which weighs the relevant preferences in the polity and may therefore yield policy outcomes that truly reflect the "public" interest. Banfield's analysis may be regarded as a classic exposition, and intellectual defense, of the pluralist policy process. Other important writings by this professor emeritus of government at Harvard University are* The Moral Basis of a Backward Society *(1958),* The Unheavenly City *(1970),* The Democratic Muse (1984), and Here the People Rule *(1985).*

Some will say that a political system such as has been described here can rarely produce outcomes that are in the public interest. If actions profoundly affecting the city's development are based not on comprehensive planning but on compromises patched up among competing parochial interests, if political heads are less concerned with the content of policy than with maintaining a voting alliance between the machine-controlled inner city and the suspicious suburbs and if the possessors of great private fortunes and the heads of big corporations cannot, despite all their talk of "civic responsibility," act concertedly for public ends—if all this be the case, the Chicago's future welfare depends (some will say) not so much upon the process of government as upon that special providence that is reserved for fools and drunkards.

The great defect of the Chicago political system (those who take this view will say) is that it does not provide sufficient central direction. There are many special interests on the scene, each of which looks after itself and cares only incidentally, if at all, for the welfare of the community as a whole. Action in public matters is largely a by-product of the struggles of these special interests for their own advantage. What is needed (the critics will conclude) is a central public authority which will survey the entire metropolitan scene, form a comprehensive, internally consistent conception of what must be done for the good of the whole, and then carry that conception into effect without compromise. This is what the advocates of "planning" and "efficient metropolitan organization" have in mind.

It seems clear that there is a tension between the nature of the political system, on the one hand, and the requirements of planning—of comprehensiveness and consistency in policy—on the other. In part, this tension arises from the decentralization so characteristic of the Chicago political system; despite the trend of recent years toward formal centralization and despite the extensive informal arrangements for overcoming decentralization, no one is in a position to survey the city—much less the metropolitan area—as a whole and to formulate and carry out a comprehensive policy. (Mayor Daley,* despite his great power as boss, can do little even in the city proper without at least tacit support from the governor.) In part, too, the tension arises from a general premise of our political culture: the belief that self-government consists, not in giving or withholding consent at infrequent intervals on matters of general principle, but rather in making influence felt in the day-to-day conduct of the public business. So long as particular interests can prevent the executive from carrying out his policy, or so long as they can place hazards and delays in the way of his carrying it out, they can demand concessions from him as the price of allowing him to act. It is the necessity of constantly making such concessions—of giving everyone something so as to generate enough support to allow of any action at all—that makes government policy so lacking in comprehensiveness and consistency.

The tendency in the United States has long been towards strengthening the executive: in Chicago as elsewhere the formal centralization of executive power is much greater than it was a decade or two ago. It seems highly unlikely, however, that this strengthening will go far enough in the forseeable future to change the essential character of the system. Chicagoans, like other Americans, want their city's policies to be comprehensive and consistent. But they also want to exercise influence in making and carrying out these policies; they want to be able to force the government to bargain with them when its policy threatens particular interests of theirs. It will be a long time, probably, before they will be willing to sacrifice as much of the second end as would be necessary to achieve the first. The tension between the nature of the system and the requirements of planning is, for all practical purposes, ineradicable.

This conclusion would be discouraging if it were perfectly clear that a comprehensive and consistent policy is necessarily better (i.e., more productive of "welfare" or "the public interest") than one which is not. We are apt to take for granted that this is the case. We are apt to suppose that a "correct" or "consistent" policy must be the product of a mind (or minds) which has addressed itself to a "problem," and, by a conscious search, "found" or "constructed" a "solution." Most of our study of political and administrative matters proceeds on the assumption that all of the elements of a problem must be brought together within the purview of some single mind (whether of a person or team) and that the task of organization is partly to assemble the elements of the problem. The more complicated the matter, the more obvious it seems that its solution must depend upon the effort of a mind which preceives a "problem" and deliberately seeks a "solution."

It will be convenient to make a fundamental distinction between "central decision," and "social choice." Both are processes by which selections are made among the action possibilities open to some group or public. A *central decision* is in some sense purposeful or deliberate: it is made by someone (leader, chairman,

**Richard Joseph Daley* (1902–1976): Democratic mayor of the city of Chicago from 1955 to 1976.

mayor, planning commission, council, committee of the whole, etc.) who, in making the selection, is trying (although perhaps ineffectually) to realize some intention for the group. From the standpoint of this decision-maker, the selection of an action, or course of action, for the group represents a "solution" to a "problem." A *social choice,* on the other hand, is the accidental by-product of the actions of two or more actors—"interested parties," they will be called—who have no common intention and who make their selections competitively or without regard to each other. In a social-choice process, each actor seeks to attain his own ends; the aggregate of all actions—the situation produced by all actions together—constitutes an outcome for the group, but it is an outcome which no one has planned as a "solution" to a "problem." It is a "resultant" rather than a "solution."

It may seem to common sense that because it is the product of intention, indeed of conscious and deliberate problem-solving, a central decision is much more likely to "work" than is a social choice. The social choice is, after all, an "accident": it was not designed to serve the needs or wishes of the group, whereas the central decision *was* so designed.

And yet, despite the presumptions of common sense, it may be that under certain circumstances the competition of forces which do not aim at a common interest produces outcomes which are more "workable," "satisfactory," or "efficient" than any that could be contrived by a central decision-maker consciously searching for solutions in the common interest. Charles E. Lindblom* has observed that while it is customary to think of the analysis of a policy problem as going on in the mind of one man or of a small group of men, it can also be seen as a social process. "Fragmentation" of analysis (i.e., analysis that goes on among many individuals or groups, each of whom approaches the problem from his distinctive and limited point of view) may be an aid to the correct weighting of values in a choice.

> Just how does the weighting take place in fragmentation? Not, I have suggested, in any one analyst's mind, nor in the minds of members of a research team, nor in the mind of any policy-maker or policy-making group. The weighting does not take place until actual policy decisions are made. At that time, the conflicting views of individuals and groups, each of whom have been concerned with a limited set of values, are brought to bear upon policy formulation. Policies are set as a resultant of such conflict, not because some one policy-making individual or group achieves an integration but because the pulling and hauling of various views accomplishes finally some kind of decision, probably different from what any one advocate of the final solution intended and probaby different from what any one advocate could comfortably defend by reference to his own limited values. The weighing or aggregation is a political process, not an intellectual process.

The evidence of the cases presented here makes it plausible to search for some such underlying logic not obvious to common sense. For if the outcomes alone of these cases are considered—that is, if the outcomes are considered apart from

**Charles E. Lindblom:* see headnote on page 485.

the seemingly "irrational" way in which they were reached—one might conclude that the political system is remarkably effective. It is impossible, of course, to come to any conclusion on this without making a large number of highly subjective judgments—not only judgments about values, but about facts and probabilities as well. Admitting this, the writer conjectures that most reasonable people who put themselves in the role of "statesman" and consider carefully all of the relevant circumstances will conclude that the outcomes are by no means indefensible. For himself, the writer can say that they are essentially what he would have favored had he been making "decisions." In every case, it seems to him "wrong" reasons (i.e., reasons which were irrelevant, illogical, or improper as a basis of a "decision" in the public interest) were controlling, but in every case these "wrong" reasons led to outcomes that were essentially "right" or "sound."

Others may not agree. But it is only necessary to establish that "obviously wrong" reasons led to outcomes that are "not obviously wrong" in order to raise the question: are such outcomes "lucky accidents" or is there some principle at work—an "invisible hand"—that leads a choice process to a result better than anyone intends?

The case for central decision rests upon the assumption that it is possible for a competent and disinterested decision-maker to find in any situation a value premise that uniquely determines the content of the public interest. If there existed several incompatible but equally desirable courses of action, a decision-maker would obviously have to employ some "arbitrary" procedure—e.g., flipping a coin, consulting his own or someone else's personal tastes, or assessing the relatives influence of the interests having a stake in the matter—in order to arrive at the decision. But the assumption of administration-minded or planning-minded persons is that this embarrassing situation seldom arises. A competent and well-intentioned decision-maker, so they suppose, can usually find in the situation some premise that clearly ought to rule. The problem of good government, therefore, is to put into office men who will look for the proper premise and use it when they find it (i.e., who seek the public interest rather than private or party advantage) and who have the technical competence necessary to apply the premise correctly in the particular circumstances.

This assumption is wrong. No matter how competent and well-intentioned, a decision-maker can never make an important decision on grounds that are not in some degree arbitrary or non-logical. He must select from among incompatible alternatives each of which is preferable in terms of a different but defensible view of the public interest. If there is a single "ultimate" value premise to which all of the lesser ones are instrumental, if its meaning is unambiguous in the concrete circumstances, and if he can know for sure which lesser premise is most instrumental to the attainment of the ultimate one, he can, indeed, make his decision in an entirely technical and non-arbitrary way. But these conditions can seldom be met, and when they can be, the matter is not "important" and usually does not require "decision." Matters come before high officials for decision precisely when it is not clear which value premises ought to be invoked, what the premises imply concretely, or what is most instrumental to their achievement. If such questions do not arise, the matter does not present itself as a "problem" at all.

In the Branch Hospital case, for example, there were at least three defensible value premises, each of which implied an altogether different decision: (*a*) "relieve overcrowding expeditiously" implied expanding on the West Side where a site was available; (*b*) "improve service" implied building on the South Side in proximity to the service area; and (*c*) "eliminate racial discrimination" implied not building at all in order to put pressure on the private hospitals. There was no higher premise to which each of these stood in an instrumental relationship and by which they could be judged. (There were slogans, of course, like "the greatest good of the greatest number," but these meant nothing concretely.) Clearly, then, the decision could not be made on technical or non-arbitrary grounds.

In such cases, where the decision-maker must select among alternatives without having any "higher" value premise by which to judge their relative importance, he must, wittingly or unwittingly, employ a criterion which has nothing to recommend it except use and wont or professional acceptance (e.g., "this is the way it is done in standard professional practice") or which expresses only his own (or someone else's) tastes or advantage, or else he must enact in imagination a choice process, imputing preference scales to the interested parties and striking, on their behalf, that compromise which he thinks "fair," productive of the most satisfaction, or the best reflection of the distribution of influence.

Thus, for example, a city-planning technician faced with the competing value premises of the Branch Hospital dispute and seeing no "higher" premise by which to decide the claims of the "lesser" ones, would, following the usual professional practice, gather a great deal of factual information on the distribution of potential hospital users, travel time, the optimal size of hospitals, etc., and then in all likelihood "find in the data" some reason—e.g., economy of travel time—for putting the hospital on the South Side. The chances are that the planner would not be as sensitive to the value, "relieve overcrowding expeditiously," as to the professionally sanctioned one, "minimize cross traffic." And it is very likely that the value, "eliminate racial discrimination," would not occur to him at all or that, if it did, it would not seem to him to be an apprioriate ultimate criterion. If it were expressly called to his attention, he might even say that it is a "political" factor which should not be allowed to influence the decision.

There is likely to be a systematic bias in a technician's choice of value premises. He will, it seems plausible to suppose, minimize the importance of those elements of the situation that are controversial, intangible, or problematic. He will favor those value premises upon the importance of which there is general agreement (e.g., travel time), and he will ignore or underrate those that are controversial or not conventionally defined (e.g., eliminating racial discrimination); he will favor those that can be measured, especially those that can be measured in money terms (e.g., the cost of transportation), and he will ignore or underrate those that are intangible and perhaps indefinable as well (e.g., the mood of a neighborhood); he will favor those that are associated with reliable predictions about the factual situation (e.g., the premise of accessibility is associated with relatively reliable predictions about population movements and consumer behavior), and he will ignore or underrate those that are associated with subjective judgments of probability (e.g., that it will be harder to get political approval for a South Side site).

In a social choice process, by contrast, there is a single ultimate criterion: the distribution of influence. The importance accorded to each alternative in a choice process depends, then, upon the relative amount of influence exercised on its behalf.

This may appear to be a highly inappropriate criterion in most situations. There are, however, a number of things that can be said in its favor:

1. The distribution of influence may be viewed as the outcome (as of a given moment) of a continuing "game" which has been going on under rules that a majority of the players have been free to change at any time. That the rules are as they are implies that they seem fair, over the long run, to most of the players. Accordingly, the outcome at any particular time is also fair, even though some players are losing. A player exerts himself to win only because winners receive rewards that are not given to losers. If, therefore, the winners have no more weight in a choice than do the losers—i.e., if the criterion does not reflect the distribution of influence—they will have that much less incentive to enter the game and to fight hard to win it. If the game is, on the whole, good for the society, it is foolish to reduce the incentive to play it. In other words, a society that wants people to exert themselves to get influence must not limit, unnecessarily, opportunities to exercise it once it has been obtained.

2. A criterion which reflects the distribution of influence also reflects, although roughly, the intensity with which the competing values are held. This is so because the choice process takes into account "real" influence, i.e., not the ability of each participant to modify the behavior of others, but the ability *which each sees fit to expend, out of his limited stock, for the sake of the particular value in question*. In the Fort Dearborn case, for example, the opponents had less influence than the Sponsors in the sense that if all had exerted themselves to the utmost, the Sponsors would have had their way. But the opponents were more intensely moved. Accordingly, they exercised a larger part of their influence potential than did the Sponsors. To the extent that the process was one of bargaining, it registered a compound of influence and intensity of interest. If it is considered appropriate to maximize "total satisfaction" of those whose views are taken into account, then it is essential to have some indication of how intensely each value is held. The choice mechanism forces each bargainer to give up something (the amount of influence he "spends"); this something can therefore be taken as a measure of the value to him of what he seeks. (If the influence distribution is "incorrect," the measure will of course be, to that extent, "wrong." But, as was maintained in the paragraph above, there is some reason to assume that the distribution is "correct.")

3. The character of the influence exercised may afford additional grounds for considering the distribution of influence to be an appropriate criterion. In one situation or set of situations, influence may consist of "forcing others to do one's will even when that will is anti-social." In another it may consist of "persuading others on reasonable grounds to accept a view of the common interest." There are circumstances in which one can exercise influence only by being (or seeming

to be) intelligently concerned with the common good ("by main force of being right"). So far as this is the case in a given society or situation, the criterion of influence has further justification.

The appropriateness of the criterion of influence is, however, only one aspect of the larger question, namely, the appropriateness of the social-choice process as a whole. It would be a point in favor of the choice process and a point against the decision process if it could be shown that while neither is clearly undesirable as a procedure for selecting an ultimate criterion, the former is more likely to bring all relevant considerations to the fore and to give them the attention they deserve.

There is indeed much reason to think that this is the case. A decision-maker, even one of long experience and great capacity, is not likely, when an issue first arises, to be fully aware of all the interests that are at stake in it or of the importance that is attached to each interest by those who hold it. He gets this information (except with regard to the most obvious matters) only as the interested parties themselves bring it to his attention. The effort an interested party makes to put its case before the decision-maker will be in proportion to *the advantage to be gained from a favorable outcome multiplied by the probability of influencing the decision*. Thus, no matter how high the stakes, an interested party will invest no effort at all in putting its case before a decision-maker who cannot be influenced. On the other hand, if there is a virtual certainty that the decision can be influenced, an interested party will have incentive to expend, in the effort to influence the decision, almost all of what may be gained from a favorable decision.

If the decision-maker is surely going to make the decision on purely public grounds, the possibilities of influencing him are relatively small. The interested party may present the facts of its case in the best possible light. It may argue that the public interest is to be understood in this way rather than that. But it cannot go much further than this. It cannot do more than try to persuade. In some cases the probability of success by persuasion may be sufficient to induce it to put forth a considerable effort. In others, however, its effort will be perfunctory because it knows that the decision-maker will pay little attention. In still others, it will make no effort at all because it knows that the decision-maker is not open to persuasion.

If, on the other hand, the official is open to influence by other means than persuasion, the probability of influencing the outcome may be vastly increased. If, indeed, it is possible, by a large enough expenditure of influence, virtually to compel him to select the favored alternative, then the incentive to make the effort is limited only by the advantage to be had from its success. In these circumstances, the affected interests will almost literally bring their cases "forcibly to the attention of" the official.

In a system of government in which the possibility of influencing outcomes is great, a vast amount of effort is spent by very able people in the attempt to do so. This expenditure of effort has some socially valuable results. It leads to the production of more information about the various alternatives and to a clarification of the values that are involved. Not only are the officials compelled to take into account more than they otherwise would, but the interests themselves are brought to examine their own and each other's positions with great care. Of course, in an instance where there exists some obviously appropriate and concretely meaningful value criterion upon which it is apparent, once the information is all at hand, that the official's decision ought to turn, the ability of an interested party to force the official to decide by some other criterion introduces error into the selection process. The argument here, however, is that such criteria almost never exist in matters of importance, and that when they do not exist, it is socially desirable that interested parties have incentive to vigorously assert value principles which will compete with those necessarily arbitrary ones (e.g., professional use and wont) which officials, wittingly or unwittingly, must fall back upon.

In a political system in which there exists no possibility whatever of influencing an outcome by an exercise of power (as distinguished from persuasion), it is unlikely that an interested party whose value position is not widely accepted as a plausible ultimate basis of decision will exert itself to put that position forward. Berry and Calloway, for example, would probably not have appeared upon the scene in the Branch Hospital dispute if the Chicago political system had been such as to make clear that the decision would be entirely in the hands of planners or technically minded people; but had they not exerted themselves, it is likely that the "race" position would have been entirely overlooked or given little weight. (The Welfare Council's planners, it will be remembered, virtually ignored it.) A "decision" reached without the racial aspects of the matter having been taken fully into account would have been deficient, although it might well have *seemed* (the deficiency not being called to anyone's attention) more "rational" than the social choice that was actually made.

In summary, then, it has been maintained: (1) that when, as is the case in important matters, there exists no concretely unambiguous criterion which clearly ought to rule, the distribution of "real" influence, as revealed in competitive exercises of influence, may be the appropriate criterion; and (2) that a selection process (or political system) which allows of the exercise of power other than that of persuasion by affected interests produces a wider canvas of policy alternatives and a more thorough scrutiny of each alternative than does a process which allows the affected interests only the opportunity to persuade. A corollary of these propositions is that the "rationality" of the process in which only persuasion is possible (i.e., the decision process) is often a simplification secured by overlooking or radically undervaluing some alternatives.

The social-choice process, however, suffers from at least two inherent limitations of great importance:

1 It takes into account only such ends as actors of influence see fit to assert, and it weights these ends according to the amount of influence behind them and without regard to their intrinsic value. In many circumstances, the distribution of influence may be an entirely inappropriate criterion. There may be ends which are not asserted in the choice process at all or which are asserted only weakly (e.g., ends which pertain to the community "as a whole") but which nevertheless ought to determine the outcome, ought to enter into it along with the ends which are asserted by influentials, or ought to serve as criteria by which the appropriateness and relative value of these and other ends are established.

2. There may exist an outcome which represents the "greatest total benefit" of the parties to the choice process but which is not likely to be found if each party seeks only his own advantage. There may, for example, be two ways in which A can attain his end equally well and between which he is indifferent. One of these ways may be advantageous to B and the other disadvantageous to him. A may not perceive the opportunity to increase total satisfaction by acting so as to benefit B; even if he does perceive it, he may have no incentive to act upon it.

It is a disadvantage of the choice process that no one has either an incentive to devise "greatest total benefit" solutions or the information about the preferences scales of the various interested parties that would be needed in order to do so.

In the Branch Hospital dispute, an arrangement whereby the county paid its clients' hospital bills in full, gave them freedom of choice in hospitals, and offered subsidies for expansions of those private hospitals which agreed not to discriminate might have represented a "greatest total benefit" solution. (It would presumably have suited both the left and the right wings of the Negro community, and the white hospitals as well.) But this solution was not likely to be devised by any of the parties to the struggle; each was too much committed to the solution implied by its own ends to look for one which would serve the ends of all.

The distribution of influence may be such as to paralyze action altogether. (In only two of the six cases described in the book—the Exhibition Hall and the Welfare Merger—was a course of action carried out as planned by its proponents; in the other cases, the outcomes were essentially the checking of action.) This tendency to paralyze action is sometimes regarded as a defect of the choice process. In certain circumstances it may be, of course. But from a general standpoint, there is no presumption that "inaction" represents a less desirable outcome than "action."

Certainly, a social-choice process is not always to be preferred to a central-decision process. Which is more appropriate will depend upon the circumstances of the case, especially the following: (*a*) the complexity of the policy problem to be solved, including especially the number of elements that must somehow be taken into account or weighted (and thus the amount of conflict in the situation) and the time and other resources that can be employed in looking for a solution; the more complicated the problem, the stronger the case for the choice mechanism; (*b*) the visibility of the factual and value elements that should be taken into account; where there is reason to believe that all relevant values (and their intensities) are not known, the play of influence should be allowed in order to assist their being made known; (*c*) the presence or absence of an appropriate "ultimate" criterion which is sufficiently definite in meaning to afford a basis for selection among the competing values that are instrumental to it; where such a criterion exists, a decision process is indicated, and the play of influence on the decision-maker is clearly undesirable; and (*d*) the appropriateness of one or another procedural criterion (e.g., that the settlement should reflect the distribution of influence, that it should accord with professional use and wont, that it should be "fair"); if the distribution of influence, or the bases upon which influence rests, are clearly undesirable, and if a decision-maker can be expected to employ procedural criteria which are *not* clearly undesirable, there is, of course, a presumption in favor of the decision process.

The discussion so far will have suggested the possibility of a selection process which combines features of both central decision and social choice and which therefore has some advantages (or, it could also be, disadvantages) of both. In a *mixed decision-choice* process, there are two or more interested parties each of whom seeks its own advantage without regard to any common intention. But there is also on the scene a central decision-maker who intervenes in the selection process to perform one or more of the following functions:

1. The central decision-maker may regulate the selection process so that "public values" are achieved or, negatively, not disregarded. He may, in the first place, decide whether the matter is one in which only the self-regarding ends of the interested parties should be taken into account (i.e., whether they are the only relevant value stuff) of whether they are corporate ends of "public values" that ought to be taken into account instead of, or along with, the self-regarding ends of the interested parties. He decides, in other words, whether selections ought to be made by social choice, central decision, or a mixed process. If he decides either that only "public values" or only "self-regarding ends" are relevant, the process then ceases to be "mixed": it becomes either central decision or social choice. But he may decide that what is appropriate is an aggregation of both public values *and* self-regarding ends—an aggregation in which certain public values and certain self-regarding ends are given greater or lesser weight. (He may, for example, decide that the matter is one in which a "qualified individualist" conception of the public interest is appropriate, and, accordingly, he may disregard "tastes" of "private-spirited" persons while giving great weight to the "settled convictions" of "public-spirited" persons.) Thus, the selection may be made through a social-choice process, but through a social-choice process *which operates within a limiting framework laid down by central direction*. The outcome of such a process is therefore both a "resultant" (from the standpoint of the interested parties) and a "solution" (from the standpoint of the central decision-maker, who decided which interested parties should be allowed to enter the process, how their ends should be weighted, and what importance should be accorded to "public values").

2. The central decision-maker may co-ordinate the activities of the interested parties in order to help them find positions optimal in terms of their (self-regarding) ends—i.e., positions such that no possible reallocation would make anyone better off without others worse off. The central decision-maker keeps track of external economies and diseconomies, which are not visible to the interested parties, and he watches for "saddle-points." He may, for example, guide the interested parties to a greater total "welfare" merely by supplying information (e.g., he may know that A is indifferent as between states *x* and *y*, whereas B much prefers state *y*; by pointing out that someone will gain and no one will lose by choosing state *y*, he increases welfare), or he may be the agent through which interpersonal comparisons of welfare are made or other agreed-upon rules are applied (e.g., if state *x* would mean great gains to A and small losses to B, he may intervene to impose the loss on B).

3. The central decision-maker merely records the relative influence exercised by the competing interested parties. In this case, he is merely an environment which facilitates the working out of a social-choice process. The interested parties make their influence known by putting pressure upon him; his action is entirely in response to these pressures (he is a weathervane, responding equally to all the breezes that blow), and it constitutes the resultant of the selection process.

In the first two of these three roles—but not in the third—the central decision-maker may eliminate inconsistences and anomalies from the outcome. Therefore, in these two types of mixed process the outcomes are both resultants (they are this insofar as they are the unintended product of competition among interested parties) and at the same time solutions (they are this insofar as they are the product of an intention—that of the central decision-maker).

It will be seen that the Chicago political system is of the type that has been called "mixed decision-choice." It has, therefore, in principle, and to a large extent in practice, the advantages of both polar types—social choice and central decision. In the writer's view, in its general features it is a reasonably close approximation of the logical model that is preferable.

One great advantage of social choice is that it involves a thorough canvas of all the elements—both the factual and the value elements—in a selection situation. The better their opportunities to influence an outcome, the more carefully will interested parties examine a situation for its effect on them, and the more vigorously will they assert their interests when they have identified them. In Chicago the opportunities to exercise influence are great enough to call into play the best abilities of many extremely able people. Nothing of importance is done in Chicago without its first being discovered what interests will be affected and how they will be affected and without the losses that will accrue to some being weighed carefully against the gains that will accrue to others. It is easy for Americans to take this kind of thing for granted, but there are cities—London, for example—where great decisions are made with little understanding of the consequences for those interests which are not plainly visible to the decision-makers.

Another great advantage of social choice is that, where there exists no concretely meaningful criterion of the public interest and where, accordingly (whether they realize it or not), central decision-makers must employ some standard (e.g., professional use and wont) that is essentially arbitrary, the competition of interested parties supplies a criterion—the distribution of "real" influence—which may be both generally acceptable and, since it puts a premium upon effort to acquire influence, serviceable to the society. In the cases reported here, there were not, in the writer's opinion, criteria from which central decision-makers could have obtained clear directions with regard to the main questions. (There was not, for example, any way by which a central decision-maker could have known whether "racial justice" or some other general end ought to be made decisive in the Branch Hospital dispute.) There being no "public values" which obviously ought to be decisive, the distribution of real influence was, it seems to the writer, as defensible a basis for decisions as any other. This judgment is strengthened by the character of the influence that is exercised in Chicago. For the most part, as previous chapters have shown, the interested parties in Chicago find it hard to take positions which cannot be defended in terms of some conception of the public interest.

The advantages of central decision are that the central decision-maker can assert the supremacy of "public values" and can find the outcome that is "best for all." On the Chicago scene there is, to be sure, no one central decision-maker who can do this in all of the most important matters. The mayor and the governor, whose tacit collaboration is essential in anything of importance, are required by the logic of their positions to disagree. Antagonism between mayor and governor, Democrat and Republican, Cook County and downstate, is the very basis of the political system. (Even in the rare intervals when the governor is a Democrat, the antagonism is not removed, for even then the Senate is dominated by downstate and is almost sure to be Republican.) There is, nevertheless, an important element of central decision in the Chicago system. The governor, the mayor, and the president of the County Board are all in positions to assert the supremacy of "public values" and, in general, to regulate the workings of the social-choice process. Although their practice is to let the social-choice process work itself out with as little interference from them as possible, each of them has in some matters the power to impose a settlement when he thinks doing so is necessary. Sometimes, as in the Fort Dearborn Project case, a political head's intervention is a conspicuous feature of the situation. At other times, a political head merely registers the influence exerted by the competing interests. (In the Branch Hospital dispute, this seemed for a long while to be Ryan's main function; in the end, however, he intervened to patch up a last-minute compromise without which all parties would have been worse off. Some observers were left with the suspicion that the clash of interests in that affair was not as important as it seemed—that it was, in fact, nothing but a public show staged by Ryan to justify a decision he had reached long before on the basis of his view of "public values.")

That the mixed–decision-choice process, as it works in Chicago, takes more time to produce an outcome than, presumably, a central decision process would take and that the outcome, when reached, is likely to be a stalemate cannot, of course, be held against it. Time spent discovering and evaluating the probable consequences of a proposal is not necessarily wasted; and if in the end nothing is done, or not much is done, that may be because it is in the public interest to do little or nothing.

31

THEODORE J. LOWI

DISTRIBUTION, REGULATION, REDISTRIBUTION: THE FUNCTIONS OF GOVERNMENT

Theodore J. Lowi, the John L. Senior Professor of American Institutions at Cornell University, was among the first political scientists to stress the two-way relationship between political process and public policy: while politics shapes policy, policy also informs politics. Lowi proposes that policies generally fit three generic categories: distributive, regulatory, or redistributive. Each generates distinctive political dynamics. This excerpt is from a highly influential article entitled "American Business, Public Policy, Case Studies, and Political Theory," published in a 1964 edition of World Politics. *Lowi is also the author of several books, including* The Politics of Disorder *(1971),* The End of Liberalism *(1969, 1979), and* The Personal President: Power Invested, Promise Unfulfilled *(1985).*

In the long run, all governmental policies may be considered redistributive, because in the long run some people pay in taxes more than they receive in services. Or, all may be thought regulatory because, in the long run, a governmental decision on the use of resources can only displace a private decision about the same resource or at least reduce private alternatives about the resource. But politics works in the short run, and in the short run certain kinds of government decisions can be made without regard to limited resources. Policies of this kind are called "distributive," a term first coined for nineteenth-century land policies, but easily extended to include most contemporary public land and resource policies; rivers and harbors ("pork barrel"*) programs; defense procurement and research and development programs: labor, business, and agricultural "clientele" services; and the traditional tariff. Distributive policies are characterized by the ease with which they can be disaggregated and dispensed unit by small unit, each unit more or less in isolation from other units and from any general rule. "Patronage" in the fullest meaning of the word can be taken as a synonym for "distributive." These are policies that are virtually not policies at all but are hightly individualized decisions that only by accumulation can be called a policy. They are policies in which the indulged and the deprived, the loser and the recipient, need never come into direct confrontation. Indeed, in many instances of distributive policy, the deprived cannot as a class be identified, because the most influential among them can be accommodated by further disaggregation of the stakes.

**Pork barrel:* term for government decisions that allocate benefits to a narrow constituency, for the chief purpose of securing its political support rather than for advancing the broader public interest.

Regulatory policies are also specific and individual in their impact, but they are not capable of the almost infinite amount of disaggregation typical of distributive policies. Although the laws are stated in general terms ("Arrange the transportation system artistically." "Thou shalt not show favoritism in pricing."), the impact of regulatory decisions is clearly one of directly raising costs and/or reducing or expanding the alternatives of private individuals ("Get off the grass!" "Produce kosher if you advertise kosher!"). Regulatory policies are distinguishable from distributive in that in the short run the regulatory decision involves a direct choice as to who will be indulged and who deprived. Not all applicants for a single television channel or an overseas air route can be propitiated. Enforcement of an unfair labor practice on the part of management weakens management in it dealings with labor. So, while implementation is firm-by-firm and case-by-case, policies cannot be disaggregated to the level of the individual or the single firm (as in distribution), because individual decisions must be made by application of a general rule and therefore become interrelated within the broader standards of law. Decisions cumulate among all individuals affected by the law in roughly the same way. Since the most stable lines of perceived common impact are the basic sectors of the economy, regulatory decisions are cumulative largely along sectoral lines; regulatory policies are usually disaggregable only down to the sector level.

Redistributive policies are like regulatory policies in the sense that relations among broad categories of private individuals are involved and, hence, individual decisions must be interrelated. But on all other counts there are great differences in the nature of impact. The categories of impact are much broader, approaching social classes. They are, crudely speaking, haves and have-nots, bigness and smallness, bourgeoisie* and proletariat.† The aim involved is not use of property but property itself, not equal treatment but equal possession, not behavior but being. The fact that our income tax is in reality only mildly redistributive does not alter the fact of the aims and the stakes involved in income tax policies. The same goes for our various "welfare state" programs, which are redistributive only for those who entered retirement or unemployment rolls without having contributed at all. The nature of a redistributive issue is not determined by the outcome of a battle over how redistributive a policy is going to be. Expectations about what it *can* be, what it threatens to be, are determinative.

ARENAS OF POWER

Once one posits the general tendency of these areas of policy or governmental activity to develop characteristic political structures, a number of hypotheses become compelling. And when the various hypotheses are accumulated, the general contours of each of the three arenas begin quickly to resemble, respectively, the three "general" theories of political process. The arena that develops

*Bourgeoisie: see footnote on page 14.

†*Proletariat:* see footnote on page 225.

around distributive policies is best characterized in the terms of E. E. Schattschneider's findings on the politics of tariff legislation in the nineteen-twenties. The regulatory arena corresponds to the pluralist school, and the school's general notions are found to be limited pretty much to this one arena. The redistributive arena most closely approximates, with some adaptation, an elitist view of the political process.

(1) The distributive arena can be identified in considerable detail from Schattschneider's case-study alone.[1] What he and his pluralist successors did not see was that the traditional structure of tariff politics is also in largest part the structure of politics of all those diverse policies identified earlier as distributive. The arena is "pluralistic" only in the sense that a large number of small, intensely organized interests are operating. In fact, there is even greater multiplicity of participants here than the pressure-group model can account for, because essentially it is a politics of every man for himself. The single person and the single firm are the major activists.

Although a generation removed, Schattschneider's conclusions about the politics of the Smoot-Hawley Tariff* are almost one-for-one applicable to rivers and harbors and land development policies, tax exemptions, defense procurement, area redevelopment, and government "services." Since there is no real basis for discriminating between those who should and those who should not be protected [indulged], says Schattschneider, Congress seeks political support by "giving a limited protection [indulgence] to all interests strong enough to furnish formidable resistance." Decision-makers become "responsive to considerations of equality, consistency, impartiality, uniformity, precedent, and moderation, however formal and insubstantial these may be." Furthermore, a "policy that is so hospitable and catholic . . . disorganizes the opposition."

When a billion-dollar issue can be disaggregated into many millions of nickel-dime items and each item can be dealt with without regard to the others, multiplication of interests and of access is inevitable, and so is reduction of conflict. All of this has the greatest bearing on the relations among participants and, therefore, the "power structure." Indeed, coalitions must be built to pass legislation and "make policy," but what of the nature and basis of the coalitions? In the distributive arena, political relationships approximate what Schattschneider called "mutual noninterference"—"a mutuality under which it is proper for each to seek duties [indulgences] for himself but improper and unfair to oppose duties [indulgences] sought by others." In the area of rivers and harbors, references are made to "pork barrel" and "log-rolling,"† but these colloquialisms have not been taken sufficiently seriously. A log-rolling coalition is not one forged of conflict, compromise, and tangential interest but, on the contrary, one

**Smoot Hawley Tariff Act of 1930:* act that imposed very high tariffs on imports to the United States. Countries throughout the world retaliated by imposing their own high tariffs and international trade was severely depressed, deepening the Great Depression.

†*Log-rolling:* game of cooperation popular among lumberjacks which challenges two people to keep their balance while standing on a floating log and turning it with short steps. In the legislative arena, log-rolling refers to the trading of favors among legislators, in which congressperson "A" will agree to vote for congressperson "B's" pet projects in exchange for "B's" support on items that are of interest mainly to "A."

composed of members who have absolutely nothing in common; and this is possible because the "pork barrel" is a container for unrelated items. This is the typical form of relationship in the distributive arena.

The structure of these log-rolling relationships lead typically, though not always, to Congress; and the structure is relatively stable because all who have access of any sort usually support whoever are the leaders. And there tend to be "elites" of a peculiar sort in the Congressional committees whose jurisdictions include the subject-matter in question. Until recently, for instance, on tariff matters the House Ways and Means Committee was virtually the government. Much the same can be said for Public Works on rivers and harbors. It is a broker leadership, but "policy" is best understood as cooptation rather than conflict and compromise.

Distributive issues individualize conflict and provide the basis for highly stable coalitions that are virtually irrelevant to the larger policy outcomes; thousands of obscure decisions are merely accumulated into a "policy" of protection or of natural-resources development or of defense subcontracting. Congress did not "give up" the tariff; as the tariff became a matter of regulation (see below), committee elites lost their power to contain the participants because obscure decisions became interrelated, therefore less obscure, and more controversy became built in and unavoidable.

(2) The regulatory arena could hardly be better identified than in the thousands of pages written for the whole polity by the pluralists. But, unfortunately, some translation is necessary to accommodate pluralism to its more limited universe. The regulatory arena appears to be composed of a multiplicity of groups organized around tangential relations or David Truman's* "shared attitudes." Within this narrower context of regulatory decisions, one can even go so far as to aceept the most extreme pluralist statement that policy tends to be a residue of the interplay of group conflict. This statement can be severely criticized only by use of examples drawn from non-regulatory decisions.

As I argued before, there is no way for regulatory policies to be disaggregated into very large numbers of unrelated items. Because individual regulatory decisions involve direct confrontations of indulged and deprived, the typical political coalition is born of conflict and compromise among tangential interests that usually involve a total sector of the economy. Thus, while the typical basis for coalition in distributive politics is uncommon interests (log-rolling), an entirely different basis is typical in regulatory politics.

Owing to the unrelatedness of issues in distributive politics, the activities of single participants need not be related but rather can be specialized as the situation warrants it. But the relatedness of regulatory issues, at least up to the sector level of the trade association, leads to the containment of all these within the association. When all the stakes are contained in one organization, constituents have no alternative but to fight against each other to shape the policies of that organization or actually to abandon it.

**David B. Truman:* political scientist whose classic analysis of interest groups, *The Governmental Process* (1951), describes how different types of groups function, interact, and affect the political system.

What this suggests is that the typical power structure in regulatory politics is far less stable than that in the distributive arena. Since coalitions form around shared interests, the coalitions will shift as the interests change or as conflicts of interest emerge. With such group-based and shifting patterns of conflict built into every regulatory issue, it is in most cases impossible for a Congressional committee, an administrative agency, a peak association* governing board, or a social elite to contain all the participants long enough to establish a stable power elite. Policy outcomes seem inevitably to be the residue remaining after all the reductions of demands by all participants have been made in order to extend support to majority size. But a majority-sized coalition of shared interests on one issue could not possibly be entirely appropriate for some other issue. In regulatory decision-making, relationships among group leadership elements and between them on any or more points of governmental access are too unstable to form a single policy-making elite. As a consequence, decision-making tends to pass from administrative agencies and Congressional committees to Congress, the place where uncertainties in the policy process have always been settled. Congress as an institution is the last resort for breakdowns in bargaining over policy, just as in the case of parties the primary is a last resort for breakdowns in bargaining over nominations. No one leadership group can contain the conflict by an almost infinite subdivision and distribution of the stakes. In the regulatory political process, Congress and the "balance of power" seem to play the classic role attributed to them by the pluralists.

Beginning with reciprocity in the 1930's, the tariff began to lose its capacity for infinite disaggregation because it slowly underwent redefinition, moving away from its purely domestic significance towards that of an instrument of international politics. In brief, the tariff, especially following World War II and our assumption of peacetime international leadership, became a means of regulating the domestic economy for international purposes. The significant feature here is not the international but the regulatory part of the redefinition. As the process of redefinition took place, a number of significant shifts in power relations took place as well, because it was no longer possible to deal with each dutiable item in isolation. Everything in Bauer, Pool, and Dexter† points toward the expansion of relationships to the level of the sector. The political problem of the South was the concentration of textile industry there. Coal, oil, and rails came closer and closer to coalition. The final shift came with the 1962 Trade Expansion Act,‡ which enabled the President for the first time to deal with broad categories (to the sector) rather than individual commodities.

Certain elements of distributive politics remain, for two obvious reasons. First, there are always efforts on the part of political leaders to disaggregate policies because this is the best way to spread the patronage and to avoid conflict. (Politi-

**Peak associations:* national professional or trade associations that have subnational units.

†*Raymond A. Bauer, Ithiel de Sola Pool,* and *Lewis Anthony Dexter:* authors of *American Business and Public Policy: The Politics of Foreign Trade* (1963, 1973).

‡*1962 Trade Expansion Act:* trade act that superseded the Reciprocal Trade Agreements Act of 1934 (see the following footnote). The act authorized the executive to negotiate further multilateral tariff reductions.

cal actors, like economic actors, probably view open competition as a necessary evil or a last resort to be avoided at almost any cost.) Second, until 1962, the basic tariff law and schedules were still contained in the Smoot-Hawley Act. This act was amended by Reciprocal Trade* but only to the extent of allowing negotiated reductions rather than reductions based on comparative costs. Until 1962, tariff politics continued to be based on commodity-by-commodity transactions, and thus until then tariff coalitions could be based upon individual firms (or even branches of large and diversified firms) and log-rolling, unrelated interests. The escape clause and peril point were maintained in the 1950's so that transactions could be made on individual items even within reciprocity. And the coalitions of strange bedfellows continued: "Offered the proper coalition, they both [New England textiles and Eastern railroads] might well have been persuaded that their interest was in the opposite direction."

But despite the persistence of certain distributive features, the true nature of tariff in the 1960's emerges as regulatory policy with a developing regulatory arena. Already we can see some changes in Congress even more clearly than the few already observed in the group structure. Out of a committee (House Ways and Means) elite, we can see the emergence of Congress in a pluralist setting. Even as early as 1954–1955, the compromises eventually ratified by Congress were worked out, not in committee through direct cooptation of interest, but in the Randall Commission,† a collection of the major interests in conflict. Those issues that could not be thrashed out through the "group process" also could not be trashed out in committee but had to pass on to Congress and the floor. After 1954 the battle centered on major categories of goods (even to the extent of a textile management-union entente) and the battle took place more or less openly on the floor. The weakening of the Ways and Means Committee as the tariff elite is seen in the fact that in 1955 Chairman Jere Cooper‡ was unable to push a closed rule through. The Rules Committee, "in line with tradition," granted a closed rule but the House voted it down 207–178. Bauer, Pool, and Dexter saw this as a victory for protectionism,§ but it is also evidence of the emerging regulatory arena—arising from the difficulty of containing conflict and policy within the governing committee. The last effort to keep the tariff as a traditional instrument of distributive politics—a motion by Daniel Reed‖ to recommit, with instructions to write in a provision that Tariff Commission rulings under the escape clause be final except

***Reciprocal Trade Agreements Act of 1934*: act aimed at correcting the imbalance caused by protectionism. It granted the president the authority to negotiate reciprocal tariff cuts with other nations. An agreement made with one country was effective for all countries that had the most-favored nation clauses in their trade agreements. Executive agreements were eventually signed with 43 countries.

†*Randall Commission*, or *Commission on Foreign Economic Policy*: commission headed by Clarence B. Randall (1891–1967), consultant on business and trade issues to Presidents Truman, Eisenhower, Kennedy, and Johnson. Randall was appointed chairman in 1953 by President Eisenhower. Eisenhower was able to secure support for only a few of the commission's recommendations.

‡*Jere Cooper* (1893–1957): Democrat from Tennessee who served in the U.S. House of Representatives from 1929 until 1957.

§*Protectionism:* governmental policy of imposing high tariffs, restrictive import quotas, or other trade restraints on imported goods to protect domestic producers and workers from foreign competition.

‖*Daniel A. Reed* (1875–1959): Republican congressman from New York who served in the U.S. House of Representatives from 1919 to 1959.

where the President finds the national security to be involved—was voted down 206–199. After that, right up to 1962, it was clear that tariff decisions would not be made piecemeal. Tariff became a regulatory policy in 1962; all that remains of distributive politics now are quotas and subsidies for producers of specific commodities injured by general tariff reductions.

(3) Compared particularly with the regulatory area, very few case-studies of redistributive decisions have ever been published. This in itself is a significant datum—which C. Wright Mills* attributed to the middle-level character of the issues that have gotten attention. But, whatever the reasons, it reduces the opportunities for elaborating upon and testing the scheme. Most of the propositions to follow are illustrated by a single case, the "welfare state" battle of the 1930's. But this case is a complex of many decisions that became one of the most important acts of policy ever achieved in the United States. A brief review of the facts of the case will be helpful. Other cases will be referred to in less detail from time to time.

As the 1934 mid-term election approached, pressures for a federal social security system began to mount. The Townsend Plan† and the Lundeen Bill‡ had become nationally prominent and were gathering widespread support. Both schemes were severly redistributive, giving all citizens access to government-based insurance as a matter of right. In response, the President created in June of 1934 a Committee on Economic Security (CES) composed of top cabinet members with Secretary of Labor Perkins as chairman. In turn, they set up an Advisory Council and a Technical Board, which held hearings, conducted massive studies, and emerged on January 17, 1935, with a bill. The insiders around the CES were representatives of large industries, business associations, unions, and the most interested government bureaucracies. And the detailed legislative histories reveal that virtually all of the debate was contained within the CES and its committees until a mature bill emerged. Since not all of the major issues had been settled in the CES's bill, its members turned to Congress with far from a common front. But the role of Congress was still not what would have been expected. Except for a short fight over committee jurisdiction (won by the more conservative Finance and Ways and Means committees) the legislative process was extraordinarily quiet, despite the import of the issues. Hearings in both Houses brought forth very few witnesses, and these were primarily CES members supporting the bill, and Treasury Department officials, led by Morgenthau,§ opposing it with "constructive criticism."

The Congressional battle was quiet because the real struggle was taking place

*C. *Wright Mills* (1916–1962): sociologist who wrote an eye-opening book *The Power Elite* (1956), which argued that an elite composed of business, military, and political leaders, ruled in America.

†*Townsend Plan:* popular program developed by Dr. Francis E. Townsend (1867–1960), proposing an old-age insurance plan through which all citizens over 60 years of age would be given a monthly $200 grant that they would be required to spend within 30 days. The program was to be funded through a 2 percent sales tax.

‡*Lundeen Bill:* workers unemployment and social insurance bill that never went to the floor of the House, introduced by Ernest Lundeen, a Minnesota representative to the U.S. House of Representatives (1917–1919, 1933–1937) and senator (1937–1943).

§*Henry Morgenthau:* see footnote on page 338.

elsewhere, essentially between the Hopkins-Perkins bureaucracies and the Treasury. The changes made in the CES bill had all been proposed by Morgenthau (the most important one being the principle of contribution, which took away the redistributive sting). And the final victory for Treasury and mild redistribution came with the removal of administrative responsibility from both Labor and Hopkins's Federal Emergency Relief Administration. Throughout all of this some public expressions of opinion were to be heard from the peak associations, but their efforts were mainly expended in the quieter proceedings in the bureaucracies. The Congress's role seems largely to have been one of ratifying agreements that arose out of the bureaucracies and the class agents represent there. Revisions attributable to Congress concerned such matters as exceptions in coverage, which are part of the distributive game that Congress plays at every opportunity. The *principle* of the Act was set in an interplay involving (quietly) top executives and business and labor leaders.

With only slight changes in the left-right positions of the participants, the same pattern has been observed in income tax decisions. Professor Stanley S. Surrey* notes: "The question, 'Who speaks for tax equity and tax fairness?,' is answered today largely in terms of only the Treasury Department." "Thus, in tax bouts . . . it is the Treasury versus percentage legislation, the Treasury versus capital gains, the Treasury versus this constituent, the Treasury versus that private group. . . . As a consequence, the congressman . . . [sees] a dispute . . . only as a contest between a private group and a government department." Congress, says Surrey, "occupies the role of mediator between the tax views of the executive and the demands of the pressure groups." And when the tax issues "are at a major political level, as are tax rates or personal exemptions, then pressure groups, labor organizations, the Chamber of Commerce, the National Association of Manufacturers, and the others, become concerned." The "average congressman does not basically believe in the present income tax in the upper-brackets," but rather than touch the principle he deals in "special hardship" and "penalizing" and waits for decisions on principle to come from abroad. Amidst the 1954–1955 tax controversies, for example, Ways and Means members decided to allow each member one bill to be favorably reported if the bill met with unanimous agreement.

Issues that involve redistribution cut closer than any others along class lines and activate interests in what are roughly class terms. If there is ever any cohesion within the peak associations, it occurs on redistributive issues, and their rhetoric suggests that they occupy themselves most of the time with these. In a ten-year period just before and after, but not including, the war years, the Manufacturers' Association of Connecticut, for example, expressed itself overwhelmingly more often on redistributive than on any other types of issues. Table 1 summarizes the pattern, showing that expressions on generalized issues involving basic relations between bourgeoisie and proletariat outnumbered expressions on regulation of business practices by 870 to 418, despite the larger number of issues in the latter

**Stanley S. Surrey:* emeritus professor of law at Harvard, and the author of *United Nations Model Convention for Tax Treaties between Developed and Developing Countries* (1980), *Pathways to Tax Reform* (1973), and *Tax Expenditures* (1985) with Paul R. McDaniel.

TABLE 1. PUBLISHED EXPRESSIONS OF MANUFACTURERS' ASSOCIATION OF CONNECTICUT ON SELECTED ISSUES

	Number of References in Ten-year Period (1934–40, 1946–48)		Per Cent of Favorable References
1. Unspecified regulation	378		7.7
2. Labor relations, general	297		0.0
3. Wages and hours	195		0.5
Total expressions, redistribution		870	
4. Trade practices	119		13.8
5. Robinson-Patman	103		18.4
6. Antitrust	72		26.4
7. Basing points	55		20.0
8. Fair-Trade (Miller-Tydings)	69		45.5
Total expressions, regulation		418	

Source: Lane, *The Regulation of Businessmen* (New Haven, 1953), 38ff. The figures are his; their arrangement is mine.

category. This pattern goes contrary to the one observed by Bauer, Pool, and Dexter in tariff politics, where they discovered, much to their surprise, that self-interest did not activate both "sides" equally. Rather, they found, the concreteness and specificity of protectionist interests activated them much more often and intensely than did the general, ideological position of the liberal-traders. This was true in tariff, as they saw, because there the "structure of the communications system favored the propagation of particular demands." But there is also a structure of communications favoring generalized and ideological demands; this structure consists of the peak associations, and it is highly effective when the issues are generalizable. This is the case consistently for redistributive issues, almost never for distributive issues, and only seldom for regulatory issues.

As the pluralists would argue, there will be a vast array of organized interests for any item on the policy agenda. But the relations among the interests and between them and government vary, and the nature of and conditions for this variation are what our political analyses should be concerned with. Let us say, in brief, that on Monday night the big associations meet in agreement and considerable cohesion on "the problem of government," the income tax, the Welfare State.* On Tuesday, facing regulatory issues, the big associations break up into their constituent trade and other specialized groups, each prepared to deal with special problems in its own special ways, usually along subject-matter lines. On Wednesday night still another fission takes place as the pork barrel and the other forms of subsidy and policy patronage come under consideration. The parent groups and "catalytic groups" still exist, but by Wednesday night they have little identity. As Bauer, Pool, and Dexter would say, they have preserved their unanimity through overlapping memberships. They gain identity to the extent that they can define the issues in redistributive terms. And when interests in issues are

**Welfare State:* a political system in which the state takes responsibility for ensuring the economic and social well-being of all its citizens. There are varying degrees of commitment to the concepts and programs of a welfare state in modern capitalist societies.

more salient in sectoral or geographic or individual terms, the common or generalized factor will be lost in abstractness and diffuseness. This is what happened to the liberal trade groups in the tariff battles of the 1950's, when "the protectionist positions was more firmly grounded in direct business considerations and . . . the liberal-trade position fitted better with the ideology of the times . . . "

Where the peak associations, led by elements of Mr. Mill's power elite, have reality, their resources and access are bound to affect power relations. Owing to their stability and the impasse (or equilibrium) in relations among broad classes of the entire society, the political structure of the redistributive arena seems to be highly stabilized, virtually institutionalized. Its stability, unlike that of the distributive arena, derives from shared interests. But in contrast to the regulatory arena, these shared interests are sufficiently stable and clear and consistent to provide the foundation for ideologies. Table 2 summarizes the hypothesized differences in political relationships drawn above.

Many of the other distinctive characteristics of this arena are related to, perhaps follow from, the special role of the peak associations. The cohesion of peak associations means that the special differences among related but competing groups are likely to be settled long before the policies reach the governmental agenda. In many respects the upperclass directors perform the functions in the redistributive arena that are performed by Congressional committees in the distributive arena and by committees and Congress in the regulatory arena. But the differences are crucial. In distributive policies there are as many "sides" as there are tariff items, bridges and dams to be built, parcels of public land to be given away or leased, and so on. And there are probably as many elites as there are Congressional committees and subcommittees which have jurisdiction over distributive policies. In redistribution, there will never be more than two sides and the sides are clear, stable, and consistent. Negotiation is possible, but only for the purpose of strengthening or softening the impact of redistribution. And there is probably one elite for each side. The elites do not correspond directly to bourgeoisie and proletariat; they are better understood under Wallace Sayre's* designation of "money-providing" and "service-demanding" groups. Nonetheless, the basis for coalition is broad, and it centers around those individuals most respected and best known for worth and wealth. If the top leaders did not know each other and develop common perspectives as a result of common schooling, as Mills would argue, these commonalities could easily develop later in life because the kinds of stakes involved in redistributive issues are always the same. So institutionalized does the conflict become that governmental bureaucracies themselves begin to reflect them, as do national party leaders and Administrations. Finally, just as the nature of redistributive policies influences politics towards the centralization and stabilization of conflict, so does it further influence the removal of decision-making from Congress. A dencentralized and bargaining Congress can cumulate

***Wallace S. Sayre* (1905–1973): Columbia University political scientist and former professor of public administration. He is the author of many books including *Your Government* (1932), *Outline of American Government* (1933), *The U.N. Secretariat* (1950), and *Governing New York City* (1952) with Herbert Kaufman.

TABLE 2. ARENAS AND POLITICAL RELATIONSHIPS: A DIAGRAMMATIC SURVEY

Arena	*Primary Political Unit*	*Relation Among Units*	*Power Structure*	*Stability of Structure*	*Primary Decisional Locus*	*Implementation*
Distribution	Individual firm, corporation	Log-rolling, mutual non-interference, uncommon interests	Non-conflictual elite with support groups	Stable	Congressional committee and/or agency**	Agency centralized to primary functional unit ("bureau")
*Regulation**	Group	"The coalition," shared subject-matter interest, bargaining	Pluralistic, multi-centered, "theory of balance"	Unstable	Congress, in classic role	Agency decentralized from center by "delegation," mixed control
Redistribution	Association	The "peak association," class, ideology	Conflictual elite, i.e., elite and counterelite	Stable	Executive and peak associations	Agency centralized toward top (above bureau"), elaborate standards

*Given the multiplicity of organized interests in the regulatory arena, there are obviously many cases of successful log-rolling coalitions that resemble the coalitions prevailing in distributive politics. In this respect, the difference between the regulatory and the distributive arenas is thus one of degree. The *predominant* form of coalition in regulatory politics is deemed to be that of common or tangential interest. Although the difference is only one of degree, it is significant because this prevailing type of coalition makes the regulatory arena so much more unstable, unpredictable, and non-elitist ("balance of power"). When we turn to the redistributive arena, however, we find differences of principle in every sense of the word.

**Distributive politics tends to stabilize around an institutional unit. In most cases, it is the Congressional committee (or subcommittee). But in others, particularly in the Department of Agriculture, the focus is the agency or the agency *and* the committee. In the cities, this is the arena where machine domination continues, if machines were in control in the first place.

but it cannot balance, and redistributive policies require complex balancing on a very large scale. What William H. Riker* has said of budget-making applies here: " . . . legislative governments cannot endure a budget. Its finances must be totted up by party leaders in the legislature itself. In a complex fiscal system, however, haphazard legislature judgments cannot bring revenue into even rough alignment with supply. So budgeting is introduced—which transfers financial control to the budget maker. . . . " Congress can provide exceptions to principles and it can implement those principles with elaborate standards of implementation as a condition for the concessions that money-providers will make. But the makers of principles of redistribution seem to be the holders of the "command posts."

None of this suggests a power elite such as Mills would have had us believe existed, but it does suggest a type of stable and continual conflict that can only be understood in class terms. The foundation upon which the social-stratification and power-elite school rested, especially when dealing with national power, was so conceptually weak and empirically unsupported that its critics were led to err in the opposite direction by denying the direct relevance of social and institutional positions and the probability of stable decision-making elites. But the relevance of that approach becomes stronger as the scope of its application is reduced and as the standards for identifying the scope are clarified. But this is equally true of the pluralist school and of those approaches based on a "politics of this-or-that policy."

NOTE

[1]E. E. Schattschneider, *Politics, Pressures, and the Tariff* (Hamden, Conn.: Shoe String, 1935).

*_William H. Riker_: political scientist at the University of Rochester and the author of numerous books including *Federalism* (1964), *Introduction to Positive Political Theory* (1973), and *Liberalism Against Populism* (1982).

Robert A. Dahl, "The American Hybrid," from A PREFACE TO DEMOCRATIC THEORY by Robert A. Dahl (The University of Chicago, 1956), pp. 124–151. Reprinted by permission of The University of Chicago Press and the author.

Richard F. Fenno, Jr., "Congressmen in Committees," from Richard F. Fenno, Jr., CONGRESSMEN IN COMMITTEES, pp. 13–14, 43–45, 79–80, 137–138, and 276–279. Copyright © 1973 by Scott, Foresman and Company. Reprinted by permission of the publisher and the author.

Morris P. Fiorina, "The Decline of Collective Responsibility in American Politics." Reprinted by permission of DAEDALUS, Journal of the American Academy of Arts and Sciences, *The End of Concensus?*, vol. 109, no. 3, Summer 1980, Cambridge, MA.

Morton Grodzins, "The Federal System," in The American Assembly, GOALS FOR AMERICANS: THE REPORT OF THE PRESIDENT'S COMMISSION ON NATIONAL GOALS, p. 265–282. Englewood Cliffs, N.J., Prentice-Hall, Inc., 1960. Reprinted by permission of the American Assembly.

Alexander Hamilton, James Madison, and John Jay, THE FEDERALIST PAPERS. Source: The New American Library, 1961 edition.

Louis Hartz, "The Concept of a Liberal Society," from THE LIBERAL TRADITION IN AMERICA, copyright © 1955, 1983 by Louis Hartz. Reprinted by permission of Harcourt Brace Jovanovich, Inc.

Samuel P. Huntington, "Congressional Responses to the Twentieth Century," in The American Assembly, THE CONGRESS AND AMERICA'S FUTURE, ed. David B. Truman, pp. 6–31, 2nd ed. Englewood Cliffs, N.J., Prentice-Hall, Inc., 1973. Reprinted by permission of the American Assembly.

V.O. Key, Jr., "The Responsible Electorate." Abridged by permission of the publishers from THE RESPONSIBLE ELECTORATE, by V.O. Key, Jr., Cambridge, Mass.: Harvard University Press, © 1966 by The President and Fellows of Harvard College.

Charles E. Lindblom, "The Science of 'Muddling Through'," from PUBLIC ADMINISTRATION REVIEW, vol. 19 (Spring 1959), pp. 79–88. Reprinted by permission of the author.

Seymour Martin Lipset, "Formulating a National Identity," from THE FIRST NEW NATION: THE UNITED STATES IN HISTORICAL AND COMPARATIVE PERSPECTIVE, by Seymour Martin Lipset. © 1963 by Seymour Martin Lipset. Reprinted by permission of Basic Books, Inc., Publishers.

Norton E. Long, "Power and Administration," PUBLIC ADMINISTRATION REVIEW, vol. 9 (Autumn 1949), pp. 257–264. Reprinted with permission from PUBLIC ADMINISTRATION REVIEW. © 1949 by The American Society for Public Administration, 1120 G Street, N.W., Suite 500, Washington, D.C. All rights reserved.

Theodore J. Lowi, "Distribution, Regulation, Redistribution: The Functions of Government," from Theodore J. Lowi, "American Business, Public Policy, Case-Studies, and Political Theory," WORLD POLITICS, vol. 16, no. 4 (July 1964). Copyright © 1964 Princeton University Press. Reprinted with permission of Princeton University Press.

Richard E. Neustadt, "The Power to Persuade." Reprinted with permission of Macmillan Publishing Company, from PRESIDENTIAL POWER: THE POLITICS OF LEADERSHIP WITH REFLECTIONS ON JOHNSON AND NIXON by Richard E. Neustadt. (New York: Macmillan 1980).

Mancur Olson, Jr., "Collective Action: The Logic," from THE RISE AND DECLINE OF NATIONS: ECONOMIC GROWTH, STAGFLATION, AND SOCIAL RIGIDITIES (New Haven: Yale University Press). Copyright © 1982 Yale University Press. Reprinted by permission.

Paul E. Peterson, "Federalism and the Great Society," pp. 257–286 in POVERTY AND PUBLIC POLICY: AN EVALUATION OF SOCIAL SCIENCE RESEARCH, ed. Vincent Covello. Copyright 1980 and reprinted with the permission of Twayne Publishers, a division of G.K. Hall & Co., Boston.

Nelson W. Polsby, "Strengthening Congress in National Policy-Making," THE YALE REVIEW, vol. LIX (June 1970), No. 4, pp. 481–497. Copyright 1970 Yale University. Reprinted by permission.

E.E. Schattschneider, "The Scope and Bias of the Pressure System" from THE SEMISOVEREIGN PEOPLE, revised by E.E. Schattschneider. Copyright © 1975 by E.E. Schattschneider and the Dryden Press. Reprinted by permission of the publisher.

Martin Shapiro, "The Presidency and the Federal Courts," in Arnold J. Meltsner, Ed., POLITICS AND THE OVAL OFFICE: TOWARDS PRESIDENTIAL GOVERNANCE (San Francisco, CA: Institute for Contemporary Studies, 1981), pp. 141–157.

James L. Sundquist, "Strengthening the National Parties," in James A. Reichley, Ed., ELECTIONS AMERICAN STYLE (Washington, D.C., The Brookings Institution, 1987), pp. 195–221.

Alexis de Tocqueville, "Equality." Source: "Equality of Condition," in Edward Handler, Ed., THE AMERICAN POLITICAL EXPERIENCE (Massachusetts: D.C. Heath and Company, 1968), pp. 13–20.

Aaron Wildavsky, "The Two Presidencies." Published by permission of Transaction Publishers, from TRANS-ACTION, vol. 4, no. 2. Copyright © 1966 by Transaction Publishers.

James Q. Wilson, "The Bureaucracy Problem," THE PUBLIC INTEREST, no. 6, Winter 1967. Reprinted by permission of the author.

Woodrow Wilson, "Congressional Government," from Woodrow Wilson, CONGRESSIONAL GOVERNMENT, pp. 193–215 (Gloucester, Mass.: Peter Smith Publisher, 1973). Reprinted by permission of the publisher.